£60

GLOBAL
Management

"To Earl Boyer Mendenhall, an expatriate's expatriate"

"To BJ's family at home in St. Vincent"

"To David's family"

GLOBAL
Management

Mark Mendenhall
University of Tennessee, Chattanooga

Betty Jane Punnett
University of Windsor

David Ricks
American Graduate School of
International Management, Thunderbird

 BLACKWELL
Publishers

First published 1995

Blackwell Publishers, a publishing imprint of Basil Blackwell Inc.
238 Main Street
Cambridge, Massachusetts 02142

Basil Blackwell Ltd.
108 Cowley Road
Oxford OX4 1JF
UK

Library of Congress Cataloging-in-Publication Data

Mendenhall, Mark E., 1956–
    Global management / Mark E. Mendenhall, Betty Jane Punnett,
  David A. Ricks.
      p.   cm.
    Includes bibliographical references and index.
    ISBN 1-55786-635-Y   ISBN 1-55786-636-8
    1. International business enterprises--Management. 2. Management.
  I. Punnett, Betty Jane. II. Ricks, David A. III. Title.
  HD62.4.M46 1995
  658'.049--dc20

British Library Cataloguing in Publication Data

A CIP catalogue record for this book is available from the British Library.

Typeset in Bodoni on 11 pt. by Benchmark Productions, Inc.

Printed in the United States of America by Quebecor

This book is printed on acid-free paper

TABLE OF CONTENTS

201-262

Chapter 3—The Cultural Environment   65

Chapter 9—Adapting Management to Foreign Environments 283

Chapter 10—Managing Operations Globally 321

Chapter 11—Organizing and Control in Global Organizations

Chapter 16—Communication and Negotiation in Global Management   531

PREFACE

Pick up any newspaper or magazine, any popular business book or academic text, and you will find attention being paid to the global dimensions of business and management. The world's economies are so interdependent that events in far-off locations must be considered by managers no matter where a particular business is situated.

The interdependence of world economies can be illustrated by almost any major event. Consider two unrelated events in 1992: in September, the United Kingdom (U.K.) pulled out of the European Monetary Union; and shortly thereafter Canada engaged in a major constitutional debate. The effects of these events were felt by businesses around the world:

- The British pound (U.K. currency) dropped in value in reaction to its withdrawal from the monetary union, and short-term investments in the U.K. sought alternative locations. High interest rates in Germany encouraged currency movements to that country, but other investors were concerned about the well-being of the European Community and chose to invest in countries outside of the European Community— including in Canada.

- Canada's debate over changes to the Canadian constitution became a major media event in Canada shortly after the U.K.'s action. Investors from Asia, Europe, and the U.S. evaluated the uncertainty associated with this process in Canada and adopted a "wait and see" attitude toward investments in Canada. To a large degree, this countered the potential increases in investment in Canada associated with the U.K.'s withdrawal from the European Monetary Union. The capital that would have come to Canada, because of the U.K.'s withdrawal from the monetary union, moved elsewhere—often to the rapidly expanding markets of the Far East.

These two unrelated events on opposite sides of the Atlantic encouraged investors to consider the Pacific Rim as a potential investment site. Many investments were initially short-term, but because of the attractive returns, some remained. In turn, these investments have helped fuel growth in the Far East.

These events exemplify why managers in the 1990s and the twenty-first century need to be aware of global issues and understand their impact on management. The interrelated nature of today's world makes it essential for managers to think globally—effective managers in this environment are not limited by national boundaries. At the same time, a global approach means that opportunities and challenges come from a variety of nations—the impact of the differences arising from inter national transactions is also important to success. Excellent firms of the coming decades will have managers who think globally while valuing diversity.

We have called this book Global Management to focus students on the need for global thinking. We recognize that global thinking results in inter national business, and much of the specific material in the book deals with diversity, and the differences that are encountered by managers in different national environments. Our aim throughout the book is to stress global approaches— encompassing the entire world—while acknowledging the importance of diversity—found around the world.

Any organization that participates in business activities that take place across national boundaries is, in essence, involved in international business. The critical factor that distinguishes this type of business from a business that could be defined as domestic is the complexity associated with operating across national boundaries. National boundaries imply varying political systems and national cultures; and these are two key factors that affect international managers.

It can be argued that the process of management remains the same, whether domestic or international. That is, managers still need to decide on strategies and plan activities, they must structure the organization to accomplish strategies, and they must have controls in place to ensure their achievement. As managers continue to rely on people to realize strategies and plans, good management relies on staffing effectively and relating to people in the organization so that they work toward desired goals. A manager in a largely domestic firm deals with a relatively well-known and well-understood environment; and understanding the impact of factors such as politics, culture, labor, and ethics at home is relatively uncomplicated. This is not true internationally.

When managers begin to think globally, they are struck by the varied environments that may be encountered around the world. A host of different customs, practices, and requirements are found in different locations. To evaluate global opportunities and threats, it is important for managers to have a basic understanding of the variations that may be experienced. In the domestic context, managers look to the environment to identify opportunities and threats; the same is true globally. This environment can vary dramatically from place to place; therefore, understanding environmental factors is a prerequisite to doing business internationally.

Once managers have a broad understanding of the global environment, they can focus on strategic and operational decisions for the firm. The manager makes strategic decisions about whether, where, and how to globalize operations. These decisions are followed by designing management, operational, organizational, and control systems.

Having made decisions about the firm's globalization strategy and operations, managers are faced with the task of ensuring that these decisions are implemented effectively. This implementation relies on people—choosing the right people, providing the appropriate training, and motivating these people to perform at a high level are all critical to successful international management.

This book explores global issues and their impact on the management process. In designing the flow of the text, the authors discussed various possibilities with students and colleagues, and sought comments from business associates. Editors and reviewers also made suggestions. All of this input was helpful in deciding on the book's organization, and we appreciate the many people who contributed in this way.

This book is designed to parallel the international manager's decision-making process. Part One focuses on the global business environment. We begin with historical developments in international business and management—to provide a context for understanding international business and its environment. We then discuss four specific aspects of the environment—cultural, political, labor, and ethical issues—viewed from a global management perspective. We have included a chapter on the ethical environment because we believe that it is vital for managers to be aware of ethical issues cross-nationally and cross-culturally when doing business internationally. Additional considerations, such as the legal environment, are clearly important but require specialized advice, which managers seek on a case by case basis; therefore, we have not discussed these topics here.

Part Two focuses on strategic issues—strategy formulation, implementation, and control considerations. We begin with an overview of global strategy, followed by a discussion of specific options for entering foreign locations. We then consider adapting the management process to international environments, operational issues, and organizational controls in global firms. The topics discussed are of a general management nature as opposed to more specialized topics such as accounting, financial, or marketing management.

Part Three addresses the task of ensuring that international decisions are successful. Here we focus on human resource issues. A substantial degree of attention is attached to these issues because it is in the management of human resources that variations in national environments often have the greatest impact. International managers cannot be effective unless they are sensitive to the differences in people that they may encounter in different locations. Part Three emphasizes choosing the best people around the world and explores ways to ensure that the staffing process is practical, constructive, and considerate of the cultural influences of people from different backgrounds.

Exhibit I depicts the flow of this book as well as the relationship between its flow, the international manager's level of analysis, and stages of the management process. The exhibit differentiates among the three parts of the book, and illustrates how these three parts encompass the management stage and the level of analysis.

In the management stage we depict the process of general management. We describe the management process as consisting of environmental understanding strategy and operations, execution, and measurement. These four boxes are analogous to the process of research, planning and organizing, staffing and directing, and controlling; thus, our management stages parallel the more traditional model of the management process.

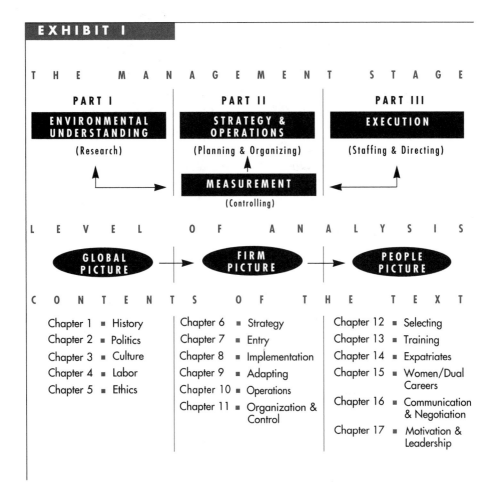

In the international manager's decision-making process, we find a progression in level of analysis from consideration of the global picture, through understanding of the firm picture, to attention to the people picture. Relating these to the management stage:

- the global picture involves environmental understanding (research).

- the firm picture involves strategy and operations (planning and organizing), and measurement (controlling).

- the people picture involves execution (staffing and directing).

In Exhibit I we also include the contents of the book, showing their relationship to the management stage and level of analysis previously described.

Each chapter of this book begins with a series of "learning objectives" that encapsulate the subjects covered in that chapter, and key discussion topics which summarize the topics students should be able to discuss after studying the chapter. Chapters conclude with "discussion questions" which generally require some outside research to complete. Some can be prepared based largely on material in the text; others require additional information and research.

Each part of the book concludes with an extensive reading list incorporating references used in preparing the chapters with many other sources. A wide variety of authors, topics, and journals are included to provide the reader with a substantial body of literature on which to draw for further understanding of the topics discussed.

The main text is complemented by a series of appendices. Appendix A considers careers in international organizations—a topic of especial interest to students. Appendix B contains a series of experiential exercises, which add an important dimension to the study of international management. Appendix C contains selected cases, which provide a realism to the understanding of international management issues, and contribute to a practical approach to international management decision making.

The need to understand the global business arena has increasingly been recognized by the academic community. This is illustrated around the world by the following developments:

- university course offerings in international and global dimensions of business.

- degree programs devoted to international and global business issues.

- executive programs that are international and global in scope.

- international student and faculty exchanges.

- new journals focusing on international and global issues.

- international and global academic conference themes.

- conferences held in foreign locations by academic institutions.

This book was written in response to these developments. It focuses on global management as a necessary complement to increased globalization of business. We hope that professors and students around the world will find that these discussions enhance understanding of the global management process. Inevitably our own backgrounds are at least partially reflected. Readers should remember this influence and reflect on their own differing international experiences. In a field as diverse and rapidly changing as international business, the best managers are those who can draw on the expertise of others as well as their own experiences and understanding.

ACKNOWLEDGMENTS

There are many people who contributed to this book directly or indirectly. Without the help of our colleagues, family, friends, and students, the book could never have been completed. These people have advised and encouraged us, and for this we owe them a great deal of gratitude. There are too many people to thank everyone individually, but we would like to identify some individuals who have been especially helpful in the process of bringing this book to fruition—Fran Adore (Thunderbird) for administrative assistance, Maria Foss (Thunderbird) for assistance in preparing bibliographies, Stephen Harper (Emory University) who authored Chapter 4, Aaron Marcotte (University of Windsor) for help with exhibits, Martin Meznar (Arizona State University West) for help preparing Chapter 6. The staff at Blackwell Publishers has also been very helpful in the process of publishing this text and we owe them all a great deal of thanks.

We gratefully acknowledge the assistance of the following individuals who reviewed the manuscript:

J. Kline Harrison
Wake Forest University

Nancy Napier
Iowa State University

Deniz S. Ones
University of Houston

William P. Anthony
Florida State University

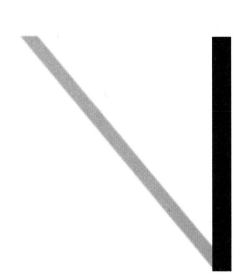

PART ONE

THE GLOBAL PICTURE: UNDERSTANDING THE INTERNATIONAL MANAGEMENT ENVIRONMENT

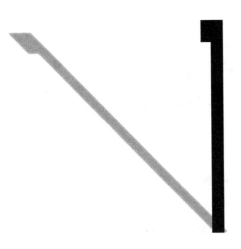

GLOBAL

MANAGEMENT:

AN OVERVIEW

3

LEARNING OBJECTIVES

IN THIS CHAPTER YOU WILL EXPLORE:

- The meaning of international business
- The history of international management
- Some current events which affect international managers
- Some likely developments in international management
- The complexity of today's international management environment
- Major forces that have shaped today's international firms
- National origins of international firms
- Stakeholder groups affected by international business
- Attributes of effective international managers
- The importance of culture in managing internationally

KEY DISCUSSION TOPICS:

- The early history of international business and trade
- The role of the new world in international business development
- The development of the Commercial Era of international business
- The Industrial Revolution's impact on international business and management
- The role of the colonies and concessions in the evolution of international business and management
- The rise of nationalism and its impact on international managers
- The emergence of today's multinational firms
- The changing nationality of international firms
- The changing actors in the international management play
- The need for cross-cultural understanding in international management
- How to develop international management expertise

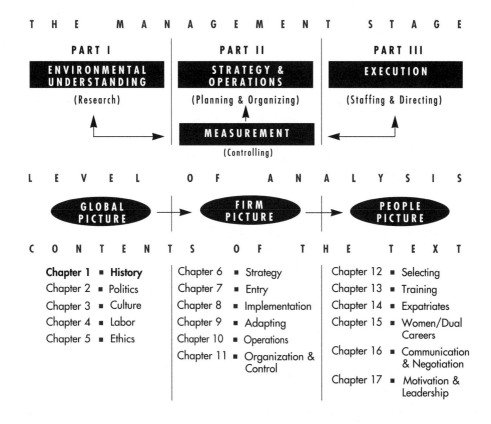

THE MANAGEMENT STAGE

PART I	PART II	PART III
ENVIRONMENTAL UNDERSTANDING	**STRATEGY & OPERATIONS**	**EXECUTION**
(Research)	(Planning & Organizing)	(Staffing & Directing)

MEASUREMENT
(Controlling)

LEVEL OF ANALYSIS

GLOBAL PICTURE → FIRM PICTURE → PEOPLE PICTURE

CONTENTS OF THE TEXT

Chapter 1 ▪ History
Chapter 2 ▪ Politics
Chapter 3 ▪ Culture
Chapter 4 ▪ Labor
Chapter 5 ▪ Ethics

Chapter 6 ▪ Strategy
Chapter 7 ▪ Entry
Chapter 8 ▪ Implementation
Chapter 9 ▪ Adapting
Chapter 10 ▪ Operations
Chapter 11 ▪ Organization & Control

Chapter 12 ▪ Selecting
Chapter 13 ▪ Training
Chapter 14 ▪ Expatriates
Chapter 15 ▪ Women/Dual Careers
Chapter 16 ▪ Communication & Negotiation
Chapter 17 ▪ Motivation & Leadership

INTRODUCTION

This chapter introduces the world of international and global management. A brief discussion of the historical development of international business management places the current state of the multinational company in perspective. Business and management across national and cultural boundaries have taken place for centuries; however, in the last half of the twentieth century the importance and complexity of international business has increased dramatically, and international firms now represent a major force in the world. As one looks to the future this can be expected to remain the case. International management is likely to grow in importance, and become global through the 1990s and the twenty-first century.

HISTORICAL DISCUSSION OF THE GLOBAL MANAGEMENT ENVIRONMENT

Managers throughout the ages have faced many challenges in international business interactions. This discussion of these challenges and how the environment has changed over time is divided into two periods. The period prior to 1900 is considered in one section. This is clearly an enormous period of history to cover in a few pages; thus the details are limited. The discussion of the twentieth century is more detailed, but still gives only an overview of events.

BEFORE 1900

International business may seem to be a recent development, but business has been international for a long time. The ancient Egyptians, Greeks, and Phoenicians all traded with foreigners, and encountered many of the same obstacles that present-day managers encounter—such as differences in language, culture, customs, and expectations; varying forms of government; and difficult transportation. In spite of these obstacles, there is evidence of extensive trade between nations as early as 3000 B.C.

Some 2,000 years ago Herod built the port of Caesarea Maritima. This served as a major east-west trade route with Byzantium and Rome, which were as much as 60 days away by sail. The harbor handled local products like wine, flax, and grain, as well as exotic products, like silk and spices, that were brought to the port from Asia by caravan. Imagine the management challenges associated with coordinating shipping schedules with the arrival of products from Asia and the purchase of local products. Caravans and sailing ships could not follow exact schedules and communication with either was very difficult. (See Hohlfelder, *National Geographic*, February 1987, for a more complete discussion.)

Closely tied to trade in silk and spices in Asia was the movement of jade. Kunlun, the original "jade mountains," were Asia's sole source of jade from prehistoric times until the 1700s. The camel caravans travelling west on the Silk Road carrying Cathay's fabrics to the Middle East passed through Kunlun. As truckers do today, they sought other cargo for the trip west and packed heavy jade boulders more than 2,000 miles to the emperors' workshops in Beijing. Marco Polo observed in 1272 that "chalcedony and jasper, which are carried for sale to Cathay, . . . form a considerable . . . commerce." (See Newman, *National Geographic*, September 1987, for a more extensive discussion.) The management challenges must have been considerable over such enormous distances with no quick means of communication. International traders also faced a host of dangers as they left home in their caravans, and the world outside was largely unknown—they constantly had to expect the unexpected.

The early Olympic Games also provide evidence of the extent of international business in earlier times. Held between 776 B.C. and 394 A.D., descriptions suggest a meeting that was part sport, part religion, and largely commerce. People travelled from all the Greek city states (each the equivalent of a small independent nation), as well as from other countries, to attend the Games every four years. Local entrepreneurs offered goods and services of all kinds— some aimed at the very wealthy, who would attend with a large contingent of servants and attendants, some aimed at the poorer visitors camped in makeshift tents. Goods and services ranged from cheap trinkets to expensive jewelry, from high-class prostitutes to prophecies of the future. Not unlike an international trade show today, this meeting provided merchants, entrepreneurs, and salespeople from all over the region an opportunity to show off their wares while making valuable contacts with people with whom they might do business in the future.

An international aspect of commerce generally developed when products available in one location were desired in other areas and where people in one location had particular skills and other local advantages. Essentially this is also true today and international business continues for most of the same reasons that it began thousands of years ago.

1500 to 1900

The discovery and exploration of the New World in the late 1400s and 1500s was fuelled by Europe's desire to facilitate trade with the Far East. The Dutch and the English, as well as other Europeans, began building worldwide business empires during this period, and these were well established by the 1700s and 1800s. The British East India Company, for example, was chartered in 1600, and soon after had established a number of foreign operations.

In North America, the first English joint stock company (the Company of Adventurers, which became the Hudson's Bay Company) was formed in 1670. This company grew out of a conviction that the way to Cathay would be found by means of a Northwest passage via Canada's Hudson's Bay (Rich 1958). When Sir George Simpson, the overseas governor of the Hudson's Bay Company, attended a state dinner in Oslo during a European tour in 1838, he was toasted as "head of the most extended Dominions in the known world—the Emperor of Russia, the Queen of England and the President of the United States excepted." This was an appropriate tribute, given that the Hudson's Bay Company encompassed nearly three million square miles, and the company's trading posts once reached from the Arctic Ocean to Hawaii and its influence far beyond that. (See Newman 1987 for a more complete discussion).

These early international businesses relied largely on trade, but there was some foreign investment among American companies beginning in the 1700s. These foreign branches were relatively short-lived until 1868, when Singer Sewing Machine built a factory in Scotland. During this period there was "a widespread expectation, especially among those engaged in commerce, that free trade would bring to an end the era of despotism and war. Merchants trading internationally were inclined to see themselves, and to be seen by others, as agents of an "individualistic and progressive liberal revolution" (Jones 1987, p.1).

The period from 1500 to 1850 has been described as the "Commercial Era" (Robinson 1964). It began with the age of the great explorers which followed Columbus's voyage to the New World. International trade during this era was very much a function of individual entrepreneurs seeking personal fortunes in distant lands. These men risked much, but the rewards were also great as they purchased exotic goods (precious metals, spices, silk, slaves) that could be sold at huge profits at home.

The Commercial Era was characterized by a close relationship between European monarchs and entrepreneurs. Once the European royalty recognized the profit potential of overseas ventures, they wanted direct involvement in order to share in the returns. Further, they used their influence to ensure maximization of profits. This resulted in the formation of the great chartered companies such as the Dutch East India Company, the Levant Company, the British Royal American Company, and the Hudson's Bay Company, which

Bev Burowicm

were granted exclusive trading rights as well as the right to perform consular functions (make alliances, appoint governors, and deploy troops).

During the period following 1850 to the end of the nineteenth century there was a shift from an emphasis on exotic goods to industrial products and an increased European influence around the world. The Industrial Revolution had changed the nature of the European enterprise and businesses sought secure and cheap sources of raw materials overseas. New business empires were built on the basis of these industrial products. By the middle of the nineteenth century a number of large-scale European-based investments had been established around the world, as shown in Exhibit 1.1.

EXHIBIT 1.1

INTERNATIONAL TRADING COMPANIES OF THE COMMERCIAL ERA AND THEIR COUNTRY OF ORIGIN

British Royal American Company (England)

Compagnie Francaise des Cent Associes (France)

Company of the East Indies (France)

English East India Company (England)

Dutch East India Company (Netherlands)
also known as Vereenidge Oost-Indische Compagnie

Dutch West India Company (Netherlands)

English United East India Company (England)

French East India Company (France)

General Company of the Trade of Brazil (Portugal)

Hudson's Bay Company (England)

Royal Company of Havana (Spain)

Royal Company of San Fernando of Seville (Spain)

Royal Company of Barcelona (Spain)

Royal Guipuzcan Company of Caracas (Spain)

The increasing number of Europeans participating in foreign ventures as well as the importance of these investments to the home economies encouraged home governments to become involved in colonial rule. Colonies became more and more dependent on foreign investment and foreign rule, and industrial and political domination became prevalent.

European investors found that local skills were often inadequate for running their enterprises. European enterprises therefore provided their own management, skilled workers, and technicians. This increased the dependence of the colonies on foreign owners. In sum, by the late nineteenth century, European influences dominated local politics, economics, and cultures in many areas of the world.

THE TWENTIETH CENTURY

While international management has been needed and accepted through the ages, there has been an explosive growth in international companies during the twentieth century, particularly during its second half.

1900 to 1950

When this period began, Western enterprises continued to assume paternalistic responsibilities in their host countries. These enterprises were increasingly based in the United States as well as Europe. Host countries often granted major concessions to the Western investors and some companies became virtually all-powerful and all-providing. Typical of these concessions were the early oil concessions in the Middle East and United Fruit's agreements in Central America, as detailed in Exhibit 1.2.

The companies provided housing, health and sanitation services, finances, education, distribution of food and other goods, transportation, and protection for their workers—all services that governments often could not provide, and were therefore happy to accept from foreigners. This dependence on foreigners seemed to Westerners to be accepted by their hosts, but rising nationalism and economic development began to take place in the 1930s.

EXHIBIT 1.2

UNITED FRUIT'S CONCESSIONS IN LATIN AMERICA

- Exemption from certain taxes and duties
  —abatement on capital equipment and process materials

- Relaxation of certain regulations
  —leeway granted on requirements to clear all foreign earning through currency controls
  —special arrangements to avoid various laws and regulations intended to prevent the monopolization of land
  —right-of-way over national lands for the construction of a railroad and the use of building materials
     found on national lands

- Right to purchase land at very low prices

Kepner Jr., & Soothill (1963, p. 209) describe these concessions as enabling banana producers such as United Fruit to dominate and control "banana production and export, railroads and radio, docks and steamships, and many phases of life of the several nations where it operates."

(May & Plaza 1958, p. 214).

A new sense of national identity combined with improved economic conditions would eventually signal the end of this era. In addition, during the Great Depression of the 1930s, many companies began to replace high-priced home nationals with trained locals and to cut back on the services they had previously provided. This encouraged local governments and businesspeople to seek independence—both political and commercial—from their colonial masters.

The 1950s and 1960s

This period was characterized by increasing hostility toward Western enterprises and antagonism toward foreign interference in local affairs. The emergence of a desire for sovereignty and self-government encouraged countries to seek independence from their former colonial masters. They also exercised their new freedom by imposing restrictions on foreign enterprises.

This was a period of instability because of the many changes in the political arena, and because many newly independent countries were in fact ill-equipped to run their internal affairs effectively. This instability did not discourage international business, however, because many companies found new opportunities around the world following World War II. In fact, it was a period of major global expansion for businesses, and during this period multinational companies, as we think of them today, emerged. Businesses began seeking both markets and productive inputs around the world, and the idea of global rationalization (producing different components in different parts of the world to achieve efficiency and cost-effectiveness) became popular. The war had encouraged the development of worldwide communication and transportation systems, as well as the development of new technologies. These developments all contributed to the pressures for businesses to take a global view of operations.

Following World War II there was an enormous pent-up demand for all types of goods and services, which fueled the development of international businesses. Activities undertaken by the U.S. government, such as the Marshall Plan to help reconstruct the European and Japanese economies, encouraged the United States to be outward looking, and U.S. firms to take a global view. In addition, U.S. firms had the capital for investment at this time. These factors combined during the 1950s and 1960s, prempting U.S. firms to embrace international business.

The multinational corporation became largely an American phenomenon in this period. There were European firms that were multinational, but U.S. firms dominated the international business scene. During this time, U.S. foreign direct investment rose from about $12 billion in 1950 to almost $80 billion in 1970.

Initially, these American companies were becoming international for defensive reasons, largely to overcome trade barriers that were widespread in the 1950s. This changed as they developed international expertise, and by the 1960s companies were aggressively seeking out international opportunities. Many seemed to feel a need to develop a global strategy if they were to remain competitive.

In the 1960s, other countries amassed sufficient capital to join the move to international expansion. By 1965, large non-American companies were investing in foreign countries at about the same annual rate as U.S. companies, and foreign direct investment in the U.S. was increasing. The Europeans were first to follow the U.S. lead, but the Japanese were not far behind. Rowthorn (1971), reported that between 1957 and 1967, Japan was the leader in international growth, followed by continental Europe, with Canada, the U.S., and the United Kingdom substantially behind.

The 1970s and 1980s

By the 1970s, some of the glamor of internationalization had worn off. This was combined with increased host government hostility toward foreign investment, which led to a period of American divestment in the early 1970s. This hostility was aimed particularly at U.S. companies, probably because they had been successful but were often culturally insensitive, believing that "the American way was the right way." American companies adopted a more wary approach to foreign operations than they had in the 1960s. Between 1971 and 1975 American companies sold almost ten percent of their subsidiaries. In addition, there was a substantial decline in the number of new subsidiaries being formed (Rose 1977).

During the same period Japanese companies were increasingly aggressive in their internationalization, and increasingly successful in selling their products in foreign markets. The mid-1970s through the mid-1980s was also a period of increased investment by foreigners in the U.S. From 1975 to 1983, U.S. investment outside its borders increased by 84 percent, while foreign investment in the U.S. increased by 280 percent.

A different shift in ownership was also occurring, which made it more difficult to identify and compare directions of investment. A number of companies were becoming truly global, and, as such, their shares were sold on stock markets around the world. Individuals and organizations investing in these markets were also increasingly global—Japanese were investing in U.S. markets, Americans were investing in European markets, Australians were investing in Association of South-East Asian Nations markets. Consequently, ownership could no longer clearly be identified as U.S. or Canadian or French, and so on.

Along with these developments, other changes are now occurring, such as the appearance of multinationals from third world countries, global alliances, and international debt-financed takeovers.

ACTORS IN THE INTERNATIONAL MANAGEMENT PLAY

An interesting way of looking at developments in global management during the second half of the twentieth century is in terms of the actors involved.

Robinson (1984) described the development as moving from two main actors to three, then four, and progressing to a multi-actor environment, as illustrated in Exhibit 1.3.

EXHIBIT 1.3

ACTORS IN THE INTERNATIONAL BUSINESS ENVIRONMENT

TWO-ACTOR STAGE

TIME PERIOD	World War II to 1955
KEY PLAYERS	Firm and foreign constituencies
CHARACTERISTICS	U.S. companies dominant
	National foreign investment policies in process of formulation
	U.S. viewed at forefront of management and technological developments

THREE-ACTOR STAGE

TIME PERIOD	1955 to 1970
KEY PLAYERS	Growing importance of host governments
CHARACTERISTICS	Countries newly independent
	Rise in nationalism
	Host governments sensitive to potential loss of power associated with foreign investment
	Japanese and European firms entering international arena

FOUR-ACTOR STAGE

TIME PERIOD	1970 to 1980
KEY PLAYERS	Growing importance of home governments
CHARACTERISTICS	Home governments seek to limit and prescribe appropriate company activities
	U.S. companies retrench

MULTI-ACTOR STAGE

TIME PERIOD	1980 onward
KEY PLAYERS	Special interest groups, international agencies, economic alliances
CHARACTERISTICS	Greater complexity. Need for awareness and assessment of changing global perspectives

Two main actors participate in the international management play from World War II through 1955. The major players were the firm itself and its foreign commercial constituencies (its customers, suppliers, and partners). This was a period of relative simplicity for the company undertaking foreign transactions, and arrangements were made with the interests of essentially these two parties to consider. For example, if a Canadian firm set up a Brazilian joint venture to supply footwear for sale in Canada, the main concern was to structure a business agreement that was mutually beneficial and satisfactory to both partners.

U.S. companies were dominant during the postwar period. Europe and Japan were under reconstruction following the war, and U.S. technology, machines, and consumer goods were in great demand. Many of the less-developed countries (LDCs) were not yet independent. National policies on foreign investment in most countries were in the process of formulation, and those regulations that did exist were poorly implemented. These factors combined to give the multinational company, particularly the U.S. multinational, a great deal of power.

Also, during this period, the success of the U.S. multinationals meant that American management was seen as the embodiment of good management. American firms were at the forefront of technological and management developments, and around the world other companies sought to copy American approaches. It is interesting to note that many of today's Japanese management approaches were adapted from American methods that were seen as particularly effective during the 1950s.

During the period from 1955 to 1970 **a third actor** became important: the host government. Many countries were newly independent, there was a rise in nationalism, and host governments were increasingly sensitive to the potential loss of power associated with foreign investment. New regulation of foreign business resulted, and this regulation was often stringently enforced. The Canadian firm dealing with a Brazilian partner was likely to find that the concerns of the Brazilian government now had an impact on the kind of arrangements that could be made. For example, the government might require a certain percentage of the Canadian partner's profits to be reinvested locally.

Japanese and European firms were now entering the international arena and communist governments were offering assistance to newly independent countries. The power base that had previously made U.S. companies virtually invincible was quickly eroding. No longer could multinationals expect to be successful by considering only the objectives of the firm and its commercial constituencies; the objectives of the host government had to be factored in as well.

From 1970 to 1980 there was a growing importance of home governments, and, thus, **a fourth actor** for international managers to consider in international business agreements. The interdependence of national economies was becoming clear and the home governments recognized that the activities of their multinationals could have a major impact at home. These home governments now sought to limit and prescribe the appropriate activities for companies. This made the situation far more complex because the multinational's decisions in foreign locations were now being questioned and regulated by a government that did not have any clear authority in the foreign location. The Canadian firm might now find the Canadian government seeking to regulate the company's activities in Brazil. For example, operations in Brazil could be seen as taking jobs out of Canada and limits might be set on the quantity of footwear that the Canadian firm was permitted to import into Canada.

A major concern that illustrates the role of the four actors is extraterritorial enforcement of laws. A United States firm (actor #1) can find a foreign partner and reach a mutually acceptable agreement with this partner (actor #2) that the host government (actor #3) finds satisfactory, and yet the U.S. government (actor #4) might object to the agreement. For example, imagine that the U.S. government prohibits U.S. companies from shipping certain chemicals to Iraq, but Jordan does not have the same requirements regarding shipments to Iraq. A U.S.–Jordanian joint venture is subject to Jordanian regulations, but the U.S. government could enforce U.S. regulations outside of the U.S. through pressure on the U.S. partner.

The **multi-actor** international business stage incorporates a variety of different interest groups, all of which consider that the activities of multinational companies affect their members. This is the environment faced by international managers today. Many groups whose membership transcends national boundaries—special interest groups (focusing for example, on environmental, racial, religious, or ethnic issues), international agencies, and economic alliances, among others—should be taken into account by the international firms of the late twentieth century.

These special interest groups have often developed a certain degree of political power, and firms can be hurt by ignoring their demands. Environmental groups around the world, for example, have influenced businesses, headquartered at home or elsewhere, to incorporate "green" issues into international strategic decisions. Similarly, other ethical issues, such as worker exploitation, may be addressed by special interest groups. The Canadian firm might now face questions associated with its impact on the rain forest in Brazil or its exploitation of children in its factories.

This latest stage is one of great complexity, where the balance of power is often not clear, and may be shifting almost continuously in response to current events around the world. To be successful in such an environment, international managers need to be aware of changing global perspectives and to assess how these may affect their firm's activities constantly.

MANAGEMENT IN THE CURRENT GLOBAL BUSINESS ENVIRONMENT

To appreciate the challenges to international managers in the current environment, we will consider some recent world developments and their impact on international business, and look at the need for effective global management. In particular, we'll look at cross-cultural interactions as a challenge to global management, and at ways to develop effective global managers.

RECENT DEVELOPMENTS

Predicting the future is a risky business and generally the responsibility of fortune tellers and soothsayers. This discussion does not attempt to predict the future. It is possible, however, to consider some of the major trends in the world and ask what these mean for international managers and what impact they are likely to have on management in coming years. For example, demographic information can be used to predict the makeup of certain populations in the future. These predictions then serve as a guide for businesses making decisions about the future.

The number of issues that could be discussed in terms of the future of global management is immense. We will consider only a few. (For a broader discussion, see *Megatrends 2000*, by John Naisbitt and Patricia Aburdene, *History of the Future: A Chronology*, by Peter Lorie and Sidd Murray-Clark, *Reinventing the Future: Global Goals for the 21st Century*, by Rushworth Kidder, and issues of *The Futurist*.) Exhibit 1.4 identifies some predictions from Naisbitt and Auberdene's *Megatrends 2000*. International managers find such predictions interesting, and they can be useful; however, they need to be tempered by other information and the manager's own judgments. Naisbitt, for example, predicts an abundance of natural resources. Many people would disagree with this. The manager needs to assess carefully the basis of such a prediction to decide on its likelihood.

Here are some other events likely to influence international managers in coming years.

Increasing speed and efficiency of global communication makes it possible to envision offices in the future that are vastly different from offices in the past. No longer is it necessary for all employees to be physically located in the same place; some employees can work just about anywhere and still be instantly in touch with others. This has implications for both large and small companies.

For some organizations, the concept of a headquarters could potentially disappear if companies have instead a network of communication across the globe. For small companies, global participation is possible without the previous overhead expense of coordinating activities from a central location. This supports a suggestion on the future of American firms in *The Futurist* that mid-sized operations are vanishing as changing market conditions favor companies that are either very large or very small (Cetron, Rocha, & Lucken 1988).

The impact of increasing speed and efficiency of communication on the management of international businesses is illustrated by one entrepreneur who lives at a farm in Vermont and runs a $7 million-a-year consulting business in Palo Alto, California. The business began by selling overseas, via a joint venture, and soon had more than 20 subcontractors around the world, from one-person shops to huge corporations, doing everything from project management to product design, packaging, and distribution. (*The Economist*, 4–10 March 1989, p. 19).

Another issue that is likely to affect international managers in the 1990s and the twenty-first century is the environment. Environmentalists and conservationists argued throughout the twentieth century that humans would not survive for long if they ignored their impact on the environment. Some effects of continuing pollution and dwindling natural resources are being felt now on a personal basis by people around the world. These effects include difficulties in disposing of toxic wastes, erratic weather conditions attributed to the

---

EXHIBIT 1.4

JOHN NAISBITT'S TEN "MILLENNIAL" MEGATRENDS

- Global Economic Boom of the 1990s - Free of the limits on growth known in the past, with an abundance of natural resources.

- Renaissance in the Arts - Arts will replace sports as society's dominant leisure activity during the 1990s.

- Emergence of Free Market Socialism - Eastern Europe heading in three directions: political pluralism, free-market economics, and, in the longer term, integration with Western Europe.

- Global Lifestyles and Cultural Nationalism - Intermingling of cultures to produce a homogeneous culture countered by small groups trying to maintain their cultural identity.

- Privatization of the Welfare State - A move from the welfare state to private ownership and private provision of services.

- Rise of the Pacific Rim - The role of the Pacific Rim countries in the global economy is expected to continue increasing.

- Women in Leadership - Women have reached a critical mass in the professions and business and their leadership role is becoming more important throughout society.

- Biotechnology - Rapid advances in biotechnology promise desirable changes but pose important ethical problems.

- Religious Revival - Religious belief is seen to be intensifying as it did a thousand years ago, and this is expected to influence all events in the coming decades.

- Role of the Individual - New technology, such as personal computers, fax machines, and cellular telephones, allows individuals the freedom to function on their own and thus make them less subject to societal pressures.

SOURCE:
From Megatrends 2000 by Naisbitt, and Aburdene. Copyright © 1990 by Megatrends Ltd. Printed by permission of William Morrow & Company, Inc.

greenhouse effect, a shortage of landfill sites for garbage disposal, and growing concern over cancers associated with chemicals in the air and food, among
others.

Consumers are increasingly being faced with choices like that posed by Lee
Iacocca in 1989: "Cheap gas or clean air—pick one. You can't have both. Not
in a consumer economy like ours, anyway" (Iacocca 1989).

If the evidence continues to mount that humans will not survive unless greater
attention is paid to damage to the environment, then it is likely that more and
more people will consider this a serious issue and factor it into their purchasing and business decisions. Environmental damage is not contained by national boundaries; therefore companies need to assess their global operations relative to environmental issues. These issues provide opportunities and challenges for international companies. There are opportunities to develop new
products and services that deal with the problems; for example, Naisbitt says
"The trend is moving sharply away from the throwaway convenience culture
that produces mountains of trash daily" and "One by-product of the trend:
As household trash-sorting proliferates, residents will be looking for new types
of kitchen and outdoor receptacles suitable for specific types of trash"
(Naisbitt 1989).

There are also many challenges associated with overcoming environmental
damages created by past and current operations. Jim MacNeil, former
Secretary General of the World Commission on Environment and
Development, says that public awareness and concern are at the highest level
ever recorded throughout the world. This awareness and concern has forced
environmental issues to the top of political agendas "in all of the major capi-
tals of the world, in the U.N., in regional bodies like the OECD, OAU, and
ASEAN, in the World Bank and other multilateral banks, and in many of the
companies listed in the Fortune 500" (MacNeil 1990, p. 48).

Concern with the environment as well as concern about other social issues has
resulted in increased calls for global regulation of social responsibility. Many
people believe that social responsibility cannot be left up to individual companies because too many companies may ignore their responsibilities. There
have been various attempts within the United Nations at regulation of multinational companies to ensure that they behave in ways that would be consid-

ered socially responsible from a global point of view. The United Nations has recently given high priority to establishing an appropriate Code of Conduct for Transnational Corporations (TNCs) through the United Nations Commission on Transnational Corporations (UNCTC). During the 1980s, there were attempts within the U.N. system to secure effective international arrangements for the operation of transnational corporations to promote TNCs' contribution to national developmental goals and world economic growth while eliminating or controlling their negative effects (Carasco & Singh 1989).

Multinational companies would generally prefer to regulate themselves than be regulated by outside bodies, and to keep outside regulations to a minimum. To the extent that managers can show that international business activities are undertaken within the framework of global social responsibility, outside agencies are less likely to intervene. At the same time, some regulation appears to be inevitable, and international managers need to be involved in developing this regulatory framework as well as maintaining awareness of the likely impact on operations. Exhibit 1.5 illustrates the benefits associated with a code of conduct for international companies, from the U.N. viewpoint.

EXHIBIT 1.5

BENEFITS ASSOCIATED WITH A CODE OF CONDUCT—U.N. VIEWPOINT

1. It would, most important, establish a balanced set of standards of good corporate conduct to be observed by transnational corporations in their operations and of standards to be observed by governments in their treatment of transnational corporations.

2. It would help ensure that the activities of transnational corporations are integrated in the development objectives of the developing countries.

3. It would establish the confidence, predictability, transparency, and stability required for expanded growth of foreign direct investment in a mutually beneficial manner.

4. It would, therefore, contribute to a reduction of friction, conflict, and painful disruption between transnational corporations and countries and permit the flow of foreign direct investment to realize its potential in the development process.

5. It would, as a consequence, encourage positive adjustment through the growth of productive capacities.

(United Nations 1987)

Changing political ideologies and affiliations are also likely to influence international managers over the next decade and beyond. The struggle between the ideologies of capitalism and communism was a major force in many of the developments of the twentieth century; both those that can be considered positive (space exploration) and those that most people see as negative (development and proliferation of nuclear weapons).

The 1980s closed and the 1990s began with an array of changes that many people found difficult to comprehend:

- Eastern European countries abandoned communism and sought ways to privatize industry and move to a capitalist economy, but many groups within these countries wanted to retain communist approaches.

- The Berlin Wall was demolished and East and West Germany reunited; this was hailed with praise yet caused hardships for many people.

- North and South Korea engaged in their first formal talks since the Korean war, and there was both optimism and pessimism as to the probable outcome of this overture.

- The USSR voted itself out of existence; this led to a larger number of smaller countries with changing allegiances.

- A U.N.-backed group of allies, including the U.S. and its NATO allies as well as most of the Arab countries, fought a successful high-technology war against Iraq.

- Israel and its Arab neighbors entered into face-to-face talks.

The news was not all good. For example, Australia, Europe, Japan, North America and, in fact, most countries of the world faced a major recession; there was growing concern over the plight of the homeless and the poor; rivalry among ethnic groups in Eastern Europe resulted in violence and civil war; thousands of children around the world died each day from starvation and mistreatment; the Chinese government suppressed thousands of student-led demonstrations calling for democracy.

Clearly, the 1990s began with a world in a state of change and these changes will have a major impact on how business is done worldwide. International companies are particularly affected by the global political climate and managers need to monitor and analyze these changing relationships.

The Economist (March 4-10 1989, pp. 19–20) described "tomorrow's companies" as operating in a world of unprecedented uncertainty. The evidence seems to indicate that the international environment is likely to become more complex and uncertain. The management answers to this uncertainty, according to *The Economist*, are "flexibility, responsiveness, adaptiveness, born of new—especially information-based—technology" and "mastering new technologies—and new forms of organization to go with them."

The successful international manager in today's environment is someone who can deal effectively with a complex and uncertain environment. In order to do this, the manager must constantly monitor and assess the environment, and be ready to change strategy to fit the changing environment.

In the 1960s, Marshall McLuhan coined the phrase "global village" to describe the contemporary world. The ease of communication and travel, taken for granted today, links virtually all of the world and makes the world seem like a village in many ways. At the same time, the world remains one of war, conflict, and misunderstanding between and among nations and cultures. Recent events in places such as the former Yugoslavian Republic or the former USSR remind the world of the continuing presence of bitter ethnic and cultural divisions. These are important for international managers to consider. To be effective in this environment, managers must be sensitive to perspectives that bind the world together and those that push people apart.

THE IMPORTANCE OF EFFECTIVE MANAGEMENT IN INTERNATIONAL BUSINESS

International managers are not the only people to deal with a complex and uncertain environment. It is likely that all managers, to some extent, face these challenges. International business is, however, by its nature complex and uncertain.

International business is often defined as doing business across national boundaries. International management, then, is managing business activities across national boundaries. Factoring national boundaries into the management process makes the process more complex and uncertain than otherwise. Consider the following illustrations of this increased complexity and uncertainty:

- Nations use different currencies. Business activities across national boundaries often involve several currencies and the conversion of these currencies from one to another. Currency values change, sometimes rapidly and unpredictably. International managers need to understand the implications of these different currencies for their activities to make appropriate decisions.

- Nations have varying trade incentives and barriers. Businesses that cross boundaries may be able to take advantage of incentives and must deal with barriers. These incentives and barriers can change and may also be subject to negotiation. International managers need to assess the impact on their ability to do business in various locations as well as on the firm's profits.

- Nations have different political and administrative systems. Business activities across borders are affected by the political system in each location as well as by the interplay of politics between locations. International managers need to be able to function within a variety of systems, and to manage the risks associated with different political ideologies.

- Cultures vary from country to country. Business activities in different countries take place in the context of these cultural variations. Management approaches that are effective in one location may not be so in another. International managers need to understand and appreciate cultural differences and be able to interact effectively with others who may see the world in unexpected ways.

It is the added complexity and uncertainty facing international managers that makes it so important to develop effective managers for international firms. Cross-cultural understanding is one of the most important challenges faced by international managers.

CROSS-CULTURAL UNDERSTANDING: A MAJOR CHALLENGE TO EFFECTIVE GLOBAL MANAGEMENT

The Economist (December 7, 1991, p. 64) discusses the question of culture relative to managers in Europe and makes the following points.

- In France, bosses tend to be Napoleonic. They are graduates of elite schools and are expected to be brilliant technical planners—equally good at industry, finance, and government. Stiff hierarchies discourage informal relations and encourage a sense of "we" and "they" that expects subordinates to respond to orders from higher up. This is in contrast to the situation in Italy, which is more flexible, and rules and regulations are often ignored. Informal networks of family and friends are important. Decisions are made secretively. What happens in a formal meeting can be less important than what happens before or after it.

- Germans like to go by the book. Board members have years of technical training and higher degrees. Most managers stay within their special fields throughout their careers. This is in contrast to the British, who identify future top managers early and send them rapidly through all departments of the firm to gain a broad overview of operations.

These contrasts illustrate a major challenge for international managers. As managers move from country to country, they inevitably encounter different ways of doing things. The contrasts discussed above are between countries that are relatively similar in geographic location, economic development, market structure, and so on, and managers from these countries have interacted for hundreds of years. Imagine how much greater the contrasts if one considers, for example, Australian and Saudi managers, Canadian and Chinese managers, or U.S. and Japanese managers.

Dealing with the cultural differences that managers encounter around the world is a major challenge because people are naturally ethnocentric. That is, people believe that the way things are done "at home" is the best way. This naturally leads to the assumption that when things are done differently they are not as good. Professor Richard Steers, in an address to the Academy of

Management, reported overhearing an American manager in Japan asking "Why do you drive on the wrong side of the road in Japan?" This clearly illustrates the assumption that different is somehow wrong. International managers need to develop the ability to accept different as simply different. The American manager above might consider the following approach: "In the U.S. we drive on the right, in Japan they drive on the left. I wonder what explains this difference."

DEVELOPING PRODUCTIVE GLOBAL MANAGERS

The complexity of international business resulting from interactions and transactions across national borders means that global management expertise is crucial to international firms. A study by Kobrin (1988) suggests that there was an increased demand for international expertise in North American firms but that fewer Americans and Canadians were gaining this expertise through foreign work experience. This suggests an ever-increasing need for colleges and universities to emphasize international aspects of management in business programs.

Professor Richard Steers, in his presidential address to the Academy of Management (entitled "The International Challenge to Management Education") in 1989, argued that global management education is particularly important in training students for today's business world. He referred to the fact that the U.S. is losing its competitive and technological edge to other countries and quoted John Young, CEO of Hewlett-Packard, as saying, "if business schools do nothing other than to train their students to think internationally, they will have accomplished an important task."

Studying global management is the beginning of the process of developing productive and effective international managers. Being a productive and effective manager requires both knowledge and experience. There is much that cannot be taught in the classroom; therefore, students should consider this book a starting point in their understanding of international and global management.

Authors (e.g. Lane & DiStefano, 1988) suggest that effective international managers need to:

- accept that knowledge and perceptions are influenced by cultural background

- be able to avoid pre-judgements about others

- accept others' questioning of their beliefs

- be able to communicate respect for different ways of behaving

- show empathy for the feelings of others

- be flexible and sensitive to cultural differences

- be able to listen to others

- be willing to admit a lack of understanding

These are skills that can be proposed in class and in text, but they can only be fully developed over time and through practice. Developing global management expertise is an ongoing endeavor in which managers constantly learn and improve.

SUMMARY

A great proportion of business management today is global, and managers face a complex and uncertain environment. This makes the study of global management both interesting and worthwhile. While complexity and uncertainty characterize today's global management environment these factors have been part of international business since the very early ventures; the explorers and traders who followed Columbus to the New World had little idea of what to expect. Throughout history international managers have been successful if they were ready to adapt to new situations and new cultures. These managers have been willing to face this uncertain and complex environment because of the rewards it offers, in terms of both economic and personal success.

This chapter has explored the development of international business over time, the various forces acting on international firms in the past and present, and the current role of global managers. The chapter concluded with a discussion of the attributes of effective global managers, and some thoughts on gaining international management expertise.

DISCUSSION QUESTIONS

1. Review your local newspaper for the past week and select a local story that has been featured during that period. Suppose you were a foreign investor considering investment in your local area, how would this news story would influence your perception of the attractiveness of the local environment?

2. Select a local store for investigation. Examine a variety of items in this store and identify their country of origin. Discuss the implications of your findings for managers at this store.

3. Identify a major international event that has occurred in the past six months. Discuss how this is likely to influence managers considering doing business abroad.

REFERENCES

Averitt, R.T. 1975. "Time's structure, Man's strategy: The American experience," in H.F. Williamson (ed.) *Evolution of International Management Structures.* Newark, Delaware: University of Delaware Press.

Carasco, E. & J.B. Singh. 1989. *Working Paper*, University of Windsor.

Center, J. "Where America was a century ago—History as a guide to the future." *The Futurist*, January–February 1990, pp. 22–28.

Cetron, M.J., W. Rocha, & R. Lucken. "Think big or think small." *The Futurist*, September–October 1988, pp. 9–16.

Copeland, L. & L. Griggs. 1985. *Going International—How to Make Friends and Deal*

Effectively in the Global Marketplace. New York: New American Library.

The Economist. "Schools brief: The Business of Europe." December 7, 1991, pp. 63–64.

Iacocca, L. "The high cost of backsliding on oil conservation." Reprinted in *Inside Guide.* Toronto: Inside Guide Magazine Limited, Fall 1989.

Jones, C.A. 1987. *International Business in the Nineteenth Century.* New York: New York University Press.

Kepner Jr., C.D., & J.H. Soothill. 1963. *The Banana Empire.* New York: Russell and Russell.

Kidder, R.M. 1989. *Reinventing the Future: Global Goals for the 21st Century.* Cambridge, MA: MIT Press.

Kobrin, S.J. 1988. "Expatriate reduction and strategic control in American multinational corporations." *Human Resources Management,* 27:1, pp. 63–75.

Lane, H.W., & J.J. DiStefano. 1988. *International Management Behavior.* Scarborough, Ont.: Nelson Canada.

Lorie, P. & S. Murray-Clark. 1989. *History of the Future: A Chronology.* New York: Doubleday.

MacNeil, J. 1990. "A threatened future and sustainable development." *Inside Guide.* Toronto: Inside Guide Magazine Limited, pp. 47–48.

May, S. & G. Plaza. 1958. *The United Fruit Company in Latin America.* New York: National Planning Association.

Naisbitt, J. "Technology fuels revolution in marketing." Reprinted in *Inside Guide.* Toronto: Inside Guide Magazine Limited, Fall 1989.

Naisbitt, J. & P. Aburdene. 1990. *Megatrends 2000.* New York: Morrow.

Newman, P.C. 1985. *Company of Adventurers.* Vol. 1. Markham, Ontario: Penguin Books Canada.

"Three centuries of the Hudson's Bay Company: Canada's fur-trading empire." *National Geographic,* 172, 1987 (2).

Company of Adventurers, Vol. 1, 1985. Markham, Ontario: Penguin Books Canada Ltd.

Rich, E.E. 1958. *The Publications of the Hudson's Bay Record Society*. Vol. 1. London: The Hudson's Bay Record Society.

Robinson, R.D. 1964. *International Business Policy*. New York: Holt, Rinehart & Winston.

"Background Concepts and Philosophy of International Business from World War II to the Present." *Journal of International Business Studies*. Spring–Summer 1981.

Ronen, S. 1986. *Comparative and Multinational Management*. New York: John Wiley & Sons.

Rose, S. "Why the multinational tide is ebbing." *Fortune*, August 1977, pp. 111–120.

Rowthorn, P. 1971. *International Big Business 1957–1967*. London: Cambridge University Press.

Steers, R.M. 1989. "The international challenge to management education." *Presidential Address to the Academy of Management Annual Meeting*.

United Nations. 1987. *General reflections on the Code of Conduct*. New York: United Nations.

Wilkins, M. 1970. *The Emergence of Multinational Enterprise: American Business Abroad from the Colonial Era to 1914*. Cambridge, MA: Harvard University Press.

Williamson, H.F. (ed.). 1975. *Evolution of International Management Structures*. Newark, Delaware: University of Delaware Press.

GLOBAL

MANAGEMENT

IN THE CONTEXT

OF POLITICS

LEARNING OBJECTIVES

IN THIS CHAPTER YOU WILL EXPLORE:

- A range of government-business relationships

- Various types of national government philosophies and ideologies

- The host country's view of foreign firms

- The potential for conflict between the host government and foreign firms

- Reasons for host country policies relative to foreign firms

- Power relationships among parties affected by foreign investment decisions

- The meaning and nature of political risk

- The political risk management process

- Varying approaches to political risk management

KEY DISCUSSION TOPICS:

- A variety of business systems and forms of government

- Current political changes and their impact on international opportunities

- The need for managers to understand potential conflict in international decisions

- Various host country policies for attracting and restricting foreign investment

- Factors that influence a firm's bargaining position

- The assessment and management of political risk

- Making judgments reflecting the political risk environment

- When defensive and integrative techniques are most effective

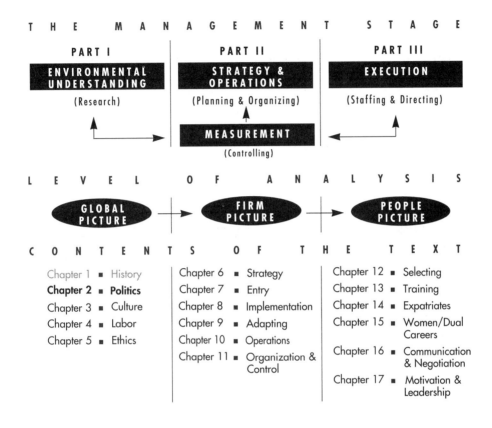

THE   MANAGEMENT   STAGE

PART I	PART II	PART III
ENVIRONMENTAL UNDERSTANDING	**STRATEGY & OPERATIONS**	**EXECUTION**
(Research)	(Planning & Organizing)	(Staffing & Directing)

MEASUREMENT
(Controlling)

LEVEL   OF   ANALYSIS

GLOBAL PICTURE → FIRM PICTURE → PEOPLE PICTURE

CONTENTS   OF   THE   TEXT

INTRODUCTION

International companies, by definition, operate across national boundaries, doing business in more than one country. Managers in international companies, therefore, have to understand different political and regulatory systems. They need to consider the impact of these systems on operations. The political environment provides both opportunities and drawbacks and is an important component of global management.

Managers in companies that are primarily domestic relate to a political system that is relatively familiar and well understood by them. However, international managers may face a number of unfamiliar political environments. The global company may even find itself the brunt of discriminatory practices in certain foreign locations. Managers in these companies must assess the possibility of discrimination and decide how they will deal with risks associated with foreign political systems.

This chapter focuses on the concept of political risk, and assessing and managing such risk. As background, we explore general business–government relationships that managers may encounter and their changing nature. Management interactions with governments are then considered. Various types of political risk are identified and specific models of political risk management presented.

GOVERNMENT-BUSINESS RELATIONS

Much of the discussion of global management assumes that countries permit private ownership and free enterprise. In fact, this is not always the case—sometimes governments prohibit some or all private ownership and free enterprise. It is important for managers to be aware of the major types of national governments that currently exist, and understand how these influence government–business relationships.

Governments can be divided into three groups: capitalist, socialist, and communist. It is important to note that the world is currently undergoing major changes in political ideologies and the classification of various political systems is changing. Nevertheless, the distinctions in viewpoint among capitalist, socialist, and communist countries are helpful in understanding the variation in business–government relationships that managers may encounter.

Capitalism is most familiar to Americans because the American system is based on the capitalist beliefs of free enterprise, a market-based economy, and the private ownership of the factors of production. The government provides necessary services that are not provided by the private sector.

The basic element of this philosophy is the primacy of individual rights and freedoms. This primacy implies the rights of individuals to enter into agreements with other individuals concerning the production and consumption of goods and services. It also means that each individual has a right to her/his own preferences, provided they do not impinge on the rights of others.

This sounds appealing, but there are limits to these rights. The government may restrict certain things "for the good of the people" (restrictions on smoking in public places is one example), and individual preferences are sometimes controlled (such as a preference for heroin).

Socialism is prevalent in Europe and many less developed countries (LDCs). This system of government combines public ownership of the basic means of production with private ownership of other factors. The basic element of this philosophy is the need for government control of those industries that directly affect the well-being of the people. The belief rests on evidence that a free market often does not provide for the unfortunate. This is appealing because it provides for the less fortunate in society, but government interference with market forces often tends to distort supply and demand, and may cause problems in the availability of goods and services.

Communism is currently followed in the People's Republic of China (PRC) and a variety of other countries. Until the breakup of the Soviet Union, communism was also found in the USSR and most of Eastern Europe. This system believes in government ownership of most, or all, factors of production.

The basic element of this philosophy is the need for a centrally planned economy to ensure that all citizens benefit equally from the country's output. The government is supplier as well as market in such a system, and makes the decisions regarding the country's needs. This is appealing to those concerned with ensuring equality for all, but the inefficiencies created by such a system are apparent in the disparities between supply and demand.

POLITICAL SYSTEMS AND GOVERNMENT-BUSINESS RELATIONSHIPS

Governments may be seen as falling along a spectrum, with communism at one extreme, capitalism at the other, and degrees of socialism in between, although all countries have some elements of socialism in their government–business relationships. The closer to communism, the more limited the role of private business; the closer to capitalism, the greater the role of private business.

In countries at the communist extreme, foreign companies have relatively limited access to markets, and trade and investment are tightly controlled.

In countries at the capitalist extreme, foreign companies have relatively free access to markets and trade, and investment are relatively open.

These systems change over time, so one cannot expect countries to maintain the same government–business relationships over long periods of time. Particularly in the early 1990s there are signs of major shifts in these relationships. Many communist countries are undergoing economic and political changes. Countries that previously embraced communist ideals (Poland, for example) are moving to a capitalist approach to private ownership and free enterprise. Even countries that adhere to the principles of communism (the People's Republic of China, for example) are liberalizing their control of private business. These events suggest an expansion in international business opportunities in the coming decades.

These three categories are helpful in understanding the types of government interactions that managers can expect based on the ideology of the country. There is always some role for government in business and therefore some interaction between managers and government representatives. The largest role for government can be expected in communist countries, and doing business in such countries consistently requires interactions with the government.

These generalizations are not always as clear-cut in reality as they are conceptually. In any country stated ideology and actual practice can differ. In China, for example, private enterprise flourishes in parts of the country while it is heavily regulated in other locations. In the United States, private enterprise is desirable but foreigners are not always welcome. Managers doing business in foreign environments need to examine both stated ideology and practice.

RELATING TO HOST GOVERNMENTS

Managing an international company inevitably involves interactions with government representatives in foreign locations. These interactions can be time-consuming and frustrating because the multinational corporation's (MNC) managers and the foreign government often see the same situation very differently. We will discuss some of the reasons for the different viewpoints and make suggestions for improving relationships.

The MNC's objective in its international activities is to establish operations that fit its overall strategy and provide a reasonable return in a relatively risk-free environment. The host government's general objective, relative to the MNC, is to gain a positive contribution to its development objectives. MNC activities can, thus, be a major concern to the host government and it may consider it necessary to regulate, at least partially, their activities.

These general objectives need not be in conflict, though differing views of a particular situation can lead to conflicts. The effective international manager wants to understand the government's objectives and find ways in which mutually beneficial operations can be established and carried out.

To achieve agreement with the host government and achieve global corporate objectives, the MNC manager needs to consider why the same situation may appear different to the two sides. The following discussion illustrates, in general terms, how the host government's view of a typical MNC investment may clash with the view of MNC management.

MNC MANAGEMENT VIEW

Typical investment by an MNC can be seen as positive. Management thinks of it as essentially beneficial to the host country. The following are some benefits the MNC manager might identify.

Capital for Growth and Development

MNC management sees the company providing needed capital, through investment, which contributes to its host's development objectives. Ambitious growth plans require capital to achieve. Often, this capital cannot be generated internally and has to be attracted from abroad.

Technology for Modernization

MNC managers often see themselves as providing the access to needed technology which most countries want. Often, advanced technology cannot be developed locally and needs to be acquired from abroad.

Skills for Local Industry

MNCs often provide needed expertise and skills, as well as training for local workers. Many countries lack sufficient numbers of people with business know-how, managerial expertise, and technical skills. It may be easier to import these skills and learn from foreign experts rather than develop them internally.

Access to Foreign Markets

MNCs can provide entry into controlled markets. MNCs often exert a fair amount of control over markets that small developing nations find difficult or impossible to enter on their own. Even sizable countries can find it difficult to access markets that are controlled by large companies.

Positive Contribution to Balance of Trade

MNC management sees the firm as having a positive effect on the host's trade balance. The MNC's products or services may be substitutes for imports or they may be exported, thus contributing either to decreased imports or increased exports.

Provision of Employment

MNC management sees local operations providing employment for host-country nationals at various levels, and may provide opportunities for employment in other MNC locations and at headquarters. Many developing countries have chronic high unemployment and any creation of employment should be beneficial. More prosperous countries also see employment creation as positive.

Provision of Foreign Exchange

MNCs provide increased foreign exchange through investment and export earnings. Many developing countries have limited amounts of the foreign currencies they need to pay for their imports, so the provision of foreign exchange may be crucial to trading relationships. Better-developed countries also see attracting foreign capital as beneficial in many cases.

Tax Revenues

Managers in MNCs believe that their companies contribute to host-country revenues. MNCs are subject to local corporate taxes and tariffs, and their employees (both local and foreign) pay income taxes. All of these payments contribute to government revenues.

Development of Entrepreneurs

MNC management believes they provide an example for host-country managers and a starting place for host-country nationals who are potential entrepreneurs. This may be particularly important in developing countries that lack skilled local managers and entrepreneurs.

From this vantage point, MNC investment appears extremely positive, and many MNC managers are surprised that they are not always welcomed and treated as benefactors by host governments. A look at how the government may view the situation illustrates some of the reasons.

HOST VIEW

The host government may see foreign investment as potentially providing the benefits outlined above, but may also see a negative side to the investment, as explained below. (These negative aspects are often magnified if the host is a developing country.)

Increased Dependence

The provision of needed resources (capital, technology, and expertise) sounds positive but can be seen as increasing dependence on foreigners. For example, many developing countries believe they need to develop their internal abilities rather than relying on others. Further, MNCs may be seen as aligned with the host-country's elite, and thus likely to retard social change by supporting the status quo.

The better-developed countries also have concerns, as can be seen in the case of Canada. Canada has always depended on outside interests for much of its economic development. During the period of rapid economic growth that followed World War II, this outside contribution was particularly extensive. In manufacturing and other key sectors, such as energy, foreign-controlled companies expanded their role, sometimes controlling as much as 75 percent of a particular industrial sector. The Canadian public's concern over the consequences of this situation resulted in the federal government setting foreign investment guidelines, followed by the establishment of the Foreign Investment Review Agency (FIRA) in 1974, and restrictions in the energy sector through the National Energy Program (NEP) in 1980.

These controls were highly publicized by the government and media, and were met by hostile foreign reactions and a drop in investment. A change in public attitudes in Canada, as well as a change in government, resulted in FIRA's replacement by Investment Canada in 1986, and an extensive campaign to persuade investors that Canada was "open for business."

Decreased Sovereignty

The provision of needed resources and consequent dependence on MNCs translates into a loss of control by the host government. Many countries, particularly small ones, feel that large MNCs can have a major, possibly dominant, and even harmful impact on their economic, social, and political systems. For example, encouragement of consumption, imposition of western values in place of traditional ones, or support of a particular political party may be seen as potentially harmful.

Consider the following comments by the Commonwealth Secretariat:

> Equity capital comes mainly through transnational corporations, whose size and economic power pose difficulties for small states in their relations with them. In terms of bargaining power, negotiating skills and access to relevant information, small states are usually seriously disadvantaged in dealing with these firms. Their economic strength tends to give the corporations considerable political influence which in some instances they have used in order to wrest special concessions, for example, favourable adjustment in tax regulations.
>
> Small states have endeavoured to alleviate some of the constraints of size through regional co-operation. In the Caribbean, Southern Africa and South Pacific, a number of these states participate in regional arrangements which extend beyond economic co-operation (Commonwealth Secretariat 1985, p. 21).

Increased Exploitation

MNCs are often seen as using up nonrenewable resources, repatriating profits rather than reinvesting them, excluding locals from valuable local resources, and generally profiting at the expense of the local community. In addition, MNCs may make new products or services available locally. This can increase consumption, and decrease local savings and investment.

The Commonwealth Secretariat's comments also illustrate this view:

> Another threat is from unscrupulous foreign business firms and 'adventurers' that are attracted to the tourist industry and off-shore financial activities on which small states increasingly rely to secure economic progress. The heart of the problem is the weak power and administration of small states and the encouragement these economic activities give to corruption, fraud, commercial crime, drug trafficking, prostitution and political interference (Commonwealth Secretariat, p. 35).

Inappropriate Technology

In many cases, the technology provided by MNCs is seen as being either outdated or too advanced. Sometimes it seems that an MNC is getting rid of its old technology by sending it to the host; in other cases, the newest technology is transferred even though the host does not have the expertise to utilize it properly. LDC hosts believe that many MNCs pay little attention to the real needs of the country from a technological point of view, and that technology is seldom adapted to local needs.

Displacement of Local Firms

Local firms may feel that they cannot compete with the MNC and may forgo local investment. At the extreme, this can mean a flight of local capital to foreign investments. Moreover, when unemployment is a concern, some governments believe that local investments would have been labor intensive, while foreign investments are capital intensive, thus the net impact of foreign direct investment (fdi) on employment is actually negative.

Outflows of Foreign Exchange

The apparent foreign exchange benefits from investment and exports can be more than offset, over time, by payments for imported machinery and parts, and repatriation of profits through dividend payments and other intrafirm transfers.

Looked at in this light, one can acknowledge that host governments have reasons to be cautious about foreign investment. If managers understand the concerns of the host, then they are in a better position to interact successfully with host-government representatives.

Different viewpoints are particularly obvious in interactions between MNCs and LDC hosts, probably because development objectives are of special importance to LDC governments. This means that negotiations with these governments may be especially time-consuming. It also means that identifying how the firm will contribute to LDC objectives can be a critical aspect of negotiations with LDC governments.

MIXED RELATIONSHIPS

The host wants the potential contributions of fdi—economic benefits of improved trade balances, increased employment, more foreign exchange, as well as increased power and prestige—but fears the potential negative consequences such as loss of sovereignty, technological dependence, and foreign control of key economic sectors. This results in a variety of host-government policies designed both to attract and confine MNCs. These usually take the form of incentives and restrictions. Exhibit 2.1 identifies the major incentives and restrictions in place in many countries. The manager needs to understand the purpose of these incentives and restrictions because they provide both opportunities and challenges for the firm.

The manager wants to minimize the negative impact of restrictions that the host government imposes and to maximize the benefits associated with incentives. The firm's local activities must conform to local regulations and restrictions, yet there is often room for negotiation.

EXHIBIT 2.1

TYPICAL GOVERNMENT
INVESTMENT INCENTIVES & RESTRICTIONS

INCENTIVES

Tax Holidays
Exemption from Duties
Tax Incentives
Monopoly Rights
Provision of Buildings
Low-Interest Loans

RESTRICTIONS

Local Ownership
Local Content
Local Personnel
Local Training
Location
Profit Repatriation
Foreign Exchange Use

The outcome of any negotiations is partially a result of the strength of each side. The strength of each side depends on how much each party needs the other and how much control each side can exert on the other. At one extreme, if a company feels a particular location is very important to its overall operations and the host has many other companies interested in locating there, the host will be strong and the company in a relatively weak position. In this situation, the company must be willing to accept most of the terms demanded by the host.

At the other extreme, where the host is anxious to attract the firm and the company has many other countries interested in it, the host is in the relatively weak position. In this situation, the company can largely dictate the terms of its investment. In most situations each side has certain strengths and weaknesses, and the negotiating skill of each side becomes very important.

The strength and bargaining position of a firm also is influenced by its home government and the relationship between the home government and the host government. A positive relationship between the two governments is likely to smooth negotiations, whereas a negative relationship may complicate issues. The likelihood of the home government supporting the firm in case of unwanted political activities, and the influence the home government can have on the host are additional factors to consider.

The interests of the home government often coincide with those of its MNCs. This is because the profit a firm earns overseas is returned to its home-country shareholders in the form of dividends and capital appreciation. Employees in the home country can also benefit from foreign operations because a profitable firm can pay higher wages. In turn, the home country benefits generally through increased taxation. Insofar as their interests are seen as compatible, the MNC can expect support from the home government.

The concerns regarding home-government influence are seen in the following case in which the overall economic interests of the home country and the MNC seem to coincide, although there is some opposition as well.

> Concern has been expressed in the Bahamas, that the neighbouring super power has attempted to exercise extraterritorial jurisdiction by compelling Bahamas-based corporate financial entities with branches in the United States to disclose information on their commercial operations, contrary to the banking laws of The Bahamas and in open breach of accepted concepts of national sovereignty. Banking is such a central segment of The Bahamas' economy that such actions could constitute a threat to the continued survival of its role as an off-shore banker (Commonwealth Secretariat, p. 29).

A decision to invest in foreign locations may be seen as not investing at home, and certain groups will be negatively affected by this decision. For example, jobs will be created in the host country rather than at home, foreign suppliers may be chosen over domestic ones, and prices of certain goods may change. Those groups feeling the adverse effects will push for home-government restrictions on MNC activities.

The government and people of the home country often expect the firm to act in the best interests of the nation rather than in the best interests of the firm. This can lead to demands by the home government which conflict with the MNC's preferences, particularly if the home government tries to control the activities of MNC subsidiaries for political reasons. The situation can become very complex for the subsidiary caught between conflicting laws and politics, as the following incident illustrates.

In the early 1980s the U.S. government wanted to impose restrictions on exports of technology-intensive products to the USSR in retaliation for the Soviet's activities in Afghanistan. This was relatively easy to accomplish with exports from the U.S. but more difficult when it was expanded to include subsidiaries of U.S. firms operating in Europe. The European hosts insisted that the subsidiaries located in their nations comply with host regulations and policies, not with those of the home country. The subsidiaries were left in a situation where any action would antagonize one or another government.

POLITICAL RISK

The need to deal with different political systems and integrate the objectives of the firm, the host government, and the home government results in substantial uncertainty in foreign operations. A particular concern of international managers is the political risk associated with foreign activities. Political risk includes a variety of factors, ranging from government confiscation of a firm's assets to government encouragement of negative attitudes toward foreign businesses. To encompass this wide range of factors, political risk can be defined as the possibility of unwanted consequences of political activity; political risk is the uncertainty associated with political activities and events. Three major categories of political risk companies face are forced divestment, unwelcome regulation, and interference with operations.

FORCED DIVESTMENT

Forced divestment occurs when a government wishes to acquire the assets of a company against the company's will. At worst, the host government may confiscate company assets—that is, take them over with no compensation. Alternatively, the host forces the company to sell its assets to local interests, usually the government itself. Forced divestment can take the form of expropriation (usually the takeover of one firm) or nationalization (generally the takeover of an entire industry). Such action on the part of a government may occur for a variety of reasons; the government may believe it can make better use of the assets; it may believe that acquisition of the assets is beneficial to the government's image; or, for defense or developmental reasons the government may want control of specific assets.

Forced divestment is legal under international law as long as it is accompanied by prompt and equitable compensation. Such a takeover does not involve the risk of a total loss of assets unless the assets are confiscated by a host government. Greater risks are that the payment will be less than what the company considers equitable, that the payment will be in nonconvertible currency or non-negotiable government bonds, and that the loss of a particular subsidiary will affect the rest of the organization's operations.

These are important risks, but, in fact, the occurrence of unwanted takeovers is relatively low in comparison to total foreign investment. Forced divestments rose during the 1970s and peaked in 1975–76 but have declined through the 1980s, and some countries have reprivatized industries that were previously nationalized. Companies should be aware of the possibility of forced divestment and its consequences, while recognizing its relatively low occurrence.

UNWELCOME REGULATION

Unwelcome regulation encompasses any government-imposed requirements that make it less profitable for a company to operate in a particular location. These include corporate or income taxes, local ownership or management requirements, restrictions on reinvestment and repatriation of profits, and limitations on employment and location. Companies expect to have to operate in the context of government regulations, and where these are known and expected they do not constitute risk. It is the unexpected imposition of such regulations that should be considered.

Governments generally impose regulations to increase revenue to the government and to encourage particular aspects of development. When a government's priorities are understood, the purpose of regulations is usually clear. For example, if a government wants to improve local managerial skills, it may impose regulations regarding the employment and training of local managers; if a government is concerned with unemployment, it is likely to establish local employment requirements; if a government wishes to establish a broad-based industrial complex, it may require maximum local sourcing and technology development.

Incidents of unwelcome regulation occur regularly, and companies should be alert to these possibilities. In contrast to forced divestment, governments do not reimburse companies for losses in profitability resulting from the imposition of regulations; therefore, the potential impact of such regulation must be carefully considered.

INTERFERENCE WITH OPERATIONS

Interference with operations refers to any government activity that makes it difficult to operate effectively. This type of risk includes government encouragement of unionization, government voicing of negative sentiments about foreigners, and discriminatory government support of locally owned and operated businesses. Governments generally engage in these kinds of activities when they believe that a foreign company's operations could be detrimental to local development or because they expect these activities to increase their support among important local constituents. Such activities may be seen as improving a government's popularity and thus enabling them to remain in power.

While forced divestment and unwelcome regulations have an immediate and identifiable impact on operations, the activities described as interference with operations may be less obvious and the effects unclear. The effects can have a great impact over time (through lost sales, increased costs, difficult labor relations, and so on); thus, companies should weigh this political risk equal attention.

Understanding the reasons for political activity enables a company to assess the likelihood of a particular outcome, and to devise ways to deal with it. Effective assessment and management of political risk begins, therefore, with an understanding of the risks that companies face and why they occur.

VULNERABILITY TO RISK

Studies suggest (Kobrin et al. 1980; Poynter 1982) that the degree of risk faced by a company is a function of both the particular country and the particular company's operations. Country characteristics—such as type of government, level of economic development, and stability of social and political systems—make a country more or less risky. Company characteristics—such as the industry, technology, ownership, and management—increase or decrease vulnerability to risk. The following are country characteristics that are generally associated with increased risk:

- Government instability

- Economic instability

- Social instability

- War and Revolution

- Terrorism

In general, instability is associated with increased risk. This is because instability implies uncertainty, which implies risk. Frequent government changes, an unstable economy, and social upheavals would obviously all increase a company's business risk in a particular location. Wars and revolution, or the prevalence of terrorism, imply personal and property risks as well as business risks. Where a gap exists (as it does in many LDCs) between what the people expect (particularly in terms of material goods) and what they can access, it may result in hostility toward foreigners who seem to be better off than local citizens.

Although relatively rare, acts of terrorism are especially worrisome to international firms. They may occur anywhere and anytime, usually unexpectedly. For example, in the summer of 1990, the Irish Republican Army struck at the heart of the British financial establishment by setting a bomb inside the London Stock Exchange. Fortunately no one was hurt because warning calls were received and the building was evacuated. In the bombing of a Pan Am flight over Scotland, the passengers and crew were not so fortunate.

Dealing with terrorism is problematic for international firms. The United States and other western countries do not allow companies to make payments for ransom to terrorists, for ethical reasons; however many companies feel that, for ethical reasons, they must protect their employees, and consequently make such payments.

While political factors imply increased risk for many companies, it is also true that certain companies benefit from them, and a fair number are not affected. At the extreme, a company whose business is selling guns or training executives to counter terrorism, benefits from situations that most companies would seek to avoid. Equally, a company that specializes in providing certain material goods at a low cost might be attracted to a location where the expectations/reality gap was high. Other companies are simply involved in businesses that are not particularly affected by changes in government, the economy, or society (for example, a company manufacturing cardboard boxes might fall into this category), and they can, to some extent, ignore these instabilities.

Certain industries appear to be more subject to political risk than others because they are seen as being important to development and the government wishes to maintain control over them. In addition, these industries are often highly visible to the local population so the government can use them as a means to maintain political control. Extractive businesses, and those that use natural resources, banking and insurance companies, as well as companies involved in infrastructure projects (railroads, airlines, or communications) have historically been most affected by direct government intervention.

Companies with complex, globally integrated operations appear to be relatively safe from government intervention. Such operations would be difficult to take over or regulate successfully because the parent company often controls sources of supply or markets, or both. This control makes it difficult for a host government to manage these operations, and also makes it possible for the parent to avoid some of the regulations imposed against it.

High-technology companies and those that have a high research and development expenditure are also relatively safe from government intervention. Local governments would be unable to manage such companies themselves, and effective regulations are difficult to impose. A company with little competition is often in a similar situation because the host government cannot turn to other sources to replace the products or services offered by this firm. The government and country may be therefore quite dependent on this particular firm and unwilling to impose undesirable restrictions for fear that the firm might choose to withdraw.

A company's ownership is also an important component of its vulnerability to risk, because local ownership is usually viewed favorably by governments. Wholly-owned subsidiaries are at risk, while joint ventures with local private partners are less risky. Such joint ventures are seen positively and local partners provide valuable local know-how. In contrast, joint ventures with the government are often more risky, presumably because the government develops the expertise to intervene in operations effectively.

Management makeup is another important consideration. All foreign management has a similar risk to one hundred percent foreign ownership; though total local management is also risky as it implies that there is no need for foreign involvement, and reduces corporate control over subsidiary activities.

The size of a company appears to have a contradictory effect on political risk. On the one hand, a large company attracts attention and may be the target of government intervention, but the large company is likely to be relatively powerful; on the other hand, a small company may be the target because of the ease of takeover or regulation, but it may not provide a politically noticeable event.

This illustrates the fact that the degree of risk in any situation is a function of both the country and the company. In assessing and managing political risk, managers must take both sets of factors into account.

DEVELOPMENT OF A POLITICAL RISK-MANAGEMENT STRATEGY

Formal systems of political risk management are relatively new to international businesses. In 1979, Kobrin found that assessment of political risk in most companies was an informal, subjective activity. Events in Iran in the 1970s resulted in substantial losses for many U.S. companies and this further established the need for a greater awareness of the political risks associated with foreign investments. Events in China in 1989 and in the Middle East during the early 1990s again underscored the need for political risk analysis and management. According to Kate Bertrand, corporate cost-cutting in the 1980s had "put political risk analysts on the endangered species list" (Donath 1990, p. 4), but in 1990 management again welcomed the risk-assessment function.

The initial focus for most companies is the assessment of political risk associated with potential investment opportunities. An equally important focus is the ongoing management of risk, assessing potential risks, then taking steps to minimize the effect of such risks on company operations.

SOURCES OF INFORMATION

Political risk strategies continue to rely heavily on subjective judgments, although risk assessment is increasingly being formalized by international companies. There are a number of methods that can help ensure that judgments are based on the best information available. Political risk assessment usually involves rating a particular location (using a scale from "very risky" to "not risky") on a number of dimensions that represent risk. Information for such ratings come from a variety of sources:

External Sources

Sources that can provide country risk information include banks, consultants, periodicals, and risk services. Each of these may provide different viewpoints so managers may want to utilize several of them. International managers also need to recognize how rapidly the world can change and how quickly information can become outdated. For instance, according to the Political and Economic Forecast Chart presented in *Planning Review* in March–April 1990, Kuwait was given a low or moderate rating for turmoil with a 60–70 percent probability of the Al-Sabah family remaining in power (Coplin & O'Leary 1990). Clearly this situation changed rather dramatically with the Iraqi invasion of Kuwait in August of 1990.

Internal Sources

Sources of information within a company include "old hands" (people with substantial international experience), subsidiary and regional managers (people with firsthand experience of a particular location), and staff personnel (people specializing in political risk analysis). Each of these provides a somewhat different viewpoint, and companies can benefit from comparing input from all of them.

Some sophisticated political risk systems are computer-based and incorporate a wide variety of country and company information, from both internal and external sources.

The Xerox political risk-management system includes the following steps:

- Each Managing Director of a major affiliate prepares a quarterly report listing the ten most salient political issues in the local environment. These issues are analyzed, in terms of their implications for Xerox, and alternative action plans for dealing with them are suggested.

- These reports go to the Operating Vice-President and the Director of International Relations at headquarters, who consider the combined implications of all the reports.

- Decisions regarding responses to political events are made by the Operating Vice-President and the Director of International Relations, incorporating the Managing Directors' recommendations. These decisions are incorporated into the company's annual plans.

Chemical Bank was reported to have a process that incorporates a political spread sheet for a given location. Significant political issues and actors are identified for each location, the actors are evaluated in terms of their stand on issues, their power to enforce a stand, and their degree of concern about it. This overview provides a rating for a given location, as well as details regarding political issues of concern. This spread sheet is completed by local managers and reviewed by headquarters.

The Royal Bank of Canada uses a ranking method to gauge the relative risk it faces in each nation (Bertrand 1990). This ranking covers the country's economic, business, and political environments. To rank a country's economy, the bank's analysts examine the country's economic structure and resources (including natural resources), its recent economic trends and policies, its foreign debt and liquidity, and its short- and long-term economic outlook. Assessing the business environment includes the quality and skills of the labor pool and business leaders, the legislative environment including rules for ownership and taxation, and the financial strengths and competitiveness of the country's top companies. Assessing the political environment involves examining the quality and stability of the government social factors, such as the impact of special interest groups or civil unrest, and its relationships with neighbors, superpowers, and Canada.

Once the bank has all the data, it ranks countries on a scale of 0 (worst) to 100 (best). The bank's Country Review Committee reviews all 80 countries in which the bank does business at least once each year.

DEVELOPING A PROCESS
FOR DEALING WITH POLITICAL RISK

The process for handling political risk comprises both assessment and management of risk. A company should estimate the degree of risk that exists in any situation and decide how to deal with that risk. For example:

- If the risk in a particular location is judged to be very high, the company should expect commensurately higher returns. These returns should be viewed in terms of the total organization, not simply the specific subsidiary.

- If higher returns are not likely to offset higher risks, the company should reconsider that opportunity or find ways to reduce its exposure to risk.

- If the returns are expected to justify the risks, the company will select methods to deal with the identified risks to limit their exposure and minimize their impact.

The political risk-management process consists of the following five steps (Gregory 1989).

Step 1: Identify Risks—The purpose of this step is to identify government policies and activities which could affect company operations. An important aspect of this step is to recognize that different policies and activities can affect different companies in different ways. Companies must concentrate their attention on those most likely to affect their operations.

Step 2: Evaluate Risks—The purpose of this step is to evaluate the likelihood of government policies and activities of interest actually occurring, as well as to determine their specific impact on company operations. Various political risk services provide information on different countries, and these can serve as a basis for estimating political events. Again, different companies, because of their differing operations, affected differently by specific events. Companies must concentrate on those events that are most likely to have the most impact on their operations.

Step 3: Select Management Techniques—The purpose of this step is to decide how to deal with the risks that have been identified. Risks can be reduced, transferred, or avoided altogether through a variety of techniques. Depending on the circumstances, companies will choose the approaches that best protect their most important interests. There are many opportunities in risky situations, but the risk must be recognized and managed. It is sometimes more risky to avoid situations than to pursue them while paying attention to the identified risks.

Many countries provide insurance to protect their own companies from losses incurred in foreign locations due to political events. The Overseas Private Insurance Corporation (OPIC) is a U.S. government agency that insures against risks of expropriation, war, or currency nonconvertibility. Similar insurance is offered in the United Kingdom by the Export Credit Guarantee Department, and in Canada by the Export Development Council. Insurance is provided by these agencies in exchange for the payment of insurance premiums.

Step 4: Implement Techniques—The purpose of this step is to put into action those techniques identified as most appropriate for a particular company. This turns risk management from analysis to action. It may not be possible to adopt all the preferred techniques, and it may be necessary to make trade-offs at this stage. Companies should insist on the approaches that protect their competitive strengths and be willing to forgo others.

Step 5: Evaluate Success—The purpose of this step is to evaluate the effectiveness of the company's political risk management. This step provides the opportunity to reassess the likelihood of various risks and to appraise the effectiveness of the risk-management techniques that have been adopted. Political risk management should be an ongoing process because the political situation embodies change. Companies that are aware of their political environment are in a better position to avoid the effects of unwanted political activity.

MANAGING VULNERABILITY TO RISK

There are basically two types of approaches to managing political risk: *defensive* and *integrative* (Gregory 1989). Defensive approaches are intended to protect a firm's strengths by reducing its dependence on any single subsidiary. Integrative approaches are designed to make a firm an integral part of the host society to protect its strengths. The two approaches are quite different and most companies use them in combination.

DEFENSIVE APPROACHES TO POLITICAL RISK MANAGEMENT

Defensive approaches generally rely on locating a crucial aspect of the company's operations beyond the reach of the host. This is intended to minimize the firm's dependence on the host, or to make it costly for the host to intervene in operations. The following is a summary of the major defensive techniques that companies employ.

Financial techniques:

- Maximize debt investment; minimize equity investment. This implies that negative host government actions will affect creditors more than the company itself.

- Raise capital from a variety of sources (including host government, local banks, international institutions, local customers and suppliers, third country institutions). This implies that a variety of parties will be affected by any unwanted government actions and the government is less likely to antagonize some of these groups.

- Enter into joint ventures with firms from third countries. This spreads the risk among several firms, each of which may have a different influence on the host government.

- Obtain host government guarantees for investment. This gives a company a good bargaining position even though the host may not always live up to these guarantees.

- Minimize local retained earnings. This reduces headquarters' costs on behalf of subsidiaries and dividend payments. Companies legitimately charge their subsidiaries for a variety of services that are provided by headquarters, and it is particularly important that these costs be identified in locations where companies want to minimize retained earnings.

Management techniques:

- Minimize the use of host nationals in strategic positions; limit locals to junior and symbolic positions. This ensures that parent country nationals are in control.

- Train and educate necessary host nationals at headquarters. This promotes an understanding of headquarters' objectives and approaches.

Logistical techniques:

- Locate a crucial segment of the company's process outside of the host. This makes the local enterprise dependent on the parent.

- Divide the production of the same components among several countries. This reduces the company's dependence on a single subsidiary.

- Concentrate R&D in the home country. This increases subsidiaries' dependence on headquarters.

Marketing techniques:

- Control markets where possible (for example, have parent or subsidiaries purchase products from other subsidiaries). This makes it difficult for the host government to take over local operations because it would have no ready-made market.

- Maintain control over transportation. This means that the host would have to develop an independent transportation system if it were to take over the subsidiary.

- Maintain a strong, single, global trademark or corporate image. This makes it difficult for anyone else to attempt to use these corporate symbols.

INTEGRATIVE APPROACHES TO POLITICAL RISK MANAGEMENT

The aim of integrative political risk-management approaches is to make the foreign company an integral part of the host society, in effect, to make it appear local. The company is seen as a good local citizen and intervention in its operations is seen as a threat to the local economy. The following is a summary of the major integrative techniques that companies use.

Management techniques:

- Employ a high percentage of local employees throughout the organization, including in top positions. This gives the subsidiary a local image and provides evidence that the company trusts its local personnel.

- Ensure that expatriates understand the host environment. This serves to avoid situations where personnel from the parent company misinterpret the local situation.

- Establish commitment among local employees. This provides a loyal work force that will react negatively to unwanted government actions.

Government relations techniques:

- Develop and maintain channels of communication with members of the political elite. This keeps the company in contact with political events and allows the company to take appropriate action to avoid unwanted actions.

- Be willing to negotiate agreements that seem fair to the host, and renegotiate those no longer perceived as fair. This ensures that a company is seen as fair and merits being treated favorably.

- Provide expert advice when asked. This helps relations with local governments when foreign companies are willing to provide expertise, *if* asked.

- Provide public services. This bolsters relations if foreign companies provide services such as education, health, or transportation, when appropriate.

Operational techniques:

- Maximize localization in terms of sourcing, employment, and R&D. This serves to enhance the subsidiary's local image and is beneficial to the local economy.

- Use local subcontractors, distributors, and professionals wherever possible. This increases dependence on locals and thus any negative impact from government is felt throughout the local economy.

Financial techniques:

- Raise equity in the host country. This involves local creditors who would consequently be affected by any negative government action. (This defensive approach shifts the risk from the company to local creditors.)

- Establish joint ventures with local participation. This ensures that local interests will be concerned with the subsidiary's success.

- Ensure that internal pricing among subsidiaries and between headquarters and subsidiaries is fair. This reassures host governments who are particularly concerned with MNCs' ability to use internal prices to move profits between subsidiaries. Companies can establish and use objective prices for goods and services to guarantee that these transfer prices are appropriate.

- Establish open reporting systems. This provides access to financial statements and bookkeeping information and can help portray the foreign company and its subsidiary in a positive light to local interests.

CHOOSING THE RIGHT COMBINATION

Both defensive and integrative approaches to political risk management have their advantages and disadvantages. In general, a globally integrated firm will emphasize defensive approaches because they fit into its overall strategy of global integration; a multidomestic firm that sees each of its foreign operations as essentially domestic entities will emphasize integrative approaches. Using largely defensive techniques tends to encourage a global or geocentric view of the firm, while relying on integrative techniques tends to encourage a fragmented and localized, or polycentric view. While certain companies may favor one or the other approach, many firms combine the two.

The specific mix of risk-management approaches that is appropriate depends on the situation and the particular company and the particular country of operations. An analysis of the company's competitive strengths and weaknesses, combined with an analysis of the political environment, leads to decisions regarding a desired mix of defensive and integrative approaches. This is often followed by bargaining with the host government and, finally, structuring corporate activities to reflect agreements reached with the government. This is illustrated in Exhibit 2.2.

A major concern for international managers is to ensure protection of firm-specific advantages. These are the strengths that allow a firm to operate successfully. These strengths vary from company to company, and can comprise a wide variety of attributes. For example, control of a particular technology, a well-known brand name, well-developed distribution systems, well-trained international managers, access to low-cost financing, familiarity with a particular country or region, could all be firm-specific advantages. Once a company identifies which aspects of its activities are most critical to its success, it can decide how to best protect them.

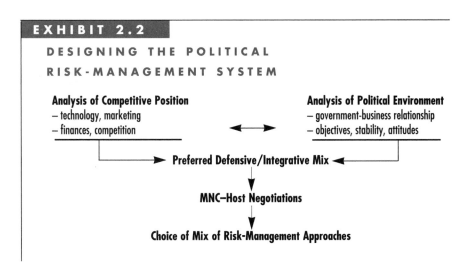

EXHIBIT 2.2

DESIGNING THE POLITICAL RISK-MANAGEMENT SYSTEM

Analysis of Competitive Position
– technology, marketing
– finances, competition

Analysis of Political Environment
– government-business relationship
– objectives, stability, attitudes

Preferred Defensive/Integrative Mix

MNC–Host Negotiations

Choice of Mix of Risk-Management Approaches

The best means of protecting firm-specific advantages depends on the country in question. Which risk-management approach to use depends on both the firm's competitive position and the political environment.

Generally, the more positive the political environment, the more integrative approaches a company is apt to employ; the more negative the environment, the more defensive approaches are appropriate. For example, European companies investing in the U.S. are often thoroughly integrated into the U.S. environment—employing U.S. managers at the highest levels, relying on U.S. sources of supply where possible, carrying out R&D in the U.S., and leaving day-to-day decisions to U.S. managers. These same companies investing in the Far East often employ quite different practices—top managers are European, supplies are coordinated from Europe, local R&D is limited, and day-to-day decisions are carefully monitored. To some extent these decisions are based on the availability of local expertise and resources, but they are also a function of the degree of risk perceived in the particular location.

A company can decide on its preferred means of political risk management but it may not necessarily be able to implement all of its preferred approaches. Negotiation with the host government is often necessary before final decisions can be made about how a company's activities will be structured. In such negotiations, the company must be willing to make concessions without jeopardizing its competitive position. For example, both IBM and Coca-Cola initially chose to forgo investments in India, even though there were attractive opportunities, in order to safeguard their firm-specific advantages.

Contractual agreements are also a part of a company's management of risk. Companies generally try to reach agreements with host interests to minimize the affect of unwanted political activities. These cannot be relied on totally, because the agreements may not be enforceable and there may be no clear mechanism for settling disputes.

SUMMARY

An inevitable aspect of international business is dealing with varying political structures and varying government–business relationships. This chapter presented the main forms of government that firms are likely to encounter as well as typical government–business interactions. These differing systems and interactions, as well as potentially conflicting views of the results of foreign direct investment, result in certain risks for international firms.

Developing an effective strategy for dealing with political risk is an important aspect of successful global management. The political environment a global company faces is complex, and therefore the assessing and managing political risk is not an easy task. Bargaining between firm and host is an integral part of managing political risk, and effective bargaining depends to some extent on understanding the objectives of the other side. Identifying contrasts between the foreign manager's view and the host's view of fdi can contribute to better understanding.

DISCUSSION QUESTIONS

1. "Ethnic differences are often a major component of political risk." Discuss this statement, using recent examples to illustrate.

2. Political parties have traditionally been defined on a spectrum of "left" or "right." Describe what is meant by each of these terms and discuss how parties at the ends of the spectrum generally view the role of business in society.

3. Using your local community as an example, identify the attitudes of local residents towards foreign investment (use local media stories, discussions with students and friends, interviews with local business managers). Discuss how the attitudes you have identified influence the degree of political risk associated with investment in your community.

REFERENCES

Bertrand, K. 1990. "Politics pushes to the marketing foreground." *Business Marketing*, March, pp. 51–55.

Brander, J.A. 1988. *Government Policy Towards Business*. Toronto: Butterworths Canada Limited.

Commonwealth Secretariat. 1985. *Vulnerability: Small States in the Global Society*. London: Commonwealth Secretariat Publications.

Coplin, W.D. & M.K. O'Leary. 1990. "1990 World political risk forecast." *Planning Review*, March-April, pp. 41–47.

Donath, B. 1990. "Coping with trade's dark side." *Business Marketing*, March, p. 4.

Gladwin, T.N. 1982. "Conflict Management in International Business," in I. Walter (ed.), *Handbook of International Business*. New York: John Wiley & Sons, Inc.

Gladwin, T.N. & I. Walter. 1980. *Multinationals under Fire: Lessons in the Management of Conflict*. New York: John Wiley & Sons, Inc.

Gregory, A. 1989. "Political Risk Management," in A. Rugman (ed.), *International Business in Canada*, pp. 310–329. Scarborough, Ont.: Prentice-Hall Canada.

Gregory, A. 1988. "Integrative and Protective Techniques in Reducing Political Risk: A Comparison of American and Canadian Firms in Indonesia," in J. Rogers (ed.), *Global Risk Assessments*, Vol. 3. Riverside, CA: Global Risk Assessments.

Grosse, R. & J. Stack 1984. "Noneconomic Risk Evaluation in Multinational Banks." *Management International Review*, Vol. 1.

Jarvis, M. & F. Kirk, Jr. (eds.). 1986. *Foreign Direct Investment in Canada: The Foreign Investor's Perspective*. International Business Study Group, School of Business, Carleton University.

Kobrin, S.J. 1979. "Political risk: A review and reconsideration." *Journal of International Business Studies*, Spring–Summer, pp. 67–80.

Kobrin, S.J., J. Basek, S. Blank, & J. LaPalombra. 1980. "The assessment and evaluation of noneconomic environment by American firms: A preliminary report." *Journal of International Business Studies*, Spring–Summer, pp. 32–47.

Mahini, A. 1988. *Making Decisions in Multinational Corporations— Managing Relations with Sovereign Governments*. New York: John Wiley & Sons, Inc.

Poynter, T.A. 1982. "Government intervention in less developed countries: The experience of multinational companies." *Journal of International Business Studies*, 13, Spring–Summer, pp. 9–25.

Rogers, J. (ed.). 1986. *Global Risk Assessments: Issues, Concepts and Applications*. Riverside, CA: Global Risk Assessments.

Simon, J.D. 1982. "Political risk assessment: Past trends and future prospects." *Columbia Journal of World Business*, Fall, pp. 62–71.

Weiss, S.E. 1987. "Creating the GM-Toyota joint venture: A case in complex negotiation." *Columbia Journal of World Business*, Summer, pp. 23–37.

Weiss-Wik, S. 1983. "Enhancing negotiators' successfulness." *Journal of Conflict Resolution*, 27 (4) pp. 706–39.

Wells, L.T. 1977. "Negotiating with third world governments." *Harvard Business Review*, January–February, pp. 72–80.

Yaprak, A. & K.T. Sheldon. 1984. "Political risk management in multinational firms: An integrative approach." *Management Decisions*, pp. 53–67.

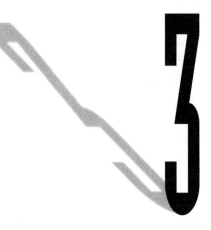

3

THE CULTURAL ENVIRONMENT

LEARNING OBJECTIVES

IN THIS CHAPTER WE WILL EXPLORE:

- The meaning of culture

- The importance of culture to international managers

- Why cultures differ

- Ethnocentric and parochial behaviors

- The importance of understanding the home culture

- Contrasts between the home country and foreign values and customs

- The relationship of culture and behavior

- The identification of important cultural factors

- The role of cultural factors in organizational effectiveness

- Differences between national and cultural characteristics

KEY DISCUSSION TOPICS:

- Reasons for studying culture in global management

- Why ethnocentrism and parochialism occur

- The difference between ethnocentric and parochial behaviors

- Some parameters that influence behavior

- The influence of language, religion, education, social systems, and economic development on global management

- The reasons for focusing on national culture in international firms

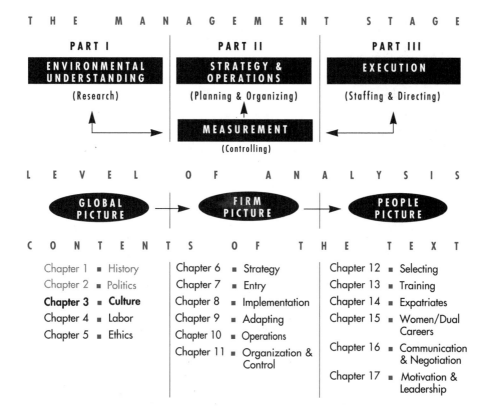

THE MANAGEMENT STAGE

PART I	PART II	PART III
ENVIRONMENTAL UNDERSTANDING	**STRATEGY & OPERATIONS**	**EXECUTION**
(Research)	(Planning & Organizing)	(Staffing & Directing)

MEASUREMENT

(Controlling)

LEVEL OF ANALYSIS

GLOBAL PICTURE → FIRM PICTURE → PEOPLE PICTURE

CONTENTS OF THE TEXT

INTRODUCTION

Gobal business, by definition, takes place across national boundaries. Managers in these businesses, therefore, have to understand and appreciate differences among nations which exhibit varying cultural profiles and environments.

In this chapter the concept of culture is defined, particularly several specific aspects of culture relevant to managers. The aim is to encourage students to be sensitive to the impact of culture on the organization. It will enable students to examine cultural differences and similarities among groups, and to determine how these similarities or differences might affect managers and their organizations.

WHY STUDY CULTURE?

The work of anthropologists, who study culture and its impact on people, is very relevant to international business. Business managers who have worked in foreign locations acknowledge that understanding the culture in those locations is necessary if one is to manage effectively. The main reason for studying culture in the context of global management is that one's management skills improve with an understanding of the cultural influences that affect colleagues and employees.

Virtually all the activities managers undertake are affected by the cultural environment. Organizations establishing and running global operations usually need to negotiate with various foreign constituencies. To be successful in negotiations managers want to understand the cultural background of the people with whom they are negotiating. For example, Graham (1985) described the almost inevitable conflicts that occur between negotiators from Japan and the United States because of their different negotiating styles which stem from their contrasting cultural backgrounds. The Japanese penchant for extensive periods of silence was found to be particularly irritating to U.S. negotiators, who tended to fill the silence by offering concessions that were often unnecessary—clearly illustrating the value of accommodating the "other side's" culture and negotiating style.

Strategic alliances are becoming more common, involving firms with different strategies and objectives. For these alliances to succeed, managers need to understand the cultural factors that influence organizational strategies and objectives. The strategic alliances orchestrated by the United States, through the United Nations, in response to Iraq's invasion of Kuwait, provides an excellent example of the varied cultural groups that may be involved in alliances. Such alliances work effectively only if the parties involved are willing to accept and accommodate the differences they encounter among allies.

Managers in foreign locations frequently find that employees behave in ways that are quite different from the managers' expectations. To lead and manage effectively it is often necessary to understand the cultural expectations that influence people's behavior. Ricks (1983) tells the following story:

An American manager in the South Pacific had hired local employees without using the traditional island status system. By hiring too many of one group, he threatened the traditional balance of power. The islanders talked over this unacceptable situation and came up with an alternative plan. It had taken them to 3 A.M. to arrive at a decision. Because time was not important in their culture, they saw no reason to wait until morning to make their suggestion to the American manager. They went to his residence and woke him. It did not occur to him that they might want to talk business at 3 A.M. Their appearance caused him to panic because he assumed they planned to attack him, so he called in the Marines. Clearly this was a situation where understanding the local culture would have been beneficial.

Expatriates, employees working in a foreign location, find that culture shock can affect their general ability to function well. Cultural understanding and adaptability have been identified as contributing to better expatriation.

One of the authors recently encountered an Irish couple who had gone to Japan when the husband was transferred. The wife believed that the firm had agreed to provide her with an acceptable job. The job was titled "procurement assistant" and entailed, almost exclusively, making and serving tea at various functions—an idea she found unacceptable. The couple found the reality of Japan very difficult to deal with because they didn't foresee the cultural differences. They thought it unlikely that they would remain for the expected period of time.

Various functional aspects of organizations, such as accounting, finance, and marketing, can differ markedly from one location to another. For an organization to be effective overseas, these functional aspects must fit the local culture. The movie *Going International* illustrates this in an encounter between a U.S. manager and a British manager who discover that their bookkeeping systems and accounting procedures differ enough that they cannot interpret one another's financial statements. Among other variations, in the U.S. the number 1,000,000,000 is called "one billion," where in Britain it is "one thousand million."

These examples illustrate the need for cultural understanding in global management. The following sections examine the concept of culture in detail and some specific attributes that can help one understand a different culture.

DEFINING CULTURE

Culture is a concept that is familiar to all of us—books, magazines, periodicals, and newspapers are filled with articles that include the word "culture." It is difficult, however, to specify what is meant by the concept. Anthropologists Kroeber and Kluckhohn (1952) catalogued 164 separate and distinct definitions. This issue is further complicated by the fact that the word "culture" has several separate meanings: it can refer to a shared, commonly held body of general beliefs and values that define what is right for a group (Kluckhohn & Strodtbeck 1961; Lane & DiStefano 1988), or it can refer to socially elitist concepts including refinement of mind, tastes, and manners based on superior education or upbringing (Heller 1988). Culture can refer to artistic output that is particular to an ethnic or regional group, and to describe a medium for growing biological specimens or a product (yogurt culture).

The word apparently originates with the Latin *cultura*, which is related to *cultus*, and can be translated to mean cult or worship. This is helpful in understanding the use of the term for our purposes because members of a cult believe in specific ways of doing things, and thus develop a culture that enshrines those beliefs; culture in this book is used in this general sense. The specific definition used is particularly relevant for international managers. The definition proposed by Terpstra and David (1985, p. 5) delineates what is meant by the word in the global management context:

> "Culture is a learned, shared, compelling, interrelated set of symbols whose meaning provides a set of orientations for members of a society. These orientations, taken together, provide solutions to problems that all societies must solve if they are to remain viable."

There are several elements of this definition that are important to understanding the relationship of cultural issues and international management:

- Culture is learned. This means that it is not innate; people are socialized from childhood to learn the rules and norms of their culture. It also means that when one goes to another culture, it is possible to learn the new culture.

- Culture is shared. This means that the focus is on those things that are shared by members of a particular group rather than on individual differences; and it is possible to study and identify group patterns.

- Culture is compelling. This means that specific behavior is determined by culture without individuals being aware of the influence of their culture. It is important to understand culture in order to understand behavior.

- Culture is interrelated. This means that while various facets of culture can be examined in isolation, these should be understood in context of the whole. A culture must be studied as a complete entity.

- Culture provides people with orientation. This means that a particular group generally reacts in the same way to a given stimulus; so that understanding a culture can help determine how group members might react in various situations.

All this suggests that culture is basic to how people behave. Running any organization in part depends on ensuring that people behave in ways appropriate for the organization. Where cultural differences exist, they must be understood and accommodated in order to achieve desired behavior and results.

The role of cultural differences in cross-cultural business encounters can best be seen through examples of cultural misunderstanding. We have provided these two:

- In India it is considered a violation of sacred hospitality rules to discuss business in the home or on social occasions. At the same time, if a businessman from India offers "come any time," he means it. In the United States this may simply be a polite expression, but in India it represents a serious invitation. The Indian is requesting a visit but is politely allowing the guest to arrange the time of the meeting. If no time is set, the Indian assumes the invitation has been refused.

- An anecdote about an American couple touring Asia illustrates the risks involved when relying on nonverbal forms of expression while in a foreign environment. A wealthy couple, accompanied by their pet poodle, was enjoying a leisurely cruise around the world. At one of the ship's Asian stops, the couple, with their inseparable pet, decided to sightsee the town. After a long walk, they chose to dine at a pleasant-looking restaurant. Since the restaurant employees could not speak English and the tourists could speak no other language, they ordered their meals by pointing to various items on the menu. Knowing the poodle was also hungry, the couple tried to order food for it. For a long time the waiter had a difficult time understanding, but after several attempts he seemed to have figured it all out. He pointed to the dog and then pointed to the kitchen. The couple interpreted this to mean that their pet could not eat in the dining area but must eat in the kitchen where the waiter had some food for it. They therefore agreed to let the waiter take the dog to the kitchen. After waiting a particularly long time, the waiter and the full staff proudly entered with the couple's order. One can imagine the tourists' horror when the chef lifted one of the lids to display how well he had cooked the poodle!

WHY CULTURES DIFFER

The previous discussion suggests that effective global management depends partially on recognizing and accommodating cultural differences found around the world. People who have worked in other countries would concur. Experiencing a foreign culture makes people conscious of cultural differences, even where the cultures are relatively similar (as is the case with Canada and the United States), but it is not immediately clear why these differences exist.

One explanation anthropologists propose is that various cultural preferences develop in order to help a group of people survive. These cultural preferences are seen as the best way to behave because they have contributed to survival in the past; clearly, any other way would not have been as good. Because these are deemed "the best way," they are passed on to future generations and perpetuated long after their initial contribution to survival. If one accepts this explanation, it is easy to see why cultures develop different preferences. Essentially, cultural differences develop because different groups of people face diverse environments and cope with them in different ways. The following examples illustrate some cultural attributes that can be related to earlier survival behavior.

- Western Europeans and North Americans shake hands with their right hands. This has been attributed to a desire to indicate a lack of aggression. Weapons, particularly swords, were drawn with the right hand, thus extending the right hand to shake hands showed that you did not intend to draw your weapon. Groups that did not carry weapons at all or carried different types of weapons did not need this custom.

- Many people use their hands to eat or to use eating implements, such as chopsticks, that are not potential weapons. Others, such as Americans, place their knives on the side of their plates after using them to cut their food. These customs may stem from the fact that animals apparently feel particularly vulnerable when eating, and need to indicate nonviolence at such times. Those who eat with knives, potentially dangerous weapons, need to indicate (by placing them on their plates) that they will not be used against others at the table. Some people adopted nonthreatening implements and did not need to indicate their lack of aggression in the same way.

- People in the tropics often seem, to their neighbors from colder climates, to lack a sense of urgency and appear to put things off for a later time. This may reflect the fact that the seasons do not change. The lack of seasonal change generally means that many crops could be grown all year long and there is less need to plant and harvest by a certain date. In cold climates, in contrast, the seasonal cycles encourage planning and a need to observe deadlines.

- Many groups have rules about what is acceptable food. Pork, for many, is not. This is probably the result of a prevalence of bacteria that (in earlier times) made pork unsafe to eat in certain locations. In other areas of the world where these bacteria were less likely to be found, pork is considered safe and therefore acceptable.

These illustrations do not provide practical guidance in understanding and dealing with different cultures. They help show that differing cultural customs, no matter how strange they may seem, originate from reasonable societal needs. Accepting this basis for cultural differences in all aspects of life is a step toward a better understanding of foreign cultures.

ETHNOCENTRISM AND PAROCHIALISM

If cultural attributes develop as a response to the environment and then become a preferred way of behaving for a group of people, it is not surprising that cultural preferences are associated with "right" and "correct" ways of behaving. Consequently, different ways of behaving are seen as "bad" and "incorrect." If "our way" somehow contributed to our survival, it is hard to accept that "their way" can also be acceptable. This is referred to as ethnocentrism—meaning that the view of our own and other cultures is centered on our own culture, and the belief that our own is superior to others.

When one thinks about it, different ways of doing things are simply different, not negative in the absolute. This is one of the first things that global managers need to accept to understand and adapt to other cultures.

Parochialism is similar to ethnocentrism and can arise when people also assume that the home culture is superior. This assumption of superiority arises not because cultures are compared but because differences are not recognized, and often occurs when someone simply lacks knowledge about other cultures.

Ethnocentrism implies that the belief in the home culture's superiority is conscious, while parochialism implies only that the home culture is seen as superior because little is known of other cultures. Both ethnocentrism and parochialism are common among managers who have to deal with people in foreign locations. Managers need not feel guilty about these attitudes; however, they do need to recognize that they are likely to exhibit either or both, and that these attitudes will inhibit their ability to work effectively in other cultures. Often the first step toward changing these prevalent attitudes is to develop a better understanding of one's home culture.

UNDERSTANDING THE HOME CULTURE

The fact that behavior is influenced by culture is relatively obvious when considering foreign behaviors. Other people dress, eat, interact, communicate, and generally act in ways that are unfamiliar, and this is often explained by their culture. The Japanese may be described as formal by North Americans, Americans can seem impatient to Mexicans, Kuwaitis may appear lazy to Canadians. In all these cases the described behavior characteristic is attributed to a different culture. It is often more difficult to identify the attributes that are part of one's own culture, yet it is important to appreciate them.

To understand how other cultures compare to one's home culture, it is necessary to understand the home culture. This is difficult to do because people are generally not aware of the cultural influences that affect their own values and behaviors. As discussed earlier, people do things the way they do because they believe this is right, and they tend to do them without thinking because they know what's expected.

The very fact that it is difficult to understand the home culture makes it particularly vital to do so. The difficulty implies a need for understanding, and self-understanding promotes sensitivity to how our behavior may be viewed by others. It is also helpful because it provides a base with which other cultures can be compared.

There are a number of approaches that can help in understanding the home culture. One can ask foreigners to describe people from the home culture. One can analyze the home culture in terms of the various cultural characteristics that are used to assess a foreign culture. One can compare and contrast the home culture to other cultures.

Foreigners' descriptions can be very enlightening because they often notice things that locals might never consider. For example, one of the authors was attending a global management class where various forms of greeting (bowing, touching, greeting) were being discussed when a non-American student said that Americans seemed to shake hands randomly, and asked if the Americans could explain when to shake hands. The Americans tried but soon realized that the rules really weren't clear, and therefore it wasn't surprising that it seemed random to a non-American who was not accustomed to the practice. The Americans found it quite enlightening to realize that one of their normal greetings seemed quite strange to others. The following examples illustrate how some foreigners view the U.S. culture.

- People from the Caribbean find U.S. colleagues impatient and rude.

- Canadians find U.S. colleagues driven by work with no time for family and friends.

- Europeans find U.S. colleagues isolated and parochial.

- The Japanese find U.S. colleagues hasty and impolite.

Assessing the home culture as one would assess a foreign culture forces consideration of many things that are taken for granted. For example, asked if religion was a major influence on Canadian culture, students in a global management class generally responded in the negative. When students gave more thought to the issue, they realized that the work week in Canada is largely determined by the Christian sabbath, that many holidays (such as Christmas) are based on Christian customs, that the legal system embodies many Christian beliefs, and so on.

Comparing and contrasting the home culture with other cultures also provides insight about the home culture (and other cultures). Because it is often easier to see how other cultures differ, this can serve as a good starting point. For example, if Australian students think that Chinese students are different because they are quiet in class, this implies something about the students who observed this fact; presumably, Australian students are more likely to speak in class than Chinese students.

It is a good idea to make comparisons with cultures where some differences are quite obvious because this highlights cultural characteristics of the home culture. For example, Japanese and Americans are often contrasted because their differences are readily apparent in some circumstances. It is also helpful to compare the home culture with more-similar cultures. This will identify similar patterns of cultural values as well as more subtle differences. Americans and Canadians provide a good example of cultures that are quite similar but do exhibit some distinct differences.

The Japanese are generally thought of as group-oriented while Americans are individualistic. This contrast in cultural values can be seen in a variety of management practices that differ between the two countries. Americans and Canadians are both individualistic, though Americans are generally seen as being somewhat more so, and they are believed to be somewhat more likely to take risks. These differences are relatively minor, but they affect management practices in the two countries.

Asking how and why we (home culture) behave the way we do increases consciousness of the home culture and an awareness of the impact of our culture on behavior. This provides a good basis for evaluating the home culture, and students should discuss their observations with others to further develop their understanding.

CULTURAL UNDERPINNINGS

The abstract and complex nature of culture makes it difficult to identify and analyze; this examination of culture is therefore simplistic and must be understood in that context. The model depicted in Exhibit 3.1 shows the factors influencing the development of individual values, and their relationship to behavior.

The model consists of the following seven parameters.

1. *National variables*. There is no clear distinction between national and societal characteristics, but national variables are depicted here as the more concrete and observable factors distinguishing one nation from another. National characteristics include such things as laws and regulations, economic conditions, and political ideology. They are generally used to describe an entire nation.

2. *Societal variables*. Tese variables may be shared with people of several nations, and there may be a variety of social groups within one nation. Societal characteristics include ethnicity, language, and religion, among others.

EXHIBIT 3.1

MODEL OF CULTURAL/NATIONAL
VARIABLES & ORGANIZATIONAL BEHAVIOR

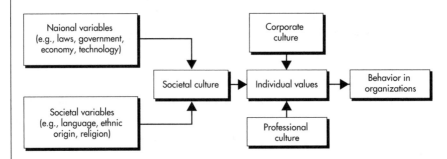

SOURCE:
Reproduced from *Experiencing International Management* with the permission of South-Western College Publishing. Copyright © 1989 by South-Western College Publishing. All rights reserved.

3. *Societal/National culture.* These characteristics, both national and societal, taken together develop a particular societal/national culture. There is a shared set of values that is typical of the people of one nation.

4. *Corporate culture.* The organization (through such characteristics as its leadership, work design, and reward systems) provides a culture of its own. There is a shared set of values typical of the people within one organization.

5. *Professional culture.* The group with which a person associates professionally (for example, accountants, managers, manual laborers) often provides a certain culture of its own. There may be a shared set of values that is typical of people within one professional grouping.

6. *Individual values.* The individual in an organization expresses specific values formed partially by societal/national cultural values

and partially by the corporate culture and the individual's professional culture, as well as personal characteristics.

7. *Behavior*. The actual behavior that individuals engage in depends on their values that are the result of a wide variety of forces.

A complete understanding of behavior in organizations is very complex, and probably impossible. An organization cannot hope to manage all of the variables, though it is possible to assess the relative similarity or dissimilarity of national cultures and deal with the major differences.

ASSESSING CULTURAL FACTORS

An organization considering entering a foreign location should assess a wide variety of cultural factors, and ongoing foreign operations must continually monitor the factors that have an impact on organizational activities. There are a wide variety of factors that could be examined in this context; we will limit our focus to the ones that seem to be of particular importance to organizational effectiveness: language, religion, education, and social systems. In each case, their impact on international organizations is discussed.

LANGUAGE

Language difficulties have been the source of many international blunders, as illustrated by some examples:

- A promotion in Quebec that was supposed to relay "Don't be half-sure, be Ponko-sure," declared instead *"Ne soyez pas DEMI-SUR, soyez PONKO-SUR."* At the root of this translation mishap was the word *"sur,"* which means sure, but if the accent over the "u" is left off, the word takes on the meaning sour. The company, therefore, was saying "Don't be half-sour, be PONKO sour."

- General Motors was troubled by the lack of enthusiasm among the Puerto Rican auto dealers for its Chevrolet Nova. The name Nova meant "star" when literally translated. However, when spoken, it sounded like *"no va"* which, in Spanish, means "it doesn't go."

- Ford encountered translation problems with two of its products. It introduced a low-cost truck called Fiera into some of the less-developed countries. Unfortunately the name meant "ugly old woman" in Spanish. Ford also experienced slow sales when it introduced the top-of-the-line Comet in Mexico under the name "Caliente," which Ford later discovered is slang for "streetwalker."

- When the Coca-Cola Company was planning its strategy for marketing in China in the 1920s, it wanted to introduce its product with the English pronunciation of Coca-Cola. A translator developed a group of Chinese characters that, when pronounced, sounded like the product name. These characters were placed on the bottles and marketed. Sales levels were low—the characters translated to mean "a wax-flattened mare" or "bite the wax tadpole."

Language problems are especially prevalent when using idioms or colloquial expressions. A Canadian working in Afghanistan was somewhat chagrined when she discovered that "out of sight, out of mind" had been interpreted to mean blind and mentally incompetent. Mistakes seem obvious once they are pointed out, yet language is such an integral part of our lives that it is often a challenge to look at it objectively. When a language is not native to any of the people communicating, extra care is necessary in encoding and decoding the message to be sent.

Language plays an important part in people's socialization, and Whorf (1956) described language as defining and perpetuating a particular world view. The important nature of language is illustrated by the belief that one cannot really speak a foreign language until one learns to think in that language. This is because the thought patterns that go with one language are different from those that accompany another; thus, language even influences the way people think. Further, the vocabulary of each language reflects the primary concerns of that society. For example, there are more than 6,000 words in Arabic for describing the camel and its equipment, and the Inuit (Eskimo) language has an extensive list of words for describing snow; while English is limited in terms of describing camels and snow. English has become accepted as the language of commerce, however, because of its extensive vocabulary dealing with business-related issues. Native English speakers are generally thought of as rather individualistic, and it is interesting to note that in English the word "I" is capitalized no matter where it appears in the sentence (another word similarly capitalized refers to God).

While it is helpful for English-speaking peoples to know that English is the most commonly spoken second language, they should not adopt the attitude that other languages are, therefore, unimportant. It may not be necessary for managers to become fluent in other languages, but it is important to understand the role of language in behavior.

Language provides people with an important means of communication; and, because communication is integral to all aspects of business, the issue of how to communicate when different languages are spoken is a key question that international companies must address. An example of the operations of a hypothetical company illustrates the language needs that a company might have.

Imagine a company, headquartered in Toronto, with a French-speaking CEO from Quebec. The company conducts the following international activities:

- a wholly-owned manufacturing subsidiary in Trinidad that supplies other Caribbean islands;

- a licensee in France who supplies the European market, including the U.K., Germany, Sweden, and Finland, from facilities in France;

- a joint venture with a Brazilian company that manufactures in Brazil and exports to the rest of South America and Central America;

- a joint venture with the Indian government that consists of small manufacturing facilities throughout India;

- negotiating a joint venture with a Japanese company to develop and exploit new technologies;

- exports from Canada to the People's Republic of China (PRC);

- considerating a merger with a U.S.-based competitor.

Communication would take place at many levels in such an organization: communications between headquarters and managers in foreign locations, headquarters and foreign partners, headquarters and foreign governments, headquarters and foreign customers, suppliers, and creditors. There would also be communications between managers in foreign locations and employees, unions, government, suppliers, customers, and local partners; and communication among managers and staff at different locations. Each of these is likely to involve more than one language.

In our example, the following languages can be identified: varieties of English (American, British, Canadian, Trinidadian), French (Canadian, Parisienne, Caribbean), Spanish, Portuguese, German, Swedish, Finnish, Japanese, Chinese (Mandarin), and several different languages in India. The international company facing such a situation has a number of options available—it can use translators and translations, language training for its employees, and outside consultants.

In facing the communication difficulties that arise because of language differences, a company must weigh carefully the benefits to be gained from improved communication against the costs associated with the improvement. For example, English is generally accepted as the common language of business and, in some cases, it may be appropriate to rely on this rather than attempt to learn a foreign language. Equally, there are situations where understanding at least some of a foreign language may provide a manager with a real advantage. The solution may involve a combination of approaches.

Organizations operating in foreign locations are often concerned not only with communicationg in a multitude of languages. Exhibit 3.2 illustrates the diversity of language in many of countries around the world.

EXHIBIT 3.2

LINGUISTICALLY HOMOGENEOUS AND HETEROGENEOUS NATIONS

LINGUISTICALLY HOMOGENEOUS NATIONS

Albania	El Salvador	Jordan	Portugal
Argentina	France	Korea, North	Rwanda
Australia	Germany, East	Korea, Republic of	Saudi Arabia
Austria	Germany, Federal	Lebanon	Somalia
Brazil	Republic of	Libya	Sweden
Burundi	Greece	Malagasy Republic	Tunisia
Chile	Haiti	Mexico	Turkey
Colombia	Honduras	Mongolia	United Kingdom
Costa Rica	Hungary	Netherlands	Uruguay
Cuba	Iceland	New Zealand	Venezuela
Denmark	Ireland	Nicaragua	Yemen
Dominican	Italy	Norway	
Republic	Jamaica	Paraguay	
Egypt	Japan	Poland	

LINGUISTICALLY HETEROGENEOUS NATIONS

Afghanistan	Ecuador	Mali	Sudan
Algeria	Ethiopia	Mauritania	Switzerland
Belgium	Finland	Morocco	Syria
Bolivia	Gabon	Nepal	Tanzania
Bulgaria	Ghana	Niger	Thailand
Burma	Guatemala	Nigeria	Togo
Cambodia	Guinea	Pakistan	Trinidad
Cameroon	India	Panama	Uganda
Canada	Indonesia	Peru	United States
Central African	Iran	Philippines	USSR
Republic	Iraq	Romania	Upper Volta
Chad	Israel	Senegal	Vietnam
Congo	Ivory Coast	Sierra Leone	Yugoslavia
Cyprus	Laos	South Africa	Zaire
Czechoslovakia	Liberia	Spain	
Dahomey	Malaysia	Sri Lanka	

SOURCE:
Arthur S. Banks and Robert B. Textor. *A Cross-Polity Survey*. Cambridge, MA: M.I.T. Press, 1963, pp. 72–75; and World Bank Atlas, 1983.

RELIGION

A lack of religious understanding has also been the cause of many international misunderstandings. The next four examples illustrate the importance of religion in intercultural relationships.

- The East India Company may have lost control of it's India operations in 1857 because it failed to modify a product it provided. In those days bullets were often encased in pig wax, and tops had to be bitten off before the bullets could be fired. The Asian soldiers were furious when they discovered the pig wax, since it was against their religion to eat pork. The soldiers revolted and hundreds were killed on both sides before peace was restored.

- One soft-drink company inadvertently offended some of its customers in the Arab world because its labels incorporated six-pointed stars. The firm considered the stars only decoration, but the Arab interpreted them as reflecting pro-Israeli sentiment.

- A refrigerator manufacturer used a picture of a refrigerator containing a centrally placed chunk of ham. The typical refrigerator advertisement often features a refrigerator full of delicious food, and because these photos are difficult to take, the photos are generally used in as many places as possible. This company used its stock photo one place too many, though, when it was used in the Middle East, where ham was prohibited. Locals considered the ad to be insensitive and unappealing.

- Saudi Arabia nearly restricted an airline from initiating flights when the company authorized "normal" newspaper advertisements. The ads featured attractive hostesses serving champagne to the happy airline passengers. Because in Saudi Arabia alcohol is illegal and unveiled women are not permitted to mix with men, the photo was viewed as an attempt to alter religious customs.

Religion has been identified as a "socially shared set of beliefs, ideas, and actions which relate to a reality that cannot be verified empirically yet is believed to affect the course of natural and human events. Because such belief conditions people's motivations and actions, it affects their actions" (Terpstra & David 1985, p. 79). Clearly, religion is closely associated with the development of cultural values, and affects many day-to-day activities in a society. International companies, therefore, need to understand the role of religion in the societies where they operate.

An international company is usually interested in four dimensions of a country's religious profile: (1) the dominant religion, or state religion; (2) the importance of religion generally in the society; (3) the degree of religious heterogeneity or homogeneity; and (4) the tolerance or intolerance of religious diversity.

The dominant religion will influence many business activities, such as opening and closing times, days off, holidays, ceremonies, and foods. A company's operations and activities must be organized with regard for religious practices that affect employees. Religious beliefs and events can affect both production and consumption, and the effective organization will make plans to accommodate these events.

It is customary in the United States to think of Sunday as a day off from work and Christmas day as a holiday for most employees. In fact, production over the entire Christmas period is often slow while consumption is at a peak. This reflects the dominance of Christian religion in the United States and U.S.-based businesses plan their operations around these events. It may seem self-evident that there will be different religious events that must be accommodated in countries that are not Christian. Unfortunately, managers often forget to consider the specifics of non-Christian religions. Exhibit 3.3 lists major holidays for a variety of religious groups, taken from the 1993 multifaith calendar.

EXHIBIT 3.3

SUMMARY OF FESTIVALS 1993

ABORIGINAL PEOPLES

June 21	First Nations Solidarity Day

BAHA'I FAITH

March 2-20	The 19-Day Fast
March 21	Naw Ruz
April 21-May 2	The Feast of Ridvan
May 23	The Declaration of the Bab
May 29	The Ascension of Bahá'u'lláh
July 9	The Martyrdom of the Bab
October 20	The Birth of the Bab
November 12	The Birth of Bahá'u'lláh
November 26	The Day of the Covenant
November 28	The Ascension of 'Abdu'l-Bahá

BUDDHISM

The following list of festivals has been devised by the Buddhist Council of Canada. It includes mainly those celebrations which are common to both Theravadins and Mahayanists; (M) indicates festivals more important to the Mahayana school, (Th) to the The ravada School. In the Western world, festivals are generally celebrated on the Sunday nearest the actual date.

January 23	Chinese/Vietnamese New Year (4691) (Year of the Cock) (M)
March 21	Spring Ohigon (Canada) (Japanese)
April 13-14	Saka New Year (Th) (Burmese, Laotian, Cambodian, Sri Lankan)
May 6	Wesak (Th, M)
July 3	Wassa (Th, M)
July 9	Dhamma Day (Th, M)
August 2	Ullambana (M)
September 21	Fall Ohigon (Canada) (Japanese)
September 30	Pavarana (Th, M)
October 16	Founder's Day (Canadian)
October 30	Kathina (Th)

HINDUISM

January 14	Makar Sankranti
January 28	Vasanta Panchami
February 20	Mahashivaratri
March 8	Holi (last day)
April 1	Ramanavami
April 13	Vaisakhi
August 2	Raksha Bandhan
August 11	Sri Krishna Jayanti
October 4	Ganesh Chaturthi
October 24	Dassehra
November 13	Diwali

ISLAM

January 19	Maraj-un-Nabi (begins in evening)
February 6	Nisfu-Shabaan (begins in evening)
February 23	First of Ramadan
March 20	Lailat-ul-Qadr (begins in evening)
March 24	Eid-ul-fitr
May 31	Day of Hajj (Day at Arafat)
June 1	Eid-ul-Adha
June 21	First of Muharram (New Year's Day, 1414 A.H.)
June 30	Ashura
August 29	Maulud-un-Nabi (begins in evening)

JAINISM

April 4	Mahavira-jayanti
April 24	Akshaya-tritiya
August 15	Paryushana-parva (Shvetambara sect)
August 22	Dashalakshani-parva (Digambara sect)
August 22	Samvatsari
August 31	Ananta-chaturdasi
September 1	Ksamavani
October 13	Mahavira Nirvana

EXHIBIT 3.3 (continued)

October 28   Lokashah Jayanti

November 23   Maunajiyaras

CHRISTIANITY

*   Julian Calendar
**   Gregorian Calendar
*** Both Julian and Gregorian Calendars

January 6   Epiphany**; Armenian Christmas

January 18-25 Week of Prayer for Christian Unity

January 24-31 Week of Prayer for Christian Unity
                              (Canada)

February 24   Ash Wednesday**

March 1   Lent Monday*

March 5   World Day of Prayer

April 4-10   Holy Week (**)

April 4   Palm Sunday**

April 8   Maundy Thursday**

April 9   Good Friday**

April 11   Easter**

April 11-17   Holy Week*

April 11   Palm Sunday*

April 15   Holy Thursday*

April 16   Holy Friday*

April 18   Pascha*

May 20   Ascension**

May 27   Ascension*

May 30   Pentecost**

June 6   Pentecost*

August 6   Transfiguration Day**

August 19   Transfiguration Day*

October 3   World Communion Sunday

November 28   First Sunday of Advent**

December 25   Christmas**

JUDAISM

March 7   Purim

April 6-13   Pesach

April 18   Yom ha-Shoah

May 26-27   Shavuot

September 16-17   Rosh Hashanah

September 25   Yom Kippur

September 30-October 7   Sukkot

October 8   Simhat Torah

December 9-16   Hanukkah

SIKHISM

January 6   Birthday of Guru Gobind Singh

April 13   Baisakhi

June 2   Martyrdom of Guru Arjan Dev

August 28   Parkash

November 11   Birthday of Guru Nanak Dev

December 1   Martyrdom of Guru Tegh Bahadur

ZOROASTRIANISM

March 16-20   Ghambar hamaspathmaedem

March 21   Naw Ruz (New Year's Day
                          in Fasli calendar)

March 26   Birthday of Prophet Zarathustra

April 30-May 4   Ghambar Maidyozarem

June 29-July 3   Ghambar Maidyoshem

August 13-22   Fravardeghan Days

August 23   Naw Ruz (New Year's Day
                         in Shenshai calendar)

September 12-16   Ghambar Paitishem

October 12-16   Ghambar Ayathrem

December 26   Death of Prophet Zarathustra

December 31-January 4   Ghambar Maidyarem

The importance of religion in a particular society is also a major consideration. In a country where religion plays a relatively minor role, people will be more flexible in terms of religious adherence, and tolerant of religious mistakes that foreigners make. In a country where religious beliefs are fundamental to the society and represent deeply held convictions of the people, there will be little flexibility or tolerance. This factor will affect a company's activities—for example, scheduling extra work on a religious holiday might be possible in the first type of country, but not in the second. Or advertising using religiously unacceptable themes might be simply corrected in the first, but may cause lasting damage in the second.

Religious diversity is also important in that a country may have one dominant religion, or may represent many different religions. It can be particularly difficult for a foreign company to accommodate the different working hours, holidays, and ceremonies of different groups of employees. If a company is aware of the necessity for treating each group according to its religious dictates, then it can devise ways to do so. If the company is not aware of the need, it may alienate some groups of employees and suffer such consequences as a poor public image, low motivation, high turnover, and absenteeism, without understanding the cause.

Religious tolerance is another serious concern for companies operating in foreign environments. In many cases, lack of tolerance for other religions is associated with religious beliefs that are held very deeply. It is not surprising that if religion is very important in a society, people in that society will believe that their religion is right and others are wrong. Such a situation clearly has the elements for conflict if employees within the same organization come from different faiths. It may not be possible to avoid some conflict, but an attentive company can make efforts to minimize the likelihood by developing approaches for managing any conflicts.

It is relatively easy to obtain information on the religious profile of a particular country; and literature on the beliefs and practices of most of the world's religions is readily available. Companies, therefore, should investigate the religious makeup of any country where they expect to conduct business. The *World Christian Encyclopedia* contains a census of the world's religions, and this can be a starting point for investigation. Here is a list of the world's most common religions (Smart 1989).

Hinduism does not insist on particular beliefs about God. It incorporates hereditary occupational groups in a caste system that dictates appropriate behaviors. Living a good life allows one to move upward in the system through reincarnation. Approximately 85 percent of Indians are Hindu and a minority of the Bangladeshi and Sri Lankans. Small groups are also found in Indonesia, Fiji, Africa, Great Britain, and the Americas.

Buddhism stems from Buddha, or "Enlightened One," a title normally associated with Prince Gautama who lived in the middle of the sixth century B.C. Buddhist traditions avoid the extremes of self-indulgence or asceticism. Enlightenment comes through the realization of the Four Noble Truths that: all existence is suffering, suffering is caused by desire, suffering ceases when desire ceases, and the Noble Eightfold Path leads to the cessation of suffering. The Noble Eightfold Path consists of accepting the Four Noble Truths, as well as the correct aspects of thought, speech, conduct, livelihood, effort, awareness, and meditation; thus, prescribing how the practicing Buddhist should live. Buddhism is practiced in Burma, China, Japan, Korea, Laos, Sri Lanka, Thailand, and Tibet.

Islam is based on the principles of the Koran. Practitioners of the Islamic religion are generally called Muslims. Islam pervades all aspects of the lives of Muslims, determining personal behavior, social relations, and community life. Consequently, in Islamic states there is no separation between church and state. A basic belief of Islam is that everything happens because of God's will. Islam is the dominant religion in a large number of countries including, Afghanistan, Algeria, Bangladesh, Egypt, Indonesia, Iran, Iraq, Jordan, Libya, Mauritania, Morocco, Pakistan, Saudi Arabia, Senegal, Somalia, Syria, Tunisia, Turkey, and Yemen (Terpstra & David 1985, p. 97). There are two sects of Islam, the Sunis and the Shiites. The Sunis are in the majority (90 percent) but the Shiites are the more orthodox fundamentalists, and are dominant in Iran and Iraq.

Christianity is based on the teachings of Jesus of Nazareth, who is called "the Christ." The Christ is believed to be the Son of God born of a woman, and thus represents the mediator between humans and god. In Christian countries today, the church is largely separate from the state. Christians normally belong to one of three groups—Roman Catholics, Orthodox, or Protestants. Australia and New Zealand, the Americas, and Europe are largely Christian.

Exhibits 3.4 and 3.5 identify the religions of the world in terms of the percentage of the world's population. According to the *World Christian Encyclopedia*, the estimates for the year 2000 have Christians as the largest group (32 percent), nonreligious next (21 percent), Muslims (19 percent), Hindus (14 percent), and Buddhists (6 percent) following, with Jewish, new religions, and nonliterate religions making up the balance.

EXHIBIT 3.4

ADHERENTS IN MILLIONS AND AS A PERCENTAGE OF THE WORLD POPULATION

	In the Year 1900	%	In the Year 1980	%	In the Year 2000 (Estimate)	%
Religion Adherents						
Buddhist	127	7.84%	274	6.29%	359	5.73%
Christian	558	34.44%	1,433	32.90%	2,020	32.27%
Roman Catholic	272	16.79%	809	18.58%	1,169	18.67%
Protestant & Anglican	153	9.44%	345	7.92%	440	7.03%
Eastern Orthodox	121	7.47%	124	2.85%	153	2.44%
Other	12	0.74%	155	3.56%	258	4.12%
Hindu	203	12.53%	583	13.39%	859	13.72%
Jewish	12	0.74%	17	0.39%	20	0.32%
Muslim	200	12.35%	723	16.60%	1,201	19.19%
New religions	6	0.37%	96	2.20%	138	2.20%
Other*	13	0.80%	17	0.39%	61	0.97%
Chinese folk religion	380	23.46%	198	4.55%	158	2.52%
Tribalist & shamanist	118	7.28%	103	2.37%	110	1.76%
Nonreligion Adherents						
Nonreligious & atheist	3	0.19%	911	20.92%	1,334	21.31%
World population	1,620	100.%	4,355	100.%	6,260	100.%

* including Sikh, Confucian, Shinto, Baha'i, Parsi

SOURCE:
World Christian Encyclopedia. Oxford University Press, 1982.

EXHIBIT 3.5

GLOBAL RELIGIONS DIVERSITY

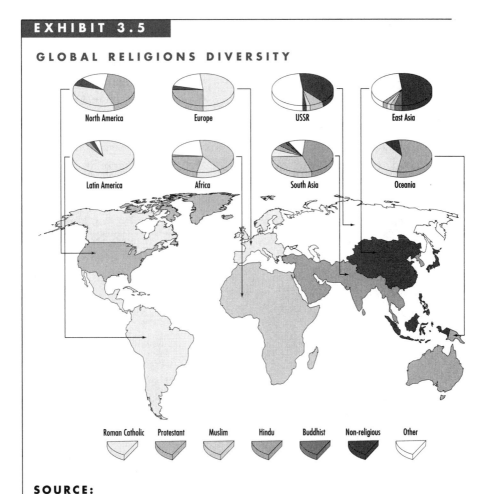

SOURCE:
Alisdair Rogers, *Atlas of Social Issues.* Oxford:Ilex Publishers Ltd. 1990. p. 59.

EDUCATION

Education plays a major role in any society, and in the interaction of international companies with specific societies. Education is a process of learning through which members of society gain information and share social expectations. Education, like language and religion, is an integral part of the development of a societal culture, and it is virtually impossible for a company to function effectively in a society without understanding its educational system.

The role education plays is seen most clearly in a company's relationships with employees. When a company decides on staffing policies, local educational systems will determine the availability of prospective employees with desired skills; they will define the degree and type of training that must be undertaken; they will influence the degree of decentralization that is possible and the communication systems that are employed.

A focus for most Western companies is the degree of educational attainment in a particular country. The higher the level of education, the more likely it is that jobs at all levels be staffed locally, the more likely that many decisions be made at the local level, the more likely that training methods be transferred, and standard written communication be adequate. A lower level of education means the company may have to consider staffing with foreigners, particularly at higher and technical levels; may need to develop extensive training programs that are adapted to be understandable and acceptable to the trainees; may find that less delegation will be possible, and that written communication is inadequate.

The more economically developed countries of the world generally have relatively high levels of education, which simplifies these staffing issues. Even in such cases, it may be important to adjust to the traditional system. Rohlen (1973) tells of a training program for a Japanese bank that incorporated Zen meditation, military training, working for strangers for no pay, time spent in an agricultural community, and a 25-mile endurance walk. This training might be met with resistance if implemented in North America. Equally, training programs that are effective in North America can be ineffective elsewhere if they depart dramatically from the type of educational system to which people are accustomed.

The role of educational systems is particularly important in relations with employees. It can also play a major role in decisions regarding customers and consumers. For example, a laundry detergent company would have benefited from local input before it initiated its promotional campaign in the Middle East. The company's advertisements pictured soiled clothes on the left, its box of soap in the middle, and clean clothes on the right.

Because in that area of the world people tend to read from right to the left, many potential customers interpreted the message to indicate the soap actually soiled the clothes.

If consumers cannot read, written descriptions of products or directions are not useful; customers will respond to pictures and interpret products in this light. In areas where many of the people are illiterate, a product label usually displays a picture of what the package contains. This very logical practice can backfire, however, as happened in the following case. A large company tried to sell baby food in an African nation by using its regular label showing a baby and stating the type of baby food in the jar. Unfortunately, the local population interpreted the labels to mean the jars contained ground-up babies.

Illiteracy can be a particularly damaging problem when products or processes are dangerous. Employees or customers who cannot read warning labels are subject to serious dangers; a number of people have even died because they were unable to read written warnings. Companies of such products must devise other effective means to warn and direct users.

Exhibit 3.6 summarizes the levels of education achieved in countries around the world.

SOCIAL SYSTEMS

Social systems encompass a wide variety of structures that delineate people's behaviors in social situations. These systems exist because human societies tend to limit the degree of individual variation allowed within a society to ensure an acceptable level of order. Social systems include such diverse activities as courting and marriage rituals, entertaining practices, interaction among people of higher and lower classes, kinship units, and business ownership, to name only a few. These examples illustrate how customs can differ:

- In some societies marriages are arranged at birth and the partners never see each other before the wedding day; in others, courtship follows a clearly defined ritual which leads, step by step, to marriage if all the steps are accomplished. In still other societies, courtship is less formal and marriage undertaken easily.

EXHIBIT 3.6

LITERACY RATES GLOBALLY

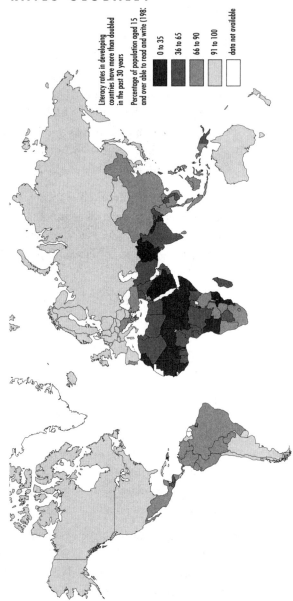

SOURCE:
Ruth Leger Sivard, *World Military and Social Expenditures 1986.* 11th Edition, World
Priorities.

- In some societies, strangers are readily invited to the home; in others, only friends are welcomed in the home; in still other societies, the home is reserved for family.

- In some societies, people of different classes are carefully segregated; in others, there is little if any class distinction, and all people meet and mix; in still other societies, there are class distinctions, but people of different classes are free to interact.

- In some societies, family units are made up of mother, father, and children; in others, the unit includes grandparents and aunts and uncles with their children; in still others, all children are considered the children of the society and belong to all of the adults.

- In some societies, business is considered the domain of the rich; in others, business is considered degrading and only appropriate for the lower classes; in still others, anyone may engage in business activities.

These contrasts in terms of social systems illustrate the variety of approaches that can exist. International managers need to appreciate that there are alternative ways of looking at the world. Rather than attempt a discussion of a complex issue, this example illustrates the importance of social systems to international managers.

The caste system of India provides an informative example of a social system and its potential impact on business activities. This system is very unlike the social systems that guide behavior in North America. Americans and Canadians generally adhere to the idea that all people are created equal. By contrast, *The Economist* (1991, p. 21) says of India, that "for the great majority the rules, rewards and punishments of social life were set in the distant past, and are systematically unfair. The idea of natural inequality remains central to their lives."

The Indian caste system is the basis for this inequality. The ancient social hierarchy consists of several layers: Brahmins (priest-intellectuals), Kshatriyas (warriors), Vaishyas (traders), Sudras (peasants and laborers), and beneath them all, Untouchables. A moral code is associated with each caste, and only by living according to this code can a person rise to a higher caste in a future life. If one is born into an upper caste it is because of virtue in an earlier life. Breaches of the code (changing occupations, or procreation with another caste) are punished by rebirth as an Untouchable. In this way the system ensures that its adherents accept inequality because acceptance is the only way to progress from lower caste to higher.

According to *The Economist*, caste shapes almost every aspect of rural Indian life: "the food they eat, and who can cook it; how they bathe; the colour of their clothes; the length of a sari; how the dhoti is tied; which way a man's moustaches are trained and whether he can carry an umbrella" (p. 22). In the cities of India the rules of the caste system are not as easy to conform to: "A Brahmin on a packed bus cannot hop off and bathe six times each time he fears the shadow of an Untouchable has fallen on him" (p. 23). Nevertheless, this system has lasted thousands of years and is not likely to disappear soon.

From a North American viewpoint, the caste system seems not only strange, but wrong, because to the North American it denies the value of equality. One reaction is to insist on changing such a system; or, alternatively, to ignore it because it does not seem possible that others would adhere to such a system. Neither of these approaches is effective. Particularly in view of the fact that India contains a quarter of the world's population, one cannot ignore their view of the world. The U.S. manager must recognize that visitors to the United States are often struck not by evidence of equality in society, but by the apparent inequality. This is exemplified by factors such as the typical secondary role of many African-Americans or the plight of the homeless in cold northern cities.

Global companies have to function within the confines of the established social systems in a particular location. This means accommodating these systems or attracting local employees who are willing to accept alternative systems. The manager needs to gather information on the social systems in foreign locations, assess the impact on operations, and then decide if and how much to adapt the organization's traditional practices to accommodate the new social systems.

LEVEL OF DEVELOPMENT

The countries of the world are often classified in terms of level of development. Level of development refers to a variety of factors, but most often economic development is the focus, and this is usually measured in terms of Gross Domestic Product (GDP) per capita. This is a crude measure because it ignores illegal and underground economic activities, and it does not take into account the quality of life achieved at different levels. Other measures worth considering are wealth distribution, daily calorie consumption, leisure time, energy consumption, and various demographic statistics (literacy, life expectancy) and health statistics (infant mortality, doctors per capita). Considerating an array of measures offers a more accurate picture of the level of a country's development. GDP per capita seems to be the most convenient to use, however, and often serves as a proxy for the others.

Countries have been classified in terms of development in a variety of ways, and these classifications are continually shifting. These terms suggest the distinctions that can be found:

Third world. The poorer countries of the world are often referred to as the third world. This is in contrast to the developed market economies (the rich countries) which constitute the first world, and the centrally planned economies, which make up the second world. The terms "first world" and "second world" are not commonly used, whereas "third world" has become a common expression for the poor countries.

Less-developed countries (LDCs). The poorer countries are also often referred to as less developed, in contrast to the more-developed (sometimes just called developed), richer countries. In the past LDCs were called "backward" or "underdeveloped," but these terms are seldom used today because they are offensive to many people.

Developing countries. Some third world countries have recently been called developing countries. This is relative to the developed, rich countries. The term developing, as opposed to third world or LDC, conveys a sense of moving forward and is preferred by some people.

Newly Industrializing Countries. These countries are moving from the poor category to the rich. These are developing countries of the third world which have experienced rapid industrial growth in the last quarter of the twentieth century. Countries such as South Korea, Taiwan, Hong Kong, Singapore, and Thailand currently fall into this category.

Centrally planned economies. These are the centrally planned, communist countries. The changes of the early 1990s suggest that only a few countries will continue to follow this economic model in coming years, and this category may be relatively small.

Developed/Industrialized Countries. These are the wealthier countries of the world. Their economies have generally been based on industrialization and free markets. Many of these countries are also referred to as "Western" (Japan being a notable exception).

From a managerial point of view, the most obvious difference of which a Western manager should be aware is that the developing countries are poor relative to the more-developed ones. This poverty is immediately apparent to managers in the way that the vast majority of people live. The general poverty has an impact on almost all aspects of management in these countries.

People in these countries are anxious to earn money and will work for very low wages. This can mean cost benefits for international companies in labor-intensive industries. McDonald (1992), for example, reported that in India, Texas Instruments' starting salary for a graduate in electrical engineering or computer science is about 5,400 rupees (U.S. $221) a month; after five years of experience monthly salaries range between 10,000 (U.S. $391) and 12,000 (US $469). In contrast, a U.S. software specialist starts at about U.S. $3,000 a month, the equivalent of about 76,000 rupees. Exhibit 3.7 illustrates the variation in earnings around the globe.

EXHIBIT 3.7

HOURLY EARNINGS IN MANUFACTURING IN SELECTED COUNTRIES

(as of November 25, 1991, in U.S. $)

Germany	13.47	South Africa	5.31
United States	13.25	Chile	1.35
Singapore	11.20	China	0.20

People in developing countries who are not poor are often disproportionately wealthy. It is this rich elite with whom international companies have to negotiate and work. In the former British colonies of the West Indies there remains a powerful white aristocracy even though whites constitute only a small percentage of the population. Although this situation is changing, it is this white minority who controls much of the wealth and resources; thus, foreign business people often work with members of this aristocracy even where this would not be their preference.

Social unrest often accompanies poverty and this results in an unsettled and sometimes dangerous environment for international companies. For example, in the Philippines unrest continues following the overthrow of the Marcos government. Up to 70 percent of the Philippine population lived below the poverty level in 1992, and the Aquino government admitted to the presence of 15,000 guerrilla fighters. The Philippine population has ousted the Spanish, the Japanese, the Americans, and a local dictator. Relentless poverty and unrest creates instability, which can prove difficult for foreign companies.

Developing countries often lag in technological capability. Transfers of technology are complex because it is difficult to determine what level of technology is appropriate. Because cameras, telephones, and computers are taken for granted in many of the more-developed countries of the world, it is often difficult for people from these countries to realize that in some poorer countries, even indoor plumbing, electricity, and refrigeration are unknown. The role of electricity in the transfer of technology is crucial and much of the technology of the developed world relies on familiarity with, and availability of, electricity. It is difficult to effectively transfer this technology where electricity is not well established.

Supplies, materials, and other resources may not be available for daily operations in developing countries. Adler, Campbell, and Laurenta (1989) discovered this when they undertook a survey in the People's Republic of China and found the respondents using small scraps of paper to respond to save the questionnaire paper for further use. One of the authors found, similarly, that respondents at a company in the Caribbean did not have access to pencils to complete a survey. It is easy for managers from the more-developed countries to make assumptions about the availability of what they see as simple resources.

In addition to poverty, common characteristics are common in the developing countries set them apart from the more-developed countries. Austin (1990) suggests that these factors be analyzed to understand a developing country:

Economic Factors

- Natural resources
- Labor
- Capital
- Infrastructure
- Technology

Political Factors

- Stability
- Ideology
- Institutions
- Geopolitical links

Cultural Factors

- Social structure and dynamics
- Human nature perspective
- Time and space orientation
- Religion
- Gender roles
- Language

Demographic Factors

- Population growth
- Age structure
- Urbanization
- Migration
- Health status

Austin (1990, p. 3) makes the point that "a distinguishing feature of more suc-cessful companies in developing countries is their superior ability to under-stand and interact with their business environment." To do this effectively takes time and patience, because the developing countries do differ from the more-developed in many of these characteristics.

We have identified some of the main characteristics that distinguish the more-developed from the developing countries. This is a helpful starting point for managers moving from one category of country to another. It is also true that within in each category countries can vary dramatically. The existence of some similar characteristics should not be interpreted to mean that all more-devel-oped countries are alike or that all developing countries share similar cultur-al characteristics. In both cases there are similarities as well as differentiating aspects of the cultures.

NATION OR CULTURE

What are the boundaries within which assessment of these factors should take place? It is possible to use national boundaries, or to identify cultural bound-aries as a basis for assessment. The following examines these two approaches from the manager's viewpoint.

Much cross-cultural organizational literature focuses on national boundaries assuming these are the same as specific cultural boundaries; that is, culture has often served simply as a synonym for nation without any further conceptu-al grounding (Bhagat & McQuaid 1982). In effect, the focus is on what might be called a national culture. This can be somewhat misleading because there are clear cases where cultures transcend national boundaries (for example, the British culture found in many former colonies); and other cases where several cultures are evident in one nation (such as in Yugoslavia in the early 1990s). On the whole, however, from the organization's viewpoint, a focus on national cultures appears appropriate.

Nations are formed, generally, as a political expression of cultural similarity. Nations composed of several different cultures with no superordinate and unit-ing values are unlikely to survive in the long run. (Yugoslavia is a recent exam-ple.) In such cases, the original nation may break up into smaller units, one group may force its values on the others, or an external threat may result in a united front. All of this suggests that, over time, it is appropriate to expect the emergence of a national culture.

Furthermore, an international firm's activities are generally constrained by national laws and regulations. The company must be structured in accordance with local requirements (which may prescribe or prohibit ownership, the makeup of the board of directors, and reporting procedures); the company must comply with local taxes (for example, import and export tariffs, income and corporate taxes); and the company must obey local laws (ranging from constraints on the use of resources to laws regarding competition and bribery). These examples illustrate that the firm is subject to national sovereignty, and must understand national laws and policies.

Human resource considerations that encourage a global firm to take a national perspective are even more important, from a cultural standpoint. The organization's work force is usually predominantly a national work force. Labor mobility within a country is usually greater than between countries; consequently, the majority of employees are generally from the country where the organization is based, even if they come from many different parts of the country. This means that management systems must be designed in view of this national character of the work force. Governments encourage this through laws and regulations. An international firm has to function in this system and should begin its cultural analysis at the national cultural level. Once overall management systems have taken the national culture into account, the company can then consider subcultures and make appropriate modifications for those groups.

It is important to realize that cultural assessment focuses on the general makeup of a nation or culture. This can be thought of as a curve—that is, most people will fall near the "norm," but there will be people in every society and who exhibit characteristics that are distinctly different from this norm. In terms of cultural antecedents, for example, a country might be generally described as religiously intolerant; this would mean that most people are intolerant of differing religions, though there may be individuals who are tolerant. International organizations can use the cultural diversity within a particular country by adapting their approaches to local norms or by seeking to attract local employees who fit the organization's culture.

SUMMARY

This chapter has defined and explored the concept of culture and its relationship to global management. Various aspects of culture, their assessment and impact on organizations were discussed. Students should now have a general appreciation of the importance of culture in managing global companies, as well as some practical guidance for assessing and managing cross-cultural encounters.

It is especially important that global managers understand of the reasons for ethnocentric and parochial attitudes. This understanding helps managers overcome these attitudes themselves, and deal with such attitudes in encounters with others. Overcoming ethnocentric and parochial attitudes begins with an understanding of your home culture and how it is similar to or different from other cultures. Many aspects of culture must be examined in this context; the focus here is cultural underpinnings affect effective global operations. While these underpinnings are described as cultural, they are often associated with nations, and firms are especially concerned with national requirements. Global firms focus initially on national cultural environments, and incorporate information on subcultures at a later stage.

DISCUSSION QUESTIONS

1. Using your local community as an example, describe its cultural characteristics. Discuss the degree of cultural homogeneity or diversity found in your community. How does this homogeneity or diversity affect foreign managers coming to your community?

2. Develop a cultural profile of your home country for foreign managers working there.

3. Select two countries that you believe to be quite different culturally. Identify the cultural differences between these two countries and discuss how the differences identified are likely to influence interactions between managers from these two countries.

REFERENCES

Adler, N. 1988. "Address to Conference on Research for Relevance in International Management," Windsor, Ontario, Canada.

Adler, N., J.N. Campbell & A. Laurent. 1989. "In search of appropriate methodology: From outside the People's Republic of China looking in." *Journal of International Business Studies*, 20 (1), pp. 61–74.

Austin, J.E. 1990. *Managing in Developing Countries: Strategic Analysis and Operating Techniques*. New York: Free Press.

Bata Shoe Organization, Corporate literature and interviews.

Bhagat, R.S. & S.J. McQuaid. 1982. "Role of subjective culture in organizations: A review and directions for future research." *Journal of Applied Psychology Monograph*, 67 (5), pp. 635–685.

The Economist, "The reincarnation of caste." June 8, pp. 21.

Graham, 1985. "The influence of culture on the process of business negotiations: An exploratory study." *Journal of International Business Studies*, 16 (1), pp. 81–96.

Heller, F.A. 1988. "Cost benefits of multinational research on organizations." *International Studies of Management and Organization*, XVIII (3), pp. 5–18.

Hofstede, G. 1980. *Culture's Consequences: International Differences in Work Related Values*. Beverly Hills: Sage Publications.

Kluckhohn, C. & F. Strodtbeck. 1961. *Variations in Value Orientations*. Westport, CT: Greenwood Press.

Kroeber, A. & C. Kluckhohn. 1952. "Culture: A critical review of concepts and definitions." Papers of the Peabody Museum of American Archaeology and Ethnology, Harvard University, pp. 1–223.

Lane, H.W. & J.J. DiStefano. 1988. *International Management Behavior*. Scarborough, Ont.: Nelson Canada.

McDonald, H. 1992. "India's silicon valley." *Far Eastern Economic Review*, December 10, p. 46.

Port Moody, B.C. 1992. *Canada: Canadian Ecumenical Action*.

Punnett, B.J. & S. Ronen. 1984. "Operationalizing cross-cultural variables." Paper delivered at the forty-fourth annual meeting of the Academy of Management, Boston.

Punnett, B.J. & S. Withane. 1990. "Hofstede's value survey module: To embrace or abandon?" S.B. Prased (ed), *Advances in International Comparative Management*, Vol. 5, Greenwich, CT: JAI Press. pp. 69–90.

Ricks, D. 1983. *Big Business Blunders*. Homewood, IL: Dow-Jones-Irwin.

Rogers, A. 1990. *Atlas of Social Issues*. Oxford: Ilex Publishers Limited.

Rohlen, T.P. "Spiritual education in a Japanese bank." *American Anthropologist*, 75 (5), 1973, pp. 1542–1562.

Ronen, S. & O. Shenkar. 1985. "Clustering countries on attitudinal dimensions: A review and synthesis." *Academy of Management Review*.

Sivard, R.L. 1986. *World Military and Social Expenditures* (11th ed.). Washington, DC: World Priorities.

Terpstra, V. & K. David. 1985. *The Cultural Environment of International Business*. Dallas: South-Western Publishing.

United Nations Statistical Yearbook 1990/91. 1993. New York.

Smart, N. 1989. *The World's Religions*. Englewood Cliffs: Prentice-Hall.

Wall Street Journal, November 25, 1991.

Whorf, B.L. 1956. "A linguistic consideration of thinking in primitive communities." In J.B. Carroll (ed.), *Language, Thought and Reality: Selected Readings of Benjamin Lee Whorf*. Cambridge, MA: MIT Press.

4

INTERNATIONAL

LABOR RELATIONS

Written by Stephen Harper

LEARNING OBJECTIVES

IN THIS CHAPTER YOU WILL EXPLORE:

- The terminology of labor relations

- The role of unions in the work place

- Labor relations practices of MNCs

- How organized labor became internationalized

- Comparative labor relations practices across cultures

- The role of quality control in modern labor relations

- The role of profit sharing and Employee Stovk Option Plans (ESOPs)

KEY DISCUSSION ISSUES:

- Do unions help or hinder productivity?

- What different roles do unions play across cultures?

- Do ESOPs and profit sharing work?

- What strategic issues must MNCs bear in mind when dealing with unions?

- Can we import union practices from other countries?

- How has the quality revolution influenced union practices?

- What accounts for cross-cultural differences in union practices?

- How can unions and management deal with work force diversity?

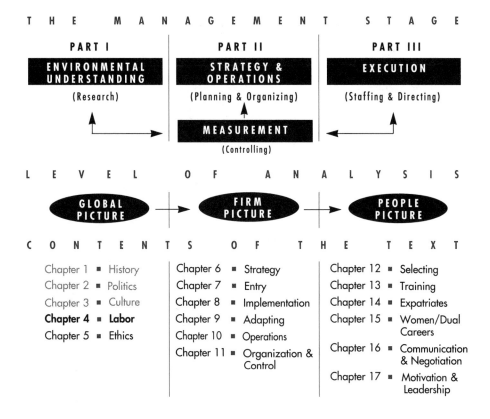

T H E   M A N A G E M E N T   S T A G E

PART I	PART II	PART III
ENVIRONMENTAL UNDERSTANDING	**STRATEGY & OPERATIONS**	**EXECUTION**
(Research)	(Planning & Organizing)	(Staffing & Directing)

MEASUREMENT
(Controlling)

L E V E L   O F   A N A L Y S I S

GLOBAL PICTURE → FIRM PICTURE → PEOPLE PICTURE

C O N T E N T S   O F   T H E   T E X T

INTRODUCTION

It is precisely because labor relations involve human relationships that labor relations are so complex within the international business context. Cultural differences impact labor relations on every level of the corporate structure—from the microlevel of a single business culture that would include aspects such as indigenous customs and habits of communication between the workers and management, to the macrolevel of a national society that would include aspects such as the legal requirements of individual nations regarding certain labor management practices and labor compensation.

This chapter will discuss international labor relations as a dynamic process that has profound implications for the strategic management of transnational businesses. While the traditional U. S. approach to labor relations will be used as a historic backdrop for the discussion of employee relations in other countries, this chapter will focus on the important aspects of labor relations when developing a management strategy for an international enterprise. From a global perspective, we look at how historic events and sociocultural attitudes affect national labor laws, comparing traditional labor relations in a few representative countries. Finally, on the level of corporate culture, we briefly examine some of the innovative strategies, such as quality control circles and employee profit-sharing plans, that have transformed employee and management interaction at the site of production.

LABOR RELATIONS TERMINOLOGY

The term labor relations can be defined as the process through which labor and management determine their relationship to their jobs. (Hodgetts & Luthans 1991) This relationship does not only include compensation, such as wages and fringe benefits for the work performed, but includes job descriptions, retirement, firing procedures, severance pay, lay-offs of redundant workers, and provisions for the duration of the agreement. The management–labor relationship may be a verbal agreement, however, when unions negotiate an agreement with management, it is usually a written contract. This process of negotiation to formalize a labor contract between workers and management is referred to as collective bargaining.

STRIKES AND LOCKOUTS

Workers and management are bound to the terms of labor contracts for a specific period; When they expire the collective bargaining process begins again. If collective bargaining fails or stalls, workers may try to force management to accept their terms by stopping their work and going on strike. Most labor contracts in the United States prohibit strikes during the period when the contract is in effect. Illicit strikes by workers that do occur while the contract is in effect are referred to as wildcat strikes (Hodgetts & Luthans 1991).

Because unions can be voted out when the workers are disillusioned with their union representation, management may respond to the strike by trying to break the union, through hiring scabs (nonunion replacement workers) or through a lockout, in which striking workers are prevented from returning to work. A strike or a lockout is expensive for both management and labor. The company continues to pay overhead without producing and some-times loses market share. Workers forfeit wages and benefits (although unions may distribute a small family maintenance stipend), and often they cannot pay their mortgages or car payments. Both sides are therefore motivated to reach a settlement (Hodgetts & Luthans 1991).

UNION RESPONSIBILITY

Generally, unions represent workers in collective bargaining with manage-ment, though the level of negotiations—whether it is on the company-site level or the national level—varies widely from country to country. In the United States, unions are charged with the responsibility to see that management lives up to its side of the labor agreement that is negotiated in collective bargaining.

In other parts of the world, such as Germany, the responsibility may fall upon works' councils comprised of both labor and management representatives. While on the industry-wide level unions have the responsibility by law for col-lective bargaining with the employers' associations, works' councils have the responsibility of negotiating at the level of the single firm. Employees elect representatives to the works' councils which also are comprised of an equal number of shareholders plus the chairperson. These works' councils decide on the working conditions and standards of employee conduct, and negotiate wage rates upward from the minimum set through union bargaining. Conflict between the labor director, who represents management, and works' councils are settled through arbitration. German works' councils are powerful com-pared to those in other European countries, and have a strong influence in the perception that employees and employers have a common welfare (Daniels & Radebargh 1992).

GRIEVANCE PROCEDURES

Part of the collective bargaining agreements are provisions for the steps that must be taken when employees have grievances. Grievances are formal complaints that an employee is not being treated fairly according to the labor agreement. The steps in the grievance procedure escalate from discussions between lower-level union representatives and management supervisors, to high-level union officials and top management. Unless both sides can agree to a solution to the grievance, the matter may be handled by a mediator or arbitrator (Hodgetts & Luthans 1991).

MEDIATORS AND ARBITRATORS

A mediator may be requested to referee the disagreement and to bring two sides together to reach an agreement that both sides will accept. If the gulf between them is too great, or the conflict too emotionally charged, the two sides may agree to use an arbitrator. Arbitrators are able to resolve differences because the conflicting parties have agreed to accept the arbitrators' decisions in advance of their hearing the arguments; thus arbitrators' decisions are binding. Mediators and arbitrators can be called in to settle individual grievances, or a company-wide or even a nation-wide strike (Hodgetts & Luthans 1991).

COMPARATIVE LABOR RELATIONS PRACTICES

Collective bargaining in the United States usually means negotiations between management and trade union locals, but in Germany or Sweden, for instance, the term refers to negotiations between trade unions at the industry level and employer's associations. Although the objectives of the talks in the U.S. are primarily financial, they are often viewed in terms of a class struggle by Europeans. The role of government or religious organizations in collective bargaining is minimal and relatively constant in the U.S., though in most other countries of the world, labor negotiations are seen as having significant social implications which require greater legal or religious restrictions than those in the United States.

To fully understand the labor relations practices of any country, it is important to be familiar with the history of organized labor movements within the sociopolitical context. Space prevents a full discussion of the topic; however, a few key points will be made about cross-cultural differences in labor relations practices of three countries: the United States, Great Britain, and Italy.

LABOR RELATIONS IN THE U.S.

The Industrial Revolution had a powerful effect on both society and labor relations in the U.S. Not only did it pull workers from the fields into the factories, but it fostered social upheavals that are yet to be reckoned with more than 150 years later (most of the poor African-Americans in urban areas of the U.S. came from or are descendants of small farmers that migrated into the cities during the 1950s). The rise of Marxist philosophy, which pits workers against the capitalist system, was probably the most important reaction to this social upheaval, and found fertile ground among workers during the Great Depression of the 1930s. Most American unions had their beginnings then, being formed under the tremendous pressure of violent confrontations with management.

During World War II, confrontational labor relations cooled as they were superseded by a wave of patriotism, and as labor and management met the demands of industrial production that were required. With the improved standard of living that most Americans enjoyed after the war, unions seemed less and less necessary. Beginning in the early fifties, or the McCarthy Era, as it is sometimes called, the Red Scare (of Communism) further eroded unions' bargaining power as the American public began to suspect that Communism was behind much of the unions' activities—a view that management encouraged.

In the late fifties, the image of unions was further tarnished when it was revealed that some large unions were involved with organized crime. More recently, organized labor in the United States has been shaken, as firms threaten to move operations to other countries where labor costs are lower. Although the number of workers represented by unions is considerably lower in the U.S. than in other developed countries, the legitimate representation of workers by unions is supported by federal laws that mandate recognition of unions as legal representatives of workers. Yet today, union membership is half of what it was in 1955. In addition, events, such as President Regan's breaking of the air traffic controller's union and the more recent lockout of United Autoworker Union employees by Caterpillar, have severely weakened unions (Poole & Jenkins 1991; Thompson 1991; Hodgetts & Luthans 1991).

Workers in the United States may unionize if: (a) 30 percent of the workers sign cards authorizing a specific union to represent them in collective bargaining with their employer; (b) that union petitions the National Labor Relations Board (NLRB) to conduct an election; or (c) 50 percent or more of the workers vote for that union to represent them. When the above conditions are met, the NLRB certifies the union as the legal representative of the workers in negotiating a written contract with management (Hodgetts & Luthans 1991).

State laws govern whether or not all workers in a firm must join the union once a union is certified. In states with right-to-work laws, workers are not required to join the certified union, and thus union solidarity can be eroded to the point that organizing unions and sustaining them in those states can be very difficult.

In the United States, most unions are organized on an industry level, though many workers are not represented by unions. While unions that are organized on the national level can influence industry-wide wage levels and can wield considerable political power, collective bargaining talks are held on a company-wide basis with them, often putting local management at a disadvantage. However, much of the responsibility for the day-to-day business of overseeing that the company lives up to their labor contract is left to union locals, which are simply local divisions of the national unions.

LABOR RELATIONS IN ITALY

The Italian system of collective bargaining is relatively complex. Not only has it undergone substantial structural changes over the past 30 years, but the collective bargaining system is not formally divided into the three typical levels: the company level, the industrial level, and the economy-wide level. Instead, significant bargaining is carried out on all levels, because the tasks and issues for each level is unclear. In addition, over time one level may become predominant, indicating the degree of centralization or decentralization of the bargaining process. This change in centralization can affect: (1) the autonomy or independence of negotiations at one level from the control, regulation, and monitoring by a higher level; (2) the extent or proportion of a given work force that is subject to collective bargaining; (3) the scope or range of the set of issues; and (4) the depth or level of involvement that trade union representatives or representatives from employer organizations have in the finalization or application of the results of the collective bargaining (Baglioni 1991).

For instance, in 1979, when many industry-wide contracts were expiring, the government intervened on the economy-wide level in an attempt to control high inflation by indexing wages. This had reverberating effects on industrial relations throughout the decade. Strike activity increased, and with a third party involved in the bargaining process, organized labor and management began talking separately with the government, often coming to agreement on issues without corresponding agreements between unions and employers. As labor relations became more politicized, company-level bargaining, which had been consistently wide-ranging, became less autonomous and narrower in scope (Baglioni 1991).

The 1986–87 round of negotiations reflected changes by both unions and management in the traditional view of collective bargaining as being confrontational. Instead, the two groups began to adapt to the changing system and meet the overall needs of the entire economy by finding many possibilities for cooperation and trade-offs. Greater autonomy returned to company-level bargaining, but it remains restricted in scope by "functional coordination" clauses which prohibit the renegotiation of issues at a lower level that had been agreed at a higher level (Baglioni 1991).

Because the government took on a larger industrial relations role and changed the old bipolar dynamics, both unions and employers are more willing to assess and modify their demands, despite their ideological differences. Strikes in the private sector have subsided. Innovations in production and economic performance now influence industrial relations more than politics and organizational strength. At the forefront of these positive changes has been the cooperative climate of relations at the company level, and the way in which agreements on that level have complemented industry-wide and economy-wide accords. However, the 1990s are bringing a significant challenge to the relative calm, as workers demand higher wages from booming corporate profits against Italian industry's insistence that it must maintain its international competitiveness through wage control (Baglioni 1991).

LABOR RELATIONS IN GREAT BRITAIN

In Great Britain union membership is widespread, especially among government employees. Because the second largest political party in Britain is the Labour party, labor is politically powerful, although during the 1980s the conservative policies of Margaret Thatcher, who took office after considerable labor unrest and economic decline, have greatly reduced the power of labor.

Compared to the United States, strikes by British unions are prevalent. This has been accounted for by some with the observation that the public believes that business has a social obligation to attend to the interests of workers, together with the facts that often grievance procedures are not formally structured, and that mediation is voluntary. Disputes can be difficult to successfully resolve, and both parties may resort to confrontation in their frustration (Rothwell 1991; Douglas & Douglas 1989; Hodgetts & Luthans 1991).

LABOR RELATIONS PRACTICES OF MNCS

Because there are profound differences in how labor and management perceive each other, a multinational corporation must deal with each group of workers according to the social, political, and religious environment of the country in which it is operating. More often than not, the labor relations strategy used in one country is of limited value in another. In some countries (such as Switzerland, Italy, and France) labor relations are seen in the larger context of a social class struggle, which can often lead to intense labor strife. Where this is the case, a firm may have a difficult time gaining cooperation in reaching its goals. In other countries (most notably Japan) conformity is now the rule, although strike activity was high just prior to World War II (Poole & Jenkins 1991).

DIVERSE ORIENTATIONS TOWARD UNIONS

To understand labor relations in the international context, it is also important to understand MNCs' various orientations toward organized labor. Because labor relations across national boundaries are so diverse, MNCs generally decentralize their labor relations. They sometimes assign the task to their foreign subsidiary, but since labor negotiations in one country can set international precedents, headquarters usually maintains some degree of supervision.

As Hamill (1984) noted in studies of British and U.S. MNCs' approaches to industrial relations, the diversity in approaches to labor relations extends beyond the question of where the subsidiary is operating, to where corporate headquarters is located. U.S.-based MNCs characteristically consolidate authority at corporate headquarters, which stress financial control and formalized reporting. They tended not to recognize trade unions or join employee associations—but at a cost. Although British MNCs cultivated less intricate and less specialized personnel departments at the subsidiary level, they usually paid less to their employees in wages and fringe benefits.

MNC's LABOR RELATIONS STRATEGIES

Because unions may strike, limit redundancy policy, or force labor costs up beyond the point that a labor market is competitive, MNCs must plan their labor relations carefully. This is particularly true for firms that rely on their foreign subsidiaries as a source for components, a strategy known as transnational sourcing. These firms are vulnerable to strikes, since halting production in a subsidiary could stop operations worldwide. To counteract the possibility that a single national union could have that much leverage, MNCs chose to dual source their supplies. However, dual-sourcing strategies permanently prevent MNCs from fully integrating and rationalizing their operations to the most efficient degree. Thus, Prahalad and Doz (1987) have concluded that:

> Union influence thus not only delays the rationalization and integration of MNCs' manufacturing networks and increases the cost of such adjustments, but also, at least in such industries as automobiles, permanently reduces the efficiency of the integrated MNC network.

Therefore, treating labor relations as incidental and relegating them to the specialists in the various countries is inappropriate. In the same way as government policies need to be integrated into strategic choices, so do labor relations.

Prahalad and Doz have touched on the labor relations dilemma for MNCs: to what degree should MNCs delegate to their subsidiaries the authority to handle labor relations? On one hand, if they try to centralize the control of labor relations at corporate headquarters, they may fail to understand cultural subtleties and run the risk of a aggravating a dispute. On the other hand, turning labor relations over to the subsidiary can prevent optimizing operations, or it could even have disastrous, unforeseen consequences.

In addition to sourcing issues when setting policy on central supervision of subsidiary labor relations, MNCs must consider environmental and safety questions, public image, and ethical practices. Recall any industrial accident that you have heard about in the past ten years, and you will probably remember questions raised about working conditions and/or poor supervision of undercompensated workers. Yet, if that firm was an MNC, its policies were probably above the legal standards of the country in which it was operating. The problem for MNCs is that the public holds them to international standards, standards often higher than those of the country in which they are operating. A poignant example of this is the horrible Union Carbide accident in Bhopal, India, in which thousands of people were severely injured or killed by leaking methyl cyanate gas. Few remember, or even care, about the defense offered by the Union Carbide manager who claimed, just after the accident, that their work and safety standards were higher than those of other local industries.

There are no pat answers to the dilemma of turning labor relations over to the subsidiary, or wading through the vastly diverse, complex, and changing labor issues faced in foreign countries in order to centralize control. Most likely a middle ground is necessary. One thing is abundantly clear transnational firms must consider labor relations central to their strategic planning.

INTERNATIONALIZATION OF ORGANIZED LABOR

As MNCs grow in size and number, labor unions feel increasingly threatened. Unlike smaller companies, the financial resources available to an MNC greatly extends the time it can endure the pressure of a strike at a subsidiary. An MNC can switch the source of its supplies, move the entire operation, or even engage in an investment strike in which the firm threatens to not reinvest in capital improvements, making the operation obsolete. Finally, the fact that the bargaining authority representing management is in another country and has better knowledge and experience means the local union is usually outgunned.

UNION RESPONSES TO MNCs

Labor unions have responded to the MNC challenge on the international level by forming International Trade Secretariats (ITS) and working through international organizations. ITS link national trade unions together to form international networks for specific industries. Their goal is to eventually organize workers transnationally to bargain as a unit with each MNC in its industry. Because MNCs tend to resist unions, their workers' remuneration is relatively high; thus, ITS has had limited success. Coupled with the resistance from the firms, ITS must face the same hurdles as the MNCs themselves, which are operating in various countries with differing labor laws and customs; and for that reason ITS does not often get support from local unions (Hodgetts & Luthans 1991).

INTERNATIONAL STANDARDS FOR LABOR PRACTICES

In 1919, the International Labor Organization (ILO) was formed to set minimum standards for humane labor conditions, including minimum wage standards, child labor practices, and legal restrictions on collective bargaining (Daniels & Radebargh 1992). Since then a number of other associations of unions representing workers from specific industries have formed to address those same issues. These include the World Confederation of Labor (WCL), the

World Federation of Trade Unions (WFTU); the International Confederation of Free Trade Unions (ICFTU); and the Organization for Economic Cooperation and Development (OECD). More recently, these groups have been concerned with labor practices of MNCs, especially the ICFTU, which has successfully lobbied the ILO, the OECD, and the United Nations Commission on Transnational Corporations (UNCTC) (Daniels & Radebargh 1992).

The OECD has issued voluntary guidelines regulating multinational behavior of corporations, including the controversial "umbrella" or *"chapeau* clause," which states that MNCs should keep to the guidelines "within the framework of the law, regulations and prevailing labor relations and employment practices, in each of the countries in which they operate." The clause is controversial because it is ambiguous: MNCs interpret the clause to mean that they must comply with national laws, while unions understand the clause to embellish national regulations, so that a corporation would be in violation even if it were in compliance with national regulations.

REDUNDANCY AND TERMINATION AGREEMENTS

Labor has also been very active on the national political level in trying to restrict MNCs with redundancy and termination laws. In an attempt to prevent jobs from being exported, termination agreements may be proscribed by law in some countries rather than by labor contracts. Also, while companies operating in the United States compensate for seasonal shifts in market demand through layoffs, elsewhere they are prohibited. Sometimes the only recourse a company may have is to fire a redundant worker, which may entail a company agreeing to make severance payments, extending benefits, and retraining and relocating the fired worker.

U.S.-BASED MNCs

In the United States, management has traditionally opposed unions, considering them to be bad for company productivity and bad for national economic performance. On the other side, labor has distrusted management, believing that management would exploit their labor force if they remained unchecked.

Although there are significant paradigm shifts in labor relations worldwide as the result of the implementation of new production strategies, attitudes rooted in ideologies change slowly. Consider the following case example:

> In 1986, Caterpillar, Inc., began a $2 billion restructuring program at its manufacturing facilities in the Peoria, Illinois, area. Besides physical refitting in the first phase, a teamwork system of labor was instituted, boosting Cat's productivity by 30 percent (Kelly 1992). The third phase of this restructuring included controlling labor costs by negotiating contracts for employee remuneration on a production-site-by-site basis with the United Auto Workers (UAW). The UAW wanted a contract with pay raises and other fringe benefits that a similar to a contract the UAW, had recently negotiated with John Deere & Co. (such contracts that are similar industry-wide are called "pattern agreements"). Although John Deere and Caterpillar were not direct competitors, they both make heavy equipment on an assembly line and were seen as comparable by the UAW who represented the workers in both corporations. The management of Caterpillar pointed out that most of John Deere's sales were domestic, while much of Caterpillar's sales are international. Thus, the management argued, Caterpillar would not be able to compete with international companies which paid lower wages if it met the UAW's contract demands.

> In the fall of 1991, during a period of high unemployment in the automotive industry, Caterpillar employees went on strike after a breakdown in negotiations between management and the UAW. After five months without an agreement with the union, the management announced that they would begin hiring permanent replacement workers or scabs. In April 1992, Caterpillar locked out 2,400 workers.

> Although the strike (but not the conflict) was ended when a third party was brought in to resolve the issues, much damage was already done. Public relations and employee goodwill suffered as Caterpillar was accused of trying to break the union. Because the UAW failed to get the contract it was seeking, the union organization was seriously weakened on an industry-wide scale. The UAW, which was stinging and bitter from the humiliation of the collapsed strike, and the workers, who were without a contract but working de facto under the terms first

offered by Caterpillar management, began to retaliate by deliberately slowing down production in a strategy called "work-to-rule." With the workers' negative emotions and distrust toward the company running high, Caterpillar, which had become increasingly dependent upon worker efficiency and quality control, is certain to be less competitive in the near future (Kelly 1992).

Should workers who are asking for pay raises at an American manufacturing plant consider the fact that their employer faces international competition which may utilize low-wage labor in another country? As a tactic for negotiating with a union, should a corporation threaten to move operations to another country with cheap labor? Should a company try to break a union by taking advantage of high unemployment within their industry? Historically in America and elsewhere, these questions were answered within a political framework that seemed to only measure whether the person was more sympathetic to "management" or to "unions."

In the past, U.S.-based MNCs have had a strong tendency to view labor relations through the filter of East–West cold war relations, in which the labor movement is related to or even equated with communism or socialism. As we have seen, this view is not shared in many countries where the corporation has a definite responsibility for the welfare of the countries' citizens. Moreover, significant changes in the global balance of power that came with reunification of Germany and dissolution of the Soviet Union have permanently altered U.S.-based MNC strategies in regard to the old political dichotomies.

As U.S.-based MNCs rethink their labor relations strategies, increasingly they are turning to successful models of industrial production that require the whole-hearted cooperation of employees. Much attention has been focused on the recent Japanese success with integrating labor relations and quality production strategies. As a result, labor issues have been pushed into the arena where questions about mutual long-term objectives must be addressed by everyone involved.

TRENDS IN LABOR RELATIONS

Although countries all have different orientations toward labor–management relations, practices that seem effective in one country are often copied by companies in other countries. This is especially the case when the production is positively impacted by a certain labor relations practice. Two recent examples of this are quality control circles and ESOPs.

QUALITY CONTROL CIRCLES AND TOTAL QUALITY CONTROL

Among the most important innovations for increasing quality and productivity in organizations are the concepts of *quality control circles (QC circles)* and *Total Quality Control (TQC)*. Importantly, the success of these strategies is completely dependent upon labor relations, especially management's attitudes toward them. The idea is that quality is produced by the way the production process is designed, so groups of workers and managers must cooperate to form QC circles whose mission is to constantly improve quality.

The QC circle is based on the work of the American W.E. Deming, who, in 1948, went to postwar Japan to teach statistically-based methods of quality control to Japanese scientists and Engineers.

The concept of TQC, that quality begins in the design stage and only ends when the services are provided to the customer, was introduced in Japan in 1954, by another American, J.M. Juran. Dr. Juran insisted that total quality is important, not just quality of manufacturing. This concept was developed into a "Japanese-style TQC" or "Company-Wide Quality Control (CWQC)."

Both QC circles and CWQC have now been widely adopted in Japan, and have greatly contributed to Japan's economic accomplishments. In the late 1970s, QC circles became the new buzzword and companies from all over the world rushed to embrace these methods. But because firms did not try to integrate the concepts into an overall management strategy, enthusiasm for QC circles waned. In an interview with the *Pacific Basin Quarterly* (1985), Dr. Deming attributes part of the difficulty with a poor understanding of the concept of quality. Perhaps his words express it best:

Americans simply have no idea of what quality is. Ask almost any plant manager in this country and he'll say it is a trade-off, that you can't have one without the other. He does not know that if you can have quality, then you can have productivity, lower costs, and a better market position. . .

The supposition of so many Americans that better quality means more gold plating or polishing, more time spent to do better work, is just not true. Quality improvement means improving the process so it produces quality without rework, quickly and directly. In other words, quality means making it right the first time so you don't have to rework it.

Additional problems that firms often encounter are unrealistic expectations about the extensive changes that must be made in labor relations, not just alterations in production techniques. Dr. Deming continues:

Many companies in America are forming QC circles without understanding what they're doing. QC circles cannot be effective in the absence of quality control, which means adopting my Fourteen Points. . .

1. Achieve constancy of purpose

2. Learn a new philosophy

3. Do not depend on mass inspections

4. Reduce the number of vendors

5. Recognize two sources of faults: management and production systems, and production workers

6. Improve on-the-job training

7. Improve supervision

8. Drive out fear

9. Improve communication

10. Eliminate fear

11. Consider work standards carefully

12. Teach statistical methods

13. Encourage new skills

14. Use statistical knowledge

> . . . the supposition [is] that quality control consists of a bag of techniques. Quality control is more than just a set of techniques. . .One of the Fourteen Points is to remove fear within a company, to make people secure. . . . Can you imagine people in a QC circle being effective when half of them will be turned out on the streets when business slacks off? Can you imagine a QC circle when half or even fewer of the people involved were rehired after being laid off during a slump?

Other Western observers have pointed to the failure to adopt *Kaizen* as root cause of the Occidental difficulty in duplicating the Japanese success with quality control. *Kaizen* means constant, gradual, and unending improvement in the workplace by everyone. For Japanese, real change means gradual and unending improvement, not the abrupt change that is commonly part of Western philosophy. For QC circles to work, management must overcome their tendency to view QC circles as ends rather than as means. Everyone must be in the program for the long haul (Watanabe 1991; Okubayashi 1989).

The primary obstacles to the implementation of quality circles lie with labor relations. Managers and workers typically are cynical, given their history of confrontation on labor issues. Workers distrust management's motives, and middle managers are frequently threatened by a perceived loss of power. Often, trade unions begrudge the friendly relationship between management and QC circles, and workers who do not participate in the program may resent those who do. Finally, top management often lacks the commitment to a QC philosophy, which can lessen the trust of those below in the hierarchy of the firm.

QC circles rely on management's commitment to improved quality and the means to get there. That means that the management–worker relationship must be one of cooperation. Management is responsible for motivating workers to cooperate by listening to their suggestions and demonstrating they are important by taking action on them. For a QC circle to be effective, labor must be committed to the quality of the final product, but that requires a reciprocal commitment of the company to the welfare of the worker. Workers easily sense when the management is making cursory gestures, rather than getting fully involved (Okubayashi 1989).

PROFIT SHARING AND ESOPs

In recent years, there has been a move to share corporate profits with labor. The most common form of profit-sharing schemes are Employee Stock Ownership Plans (ESOPs). Adoption of these plans extend worldwide to Australia, Japan, Italy, France, Spain, Sweden, Norway, and especially the United Kingdom and United States (*International Management* 1989). American involvement is the most extensive, encouraged by the 1986 tax incentives which provide tax deductions for businesses and tax exemptions for employees. Under ESOPs, workers are compensated for their work, both with a base wage and a wage that is linked with profits.

Have companies suddenly become more altruistic? Why would they be inclined to share their profits with workers? The answer is that management views profit sharing as being in their own self-interest on a number of levels. Profit sharing will motivate workers to improve quality, productivity, and profitability due to reduced conflict, labor turnover, and absenteeism. They can form part of the managerial human resources strategy to influence the level of the output, the degree of commitment, and the level of joint decision making between management and employees. ESOPs offer employee shareholders the opportunity to increase their involvement in the workplace, and to raise their level of understanding about the fiscal conditions that drive decision making. Because ownership confers a legitimate right to participate in decision making, it increases organization identification (*International Management* 1989).

Theoretically, profit-sharing schemes can have an effect on macroeconomics by reducing inflation and unemployment. Under this plan a worker's wages are tied to profits (and indirectly to production) rather than to a fixed annual percentage increase. Thus, inflation is curbed, and the company is automatically able to control the costs of added employees. This motivates the company to hire more workers because the added revenue cost of hiring another worker is less than the additional revenue that worker will generate. Hiring more workers reduces the profit per worker, but total profits rise (*International Management* 1989).

In practice, however, the story is more complex. Because reducing the profit per worker will reduce the wage per worker, workers will oppose hiring. Furthermore, if profit sharing is added to normal wages, it can fuel inflation. Thus, the macroeconomic impact of profit sharing is mixed. However, it is clear that because employee participation in hiring policies can conflict with the interests of long-term corporate goals, worker participation in hiring practices should be curbed by management (*International Management* 1989).

Are ESOPs a threat to unions? When employees change their status to employee shareholders, existing channels of employee representation and participation in the decision-making process are impacted. Usually this means a rethinking of union representation. In opposition to the historical mission of unions, a shift in status of the employee alters the traditional role of the union from protecting the rights of workers to protecting the rights of shareholders (*International Management* 1989). As employee shareholders' interests begin to match management interest, the need for union representation may be questioned. Furthermore, profit-sharing schemes can be uneven, dividing employees into groups of those with and without profit sharing. Hence, in the short term, trade union solidarity may be fractured, and bargaining power diminished (*International Management* 1989).

In the long run, if unions are flexible and responsive to their membership, they may be strengthened by ESOPs. The improved status of union members as shareholders includes the right to financial information about the company that is not typically available to employees and unions. Such information can give unions a distinct advantage during bargaining talks with management. Also, unions would remain instrumental for employee shareholders in bargaining talks because individual employees acting on their own behalf may find it difficult or impossible to confirm their fair share of profits without the union's access to accounting expertise and bargaining power (*International Management* 1989).

From a certain perspective, introduction of an ESOP seems to invert the relation of the employee to management, with the employee placed in a position to delegate the operations of the firm to management. In reality, an employee shareholder has little more impact in running the company than another small investor, although the collective representation of employee shareholders has the potential to challenge managerial expertise. Despite the intention of linking employee financial participation with decision-making, management rarely relinquishes control to the extent of cooperatives or worker-owned businesses. However, worker decision-making is important, for studies have shown that the success of profit-sharing schemes depends on the extent of management's commitment to its introduction, along with "actual routines of participation;" that is, the number of meetings held in which management and workers solve problems and make corporate plans (*International Management* 1989).

Among the benefits of ESOPs for management are the increased level of employee involvement and the extent to which employees share the goals of the firm. By giving employees a voice in the decisions that affect them, employees become more committed and feel as though they have a stake in the company's success.

Traditionally, management rewards an individual worker's effort with incentives. The innovation of ESOPs is linking the efforts of all employees as a group to the incentives, thereby creating peer review of other workers' performance. The impact of peer review on productivity is strongest where the group is small enough so that they can witness the impact of their efforts on profits. This is why, it is important for management to have regular decision-making meetings with employees, to make them aware of their impact and to listen to their suggestions (International Management 1989; Rosen & Quarrey 1987).

An ESOP is not a magic pill. In fact, management must be strongly committed to make profit sharing work by supporting it with positive attitudes and formalized methods for employee input into decision-making. Management and employees must come to view their relationship as a partnership in which they have common goals.

ESOPs can be risky for employees. Because part of an employee's wages are derived from profits, an employee is exposed to substantial financial risk. If the share price declines, so does the remuneration to the employee. This can be unfair if the cause of the decline of profits has nothing to do with the employee's decision-making or work effort.

Yet the effects of ESOPs are clearly worthwhile. ESOP companies that instituted participation plans grew at a rate three to four times faster than those that did not have those plans (Rosen & Quarrey 1987). They are likely to give greater security to both management and employees, and to foster increased profitability and productivity. Companies with profit-sharing arrangements have been shown to outperform non-profit-sharing firms. There is clear link between the adoption of schemes, and trends in business volume and annual turnover of companies. As long as expectations are realistic and ESOPs are part of a larger and integrated program of human resource management in the firm, profit sharing can produce significant results.

SUMMARY

The country differences in laws, customs, values, and norms regarding labor-management relations cannot be ignored by companies when operating overseas. This chapter summarized and defined important terminology used in the field of labor relations. Labor relations practices from different countries (U.S., Italy, Great Britain, and Germany) were compared and contrasted.

Labor relations issues were then viewed from the perspective of MNCs, and how MNCs' view of unions, strategize in their relationships with local unions, and manage their labor capital across borders, were discussed. Union responses to MNCs' strategies, international standards for labor practices, and other international organized labor issues were also discussed.

Finally, recent trends that affect labor relations around the world were discussed: the quality movement, profit sharing, and ESOPs. In-depth analyses of the labor dimension must be part of any global strategic plan. Consider the following thought process a North American human resource manager might go through to consider the labor implications of opening up a subsidiary overseas:

I wonder if unions will be a problem for us? I remember reading somewhere that in order to shut down a manufacturing facility in France (or was it Germany or Sweden?), management had to give the workers a full year's notice, retrain them, and then find them new jobs...Well, maybe the Asian labor markets are less unionized and won't be as problematic...Wait a minute...what about that American toy company I read about a couple of years ago that put pressure on its contract manufacturers in Hong Kong and the PRC to increase production dramatically in order to fill their unforeseen needs during the Christmas season? The press had gotten hold of stories about female workers who were working sixteen hour days with no breaks; if they complained, they were terminated on the spot. Some of the women had even miscarried. Maybe dealing with unions wouldn't be all bad. Maybe unions will protect us from questionable ethical nightmares....But the thought of co-determination laws in countries like Germany and worker's representatives sitting on the local boards of directors— that would not be easy for American managers to stomach.....(Mendenhall & Oddou 1991).

Future challenges in the labor relations—will be of utmost concern to everyone; it will be interesting to view how things evolve during the next ten years.

DISCUSSION QUESTIONS

1. Select two countries and discuss contrasts in their approaches to labor relations.

2. Identify evidence of cultural diversity in your local work force. Discuss how this diversity is likely to affect management approaches.

3. Discuss ways in which the internationalization of the labor union movement has kept pace with the internationalization of business. Discuss.

REFERENCES

Badham, R. 1991. "The social dimension of computer-integrated manufacturing." *International Labour Review*, 130, (3), pp. 373–92.

Baglioni, G. 1991. "An Italian mosaic: Collective bargaining patterns in the 1980s." *International Labour Review*, 130 (1), pp. 81–112.

Campbell, A., A. Sorge & M. Warner. 1990. "Technological change, product strategies and human resources: Defining Anglo-German differences." *Journal of General Management*, 15 (3), pp. 39–54.

Chatak, E. 1991. "A unionist's perspective on the future of American unions." *Journal of Labor Research*, 12 (4), pp. 327-32.

Craft, J. A. 1991. "Unions, bureaucracy, and change: Old dogs learn new tricks very slowly." *Journal of Labor Research*, 12 (4), pp. 393–405.

Daniels, J.D. & Radebargh, L.H. (1992) *International Business: Environments and Operations.* (6th Ed.) Reading, MA: Addison-Wesley Publishing Company.

Delaney, J.T. 1991. "The future of unions as political organizations." *Journal of Labor Research*, 12 (4), pp. 373–87.

Douglas, M. & J. Douglas. 1989. "Institutions of the third kind: British and Swedish labor markets compared." *Journal of General Management*, 14 (4), pp. 34–52.

Edwards, Deming. 1985. *Pacific Basin Quarterly*, 12, Spring–Summer, pp. 1–4.

Hamill, J. 1984. "Labor relations practices and multinational corporations and industrial relations." *Industrial Relations Journal*, 15 (2), pp. 30–4.

Hodgetts, R.M. & F. Luthans. 1991. *International Management.* New York: McGraw Hill.

Jarley, P. & J. Fiorito. 1991. "Unionism and changing employee views toward work." *Journal of Labor Research*, 12 (3), pp. 223–9.

Kelly, K. 1992. "Caterpillar's Don Fites: Why he didn't blink." *Business Week*, 3278, August 10, pp. 56–7.

Mendenhall, M. & G. Oddou. 1991. "The white water rapids of International human resource management." In (M. Mendenhall and G. Oddou) *Readings and Cases in International Human Resource Management.* Boston: PWS-Kent.

Okubayashi, K. 1989. "The Japanese industrial relations system." *Journal of General Management*, 14 (3), pp. 67–88.

"The roots of quality control in Japan: An interview with W. Parry, J." (1989). Paying guests. *International Management*, 46 (1), pp. 38–41.

Poole, M. & G. Jenkins. 1991. "The impact of profit-sharing and employee shareholding schemes." *Journal of General Management*, 16 (3), pp. 52–72.

Poole, M. 1986. "Managerial strategies and styles in industrial relations: A comparative analysis." *Journal of General Management*, 12 (1), pp. 40–53.

Prahalad, C.K. & Y.L. Doz. 1987. *The Multinational Mission: Balancing Local Demands and Global Vision*. New York: The Free Press.

Rosen, C. & M. Quarrey. 1987. "How well is employee ownership working?" *Harvard Business Review*, September–October, pp. 126–129.

Rothwell, S. 1989. "Is there a real change in industrial relations in Britain?" *Manager Update*, 1 (1), pp. 16–23.

Rubin, P.H. 1991. "Unions, bureaucracy, and change: Comment." *Journal of Labor Research*, 12 (4), pp. 406–409.

Thompson, R.T. 1991. "The changing character of employee relations." *Journal of Labor Research*, 12 (4), pp. 311–321.

Watanabe, S. 1991. "The Japanese quality control circle: Why it works." *International Labour Review*, 130 (1), pp. 57–80.

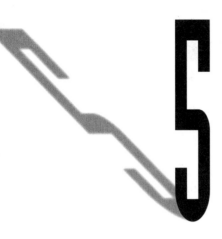

5

THE GLOBAL

ETHICAL

ENVIRONMENT

LEARNING OBJECTIVES

IN THIS CHAPTER YOU WILL EXPLORE:

- The role of ethical issues in international business

- Ethical philosophies that impinge on management practices

- The Foreign Corrupt Practices Act (FCPA)

- The nature of unethical activities in international management

- Ethical dilemmas MNC managers face

- The Civil Rights Act of 1991

- Ethical issues about the use of guest workers

KEY DISCUSSION ISSUES:

- How does culture influence ethical issues in business?

- What are the implications of cultural relativism vs. universalism?

- Does the FCPA hinder success in the international marketplace?

- Why does bribery occur, and what can be done about it?

- How can MNCs resolve ethical dilemmas they encounter?

- How should governments and businesses view and treat guest workers?

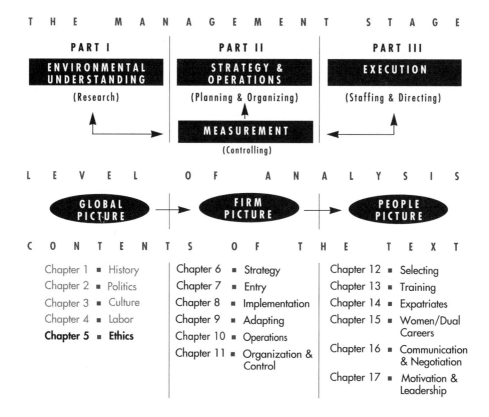

THE MANAGEMENT STAGE

PART I	PART II	PART III
ENVIRONMENTAL UNDERSTANDING	**STRATEGY & OPERATIONS**	**EXECUTION**
(Research)	(Planning & Organizing)	(Staffing & Directing)

MEASUREMENT

(Controlling)

LEVEL OF ANALYSIS

GLOBAL PICTURE → **FIRM PICTURE** → **PEOPLE PICTURE**

CONTENTS OF THE TEXT

INTRODUCTION

Anyone who has done much travelling around the world knows that countries differ in their approach to punishing certain kinds of behaviors. Many countries have laws "on the books" regarding the criminal nature of certain behaviors, yet the daily practice is to disregard the law. Everyone—the police, the government, and the population, quietly accepts the daily reality over the law on the books. Consider the following:

> Government spending [in India] . . . has multiplied 50 times in the past three decades and now accounts for almost a quarter of GNP . . . [However, it is reported that] in many public works projects, 10 percent–50 percemt of the budgets disappear into the pockets of contractors and bureaucrats . . . Significant cuts and kickbacks to key decision makers has become the rule rather than the exception. (Spaeth 1988).

When an expatriate enters a new country and begins doing business there, he/she may be confronted with business practices that are not just different, but unethical from his/her perspective. The expatriate might also act in a manner that is deemed illegal locally, though considered legal at home. This chapter will discuss some of the troubling issues that can arise when doing business internationally, and possible courses one can take to behave ethically overseas.

THE IMPORTANCE OF BUSINESS ETHICS

Virtually all societies have developed rules and regulations about how business should be transacted and how business organizations should be managed. In other words, based on experience and the philosophical and/or religious values of a society, rules of acceptable and nonacceptable behaviors evolve and are encoded into society. For example, in every society we are aware of, it is illegal, wrong, and unethical to murder one's subordinates if they make a mistake at work. This may sound like a ridiculous example, but the restraining rule forbidding this managerial conduct—including the penalty associated with it—is based on basic beliefs about human beings, their proper relationships, and the value of human life. Thus, business ethics can be defined as "the moral principles and standards that guide behavior in the world of business" (Ferrell & Fraedrich 1991, p. 5).

F. Neil Brady suggests that many of us think of business ethics as a tangential issue in the life of a business manager. However, the reality is that managerial decisions are woven through with ethical issues. Brady lists several reasons why managers—both international and domestic—should be concerned with ethics. (The following four points with lists of questions, and quotes come from Brady 1990, pp. 2–5.)

1. *Managerial decisions affect people's lives and well being.*

Consider this list of managerial concerns:

- Which one of five eligible individuals should get the promotion?

- How can I diffuse the discontent on the shop floor among angry and frustrated workers?

- What position should I take in negotiating with the union?

- Should I try to arrange a private office for a particularly successful employee?

- Should I assign two people whose personalities differ to the same project team?

Brady notes that in each case a poor or unwise decision on the part of the manager can adversely affect the lives of many people. Often the answers to such questions are not clear, yet they always involve issues of what is right or wrong, and what would be good or bad for employees.

2. *Managers must distribute organizational resources fairly.*

This managerial responsibility is clearly influenced by ethical concerns, as can be seen by considering the questions:

- How should I use our profits this year—to increase employee benefits, to lower the prices of our products, or to invest in new equipment?

- Which of my employees should get the new chairs sent to us from the purchasing department?

- How much time should I give to interviews with outside groups, such as consumer groups, reporters, and community leaders?

- How much money should the organization donate this year to community and political causes?

Such questions are just as relevant to an expatriate manager in Brussels as they are to his/her counterpart in Baltimore.

Brady notes that "such decisions are ethical because of the need to be fair, and fairness is a strong component of the daily managerial routine. But this is not as simple as it sounds. A fair distribution is not always an equal one . . . where special ethical needs exist, there may be ethical justification for skewing an otherwise equal distribution in favor of those needs."

3. *Managers create rules and policies.*

Managers create, implement, and enforce rules and policies in companies—as one of their major roles. Brady notes that "the relationship of a manager to the rules is not merely mechanical. If it were, there would be no discretionary power, and there would be less reason for supposing the situation to be ethical. But because most managers do have discretion to waive rules or to change them, or at least to decide in any particular case whether a rule applies, therefore we hold managers responsible for the proper development and application of organizational rules."

Consider the issues these examples raise:

- Should the dress and grooming policy apply only to personnel who have contact with the public, or should it apply to all employees?

- Are employees abusing their sick leave, and if so, what should I do about it?

- Should we adopt a policy regarding tardiness?

    These questions are difficult enough to sort out in a domestic situation, let alone a cross-cultural one. "The ethical responsibility in all of these situations is to produce a system of shared values and expectations that is realistic and fair."

4. *Managerial-decision making tests one's personal values.*

Managers sometimes are faced with decisions that test their own personal values; that is, the decision that seems best for the organization or the situation conflicts with their own sense of right and wrong.

For example:

- Should this report reflect my professional judgment or the requests of my boss?

- Should I simply do what I'm told, even though I feel strongly otherwise?

- Should I object to sexual harassment in the office?

- Should I sacrifice time with my family to get ahead in my career?

- My best friend is not well-liked in the company; should I come to his defense in meetings even though I might be seen as a persona non grata by others?

Brady further notes that "it is in the managerial arena that organizational dominance over personal judgment may be most intense." This incongruence between the organizational, situational needs and personal values can be especially marked in cross-cultural situations, when managers and employees have differing value systems. Thus, the issue of business ethics permeates organizational life—especially the organizational life of the manager. With this in mind, we will explore some of the common challenges of managing ethically in an international environment.

ETHICS IN THE INTERNATIONAL BUSINESS ARENA

To explore the issues associated with international business ethics, it is helpful to distinguish between three concepts: individual relativism, cultural relativism, and universalism.

The idea of *individual relativism*, in its extreme position, is that there is no absolute principle of right and wrong, good or bad, in any social situation. What is right and what is wrong should be left up to the individual or individuals involved in the situation at hand. A pure individual relativist might claim that practices that are universally banned by most societies (such as incest, cannibalism, or grave-robbing) are neither right nor wrong—they simply depend on the beliefs of each individual and each individual alone.

Cultural relativism is, according to Norman Bowie (1990), "the doctrine that what is right or wrong, good or bad, depends on one's culture. If the Irish consider abortion to be morally wrong, abortion is morally wrong in Ireland. If the Swedes do not consider abortion to be morally wrong, then abortion is not morally wrong in Sweden. There is no universal principle to which the Swedes and the Irish can appeal that determines whether abortion really is wrong or not."

Societies, through experience, have developed rules that benefit most of the people, most of the time. And because each society has faced different situations over time, each society has evolved different rules to create order, justice, predictability, and ensure smooth commerce. Thus, applied to business, cultural relativism holds that business people operating in foreign countries should follow the practices in that country; that is, "When in Rome, do as the Romans do."

One of the authors once invited a successful international businessman to speak at an MBA class. After the presentation, the question was asked of him: "What's the first thing you do when you arrive in a new foreign country to do business?" He answered without hesitation: "I find out who the key people are to my success and how to best bribe them." The class was shocked at his philosophy. He was an unabashed cultural relativist and expanded on his statement with a discussion of "When in Rome, do as the Romans do." His view was: "What right to North Americans have to enter a country as guests and push their values and ways of doing things on others? One should respect the values and standards of other cultures and conform to them when on their soil."

Universalism holds that there are "universal and objective ethical rules . . . and that, without such an ethical framework, which is already supplied by a number of established treaties and conventions . . . multinational business dealings could not be possible at all" (Bowie 1990). The assumption within universalism is that there are core, universal ethical principles that guide societies' social behaviors and that, often, apparent differences in rules between societies really come from the same core ethical principle. As Bowie explains:

> . . . in some cultures, after a certain age parents are put to death. In [the North American] culture such behavior would be murder. We take care of our parents. Does this difference in behavior prove that the two cultures disagree about matters of ethics? No, it does not. Suppose the other culture believes that people exist in the afterlife in the same condition that they leave their present life. It would be very cruel to have one's parents exist eternally in an unhealthy state. By killing them when they are relatively active and vigorous, [the children] insure their [parents'] happiness for all eternity. The underlying ethical principle of this culture is that children have duties to their parents, including the duty to be concerned with their parents' happiness . . . This ethical principle is identical with our own. What looked like a difference in ethics . . . turned out, upon close examination, to be a difference based on factual evidence alone (Bowie 1990).

Those who take the universalist position observe that there is a wide acceptance of many core business principles around the world. Take bribery, for example. Michael Bogdan (1979) has shown that bribery is prohibited officially in laws in virtually every nation of the world. Some governments may not enforce those laws as rigidly as others—but universalists believe that there is widespread conceptual agreement among all people regarding the ethicality of this.

Another contention of the universalists is that, if the world is to have any hope of enduring social stability, values will have to be negotiated and adopted globally. Thus, for the universalist, international social stability, especially in the business world, depends on a universal view as the best approach.

Interestingly, the "social stability requires the negotiation of shared values" argument is what cultural relativists use against individual relativists: How can society function if everyone does whatever he or she wants? Universalists would use the same argument against the cultural relativist: How can world stability occur if every nation does whatever it wants?

This has been a conceptual discussion of the differing approaches to viewing cross-cultural differences in ethics. However, international business people operate in the real world. The following sections will deal with issues that confront the international manager. We shall see that "doing as the Romans do" can often backfire, as a strategy, when doing business overseas.

BRIBERY

Bribery is a practice that can be found in almost all cultures around the world. In the Middle East, the word used for bribery is *baksheesh*, which technically is defined as the tip or gratuity given by a boss to his/her subordinate. Now, it has come to mean influence that can be had by giving money. Its origins come from the word's first usage, which referred to the money that a new sultan would give to his troops upon acquiring his position.

In most Spanish-speaking countries bribery is referred to as *el soborno*, meaning "payoff." In Mexico, bribery is often called *la mordida*, which means "the bite." In Germany bribery is called *Schmiergeld* which literally translates into English as "grease money." Sometimes Germans simply refer to bribery as "N.A.," a colloquial abbreviation of *nutzliche Abgabe* which means "useful contribution." In France bribery is referred to as *pot-de-vin* (jug of wine); in Italy, the word for a bribe is *bastarella* (little envelope) (*Time* 1981).

Bribery can take other forms than money. In Mexico bribery can include lavish entertainment in exclusive restaurants and weekend trips to resorts. In Argentina, bribery can take the form of expensive gifts, such as post-impressionistic paintings or jewelry. In Malaysia, bribery can be conducted by wisely losing games of chance. Whatever form it takes, it can add significantly to the cost of doing business. It has been estimated that the approximate markup of contracts due to bribery often ranges from 5 to 10 percent in some countries where bribery is tolerated (*Time* 1981).

Before one concedes that the easiest way out is to simply follow the dictum of the cultural relativists, it is important to understand that obeying it can sometimes lead to a career downfall overseas; for in many cases, "doing what the Romans do" means breaking U.S. law. Consider the Foreign Corrupt Practices Act.

THE FOREIGN CORRUPT PRACTICES ACT

U.S. business managers who are U.S. citizens are held accountable by the U.S. government via the Foreign Corrupt Practices Act (FCPA). In 1977, President Carter signed into the lawbooks S.305, the FCPA. Under its provisions, it is illegal for American companies to offer payments to officials of foreign governments to gain business contracts. This law makes three distinctions about bribery:

1. *Bribery vs. extortion.* Bribes are voluntarily offered to encourage unlawful special treatment; extortion is payment made under duress to someone seeking only treatment to which he/she is entitled. Example: If terrorists operating in a country approach an American company and demand that the company pay a "revolutionary tax," the company may feel it has to pay in order to avoid violence and other trouble. This "revolutionary tax" constitutes payment made under duress for treatment the company was entitled to as a legitimate business.

2. *Bribery vs. lubrication or grease payments.* A lubrication payment is a small payment to low-level business people or government officials to "grease the wheels" of business. The purpose is to encourage prompt performance of functions that should be lawfully carried out by these individuals, but which they refuse until they are offered remuneration for doing so. In essence, a grease payment differs from a bribe in two important ways: the amount of money involved is small, and it is not designed to seek after unlawful

competitive advantage. Example: In Nigeria an American cosmetics firm was trying to finish the paperwork necessary to gain permission for the agents to operate in a district of that country. Time went by and the official documents were still not ready. When confronted by the American representative of the company, the government official hinted that he would love a box of Havana cigars. When presented with the box of cigars, the paperwork magically appeared, and the company was able to operate legally in that area of the country. Under U.S. law, that company did nothing illegal, for the box of Havana cigars constituted a "lubrication payment" (Vassel 1983).

3. *Bribes vs. agents fees.* Companies often will employ business agents to help them do business in a foreign country. The business agent is usually a native of the foreign country who knows how business is done there. For a fee, the agent will help the company set up interviews with key government and business officials, help the company in their business negotiations, and so on. If a U.S. company has "reason to know" that part of the fee they pay the agent will be used by the agent to in turn bribe local officials on behalf of the company, the company is in violation of the FCPA. Example: An American firm hires an agent who they understand can "deliver the goods," and that part of his modus operandi is asking for high fees so that he can use part of those fees to bribe key players in the local government. Entering into a contract with this agent knowing that he will use part of his fee as bribes, constitutes a violation of the FCPA.

Barry Richman (1979) offers some measures for preventing questionable payments via agents. Companies should:

- Conduct thorough checks on the backgrounds, qualifications, and past behavior of foreign agents the company is considering using in selling their product or for representing the company.

- Include government and/or public disclosure clauses in contracts or agreements involving potentially sensitive terms and conditions.

- Require agreement by foreign agents to abide by the applicable corporate ethical and legal policies of the company, and to provide periodic compliance letters to company officials.

- Require that foreign agents agree to allow company auditors access to their books and records if questions of impropriety arise.

To comply with the FCPA, a company must:

- Set up and enforce an antibribery company policy with the full backing of top management, both orally and in writing.

- Set up guidelines to assist the company's sales and accounting personnel develop appropriate international sales strategies and corresponding accounting policies.

- Design, implement, and maintain a system of internal accounting controls which correspond to the company's antibribery policy.

- Seek advice from government agencies if the legality of certain payments is questioned.

- Reward and punish employees based on their adherence to the company's antibribery policy.

If convicted of violating this law, companies face fines of up to $1 million, and individual offenders within the company face jail sentences of up to five years and/or personal fines of $10,000. Interestingly, the FCPA does not ban "grease payments," bribes to low-ranking officials or clerical workers who can hold up the normal flow of business by demanding bribes. The U.S. government felt that it would be unreasonable to ask U.S. business people to suffer business losses due to demands made on them for bribes by such people. Thus, the law is designed to prevent exorbitant bribes to high-ranking officials only.

One weakness of the FCPA is that it does not spell out how much money constitutes an exorbitant bribe, and who exactly a high-ranking official is. This is one weakness critics print out. Many feel the law should be explicit in its statutes.

After the law was enacted, the Securities and Exchange Commission (SEC) created a "voluntary disclosure" program, whose purpose was simply to ask companies to indicate, anonymously, to what degree they had been involved in bribery during the decade preceding the birth of the FCPA. More than 400 companies (117 of which were Fortune 500 companies) reported having given out over $300 million in various payments that would have been illegal under the FCPA (Ferrell & Fraedrich 1991). This, of course, does not reflect the entire picture of international bribery carried out by American firms during this period; it represents only the 400 companies who volunteered information to the SEC. The extent of the bribery during that time was probably much greater. For example, in the 1970s, PEMEX, Mexico's national oil company, received bribes from a single Texas businessman that involved contracts worth $293 million (*The Economist* 1990, p. 392). From 1970 to 1975, Lockheed paid $22 million in bribes to Japanese foreign officials, the bulk of which went to the prime minister, Kakuei Tanaka.

There have been many critics of the FCPA. Probably the biggest criticism of this law is that it places American companies at a disadvantage when competing with foreign firms. Other countries have laws against bribery within their domestic business context, yet allow their companies to bribe when doing business overseas. For example, in Switzerland, Germany, and many other countries, bribery is seen simply as a cost of doing business, and can be claimed as a corporate tax deduction. Has the law hurt American competitiveness abroad?

John Graham and Mark McKean (*The Economist* 1990) looked at information from American embassies in 51 countries that accounted for four-fifths of U.S. exports. These countries were then divided into two groups: countries where bribery was considered part of the business culture and countries where bribery was not accepted. After eight years of the passage of the FCPA, they found that the U.S. share of the imports of countries labeled as corrupt increased as fast as its share of the imports of countries labeled as law-abiding. This and other studies done since the FCPA seem to indicate that the law has not seriously curtailed American sales overseas. John Graham (1983, p. 89–94) concludes from his research that:

From a legal standpoint, the recommendation is clear—avoid questionable deals. The loss of the few "questionable" contracts probably is not worth the risk of indictment, prosecution, conviction. . . . Moreover, if you are indicted, will your company support you or opt to plead guilty and accept the fine? From an ethical perspective, making a bribe represents a personal choice . . . and as Peter Drucker puts it, only you have to live with your reflection in the mirror.

Many firms have policies regarding "questionable payments" in foreign countries. These provide guidance for managers faced with situations where they are unsure how to respond to a request for payment. These guidelines can themselves pose ethical dilemmas, as this case illustrates:

A Canadian firm had a very strict set of regulations that required managers to report any payments, no matter how small, made to host-government representatives. Apparently this resulted in no such payments, which was the firm's goal. Unfortunately this record was broken when the president of the Mexican subsidiary, a Canadian, was arrested by the Mexican police, following a party. Headquarters in Canada was faced with the choice between allowing its representative in Mexico to remain in a Mexican jail or making what was considered a questionable payment to the police. They chose the second option.

SOCIAL RESPONSIBILITY

From 1960 to 1970, social changes occurred in the U.S. that affected business. The issues of civil rights, equal rights, environmental awareness, and various consumer issues all influenced how businesses within the U.S. dealt with their employees and their surrounding communities. From this time period, the term "social responsibility" came into being. Rogene Bucholz (1989, p. 5) notes that:

There are many definitions of social responsibility, but in general it means that a private corporation has responsibilities to society that go beyond the production of goods and services at a profit—that a corporation has a broader constituency to serve than stockholders alone. . . .Corporations are more than economic institutions and have

a responsibility to devote some of their resources to helping solve
some of the most pressing social problems, many of which corporations helped to cause.

Many people do not subscribe to this view; nevertheless, significant pressure
is put on corporations to consider the social impact of their products, services,
and practices. A cultural relativist might argue that this aspect of corporate
responsibility is limited to North America; thus, when a company operates
overseas all it has to do is conform to local regulations and all will be fine.
Things are not that simple; the Bhopal incident provides a striking example of
why:

Conforming to local laws is exactly what Union Carbide did when it constructed a plant in Bhopal, India. The Indian government's desire to produce
pesticides and fertilizers to increase the agricultural productivity of their
country led to Union Carbide's venture in India. This plant brought many jobs
to the area, and until the accident, the relationship between the local government and community and Union Carbide was a positive one.

However, on December 3, 1984, a methyl-isocyanate gas leak at the plant
killed more than 1,600 people immediately and roughly 700 people subsequently from the effects of the accident. Survivors suffered from lung problems, shortness of breath, depression, eye irritation, and stomach pains.
Eventually, over 2,700 lawsuits were filed in India against Union Carbide.
Union Carbide was sued for not adhering to U.S. safety standards in the construction of the plant, and received censure in the foreign and U.S. press for
having lowered what it knew to be necessary safety standards, simply to save
money by adhering to less stringent local standards. Union Carbide contend-
ed that the gas leakage was due to sabotage.

On February 14, 1989, the Indian government reached settlement with Union
Carbide. The Indian Supreme Court ordered Union Carbide to pay $470 mil-
lion in damages to the Indian government on behalf of the victims of Bhopal.
All criminal charges and civil suits in India were dropped in return
(Asheghian & Ebrahimi 1990).

Looking beyond cultural relativistic solutions to issues of corporate responsibility toward a more universalistic approach is also fraught with dilemmas. The next section is not an exhaustive discussion, but to the challenge of managing the ethical dimension of an overseas operation—an ongoing, dynamic process.

ETHICAL DILEMMAS MNCs FACE

The objective of the MNC is to optimize its operations globally; conversely, the policy of the host country's government is to optimize its operations locally. In essence, the implication of this dilemma is that often a MNC cannot simply come into a country, set up shop, and organize itself to make the company as efficient as possible. Host governments may fear the MNC inherent economic power. Thus, the host government may try to gain control over MNCs—and make use of MNCs—to meet their own goals, which may include creating a more equitable distribution of wealth or increasing their country's economic self-determination (Garland, Farmer, & Taylor 1990). Sometimes, to facilitate the latter goal, the host government may require that MNCs hire a high percentage of host country managers to staff the MNC's subsidiary rather than allowing expatriate managers to do so.

The following examples from Garland, Farmer, & Taylor (1990, pp. 201–2), illustrate other issues involving ethical dilemmas:

- If a MNC installs state-of-the-art, labor-saving technology in a foreign subsidiary, the host government may not be very pleased. If there is a high incidence of unemployment or underemployment in the country, the government may prefer the MNC to use older, more labor-intensive technology to create more jobs for its people. Such provisions may even be part of the agreement in the initial negotiations with the government. Once the MNC decides to use labor-intensive technology, over time, the government may begin to criticize the MNC for not gradually introducing more labor-reducing technology. The MNC may, over time, begin to be accused of not assisting the country in developing its technological base.

- If the MNC repatriates most of its profits, it is accused of depriving the host country of money that was generated within the host country. However, if a decision to reinvest profits in the host country is made, the MNC might be perceived to be adding to its economic control of the local economy or in a sector of the local economy.

- If the MNC pays local wages to its workers, it might be seen as an exploiter of low-cost labor; however, if it pays above-average wages to local workers it might be accused of emasculating the competitiveness of local firms and hoarding the brightest talent from the labor pool.

- If the MNC does not promote local managerial talent, it might be seen as being discriminatory. If it does, however, it might be seen as creating a "brain drain," that is, taking out of the country some of the country's brightest people.

Positive relationships between the MNC and local government, business and labor leaders are a key to the success of an overseas subsidiary. Usually, MNCs want to keep a low profile overseas. However, the more successful an MNC is overseas, the less likely it will be able to keep a low profile. The results of success are high visibility and being forced to play a major role in the society of that country. In other words, there may simply be no way to get away from the influence, expectations, desires, and needs of the local communities in which subsidiaries operate.

In the end, MNCs are tolerated when the local institutions of power perceive their net contribution to the economy and society to be greater than their costs. There are no easy solutions to these dilemmas. For example, consider an MNC who decides to pay local workers in excess of the average salary of that country. Such a step may be lauded by the press and other watchdog groups in the home country, yet such a step may lead to other problems:

> The higher wages paid to MNC workers in the industrial sector may lure farmers from the agricultural sector in the LDC. This may lead to a decline in the production of food and raw materials that could severely harm the LDC's economic development in the long run. . . .

The local merchants may perceive the higher purchasing power of this small group as an indication of the total community's purchasing capability. As a result, the merchants may raise prices, which will damage the poorer majority's ability to buy goods. This, in turn, may lead to social conflicts (Asheghian & Ebrahimi 1990, p. 632).

When the tension between the MNCs' interests and those of the local community become strained and out of balance, it can result in a public relations nightmare, which in turn can influence profits negatively (recall the Bhopal incident). Garland, Farmer, and Taylor (1990, p. 202) suggest these four reasons for this tension. We illustrate each point with examples.

1. "Multinationals serve as convenient targets when governments are unable to satisfy the needs and aspirations of their people." Examples: Scenes such as U.S. congressmen/women bashing a Japanese car with a sledgehammer because of their frustration with the U.S.–Japan trade imbalance is an example of larger, complex issues being taken out on the nearest symbol associated with the perceived adversary—a company from that country. Likewise, North American companies have been targets of terrorist activities in Europe by groups that have ideological differences with U.S. policies, showing that companies thus become symbols of the main adversary—the policies of the country's government.

2. "The multinational is foreign, and is seen as an alien influence subverting the indigenous culture and acting as a tool of its home state." Example: When Disney was negotiating the building of Euro-Disney, many in the French media and special interest groups displayed their displeasure with "American neoprovincialism" and the "cultural Chernobyl" that Euro-Disney would wreak upon French society. Also, the fear that Disney would cause children to adopt a "consumer mentality" was raised. Disney needed to do public relations campaigning to overcome the local criticisms of its venture.

3. "The multinational is typically private, and is viewed as a rapacious pursuer of its own gain at the expense of the public welfare." Examples: This fear is not without some grounding in fact, as when Malaysia and Liberia were almost totally economically dependent on companies such as Firestone Tire & Rubber Company and United Fruit Company. Some companies have even tried to influence political boundaries, such as the Belgian mining company Union Miniere S.A., which helped to finance the attempted breakaway of Katanga after Zaire attained independence (Ferrell & Fraedrich 1991, pp. 154–5).

4. The multinational is "the most visible symbol of a world order that allegedly systematically discriminates against the less-developed countries, and in that sense the legitimacy of the multinational corporation is inherently subject to dispute." Example: Again, there is some justification for this a view, such as when MNCs pay a low price for the right to remove minerals and other natural resources, and then sell their products made from those resources at a much higher price with only a small portion going back to the country of origin; this kind of problem led to the formation of the Organization of Petroleum Exporting Countries (OPEC) in the 1960s when the member countries tried to gain control over the revenues from oil produced in their countries (Ferrell & Fraedrich 1991, p. 155).

Because of these perceptions, multinationals should pay constant attention to the quality of their relationships with the local communities around the world in which they have set up operations. What this really means is that the managers of those subsidiaries must do the work of maintaining good relations with the key players in the community in which they work, such as government leaders, labor leaders, activist groups, the media, charitable organizations, and religious organizations. The role of "bridge builder" is a significant one in the job description of an expatriate manager.

INTRA-COMPANY ETHICAL ISSUES IN INTERNATIONAL BUSINESS

So far our discussion has focused on ethical issues that arise from the relationship between MNCs and other institutions and people. We now explore the ethical issues within MNCs, and the people who work there.

Consider this hypothetical situation (Taylor & Eder 1994):

> A large U.S. teaching hospital has a cooperative program with a major teaching hospital in Saudi Arabia. Each year several doctors from the U.S. hospital spend the year in Saudi Arabia teaching and doing research. The stay in Saudi Arabia is generally considered both lucrative as well as professionally rewarding. Two well-qualified doctors in the hospital are upset because they were rejected for assignment to Saudi Arabia. The director of human resources explained to them that while the selection committee was impressed with their abilities, the committee decided that because they were Jewish, it would be best if they were disqualified from consideration. In spite of vigorous protest from the two doctors, the director supported the committee's decision. Is the director correct in supporting the committee's decision? By what criteria should the committee, and the director, base a decision? Do the doctors have any legal recourse?

It is questions like these that Sully Taylor and Robert Eder (1994) pose in their research on how companies should legally treat their expatriates. They note that the U.S. alone has roughly 3,500 multinational corporations and 25,000 companies with some overseas branches and affiliates. Over 40,000 U.S. companies do business abroad in some fashion. Because overseas assignments are important to a company's success, and also provide future company leaders with international experience, companies obviously desire to send overseas people they feel they can trust to do a good job. Taylor and Eder note that recent changes in the Civil Rights Act have important implications for how U.S. expatriates should be selected.

In essence, the Civil Rights Act of 1991, Section 109 (P.L. 102–199, Section 109 105 STAT. 1077–1078) ensures that American citizens who are employed in a foreign country are covered by U.S. civil rights laws. Companies must comply with the provisions of these laws. The only exception is when a company's compliance to the law, would violate the law of the country in which the work place is located. Also, the U.S. citizen must be employed overseas by a firm that is controlled by a U.S. employer.

Taylor and Eder (1994) note that control can be determined in several ways: interrelation of operations between the American firm and the operation overseas; common management practices; centralized control of labor relations; and common ownership or financial control of the corporation and the employer. They suggest that to obey this law, companies are likely to engage in two types of behaviors.

1. *Fill positions overseas with host-national managers.*

   One way to avoid worrying whether one can use gender, ethnic background, or race as criteria when selecting for overseas assignments, is to hire host-nationals to fill those slots. Many companies have been doing this anyway; yet, it is difficult to direct a MNC if one has never been overseas and gained international experience. International business experience and expertise are critical to managerial success; thus, the strategy of eliminating all expatriates is difficult. The challenge of dealing with the civil rights law in international business assignments will always be there. Even if a company could eliminate 80 percent of its expatriates—for the remaining 20 percent the law would still be in effect.

2. *Increase complexity in the recruitment and selection process.*

   The Civil Rights Act of 1991 requires companies to be more methodical and careful in the selection process to comply with the legal standards of the law. Taylor and Eder (p.17) note that: "The practice of a few key executives meeting behind closed doors to discuss an overseas selection, meeting with the pre-ordained choice, and quickly preparing the individual to go abroad would appear to be inconsistent with legal expectations for equal opportunity to all those able and willing to be considered." Companies will have to make the following changes:

- Firms must post available overseas positions in a more open manner, in the same way required for domestic positions.

- People will no longer be able to agree to "deals" involving promises that they will be sent overseas in the future as part of a career-enhancing strategy.

- Advertisements for expatriate assignments, wherever they are placed (in the U.S. or in overseas subsidiaries) will need to comply with U.S. civil rights laws.

- Unless the local laws clearly allow for such discrimination, references to race, gender, age, or religion will be illegal when circulating information about overseas job opportunities.

The shift from a behind-closed-doors style of selection for overseas assignments to a more structured, open, and formal approach may be a blessing in disguise for companies. Taylor and Eder (p.18) note that:

> On the positive side, a move to a more open job posting system would require firms to integrate overseas assignments with managerial career planning, which would require a longer term perspective to be taken in the overseas staffing decision. As employees see the postings for overseas positions, they will seek information on how to acquire experience and training that makes such assignments attainable, leading to greater career planning. Moreover, this long-term perspective could potentially reduce part of the repatriation problem.

U.S. laws attempt to reinforce and ensure that fairness in job selection and promotion will exist in the work place. In the past these laws did not apply to overseas assignments—now they do. Many managers are unaware of the implications of these relatively recent laws on their practices of expatriate selection and recruitment. It will be interesting to see how things evolve with increasing awareness in companies and their employees about this issue.

There are laws in many other countries (for example, Australia, Canada, and Europe) that equally try to reinforce and ensure fairness in terms of job selection and promotion in the work place. Firms based in these countriesface issues similar to those faced by U.S. firms. In addition, international firms often face the challenge of complying with two sets of regulations—home and host—which are sometimes incongruent.

A problem arises where "fairness" means different things in different locations. A major concern when regulations are applied extraterritorially is that they may be applied in countries where values are vastly different. Iran's death penalty for the author Salmon Rushdie, no matter where he is located, apparently conforms to Iran's Islamic Law and, presumably, is seen as "fair." Clearly it is not seen in the same way in the United Kingdom, where Rushdie resides, (or in the western world).

TRAINING REQUIREMENTS

As will be explained in Chapter 13, expatriate managers and their families often do not receive adequate cross-cultural training before going abroad. The challenges an overseas assignment brings can cause high levels of stress, which in turn can adversely affect family relationships and consequently the manager's performance at work.

All jobs have a stressful component to them, but it is common sense to train someone before he or she undertakes a new task. The military would never send untrained soldiers into combat. It would be foolhardy as well as unethical from a "productivity" standpoint. A university professor would be disciplined severely if that professor were to announce at the beginning of the semester: "This class in global management won't be meeting anymore this semester, except when I give you the mid-term and the final exams. You are all bright and self-motivated students, so I'm sure you will do fine if you apply yourselves and take the responsibility for figuring out what you will need to know and using it in your existing knowledge about how businesses operate. Good luck. I will see you at the exams."

This is, in essence, what many companies do. They send people to operate in a new business culture, with different business norms and customs, with little or no preparation, and expect them to perform well immediately upon arrival. One can argue that it is unethical not to provide employees with the training they need to perform their jobs well. Without training, it is unethical and irrational to expect high levels of performance. Further, it is unethical to expose employees to the negative emotional and psychological side effects that result from lack of training. It is important to understand that internal company policies can affect people adversely just as much as the external environment of the international business world.

ETHICAL ISSUES IN THE USE OF GUEST WORKERS AND IMMIGRANTS

Throughout the world, there are many "guest workers" (including migrant workers, immigrants, and illegal aliens) who have left their country of birth to work in a country which offers higher pay and a better standard of living. These guest workers are brought in to work in jobs that the local populace choose not to hold: for example, garbage collection, maid service, repetitive factory work, and manual labor.

The ethical dilemma concerning guest workers in foreign countries is illustrated by the following example:

> A vice-president of an international construction firm was assigned the staffing responsibility of a major reconstruction project in Kuwait following Operation Desert Storm. During that period there was an enormous need for construction workers to rebuild the country. However, the Kuwaiti standard of living is so high, and jobs so plentiful, that very few Kuwaitis need to work in manual labor jobs so the supply of Kuwaiti construction workers was small. To staff the project, the vice president went to the Philippines to hire laborers. The Filipino laborers would make more money than they could in the Philippines, but would be separated from their families for long periods of time and would not be accepted into the mainstream culture of Kuwait.

Guest workers increasingly make up large portions of the labor force around the world, yet they are almost always denied citizenship in the country in which they work. They can be deported in an economic downturn; their career mobility is often limited; and their quality of life is usually much lower than that of most of the citizens of the country in which they work, even though they may contribute significantly to the GNP and are often the foundation upon which many industries' profits rest. Whether they are illegal aliens or legal short-term residents, the life of a foreign guest worker tends to be one of uncertainty, unequal treatment compared to the country's citizens, and poor upward mobility. They usually live in isolated "ghettos" and because they hold different religious beliefs, eat different foods, wear different clothes, and hold cultural preferences that differ from the local citizens, conflict between them usually occurs.

This treatment of guest workers is clearly inequitable because they are not considered equal to the citizens of the country. To many people, this treatment is therefore unethical, but, at the same time the guest workers themselves choose to work in spite of the treatment. Managers in these countries are faced with the issue of whether they should provide work for these guest workers when the differential treatment is seen as unethical.

One might assume that while legal immigrants, guest workers, and illegal aliens may be treated rather badly in some countries, this would not be true in the United States, where civil rights is an important and serious issue. However, this is not strictly the case. Martin West and Erin Moore (1989) compared the treatment of undocumented workers in both the United States and South Africa. While the differences between these two countries is striking—because the United States ardently supports civil rights while South Africa retained its legacy of apartheid, or legally instituted system of discrimination based on race—the similarities are also remarkable. Both countries have dominant economies that attract workers from beyond their borders; both have employers who house the workers in conditions that are far from typical of the general population; and both provide minimal access to medical care.

This usage of guest workers is also seen in Asia, where China, Indonesia, and the Philippines supply unskilled workers to Australia, Singapore, Brunei, Malaysia, and Thailand (Rees and Lau 1990, do Rosario et al 1992, Cohen 1990, Tasker, Hoon, & Moore 1990); and is similar in Europe with immigrant and migrant workers playing a vital role in Western Europe's economies (Parry 1992, Reier 1992). During the 1950s and 1960s countries such as France,

Germany, Austria, and Italy relied heavily upon guest workers from Algeria and Turkey, who created social problems because they often did not return home. More recently, migrant workers from Eastern Europe are arriving in large numbers in Western Europe, as their own countries undergo tumultuous political, economic, and social upheavals. Ironically, in the face of attempts by leaders in the European Community (EC) to create a union of free and equal Western Europeans, some Western European firms are attempting to stay competitive by hiring cheap labor, driving the mushrooming demand for both legal and illegal guest workers. Well-educated and trained Eastern Europeans are willing to take undocumented jobs, accept a fraction of the going wage with no benefits, live in crowded quarters, and do without legal rights because conditions in their own country are worse (Reichlin 1992).

High unemployment in Western Europe has recently rekindled xenophobic reactions, with right-wing politicos blaming job losses on immigrants and migrant workers, and racist neo-nazi and "skin-head" attacks on ethnic minorities. But as Sharon Reier (1992) notes, it is the lavish unemployment-compensation policies that are responsible for the fact that during the 1980s, long-term unemployment did not abate in concert with the revival of European economies. The unemployed have little incentive to return to work when, for years, they have been able to receive as much as 90 percent of their former salary in unemployment compensation.

Some governments are rethinking their policies toward the use of guest workers because of concerns about social issues surrounding their working conditions and about indigenous unemployment. To stem the tide of migrant workers, political pressure is mounting for the EC to adopt a migrant-labor policy (Reichlin 1992) and various countries are adopting quotas and instituting sanctions on businesses that hire undocumented workers. However, these quotas remain ineffective as long as there is a demand for cheap labor and workers who will take the jobs. For instance, in 1986, the United States passed the Immigration Reform and Control Act (IRCA) to curtail, but not halt, the influx of legal and illegal immigrants; yet, there is little evidence that IRCA has significantly deterred Mexicans from entering the U.S. On the contrary, there is evidence that migrants stay longer in the U.S. (Kossoudji 1992) and evidence that supports the view that international migration operates as a self-sustaining social process (Donato, Durand, & Massey 1992).

As an approach to regulate immigration in Europe with its constant traffic of qualified workers, W.R. Bohning (1991) suggests that quota policies be combined with project-tied migration. He recommends direct foreign investment in migrant-sending countries, a reduction of the need of people from poor countries to move to rich countries by increasing trade flows, and official development assistance. Similar approaches are being taken by the U.S., Mexico, and Canada, with the North American Free Trade Agreement (NAFTA). These trends are also evident in the U.S. agricultural industry:

> Relief from the more oppressive aspects of migrant agricultural work may be forthcoming as the agricultural industry realizes that it is in its own self-interest to invest in its work force. Growers are beginning to meet the needs of migrants for adequate shelter and are offering fair payroll compensation and benefits. A. Duda & Sons is a grower that has developed a full human resources program that reflects its serious business, financial, and social commitment to improve the living and working conditions of its employees. Taylor & Fulton Inc. is another grower that is responding to its employee needs by donating to charity organizations that provide day care for the workers' children. Though problems with transportation, Social Security, and insurance still remain, enlightened growers that are aware of these human resource issues benefit by a healthier, more stable work force that requires less supervision and less training. (Stuart 1992).

The utilization of guest workers around the world touches on the core of societies' values, which in turn are the foundation of ethical systems. Standards of fairness, equality, and human dignity come into play when governments and managers try to wrestle with the guest worker issue. Should guest workers' conditions be judged against the standards and values of their home cultures or the culture in which they are presently living and working? If they contribute to the economy, should they be given the same rights and privileges of the local citizenry who also contribute to the economy? And what about guest workers who are willing to work in very low-paying jobs versus citizens who accept public welfare rather than work in such jobs? Who is more of a drain on the economy in this case, and what does that imply for granting guest workers more legal status under the law? Many governments are wrestling with these issues, all of which concern the question: What is the right thing to do?

Ethical dimensions are interwoven throughout the world of international business. So, what is a manager to do? Manuel Velasquez, an expert in the field of business ethics, contends that when faced with a difficult situation, one must analyze it carefully from an ethical approach (1990). He suggests that when faced with an ethical dilemma, one should ask:

- What are the facts; what are my alternatives?

- What parties will be affected?

- What do I owe each of these parties?

- What would produce the greatest benefits for all parties?

- What rights does each party have, and how can these rights best be respected?

- Are all parties treated fairly and justly?

- On balance, what is the most ethical alternative?

- How do I best implement this alternative?

SUMMARY

One of the key points made in this chapter was that virtually every decision an international manager makes involves issues of justice, legality, fairness, equity, right vs. wrong, and human decency. Making those decisions in cross-cultural contexts can be exceedingly difficult due to differing beliefs of those involved.

The field of business ethics was delineated, and the idea of business ethics was defined. To help students grasp the issues involved in international business ethics two concepts were discussed: Relativism and universalism. These two ideas were given as conceptual frames around which ethical dimensions of international business practices can be understood.

The problem of bribery, in many of its cross-cultural manifestations, was described along with a U.S. law, the Foreign Corrupt Practices Act, that forbids engaging in that act. Differing viewpoints were offered regarding the viability and necessity of this law, and how it affects U.S. businesses abroad. Research studies investigating these issues were also reported.

The inherent ethical tensions associated with social responsibility issues in MNCS were described and illustrated, and the impact of the Civil Rights Act of 1991 on MNCs was explored in detail. An understanding of the ethical tensions associated with operating overseas is crucial for managers to comprehend in this day and age of global economic interdependency. Managing these tensions is one of the most important aspects of an international manager's job.

Intra-company ethical issues that revolve around international aspects of business were discussed as well. The legal ramifications of the Civil Rights Act of 1991, for expatriate selection, were discussed in detail. The ethical problems of managing guest workers and immigrants were also discussed. For North American managers, these issues present daily challenges. Finally, some suggestions and guidelines were offered to help managers deal with ethical dilemmas.

DISCUSSION QUESTIONS

1. Discuss the two main contrasting approaches of ethics presented here. What are your personal reactions to these approaches?

2. Review recent newspaper articles and identify one current ethical issue faced by an international company. Discuss and evaluate the company's reactions.

3. Interview company managers in the local community to identify their ethical concerns.

REFERENCES

Anonymous. 1991. "How to manage a diverse workforce," *ABA Banking Journal*, 83 (10),. pp. 122, 124.

Badham, R. 1991. "The social dimension of computer-integrated manufacturing," *International Labour Review*, 130, (3), pp. 373–392.

Baglioni, G. 1991. "An Italian mosiac: Collective bargaining patterns in the 1980s," *International Labour Review*, 130, (1), pp. 81–112.

Bohning, W. 1991. "Integration and immigration pressures in Western Europe," *International Labour Review*, 130 (4), pp. 445–458.

Bronstein, A.S., "Temporary work in Western Europe: Threat or complement to permanent employment?," *International Labour Review*, 130 (3), 1991, pp. 291–310.

Campbell, A., A. Sorge, and M. Warner, "Technological change, product strategies and human resources: Defining Anglo-German differences, " *Journal of General Management*, 15 (3), 1990, pp. 39–54.

Chatak, E. "A unionist's perspective on the future of American unions," *Journal of Labor Research*. 12 (4), 1991, pp. 327–332.

Cohen, M. 1990. "Philippines: Labour pains—A worker's diaspora leaves behind a trail of broken homes," *Far Eastern Economic Review*, 147 (10), pp. 32–33.

Craft, J.A. 1991. "Unions, bureaucracy, and change: Old dogs learn new tricks very slowly," *Journal of Labor Research*, 12 (4), pp. 394–405.

Delaney, J.T., "The future of unions as political organizations," *Journal of Labor Research*, 12 (4), 1991, pp. 373–387.

Do Rosario, L., G. Fairclough, L. Kaye, F. Jiang, M. Vatikiotis, and S. Ali. 1992. "Migrant labour: Toilers of the East," *Far Eastern Economic Review*, 155 (13), pp. 20–27.

Dominguez, C. 1991–1992. "The challenge of workforce 2000," *Bureaucrat*, 20 (4), Winter, pp. 15–18.

Donato, K., J. Durand, and D. Massey. 1992. "Stemming the tide? Assessing the deterrent effects of the Immigration Reform and Control Act," *Demography*, 29 (2), pp. 139–157.

Douglas, M. & J. Douglas. 1989. "Institutions of the third kind: British and Swedish labor markets compared," *Journal of General Management*, 14 (4), pp. 34-52.

Enshassi, A. & R. Burgess. 1991. "Managerial Effectiveness and the Style of Management in the Middle East: An Empirical Analysis," *Construction Management & Economics*, 9 (1), pp. 79–92.

Hamill, J. 1984. "Labor Relations Practices" and "Multinational Corporations and Industrial Relations," *Industrial Relations Journal*, 15 (2), pp. 30–34.

Hurt, R. 1991. "How workforce 2000 will get paid," *HRMagazine*, 36 (10), pp. 110, 112

Jarley, P. & J. Fiorito. 1991. "Unionism and changing employee views toward work," *Journal of Labor Research*, 12 (3), pp. 223–229.

Johnston, W.B. 1991. "Global work force 2000: The new world labor market," *Harvard Business Review*, March–April. pp. 115–127.

Junkins, J. 1991. "Diversity, yes—Drugs, no," *Executive Excellence*, 8 (3), pp. 12–13.

Kelly, K. 1992. "Caterpillar's Don Fites: Why he didn't blink," *Business Week*, 3278, August 10. pp. 56–57.

Kossoudji, S. 1992. "Playing cat and mouse at the U.S.-Mexican border," *Demography*, 29 (2), pp. 159–180.

McBride, M. 1992. "Management development in the global village: Beyond culture—a microworld approach," *Journal of Management Development*, 11 (7), pp. 48–57.

Okubayashi, K. 1989. "The Japanese industrial relations system," *Journal of General Management*, 14 (3), pp. 67–88.

Parry, J. 1989. "Paying guests," *International Management,* 46 (1), pp. 38–41.

Poole, M. & G. Jenkins. 1991. "The impact of profit-sharing and employee shareholding schemes," *Journal of General Management,* 16 (3), pp. 52-72.

Poole, M. 1986. "Managerial strategies and 'styles' in industrial relations: A comparative analysis," *Journal of General Management,* 12 (1), pp. 40–53.

Prahalad, C.K. & Y.L. Doz. 1987. *The Multinational Mission: Balancing Local Demands and Global Vision.* New York: The Free Press.

Rees, J. & E. Lau. 1990. "Zone of exploitation: Chinese guest workers hit problems in Australia," *Far Eastern Economic Review,* 148 (16), pp. 20–21.

Reichlin, I. 1992. "Long days, low pay, and a moldy cot," *Business Week,* 3249, January 27. pp. 44–45.

Reier, S. 1992. "Xenophobia," *Financial World,* 161 (5), pp. 34–36.

"The roots of quality control in Japan: An interview with W. Edwards Deming." 1985 *Pacific Basin Quarterly,* 12, Spring/Summer 1985, pp. 1–4.

Rosen, C. & M. Quarrey. 1987. "How well is employee ownership working?," *Harvard Business Review,* September–October. pp. 126–129.

Rothwell, S. 1991. "Human resources management," *Manager Update,* 2 (30), pp. 22–31.

Rothwell, S. 1989. "Is there a real change in industrial relations in Britain?," *Manager Update,* 1 (1), pp. 16–23.

Rubin, P.H. 1991. "Unions, bureaucracy, and change: Comment," *Journal of Labor Research,* 12 (4), pp. 406–409.

Stuart, P. 1992. "A better future for migrant workers," *Personnel Journal,* 71 (12), pp. 65–74.

Tasker, R., S. Hoon, & J. Moore, "Labour: The lure of jobs; won world; grist to the mill," 1990. *Far Eastern Economic Review,* 148 (14), pp. 18–20.

Thomas, R.R., Jr. 1990. "From Affirmative Action to affirmative diversity." *Harvard Business Review,* March–April. pp. 107–117.

Thompson, R.T. 1991. "The changing character of employee relations," *Journal of Labor Research,* 12 (4), pp. 311–321.

Watanabe, S. 1991. "The Japanese quality control circle: Why it works," *International Labour Review,* 130 (1), pp. 57–80.

West, M. & E. Moore. "Undocumented workers in the United States and South Africa: A comparative study of changing control," *Human Organization,* 48 (1), pp. 1–10.

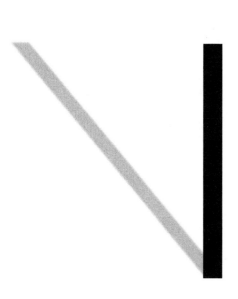

PART ONE:

MAJOR

REFERENCES

Adler, N.J. 1983. "Cross-cultural management research: The ostrich and the trend." *Academy of Management Review*, 8(2), pp. 226–232.

Adler, N.J. 1983. "A typology of management studies involving culture." *Journal of International Business Studies*, 14(2), pp. 29–47.

Adler N.J. & R. Doktor (with S.G. Redding). 1986. "From the Atlantic to the Pacific century: Cross-cultural management reviewed." *Journal of Management*, 12(2), pp. 295–318

Adler, N.J. & J.L. Graham. 1989. "Cross-cultural interaction: The international comparison fallacy?" *Journal of International Business Studies*, 20(3), pp. 515–537.

Adler, N.J. & M. Jelinek. 1986. "Is 'organizational culture' culture bound?" *Human Resource Management*, 25(1), pp. 73–90.

Austin, J.E. 1990. *Managing in Developing Countries: Strategic Analysis and Operating Techniques*. New York: Free Press.

Axtell, R.E. 1993. *Do's and Taboos Around the World*. 3rd ed. New York: John Wiley & Sons, Inc.

Babbar, S. & A. Rai. 1993. "Competitive intelligence for international business." *Long Range Planning*, 26(3), June, pp. 103–113.

Barham, K. 1992. "Overseas Assets." *International Management*, 47(9), October, pp. 56–59.

Bartlett, C.A. & Sumantra Ghoshal. 1989. *Managing Across Borders: The Transnational Solution*. Boston: Harvard Business School Press.

Bartlett, C.A. & Sumantra Ghoshal. 1991. *Transnational Management: Text, Cases, and Reading in Cross-Border Management*. Homewood, IL: Irwin.

Baruch, H. 1979. The Foreign Corrupt Practices Act. *Harvard Business Review*, Vol. 57, pp. 32–50.

Beamish, P.W., J.P. Killing, D.J. LeCraw, & H. Crookell. 1991. *International Management Text and Cases*. Homewood, IL: Irwin.

Bertrand K. 1990. "Politics pushes to the marketing foreground." *Business Marketing*, March, pp. 51–55.

Bhagat, R.S. & S.J. McQuaid. 1982. "The role of subjective culture in organizations: A review and directions for future research." *Journal of Applied Psychology Monograph*, 67(5), pp. 635–685.

Boddewyn, J. 1988. "Political aspects of MNE theory." *Journal of International Business Studies*, 19(3), pp. 341–364.

Brandler, J.A. 1988. *Government Policy Towards Business*. Toronto: Butterworths Canada.

Brewer, T.L. 1993. "Government policies, market imperfections, and foreign direct investment in the Caribbean Basin." *Journal of International Business Studies*, 24(1), First Quarter, pp. 101–120.

Brislin, R.W. 1981. *Cross-cultural Encounters*. New York: Pergamon Press.

Carson, T.L. 1987. "Bribery and implicit agreement: A reply to Philips." *Journal of Business Ethics*, February, pp. 123–125.

Cartwright, S. & C.L. Cooper. 1993. "The role of culture compatibility in successful organization marriage." *Academy of Management Executive*, 7(2), pp. 57–70.

Casse, P. 1982. *Training for the Multicultural Manager*. Washington, DC: Society of Intercultural Education, Training, and Research.

Child, J. 1981. "Culture, contingency and capitalism in the cross-national study of organizations." In L.L. Cummings & F.M Staw (Eds.), *Research in Organizational Behavior*, Greenwich, CT: JAI Press, Vol. 3, pp. 303–356.

Commonwealth Secretariat. 1985. *Vulnerability: Small States in the Global Society*. London: Commonwealth Secretariat Publications.

Copeland, L. & L. Griggs. 1985. *Going International: How to Make Friends and Deal Effectively in the Global Marketplace*. New York: Random House.

Coplin, W.D. & M.K. O'Leary. 1990 "World political forecast." *Planning Review*, April, pp. 41–47.

Cosset, J. & J. Roy. 1991. "The determinants of country risk ratings." *Journal of International Business Studies*, 22(1), First Quarter, pp. 135–142.

Coye, R. 1986. "Individual values and business ethics." *Journal of Business Ethics*, Vol. 5, No. 1, pp. 45–49.

D'Andrale, K. 1985. Bribery. *Journal of Business Ethics*, 4, pp. 239–248.

Davidson, W.H. & J. de la Torre. 1989. *Managing the Global Corporation*. New York: McGraw-Hill.

Deresky, H. 1994. *International Management: Managing Across Borders and Cultures*. New York: Harper Collins College Publishers.

Donath, B. 1990. "Coping with trade's dark side." *Business Marketing*, March, p. 4

Doz, Y. 1986. "Government policies and global industries." In M. Porter (ed), *Competition in Global Industries*. Boston: Harvard Business School.

Dunning, J.H. 1993. *The Globalization of Business: The Challenge of the 1900s*. New York: Routledge.

England, G.W. 1978. "Managers and their value systems: A five-country comparative study." *Columbia Journal of World Business*, Summer, pp. 35–44.

Fadiman, J.A. 1986. "A traveler's guide to gifts and bribes." *Harvard Business Review*, July–August, pp. 122–136.

Fagre, N. & L.T. Wells, Jr. 1982. "Bargaining power of multinationals and host governments." *Journal of International Business Studies*, 13(2), pp. 9–23.

Farmer, R. & B. Richman. 1965. *Comparative Management and Economic Progress*. New York: Irwin.

Fitzpatrick, M. 1983. "The definition and assessment of political risk in international business: A review of literature." *Academy of Management Review*, 8(2), pp. 249–254.

Francis, J.N. 1991. "When in Rome? The effects of cultural adaptations on the intercultural business negotiations." *Journal of International Business Studies*, 22(3), Third Quarter, pp. 403–428.

Gellerman, S.W. 1986. "Why good managers make bad ethical choices." *Harvard Business Review*, July–August, p. 85.

Gillespie, K. 1987. "The Middle East response to the U.S. Foreign Corrupt Practices Act." *Management Review*, Summer, Vol. 29, No. 4, pp.9-30.

Gladwin, T.N. 1982. "Conflict management in international business." In I. Walter (Ed.), *Handbook of International Business*. New York: John Wiley & Sons, Inc.

Gladwin, T.N. & I. Walter. 1980. *Multinationals under Fire: Lessons in the Management of Conflict*. New York: John Wiley & Sons, Inc.

Graham, J.L. 1985. "The influence of culture on the process of business negotiations: An exploratory study." *Journal of International Business Studies*, 16(1), pp. 81–96.

Graham, J.L. 1983. "Foreign corrupt practices: A manager's guide." *Columbia Journal of World Business*, Fall, pp. 89–94.

Graham, J.L. 1984. "The Foreign Corrupt Policies Act: A new perspective." *Journal of International Studies*, Winter, p. 120.

Green, R.T. & C.H. Smith. 1972. "Multinational profitability as a function of political instability." *Management International Review*, 12(6), pp. 23–29.

Gregory, A. 1988. "Integrative and protective techniques in reducing political risk: A comparison of American and Canadian firms in Indonesia." In J. Rogers (ed.), *Global Risk Assessments*, Vol. 3. Riverside, CA: Global Risk Assessment.

Gregory, A. 1989. "Political risk management." In A Rugman (ed.), *Intentional Business in Canada*. Scarborough, Ont.: Prentice-Hall Canada.

Grosse, R. & J. Stack. 1984. "Noneconomic risk evaluation in multinationals bands." *Management International Review*, Vol. 24, No. 1, pp. 41-59.

Harris, P. & R. Moran. 1991. *Managing Cultural Differences* (3rd ed.). Houston: Gulf Publishing Co.

Hayes J. & C.W. Allison. 1988. "Cultural differences in the learning styles of managers." *Management International Review*, 28(3), pp. 75–80.

Heller, F.A. 1988. "Cost benefits of multinational research on organizations." *International Studies of Management and Organization*, 18(3), pp. 5–18.

Hodgetts, R.M. & E. Luthans. 1991. *International Management*. New York: McGraw-Hill.

Hofstede, G. 1993. "Cultural constraints in management theories." *Academy of Management Executive*, 7(1), pp. 81–93.

Hofstede, G. 1991. *Cultures and Organization—Software of the Mind*. London: McGraw-Hill.

Hofstede, G. 1983. "The cultural relativity of organization practices and theories." *Journal of International Business Studies*, 14(2), pp. 75–90.

Hofstede G. 1980. *Culture's Consequences: International Differences in Work Related Values*. Beverly Hills, CA: Sage Publications.

Hooker, M. & M. Pastin. 1980. Ethics and the Foreign Corrupt Practices Act. *Business Horizons*, December, pp. 43–47.

Jaeger, A.M. 1986. "Organization development and national culture: Where's the fit?" *Academy of Management Review* 11(1), pp. 178–190.

Jaeger, A.M. & R.N. Kanungo, (eds.). 1990. *Management in Developing Countries*. London: Routledge.

Jarvis, M. & F. Kirk, Jr. (eds.). 1986. *Foreign Direct Investment in Canada: The Foreign Investor's Perspective*. Ottawa, Ont.: International Business Study Group, School of Business, Carleton University.

Jodice, D.A. 1985. *Political Risk Assessment: An Annoted Bibliography*. Westport, CT: Greenwood Press.

Jones, C.A. 1987. *International Business in the Nineteenth Century*. New York: New York University Press.

Johnson, H.L. 1985. "Bribery in international markets: diagnosis, clarification and remedy." *Journal of Business Ethics*, May, pp. 447–455.

Johnson, M. & R.T. Moran. 1992 *Robert T. Moran's Cultural Guide to Doing Business in Europe* (2nd ed.). Oxford: Butterworth-Heinemann Ltd.

Joynt, P. & M. Warner. 1985. *Managing in Different Cultures*. Oslo, Norway: Universitetsforlaget.

Kaikati, J.G. 1977. "The phenomenon of international bribery." *Business Horizons*, February, pp. 25–37.

Kedia, B. & R. Bhagat. 1988. "Cultural constraints on the transfer of technology across nations: Implications for research in international and comparative management." *Academy of Management Review*, 13 October, pp. 559–571.

Kelley, L., A. Whatley, & R. Worthley. 1987. "Assessing the effects of culture on managerial attitude: A three-culture test." *Journal of International Business Studies*, 18(2), pp. 17–31.

Kennedy, C.R., Jr. 1991. *Managing the International Business Environment: Cases in Political and Country Risk*. Englewood Cliffs, NJ: Prentice-Hall.

Kennedy, C.R., Jr. 1987. "Political risk management: A portfolio planning model." *Business Horizons*, 31(6), pp. 26–33.

Keys, J.B., R. Wells, & A. Edge. 1993. "International management games: Laboratories for performance-based intercultural learning." *Leadership & Organization Development Journal*, 14(3), pp. 25–30.

Kim, W.C. 1987. "Competition and the host government intervention." *Sloan Management Review*, 28(3), pp. 33–39.

Kim, W.C. 1988. "The effects of competition and corporate political responsiveness on multinational bargaining power." *Strategic Management Journal*, (28(2), pp. 289–295.

Kim, W.C. 1988. "Industry competition, corporate variables, and host government intervention in developing nations." *Management International Review*, 28(2), pp. 16–27.

Kluckhohn, A. & F. Strodbeck. 1961. *Variations in Value Orientations*. Westport, CT: Greenwood Press.

Kobrin, S.J. 1982. *Managing Political Risk Assessment*. Berkeley, CA: University of California Press.

Kobrin, S.J. 1979. "Political risk: A review and reconsideration." *Journal of International Business Studies*, Spring–Summer, pp. 67–80.

Kobrin, S.J. 1976. "Morality, political power and illegal payment by multinational corporations." *Columbia Journal of World Business*, Winter, pp. 105–110.

Kobrin, S.J. 1987. "Testing the bargaining hypothesis in the manufacturing sector in developing countries." *International Organization*, Autumn, pp. 609–638.

Kobrin, W.J., J. Basek, S. Blank, & J. LaPalombra. 1980. "The assessment and evaluation of noneconomic environment by American firms: A preliminary report." *Journal of International Business Studies*, Spring–Summer, pp. 32–47.

Kogut, B. & H. Singh. 1988. "The effect of national culture on the choice of entry mode." *Journal of International Business Studies*, 19(3), pp. 411–432.

Kluckhohn, C. & F. Strodtbeck. 1961. *Variations in Value Orientations*. Westport, CT: Greenwood Press.

Kroeber, A. & C. Kluckhohn. 1952. "Culture: A critical review of concepts and definitions." Papers of the Peabody Museum of American Archaeology and Ethnology, Harvard University, pp. 1–223.

Lane, H.W. & J.J. DiStefano. 1988. *Intentional Management Behavior*. Scarborough, Ont.: Nelson Canada.

Lane, H.W. & D.G. Simpson. 1984. "Bribery in international business: Whose problem is it?" *Journal of Business Ethics*, February, pp. 35–42.

Lasserre, P. 1993. "Gathering and Interpreting strategic intelligence in Asia Pacific." *Long Range Planning*, 26(3), June, pp. 56–66.

Laurent, A. 1983. "The cultural diversity of Western management conceptions." *International Studies of Management and Organizations*, 8(1-2), pp. 75–96.

LeCraw, D.J. 1984. "Bargaining power, ownership, and profitability of transnational corporations in developing countries." *Journal of International Business Studies*, 15(1), pp. 27–43.

Lessem, R. 1989. *Global Management Principles*. London: Prentice-Hall International (UK) Ltd.

Linowes, R.G. 1993. "The Japanese manager's traumatic entry into the United States: Understanding the American-Japanese cultural divide." *Academy of Management Executive*, 7(4), pp. 21–37.

Maddox, R.C. & D. Short. 1988. "The cultural integrator." *Business Horizons*, November–December, pp. 57–59.

Mahini, A. 1988. *Making Decision in Multinational Corporations— Managing Relations with Sovereign Governments*. New York: John Wiley & Sons.

Marchione, A.R. 1987. "Illegal payments: Unnecessary cost of free enterprise." *University of Michigan Business Review*, July 22, pp. 22–26.

Maruyama, M. 1992. "Changing dimensions in international business." *Academy of Management Executive*, 6(3), pp. 88–96.

Maruyama, M. 1992. "Lessons from Japanese management failures in foreign countries." *Human Systems Management*, 11(1), pp. 41–48.

Mascarenhas, B. & O.C. Sand. 1985. "Country-risk assessment systems in banks: Patterns and performance." *Journal of International Business Studies*, 16(1), pp. 19–36.

McNutty, N.G. 1992. "Management education in Eastern Europe: 'fore and after." *Academy of Management Executive*, 6(4), pp. 78–87.

Miller, K.D. 1992. "A framework for integrated risk management in international business." *Journal of International Business Studies*, 23(2), Second Quarter, pp. 311–331.

Miller, K.D. 1993. "Industry and country effects on managers' perceptions on environmental uncertainties." *Journal of International Business Studies*, 24(4), Fourth Quarter, pp. 693–714.

Moran, T. 1985. *Multinational Corporations: The Political Economy of Foreign Direct Investment*. Lexington, MA: Lexington Books.

Moran, R.T., P.R. Harris, & W.G. Stripp. 1993. *Developing the Global Organizations: Strategies for Human Resource Professionals*. Houston: Gulf Publishing Co.

Murray, A. 1993. "The global economy bungled." *Foreign Affairs*, 72(1), pp. 158–166.

Negandhi, A.R. 1983. "Cross-cultural management research: Trend and future directions." *Journal of International Business Studies* 14(2), pp. 17–28.

Nigh, C. 1985. "The effects of political events on United States' direct foreign investment: A pooled time-series cross-sectional analysis." *Journal of International Business Studies*, 16(1), pp. 1–18.

Norburn, D. 1987. "Corporate leaders in Britain and America: A cross-national analysis." *Journal of International Business Studies*, 18(3), pp. 15–32.

Ohmae, K. 1985. *Triad Power: The Coming Shape of Global Competition*. New York: The Free Press.

Phatak, A.V. 1992. *International Dimensions of Management* (3rd ed.) Boston: PWS-Kent.

Philips, M. 1987. "Bribery, consent, and prima facie duty: A rejoinder to Carson." *Journal of Business Ethics*, July, pp. 361–364.

Porter, M. 1991. *Canada at the Crossroads: The Reality of the New Competitive Environment*. Ottawa, Ont: The Monitor Group,

Poynter, T.A. 1982. "Government intervention in less developed countries: The experience of multinational companies." *Journal of International Business Studies*, Spring-Summer, pp. 9–25.

Poynter, T.A. 1986. "Managing government interventions: A strategy for defending the subsidiary." *Columbia Journal of World Business*, 21(4), pp. 55–65.

Poynter, T.A. 1985. *Multinational Enterprises and Government Intervention*. New York: St. Martin's Press.

Preble, J., P. Rau, & A. Reichel. 1988. "The environmental scanning practices of U.S. multinational in the late 1980's." *Management International Review*, 28(4), pp. 4–14.

Punnet, B.J. 1995. "Cross-national culture and management." Forthcoming in M. Warner (ed.) *International Encyclopedia of Business and Management*. London: Routledge.

Punnet, B.J. & D.A. Ricks. 1992. *International Business*. Boston: PWS-Kent.

Punnet, B.J. & S. Ronen. 1984. "Operationalizing cross-culture variables." Paper delivered at the 44th annual meeting of the Academy of Management, Boston.

Punnet, B.J. & S. Withane. 1990. "Hofstede's value survey module: To embrace or abandon?" *Advances in Intentional Comparative Management*. Greenwich, CT: JAI Press.

Richman, B. 1979. "Can we prevent questionable foreign payments?" *Business Horizons*, July, pp. 14–19.

Ricks, D.A. 1983. *Big Business Blunders: Mistakes in Multinational Marketing*. Homewood, IL: Dow Jones-Irwin.

Ricks, D.A. 1993. *Blunders in International Business*. Cambridge, MA: Blackwell Publishers.

Ricks, D.A., M.Y.C. Fu, & J.S. Arpan. 1974. *International Business Blunders*. Columbus, OH: Grid.

Rieger, F. & D. Wong-Rieger. 1990. "The development of culturally-based organizational configurations." In S.B. Prasad, *Advances in International Comparative Management*, Vol. 5, pp. 21–50, Greenwich, CT: JAI Press.

Robinson, R.D. 1964. *International Business Policy*. New York: Holt, Rinehart, & Winston.

Rogers, J. (ed.). 1986. *Global Risk Assessments: Issues, Concepts, and Applications*. Riverside, CA: Global Risk Assessments.

Ronen, S. 1984. *Comparative and Multinational Management*. New York: John Wiley & Sons, Inc.

Ronen, S. & O. Shenkar. 1985. "Clustering countries on attitudinal dimensions: A review and synthesis." *Academy of Management Review*, Vol. 10, pp. 435–454.

Rugman, A.M. & J. D'Cruz. 1991. "Canadian strategies for competitiveness." *Business in the Contemporary World*, 3(1), pp. 93–100.

Schneider, S.C. 1988. "National vs. corporate culture: Implications for human resource management." *Human Resource Management*, 27(2), pp. 231–246.

Schollhammer, H. & D. Nigh. 1984. "The effects of political events on foreign direct investments by German multinational corporations." *Management International Review*, 28(1), pp. 60–74.

Scott, B. & G. Lodge. 1985. *U.S. Competitiveness in the World Economy.* Cambridge, MA: Harvard Business School Press.

Sera, K. 1992. "Corporate globalization: A new trend." *Academy of Management Executive*, 6(1), pp. 89–96.

Sethi, S. & K. Luther. 1986. "Political risk analysis and direct foreign investment: Some problems of definition and measurement." *California Management Review*, 28, pp. 57–68.

Shan, W. 1991. "Environmental risks and joint venture sharing arrangements." *Journal of International Business Studies*, 22(4), Fourth Quarter, pp. 555–578.

Shane, S.A. 1992. "The effect of cultural difference in perceptions of transaction costs on national differences in the preference for licensing." *Management International Review*, 32(4), Fourth Quarter, pp. 295–311.

Simon J.D. 1987. "Political risk assessment: Past trends and future prospects." *Columbia Journal of World Business*, Summer, pp. 23–27.

Stonham, P. 1992. "European management unlimited: Dynamics of an emerging process," *European Management Journal* 10(4), December, pp. 501–502.

Stopford, J.M. & L.T. Wells. 1972. Managing the *Multinational Enterprise.* New York: Basic Books.

Terpstra, V. & K. David. 1985. *The Cultural Environment of International Business.* Cincinnati: South-Western.

Tong, H. 1982. "What American business managers should know and do about international bribery." *Baylor Business Studies*, November, pp. 7–18.

Tse, D.K., K. Lee, I. Vertinsky, & D.A. Wehrung. 1988. "Does culture matter? A cross-cultural study of executives choice, decisiveness, and risk adjustments in international marketing." *Journal of Marketing*, 52(4), pp. 81–95.

Turrow, S. 1985. "What's wrong with bribery." *Journal of Business Ethics,* August, pp. 249–51.

Weiss, S.E. 1987. "Creating the GM-Toyota joint venture: A case in complex negotiation." *Columbia Journal of World Business.* Summer, pp. 23–27.

Weiss-Wik, S. 1983. "Enhancing negotiators' successfulness." *Journal of Conflict Resolution,* 27(4), pp. 706–739.

Wells, L.T. 1977. "Negotiating with third world governments." *Harvard Business Review,* January–February, pp. 72–80.

Whorf, B.L. 1967. *Language, Thought, and Reality*: Cambridge, MA: MIT Press.

Whorf, B.L. 1956. "A linguistic consideration of thinking in primitive communities." In *Language, Thought, and Reality: Selected Readings of Benjamin Lee Whorf,* J.B. Carroll (ed.). Cambridge, MA: MIT Press.

Wilkins, M. 1970. *The Emergence of Multinational Enterprise: American Business Abroad from the Colonial Era to 1914.* Cambridge, MA: Harvard University Press.

Williamson, H.F. (ed.). 1975. *Evolution of International Management Structures.* Newark, DE: University of Delaware Press.

Yaprak, A. & K.T. Sheldon. 1984. "Political risk management in multinational firms: An integrative approach." *Management Decisions,* Vol. 22, No. 6, pp. 53–67.

THE FIRM PICTURE: INTERNATIONAL STRATEGIC MANAGEMENT AND OPERATIONS

GLOBAL

STRATEGY

OVERVIEW

This chapter was prepared with the assistance of Dr. Martin Meznar, Assistant Professor of International Business at Arizona State University – West.

LEARNING OBJECTIVES

IN THIS CHAPTER WE WILL EXPLORE:

- The meaning of strategy and strategic decisions

- Aspects of international strategy

- How firms create a competitive advantage internationally

- Trade-offs in approaches to competitive advantage

- Matching strategic choices to industry characteristics

- Strategic possibilities of national responsiveness and worldwide integration

- The importance of management skills in gaining competitive advantage

- Avoiding disadvantage as global strategy

- Porter's four generic strategies

- Synthesizing strategic approaches

KEY DISCUSSION TOPICS:

- What makes decisions strategic

- Factors that give firms a competitive advantage

- National responsiveness and worldwide integration as strategic choices

- The management skills that enhance competitive advantage

- Oligopolies and competitive advantage

- Choosing among strategic responses

- Integrating approaches in a strategic stance

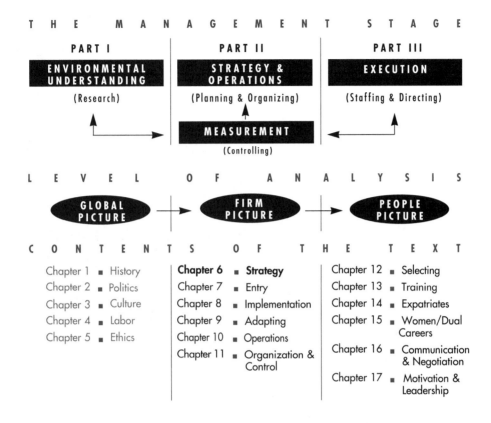

T H E   M A N A G E M E N T   S T A G E

PART I	PART II	PART III
ENVIRONMENTAL UNDERSTANDING	**STRATEGY & OPERATIONS**	**EXECUTION**
(Research)	(Planning & Organizing)	(Staffing & Directing)

MEASUREMENT
(Controlling)

L E V E L   O F   A N A L Y S I S

GLOBAL PICTURE → FIRM PICTURE → PEOPLE PICTURE

C O N T E N T S   O F   T H E   T E X T

Chapter 1 ▪ History	**Chapter 6 ▪ Strategy**	Chapter 12 ▪ Selecting
Chapter 2 ▪ Politics	Chapter 7 ▪ Entry	Chapter 13 ▪ Training
Chapter 3 ▪ Culture	Chapter 8 ▪ Implementation	Chapter 14 ▪ Expatriates
Chapter 4 ▪ Labor	Chapter 9 ▪ Adapting	Chapter 15 ▪ Women/Dual Careers
Chapter 5 ▪ Ethics	Chapter 10 ▪ Operations	Chapter 16 ▪ Communication & Negotiation
	Chapter 11 ▪ Organization & Control	Chapter 17 ▪ Motivation & Leadership

INTRODUCTION

Strategic decisions are complex in any case, and increasingly so for international firms. These firms are faced with the traditional task of assessing their strengths and weaknesses, and matching them to the environment, but they have to do so within the context of the varied political, cultural, labor, and ethical environments around the world. Strengths at home can become weaknesses elsewhere or the converse: weaknesses may suddenly be seen as strengths. For example, some U.S. companies that pride themselves on their distribution systems in North America have been at a loss to make inroads into the Japanese market because of the distribution systems there. In contrast, some firms whose products face declining markets at home can find new opportunities in foreign locations.

This chapter provides an overview of what is meant by "global strategy;" what strategies multinational corporations typically pursue, and what trade-offs a firm faces by selecting one strategy over another. The following chapters discuss specific strategic decisions a firm faces when competing in the international arena.

Strategy involves the critical decisions a firm makes about how to match its resources and strengths with its environment to create an advantage over its competitors. A firm's strategy is essentially the way it goes about seeking to compete successfully. It could be argued that everything a firm does—from deciding on the raise to give its hourly employees, to deciding to build a plant overseas—is associated with trying to compete successfully. To narrow the scope we will discuss strategy in terms of critical decisions: decisions that have far-reaching effects on the way a firm does business. The decision to "go international," for example, is strategic. The decision to change from one supplier of raw materials to another may not be.

GLOBAL STRATEGIES

The importance of a global perspective is seen in the experience of U.S. firms. In the past, U.S. firms have been able to achieve success by simply catering to the large, affluent consumer market in the United States. After World War II, the U.S. was the supreme industrial power because many other countries were busy rebuilding from the devastating consequences of the war. Competitive threats from manufacturers outside the U.S. were few. In recent years, a number of developments have made it important that American firms consider their operations from a global perspective:

- The large consumer pool and reduced regulation created by the European Community's integration

- The international orientation of Japanese producers, and the lowering of trade barriers between the U.S., Canada, and Mexico

- The continuing General Agreement on Trade and Tariffs (GATT) tariff-reduction negotiations

- Technological advances in transportation and communication.

These events all serve to facilitate and promote international business. Naturally, these recent events affect firms outside of the U.S. as well. Firms around the world are internationalizing. These changes make it critical that U.S. firms consider the global environment in developing their strategies. Our discussion focuses on the strategies of firms operating in multiple countries, but the solely domestic firm must also keep a global perspective to be prepared for foreign competitors entering its market.

Once a firm has made the decision to become international, it must deal with a number of strategic issues as it seeks to create or maintain an advantage over its competitors. A firm's global strategy is a reflection of how the firm has configured its resources and strengths in pursuit of that advantage.

The way a firm decides to deploy its resources and compete globally is affected by a number of factors. We will consider a firm's global strategy to be the result of both its efforts to create a competitive advantage for itself over other firms, and to avoid being placed at a competitive disadvantage by others.

CREATING A COMPETITIVE ADVANTAGE

Once a firm has made the decision to compete in the global environment, it subjects itself to pressures single-country firms often do not face. Single-country firms normally operate in a relatively homogeneous market for their products and services. Consequently, product design and production can often be fairly standardized, allowing the firm to achieve economies of scale in production, and deliver a product that appeals to its entire market. Furthermore, strictly domestic firms typically don't have to concern themselves with differences in industry and trade regulations from other countries.

The international firm, in contrast, often faces a trade-off between seeking competitive advantage through the lower production costs that global economies of scale allow, and seeking competitive advantage by tailoring its products to specific national markets—forgoing economies of scale but providing a product more tailored to local tastes. Furthermore, the international firm must determine how to balance the demands and practices in one country with the demands and practices of other countries. These pressures illustrate the trade-off firms often must make between national responsiveness, and worldwide integration of activities.

CREATING COMPETITIVE ADVANTAGE THROUGH A WORLDWIDE INTEGRATION STRATEGY

International firms may possess an advantage over domestic firms because the global market they serve is larger than any single domestic market, and they can achieve greater economies of scale if they offer similar products to customers around the globe. Global economies of scale can be found in production—as production volume increases, per-unit cost drops. International firms may also be able to obtain scale economies in purchasing. The high volume of raw material they purchase allows the international firm to take advantage of volume discounts and gives the firm increased bargaining power with suppliers. Economies of scale also exist in marketing and logistics. Ford's attempt to make the Escort a "world car" illustrates the use of economies of scale. As depicted in Exhibit 6.1, the production of each major component for the car is limited to a few locations. Thus, economies of scale can be captured by manufacturing most cylinder heads in Italy and France, while producing most transmission cases in Germany. The economies of scale resulting from this strategy enable Ford to produce the Escort at a lower cost, and thereby gain an advantage over competitors.

The internationally integrated firm also has more options as it seeks to configure its production process. It is better able to scan the globe for the least expensive sources of raw materials. It can shift labor-intensive production operations to countries where labor is abundant and inexpensive, and can produce particular components in the countries most skilled in the necessary techniques. Differences in tax structures and financial markets across countries permit the

EXHIBIT 6.1

ASSEMBLING A WORLD CAR

Glass, radio — **Canada**

Carburetor rocker arm, clutch, ignition, exhaust, oil pump, distributor, cylinder bolt, cylinder head, flywheel ring gear, heater, speedometer, battery, rear wheel spindle, intake manifold, fuel tank, switches, lamps, front disc, steering wheel, steering column, glass, locks, weatherstrips — **Great Britain**

Exhaust flanges, tires — **Norway**

Locks, pistons, exhaust, ignition, switches, front disc, distributor, weatherstrips, rocker arm, speedometer, fuel tank, cylinder bolt, cylinder head gasket, front wheel knuckles, rear wheel spindle, transmission cases, clutch, steering column, battery, glass — **Germany**

Fan Belt — **Denmark**

Tires, paint, hardware — **Netherlands**

THE FORD ESCORT

Tires, radiator and heater hoses — **Austria**

Tires, tubes, seat pads, brakes, trim — **Belgium**

Starter, alternator, cone and roller bearing, windshield screen washer pump — **Japan**

Hose clamps, cylinder bolt, exhaust down pipes, pressings, hardware — **Sweden**

Underbody coating, speedometer gears — **Switzerland**

Alternator, cylinder head, master cylinder, brakes, underbody coating, seat pads and frames, clutch release bearings, steering shaft and joints, transmission cases, clutch cases, tires, suspension bushes, ventilation units, heater hose clamps, scalers — **France**

Wiring harness, radiator and heater hoses, air filter, fork clutch release, battery, mirrors — **Spain**

Cylinder head, carburator, glass, lamps, defroster grills — **Italy**

EGR valves, wheel nuts, hydraulic tappet, glass — **United States**

SOURCE:

World Development Report 1987 (New York: Oxford University Press, 1987), p. 39. Adapted from John Daniels and Lee H. Radebaugh, *International Business, Updated Sixth Edition* (pg. 517), © 1994 by Addison-Wesley Publishing Company, Inc. Reprinted by permission of the publisher.

international firm to structure itself in a way that minimizes its tax burden and takes advantage of interest rate and currency value fluctuations around the globe. These opportunities can give the firm pursuing a worldwide integration strategy a competitive advantage over domestic firms.

The fact that the international firm has these potential advantages does not necessarily mean it can always successfully utilize them. Rather, managing the international firm in a way that allows it to quickly respond to such opportunities is a great challenge, which we will address later in this chapter. While these advantages may allow an international firm to compete successfully against a domestic firm in terms of production cost, it is the skill of its management in turning these potential advantages into actual ones that will enable the firm to successfully compete against other international firms that are also pursuing a worldwide integration strategy.

By the nature of the way it chooses to compete, an international firm pursuing a worldwide integration strategy may find itself at a disadvantage against some purely domestic firms, or against international firms pursuing a national responsiveness strategy. This will occur in industries where consumer preferences vary greatly across national boundaries and products must be tailored for each market, or in industries where global economies of scale cannot be achieved. The worldwide integration strategy emphasizes flexibility in configuring global operations but limits a firm's flexibility to respond to specific country preferences. It is clear that a firm's choice of global strategy must take into account the nature of the industry in which it is competing. To be successful, the firm must match its strategy with the industry environment in which it operates. Industries characterized by large economies of scale, standardized products worldwide, low tariff and nontariff barriers to trade, and high factor (labor, land, and capital) cost differences across countries are likely to lend themselves to a worldwide integration strategy. Such industries are often called global industries. If the industry does not possess such characteristics, a different global strategy may be more appropriate.

The operations of a highly integrated firm tend to be highly interdependent. By centralizing the production of particular components to achieve economies of scale, the firm becomes more vulnerable to serious disruptions of the production process. For example, if Ford produced all Escort carburetors in England and British workers went on strike, the entire Escort production would come to a halt. Therefore, even firms pursing a worldwide integration strategy usually try to retain some duplication in their operations, even if this somewhat reduces their economies of scale.

Caterpillar Tractor Company has been identified as a firm with a worldwide integration strategy. Punnett and Ricks (1992) describe their operations:

> Caterpillar has chosen the advantages offered by a global approach to its multinational operation. The company's main advantages stem from its ability to establish major barriers to entry into the industry through globally independent distribution system and worldwide production scale. The company first established independent dealerships to service fleets of Caterpillar equipment left overseas after World War II; these dealerships formed the basis of the current dealership network, which is larger and better financed than its competitors' distribution systems. Economies of scale have been achieved because product lines are limited and use identical components, allowing a few large-scale manufacturing facilities to fill worldwide demand. These facilities are augmented by assembly and production of local adaptations in its major markets. The very strength of this approach can be its weakness, however. In a globally integrated company, the entire organization can suffer because of events that affect only one part.

In the case of Caterpillar, Inc., the company went from forty-eight years of continuous profits in 1982, to three years of losses totaling almost $1 billion. Some of the company's main customers were in third world nations, and when they experienced extremely bad economic conditions, combined with enormous international debt payments, their purchases declined. At the same time, the U.S. dollar's value was rising and Caterpillar's large-scale facilities in the United States were manufacturing products that were increasingly expensive, forcing its overseas customers to consider other suppliers (Punnett & Ricks 1992, pp. 247–248).

CREATING COMPETITIVE ADVANTAGE THROUGH A NATIONAL RESPONSIVENESS STRATEGY

On the other end of the spectrum from firms pursuing a worldwide integration strategy are the international firms that pursue a national responsiveness strategy. These firms give their subsidiaries much more autonomy to respond to local market conditions. The ability to quickly respond to differing preferences and regulatory changes across countries gives the nationally responsive firm an advantage over the international firm pursuing a worldwide integration strategy. While the integrated firm cannot quickly alter its operations in one country without threatening the operations of other subsidiaries, the responsive firm can. A problem in Britain might threaten the entire production of a "world" car, whereas if completely different cars were produced in each country (a nationally responsive approach), problems in Britain would be limited to Britain and not affect the entire firm's global operations.

Given that each of the subsidiaries of a nationally responsive firm operates almost as if it were a local company, one might wonder what advantage an international firm following this strategy would have over purely domestic competitors who have a better understanding of local tastes, customs, and culture. The international firm has at least four advantages:

1. It can pool financial risks across subsidiaries in many different countries.

2. It can spread its research and development costs over a larger volume of sales.

3. It can coordinate exporting from local markets more easily, owing to its international experience.

4. Specific skills and technology learned in one subsidiary can be transferred to another, increasing the overall learning that takes place in the firm.

By emphasizing local flexibility, the responsive firm often forgoes the advantages made possible under worldwide integration (such as economies of scale). A national responsiveness strategy saves firms in industries with characteristics that would make worldwide integration difficult. Industries where product preferences vary considerably across national markets (such as foods or clothing), where economies of scale are small or nonexistent, or where high barriers to international trade exist, often lend themselves to competition under a nationally responsive strategy. Because international firms in these industries often try to operate as if they were domestic in each country where they operate, these are called multidomestic industries.

The Bata Shoe Organization is one firm that follows a national responsiveness or multi-domestic strategy. Bata is the world's largest manufacturer and marketer of footwear, and, according to its corporate literature, it has operations in more than 100 countries. Bata is a family owned firm which describes itself as a "multi-domestic" firm—with each of its subsidiaries essentially indepentent. This multi-domestic strategy has resulted in Bata subsidiaries being viewed as local companies in many locations.

Bata prides itelf in contributing to the development of the countries in which it operates, and to the extent possible, each local operation is self-sufficient in production and safety. At the same time, Bata benefits from sharing information among subsidiaries, and a critical strength of the firm appears to be intentionally oriented managers and personnel. Bata is seen by many as the quintessential multi-domestic that exploits global advantages.

ADMINISTRATION COORDINATION STRATEGY: COMBINING RESPONSIVENESS AND INTEGRATION

To effectively implement any global strategy, firms use national differences, scale economies, and synergies between different activities to attain and maintain a competitive advantage. The strategic task of managing globally is to use these sources of competitive advantage to the fullest extent. Since most industries are not entirely global or entirely multidomestic, it is often necessary that firms develop the ability to both integrate globally and be locally responsive. According to Doz (1980), firms that concentrate on integrating and being responsive are following an "administrative coordination strategy." In one sense, this approach requires that the firm follow both strategies simultaneously; in another, it requires that the firm make each strategic decision according to its own merits. While the rewards of this "ultimately flexible" approach are clear, it is very difficult to carry out. Instead of taking a clear cut strategy, continual administrative changes continually are required to deal with each new situation. Local responsiveness and worldwide integration are trade-offs between flexibility across countries and flexibility within countries, while the firm concentrates on internal efficiency. The administrative coordination strategy, on the other hand, pursues external flexibility (within and across countries), often at the expense of international efficiency, as depicted in Exhibit 6.2.

The strength of this approach is that, in theory, the firm can benefit from the advantages of both the worldwide integration and the national responsiveness strategies. The difficulty is in having the necessary management skills and flexible organizational structure to respond adequately both to pressures for integration and responsiveness. *Business Week* (1990, p. 102) recently described how some firms are trying to be both locally responsive and globally integrated:

EXHIBIT 6.2

STRATEGIC OBJECTIVES

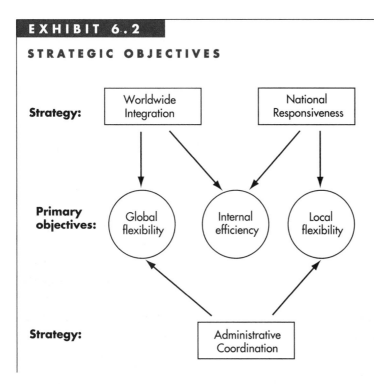

Maintaining a balance between functioning as a global organization while customizing products to local tastes requires creative managers. World companies are developing a cadre of bosses of different nationalities who have all had several foreign postings. Of Dow Chemical's top 25 executives, 20, including CEO Frank Popoff, have had foreign experience. For GE Plastics, the general manager of auto marketing worldwide is Dutch, and the manager of plastics marketing is German. Says Peter Mercer, a human resources executive for GE Plastics-in Pittsfield, MA: "Nationality really doesn't make a difference."

It's not so much that world companies are abandoning identification with a single nation as much as they are trying to become local companies in many countries. As the new global companies juggle identities, they are shaking up old-style matrix management. In short, the old-fashioned matrix is "too bureaucratic, too slow, and too expensive in today's market," says Richard Dulude a member of Corning Glass Works' board of directors.

MANAGEMENT SKILLS
AND COMPETITIVE ADVANTAGE

Much of the discussion concerning which global strategy is most appropriate for a particular firm relies on the assumption that inconsistencies across countries provide opportunities for firms to gain a competitive advantage. For example, differences in labor costs create an opportunity for international firms to gain an advantage by locating production facilities in low-labor-cost countries. Differences in customer tastes lead to opportunities for the nationally responsive firm. To the extent that such differences are either disappearing or becoming less important because of changes in technology (such as automated production, ability to efficiently handle small production runs, increased ease of raising capital in any financial market) competitive advantages based on "imperfections" (or differences) in financial and product markets will become increasingly difficult to maintain. Ultimately, the quality of the international firm's management may be the deciding factor in gaining and maintaining an advantage over competitors. Doz and Prahalad (1988) identify seven dimensions of quality management that make any international strategy succeed.

1. Having information-processing capability. International managers must have access to multiple types of accurate data, must be able to analyze the data in a sophisticated fashion, and must be able to respond quickly.

2. Using a differentiated management system. The management system, or structure, of the organization must be flexible and varied. Quality management implies being able to deal with different lines of business and subsidiaries in different and unique ways.

3. Managing interdependencies. Different interrelated activities carried out throughout the MNCs must be managed to promote synergy and learning throughout the organization.

4. Managing strategic change. In the constantly changing global environment, managers must be able to shift strategies and refocus attention quickly.

5. Managing innovation. Managers must have the skill to identify and take advantage of new opportunities to increase internal competencies (office automation, production automation) and to identify new business opportunities.

6. Establishing pivots. Managers must be alert to finding key themes to promote unity of purpose and motivation in a widely dispersed organization.

7. Ensuring executive process quality. Managers must recognize the legitimacy of dissent within the organization. They must be equitable and build trust, and they must align corporate and individual interests.

AVOIDING COMPETITIVE DISADVANTAGE

Not all strategic decisions a firm makes are geared toward creating a competitive advantage. Often, far-reaching decisions are made in an attempt to avoid letting a competitor gain an advantage.

OLIGOPOLISTIC REACTION

In highly concentrated industries (where a few firms account for the majority of production and sales—also known as "oligopolies") the moves of a major competitor often lead to reactions by the other firms. F.T. Knickerbocker (1974) noted that in such industries, when one firm moved into a new foreign market, other major industry players were quick to move into that market as well. He called this phenomenon "oligopolistic reaction." One rationale for this phenomenon is that if one firm were able to dominate the industry in a particular foreign country, its preeminence there might so disrupt the balance in the industry that competitors would find their global market shares diminishing. Since the smaller market shares might place them at a competitive disadvantage, competitors tend to follow each other into new markets to maintain the industry status quo in terms of each firm's share of the market.

PRESENCE IN COMPETITORS' HOME MARKETS

Global expansion can also help avoid a competitive disadvantage in another way. Consider this simplified scenario. Suppose Firm A is an Australian company that does 70 percent of its $1 billion in sales in Australia and has captured 50 percent of the Australian market but does no business in Japan. Firm B is a Japanese firm much like Firm A. It operates in the same industry as firm A, with 70 percent of its $1 billion sales in Japan (where it has a market share of 50 percent). Firm B expands into the Australian market. Knowing that Firm A sells its product in Australia for $100, Firm B will sell its product in Australia for $90 to gain a share of the Australian market. This low price will have a minimal impact on Firm B because almost all of its revenue comes from its sales in Japan. However, if Firm A wants to keep its 50 percent of the Australian market it will have to lower the price of its product $90. This 10 percent decrease on Australian sales of $700 million would cost Firm A around $70 million. The loss of revenue would place Firm A at a disadvantage to Firm B in terms of worldwide sales.

If Firm A had even a small operation in Japan, it could counteract Firm B's tactic in Australia by lowering the price of its own product in Firm B's home market of Japan. The simple presence of Firm A in Japan, even on a relatively small scale, may pose a sufficient threat to Firm B to keep it from attacking Firm A's primary market.

PRESENCE IN KEY GLOBAL MARKETS

The United States, Japan, and Western Europe account for about half of the world's total consumption, and they share certain important economic and demographic conditions (such as high income levels and high GNP values). It has been argued (Ohmae 1985) that a firm cannot truly compete on a global scale if it is not present in this "triad."

If a firm does not have operations in all three areas of the triad, it may not be able to achieve maximum economies of scale. Furthermore, since the three areas are often the source of technological and product innovations, a firm not present in all triad areas would have difficulty keeping abreast of technological developments in its industry. Finally, since the triad accounts for one-half of the world's consumers (even more in some industries), presence in the triad is necessary to keep abreast of consumer preferences and changes in consumer trends. Therefore, some people have suggested that to remain competitive, multinationals must pursue a "triad strategy." Of course, there are other arguments about key global markets. For example, China, with a billion people, a rapidly growing economy, and poorly served consumers, is seen by some as a key market of the future.

COMPETITIVE STRATEGIES AND INTERNATIONAL SCOPE

The worldwide integration and nationally responsive strategies discussed above are closely related to Michael Porter's work on competitive strategies (1980). According to Porter, firms international or domestic can gain an advantage over competitors in three ways: by cost leadership, differentiation, or focus. Porter calls each of the three approaches a "generic" competitive strategy.

1. Cost leadership. The goal of this strategy is to so well manage the costs associated with development, production, and marketing of a product that the firm is able to gain an advantage by underpricing competitors, or, if the firm so chooses, to sell at the same price as competitors but have a higher profit margin. This strategy requires the firm to take advantage of economies of scale and to vigorously pursue cost reduction in areas such as overhead, research and development, service, advertising, and so on.

2. Differentiation. This second strategy is based on the firm fielding products that consumers perceive as unique. This uniqueness can be achieved in many ways: by using a distinctive brand name, by concentrating on providing specific product features, by differentiating themselves on the basis of after-sales customer service, by providing a higher quality product than competitors, and so forth. While the firm pursuing a differentiation strategy cannot ignore costs, the concern with costs is not the ultimate driving force.

Rather, it is through the uniqueness of its product(s) that the firm is able to command a premium for its goods and secure a higher-than-average profit margin.

3. Focus. Porter's third competitive strategy can be thought of in terms the scope of the firm's operations. While some firms provide full product lines designed to reach a very broad customer base, others focus on much narrower market segments. The broad-scope companies can compete either on the basis of cost or differentiation. The firms that target a smaller segment of the market are using a focus strategy. Firms that may be unable to compete strictly in terms of cost or differentiation can still gain above-average returns by concentrating on serving the idiosyncrasies of a particular market subgroup ill-served by the broad-scope companies.

INTERNATIONAL SCOPE

Building on his generic competitive strategies, Porter suggests four alternative strategies that firms involved in global industries may follow. Once again, these strategies are defined in terms of the scope of the firm's operations. Porter's strategies are analogous to the worldwide integration, national responsiveness, and administrative coordination strategies described earlier. However, Porter's approach helps amplify the earlier discussion by pointing out the different competitive strategies available to international firms and the alternatives the international firm faces in selecting the scope of its operations. Porter's four strategies for global competition are: broad-line global competition, global focus, national focus, and protected niche.

1. Broad-line global competition. Under this strategy, firms compete on a worldwide basis and offer a wide range of products in a given industry. For example, IBM competes in all segments of the computer market (mainframes, minis, and micros) and its products are available around the globe. Broad-line global competitors can gain a competitive advantage either by capitalizing on scale economies and achieving cost leadership, or through differentiation. IBM

appears to pursue the latter strategy, as its products are sold at a premium, owing to the unique quality and customer service it provides.

2. Global focus. This strategy implies competing worldwide, but only in a part of the industry. Many of IBM's competitors appear to follow this strategy. For example, Burroughs is primarily involved with mainframes, DEC focuses on minis, and Compaq and Apple compete in the microcomputer segment. These firms identify a particular slice of the industry where they possess particular strengths, and barriers to globalization are low. They then compete in that segment using either a cost leadership or differentiation strategy, depending on the competitive environment. Compaq has successful in built a reputation for quality in the microcomputer segment of the industry, and is able to command a premium for its products on that basis. Though, given IBM's strength, it would be very difficult for Compaq to compete on that basis industry-wide, Compaq is successful in implementing a global focus strategy based on differentiation. Liggett & Myers, on the other hand, has taken advantage of global economies of scale in cigarette production to successfully compete, using a cost leadership strategy, in the generic segment of the tobacco industry.

3. National focus. Firms following this strategy focus on one or a few particular national markets and try to outperform global firms by concentrating on keeping costs low or differentiating themselves within those few markets. Porter's national focus approach is similar to the nationally responsive strategy discussed earlier. Note that an international firm adopting a national focus strategy does not necessarily rely entirely on differentiation to gain a competitive advantage. For example, in countries where import barriers are high, an international firm may set up a relatively self-contained local operation (a nationally responsive approach), in order to be able to produce as cheaply as possible (by avoiding trade barriers) and gain a cost leadership advantage over global competitors in that country. Thus, when cost advantages are associated with the

economies of scale afforded by competing globally, there are enough imperfections in international markets to allow for considerable diversity in selecting and implementing competitive strategies.

4. Protected niche. Firms following this strategy seek governmental protection from competition in certain countries to gain a competitive advantage. One could argue that they are not really gaining a competitive advantage; rather, they are isolating themselves from competition through the use of government protection. Thus, questions of cost versus differentiation strategies do not really apply. A number of multinationals in important industries are able to negotiate favorable deals for setting up operations, particularly in third world countries. However, such governmental protection is difficult to negotiate from countries belonging to the triad, and consequently the protected niche approach is difficult to implement on a global basis. Firms from smaller countries and developing countries may find this approach particularly advantageous.

AN INTERNATIONAL COMPETITIVE STRATEGIES FRAMEWORK

We now briefly combine some of the issues addressed thus far. As explained earlier, the way an international firm competes is largely contingent on the characteristics of the industry in which the firm operates. Some industries lend themselves to global approaches, other industries require a multidomestic emphasis. By the same token, some industries are more conducive to broad-line global competition, while others are better suited to a focused approach. However, most industries cannot be clearly categorized as either global or multidomestic. To varying degrees each industry comprises characteristics of both. Semiconductors and airplane parts may fall heavily toward the global side, while processed foods and footwear are more multidomestic, yet there is enough diversity within each industry to allow the firm discretion in tailoring its strategy to match its own strengths and operating philosophy. Industry characteristics alone cannot dictate how the firm should compete, but the firm cannot afford to, disregard these characteristics. It is in properly matching the strengths and resources of the firm with particular elements of its environment that a competitive advantage is attained. It is management's role to identify the appropriate mix.

Exhibit 6.3 synthesizes some of the arguments presented so far. However, it must be remembered that these are general principles, not hard and fast rules. The first column in the exhibit is comprised of the international strategies dis-

EXHIBIT 6.3

AN INTERNATIONAL STRATEGY FRAMEWORK

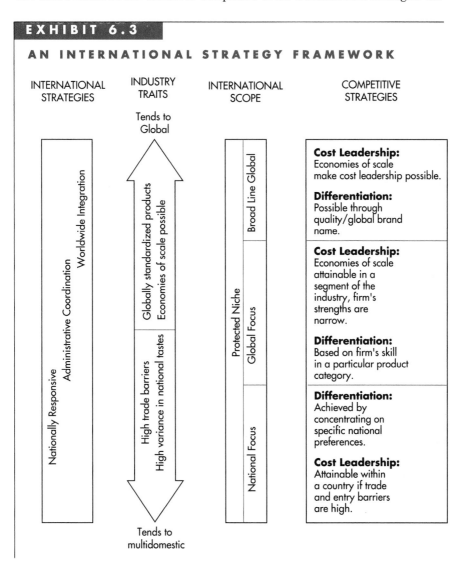

| INTERNATIONAL STRATEGIES | INDUSTRY TRAITS | INTERNATIONAL SCOPE | COMPETITIVE STRATEGIES |

cussed earlier in this chapter. Each strategy is associated with particular industry characteristics, some of which are identified in the second column. Likewise, as depicted in column three, certain of the scopes of international activities identified by Porter are more readily reconcilable with certain industry characteristics. The fourth column briefly summarizes how different competitive strategies may be appropriate despite differences in industry traits, international scope, and global strategies.

It should be emphasized however, that competitive advantage often results from firms finding a new way to implement a particular strategy in an environment where competitors have taken a different approach. Exhibit 6.3 depicts only the general way firms seem to operate. It is often in finding a new way to break out from the mold that firms achieve success.

INTERNATIONAL EFFECTIVENESS

The U.S. trade deficit, particularly with Japan, suggests that Americans often prefer foreign goods to those made at home, and that "made in America" no longer implies a product that is the best available. Managers in the United States have become acutely aware of the need to be more effective in meeting the needs and expectations of their customers. This has resulted in a renewed emphasis on quality and continuous improvement of outputs and processes. Recently a variety of books and papers have focused on this issue using the phrase "total quality management." The need to strive for quality and continuous improvement is by no means unique to the U.S. firm. For example:

- The Japanese have accomplished much of their global expansion since World War II through their efforts to provide quality products and services.

- The European community sees quality management as a fundamental aspect of its competitiveness.

- Third world countries have recognized that their inability to produce quality can be a major barrier to development.

International firms may expand internationally partly to respond to the pressure for improved quality. For example:

- Firms seek resources and skills in foreign locations because they are believed to be better than those at home.

- Firms establish operations in locations that help minimize costs of inputs and transportation.

- Firms seek foreign markets that need their products or services.

- Firms adapt their processes, products, and services to meet the conditions and needs of foreign locations.

The international business environment is particularly competitive because competition can come from virtually anywhere and may appear in unexpected forms. International managers must therefore be particularly concerned with achieving quality and continuous improvement in their operations around the world. Understanding the needs and expectations of customers, as well as the other stakeholders in an organization, is fundamental to achieving appropriate quality and improvement.

International firms and managers face an extraordinarily complex task in analyzing, understanding, and meeting the needs and expectations of stakeholders, including such diverse groups as home and host governments, employees in different locations, expatriate managers, worldwide customers, and diverse shareholders. The need for achieving this understanding underlies all the discussions in this book. We believe that understanding the global environment and international human resource issues is fundamental to developing an effective strategy that can achieve quality and continuous improvement on a worldwide scale.

CONCLUSIONS

Most of our discussion in this chapter has centered around strategic choices made by top management of the MNC as they consider the characteristics of their industry worldwide. However, selecting and implementing an appropriate strategy requires not only an understanding of the MNC's industry (or industries) but also an understanding of how the MNC itself is structured and operates. Proper coordination between subsidiaries and between subsidiaries and headquarters is vital if the MNC is to secure a competitive advantage. Lack of proper coordination within the MNC will limit its synergy and learning opportunities.

Exhibit 6.4 shows the simplest possible representation of N.V. Philips, a multinational company headquartered in the Netherlands. The company has its own operating units in 60 countries as diverse as the United States, France, Japan, South Korea, Nigeria, Uruguay, and Bangladesh. Some of these units are large, fully integrated companies developing, manufacturing, and marketing a diverse range of products from light bulbs to defense systems. Such subsidiaries might have 5,000 or more employees and might be among the largest companies in their host countries. Others are small, single-function operations responsible for only R&D, or manufacturing, or marketing for only one or a few of these different businesses. Some such units might employ 50 or fewer people. In some cases, the units have been in operation for more than 50 years; a few began their organizational lives less than 10 years ago. Some of these units are tightly controlled from headquarters; others enjoy relationships with the headquarters akin to those between equal partners.

The issue of coordination is addressed in other chapters of this book. At this point, however, one should realize how important and difficult it is to properly manage a truly global firm. Exhibit 6.4 illustrates some of these difficulties.

Trying to identify the appropriate strategy for a company like N.V. Philips would certainly be difficult, considering the breadth of industries the firm spans as well as the variety of skills and relationships across different units of the firm. Even more difficult would be implementing any one strategy, given the multitude of subsidiary characteristics.

A major difficulty facing experienced global firms is balancing the use of traditionally straightforward but increasingly inadequate organizational structures with more flexible yet more unmanageable means of coordination. It has been argued that instead of thinking of the firm as a hierarchy in the traditional sense, it should be thought of as a "heterarchy"—that is, a network of

EXHIBIT 6.4

INTERORGANIZATIONAL LINKAGES WITHIN N.V. PHILIPS

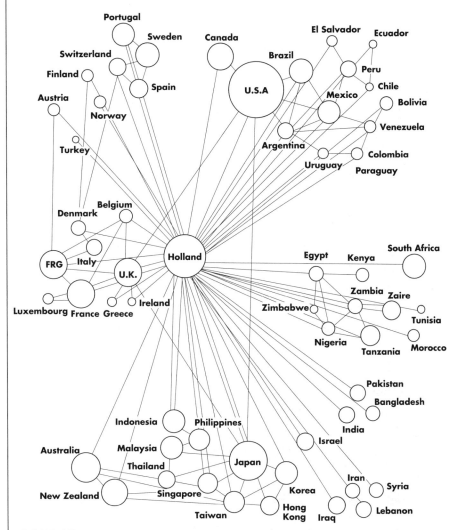

SOURCE:

Reprinted from "Strategic Management in Multinational Companies" by Y. Doz, *Sloan Management Review*, 1980, pp. 27-46, by permission of the publisher. Copyright © 1980 by the Sloan Management Review Association. All rights reserved.

operating units where the notion of a "headquarters" carries little meaning. Gunnar Hedlund (Hedlund & Rolander 1990) suggests that more and more international firms will be characterized by these four traits:

1. Functions typically associated with headquarters are geographically diffused across subsidiaries and the firm's structure varies continuously.

2. Subsidiaries increasingly have a strategic role of their own, not just a role determined by their head office.

3. Greater variety exists in structuring operations; that is, there is simultaneous use of joint ventures, market transactions, in-house transactions at arm's length, internal transfers, and so on.

4. Operations are increasingly integrated through the use of "normative" methods—such as "corporate culture," "management ethics," and "style," instead of formal mechanisms—such as reports, schedules, budgets, and so on.

In this way of thinking, a firm's global strategy takes on an entirely different meaning. Strategy is not a premeditated approach the MNC adopts. Premeditated approaches are thought of as being too restrictive. Rather, strategy becomes the firm's pattern of reaction to opportunities over time. Competitive advantage is derived almost entirely by how flexibly the firm is structured.

There is little doubt that most firms today, international or not, still reflect more closely a hierarchy with an identifiable head office in a specific home country, than the headquarterless network of the heterarchical firm. However, as Exhibit 6.5 illustrates, many companies are becoming so international that eventually their home office may be little more than just that: an office. The day may be coming when the country where the MNC is headquartered will mean little in terms of where it actually conducts its business.

It is difficult to predict what direction the MNC will take and what impact new organizational firms will have on the interpretation of global strategy. Gaining a competitive advantage in international business is a challenging task, and flexibility and creativity are increasingly important in achieving it.

EXHIBIT 6.5

HIGHLY INTERNATIONALIZED FIRMS

This is a sampling of manufacturing companies with a minimum $3 billion in annual sales that derive at least 40% of those sales from countries other than their home country. It does not include state-owned companies or holding companies.

Company	Home country	1989 Total sales Billions	Sales outside home country	Assets outside home country	Shares held outside country	Management approach
NESTLÉ	SWITZERLAND	32.9*	98.0%	95.0%	Few	CEO is German, has 10 general managers, of whom five are not Swiss
SANDOZ	SWITZERLAND	8.6*	96.0	94.0	5.0%	All Swiss at top, more conservative in style than other Swiss companies
SKF	SWEDEN	4.1	96.0	90.0	20.0	Foreigners have cracked board and top management group
HOFFMAN-LA ROCHE	SWITZERLAND	6.7*	96.0	60.0	0.0	All-Swiss board, but next level of managers mixed
PHILIPS	NETHERLANDS	30.0	94.0	85.0*	46.0	Solidly Dutch company, but number of senior foreign managers is Increasing
SMITHKLINE BEECHAM	BRITAIN	7.0	89.0	75.0	46.0	Joint U.S.-British management of all levels
AUP	SWEDEN	20.6	85.0*	NA	50.0	Moved headquarters to Switzerland, managers are Swedish, Swiss, German
ELECTROLUX	SWEDEN	13.8	83.0	80.0	20.0	Of 50 top managers outside Sweden, only five are Swedish
VOLVO	SWEDEN	14.8	80.0	30.0	10.0	Solidly Swedish at all top management levels
ICI	BRITAIN	22.1	78.0	50.0	16.0	40% of top 170 executives are not British, top ranks include four other nationalities
MICHELIN	FRANCE	9.4	78.0	NA	0.0	Secretive, centralized, with top management almost entirely French
NOECHST	W. GERMANY	27.3	77.0	NA	42.0	No foreigners on board, but most foreign operations are run by locals
UNILEVER	BRITAIN/NETH.	35.3	75.0*	70.0*	27.0	Five nationalities on board, thoroughly stateless management

EXHIBIT 6.5 (continued)

AIR LIQUIDE	FRANCE	5.0	70.0	66.0	6.0	English is official language, but it considers itself thoroughly French
CANON	JAPAN	9.4	69.0	32.0	14.0	Foreigners run many sales subsidiaries, but none in top ranks
NORTHERN TELECOM	CANADA	6.1	67.1	70.5	16.0	Thoroughly Canadian, but has assumed U.S. identity
SONY	JAPAN	16.3	66.0	NA	13.6	Only major Japanese manufacturer with foreigners on board
BAYER	W. GERMANY	25.8	65.4	NA	48.0	No foreigners on board, but six of 25 business groups run by foreigners
BASF	W. GERMANY	13.3	65.0	NA	NA	Relies on local managers to run foreign operations, but none in the top ranks
GILLETTE	U.S.	3.8	65.0	63.0	10.0*	Three foreigners among top 21 officers
COLGATE	U.S.	5.0	64.0	47.0	10.0*	CEO, other top execs have had several foreign posts, many multilingual
HONDA	JAPAN	26.4	63.0	35.7	6.9	Foreigners running offshore plant, but none at the top levels at home
DAIMLER BENZ	W. GERMANY	45.5	61.0	NA	25.0*	Similar to other German plants
IBM	U.S.	62.7	59.0	NA	NA	Relies on locals to manage non-U.S. operations, increasing number of foreigners in top ranks
NCR	U.S.	6.0	58.9	40.5	NA	Nationals run foreign operations, but none in top ranks
CPC INTERNATIONAL	U.S.	5.1	56.0	62.0	5.0*	One-third of officers are foreign nationals
COCA-COLA	U.S.	9.0	54.0	45.0	0.0	Thoroughly multinational management group making big international push
DIGITAL	U.S.	12.7	54.0	44.0	NA	Five of top 37 officers are foreign, most foreign operations run by locals
DOW CHEMICAL	U.S.	17.6	54.0	45.0	5.0	Out of top 25 managers, 20 have experience outside U.S.
SAINT GOBAIN	FRANCE	11.6	54.0	50.0	13.0	Of 25 top managers, only two are not French
XEROX	U.S.	12.4	54.0	51.8	0.0	Major joint ventures with Ronk, Fuji have shaped top management thinking

EXHIBIT 6.5 (continued)						
CATERPILLAR	U.S.	11.1	53.0	NA	NA	Of top five executives, four have foreign experience, including CEO-elect
HEWLETT-PACKARD	U.S.	11.9	53.0	38.6	8.0	Five of top 25 officers not U.S. citizens; many units managed offshore
SIEMENS	W. GERMANY	36.3	51.0	NA	44.0	Some business groups managed from outside Germany by non-Germans but none on management board
CORNING	U.S.	3.1*	50.0*	45.0*	NA	Company is leader in use of joint ventures to penetrate markets
JOHNSON & JOHNSON	U.S.	9.8	50.0	48.0	NA	First foreign national on board in 1989, senior managers include foreign born
UNITED-TECHNOLOGIES	U.S.	19.8	49.7	26.7	NA	Because of U.S. defense business, few foreigners at top
UNISYS	U.S.	10.1	49.0	31.0	10.0	Aside from Japanese joint venture, management is largely American
MERCK	U.S.	6.0	47.0	NA	NA	Top management is American but foreign nationals run overseas operations
NISSAN	JAPAN	36.5	47.0	20.0	2.9	Foreign operations managed by locals, completely Japanese at headquarters
3M	U.S.	12.0	46.0	42.0	15.0	CEO pushing to raise foreign sales to 50% of total by 1992
DU PONT	U.S.	35.5	44.0	20.0	24.0	Has two foreign directors, both Canadians, but top management is heavily American
MATSUSHITA	JAPAN	41.7	42.0	NA	7.0	American named No. 2 for North America, but no foreigners in top ranks
HEINZ	U.S.	6.0	40.0	41.0	0.6	CEO is Irish citizen, management thoroughly mixed
P&G	U.S.	21.4	40.0	32.0	NA	International operations chief recently named CEO

NA = not available
Data Company Reports
*BW estimates

SOURCE:

Reprinted from May 14, 1990 issue of *Business Week* by special permission, Copyright © 1990 by McGraw-Hill, Inc.

SUMMARY

This chapter gives an overview of what is meant by international strategy. Specific strategies were identified and discussed in light of their appropriateness for industries with particular characteristics. The role of global strategies in creating a sustainable competitive advantage was discussed, as was global strategic decisions made to prevent a competitor from gaining an advantage. This chapter also discussed the relationship between global strategies, international scope, and competitive strategies. The chapter concluded by highlighting the difficulties associated with managing a diversified multinational, and by suggesting new ways global businesses might structure themselves, with significant implications for the strategy formulation and implementation process. Developing an effective strategy requires care and attention. This chapter introduced students to the complexity of global strategic management by illustrating the many issues that firms face in making strategic decisions. The following chapters examine various foreign entry decisions.

DISCUSSION QUESTIONS

1. Identify a successful local firm and identify the strengths that have contributed to its success. Discuss whether these strengths can be employed internationally.

2. Suppose a foreign firm were seeking a joint-venture partner in your local community. Discuss how this foreign firm should identify and contact potential partners.

3. Identify a firm that has been successful in international franchising and discuss what factors account for its success.

REFERENCES

Beamish, P.W., J.P. Killing, D.J. Lecraw, and H. Crookell, 1991. *International Management.* Homewood, IL: Irwin.

Business Week, May 14, 1990, p. 102.

Doz, Y. 1980. "Strategic Management in Multinational Companies." *Sloan Management Review*, Winter, pp. 27–45.

Doz, Y. & C. Prahalad. 1988. "Quality of management: An emergent source of global competitive advantage?"

Ghoshal S. & A. Bartlett. 1990. "The Multinational Corporation as an Interorganizational Network." *Academy of Management Review*, October, pp. 603–625.

Hedlund & Rolander. 1990. *Action in Heterarchies—New Approaches to Managing the MNC.*

Knickerbocker, F.T. 1974. *Oligopolistic Reaction and Multinational Enterprise.* Cambridge, MA: Harvard Business School Division of Research.

Ohmae, K. 1985. *Triad Power: The Coming Shape of Global Competition.* New York: Free Press.

Porter, M.E. 1980. *Competitive Strategy.* New York: Free Press.

Punnett, B.J. & D.A. Ricks, 1992. *International Business.* Boston: PWS-Kent Publishing Company. Used with permission by South-Western College Publishing.

THE FOREIGN

ENTRY DECISION

LEARNING OBJECTIVES

IN THIS CHAPTER WE WILL EXPLORE:

- Reasons for globalizing

- Benefits and risks associated with globalizing

- Forces that influence strategic global decisions

- Entry into foreign locations

- Advantages and disadvantages of various forms of entry

- Matching the firm's strengths to the environment for the best entry

- Ownership options

- A strategic entry model

KEY DISCUSSION TOPICS:

- External and internal forces influencing global decisions

- The pros and cons of entry options

- The advantages and disadvantages of ownership options

- Evaluation of joint ventures and strategic alliances

- How to make the best entry

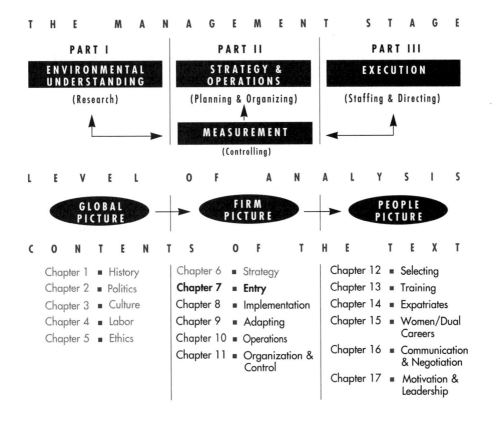

THE MANAGEMENT STAGE

PART I
ENVIRONMENTAL
UNDERSTANDING
(Research)

PART II
STRATEGY &
OPERATIONS
(Planning & Organizing)

PART III
EXECUTION
(Staffing & Directing)

MEASUREMENT
(Controlling)

LEVEL OF ANALYSIS

GLOBAL
PICTURE

FIRM
PICTURE

PEOPLE
PICTURE

CONTENTS OF THE TEXT

Chapter 1 ■ History
Chapter 2 ■ Politics
Chapter 3 ■ Culture
Chapter 4 ■ Labor
Chapter 5 ■ Ethics

Chapter 6 ■ Strategy
Chapter 7 ■ Entry
Chapter 8 ■ Implementation
Chapter 9 ■ Adapting
Chapter 10 ■ Operations
Chapter 11 ■ Organization &
Control

Chapter 12 ■ Selecting
Chapter 13 ■ Training
Chapter 14 ■ Expatriates
Chapter 15 ■ Women/Dual
Careers
Chapter 16 ■ Communication
& Negotiation
Chapter 17 ■ Motivation &
Leadership

INTRODUCTION

The global business environment has been growing constantly and dramatically since World War II, and the number of enterprises considered international is now very large. Foreign direct investment (investment outside of the home country) is a major force in today's world. According to the United Nations Center on Transnational Corporations (1988, pp. 33–34), in 1985, the 600 largest transnational corporations engaged in industrial or agricultural production had total sales of about three trillion U.S. dollars. These large multinationals, with affiliates scattered throughout the world, generated more than one-fifth of the total industrial and agricultural value-added products made in both the developed market economies and the developing countries. The primary lines of business for these companies were: petroleum and gas

(24.6 percent); machinery and equipment (24.5 percent); chemicals (13.5 percent); motor vehicles (12.6 percent); food, beverages and tobacco (10.4 percent); basic metals (6.6 percent); paper and printing (3.8 percent); and mining (1.6 percent).

A small number of multinational corporations was responsible for a large share of economic activity: only 69 corporations accounted for half of the total sales. Nevertheless, the contribution of small and medium-sized companies is considerable, representing half of the total number of firms investing abroad.

Why is there such a large number of global enterprises and why has international business become such a widespread phenomenon? To address these issues, it is important to examine the reasons why companies expand beyond their home-country borders. This chapter examines issues from the perspective of the individual company. The focus is on management's decisions to expand internationally, and the options they chose to accomplish such expansion.

WHY FIRMS GO OVERSEAS

Many benefits are available to companies in the global arena; however, the complexity of the global business environment means that international ventures are inherently more risky than purely domestic ones. For rational business decisions to justify international activities, the perceived benefits must outweigh the anticipated risks.

Companies that "go international" or expand their international presence, do so to gain from the perceived benefits. They want also to minimize the risks to which they are exposed. The decision is made in the context of their particular internal and external environment. Simply: internally, they consider strengths and weaknesses; externally, they consider opportunities and threats.

A company's reasons for expanding internationally can be both reactive and proactive. Reactive implies that managers are responding to something in the firm's external environment, generally something outside their control. Proactive implies that managers are seeking advantages and benefits to give the firm a competitive edge. We consider these as two distinct categories for simplicity, but in many cases managers make decisions that are reactive and proactive at the same time.

REACTING TO THE ENVIRONMENT

Many companies do not actively seek international involvement, eiter because the risks and costs are seen as too high, the payoffs as relatively low, or the company does not have adequate resources to pursue such opportunities actively. These companies, nevertheless, often find that globalization is forced on them by events outside their control. This form of reactive internationalization is summarized in Exhibit 7.1.

Trade barriers imposed by trading partners who are customers for a company's product or services often encourage that company to initiate international operations. These trade barriers can make a product or service too expensive because of tariffs (taxes on the import price of a product), unavailable because of quotas (limitations on the quantities that can be imported), or unattractive because of programs such as "buy local" campaigns (encouragements to buy products made locally). If the product or service is produced locally, it is not subject to the same trade barriers and can benefit from its local status.

If a company's customers choose to become international, the company may have to follow their lead to keep them as customers. Many international companies prefer to deal with a smaller number of suppliers worldwide; thus, if a supplier cannot meet customer needs in foreign locations, it may lose them as domestic customers as well.

Here is a good example:

> When a client of an accounting firm sets up operations in a foreign location, that client wants to deal with a branch of its current accounting firm. If that firm does not have a branch in a particular location, it may want to set one up to avoid the risk of the client having to go to a competitor.

When competitors become international, a company may have to follow their lead to remain competitive. If international competitors become well-established in foreign environments, this may put them in a position to attack the domestic market via lower costs of operation. In addition, if competitors become well-established in international markets, the domestic company may find it difficult to compete in these markets at a later date. Many companies, therefore, follow the international lead of their competitors.

Home governments can impose regulations and restrictions that increase the costs of operating domestically. These include environmental, health and safety, and insurance regulations, among others. If less-rigorous regulations and restrictions exist elsewhere, other factors being equal, companies may decide to operate in the less-restrictive environment. For example, in the late 1980s, many Hong Kong capitalists decided to invest in business ventures and real estate outside of Hong Kong. This outflow of capital was prompted by anticipation of regulations changing from the transfer of control to the People's Republic of China.

EXHIBIT 7.1

SUMMARY OF REACTIVE REASONS FOR EXPANDING BUSINESS INTERNATIONALLY

OUTSIDE OCCURRENCE	EXPLANATION OF REACTION
Trade barriers	Restrictive trade practices can make exports to foreign markets less attractive; local operations in foreign locations thus become more attractive.
International customers	If a company's customer base becomes international and the company wants to continue to serve it, local operations in foreign locations may be necessary.
International competition	If a company's competitors become international and the company wants to remain competitive, foreign operations may be necessary.
Regulations	Regulations and restrictions imposed by the home government may increase the cost of operating at home; it may be possible to avoid these by establishing foreign operations.
Chance	Unexpected events can prompt a company to enter foreign locations.

Many companies seem to become international purely by chance. A chance meeting between a company's CEO and a potential foreign associate on a plane trip can result in the decision to set up foreign operations of some kind. For example, the Silver Leaf Tobacco Company [according to the case Silver Leaf Tobacco (Kush) Limited (A) (Punnett & Ricks 1992] initiated operations in the African country of Kush because of a chance airplane stopover.

SEEKING COMPETITIVE ADVANTAGE

International differences in customs and cultures, as well as differing factor endowments, often provide opportunities for companies outside of their home borders. This engenders proactive management decisions, as summarized in Exhibit 7.2.

Resources are more readily available in some locations than in others because they are more accessible, cheaper, or subject to fewer restrictions. This is true of natural, human, technological, and financial resources. If a company needs a resource that is scarce at home, it will seek out that resource elsewhere; and, if the resource cannot be readily transported, the company will move operations overseas. For example, Chinese silk rugs are renowned around the world, and foreign firms who want to sell these rugs may choose to locate a facility in China to take advantage of this source.

Just as natural resources are less expensive where they are plentiful, the costs of labor are lower where labor is abundant. Costs such as energy and transportation also may differ depending on the location of production facilities relative to markets. In addition, the costs of doing business, including interest rates and taxes, vary from country to country. Companies can take advantage of these cost differentials by locating facilities in countries where particular costs are low. If a natural resource (such as lumber) is an important component of a product, it is logical for the company to seek out locations, either at home or abroad, where this resource is least costly. Similarly, if a product or service is labor intensive, it is logical to seek out locations where wages are low. This holds true for any input that is a major part of the cost of a product or service. For example, as costs of labor have increased in North America, many North

EXHIBIT 7.2

SUMMARY OF PROACTIVE REASONS FOR INTERNATIONAL BUSINESS

ADVANTAGE/OPPORTUNITY	EXPLANATION OF ACTION
Additional resources	Various inputs, including natural resources, technologies, skilled personnel, and materials may be obtained more readily outside the home country.
Lower costs	Various costs, including labor, materials, transport, and financing may be lower outside the home country.
Incentives	Various incentives may be available from the host government or the home government to encourage foreign investment in specific locations.
New, expanded markets	New and different markets may be available outside the home country; excess resources, including management, skills, machinery, and money can be utilized in foreign locations.
Exploitation of firm specific strengths	Technologies, brands, and recognized names are advantages that can provide opportunities in foreign locations.
Taxes	Differing corporate tax rates and tax systems in different locations provide opportunities for companies to maximize their after-tax worldwide profits.
Economies of scale	National markets may be too small to support efficient production, while sales from several, combined, allow for larger-scale production.
Synergy	Operations in more than one national environment provide opportunities to combine benefits from one location with another which is impossible without both of them.
Power and prestige	The image of being international may increase a company's power and prestige and improve its domestic sales and relations with various stakeholder groups.
Protect home market through offense in competitor's home	A strong offense in a competitor's market can put pressure on the competitor that results in a pull back from foreign activities to protect itself at home.

American companies have moved operations overseas to take advantage of low labor costs in other areas such as the Caribbean, the Far East, or Latin America.

Many countries feel that they benefit from foreign investment. This investment may be seen as providing needed foreign exchange, employment, technology, skills, training, and so forth. Governments offer incentives to entice foreign investors. Incentives include such things as provision of industrial buildings, insurance, tax exemptions, tax holidays, and interest-free loans. The home government may also want to encourage domestic companies to choose certain foreign locations over others and may offer its own incentives—trade assistance, subsidies, low-interest loans, and risk insurance. Such incentives can increase profits and decrease risks, making foreign operations more attractive. Managers often seek these opportunities around the world to maximize their net returns.

Different levels of economic development and different lifestyles, customs, and conditions throughout the world all provide reasons to consider foreign investment. A mature product in a declining market at home may be an innovative product in a growth market somewhere else. Outdated technology at home may be welcomed elsewhere. New products not suited to the home market may be appropriate for foreign locations. Conditions elsewhere may be more suitable for certain processes. The opportunities are almost endless. For example, a British manufacturer of heaters was surprised to find that Venezuela, Brazil, and Jordan, imported large quantities of heaters. It turned out that, in Jordan, they were used at night when the temperature dropped rapidly, but in Venezuela and Brazil, they were used for drying coffee. ("Marketing Strategy" in *International Business*, p.10)

Company strengths that originate at home can easily be advantageous in the global environment. A well-known brand name, a technological lead, a recognized company image are all potential global strengths. Many companies have been able to take turn domestic strengths into global advantages. The Coca-Cola company has been able to use its well-known trademark in many parts of the world. Coke is distributed in at least 155 countries around the world, and is consumed more than 303 million times each day (Oliver 1986). The Coca-Cola company makes its profits from sales of its concentrate to bottlers; it is therefore important to retain control of its secret formula. The importance of this formula is illustrated by the company's willingness to forgo the substantial Indian market rather than put production of the formula in the hands of a subsidiary with less than 100 percent ownership.

The tax differential among countries is another important aspect for companies that operate internationally. A company can minimize the corporate taxes it pays globally by locating its various operations in appropriate countries. In essence, an international company aims to maximize its profits in low-corporate-tax countries and minimize them in high-corporate-tax countries. They can accomplish this by establishing operations in countries that offer these tax advantages. For example, corporate taxes in Hong Kong (prior to 1997) were among the lowest in the world, and many foreign companies located "paper offices" (that is, legal corporate offices rather than physical presence) there to take advantage of the low rates.

Economies of scale unavailable in a single market may be possible on a global scale. The sheer size of the potential global markets means that, for those products or services that can benefit from economies of scale, there is great potential. Car makers have found that their markets are essentially global. Rather than produce locally for local markets, they can achieve substantial cost savings and efficiencies by producing for this worldwide market.

International operations create a certain degree of synergy. Having operations in more than one country provides opportunities to transfer learning from one location to another. In the early 1960s, IBM was pressured by Japan to offer its basic patents to Japanese companies. By 1985, when Japan had developed its own leading technologies, IBM was able to win access to Japan's government patents.

A search for increased power and prestige also may provide a reason for seeking international activities. Being international can increase a company's image as powerful and prestigious; and this can improve its domestic sales, as well as relations with various stakeholder groups. Customers at home may feel that if a company is international, its products or services must be world class; suppliers may feel that relations with an international company are more important than those with a purely domestic company; and shareholders may feel that share value is enhanced by global recognition. Many companies, in their domestic literature (advertising, corporate reports, public relations announcements), stress their global nature to enhance their image. Power and prestige is not purely a function of corporate advantage, it may well be the CEO and top managers who seek personal power and prestige through globalization.

Some firms have found that the best defense of the home market is a strong offense in the foreign competitor's home market. If a firm can put enough pressure on the competitor in the competitor's own home market, then that competitor may need to pull back from its foreign activities to protect itself at home.

MAKING THE DECISION TO GLOBALIZE

In sum, the manager's decision-making process regarding new or increased international operations involves reacting to the environment, seeking competitive advantage globally, and assessing the company's capability in the global context. The process can be seen as a series of questions.

> Question 1. Must we be more international? To answer this question, the manager assesses these factors: its home market, the competition, trade policies, and the regulatory environment. If its home market is limited or its customers are becoming international and want to use the same supplier worldwide, the answer is "yes." If the domestic

competition is becoming international or foreign competition is increasing, the answer is probably "yes." If there is a high probability of increased trade barriers that will affect the company's export markets, the answer is "yes." If the regulatory environment is making current operations less attractive, the answer is probably "yes." If none of these are occurring, the answer is probably "no."

Question 2. If the answer to Question 1 is "no," the manager asks: Should we be more international? To answer this question, the manager assesses factors that offer the company potential advantages— examining the reasons for internationalization. If specific global opportunities are identified, the answer is "yes." If none are compelling, the answer is probably "no," and the company should concentrate on domestic opportunities.

With the pressures for globalization in today's business environment, the likelihood of answering "no" to both Questions 1 and 2 is slim.

Question 3. If the answers to 1 or 2 are "yes," the manager then asks: Are we capable of becoming more international? To answer, the manager assesses the firm's strengths and weaknesses. The assessment is essentially an internal inventory and should include factors such as management, finances, products, equipment, expertise, technology, and distribution. It is important for this assessment to be internationally oriented. A strength at home may prove to be a weakness internationally, and vice versa. For example:

- An employee's facility with foreign languages might not be considered important in domestic operations but might be of critical importance in certain foreign operations.

- Participatory management approaches that work well at home may be ineffective in some foreign locations.

- Outdated machinery might be considered a liability in domestic operations, but could prove to be the most adaptable in less technologically advanced countries.

If the company is generally strong in assets that will be useful internationally, and if no critical weaknesses are uncovered in the assessment, the answer to Question 3 is "yes." If there are critical weaknesses or a general lack of strength, then the answer is "no.".

Question 4. If the answer is "no," the manager asks: How can we improve our capability? The manager has previously determined that the firm should expand internationally. The issue now is how to do so successfully. The previous assessment will have identified specific weak areas and/or a general lack of strength. The focus now shifts to creating programs to strengthen weak areas before undertaking global expansion. These may include internal changes as well as linkages with other organizations that can help provide the desired result.

Question 5. If the answer to Question 3 is "yes," the manager asks: What opportunities should we pursue? The answer depends on the identified reasons for expansion. Only a limited number of options can be explored in detail because analysis is both time-consuming and costly, therefore, those to be examined, should be chosen with care. If, for example, the company is reacting to government regulations and also seeking locations where specific raw materials are available, regions or countries where different regulations are in effect and the particular raw materials are available would be identified. If, in contrast, the company is seeking new markets for products that are mature at home, then regions or countries where the products are likely to be in the growth stage can be identified. If the company is reacting to competitors' moves, the specific actions taken by the competition must be examined to determine regions or countries to be assessed.

Question 6. The manager finally asks: How should we enter a specific location? The manager must now assess the costs and benefits of various possible modes of entry into a particular location. In general, the choices can be seen as ranging from no ownership in foreign locations, to joint ventures, to sole ownership of a foreign subsidiary.

Each of these options has benefits as well as drawbacks (as discussed in the next section) that the manager must weigh to make an appropriate choice. Once a choice is made, an action plan is designed to achieve the desired foreign activity.

The decision process should be thought of as an iterative process—that is, having been through the model once, a manager will periodically return to the first question and repeat the process. This has the effect of converting a reactive strategy to a proactive one.

FOREIGN ENTRY CHOICES

One of the most important decisions for many companies is the appropriate form of entry into a given foreign location. Companies can enter foreign locations in a variety of ways, through exports, licenses and contracts, or ownership of foreign operations. Entry decisions are not necessarily either/or decisions; they may involve a variety of forms in combination.

The nature of business activities that a company undertakes in a given location is a function of that company's situation. This sample of companies doing business internationally illustrates a variety of entry choices:

- Avis rents and leases vehicles worldwide through a group of largely independent franchises. About 70 percent of its international operations are independently owned, about 20 percent are wholly owned by Avis, and the remainder are joint ventures.

- Overseas Keyboarding Services provides a computer data entry service and sells contracts for data entry from Philadelphia to companies all over North America, for work done in India.

- Moore Corporation (a forms supplier) prefers to retain 100 percent ownership in subsidiaries in about 50 countries around the world, but has set up joint ventures in Japan, Venezuela, Barbados, Jamaica, and Central America, partly because of perceived political risks, and partly in response to restrictions on foreign investment.

We will discuss the most common forms of foreign entry, citing the general benefits and drawbacks of each option: those involving no foreign ownership, joint ventures, or sole ownership.

NO OWNERSHIP OF FOREIGN ASSETS

There are many ways in which companies can be involved in foreign locations, and even generate most of their revenue and profits from foreign markets, without ownership or direct investment. Here we identify five major opportunities of this type.

EXPORTING

A firm can supply foreign demand from home production by exporting. This approach is appropriate where capacity exists at home and the product reaches the foreign markets in a timely manner and at a competitive price. Exports are relatively easy to undertake and are often the first international step for a company. The company essentially continues operations as when purely domestic, however, now some output is exported to foreign markets.

The company benefits from increased sales and can test its products or services in foreign markets with relatively little risk because there is little change in operations. There are financial risks because of potential changes in exchange rates, but these can be minimized through currency markets or contracts.

Exporting can be appropriate for certain products, yet there are factors which may make exporting undesirable. For example, if transportation costs are high or tariffs apply to the product, the final price to customers may be too high to be competitive. This occurred following World War II, when the high cost of transporting U.S. automobiles to Australia, combined with tariffs of up to 100 percent, made U.S. cars too expensive in Australia and gave rise to Australia's car manufacturing industry. Other situations that may curtail export are: if products are perishable or delicate, it may not be possible to transport them any substantial distance; if non-tariff barriers exist in the foreign market, then it may be difficult to access the market; or if after-sales service is important, a local presence may be necessary.

While exports provide a relatively risk-free means of testing the international waters, the company may not realize the full market that exists in a foreign location through exports. In most cases, companies rely on the foreign importer to distribute and promote their product, and they may not do this adequately. Or even worse, if the foreign importer fails, this can reflect badly on the company and make future ventures more difficult, so it is important that an exporter consider its corporate trading partner carefully. In addition, an exporter must assess which export route would be most appropriate for its product(s) and market(s). Exhibit 7.3 illustrates a variety of potential routes.

Licenses

In this form of foreign entry, a firm (the licensor) grants the rights on some intangible property (patents, processes, copyrights, trademarks) to a foreign

---

EXHIBIT 7.3

POTENTIAL EXPORT ROUTES

The exporting company can go directly to the customer or through home-country agents, such as:

- export houses
- resident foreign buyers
- export commission houses
- export associations
- export brokers

The exporting company, the home-country agent, or both can go directly to the customer or through foreign agents, such as:

- individuals
- import brokers
- import houses
- distributors
- sales branches
- sales subsidiaries

Some combination is often used; e.g., export company to export house to export broker to import broker to import house to distributor.

firm (the licensee) for an agreed-upon compensation (a royalty). This approach is appropriate where foreign production is preferable to production at home, but the licensor does not wish to engage in foreign production itself. A licensing agreement gives the company access to foreign markets and foreign production, without demanding investment in the foreign location.

Licensing agreements vary, depending on the bargaining power of the two parties and the assistance provided by the licensor. Often, the licensee pays a sum when signing the agreement, then pays a periodic percentage of sales for the period of the contract. The licensing company benefits from sales in the foreign location and increased revenues through royalties, without having to provide capital or management. This is particularly attractive for a company that wants to access foreign markets through local production but does not have the financial or managerial capacity to do so on its own.

The drawbacks to licensing arrangements are that:

- If the product or service is successful, the company's revenue is less than it would have been had the company set up operations itself.

- The company is dependent on the foreign licensee for quality, efficiency, and promotion of the product or service, and if the licensee is not effective this will reflect on the licensor.

- The company may be creating a potential competitor.

- A certain amount of technology sharing is necessary and the company may risk losing its technological edge.

These disadvantages mean that the licensor should choose a licensee who will perform at an acceptable level and is trustworthy. The agreement that is reached is very important to both parties; it should ensure that the licensee is encouraged to be efficient, that the licensor benefits from increased profits, and that the licensor's technology is adequately protected.

The decision not to license can be as traumatic as the decision to license. Some examples from Ricks (1983) illustrate the pitfalls associated with the licensing decision:

- A U.S. manufacturer not only licensed the manufacture and sale of its products to an English firm but also granted the firm the exclusive right to sublicense the U.S. expertise to other countries. At the time the decision was made, the company was not interested in expanding overseas. The firm believed that it was best to simply collect the royalties and thus eliminate the need to provide additional investment money. Within a few years, worldwide markets for the firm's products developed. Naturally, the company greatly regretted its earlier decision permitting exclusive licensing.

- A U.S. pharmaceutical firm licensed its manufacturing techniques to an Asian company. The Asian company heavily promoted the products and enjoyed great success. As a result of the licensing terms, however, almost all of the profits were reaped by the Asian company. The U.S. company had permitted the licensing never having realized the product's potential. If the U.S. firm had committed to a more direct form of involvement, such as equity participation, it could have earned greater profits.

- One U.S. firm granted an exclusive license to a Japanese company. Market studies indicated the product was destined to replace some of the more conventional materials currently in use in Japan. The U.S. firm had carefully studied its potential licensees and had chosen the Japanese company because of its strength of distribution, size, and record of profit performance. However, the Japanese company continued to push the more conventional materials and failed to promote the new product actively. Since the contract contained no agreement concerning minimum royalties, the U.S. company earned no income for the first ten years of a twenty-year agreement.

Franchising

In a franchised foreign entry, for a fee, the franchiser grants, an independent foreign firm (the franchisee), the use of a trademark or other asset essential to the operation of the franchised business. This approach is appropriate for firms that have developed such an asset (such as McDonald's or Kentucky Fried Chicken) and can locate appropriate foreign franchises.

The benefit for the franchising firm is the ability to expand rapidly without investing its own resources. In addition, the franchiser does not need to have local knowledge—that is left up to the franchisee. The drawbacks are the need for appropriate franchisees, and the difficulty of maintaining control over a specific asset. Franchisees must be able to contribute the capital necessary to set up operations, and be capable of running the franchised business. Such individuals may be difficult to find, particularly in unfamiliar environments. A franchise is only workable where the franchiser can maintain control of a needed asset; otherwise, the company simply creates a competitor in the franchisee.

Fast-food operations that started as franchises in the domestic market have successfully expanded the concept to international markets. McDonald's, for example, has franchisees around the world, including its very successful Moscow restaurant. The franchising approach has worked well for McDonald's because it has a name and an overall look (the Golden Arches) that is so well-marketed and publicized that it is known worldwide. In addition, their procedures and marketing strategy are well-developed and controlled by the franchiser. This means that McDonald's franchises are in demand around the world, and franchisees cannot simply learn from McDonald's and then set up in competition, because they cannot hope to be successful without the support of the franchiser.

Companies considering franchising internationally should probably be those that have experience franchising at home. Success at home does not, however, guarantee success in other environments. The Canadian Tire Company found, for example, that its Canadian franchising formula was not successful when it tried to expand to the United States. In order to franchise successfully around the world, a company must have a formula that can be transferred successfully across national and cultural boundaries. Even successful global franchisers have run into difficulties in certain locations; as when McDonald's encountered significant problems in obtaining needed supplies, including food ingredients and paper napkins, in its Moscow venture.

Contracts

In a contractual foreign entry a firm provides general and specialized services (including management, technical expertise, and operational know-how) in a foreign location for a specified time period, for a fee. This is appropriate for firms that have talents which are not being fully utilized at home and which are in demand in foreign locations.

Manufacturing contracts are also possible. Australia's Coles-Meyer, which became the world's fifteenth largest retailer in 1985, sources many of its product lines by means of contract manufacturing in Asia. Similarly, Italian clothes designers contract production of designer silk fashions in Nepal. Such contracts allow a firm to benefit from advantages in the foreign location without investing itself, while maintaining control of important aspects of production by specifying acceptable product parameters.

Contracts are attractive because they allow a company to use their resources effectively, they are relatively short-term, and revenues are specified in the contract. The major drawback is their short-term nature; this means the company must constantly be developing new business and negotiating new contracts—which is time-consuming, costly,, and requires skill at cross-cultural negotiation. The company's revenues from international contracts are likely to be uneven and the company must be in a position to weather periods when new contracts do not materialize. Further, the company's revenues can be affected if the customer faces an economic downturn. It may be difficult to collect fees, restrictions on the movement of foreign exchange may be imposed, and currency values may change. The form of each contract is therefore important in protecting the company's economic interests.

Turnkey Operations

In this type of foreign entry a firm provides construction of a facility, start-up operations, and training of local personnel. Then the facility is transferred (the keys are turned over) to the foreign owner when ready to commence operations, or when running smoothly. Projects of this kind are generally undertaken in less-developed countries by companies from developed countries. In many cases they are financed by global organizations, such as the World Bank, and they tend to be megaprojects with specialized requirements (therefore, suitable only for a few large companies). These companies often have control over assets or resources, which makes it difficult for other companies to compete against them in bidding for projects.

Typical projects include airports, ports, power stations, dams, or large plants. Turnkey operations, because of their size, can produce substantial revenues for the company providing the service. Equally, in the event of if cost overruns, there can be substantial losses. Cost overruns can be the result of inadequate understanding of, and preparation for, working in the host-country environment.

Joint Ventures

Broadly, a joint venture consists of two or more partners sharing in a project. Joint ventures can take many forms, depending on what is shared, the degree of sharing, the number of partners involved, the type of project, and the time frame. As such, it is impossible to identify discrete opportunities; rather, we will discuss options in view of each variable.

What to Share

Most commonly, joint ventures involve shared ownership. Two or more parties contribute capital, or other resources with a specified value, to create a separate entity that is jointly owned by the partners. Sharing ownership with locals is required by law in many countries. It is equally appropriate when one company wishes to establish a viable foreign operation but is unable to do so on its own.

In conjunction with sharing ownership, companies may share technology or other specialized inputs. Two or more companies each can provide specialized technology to one project, in a situation where no one company has access to all of the technologies required for a project. Similarly, companies can each provide specialized inputs (raw materials, access to markets, distribution systems, management) to one project; this is appropriate where each of the different inputs is essential to the project but no one company controls all of them.

Sharing ownership, technology, or other inputs is often the only way to make a project viable; thus, it offers the benefit of initiating a foreign operation that could not otherwise be established. For example, the North–West shelf project, off the northwest coast of the state of Western Australia, the largest offshore energy investment in the world, cost eight billion dollars and took ten years to complete. This project was made possible because Woodside Petroleum, BHP, BP, and Shell formed a joint venture. The partners contributed capital, technology, management, and market access to make the venture a reality.

One advantage is that the risk is shared by the partners. Companies involved in a joint venture can gain from each other and develop a certain synergy. Sharing usually involves conflict, however, and companies have concerns about entering joint ventures.

Major concerns are lower profits, less control, and the potential for loss of technology. First, profits must be shared among the partners; thus, the profit potential may be lower than if the company were the sole owner of the subsidiary. Second, when ownership is shared, decision-making may be shared as well, and there may be disagreement among partners, stemming from different objectives and values, particularly where partners come from different political and cultural backgrounds. Third, the major concern regarding sharing of technology or other inputs, is that another party, possibly a rival, has access to proprietary information. Given these concerns, companies must carefully weigh the potential benefits against losses that may accrue from a joint venture in order to decide what they are willing to share.

How Much to Share

Each joint venture project involves decisions about how much each partner contributes and what each partner gets in return for that contribution. In the case of ownership, there is a range from very low ownership (say ten percent of equity), through equal shares (50–50), to high ownership (ninety percent of equity). The degree of ownership implies—but does not invariably guarantee—a certain degree of control and decision-making, and a certain share in profits.

With Whom to Share

The choice of partners is extremely important to the success of a joint venture. Joint ventures have often been compared to marriages: they are most successful when the partners work well together. There are many potential partners for a joint venture. They can be from the home country, the host country, third countries, or some combination. Partners may be individuals, local companies, multinational companies, governments, international organizations, or some combination. Finally, there may be few partners or many, and partners can take many roles, from silent to active. The choice of appropriate partners depends on the project and the location as well as the availability of potential partners.

How Long to Share

Joint ventures have been found to be generally unstable. This may be because most joint venture partnerships are formed for a specific undertaking; thus, implicitly, they are intended to last for only a limited period of time. It is appropriate for partners to give explicit attention to this point when forming a joint venture. Further, the partners should deal specifically with the question of what to do if the venture fails, deciding how to dissolve the partnership, and who gets what in the settlement.

Total Ownership

In this choice, a company establishes a subsidiary that is entirely owned by the parent company. This approach is appropriate where control of decisions and policies is important to the parent, and the parent can provide the needed resources to operate the subsidiary effectively. The company choosing this mode of entry has access to all of the subsidiary's profits and, subject to government regulations, retains control of decision-making; equally, the company assumes all of the risk associated with the subsidiary's operation.

Sole ownership was the preferred entry mode of U.S. companies in the past, because of the desire for parent control. More recently a variety of strategic alliances as well as combined approaches are more common. This shift seems to have occurred for three reasons—the necessity of local involvement imposed by host governments, greater recognition of the potential benefits of other forms of entry, and the competitive advantages offered by global strategic alliances.

Although other forms of international entry are increasingly used by global firms, the wholly-owned subsidiary is still a common form of international entry. Wholly-owned subsidiaries eliminate many of the problems associated with other forms of entry and so can be very attractive.

Making the Right Entry Choice

The view that sole ownership was generally the "best" entry mode, and that other options should be examined only when sole ownership was not possible, simplified the entry decision for many companies. The changing emphasis in terms of preferred forms of entry makes the decision more complex, and an assessment of the options plays an important part in choosing the optimal approach in each case.

There are three dimensions to examine in reaching an entry decision: the company's international strengths and weaknesses (company capability); the attractiveness of a particular (location); and assessment of perceived risk. The entry choice is discussed in terms of degree of involvement desired for a particular location. A company's desired level of involvement in a particular foreign location is a function of the company's capability in conjunction with decisions regarding the attractiveness of the location, and the perceived risk. Assessment of company capability has been previously described in this chapter under Question 3: "Are we capable of becoming more international?" This analysis would lead to a judgment of the company's overall capability to undertake an international venture.

Attractiveness of Location

Assessment of location attractiveness involves considering the net benefit to the company of operations in a given location. Important aspects of a location assessment include the political and cultural conditions, as well as consideration of competition, entry and exit barriers, incentives, potential markets, regulations, supplies, and taxes. The assessment should focus on both the opportunities and threats that operations in a location would encounter. Assessment of a particular location should be based on its potential as a market or a source of supply (or both) and should be considered as part of the overall company's operations. While profit potential is an important part of this assessment, the focus is not necessarily on profits from a particular location, but rather on the impact that operations in this location will have on overall corporate profits.

The attractiveness of a location depends on the company that is doing the analysis; that is, beauty is in the eye of the beholder. For example:

- A company seeking increased markets for a low-cost product (such as toilet paper) considers a country with a large population and low income attractive; whereas one with a relatively expensive product consider, this location less attractive.

- A company seeking low-cost labor considers a country in which unskilled labor is abundant and wage rates are low (for example, The Philippines) attractive; while one that needs skilled labor might consider it less attractive.

- A company seeking rare raw materials considers any location where they are available attractive in spite of conditions (say, the extreme cold of Siberia) that might make it unattractive to most other companies.

Perceived Risk

Assessment of risk involves consideration of how safe operations are likely to be in a particular location. This includes the social environment, the economic environment, and the political environment.

A location analysis should examine stability and compatibility. Stability can be thought of in terms of the degree and frequency of unplanned change; the greater the likelihood of such change, the greater the risk. Compatibility can be thought of as the degree of divergence between the company and country in terms of objectives, culture, and systems. The more compatible (similar) the company and country are, the more likely that operations will be relatively safe; the less compatible (different), the more potential for disagreement and unwelcome conflicts.

The degree of risk in any situation depends on the company. A risky situation for one company may be quite safe for another. For example:

- Frequent changes in government would suggest a risky environment for a company that relies on government support, but would be relatively safe for a company whose operations are of little interest to the host government.

- Anti-American feelings would be a risky environment for an American owned and operated company, but could be quite safe for an Australian company.

An assessment of company capability, location attractiveness, and perceived risk should result in identifying external opportunities and threats, and internal strengths and weaknesses. These can then be related to the company's entry options. The company should choose a form of entry, in a particular location, to maximize the benefits and minimize the drawbacks identified.

The entry choice should reflect the degree of involvement that a company would like in a location. Specifically, involvement increases as capability and attractiveness increase and risk decreases. If the situation is very favorable, then the company may maximize its involvement; if it is unfavorable, it aims to minimize involvement. It is important to note that degree of involvement and ownership are not necessarily the same (although increased ownership often implies increased involvement). Joint ventures and other forms of foreign participation can also be undertaken at varying levels. The entry modes considered for a particular location are limited to those that are permitted within the regulations that exist for a given location.

Classifying company capability (CC), location attractiveness (LA), and perceived risk (PR) on a scale from "high" to "low," helps to guide decision-making. Consider the following possibilities:

1. High CC, High LA, High PR: A manager wants to take advantage of this situation because the firm's capability is considered more than adequate and the location is very attractive, but there is concern

because of perceived risk. The manager's focus will thus be on reducing and managing the perceived risk. The exact option will depend on the type of risk foreseen. If the concern is foreign exchange risk, investments can be structured to minimize the assets exposed to changes in exchange rates. If the concern is social, such as lack of acceptance by local groups, a joint venture with local participation may be desirable. If the concern is a political risk, such as feared nationalization of assets, limited ownership might be considered, or external location of key aspects of the business.

2. High CC, High LA, Low PR: This is the ideal situation from the manager's viewpoint and maximization of the company's presence in this location will be the aim. The specific choice will be governed by the regulations that exist. If wholly-owned subsidiaries are permitted, this will be the most desirable option; if not, the company will want to maximize ownership within existing regulations.

3. High CC, Low LA, High PR: Here the firm is strong, but relatively low location attractiveness and high perceived risk suggest that the company can use its capabilities more effectively and safely elsewhere. If the company chooses to maintain a presence in this location because it feels the situation may change, then it should do so in a way that minimizes its exposure, perhaps through exports or licensing.

4. High CC, Low LA, Low PR: The concern for the manager here is the limited attractiveness of the location. It is, however, a safe environment and the company may want to maintain a presence, to be ready in case the location becomes more attractive later. A company in this situation will opt for limited involvement—probably exports or a licensing arrangement, and possibly a sales branch.

5. Low CC, High LA, High PR: In this situation the company's capability and the perceived risks are both concerns. The attractiveness of the location means, however, that the manager would like to maintain some presence there. The manager might consider a joint venture, which would offset its weaknesses and limit its exposure.

Choice of partner is very important relative to the degree of risk to which the company is exposed. In all low capability situations, the company should be pursuing programs to improve its capability.

6. Low CC, High LA, Low PR: This is an attractive situation, but the company's capability is questionable. The manager should consider a joint venture with a partner who can provide specific complementary strengths, and will want to maximize company ownership.

7. Low CC, Low LA, High PR: This situation is the least interesting from the manager's point of view, and no presence is probably the appropriate choice.

8. Low CC, Low LA, Low PR: This situation is unattractive but the safe environment might suggest maintaining a minimal presence. Such a presence might be maintained through exports or a licensing agreement that do not place undue strain on the company's capabilities.

In general terms, a manager might react to the three dimensions as follows:

- If the company is capable of international investment and operations, it should aggressively seek out opportunities. If, in contrast, important deficiencies in its abilities have been identified, it should seek to rectify these through partners or by building up its own resources.

- If a location is attractive to a company, it should maintain as high a presence as possible, given the constraints that it faces, and seek to expand its involvement over time. If, in contrast, a location is unattractive, the company should maintain only enough presence to allow it to increase its involvement if the situation changes positively.

- If a situation is relatively safe, the company should maintain a presence appropriate to the attractiveness of the location and its capability. If a situation is seen as risky, the reduction and management of risk become a primary concern in that location.

The assessment approach presented here in this simple form delineates the foreign entry decision process to assist managers in making the appropriate choice.

SUMMARY

This chapter examined the foreign entry decision from the point of view of the individual firm and its managers. Reasons for globalizing, or expanding international operations, were explained and options for entry assessed. The emphasis was on decision-making as applied to a company in a specific situation. The model presented to illustrate the decision-making process can serve as a guide for real decisions about real companies. An approach that can be used for further assessment of specific entry choices was also presented to serve as a guide for decision-making.

DISCUSSION QUESTIONS

1. Suppose a foreign firm wants to sell its products in your local community (that is, the product will be exported from the foreign location and imported into your country). Identify and discuss the regulations with which the foreign firm must comply.

2. Identify and discuss different ways for establishing license fees.

3. Discuss how cultural differences are likely to affect the formation of a joint venture.

REFERENCES

Boddewyn, J.J. 1993. "Foreign direct divestment theory: Is it the reverse of FDI theory?" *Weltwirtschfliches Archiv*, pp. 345–355.

Czinkota, M.R. & W.J. Johnston. 1983. "Exporting: Does sales volume make a difference?" *Journal of International Business Studies*, Spring–Summer, pp. 147–153.

Contractor, F.J. 1981. "In defense of licensing: Its increased role in international operations." *Columbia Journal of World Business*.

Grosse, R. 1980. *Foreign Investment Codes and Location of Direct Investment.* New York: Praeger.

Hout, T., M.E. Porter & E. Rudden. 1982. *How Global Companies Win Out. Harvard Business Review*, September–October, pp. 98–103.

Meyers, G.C., with J. Holusha. 1986. *When It Hits the Fan—Managing the Nine Crises of Business.* New York: Mentor Books.

Porter, M.E. & M.B. Fuller. 1986. "Coalitions in Global Strategy," in *Competition in Global Industries*, M.E. Porter (ed.). Boston: Harvard Business School Press.

Punnett, B.J. "International human resource management," in *International Business in Canada: Strategic Approaches to Management*, A. Rugman (ed.). Toronto: Prentice-Hall Canada, in press.

Punnett, B.J. & D.A. Ricks. 1992. *International Business*, Boston: PWS-Kent Publishing Company.

Ricks, D.A. 1993. *Big Business Blunders—Mistakes in Multinational Marketing*, Homewood, IL: Dow-Jones Irwin.

Ricks, D.A., M. Fu & J. Arpan. 1974. *International Big Business Blunders*, Columbus, Ohio: Grid.

Stopford, J.M. 1976. "Changing perspectives on investment by British manufacturing multinationals." *Journal of International Business Studies*, Winter.

"United Nations Centre on Transnational Corporations," 1988. *Transnational Corporations in World Development: Trends and Prospects*, New York: United Nations.

IMPLEMENTING

FOREIGN ENTRY

DECISIONS

LEARNING OBJECTIVES

IN THIS CHAPTER WE WILL EXPLORE:

- Practical issues associated with international entry

- Various exporting and importing routes

- Transportation options

- Payment methods, documentation requirements, and product preparation needs

- Pros and cons of licensing, contracting, and franchising

- Advantages and disadvantages of various levels of ownership

- The relationship of ownership and control

- Benefits of various joint venture partners

- Reasons for the growth of strategic alliances

- Ways to make joint ventures and strategic alliances succeed

- Relationships between firms and host governments

- The impact of ethics on international success

KEY DISCUSSION TOPICS:

- The complexities of exporting/importing

- Trade-offs between licensing, contracting, and franchising

- The elements of a successful license, contract, or franchise

- Benefits and drawbacks of ownership options

- Why joint ventures and strategic alliances succeed or fail

- Interacting with foreign governments

T H E   M A N A G E M E N T   S T A G E

PART I	PART II	PART III
ENVIRONMENTAL UNDERSTANDING	**STRATEGY & OPERATIONS**	**EXECUTION**
(Research)	(Planning & Organizing)	(Staffing & Directing)

MEASUREMENT

(Controlling)

L E V E L   O F   A N A L Y S I S

GLOBAL PICTURE → FIRM PICTURE → PEOPLE PICTURE

C O N T E N T S   O F   T H E   T E X T

Chapter 1 ■ History	Chapter 6 ■ Strategy	Chapter 12 ■ Selecting
Chapter 2 ■ Politics	Chapter 7 ■ Entry	Chapter 13 ■ Training
Chapter 3 ■ Culture	**Chapter 8 ■ Implementation**	Chapter 14 ■ Expatriates
Chapter 4 ■ Labor	Chapter 9 ■ Adapting	Chapter 15 ■ Women/Dual Careers
Chapter 5 ■ Ethics	Chapter 10 ■ Operations	Chapter 16 ■ Communication & Negotiation
	Chapter 11 ■ Organization & Control	Chapter 17 ■ Motivation & Leadership

INTRODUCTION

Chapter 7 focused on the reasons for international expansion, the forms of entry into foreign locations, and suggestions for making an effective choice among options. Once the decision to become international has been made and avenues of internationalization identified, the company turns its attention to putting these decisions into practice. The focus of this chapter is on implementing the choices made.

The major considerations associated with entry into foreign locations are: imports and exports, licensing and contracting, and ownership. The ownership decision is discussed in terms of the benefits and drawbacks of various forms and degrees of ownership. The discussion of joint ventures presents considerations of the process of selecting a joint venture partner and offers suggestions for making a joint venture successful. Strategic alliances are considered a separate form of doing business internationally. The chapter concludes with a discussion of company-government interactions, an unavoidable aspect of implementing almost any international strategy.

We provide an overview and appreciation of the practical issues to be dealt with in implementing international investment plans in this chapter, but we do not address the legal, accounting, and tax issues associated with implementation. These issues are specialized and differ from one decision to another; therefore, companies often use specialists to assess these aspects of international management.

EXPORTS AND IMPORTS

Companies typically begin an international involvement through exports or imports, and these aspects of doing business internationally often remain important to companies even after they become involved in other forms of international business. To some degree, exporting and importing are relatively simple forms of international business, though they are more complex than many people realize. Robinson (1978, p. 69) discusses this complexity: "It should be clearly understood that export requires a set of highly specialized skills having to do with packaging, marking, documentation, selection of carriers, insurance, foreign import regulations, foreign export finance, and the selection of overseas commission houses, representatives, and/or agencies; as well as the sensitivity to know when direct entry into a foreign sales branch or subsidiary is advantageous."

An event that occurred in a small island in the Caribbean (population 90,000) illustrates the challenges of exports and imports:

> A small shop ordered a variety of sizes of men's trousers from a company in Britain. The shop's owners wanted about two dozen pairs of trousers in total, but their order was interpreted to mean two dozen in each size available. When the order of several thousand trousers arrived, the owners were completely overwhelmed. Not only could they not hope to sell this number of rather expensive trousers, they could not afford to pay for them. To make matters worse, the costs of

shipping them back to Britain meant that the option of returning them was not practical. Needless to say, the relationship between the Caribbean shop and its British supplier were not good after this event.

A company generally chooses to export its products or services when it has the capacity to do so and there are profits to be made. A company chooses to import products or services because it can secure a better source of supply outside of domestic sources. This sounds simple, and because exports and imports involve relatively limited interaction with other countries, some of the risks of international interactions are minimized; but, as Robinson noted in the above quote, many decisions remain to be made to approach exports and imports effectively. The major concerns regarding intermediaries, transportation, payment methods, documentation, and product preparation all need attention. Here we will discuss them from the exporting point of view, though they are equally important considerations for importers.

EXPORT INTERMEDIARY OPTIONS

We will start by looking at the advantages and disadvantages of four major options: (1) direct from exporter to foreign buyer; (2) from exporter, through a domestic export intermediary, to foreign buyer; (3) from exporter, through a foreign import intermediary, to foreign buyer; and (4) from exporter, through domestic export intermediary and foreign import intermediary, to buyer. Each option will be followed by its benefits and drawbacks.

1. **Direct from the exporter.** This can be the simplest option because it involves two parties only—the exporter and the foreign buyer. This approach minimizes certain costs and provides certain benefits, but increases other risks.

   Benefits:

   - Costs associated with intermediaries are minimized.

   - The parties communicate directly.

   - The firm develops exporting skills internally.

- The firm becomes familiar with its export markets.

- The exporter's interests can be the dominant focus.

Drawbacks:

- Internal specialists are needed.

- Internal specialists may be costly to find or develop.

- The foreign buyer may not be a competent importer.

- The exporter assumes much of the financial risk.

2. **Through a home-country exporting firm.** The second option involves a third party in the export transaction. The third party is based in the exporter's home country and acts as an intermediary. This adds certain costs but provides other benefits and decreases some risks.

Benefits:

- Specialized outside expertise is utilized.

- The intermediary may have established access to certain locations and good working relationships with relevant local people.

- The firm's internal resources not tied up with exporting details.

- Some financial risk may be transferred to the outside specialists.

Drawbacks:

- There are added costs of the intermediary.

- The intermediary deals with many exporters and markets, which can lead to difficulty in attaining/retaining priority status where there are conflicting interests.

- No development of internal expertise takes place.

- The intermediary may not have in-depth knowledge of a specific foreign buyer or location.

3. **Through a foreign importing firm.** This option involves a third party as well, but in this case the third party is located in the foreign buyer's country. This again adds certain costs but provides benefits and decreases risks.

Benefits:

- Specialized knowledge of a particular foreign environment is provided.

- The intermediary is likely to have desired contacts with a variety of government officials, potential customers, and transport companies in the foreign location.

Drawbacks:

- Interactions may be difficult owing to language and other communication barriers.

- The firm must still provide export expertise.

- The added costs of the intermediary become part of the transaction.

4. **Using home and foreign intermediaries.** The fourth option combines Options two and three. This option is the most complex because it involves several players. This option removes the exporting firm from the export process and relies on the expertise of outsiders. As might be expected, the benefits and drawbacks are a combination of two and three. Specialized know-how regarding exporting and the foreign location, and a transfer of some of the risk from the exporting firm to the intermediaries, are the major benefits. In contrast, the costs may be high, and the firm's distance from the process can mean that its best interests are not always served.

To make the most effective choice, the exporting firm should weigh the costs and benefits of the available exporting options against its own position in a particular location. Factors such as the need for adaptation, the degree of standardization, the firm's familiarity with the foreign market, the complexity of the foreign environment, and the maturity of the market should to be factored into the decision, although these factors will affect firms in different ways. For example, if a product must be substantially adapted for a particular market, one firm might decide that its lack of knowledge of the local market suggests the need for an intermediary who is more familiar with this location, while another firm might feel the need to develop this local expertise itself to make appropriate adaptations.

TRANSPORTATION ISSUES

A major consideration in exporting goods is the physical movement of products from the point of production to the foreign buyer. Transportation choices involve trade-offs in terms of costs, speed, safety, reliability, and convenience. The forms of transportation firms normally consider are ocean, air, rail, truck, and electronic transfer. Each offers different benefits and drawbacks that must be related to the product and location in question.

Ocean transportation is relatively inexpensive and appropriate for products of varying sizes and weights, and may be particularly appropriate for large items. Ocean routes are often slow and indirect because ships stop at many ports and shipping lines differ in terms of of safety and reliability. In addition, ground transportation must be arranged to and from the docks. Convenience of these routes often depends on the location of the exporting firm and the foreign buyer.

Air transportation is quick and direct but it is relatively expensive and may be appropriate only for smaller or high-value items. Air transportation is relatively safe, reliable, and more convenient to major locations than remote locations. Ground link transportation also must be arranged, often separately.

Rail transportation is relatively inexpensive, safe, and reliable. It is slower than air and depends on the availability of rail lines and spurs to serve specific customers. If spurs are not available, transportation to and from rail lines must be arranged.

Truck transportation is versatile and provides door-to-door pick-up and delivery, and trucks can often service locations that cannot be served by other means. Although off-road vehicles and helicopters are available for inaccessible areas, most truck transportation relies on an adequate system of roads and receiving facilities.

Electronic transportation is quick and direct but it is expensive and limited to rather specific items. Some items that can be transmitted electronically are contracts, plans, reports, computer programs, and data lists. Where the product is appropriate and the technology available, electronic transfers can be reliable and convenient; however, there may be problems protecting the privacy of such transfers.

PAYMENT METHODS

The means by which the exporting firm receives payment for its products is an important consideration in the export process. Payment can be taken in a variety of forms and at different times. These choices depend on the relationship between the buyer and seller. A seller that wishes to eliminate the risks associated with payments can ask for payment in advance, but this may discourage the buyer. A firm that wants to encourage sales can extend credit to its customers, but it takes the risk of not receiving the expected payment. As in all exporting decisions, the firm must consider the trade-offs to make an appropriate choice. Generally, a seller that is in a strong position to a buyer can arrange terms that are in the seller's favor, while a seller that is in a relatively weak position may accept terms that are more in the buyer's favor.

Export arrangements also specify of the currency in which payment is to be made. If it is made in the seller's currency, the seller knows exactly how much will be received and does not face the uncertainty of receiving a foreign currency. If payment is made in the buyer's currency and the seller plans to convert it, there is uncertainty about the exact amount that will be received. If payment is in a third currency and each party is converting this currency, both are unsure of the exact payment.

DOCUMENTATION

Export documentation is a necessary part of the export process. There are a forms to be completed and procedures with which the exporting firm must comply before it can actually move its goods from the domestic to the foreign location. These forms and procedures relate to products leaving the home country as well as those arriving in the foreign country, as well as passage through other countries. Each country has its own regulations about the movement of products in and out of its borders, and all regulations must be met if an export transaction is to be completed satisfactorily. Prior to undertaking an export obligation, a firm should ascertain the required documentation to complete its obligation, and ensure that it can comply with the necessary procedures. There are specialists who can provide information on export documentation. Firms that plan not to use intermediaries may need to seek advice from such specialists.

Among the documents that may have to be prepared are bills of lading, commercial invoices, export licenses, insurance certificates, certificates of product origin, and inspection certificates. Overlooking even one required form will delay the entire export transaction; therefore, companies must be sure that they have accurately identified all of the documents required at both ends of the export process, as well as in transit. Not all documents are required for all shipments, so the exporter must identify which documents are needed for a particular shipment. This depends on factors such as the type of goods being shipped, the method of shipment, the origin and destination of the shipment. The main documents required are:

- *Bills of lading*. These are issued by the shipping company or its agent and used as evidence of a contract to ship the goods. The bill of lading shows that the exporter delivered the goods to the shipping company. Shipments by air use air way-bills and shipments involving several types of transportation (e.g., rail to air to truck) may use a combined transport document.

- *Commercial invoices*. These are invoices written by the exporter that describe the details of the merchandise and the terms of payment.

- *Export licenses*. These licenses are issued by the regulatory agency in the country of origin, and give the exporter the right to legally export the goods being shipped.

- *Insurance certificates*. These are issued by the insuring company and specify the goods that are insured and the terms of the insurance contract.

- *Certificates of product origin*. These are issued by regulatory agencies in the country of origin and provide evidence that the goods were made in a particular country. These are also required to assess various tariffs and regulations imposed by the importing country.

- *Inspection certificates*. These can be issued by regulatory agencies either in the exporting country or the importing country, and provide evidence that the goods have been inspected and meet the prescribed standards for goods of this type.

- *Payment documents*. These ensure that the exporter receives payment for the goods. The most common form of payment is a letter of credit. An export letter of credit is issued by a buyer/importer's bank and promises to pay the seller/exporter a specified amount when the bank has received certain documents, specified in the letter, by a specified time. Most letters of credit are designated as "confirmed and irrevocable," which means that once accepted, they cannot be changed.

PRODUCT PREPARATION

Production of any product is but one phase in exporting. Another important phase is getting the product ready for the exporting process and foreign markets. The major issues to be considered are foreign requirements, language, and packaging for shipment. Dealing with each of these issues can involve some modifications and thus increase costs. Any cost increases must be examined as part of the overall decision to export.

Foreign requirements regarding product standards, labeling, and so forth, should be determined before exporting. These requirements are often different from those at home and, thus, modification of the product or the label may be necessary to comply with foreign requirements. Definition of the product for customs purposes may be critical to ensure clearance through customs and correct classification for duty purposes.

Labeling language is also an important consideration for exporters. If a firm exports to a country where a different language is spoken, the firm must translate its labels and product information. This can be an expensive and time-consuming process, particularly where product information is extensive and/or complex.

Packaging for shipment must also be resolved before the exporting process can be undertaken. Packaging can be extremely important to a product's arrival at its destination in an acceptable condition. Appropriate packaging depends on the product, the method of shipment, and the country to which the product is being shipped. It may be necessary to develop a new form of packaging, or to modify the existing packing, which can be costly and time-consuming.

LICENSING, CONTRACTING, AND FRANCHISING

Licensing, contracting, and franchising represent intermediate levels of foreign involvement relative to exports/imports and foreign ownership. These can take many forms, but our discussion will give the student an idea of the practical considerations of such strategies.

LICENSES

Generally, a licensing agreement involves the granting of rights to intangible property, such as patents, copyrights, trademarks, or procedures. An agreement is made between the owner (licenser) of the property and a user (licensee) to specify the terms of use and the payment for use. A firm, as owner or licenser, must consider several issues prior to entering into a licensing agreement. Major considerations are choice of the licenser, payment terms and time frames, and protection of assets. These are complex issues, and firms generally obtain legal advice (either internal or external) prior to finalizing a licensing agreement. The following points to be considered are:

- The licenser should be trustworthy and capable of using the licensed asset effectively. License agreements should be finalized only after the licensee has been qualified thoroughly, and it may be advisable to consider several licensees before reaching a choice.

- Payment terms should provide an adequate return to both the licenser and licensee. It may be appropriate to provide for renegotiation of payment terms once both parties evaluate the potential of the licensing agreement. Time frames are closely tied into payment terms and should be of reasonable duration for both parties. Again, it may be appropriate to renegotiate the agreement at specified times.

- Protection of licensed assets can be vital from the licenser's viewpoint because these assets can cost millions of dollars to develop, and the licenser must assure that they cannot be lost through the granting of a license. Firms limit the extent to which they give licensers access to key aspects of their technology and try to legally protect the safety of their assets.

- Not all countries are signatories to international agreements regarding matters of patents or copyrights. The firm's legal rights should be carefully established to ensure protection of its vulnerable assets.

To point out the complexity and importance of international licensing, we offer an example that nearly cost a company its market: The Gillette company had developed a superior stainless steel blade, but because the new blade was so outstanding and would require fewer replacements, the company was afraid to market it. So Gillette sold the technology to a British garden-tool manufacturer, Wilkinson. Because Gillette had assumed that Wilkinson would only use the new technology in the production of its garden tools, the licensing arrangement failed to restrict Wilkinson from competing in the razor-blade market. However, Wilkinson Sword Blades were promptly introduced and sold as quickly as they could be made.

CONTRACTS

Many companies provide services to foreign buyers based on their particular expertise and skills (for example, computer, economic, engineering, management, or marketing skills). These skills are generally provided on a contract basis, where deliverables and time frames are specified and associated with specific payments.

Firms considering contracting their services internationally face a number of complex decisions, as do their licensing counterparts. These firms need to invest substantially in business development activities if they are to be selected as contractors. They must assess the contracting organization and its ability to fulfill its end of a contract; and they must be culturally sensitive because the nature of their business necessitates cross-cultural interactions.

Many firms invest hundreds of thousands of dollars in business development activities in their efforts to land a particular contract. Business development can involve extensive worldwide travel and substantial preliminary project design. Prior to incurring these costs, the firm must understand the contracting organization and the project in question. It is important to estimate whether the contract is actually open to all firms and has not been promised to another firm because of its relationship with the contracting organization. It is also important to determine the contracting organization's objectives and whether the firm can meet those objectives in an efficient and effective manner. The contracting organization's ability to live up to its side of the contract—in terms of provision of services, and materials, and prompt payments—should also be assessed. If the assessment of the contracting organization is positive, then the time and money necessary to bid for the contract can be compared to the expected returns. In addition, one must consider obtaining work permits, income tax responsibilities, and other issues related to working in a foreign location.

Contracting firms rely on their communicating and negotiating ability throughout the process of bidding for, signing, and completing a contract. Many firms are very successful international contractors but many more find that the costs often outweigh the benefits. Contracting provides unique opportunities for firms who offer specialized skills that are in demand internationally, but firms should not make the mistake of thinking that international contracts are easy to obtain.

FRANCHISES

Many firms have been able to develop a company image and name that is identified with desirable qualities such as quality, service, cleanliness, or good value. Once this image is established, the chain is in a good position to consider franchising.

The first issue to be addressed is whether the established image can be transferred to other locations around the world. Success at home is based on providing a particular product or service that appeals to consumers in the home culture (for example, speed, and quality at McDonald's). The company considering franchising in foreign locations needs to determine if this product or service will be desirable in these locations. The second issue is whether the factors contributing to success at home can be transferred. Franchising success is often attributable to standardization, high identification because of aggressive promotion, and cost controls. The company considering franchising in foreign locations must consider whether these will be equally possible in these locations, or whether there are local conditions and regulations that can make it difficult to achieve the necessary degree of standardization, identification, and cost control.

If a company believes it has the potential for successful franchising in foreign locations, the benefits and costs must be carefully evaluated. Franchising provides many benefits: it provides the opportunity to expand internationally with relatively little investment; it shares the risk of international operations with the foreign franchisees; and it draws on the local knowledge and input of the franchisees. There are also costs: the costs associated with identifying and assessing potential franchisees; the risks of establishing foreign franchises that fail, causing repercussions at home; and the legal costs of establishing and enforcing franchise agreements. The costs and benefits will vary from company to company and location to location; therefore, a cost/benefit analysis must be undertaken for each new location.

Franchising is more common in the United States than elsewhere in the world, and currently U.S. companies represent the major international franchisers; however, many other countries have generated franchise operations and growth in international franchising appears likely. Among U.S. restaurant chains that have expanded internationally through franchises are Burger King, Dairy

Queen, Dunkin' Donuts, Kentucky Fried Chicken, McDonald's, and Pizza Hut. The fastest-growth areas for U.S. companies have been Canada, Japan, and the United Kingdom, but there are franchises in most parts of the world (for example, Kentucky Fried Chicken's largest restaurant is in Beijing).

Foreign franchising opportunities may be tempered by the fact that franchising is not common in some locations, and that local financing may be difficult for franchisees to secure. Firms that pursue the franchise approach globally may have to develop promotional packages to explain the concept and opportunities both to potential franchisees and financing organizations. In addition, firms often have to modify their traditional operations to deal with local customs, regulations, and constraints. Overall, franchising internationally provides benefits for the right companies, but specific costs and benefits must be carefully evaluated to determine if this approach can work for a particular company.

VARIOUS OWNERSHIP DECISIONS

Many businesses opt for ownership in some or all of their global ventures. In many ways, the decision to adopt ownership arrangements is a natural progression as companies become more familiar with the global environment. Once a company establishes subsidiaries or associated organizations in which it participates through ownership, its commitment to international operations increases. By contrast, operations based solely on exports and imports can be eliminated relatively easily if a decision is made to focus more on domestic markets and supplies, and agreements such as licenses and contracts are usually of limited duration and need not be renewed if the firm's global strategy changes.

Ownership implies a longer-term commitment, and it is more difficult, costly, and time-consuming to divest from ownership than from other forms of involvement. This implied commitment means that ownership options must be considered carefully and ownership decisions made deliberately and strategically, after weighing the advantages and disadvantages.

Ownership can vary from 100 percent (wholly owned) to low ownership (of as little as 5 or 10 percent). There are many possibilities, but the major ones are: total ownership; public sale of shares; ownership fadeout; little ownership; and joint ventures. We will discuss forms of ownership and the benefits and drawbacks of each.

TOTAL OWNERSHIP

Many companies prefer to have a 100 percent interest in their foreign operations because they believe that control of operations can be more closely retained by the parent company with this arrangement. On the benefits side, the wholly-owned option does give the parent company more decision-making control about foreign operations, and this can be a major consideration when centralized control is necessary or desirable (for example, in globally integrated operations). Total ownership also eliminates the need to bargain with local or other shareholders, who can have different views or objectives than the parent. The parent can rationalize its operations on a global basis even when this involves decisions that do not favor a particular subsidiary. An additional benefit is that there is no sharing of profits and, particularly when profit potential is substantial, the parent may not want to accept lower profits.

There are drawbacks to this option as well. No sharing of profits implies no sharing of losses; and thus, the wholly-owned option involves assuming all the risks associated with a foreign venture. It also means that the parent undertakes the entire initial investment, which may be high. A bigger potential drawback is the fact that wholly-owned foreign subsidiaries may be viewed negatively and resented by local groups. This can result in difficult local relationships with local managers, employees, suppliers, creditors, as well as with the host government. In the worst case, these negative views and difficult relationships can single the company out for government intervention and thus increase the political risk associated with a particular location.

The story of a major U.S. manufacturer of mixed feed for poultry illustrates these disadvantages:

> The company decided to establish a market in Spain after receiving encouraging results from a preliminary market study. Although local business people advised the firm against forming a subsidiary that was

wholly-owned, the company went ahead with its plans. A factory was built, a technical staff was brought in, and operations were set up. However, once production began, the firm discovered that it could not sell its products. Why? The Spanish poultry growers and feed producers comprised a closely knit family, and newcomers were not welcome. So to overcome this obstacle, the firm bought a series of chicken farms. To its dismay, the company discovered that no one would buy its chickens either! (Ricks, Fu, & Arpan 1974, p. 119).

PUBLIC SALE OF SHARES

Companies may choose to sell shares in foreign operations on the open market. Where stock markets exist, such sales would be made through the market; however, public offerings can be made using other local arrangements if there is no formal stock market. Companies may choose this option if they want to raise outside capital and spread the risks but maintain a fair degree of control. Stock offerings may be limited to local participation or may be global.

On the benefits side, this option allows the company to raise capital and share the risks of the foreign operation while maintaining a relatively high degree of control. Decision-making control is maintained because the ownership is usually spread out over a fairly large number of small minority stockholders. This means that the parent usually can exert control even with a relatively small percentage of the shares because the minority stockholders are not likely to act in concert against the major stockholder, as long as satisfactory results are being achieved.

A sale of shares to local individuals and groups means that the company may be viewed in a favorable light by the local community because it is essentially seen as a local company. This, in turn, can enhance local relationships and reduce political risk. This option retains some of the benefits of 100 percent ownership while overcoming some of the disadvantages. However, it has its own set of disadvantages.

A major disadvantage to this option is the lack of stock markets in many countries, especially developing countries. While other means for making a public offering of sales do exist, they may be cumbersome and inefficient, and can result in unwanted concentration of ownership in the hands of a few powerful local groups. This approach also involves specific costs associated with a stock offering; therefore, the size of the offering must be large enough to warrant such an offering, and it could be difficult to find buyers for a large offering in a small or relatively poor foreign country. In addition, it is possible that even a diverse group of stockholders will decide to act together and wrest control from the parent company, or, alternatively, that one stockholder will buy out others and establish majority ownership this way. Finally, most countries have laws that deal with the rights of minority shareholders. Thus, a company choosing this option cannot make decisions that would negatively affect these stockholders, although such decisions might be in the parent's best interests.

OWNERSHIP FADEOUT

The concept of a fadeout is that the company begins with 100 percent of the equity, or at least a majority share, and, over time sells shares in the company until its ownership is reduced to a minority position, or no ownership. Although they are not common, there are some situations where this approach may be attractive. This ownership option allows the company to retain decision-making control in the early stages of foreign operations and gives the parent access to all profits initially, while appealing to local interests because it is clear that over time the subsidiary will be localized. In a situation where control is particularly important in the start-up phase and less so later on, or one where a continuing infusion of capital will be needed after start-up and the company does not wish to commit itself to additional investment, this arrangement would be appropriate. In such an arrangement, the company makes its profits early and does not incur a long-term risk.

The obvious disadvantage to this approach is that the company gives up control over time and participates less and less in the profits. If the company can accurately forecast the need for control and expected profits, it can structure the fadeout to its advantage; unfortunately, if its forecasts are incorrect, it may find it has chosen an undesirable ownership option. There is a natural tendency in such an arrangement, because of the short-term commitment, to focus on short-term profits, which is often detrimental to the foreign entity itself.

LITTLE OWNERSHIP

A company might choose this option if it wanted to participate in an attractive foreign venture but was not in a position financially or managerially to take a greater share of ownership. The company in a minority position benefits from the successes of the foreign venture but may not need to make a substantial investment or tie up its own management in day-to-day operations. Such a position might be particularly attractive if the foreign operation was likely to become a customer or supplier. Of course, to a large extent, the company choosing to accept a minority share limits its ability to influence the direction of the foreign entity. The minority position also means that the company participates in profits only to a limited degree while it will still suffer the consequence of losses. This can be a very difficult situation if the losses appear to be attributable to its inability to influence the direction of the foreign entity.

The degree of ownership sought by particular companies in foreign locations are influenced by legal and tax issues as well. Each choice will have different tax implications and will affect shareholders in the parent company and other subsidiaries. These issues should be examined by experts in the relevant fields before a final ownership decision is made.

JOINT VENTURES

Joint ventures involve shared ownership. They are differentiated from sharing ownership through a public sale of shares or by taking a minority position in a foreign entity, however, because they are discussed here in terms of partnerships (although they may not take the legal form of a partnership). This implies an agreement between the partners regarding their respective rights and responsibilities.

Joint ventures or partnerships have become reasonably common in international business because there are a number of economic, social, and political factors that encourage their use. In broad terms, joint ventures provide needed capital and expertise, and allow companies to blend their respective strengths while sharing the risk in foreign undertakings. Joint ventures often improve the local image when they involve local partners, and satisfy government regulations and incentives that mandate or encourage the involvement of local partners. According to the United Nations Center on Transnational Corporations (1988), a major proportion of expansion is done through joint ventures.

The importance of host-government approval of a joint venture is illustrated by the following account. Massey-Ferguson reportedly experienced some difficulties after it entered into a 51 percent ownership venture in Turkey to produce tractors. A large-scale plan was developed for an initial annual production capacity of 50,000 engines, and called for the later addition of a second facility that would produce another 30,000 tractors a year. The company's high hopes were never realized. Massey-Ferguson reportedly failed to investigate thoroughly the implications of the economic and political pressures present in Turkey and the stability of the government. To assure its market success, the company needed strong governmental backing. This support never fully materialized and the venture had to be terminated (Ricks, Fu, & Arpan 1974, p. 121).

Joint ventures, as with other forms of ownership, have benefits and drawbacks. As a benefit, joint ventures provide a means to spread large capital needs over a number of parties, and often major projects are feasible only under a partnership. This spreading of the initial investment also spreads the risks among the partners. Different parties can bring specific skills and know-how to the partnership, making the foreign operation more effective than it would be with one party alone. Overall, a successful joint venture provides synergy—that is, it is a better undertaking because of the combined resources of the partnership.

The benefits of joint ventures can easily be negated. There is potential for conflicting objectives, which lead to disputes between the interested parties. Once disputes arise, decision-making slows down and foreign operations can become unresponsive and inefficient. Even without disputes, decision-making can be slow because all parties must agree on major issues, and differing viewpoints can make this process complex.

The more general benefits and drawbacks vary, depending on the makeup of a joint venture. There are a variety of partners from whom to choose, and each can be helpful or cause problems in different ways. The ability of partners to work well with each other is critical to joint-venture success, therefore choosing the right partner is an extremely important step. Consider this case:

> A U.S. firm that entered into a joint venture with some South American capitalists did not fully comprehend its initial errors until some five years later. At the time of the company's commitment, its South American partners were in favor with those in the local government. However, the joint venture began to gradually experience various forms of host-government harassment and, consequently, profits slowly declined. Investment money, effort, and time were lost by the U.S. partner. What had happened? The U.S. company had failed to analyze the situation thoroughly. Early analyses should have revealed the existence of a volatile political scene and the degree of political involvement in local business practices (Ricks, Fu, & Arpan 1974, p. 102).

There are a number of groups from which a partner, or partners, may be chosen. The main groups considered here are host governments, private host parties, and other MNCs.

Host governments often act as the local partner in a joint venture. This is likely to be the case if the host government controls the resources the joint venture needs to function, or if no suitable private partners are available and the country does not allow wholly-owned foreign operations. Joint ventures with host governments are inevitable where most commerce is centrally controlled, and they are common in resource-based industries where the government controls the natural resources the venture will be using.

In some respects a joint venture with the host government is appealing because this clearly puts the foreign partner in touch with the people currently in control. The government can be expected to smooth the way for the joint venture because it is as interested in its success as the foreign partner.

This is true in some cases, but there are many situations where it is not. First, there is the difficulty of changes in government. When this occurs, the joint venture can be associated with the previous regime and may be singled out for harassment by the new government. Second, the government, as partner, has access to the joint venture's policies, procedures, techniques, and technology. Once familiar with these factors, the government may conclude that there is no need for foreign involvement and choose to nationalize the venture. Third, the objectives of the government and the foreign parent company will probably clash at some point because the fundamental nature of their strategies is different; for example, the government might want to expand domestic employment to support its development priorities, whereas the foreign company believes that automation will cut costs over time and will result in better quality and higher profits. Governments are not structured for the same kind of decision-making as private firms, and bureaucratic complexities may become a problem in these partnerships.

On balance, it appears that host governments are not particularly good joint venture partners, thus companies may prefer to avoid these partnerships, if possible. There will, nevertheless, be instances where companies find such alliances desirable. Companies entering into such joint ventures must be particularly aware of the potential problems inherent in such alliances so that they are prepared to deal with them.

Many companies seek out *private partners* in the host environment. These partners can be described, broadly, as silent or active. A silent partner is one who has shares in the local company but does not become actively involved in its operations. An active partner participates in terms of ownership as well as management. Some investing companies choose silent partners, others see greater benefits from active partners.

A local private partner usually provides local know-how to creditors, employees, government, markets, suppliers, unions, and so on. At the same time, involvement of a local partner increases the likelihood of differing objectives and dilution of profits. An enterprise that incorporates local ownership is apt to be viewed positively by the host government and people, but it suggests the sharing of decisions, expertise, and technology.

Silent partners are advantageous because they provide local acceptance, local knowledge, and local capital, while agreeing to remain outside the day-to-day decision-making. For some foreign enterprises, a silent partner allows the parent company to take advantage of the benefits of localization without losing control over decisions. This may be especially important where the foreign parent needs to protect some firm-specific advantage (such as proprietary technology) that will be exposed in the joint enterprise. Silent partnerships can backfire if the partner who was expected to be silent demands an active role in the enterprise, or if the host government decides that the enterprise is not truly localized because the silent partner is merely a front to mask real control by the foreign firm.

Active local partners provide more detailed local knowledge because of active involvement in operations, and this expertise is vital to many enterprises. Many multinational companies seek out this knowledge in local partners and find that with it, they can be more responsive to local markets. The price is a decrease in decision-making control and decisions that take more time. Slower decision-making, however, does have some benefits. A high degree of involvement of locals in the process often means that the reasons for decisions are clearly understood and the decisions are supported by locals. In turn, it enhances cooperation and implements decisions more quickly and smoothly, in compensation.

Joint ventures *between multinational companies* are also fairly common. These arrangements are generally entered into when the skills of each of the multinational companies is needed to ensure the success of a particular venture. This choice is often appropriate where the project is large and no one company can undertake the entire project effectively.

A joint venture among a group of multinational companies provides security for any one member, because resources are pooled and there is strength in numbers. This approach suggests, however, possible disputes over respective roles and increased visibility, which can result in increased local resentment.

Making a Joint Venture Sucessful

Once a company has decided upon its preferred partner for a joint venture, it should then move to a detailed examination of various partners. Joint ventures have often been compared to marriages, and the analogy is particularly apt in terms of choosing the right partner. Marriages between people who have conflicting objectives are not as likely to succeed as those where basic objectives are complementary; the same is true of a joint-venture partnership. People considering marriage are often advised to consider more than one partner before making a final selection, and, further, to get to know the anticipated partner well before taking the vows. The advice to companies entering into joint ventures is parallel—look closely at a variety of possible partners and don't rush into an agreement. The first advice to companies contemplating a joint-venture arrangement is choose partner(s) carefully.

The choice of a partner is complicated in international joint ventures because the negotiators of the agreement may not be the people responsible for carrying it through. It is possible for negotiators to develop a trusting relationship that suggests a joint undertaking will be a success, only to have the deal fall apart because the managers selected by each side do not relate well. Clearly, it is important to establish good relationships at both levels before proceeding.

A substantial number of joint ventures end unhappily, and such endings, like divorces, can be messy and costly. Companies entering into joint ventures should do everything possible to avoid an unhappy ending. Potential problems must be addressed prior to undertaking the agreement if the venture is to succeed. Harrigan (1984) advises:

- Don't accept a joint-venture agreement too quickly; weigh the pros and cons.

- Get to know a partner by initially doing a limited project together; if a small project is successful, bigger projects are more feasible.

- Small companies are vulnerable to having their expertise lost to larger joint-venture partners; small companies must structure such deals with great care and guard against potential losses.

- Companies with similar cultures and relatively equal financial resources work best together; keep this in mind when looking for an appropriate partner.

- Protect the company's core business through legal means, such as unassailable patents; if this is not possible, don't let the partner learn your methods.

- The joint enterprise must fit the corporate strategy of both parents; if this is not the case, there will inevitably be conflicts.

- Keep the mission of the joint enterprise small and well-defined; ensure that it does not compete with the parents.

- Give the joint enterprise autonomy to function on its own and set up mechanisms to monitor its results; it should be a separate entity from both parents.

- Learn from the joint enterprise and use this in the parent organization.

- Limit the time frame of the joint enterprise and review its progress often (as often as every three months).

To succeed, a joint venture should have clearly defined goals as well as established measures of performance to which the parents have agreed. The exact nature of each parent's contribution in terms of finances, management, technology, and know-how should be established to both parties' satisfaction. Conflicts are almost inevitable in a joint venture, therefore a conflict-resolution mechanism should be in place. In addition a "pre-nuptial" agreement that specifies the conditions for dissolution of the venture, and division of assets in case of a divorce, is a good idea. Establishing agreement on these issues prior to undertaking a joint venture eliminates many potential causes of conflict.

Joint-venture success cannot always be judged on the basis of longevity. The description of a joint venture in the Caribbean illustrates this point:

> A local businessman wished to purchase a parcel of land locally as a tourist development. He was unable to raise the capital on his own and felt that outside expertise would be helpful in planning and implementing the development project. A joint venture was formed with a U.S. firm to undertake the project, which continued for more than 15 years. On the surface, the joint venture was a success because a divorce did not take place; yet, very little profitable development took place, and the project did not live up to local expectations. It seemed that the U.S. partner viewed the property as a vacation spot that would be "spoiled" if others were attracted to it. The final outcome was that the local government acquired the property because they believed it was not being properly utilized.

STRATEGIC ALLIANCES

Joint ventures, as discussed here, imply shared equity by two or more partners. Strategic alliances are different from joint ventures in that they involve non-equity arrangements. Strategic alliances can be thought of simply as cooperative ventures, where two or more organizations choose to cooperate with each other for specific purposes for a defined period of time. This concept of a strategic alliance incorporates a wide variety of possible cooperative ventures. For example, two companies might pool their R&D expertise to develop a technology that would benefit both companies; or a company with a good product might cooperate with another company that has a well-developed distribution or marketing network; or one company with expertise in one location might work with a supplier company to establish operations in that location. In none of these cases is there a separate entity established with joint ownership. Rather, companies cooperate because each believes that it can benefit from it. Strategic alliances or cooperative ventures are different from traditional joint ventures but involve many of the same problems and must be handled with equal care. Certainly, the risk of losing firm-specific advantages is as present in these alliances as in joint ventures, and the likelihood of conflict also exists. The joint venture may actually be less risky because the parents are establishing a separate entity that can be dissolved or taken over by one partner, if that is desirable. This option does not exist for a strategic alliance, where no separate entity is created. Dissolving such agreements prematurely can fundamentally affect one or another partner's ability to operate effectively.

Choosing the right partner with whom to ally or cooperate is a key element of success in these arrangements. Each party must trust the others. To develop trust it is necessary to get to know potential partners as the risks are too great to enter into such arrangements without first establishing a relationship with which all partners are comfortable.

Strategic alliances of all kinds appear to be increasing in number. The rate of technological change and global competition in the last decades of the twentieth century have increased to a level where such alliances have become necessary for certain global operations, and this trend shows no signs of abating.

It is important, therefore, that international companies have a sound understanding of the implications of such alliances.

Strategic alliances may be beneficial from a firm's point of view but not in the opinion of governments. In the United States, for example, antitrust legislation may prevent the formation of such alliances. In other countries, legislation may either prohibit or encourage alliances of various kinds. The legal dimensions of these decisions, both at home and aboard, should be carefully examined prior to entering into any agreement.

COMPANY INTERACTIONS WITH HOST GOVERNMENTS

Company interactions with the host government are almost inevitable, no matter which form of entry into a foreign location a company chooses. These interactions may be minor if a company is exporting through intermediaries, but, even in this case, a company needs to understand the host government's requirements regarding its exports. Interactions may be significant if a subsidiary is established in the foreign location. Foreign direct investment of any kind is usually subject to host-government review and various approvals.

Companies often find themselves negotiating the terms of their investment with the host government, including the degree of investment, ownership and management structure, employment levels, location, and level of exports and imports. They may have to negotiate incentives with the host government as well, including tax and tariff exemptions, favorable loan terms, subsidies, government services, and provision of land or buildings.

The host-government literature, and even legislation, may serve only as a starting point for possible arrangements. In many cases unique conditions can be negotiated. Further, many of the questions a company has, or the issues it needs to have clarified prior to investment may not be covered in official government communications, and these must be addressed in personal interactions. Companies can, therefore, expect to be involved in substantial interactions with host governments in the initial stages of foreign expansion.

Interactions with host governments are apt be ongoing throughout the life of the company's involvement in a foreign location. This is because the company and the government's situation will change over time and changes lead to the need to negotiate new agreements or renegotiate existing ones.

To have productive interactions with host governments, companies must consider two important points. First, a successful relationship is more likely if both parties feel that the deal is fair. Second, the company and the host government have different cultures and a relationship will be most effective where this is acknowledged.

The first point means that the company must seek to understand the host government's objectives and strategies so that it can structure its project to contribute to these while achieving its own objectives. The second means that the company must seek to understand the host culture and establish its negotiating style in light of this. Successful companies have a clear sense of what they want from a foreign venture and ensure that they attain these goals by establishing good relations with the host government.

ETHICAL ISSUES

Questions of ethics often arise when international firms make decisions and implement them. Although ethical issues are discussed in detail in Chapter 5, our brief reiteration here emphasizes the importance of ethics in implementing a foreign entry decision. Global firms have been the subject of much ethical criticism. Their decisions tend to have wide-ranging repercussions, and this accounts for the attention paid to the ethical characteristics of their activities.

Ethical questions arise in a wide variety of behaviors, and many global firms have been accused of acting unethically. The outcome of such accusations is usually negative, including lawsuits, consumer boycotts, bad publicity, and government intervention. To illustrate the variety of decisions that raise ethical questions, a number of examples of allegedly unethical behavior are presented

below. These examples present only one side of the situation; there may be
equally good ethical arguments on the other side. The intent is simply to illustrate ethical issues, not to evaluate moral arguments.

- The Nestlé Company has marketed infant formula to mothers in the
  third world. Some people argued this was unethical because these
  uneducated, poor women and their infants have been hurt by the use
  of formula. These women discontinued breast-feeding and substituted
  formula in response to "aggressive marketing techniques." Formula
  cost them more than breast-feeding (costs the poor could ill-afford), it
  may not have been as healthy for the infants, and, further, it may have
  been mixed incorrectly by mothers who were seeking to stretch the formula or who were unable to read the directions.

- Union Carbide suffered a major chemical accident in Bhopal, India.
  This has been reported as the result of unethical behavior and a lack
  of concern for Indian workers. The argument is that the facilities did
  not meet safety standards required in more-developed countries, and
  the workers were not supervised adequately.

- The Vanguard Corporation was reported to have continued manufacturing and exporting pesticides to third world countries after their use
  was prohibited in the United States. This has been considered unethical because it endangers the environment and the health of the people in third world communities.

- Lockheed executives were accused of engaging in payments to officials in foreign countries. This was considered bribery, corrupt practice, and therefore unethical.

- Firestone Tire & Rubber Company dominated the rubber economies of
  Malaysia and Liberia. Such reliance on a foreign company has been
  considered potentially damaging to these countries, and therefore
  unethical on the part of the company.

Companies have also been accused of unethical behavior for continuing operations in countries that violate human rights, for influencing the outcome of

elections, for transferring jobs overseas where wage rates are lower, for operating in countries with few environmental regulations, and for a variety of other activities.

International firms must act in ways that are socially and morally acceptable, or ethical, both because this is the right way to behave, and because it avoids the negative consequences of unethical behavior. There are difficulties, however, because what is considered ethical in one location may be seen as unethical elsewhere. Two examples illustrate this dilemma:

- Continued manufacture and sales of a banned pesticide seems unethical from the U.S. viewpoint, but a poor country might knowingly choose to continue use of the pesticide if it increases agricultural yields. The poor country might argue that feeding its people now is more important than longer-term concerns with their health or the environment.

- Unrecorded payments to facilitate projects are considered unacceptable in North America, and are seen as bribes, but they are the norm in some other countries, where they are seen as "facilitative payments." Foreigners argue that activities that are normal in North America, such as taking business colleagues out to restaurants, are in fact "payments" to facilitate projects.

To determine what is ethically appropriate, companies must consider the impact of their decisions on a variety of stakeholders—groups that are affected by a particular decision—both at home and in foreign locations. It is not practical to expect to find decisions that will be acceptable to all stakeholders (because, as illustrated in the previous examples, there may be conflicting issues and views). However, by considering the impact on the major stakeholders, companies can make informed judgments. Many companies have developed guidelines to help international managers evaluate the ethical aspects of various decisions.

In the area of questionable payments, U.S. firms have guidance in the Foreign Corrupt Practices Act (FCPA) of 1977. The objective of the FCPA is to stop U.S. multinational companies from initiating or perpetuating what are believed in the U.S. to be corrupt practices in foreign locations by requiring companies to report all payments made in foreign locations. The Justice Department prosecutes firms for contravening the FCPA, so global firms must be aware of the details of the act. The United Nations Committee on Transnational Corporations (UNCTC) has developed Codes of Conduct for international companies, which can also be helpful to firms in defining what is ethical and what is not.

Arguments continue over the appropriateness of legislating morality based on a particular cultural viewpoint. There are some who believe that ethics should be governed by local customs, and others who believe that the developed countries and their companies should take the lead in establishing ethical standards on a worldwide basis.

SUMMARY

This chapter has explored some of the issues associated with implementing global expansion decisions. Specifically, concerns about exports and imports, licensing/contracting/franchising, and ownership were addressed. Joint ventures were considered as well as strategic alliances. The final focus was on interactions with host governments and ethical issues. These are all issues that international companies face continually. Companies do not normally make decisions that are unchanging. The global expansion decision is an ongoing one that is reviewed again and again. Each of the concerns addressed in this chapter will probably affect every global company at one time or another. In addition, companies often face many of these issues at the same time and must be prepared to deal with the implications.

This chapter outlined the major considerations that affect implementing global decisions. They have been examined in a general sense only; each company will have specific concerns and will face unique situations. Legal advice is, therefore, often necessary before proceeding with the a course of action. Similarly, each decision has implications from an accounting and tax perspective which must be considered prior to executing expansion decisions.

DISCUSSION QUESTIONS

1. Both goods and services can be imported or exported. Identify and discuss some of the differences in exporting goods (a physical product) versus a service.

2. Discuss how the North American Free Trade Agreement will influence decisions regarding facility locations within North American.

3. Assume you are exporting a perishable product from the United States to the People's Republic of China. Identify the available options and discuss the advantages and disadvantages of each.

REFERENCES

Adler, N. & J.L Graham. 1987. "Business negotiations: Canadians are not just like Americans." *Canadian Journal of Administrative Sciences*, 4(3), pp. 211–238.

Bilkey, W.J. 1978. "An attempted integration of the literature on export behavior of firms." *Journal of International Business Studies*, Summer, pp. 33–46.

Bowie, Norman. 1986. "The moral obligations of multinational corporations." *Hilton Business Ethics Day*, Loyola Marymount University, Vol. III, Fall.

Contractor, F.J. 1986. "Strategies for structuring joint-ventures: A negotiations planning paradigm." *Columbia Journal of World Business*, Summer, pp. 30–39.

Franko, L.G. 1971. *Joint Venture Survival in Multinational Corporations*. New York: Praeger.

Ferrel, O.C. & John Fraedrich. 1991. "International business ethics." In *Business Ethics—Ethical Decision-Making and Cases*. Boston: Houghton Mifflin Company.

Graham, J.L. 1985. "The influence of culture on the process of business negotiations: An exploratory study." *Journal of International Business Studies*, 16 (1), pp. 81–96.

Graham, J.L. 1981. "A hidden cause of America's trade deficit with Japan," *Columbia Journal of World Business*, Fall, pp. 5-15.

Harrigan, K.R. 1981. "Joint ventures and global strategies". *Columbia Journal of World Business*, 19 (1), Summer, pp. 7–16.

Killing, J.P. 1982. "How to make a joint venture work." *Harvard Business Review*, pp. 120–127.

Lyles, M.A. 1987. "Common mistakes of joint venture experienced firms." *Columbia Journal of World Business*, 22 (2), pp. 79–85.

Poynter, T.A. 1982 "Government intervention in the less developed countries: The experience of multinational companies." *Journal of International Business Studies*, Spring–Summer, 13 (1), pp. 19–26.

Ricks, D.A., M.Fu & J. Arpan 1974. *International Business Blunders*, Columbus, OH: Grid.

Robinson, R.D. 1978. *International Business Management—A Guide to Decision-Making*, Hinsdale, IL: Dryden Press.

Shenkar, O. & S. Ronen. 1987. "The cultural context of negotiations: The implications of Chinese interpersonal norms." *Journal of Applied Behavioral Science*, 23 (20), pp. 263–275.

Shenkar, O. & Y. Zeira. 1987. "Human resource management in international joint ventures: Directions for research." *Academy of Management Review*, 12 (3), pp. 546–557.

Weigand, R. 1983. "International investments: Weighing the incentives." *Harvard Business Review*, July–August, pp. 146–152.

Weiss, S. 1987. "Creating the GM-Toyota joint venture: A case in complex negotiation." *Columbia Journal of World Business*, Summer, pp. 23–37.

Weiss-Wik, S. 1983. "Enhancing negotiators successfulness." *Journal of Conflict Resolution*, 27 (4), pp. 706–739.

Wells, L.T. 1977. "Negotiating with third world governments." *Harvard Business Review*, January–February, pp. 72–80.

9

ADAPTING

MANAGEMENT

TO FOREIGN

ENVIRONMENTS

LEARNING OBJECTIVES

IN THIS CHAPTER WE WILL EXPLORE:

- The definitions of values, needs, attitudes, and norms

- The importance of values for international managers

- Models of cultural values

- Biases in models of cultural values

- Using cultural models effectively

- The role of individual differences in behavior

- Relating cultural models to aspects of global management

- National cultures, subcultures, and overlapping cultures

- Convergent and divergent forces influencing management

KEY DISCUSSION TOPICS:

- The relationship of values and behavior

- Differences among values, norms, attitudes, and needs

- The appropriate use of management models and theories

- The importance of managers' openness to new ways of thinking

- Modifying management based on cultural models

- Country clusters and their relationship to global decisions

- How cultures change

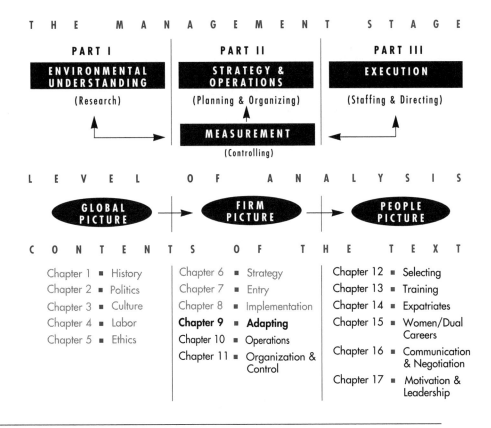

THE MANAGEMENT STAGE

PART I	PART II	PART III
ENVIRONMENTAL UNDERSTANDING	**STRATEGY & OPERATIONS**	**EXECUTION**
(Research)	(Planning & Organizing)	(Staffing & Directing)

MEASUREMENT

(Controlling)

LEVEL OF ANALYSIS

GLOBAL PICTURE → **FIRM PICTURE** → **PEOPLE PICTURE**

CONTENTS OF THE TEXT

INTRODUCTION

This chapter considers cultural values as an expression of cultural differences and suggests ways to assess and understand them and their relationship to management. We define values and distinguish between values and other concepts, while relating values to these other concepts. Models are presented to help students understand cultural similarities and differences and their implications for international managers. The chapter gives students a thorough appreciation of the role of cultural values in organizations and provides suggestions for working with differences and similarities among cultures. The chapter also warns of the inherent Western biases in these discussions of culture and management and identifies the limitations of the models discussed. Subcultures, overlapping cultures, and forces leading to the convergence or divergence of cultures are also considered.

THE IMPORTANCE OF CULTURAL VALUES FOR INTERNATIONAL MANAGERS

Cultural values are important in effective global management. A major challenge for all international managers is working with people from a variety of national cultures. The varied backgrounds of people often means that problems are approached from unfamiliar angles, priorities differ, the nature of rewards and punishments vary, and so on.

Values are useful in explaining and understanding similarities and differences in behavior. Thus, understanding values and their cultural basis is helpful to international managers. If international managers understand how values can vary from culture to culture, they are more likely to accept and correctly interpret behavioral differences. This acceptance and correct interpretation, in turn, enables managers to interact effectively with others whose values and behaviors are unfamiliar.

DEFINING AND UNDERSTANDING CULTURAL VALUES

Before cultural values can be understood, it is helpful to define the concept as well as to distinguish it from, and relate it to, other social concepts. The concepts of *needs*, *attitudes*, and *norms* are all similar to cultural values, but they are not identical. Therefore, it is worthwhile to distinguish among them.

Values have been described as enduring beliefs that specific modes of conduct or states of existence are socially preferable to their opposites (Rokeach 1973). A value system is seen as a relatively permanent perceptual framework that influences an individual's behavior (England 1978). Values establish the standards by which everything in society is judged. The pertinent point for global management in these definitions is the role of social values in behavior. In general, values are societal, while needs, attitudes, and norms are more specific to individuals and situations.

Needs are forces motivating an individual to act in a certain way; once satisfied, needs no longer have an impact on behavior. For example, a need for food motivates people to seek food; once people have eaten, they normally no longer seek food (unless motivated by other needs). Societal values interact with individual needs because they influence how people choose to satisfy their needs.

Two of the most basic and universal human needs are food and sex, yet satisfaction of these needs differs because of societal values. In most societies the value of human life precludes cannibalism to satisfy a need for food. Societies often have accepted time periods for eating, and even when people are hungry, they observe these time frames. Similarly, social customs regarding sexual partners limit satisfaction of sexual needs.

Many societies practice restrictions regarding food associated with religious rituals. For example, during Lent, Christians often forgo favorite foods or limit their intake of meat; during the Month of Ramadan, Muslims fast completely during daylight hours. Some sects eat no meat, some do not allow beef, others prohibit shellfish, others do not eat pork, and still others do not allow certain combinations of foods. Individual needs are put aside to observe these restrictions.

Many societies also have customs regarding the timing and selection of sexual partners. Some societies allow men to have multiple wives; others have group marriages where any partner may have sex with any other. In some locations marriages are arranged for girls at birth, and they must remain virgins until marriage. In others men and women select their own sexual and marriage partners. As with food, individual needs are put aside to observe these restrictions.

Attitudes are a tendency to respond favorably or unfavorably to objects or situations, based on beliefs about them. Societal values influence what we respond to favorably and unfavorably.

For example, in business dress can mean different things depending on what the society values and how different types of dress are interpreted. If wearing a suit and tie indicates a conservative business perspective and conservatism is valued, then someone in this attire would be viewed favorably. If innovation in business was more highly valued and wearing a brightly colored T-shirt and jeans was seen as indicating an innovative perspective, these clothes might be viewed positively. Similarly, in some societies males with long hair are seen negatively, while in others long hair represents virtue:

> The ancients believed a hairy man a strong man. The Greeks and Romans shaved or tore out their hair as offerings to the gods. Orthodox Jews are forbidden to shave "the four corners of the face." In battle, ancient Britons wore drooping moustaches dyed green blue to irk Caesar's legions. The Franks of the fifth and sixth centuries chose their kings from the hairiest of their warriors. Shaving of beards and heads has been a common punishment in many cultures. Chinese males in the sixteenth and seventeenth centuries had to wear pigtails and shave their foreheads as a sign of loyalty—under pain of death. (*Globe & Mail* 1990)

Norms prescribe or proscribe specific behaviors in specific situations and result in standardized, distinctive ways of behaving. They are seen as normal (thus the word "norms") and appropriate behavior. A typical U.S. norm involves eating with the fork in the right hand. This seems acceptable and normal to people who have lived in the U.S. for extended periods. People in many other countries hold their forks in the left hand, and in other places forks are not used at all. For those accustomed to using the right hand for a fork, the reverse can be quite uncomfortable, and using chopsticks in place of a fork quite difficult.

Norms probably originated from values that they no longer clearly represent. The U.S. norm of eating with the fork in the right hand would not be described as a societal value; it is simply the accepted way of behaving in the U.S. According to Visser (1991) this particular norm is related to the U.S. wish to differentiate its customs from the British. The value of independence thus was translated to something that is today a norm.

CULTURAL VALUE DIMENSIONS

In order to assess cultural similarities and differences, it is necessary to have a framework from which to work. A variety of proposed models are helpful in analyzing cultural values. The models examine dimensions of cultural values and compare various national cultures on these dimensions. The models are not mutually exclusive nor are they all-encompassing; rather, they provide a variety of ways of examining cultural similarities and differences. Each approach provides different insights and can be useful on its own and in combination with others. Due to space limitations we can only examine a limited number of models, but students are encouraged to identify others. Those selected for consideration are well-known in the management literature, and we believe they provide practical information for international managers. Before we examine these cultural models, a word of caution about such models.

WESTERN BIASES INHERENT IN THESE DISCUSSIONS

Western biases are inherent in these discussions of culture and management. The management process and the activities discussed are helpful because they will be familiar to most readers: that is how business and management are usually approached in North America and Europe. There is, thus, an inherent Western bias in these discussions.

It would be difficult for most Westerners to discuss management in non-Western terms. Using a Western framework is thus a necessity. In spite of this, students and managers should constantly question even the most basic assumptions about the management process and activities. Consider the following assumptions about possible variations in views; these are not meant to represent real or specific views, merely possibilities.

- Is planning a necessary part of management? If events are predetermined, planning may at best be a waste of time, and at worst a questioning of a higher power.

- Should firms be formally organized? If personal influence is important in day-to-day activities, it may not be appropriate to identify positions within the firm.

- Can people be allocated to fill positions within the firm? If people prefer to work at tasks as they arise, it may not be helpful to allocate them
  to specific slots.

- Does management actively seek to direct and motivate subordinates?
  If people believe that they should work hard only for personal achievement, it may be counterproductive for management to actively direct
  and motivate them.

This inherent Western bias in thinking about management reveals a major
challenge for cross-cultural management. Effective managers cannot take anything for granted. Openness to the possibility that the world is not the world you
know and accept is constantly necessary.

Models of cultural values are helpful in understanding cultural similarities and
differences. In essence, however, they are stereotypes providing only a simplified way of examining cultures. Any culture is far more complex than such
models would suggest, and it is important that this complexity be recognized.
One can think of these cultural stereotypes as describing the values of a typical member of a particular culture, but acknowledge that any culture is made
up of individuals, many of whom will not share the typical values. In working
with people from other cultures, both cultural prefernce and individual variation to be considered. To illustrate: consider two hypothetical cultures, Alpha
and Beta. Alpha might be a culture described as valuing personal initiative,
and Beta as valuing group harmony (the United States and Japan, respective-
ly, would fit these descriptions to some degree). These values are measured on
an individualism scale.

If these preferences are considered as describing the average in these two societies, these cultural values can be pictured graphically as normal curves, as in
exhibit 9.1. In these diagrams the y axis represents the relative frequency of
occurrence of individualism in society, and the x axis represents a continuum
from low individualism to high individualism.

As diagram A illustrates, there are some Alphans who are concerned with
group harmony (contrary to their average), and there are some Betans who
are concerned with personal initiative (contrary to their average). It is possible to talk of the Alphans as generally being high in individualism and
concerned with personal initiative, and the Betans as generally being low in

individualism and concerned with group harmony. At the same time, individuals within each culture can vary from the general preference, thus producing a moderate overlap.

In contrast, it is possible, although unlikely, that there could be virtually no overlap between two cultures as shown in diagram B of Exhibit 9.1. Or two cultures can also be similar and yet reflect a subtle difference in preferences, as displayed in diagram C. This would be the case in comparing Canada and the United States, where there is a great deal of overlap between the cultures, yet the norm for each country are slightly different.

HOFSTEDE'S VALUE SURVEY MODEL (VSM)

This model has been widely discussed in global management literature because it provides information relevant to managers. In other words, variations in the values described in the model can be related to management processes. Although Hofstede's model can be helpful in understanding the relationship between culture and global management, its limitations will also be brought out in our discussion.

The Hofstede (1980) model proposes four dimensions of culture, called *cultural indices*. These were developed on the basis of a worldwide survey of employees in a large U.S. multinational company. The indices are termed (by Hofstede): individualism (IDV), uncertainty avoidance (UAI), power distance (PDI), and masculinity (MAS). Scores on each index can range from 0 to 100. These scores describe the cultural values of a national group and should be interpreted as giving a general sense of the values likely to be found in a particular country.

Individualism (IDV) refers to the degree to which individual decision making and action are accepted and encouraged by the society. Where IDV is high, the society emphasizes the role of the individual; where IDV is low, the society emphasizes the role of the group. Some societies view individualism positively and see it as the basis for creativity and achievement; others view it with disapproval and see it as disruptive to group harmony and cooperation. Effective

EXHIBIT 9.1

CULTURAL VALUES: LEVELS OF INDIVIDUALISM IN ALPHA AND BETA

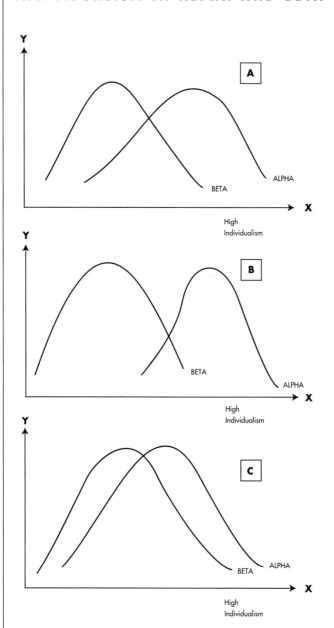

management in high-IDV countries incorporates policies, practices, and procedures that allow individuals to take initiative, make decisions, and work on their own. In low-IDV countries, the reverse is appropriate and group decisions, group action, and group work are preferred.

Uncertainty avoidance (UAI) refers to the degree to which the society is willing to accept and deal with uncertainty. Where UAI is high, the society is concerned with certainty and security and seeks to avoid uncertainty; where UAI is low, the society is comfortable with a high degree of uncertainty and is open to the unknown. Some societies view certainty as necessary, so that people can function without worrying about the consequences of uncertainty. Others view uncertainty as providing excitement and opportunities for innovation and change. Effective management in high-UAI countries provides job security, a well-defined work role, and opportunities to decrease uncertainty through consensus building. In low-UAI countries, the reverse is true. Job security is not stressed, risk-taking is encouraged, and decisions are often made quickly and with relatively little information.

Power distance (PDI) refers to the degree to which power differences are accepted and sanctioned by society. Where PDI is high, the society believes that there should be a well-defined order of inequality in which everyone has a rightful place. Where PDI is low, the prevalent belief is that all people should have equal rights and the opportunity to change their position in society. Some societies view a well-ordered distribution of power as contributing to a well-managed society because each person knows what her/his position is, and people are, in fact, protected by this order. Other societies view power as corrupting and believe that those with less power will inevitably suffer at the hands of those with more. Effective management in high-PDI countries incorporates a well-defined hierarchy, centralized decision making, and authoritarian leadership. In low-PDI countries, the reverse is true; flatter organizations, fewer supervisors, and democratic leadership would be more successful.

Masculinity (MAS) refers to the degree to which traditional male values are important to a society. Traditional male values include assertiveness, performance, ambition, achievement, and material possessions while traditional female values focus on the quality of life, the environment, nurturance, and concern for the less fortunate. In societies that are high in MAS, sex roles are clearly differentiated, and men dominate in low-MAS societies, sex roles are more fluid, and feminine values predominate. Some societies see traditional male values as necessary for survival. This implies men must be aggressive, and women must be protected. Others view both sexes as equal contributors to society and believe that a dominance by traditional male values is destructive. Effective management in societies where MAS is high would differentiate work roles, stress achievement, and reward high performers with money. Where MAS was low, sex equity would be expected, quality of work life would be important, and rewards would not be based purely on performance and could be less tangible.

The extremes of each of these indices has been described. Most countries are not at an extreme, but may be moderately high or moderately low. Thus, effective management practices will not usually reflect an extreme but rather a sensitivity to a tendency.

The original Hofstede data covered many countries. While there are scores available for each country on each of the indices, it is interesting to group countries into four quartiles: high, moderately high, moderately low, and low. Exhibit 9.2 presents the countries examined by Hofstede using the quartile format.

Examination of profiles of different countries shows the variety possible in these four dimensions. Some examples illustrate their possible influence on management practices:

- New Zealand as a society is individualistic, does not avoid uncertainty, and believes in equality and traditional male values. This would suggest that organizational structures will be relatively flat with individuals making decisions on their own and competing for scarce resources.

- Italy as a society is individualistic, avoids uncertainty, and believes in equality (within the confines of sex distinctions) and traditional male values. This would suggest a structure similar to that of New Zealand, but with a reliance on gathering information for decisions and an emphasis on job security and seniority as important components of the management system.

EXHIBIT 9.2

COUNTRY SCORES ON THE HOFSTEDE VSM

Cluster	IDV	UAI	PDI	MAS
Anglo				
Australia	H	ML	ML	MH
Canada	H	ML	ML	MH
Ireland	MH	L	L	MH
New Zealand	H	ML	L	MH
South Africa	MH	ML	ML	MH
United Kingdom	H	L	ML	MH
United States	H	ML	ML	MH
Germanic				
Austria	MH	MH	L	H
Germany (East and West)	MH	MH	ML	MH
Switzerland	MH	ML	ML	H
Latin European				
Belgium	MH	H	MH	MH
France	MH	MH	MH	ML
Italy	H	MH	ML	H
Portugal	ML	H	MH	ML
Spain	MH	MH	MH	ML
Nordic				
Denmark	MH	L	L	L
Finland	MH	ML	ML	L
Norway	MH	ML	L	L
Sweden	MH	L	L	L
Latin American				
Argentina	ML	MH	ML	MH
Chile	L	MH	MH	L
Colombia	L	MH	MH	MH
Peru	L	MH	MH	ML
Venezuela	MH	MH	L	H
Far Eastern				
Hong Kong	L	L	MH	MH
Philippines	ML	ML	H	MH
Singapore	L	L	H	ML
Taiwan	L	MH	MH	ML
Thailand	L	MH	MH	ML
Near Eastern				
Greece	ML	H	MH	MH
Iran	ML	ML	MH	ML
Pakistan	L	MH	MH	MH
Turkey	ML	MH	MH	ML
Independent				
Brazil	ML	MH	MH	ML
India	ML	ML	H	MH
Israel	MH	MH	L	ML
Japan	ML	H	MH	H

Note: H = high (1st quartile); MH = moderately high (2nd quartile); ML = moderately low
(3rd quartile); L = low (4th quartile)

SOURCE:

Reproduced from *Experiencing International Management*, p. 19 with the permission of
South-Western College Publishing. Copyright © 1989 by South-Western College Publishing.
All rights reserved.

- Singapore as a society is collectivist, does not avoid uncertainty, believes in power distinctions, and is relatively low on masculinity. This suggests a paternalistic system, with the leader expressing concern for subordinates and the quality of life, but without a stress on job security.

- Japan as a society is collectivist and high in uncertainty avoidance as well as masculinity, and relatively high in power distance. This would suggest a system that seeks consensus among group members but is competitive and has clear distinctions in power. Job security would be stressed and jobs allocated on the basis of sex.

LIMITATIONS OF THE VSM

It is important to stress that the scores reported by Hofstede are based on employees within one organization—a large U.S. multinational company. Certain types of individuals will be attracted to such an organization, and this will be reflected in these scores. These scores should not, therefore, be interpreted as an accurate description of a national culture as a whole; rather, they should be seen as indicating similarities and differences that one might expect to find among employees in this type of organization in different countries.

In addition, these scores represent a central tendency in a particular population, but there is probably a wide array of values in any country. Organizations and industries will attract and retain individuals with value systems that fit into the organizational culture. For example, a study of fast-food restaurant managers in Canada and the United States revealed a low level of individualism, combined with no uncertainty avoidance and high power distance and masculinity, as shown in Exhibit 9.3 (Punnett & Withane 1989). This is quite dissimilar from the Canadian and U.S. value profile presented in Exhibit 9.2. But, it appears to match the needs of an industry where people must work in close coordination, where there is little job security, and where there are clear distinctions of power and a great deal of competition.

EXHIBIT 9.3

GRAPHICAL COMPARISON: FAST-FOOD
SAMPLE WITH SELECTED HOFSTEDE SCORES

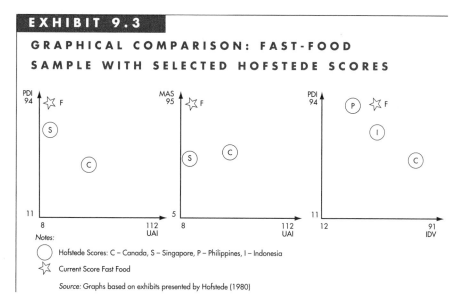

Notes:

◯ Hofstede Scores: C – Canada, S – Singapore, P – Philippines, I – Indonesia

☆ Current Score Fast Food

Source: Graphs based on exhibits presented by Hofstede (1980)

Researchers have also expressed concerns regarding the survey instrument used in Hofstede's research, and the validity of the measure has been questioned. Researchers question whether the country scores provided are representative of the normal population and whether the important cultural variables are the ones being measured.

These concerns should all be kept in mind when interpreting the results of Hofstede's study. In spite of these concerns, from a practical perspective, the cultural variables described by the model are appealing because of their apparent relationship to the management process.

USING THE VSM IN GLOBAL MANAGEMENT

The management process is often described as planning, organizing, staffing, directing, and controlling. These phases of management probably occur in some form in all businesses, but the form may differ depending on the environment. In particular, the cultural values typical of a particular society can influence what is effective in this process. International managers may find that they have to adapt their thinking to deal with these differences. The following numbered paragraphs illustrate the extremes of the Hofstede dimensions as they might relate to aspects of management.

1. Where individualism is high, individual input is sought from those who have particular knowledge or expertise. Superiors are expected to make day-to-day decisions and communicate these to subordinates who are expected to carry them out. Input may be sought from subordinates, or others, who will be affected by decisions, or who have particular knowledge or expertise. Individuals may disagree with particular decisions, but will generally go along if the majority agrees or if the decision has been made by a person in power. Individuals are given specific responsibility for completing tasks and achieving goals and objectives. The individual is expected to make the necessary decisions to carry through with a given assignment. Management by objectives (MBO) is a popular approach because it incorporates the idea of top management setting strategic directions, lower levels developing action plans to achieve these, and individuals accepting and working toward individual goals.

2. Where collectivism is high, organizational plans are formulated on the basis of the larger societal direction, with input from all organizational members. The overall direction of the organization is discussed and agreed to throughout the organization. Decisions are made collectively with all those affected participating in the process. Disagreements are dealt with throughout the process, and consensus from all members is sought. Tasks and assignments are carried out by groups. There is pressure from the group for conformity to acceptable standards. When decisions need to be made, they are made by the group as a whole. The quality circle approach is popular because it incorporates the idea of bottom-up decision making, consensus among members, and group involvement.

3. Where uncertainty avoidance is high, uncertainty can be avoided by having group members share responsibility for planning and decisions, or, alternatively, by having one person in a position of power take the responsibility. The advice of experts is likely to be important in formulating plans and making decisions. Planning provides security and is well accepted. Plans are likely to be detailed and complex, incorporating priorities and contingencies. Specific plans provide direction with little ambiguity. Strategic planning is as long-term in scope as practical. Checks and balances ensure that performance is at the planned level and allow for correction before a major departure occurs. Decisions are reached slowly. If responsibility is shared, then group agreement is important to the planning process. If a powerful individual makes the decisions, then these are imparted to subordinates as absolutes. In both cases, disagreement is discouraged.

4. Where uncertainty avoidance is low, planning is flexible and relatively short term. Uncertainty is seen as inevitable, and therefore the organization must be able to change direction quickly. Planning is accepted as providing guidance but not constraints. Formal planning is most likely to take place at top levels and be, at least partially, based on a subjective evaluation of opportunities. Personal preferences are likely to be evident in strategic directions. A certain amount of risk taking will be encouraged. Individuals are likely to accept the risk of decision making, and the need for making quick decisions will be stressed.

5. Where power distance is high, planning and decision making are done at the top. Input is accepted from those in power, but no input is expected from those at lower levels. Long-term plans are kept secret. Operational decisions are made on a daily basis by superiors, and work is assigned to subordinates. All decisions are referred to the superior, and subordinates are discouraged from taking the initiative and making decisions. Subordinates accept assigned work

and carry out tasks as instructed. Those in positions of power are respected, and those in inferior positions expect that more powerful individuals will take responsibility for decision making.

6. Where power distance is low, everyone is seen as capable of contributing to the planning process, and input from a variety of organizational levels is sought in developing strategic plans. Decision making in general is participative, and long-term plans are likely to be shared among organizational members. Operational decisions incorporate the views of those who must carry them out. The people involved in particular tasks are expected to make the routine decisions necessary to complete the task, and decisions are only referred to the superior when they involve unusual circumstances. Power differences exist but are minimized, and friendly relationships between superiors and subordinates are normal.

7. Where traditional masculine values predominate, strategic plans emphasize specific, measurable achievements by the organization (such as increases in market share or profitability). These achievements are believed to be difficult but possible, with tangible results. Strategic choices are made at the top level. Operational decisions will focus on task accomplishment, and tasks will be undertaken by those people most likely to perform them at the desired level. Certain tasks will be seen as more suitable for males, others as more suitable for females. Responsibility for different types of decisions will be based on gender.

8. Where traditional feminine values predominate, strategic plans will take into account the environment, the quality of working life, and concern for the less fortunate. Factors such as profitability and market share will be defined within this context. Operational decisions will focus on satisfaction with work and development of a congenial and nurturing work environment. Task accomplishment will be within this framework. Work will be seen as generally suitable for either sex with more concern for assigning work according to individual abilities and preferences. Decision making will be shared between the sexes. Decision-making responsibility will depend on

ability and preferences rather than on gender. The "male" values of achievement, money, and performance will rank equally with the "female" values of nurturance, quality of life, and caring for the less fortunate.

KLUCKHOHN AND STRODTBECK'S VALUE ORIENTATION MODEL

The anthropologists Kluckhohn and Strodtbeck (1961) explained cultural similarities and differences in terms of five basic problems that all societies face. These are relationship to nature, time orientation, basic human nature, activity orientation, and human relationships. Cultural differences are explained by varying ways of coping with these problems, as different societies adopt different solutions. Like the Hofstede framework, these ways of coping represent the central tendency in a society though individuals will deviate from this general preference. This approach has been used by a number of global management authors, and it provides a helpful alternative to the Hofstede model.

We will examine the Kluckhohn & Strodtbeck model and discuss its relationship to a variety of management activities. We begin by describing the various solutions that societies have developed for the five problems identified by these anthropologists.

Relationship to nature means either subjugation, harmony, or mastery of nature. Societies that view themselves as subjugated to nature view life as essentially preordained; people are not masters of their own destinies, and trying to change the inevitable is futile. Societies that view themselves as living in harmony with nature believe that people must alter their behavior to accommodate nature. Societies that view themselves as able to master nature think in terms of the supremacy of the human race and harnessing the forces of nature.

The Muslim view of events as "occurring if God wills them" exemplifies the first view. The North American Indian wish to preserve nature as it is, is a good example of the second. The third is seen in the English-speaking world's desire to conquer natural phenomena.

Time orientation is the relationship to past, present, and future. Societies oriented toward the past look for solutions in the past: what would our forefathers have done? Societies that are present-oriented consider the immediate effects of their actions: what will happen if I do this? Societies that are future-oriented look to the long-term results of today's events: what will happen to future generations if we do these things today?

The Chinese veneration for older people suggests an orientation to the past. The reported American desire for instant gratification suggests an orientation toward the present. The Japanese emphasis on long-term planning might be considered an orientation toward the future.

Basic human nature indicates seeing human beings as evil, good, or mixed. Societies that believe people are primarily evil focus on controlling their behaviour through specified codes of conduct and sanctions for wrong-doing. Societies that believe people are essentially good would exhibit trust and rely on verbal agreements. Societies that see people as mixed probably also see people as changeable and would focus on means to modify behaviour, to encourage desired behavior, and discourage behaviors that are not desirable.

North Americans probably see people as mixed, and this is reflected in the treatment of employees. There is a general emphasis on rewarding "good" behavior and punishing "bad" (the same might be said of the penal system). The Japanese work environment suggests they hold the attitude that people are "good"; an employee is not singled out for good performance because this is simply living up to expectations. Islamic punishments that clearly relate the penalty to the crime—for example, theft punished by the amputation of the hand—may suggest a belief that evil cannot be changed but must be eliminated.

Activity orientation concerns the ideas of being, containing and controlling, and doing. Societies that are primarily "being" oriented are emotional; people react spontaneously based on what they feel at the time. Those concerned with containing and controlling focus on moderation and orderliness; people seek to achieve a balance in life and in society. Those which are "doing" oriented are constantly striving to achieve; people are driven by a need to accomplish difficult tasks.

The Latin temperament might illustrate "being" because strong emotional reactions are acceptable. The Chinese, on the other hand, could be seen as "controlling" because they stress moderation and order. The American view that work is good, and that "idle hands make mischief" would represent the "doing" orientation.

Human relationships are viewed as individual, lineal, or colineal. Societies that are primarily individual believe that individuals should be independent and take responsibility for their own actions. Those that are lineal are concerned with the family line and the power structure that underlies a hierarchy. Those that are colineal are group-oriented and emphasize group interactions and actions.

English-speaking societies tend to be individualistic, stressing the role of the individual in society. Indian society is probably largely lineal, placing emphasis on the individual's lineage. The Japanese may be considered predominantly colineal because of their concern with intragroup relationships.

Now that we have defined the types of value orientations to basic societal problems, we can relate them to effective global management. Some brief suggestions illustrate how these orientations may be related to management:

- In a society that believes humans are subjugated by nature, planning would be futile because the future is viewed as preordained.

- In a society that is present-oriented, rewards would be closely tied to current performance.

- In a society that believes in the basic goodness of humans, participative management is likely to be normal.

- In a society that is primarily "being" oriented, decisions are likely to be intuitive with less concern for logic.

- In a society that is hierarchical, the organization structure might be a formal, authority-based hierarchy.

Understanding the value dimensions of a culture can provide international managers with insights into people's behavior in foreign locations, and allow these managers to adapt their own style and adjust their organization's practices to accommodate cultural differences. Some relationships between value orientations and global management are considered up in the following general statements.

- In a society that thinks in terms of mastery over nature, technology is likely to be admired, and people will be willing to work toward production goals and objectives set by management. In a society that emphasizes harmony with nature, there will be concern over the impact of technology on nature, and goals and objectives that will be acceptable will relate to both productivity and the environment. In a society that sees itself as subject to nature, mastery of technology may be viewed with caution and specific goals and objectives disliked.

- In a past-oriented society, market research will focus on the past, and customer tastes will not be expected to change dramatically or quickly. Sales efforts will emphasize past quality and performance and use familiar approaches. In a present-oriented society, market research will focus on identifying what is current and identify products and services with practical immediate benefits. Sales efforts will use topical references and up-to-date approaches. In a future-oriented society, market research will be concerned with expectations of the future and try to identify tomorrow's tastes and needs. Sales efforts will emphasize the long-term benefits of products and services and use futuristic references and images.

- In a society where people are believed to be basically good, a firm can portray itself as working for the benefit of it peoples constituencies. If errors occur, they can be explained best as happening in spite of people's efforts. In a society where people are believed to be basically evil, a firm is better portrayed as an entity of its own without emphasis on individuals. Errors can be explained in terms of individual human error, disassociated from the firm. In a society where people are seen as a mixture of good and evil, the selection of the best people to work in the firm might be emphasized. Errors can be admitted readily, and the actions taken to correct and avoid them in the future can be explained.

- In a being-oriented society (where people are spontaneous and react emotionally), accounting and financial systems will need to be relatively flexible, allowing for alternative ways of carrying out needed activities. Policies and procedures will be general and provide guidelines rather than specific and detailed instructions. In a containing-and-controlling society the emphasis will be on logic. Systems will be rationally designed and explained, assuming that people will comply with logic. Policies and procedures will be complex and include both qualitative and quantitative guidelines and instructions. In a doing-oriented society (where there is concern for activity and accomplishment), systems will be pragmatic and emphasize expected results. Policies and procedures will be relatively simple and described in operational, active terms.

- In a society that is primarily individual, the individual person will be the focus of management activities. This will be true of decision making, leadership, work design, rewards, and so on. In a society that is lineal, the hierarchy of power and authority will be important in all management activities. Leadership is associated with level in the organization, which is accompanied by power and authority. Vertical differentiation will be stressed, and decisions, work design, and reward system will conform to the hierarchical structure. In a society that is colineal, group activities are normal and preferred. The group becomes the focus in terms of decisions, leadership, work design, rewards, and so on.

COUNTRY CLUSTERS

In addition to the cultural models discussed so far, examining clusters of countries that share similar values can be useful for international managers. One of the most extensive studies resulting in country clusters was carried out by Ronen and Shenkar (1985). This was a synthesis of previous research and identified eight clusters of countries (see Exhibit 9.4). They named these eight Nordic, Germanic, Anglo, Latin European, Latin American, Far Eastern, Arab, and Near Eastern. A number of countries that did not fall into one of the clusters were identified as independent.

EXHIBIT 9.4

COUNTRY CLUSTERS BASED
ON EMPLOYEE ATTITUDE

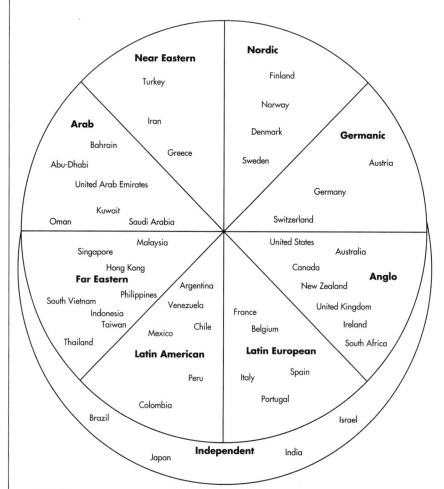

SOURCE:
S. Ronen and O. Shenkar. 1985. "Clustering countries on attitudinal dimensions: A review and synthesis." *Academy of Management Review*. Vol. 10, No. 3.

The specific countries included in Exhibit 9.4 reflect available research. Students will note that regions such as Africa and Eastern Europe are not represented at all, and that within other clusters, major countries are missing. (Brazil is missing from Latin America, and the People's Republic of China from the Far East.) This missing information is a major limitation of current research because managers may be particularly interested in one of these countries or regions. In spite of this limitation, the clusters can be helpful to managers deciding on the degree to which cultural adaptation is needed when moving cross-culturally. A manager interacting with colleagues from within the home cluster can expect relatively similar values and relatively easy adaptation—for example, Australians interacting with Canadians will be in relatively familiar territory. Moving outside the home cluster can be relatively more difficult because of the likely diversity of values and greater need for adaptation—for example, a Mexican going to Saudi Arabia is likely to be faced with more cultural adaptation than the Australian.

Exhibit 9.5, using information from Punnett and Ronen (1984), shows similarities and differences in cultural factors that shape cultural values (these are labelled "cultural antecedents"). The cultural antecedents are compared for each cluster of countries, showing that countries in the Anglo cluster share, to a large extent, their language, religion, race, and level of economic development. Other clusters are similar to the Anglo cluster in some of these cultural traits, and still others do not overlap with the Anglo group at all. It would seem that where all antecedents are shared, there will be relative cultural similarity; where none are shared, there will be a relative cultural dissimilarity. For example, the Arab cluster differs from the Anglo cluster in language, religion, race, and level of economic development. This suggests that national cultures in this cluster would be different from countries in the Anglo cluster.

EXHIBIT 9.5

CULTURAL ANTECEDENTS AMONG
COUNTRY CLUSTERS/RELATIVE TO ANGLO VALUES

	Germanic	Latin European	Nordic	Latin American	Near Eastern	Far Eastern	Arab	Independent
Anglo								
Language (English)	*	x	x	x	x	x	x	India?*
Religion (Judeo-Christian)	*	*	*	*	x	x	x	x
Race (Caucasian)	*	*	*	?	x	x	x	x
Economy (Industrial)	*	*	*	x	x	x	x	Japan

Similarities are indicated by an *, differences by an x, and some overlap by a ?

English is a commonly spoken language in India.

SOURCE:

Betty Jane Punnett. 1984. *Experiencing International Management*. Boston: PWS-KENT, p. 18. Based on information presented by Punnett and Ronen 1984.

The degrees of similarity are identified in Exhibit 9.6. Countries within a cluster are considered similar with regard to their cultural values. Clusters are arranged in an approximate order of cluster similarity; for example, the Anglo cluster is more similar to the European clusters (Germanic, Latin European, and Nordic) than it is to the Latin American, Near Eastern, Far Eastern, and Arab clusters.

EXHIBIT 9.6

RELATIVE SIMILARITY OF COUNTRY CLUSTERS TO ANGLO

Cluster 1 — Anglo

Canada, Australia, New Zealand, United Kingdom, United States

Cluster 2 — Germanic

Austria, Germany, Switzerland

Cluster 3 — Latin European

Belgium, France, Italy, Portugal, Spain

Cluster 4 — Nordic

Denmark, Finland, Norway, Sweden

Cluster 5 — Latin American

Argentina, Chile, Colombia, Mexico, Peru, Venezuela

Cluster 6 — Near Eastern

Greece, Iran, Turkey

Cluster 7 — Far Eastern

Hong Kong, Indonesia, Malaysia, Philippines, Singapore, South Vietnam, Taiwan

Cluster 8 — Arab

Bahrain, Kuwait, Saudi Arabia, United Arab Emirates

Independent (not closely related to other countries)

Japan, India, Israel

SOURCE:

B.J. Punnett. *Experiencing International Management* (Boston: PWS-KENT, 1989), p. 17. Used with permission. Based on information presented by S. Ronen. 1984. *Comparative and International Management*. (New York: John Wiley & Sons, Inc.).

As noted earlier, the clusters are based on available research, and the countries included in the list are, therefore, only those countries where there has been appropriate research. Sometimes it is possible to make informed judgments regarding the likely position of countries that are not represented, based on information about their cultural antecedents and neighbors.

If you are faced with going to a new country and you want to identify how similar or different it is from others that are familiar, try this approach: dress and pack as you would normally for a trip lasting a couple of days. Take the next available plane to the country of interest and arrange to stay for a couple of days. If you feel comfortable when you arrive, have no difficulty dealing with immigration, customs, and other airport authorities, and find making arrangements to stay relatively easy, you can probably assume the country of interest will not be a major cultural challenge. The more uncomfortable you feel, and the more difficulties you encounter, the more likely it is that the cross-cultural adjustment will be difficult as well.

THE ROLE OF COUNTRY CLUSTERS IN GLOBAL DECISIONS

Grouping countries into culturally similar clusters is helpful to international managers in a number of ways. If we consider some typical concerns of international managers, we can see how country clusters might be used. Our discussion here is by no means all inclusive since there are many additional ways in which country cluster information can be used by international managers. However, it does give a sense of how this information may be factored into global management decisions.

Members of a cluster can be expected to share basic cultural values, and people in all the countries in a cluster are likely to behave in relatively similar ways. Managers with experience in one country (say, Norway) can then move relatively easily to another country in the same cluster (say, Finland). This does not mean that everything in Finland will be the same as in Norway. Rather, it means that the experience gained in Norway will likely be helpful in adjusting to Finland.

Managers in one country in a cluster can move to others in the same cluster with a minimum of culture shock and with relatively little need for adaptation. Movement from one cultural cluster to another can be expected to be more difficult. Managers in one cluster moving to another cluster need to be particularly aware of the cultural differences. They may experience culture shock and should be prepared to adapt to the new culture.

Counties in different clusters are likely to exhibit different cultural values, and the people will behave in relatively dissimilar ways. Managers moving from a country in one cluster (say, Australia) to a country in a different cluster (say, Argentina) can expect that they will encounter substantial differences. They can be prepared and adapt their management style as needed.

Decisions regarding locations for international subsidiaries can take advantage of information provided by country clusters. A firm seeking to expand internationally might initially want to gain experience in culturally similar locations. For example, a Canadian firm might expand to other countries in the Anglo cluster. Alternatively, an international firm with substantial experience may feel there is potential benefit in expanding to countries that are culturally different. In this case, the Canadian firm could consider places like Saudi Arabia, Portugal, or Indonesia.

International staffing decisions can benefit from considering country clusters. Allocating personnel to relatively similar cultures (for example, moving French personnel to Belgium) minimizes the culture shock they should experience. Such a move can be relatively easy, and extensive cross-cultural training and support are not needed. In contrast, a move to a country in a different cluster (for example, French personnel to the United States) may present a greater challenge. In this move a greater degree of culture shock is likely, and, therefore, appropriate training and support need to be provided.

International managers can consider country clusters in relation to joint ventures and strategic alliances. Many alliances fail because of the differing objectives of the parties involved, and, to some extent, these objectives reflect the national culture. (For example, Japanese managers are generally believed to take a longer-term view than U.S. managers.) Firms entering alliances within a familiar cluster may be able to reach agreement on objectives more easily than in an unfamiliar cluster. When entering an alliance in an unfamiliar cluster, it is important to allow adequate time to discuss objectives in detail, and it may be necessary to consider innovative proposals.

Managers may find negotiations follow similar procedures within clusters but can change dramatically between clusters. Managers who are aware of this are likely to be better negotiators because they will prepare for and use the similarities and differences that exist.

Managers also need to consider whether management practices and approaches can be transferred from one country to another. Management practices are more likely to be generally similar within cultural clusters. Managers who have successfully worked in one country can have some confidence that they can be effective in other countries in the same cluster.

International managers often make decisions about expanding to new locations, and when making a choice between two locations that are equally attractive in other ways, cultural similarities and differences may be a deciding factor. Expansion to new locations within a familiar cluster is likely to involve fewer unexpected occurrences than expanding to an unfamiliar cluster. In contrast, the differences that are inherent in a new cluster may provide opportunities that do not exist in culturally similar locations.

Subsidiaries of international firms are often grouped based on similarities of activities, and regional groupings are fairly common. Country clusters provide one basis for deciding on regional groupings. Countries within a cluster can be expected to share some characteristics such as language, or religion and to express relatively similar values. These similarities suggest that taking a common approach to countries within a cluster may be appropriate.

The decisions regarding marketing in different countries can be a challenge. A major concern for marketers is taking advantage of efficiencies offered by standardized marketing approaches while adapting to cultural differences. Country clusters provide input into decisions regarding marketing standardization and adaptation. The relative similarity of countries within a cluster suggests that greater standardization may be appropriate, while differences between clusters highlights the need for adaptation.

LIMITATIONS OF COUNTRY CLUSTER INFORMATION

The clusters of countries identified by Ronen and Shenkar provide some help to international managers, but there are some limitations to consider. For example:

- As previously noted, the countries included are limited to those that have been studied; therefore, there are notable absences such as the African countries and many of the developing countries.

- The clusters are based on variables studied in the past; it is possible that different clusters would emerge if studying different variables.

- These clusters do not identify the relative similarity between clusters; this may be an important consideration for international managers.

- The clusters may overemphasize similarity within a cluster or dissimilarity between clusters. Countries within a cluster do differ, and those in different clusters can exhibit some similarities.

These clusters should be thought of as providing helpful insight into cross-cultural interactions and adding to the international manager's store of information. As with all of the models discussed, the clusters are more helpful in some global management decisions and than others.

VARIATION WITHIN CULTURES

Much literature on cross-cultural organizations focuses on national boundaries rather than specific cultural boundaries. As previously noted, "culture has often served simply as a synonym for nation without any further conceptual grounding" (Bhagat & McQuaid, 1982). In effect, the focus is on what might be called a national culture. This can be somewhat misleading because there are clear cases where cultures transcend national boundaries, and other cases where several cultures are evident in one nation. As discussed in Chapter 3, from the organization's viewpoint, a focus on national cultures is an appropriate beginning. Within this framework, subcultures, overlapping cultures, and forces for convergence and divergence need to be considered.

UNDERSTANDING SUBCULTURES

It is also important to recognize the existence of subcultures within any national culture. Identifying subcultures and their values is necessary in some situations and can be particularly useful to international managers.

A subculture may hold values in sharp contrast to those of the broader national culture. If a manager is interacting substantially with members of a subculture, he or she will need to appreciate and accommodate these differences. For example, Sikh immigrants to Canada still maintain their cultural heritage and believe in the importance of wearing turbans. The Royal Canadian Mounted Police found it was necessary to accommodate this custom in order to attract and retain Sikhs in the force.

The values of a subculture can be more similar to a foreign manager's own cultural values than those of the broader national culture of which it is a part. A manager might want to seek out members of such a subculture in situations where similar values are desired. A manager from a largely Christian country such as the United Kingdom might find some similarity of values with the Christian minority in Japan might seek out this group at certain times, particularly, say, in times of grief.

Members of a subculture whose values are in conflict with the broader national culture may not be integrated into the work force easily. Contrasting values may cause personal conflicts among employees from different groups. A manager must be sensitive to these potential conflicts and identify ways of dealing with them. Malaysia is a case in point. The indigenous Malays and the Chinese in Malaysia have been described as exhibiting sometimes radically different values that can lead to conflicts at work. These are partially due to conflicting religious practices (the Malays, for the most part, are Muslims while the Chinese are Confucian and Buddhists), and partially due to attitudes toward work (the Malays are seen as easy-going people who are working to live, while the Chinese are described as concerned with getting ahead so work is more central to their lives).

Synergy can develop where employees with different values work together because they may view the same situation from varying perspectives. Managers who can effectively control interactions among employees with different values can benefit from the development of new and innovative ways of thinking. For example, the Bata Shoe Company has subsidiaries throughout the world and finds that by bringing its diverse marketing managers together in Canada, new ideas for products and marketing approaches can be developed.

Working with a variety of subcultures within one national location provides many of the same experiences as working in a new national culture. Managers can increase their cross-cultural sensitivity by seeking out members of different cultural minorities and interacting and working with them on an ongoing basis. The United States is made up of many groups that maintain their cultural heritage in spite of being Americans. Some companies have made a virtue of this cultural diversity. For example, it has been reported that Monsanto employees must deal with local diversity and work effectively throughout the world, and the company has developed a number of programs to ensure that all employees are culturally aware.

UNDERSTANDING OVERLAPPING CULTURES

Subcultures are often encountered and cannot be ignored by international managers. The same is true of cultures that overlap national boundaries. In many situations groups in different countries share similar values. In fact, some subcultures identified previously (for example, the Sikhs) can be found in many countries, and their values will be somewhat similar in each location. The similarities in values are often attributable to shared ethnicity or religion. Some examples illustrate this potential overlap:

- Rastafarians (members of a religious sect originating in Jamaica) can be found throughout the Caribbean and in Canada, the United Kingdom, and the United States. The values and customs associated with their religious beliefs remain similar even when they have been integrated into societies outside Jamaica.

- The Jewish people often exhibit similar values no matter where in the world they have settled. To some extent this is because of shared religious beliefs. But even nonpracticing Jews feel a kinship with other Jews in different parts of the world, and many Jews see this as a shared cultural heritage, not simply a religious similarity.

- The British left a clear mark on many of their colonies, and the governing classes in former British colonies retain many British characteristics.

- The boundaries of many nations have been identified so that cultural groups have been divided. These groups often share more culturally with their counterparts in other countries than with the nation in which they live. The Kurdish people of Iran, Iraq, and Turkey provide a good example.

It can be helpful for international managers to identify overlapping cultural values found in different locations. Familiarity with the cultural values of a group in one location can then be useful in identifying values of a counterpart elsewhere.

In countries with a strong national culture that culture will have an impact on all the people who choose to live in that nation. Subcultures will differ from the national culture in some aspects, but members will share some national values. Similarly, overlapping cultures will share certain values but will differ on others because of national cultural differences.

Clearly the task of understanding culture is not easy. In addition to subcultures and overlapping cultures, there are also forces that encourage convergence and divergence of cultures, and these have to be considered as well.

CONVERGENCE AND DIVERGENCE OF CULTURES

Some people argue that there are many forces in the world that encourage countries to become more alike and to share common values. For example, the ease of global communication and travel exposes people to foreigners and foreign media. People in the U.S. can watch French television, listen to radio broadcasts from the PRC, and attend Indian movies. Without ever leaving home, they can meet Japanese tourists, talk with Saudi business people, and have dinner with African students in Balinese restaurants. Similarly, products that originated in the U.S. are sought around the world—Levi jeans, Coca-Cola, Elvis Presley records, and Rambo movies, among others. The British rock group, the Beatles, has been popular in countries as diverse as the United

States, the Soviet Union, and Japan. Over time, it would seem that if people are exposed to similar experiences and interact with others from different cultures, there might be a convergence of values.

The current worldwide concern with the environment also suggests a potential converging of values. If cultural values develop in response to perceived survival needs, then global concerns not defined by national boundaries may lead to global solutions and shared values.

In addition, the existence of multinational and global companies may contribute to the convergence of cultures. These organizations inevitably take features of the home culture with them to foreign locations, and subsidiaries will to some extent share a corporate culture and perhaps a professional culture. At the same time, as the firm draws its leaders from around the world, there is a sharing of values. Over time, this would suggest an increasing importance of the corporate influence and some convergence of values.

In contrast to this view, there are arguments that cultural values are not converging, but may be diverging. The ease of communication and travel may have this effect rather that the former. Extensive exposure to foreigners and foreign media may increase awareness of the home values, which may be seen as particularly "good" in contrast to foreign values. A sense of domination by foreigners can result in a determination to maintain one's own value system. Canadians, for example, feel they are influenced by the U.S. and react by being more Canadian. Some people in the U.S. are concerned about the Japanese influence and react by perceiving Japanese ways as negative.

Recent events such as the collapse of the Soviet Union suggest that strong cultural value differences have been maintained by groups there in spite of efforts to eliminate these differences. Similarly, the French Canadian wish to be recognized as a "distinct society" and native American groups' arguments for self-government focus around cultural uniqueness and suggest divergence rather than convergence.

It could also be argued that the activities of multinational and global companies can contribute to divergence. Some of these companies provide products or services specifically developed for particular countries or regions, and they adapt their decisions to fit the needs of different locations. This sensitivity to cultural differences can, in effect, perpetuate the differences.

The arguments for convergence and divergence are both reasonable. Perhaps one can conclude that convergence will occur in some aspects of culture and divergence in others. International managers should be aware of the forces leading to both and consider their likely impact in specific situations.

SUMMARY

In this chapter we looked at three models that are useful in understanding the relationship of culture and management: the Hofstede VSM, Kluckhohn and Strodtbeck's value orientation model, and Ronen and Shenkar's country clusters. These were described and their relationships to global management explored. There are others that could have been included. However, these three have been widely discussed in global management literature, and they illustrate contrasting approaches that can be helpful to international managers.

However, their limitations need to be recognized, and the inherent Western biases of the discussion considered. In addition, these models focus essentially on national cultures. Issues associated with subcultures, overlapping cultures, and the convergence and divergence of cultures should also be considered by international managers.

Understanding cultural similarities and differences is important for international managers because these similarities and differences can be used to make the global firm more effective. Cultural values pervade the global firm's decisions, and, therefore, it is vital for managers to have a good understanding of why cultural values differ and how they relate to management.

DISCUSSION QUESTIONS

1. Select one of Hofstede's cultural value dimensions (for example, individualism). Identify two countries that are at opposite extremes on this dimension—one high and one low. Discuss how this difference would be likely to show up in a meeting between managers from these two countries.

2. Suppose you have been asked to design a training program for employees in a foreign subsidiary of your firm. Computers are being introduced to these employees, and your initial task is to train the employees in their basic use. You have done some research and found that people in the foreign location are usually oriented to the past and see their relationship to nature as subjugation. Discuss how these cultural characteristics would influence the training program.

3. "A group of local Brazilian accountants working for the ABC corporation in Brazil will behave in the same way." Discuss the validity of this statement.

REFERENCES

Adler, N. 1991. *International Dimensions of Organizational Behavior*. Boston: PWS-Kent Publishing Company.

Bata Shoe Organization. 1989. *Corporate Literature*.

Bhagat, R.S. & S.J. McQuaid. 1982. "Role of subjective culture in organizations: A review and directions for future research." *Journal of Applied Psychology Monograph*, 67 (5), pp. 635–685.

Copeland, L. & L. Griggs. 1986. *Going International—How to Make Friends and Deal Effectively in the Global Marketplace*. New York: New American Library.

England, G.W. 1978. "Managers and their value systems: A five country comparative study." *Columbia Journal of World Business*, 13 (2) pp. 35–44.

Ferraro, G.P. 1990. *The Cultural Dimensions of International Business.* Englewood Cliffs, NJ: Prentice Hall.

Globe and Mail. 1990. "Social Studies," November 19, p. A16.

Heller, F.A. 1988. "Cost benefits of multinational research on organizations." *International Studies of Management and Organization,* XVIII (3), pp. 5–18.

Hofstede, G. 1991. *Cultures and Organizations.* London: McGraw-Hill Book Company.

Hofstede G. 1980. *Cultures Consequences: International Differences in Work Related Values.* Beverly Hills: Sage Publications.

Kluckhohn, C. & F. Strodtbeck. 1961). *Variations in Value Orientations.* Westport, CT: Greenwood Press.

Kroeber, A. & C. Kluckhohn. 1952. "Culture: A critical review of concepts and definitions." *Papers of the Peabody Museum of American Archaeology and Ethnology,* Harvard University, pp. 1–223.

Lane H.W. & J.J. DiStefano. 1988. *International Management Behavior.* Scarborough, Ont.: Nelson Canada.

Punnett, B.J. & S. Ronen. 1984. "Operationalizing cross-cultural variables." A paper delivered at the forty-fourth Annual Meeting of the Academy of Management, Boston.

Punnett, B.J. & S. Withane. 1989. "Hofstede's value survey module: To embrace or abandon?" B. Prasad (Ed.) *Advances in International Comparative Management.* Greenwich, CT: JAI Press.

Ronen, S. & O. Shenkar. 1985. "Clustering countries on attitudinal dimensions: A review and synthesis." *Academy of Management Review.* Vol. 10 (3).

Rokeach, J. 1973. *The Nature of Human Values.* New York: The Free Press.

Terpstra, V. & K. David. 1985. *The Cultural Environment of International Business.* Dallas: South-Western Publishing.

Visser, M. 1991. *The Rituals of Dinner: The Origins, Evolution, Eccentricities and Meaning of Table Manners.* New York: Grove Press.

10

MANAGING

OPERATIONS

GLOBALLY

LEARNING OBJECTIVES

IN THIS CHAPTER WE WILL EXPLORE:

- Components of the operational system

- Adapting operational decisions internationally

- International options in terms of access to supplies

- Balancing local and global operational requirements

- Achieving quality in international production

- Trade-offs in choosing production locations

- Selecting the most effective facilities

- A systems approach to international operations

- Operational differences for goods and services

KEY DISCUSSION ISSUES:

- A comparison of global and multinational perspectives on operations

- Access to inputs versus access to markets

- The benefits and drawbacks of integration

- The selection of national suppliers

- How TQM changes at the international level

- The benefits and drawbacks of small and large facilities

- Adapting production to local conditions

- Understanding differences between goods and services

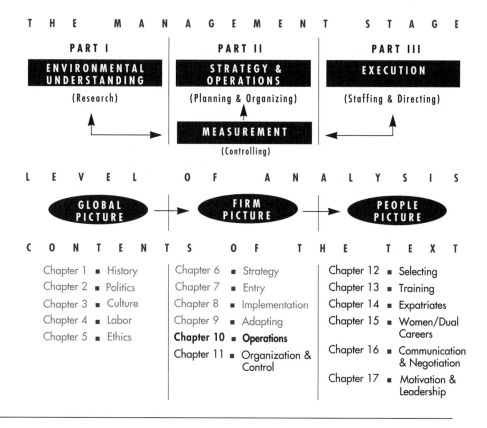

THE MANAGEMENT STAGE

PART I	PART II	PART III
ENVIRONMENTAL UNDERSTANDING	**STRATEGY & OPERATIONS**	**EXECUTION**
(Research)	(Planning & Organizing)	(Staffing & Directing)

MEASUREMENT
(Controlling)

LEVEL OF ANALYSIS

GLOBAL PICTURE → FIRM PICTURE → PEOPLE PICTURE

CONTENTS OF THE TEXT

INTRODUCTION

This chapter examines operational decisions from a global perspective. Operational decisions can be both strategic and tactical. These decisions encompass long term decisions such as plant locations and size of facilities, as well as day-to-day decisions such as production schedules and delivery timetables. Operational managers, in other words, sometimes take a long-term view and at other times take a short-term view. Strategic operational decisions may lock a company into a particular arrangement for many years, but day-to-day operational decisions often need to be made quickly with the needs of the current situation as the paramount consideration. Thus, there is a dual nature to operational management.

Operational managers in international companies often face another dilemma as well: a trade-off between a global perspective and a multinational perspective. In thinking from a global perspective, managers consider the availability and costs of resources around the world in order to choose optimal sites for operations: they think in terms of unified, globally rationalized operations. In thinking from a multinational perspective, managers tailor operations to fit the unique aspects of various locations and adapt company operations to local requirements: they think in terms of individual, nationally adapted operations. There are advantages and disadvantages to both the global approach and the multinational one. These will depend on the individual company, industry and market characteristics, and the available operational locations. Managers often combine global and local approaches in a variety of ways and through a variety of operational choices and trade-offs.

Three major topics will be covered: procurement, production, and delivery. Procurement involves decisions about the source, timing, and means of obtaining needed inputs. Production involves the location, type, and coordination of facilities, as well as total quality management. Delivery involves getting the finished product to the customer and logistical networks as they apply to the entire operational system. We will also discuss the difference between goods and services as two classes of products.

PROCUREMENT ISSUES

In order to provide a product, a firm needs certain inputs, including raw materials, labor, and energy. Managers have to select the best source for these inputs, decide on the most effective means of obtaining them, and determine the timing for acquiring them. The firm's overall objective is to obtain the best inputs from around the world in order to produce components and products efficiently. The manager needs to adjust this objective in light of the constraints of different political and cultural environments. We consider two major issues that managers face relative to obtaining inputs: the degree of vertical integration that is desirable and the national origin of inputs and suppliers of these inputs.

DEGREE OF INTEGRATION

The degree of vertical integration depends on the degree to which a firm is its own supplier and market. The focus in procurement is on the supplier. In effect, therefore, decisions regarding vertical integration are make-versus-buy decisions. At one extreme, a firm can seek to make all of its own inputs (also called "backward integration") and be its own supplier; at the other extreme, it can choose to buy virtually all the inputs it needs and rely on others as suppliers. Partial integration is also possible, with some inputs being bought while others are made.

From the manager's perspective, the benefit of making the inputs is the control maintained over them (in terms of costs, quality, timeliness, and so on). The major costs are the investment and expertise needed to provide these inputs. A benefit of buying is the ability to choose among suppliers and thus avoid the risks associated with the suppliers' businesses. A major cost is this reliance on others for needed inputs. There are, of course, other benefits and costs to be evaluated. The examples given in Exhibit 10.1 indicate the kinds of trade-offs that exist.

EXHIBIT 10.1

SOME MAKE-VERSUS-BUY TRADE-OFFS

	MAKE	BUY
ADVANTAGES	Control over costs	Increased choice
	Control over quality	Business risks down
	Control over delivery	No additional investment
	Manage supply	No need for expertise
	Develop new expertise	
DRAWBACKS	Investment increases	Relies on outsiders
	Need for expertise	Competing for supplies
	Need for management	Supplier may go out of business
	May be inefficient	Overspecialization

The make-or-buy decision is complex in an international company because it has to be made relative both to the company as a whole and to each of its subsidiaries. Many combinations of factors affect this decision. To simplify the matter, we will consider three options:

1. A subsidiary can be vertically integrated itself: that is, it makes its own inputs.

2. A subsidiary can be vertically integrated with other parts of the company: that is, it purchases inputs from other subsidiaries or from the parent.

3. No backward integration occurs: that is, supplies are obtained outside of the company.

Each of these decisions can have different consequences for the subsidiary, its associated subsidiaries, and the company as a whole. For example, consider an Australian wire producer with one subsidiary in Indonesia that assembles cellular phones and a second subsidiary in the U.S. that produces wire used in assembling the phones. The Australian company could supply the Indonesian subsidiary with wire from the U.S. subsidiary, its Australian headquarters, or external sources. The decision has consequences for each of the parties, and the "best" decision can be different for each party.

The Indonesian subsidiary probably wants a stable and cost-effective source of supply. The U.S. subsidiary probably wants sales at the best price it can obtain. And the Australian parent wants to maximize overall returns while minimizing exposure to risk. The difficulty is that these objectives may be achieved in different ways as these scenarios illustrate:

- The Indonesian subsidiary may want to purchase wire from the U.S. subsidiary because of its quality and availability. But the U.S. subsidiary may be able to sell its wire at a better price elsewhere.

- The Australian parent may choose to sell wire to Indonesia itself, at a high price in order to minimize profits in Indonesia. But the Indonesian managers might prefer to purchase inexpensive local wire to maximize local profits.

- The U.S. subsidiary may want to sell to Indonesia because this gives it a known and captive market. But the Indonesian managers might prefer to have the flexibility of buying wire outside of the company to get the best possible price and quality.

These are only a few of the possible management conflicts that can arise. Complicating the decision further are factors besides financial expenditures and returns that need to be taken into account. There are political implications to the decision as well. For example, guidelines and regulations in many countries encourage or specify the use of local suppliers or give preference to suppliers from favored trading partners. Such considerations need to be balanced in making the final choice.

Another factor is the company's political risk-management strategy. This may promote or discourage the use of certain suppliers. In the situation described, the Indonesian government may encourage the use of local suppliers, the U.S. government may have incentives associated with exports to the Far East, and the Australian parent may believe it can minimize its political risk exposure if it controls supplies to Indonesia from Australia. Decisions made in terms of the political situation in one location can also have negative repercussions at home and abroad. For example, if the Australian parent obtained some of its raw materials from Vietnam, and these in turn became components in the telephones assembled in Indonesia and shipped to the U.S., this indirect association with Vietnam could have negative consequences for the U.S. subsidiary selling in the U.S.

The example used here is simple, involving only three locations and one input. For global companies the situation can be more complex, involving a large number of locations, inputs, and potential suppliers.

Clearly, it is difficult to reconcile the various objectives and views that are likely to have an impact on an international manager's choice of suppliers. One approach is to consider the problem initially from the point of view of overall corporate efficiency and develop a procurement model based on costs and efficiencies. This model can then be used as a basis on which to build. Final decisions can be adjusted based on national and political characteristics as well as local, regional, and headquarters' objectives and management preferences. In this way, the trade-offs can be clearly identified and the costs estimated and compared with the benefits.

Overall, the global firm's aim is to obtain inputs from around the world in an efficient manner. The firm wants to ensure that inputs of a desired standard are available when needed and at a competitive cost. Managers have many supply options available to them, and these can give them a competitive advantage. At the same time, the variety of options increases the complexity of the procurement decision. This complexity means that the most efficient procurement decision is not always practical. The procurement decision, therefore, often combines objective programming models and subjective management judgments.

NATIONAL ORIGINS

The vertical integration decision involves issues related to location of suppliers, as the previous examples showed. There are some other considerations as well. In selecting suppliers, whether internal or external, international managers can often choose among suppliers from different nations. This provides both opportunities and difficulties.

Opportunities arise because the manager has a larger base of suppliers from which to select. Suppliers from different locations may offer variations in quality and service, and a manager may be able to match suppliers to the firm's specific needs more exactly than if limited to suppliers from the same country of origin. These variations in quality and service can also be the cause of difficulties because the quality or service offered by suppliers in foreign locations may differ from the manager's expectations. Before selecting a foreign supplier, the manager needs to investigate thoroughly the foreign firm's ability to provide the desired inputs.

Specifications and regulations come into play in this decision as well. Variations in national standards can be important in choosing a supplier. The supplier must comply with its local standards, and these may not correspond with the requirements for another location. For example, the U.S. does not use the metric system while most other countries do. This causes numerous complications for companies that must convert inches to centimeters, gallons to liters, Fahrenheit to Celsius, and so on. The conversion can be crucial when dealing with parts that must fit with precision.

National origin of suppliers can have political and social implications as well. Certain countries may be looked on unfavorably, and any association with suppliers in those countries can have negative repercussions in other locations. Consumer boycotts have often been organized against a company's products because the company uses inputs originating in a foreign location viewed negatively by consumers.

The procurement decision is further complicated when moving products from one country to another requires going through additional countries. Each country's political relationships, regulations, and dependability have to be taken into account. Even relatively minor problems in an intermediary country can disrupt an otherwise efficient and effective procurement system. For example, truckers going from the West Coast of the U.S. to the East Coast sometimes find it convenient to take Canada's Highway 401; but this route involves crossing the border into Canada and back into the U.S. as well as ensuring compliance with Canada's highway regulations, which are different from those in the U.S.

Problems arising in intermediary countries can be particularly difficult to deal with because both the supplier and the buyer may be unfamiliar with the third country. Companies are generally reasonably well-informed about the environments in their home country, and thus they are equipped to operate in this environment and to solve problems as they arise. It is much more difficult to find solutions to problems in an unfamiliar environment. If an Irish supplier of raw materials is selling to a Spanish company, each partner in the transaction faces both a familiar and an unfamiliar environment. The Irish company relies on its Spanish partner to deal with the Spanish environment, and vice versa. If the transaction is complicated by the need to ship the materials through a third country such as France, neither the Irish nor the Spanish company is on home ground, and both may find problems in dealing with this third country. They cannot rely on their instinctive know-how or on established patterns. In this situation the companies need to turn to other parties with the needed expertise in the third country or to develop the expertise themselves. This adds to the cost of doing business together.

TIMING ISSUES

Timing of shipments and receipt of supplies are also important considerations. This is essentially an inventory and stock issue. Companies can choose to maintain varying quantities of needed inputs. The trade-offs are among shipping costs, carrying costs, and the risks of being out of stock of needed items. These are issues faced by all companies, and there are models designed to identify optimum inventory levels. International managers find that the situation is more complex, however, because of border crossings. These can lead to unanticipated delays in transporting products, and such delays cannot always be factored into the inventory equation.

The auto industries of Canada and the United States exemplify the potential difficulties of border crossings. Many U.S. and Canadian auto plants adopted a "just-in-time" inventory system in the late 1980s. This system relies on suppliers getting parts to the plants just in time to be used by the plant. In essence, the auto manufacturers do not keep any inventory on hand. This system is cost-efficient, and because of the trade agreements between Canada and the U.S., parts suppliers in both countries are used, and parts cross the Canada–U.S. border regularly. In 1990 Canadian independent truckers established a blockade of major border crossings on several occasions to protest Canadian trucking regulations. The result for the auto plants was no just-in-time delivery of parts, and several were forced to shut down for several hours, or even days in some cases, until deliveries resumed.

In other cases, handling deliveries may cause difficulties, as the following story illustrates:

> Nigeria probably experienced the largest purchasing blunder. Due to increased oil revenues that resulted from the sharp rise of oil prices in the mid-1970s, Nigeria began to initiate major modernization programs. An economically minded bureaucrat decided to purchase the total amount of cement needed to construct all of the new buildings being planned. Because Nigeria did not have its own cement plant, the cement was ordered from other countries. Soon it began to arrive by the shipload. The dock workers were unable to unload the cement as fast as it arrived, so the ships were forced to await their turn for unloading. Within weeks, there were so many shiploads of unloaded cement that someone computed the length of time required to unload

all of the ships. Even with an expanded dock in Lagos, it was discovered that the 20 million tons of cement could not be fully unloaded for 40 years! Much of the cement had to be dumped overboard; the cost to hold the ships until unloading was greater than the cost of reordering the cement (Ricks 1983, p. 98).

The efficient management of supply networks can contribute greatly to a company's ability to compete internationally, but the previous discussion and examples illustrate some of the complexities inherent in such a network. Designing and managing an effective international supply network is part science and part subjective judgment. Scientific linear programming models can be used to identify optimum solutions, and these can serve as the basis for establishing a network. In order to function in the real world of national boundaries, however, these solutions may need to be modified based on managerial judgments, which are often subjective in nature. A globally efficient sourcing network essentially means that the international company is functioning as a global citizen, but this may conflict with with particular local concerns. International managers are faced with the need to find a balance between global and local needs.

International corporate interactions require careful consideration of all aspects of suppliers and buyers. For example:

> Fruehauf, a large U.S. truck manufacturer, had problems with its French subsidiary because of sales to the People's Republic of China at a time when U.S. regulations prohibited such sales. The Fruehauf subsidiary sold truck bodies to Berliet, an independent French truck manufacturer, who then sold the finished trucks to mainland Chinese. Fruehauf U.S.A. was adjudged in violation of the "Trading with the Enemy Act" because, according to the U.S. government, it had control of the French subsidiary and was therefore responsible for the sale (even though their subsidiary did not sell directly to the Chinese). The French government, on the other hand, held that Fruehauf France would be in violation of French law if it did not honor and fulfill the sales contract to Berliet. The French court took temporary control of Fruehauf's French subsidiary and it suffered substantial monetary losses in a French suit filed by Berliet for default of contract. Fruehauf U.S.A. found itself embroiled in an international political and legal dispute between two governments and lost money and prestige on both sides (Ricks, Fu, & Arpan 1974, p. 55).

PRODUCTION ISSUES

So far we have focused on the acquisition of inputs needed for a product. We will now look at the issues of converting inputs into a final product. Production issues involve the location and type of production facilities as well as coordinating facilities. Before we discuss the different operational strategies that managers can consider and the cost/benefit trade-offs associated with these strategies, we need to identify a concept that increasingly underpins all production decisions: total quality management.

TOTAL QUALITY MANAGEMENT

Total quality management (TQM) has been described as "continuous improvement of every output, whether it be a product or a service, by removing unwanted variation and by improving the underlying work processes" (Tenner & DeToro 1992, p. 24). International managers, like their domestic counterparts, find that incorporating the idea of total quality management into their management process can give a competitive advantage.

A model developed by Tenner and DeToro will be helpful in discussing the process of establishing a competitive advantage through TQM. This model identifies continuous improvement as the essential aim of the firm and proposes three basic ways to achieving this—customer focus, process improvement, and total involvement.

Customer focus means the firm needs to know its customers and what they want in order to provide quality. This may sound simple and self-evident, but it is not always so in reality. The model identifies both internal and external customers and makes the point that within the organization employees serve other employees and that these "internal customers" must be part of the quality process. Tenner and DeToro discuss how to establish the country focus:

> The first step in developing such a framework is to identify the output—a product or service that an individual produces. Next, we pose the question, "Who is the person to whom I will pass this output?" If no person can be identified, then, obviously, scrap is being produced and an immediate decision can be made to stop! . . .

If however, we can identify the person to whom we pass the output of our work, then we can secure from that person a list of needs, expectations, and requirements that we as the supplier must meet (p. 53).

Process improvement is defined as "the sequential integration of people, methods, and machines in an environment to produce value-added outputs for customers" (p. 99). In order to achieve the customer satisfaction that is essential to a customer focus, effective process management is vital. Key processes in the firm have to be identified and analyzed in order to design ways of improving them and maximizing their usefulness.

Total involvement indicates that customer satisfaction and process improvement depend on the efforts of those within the organization as well as those who interact with it. Total involvement focuses on the need to integrate the activities of all the people who contribute to the firm's product or service. Points of focus are senior management leadership, empowering the work force, and establishing quality suppliers.

This brief description of a TQM system illustrates that quality is achieved by clearly understanding the firm's reasons for existing and by identifying how it achieves its objectives. This understanding is even more important in an international firm. The complexities of the international firm's internal and external environment mean that the task is likely to be complicated. In particular, in the international environment, it is important to recognize that "quality" can mean different things to different people. The international firm achieves TQM by identifying both similarities and differences in its worldwide operations and uses these to create quality.

LOCATION OF FACILITIES

Facilities can be located to take advantage of inputs or of markets and can be concentrated or dispersed. We will discuss the trade-offs between these choices.

Inputs versus Markets If sources of inputs are relatively close to major markets, then facilities can be located convenient to both. For many international companies this is not the case because inputs can come from around the world and markets may be in various parts of the world. The major factor that determines the appropriate location of facilities relative to inputs and markets is the ease with which inputs and finished goods can be moved from one location to another. This depends on factors such as mobility, size and weight, ability to withstand transportation, and need to preserve freshness. These factors need to be examined relative to inputs as well as to intermediate and finished products in order to select appropriate locations for production facilities. The following examples illustrate some of these considerations:

- Many products are assembled by unskilled labor in countries where labor costs are low. It is often difficult to move people around the world and if labor is an important input into a product, facilities will generally be located close to the source of the needed labor.

- The wire, beads, and coils used to produce electronic parts are small and easy to transport around the world, as are the finished parts. Companies that assemble these parts often have their facilities located close to labor sources and remote from other inputs and markets.

- Precision scientific equipment often cannot be moved once it is assembled because movement can affect the delicate balance needed for accuracy. Companies that provide such equipment will need to have at least some facilities located close to their customers.

- Produce retains its freshness for only a limited period. Companies that use such produce will tend to locate their facilities close to the source of supply. Many companies that can fruit and vegetables are located in small farming communities where fresh produce can be brought to the factory within hours of harvest.

- Harvesting fresh produce in some developed countries relies on unskilled, low-cost labor, which is unavailable locally. The growing location cannot be changed easily; therefore, seasonal labor is brought from other locations in spite of the difficulties associated with moving people.

- Automobile components are smaller and cheaper to transport than completed automobiles. Components may be produced in a variety of locations to take advantage of local conditions and shipped to a location close to major markets for assembly.

■ Precious stones for jewelry must be obtained in locations where they are available. But they may be shipped to other locations for polishing and setting and to still other locations where the major markets exist.

The previously mentioned U.S. food processor attempting to combine the advantages of a fresh source of supply with ease of shipment to markets illustrates the difficulties inherent in decisions about locations. The company located a cannery at the delta of a river in Mexico which was downstream from a large pineapple plantation. The plan was to barge the ripe fruit downstream for canning, load it directly onto ocean liners, and ship it to the company's various markets. When the pineapples were ripe, the company found itself in trouble: the time of crop maturity coincided with the flood stage of the river. The current in the river during this period was too strong to permit the backhauling of barges upstream. Thus the plan for transporting the fruit with barges could not be implemented. With no alternatively feasible means of transport, the company was forced to close the operation. Its new equipment was sold for five percent of original cost to a Mexican group, which immediately relocated the cannery. A seemingly simple, harmless oversight of weather and navigation conditions became costly and, in fact, the primary cause of major losses to the company (Ricks, Fu, & Arpan 1974, p. 50).

Consider the earlier example of an Australian firm with a subsidiary in Indonesia and sources of raw materials in both Australia and the U.S. If this company sells the finished cellular telephones to a distributor in the U.S., initially it might seem inefficient to locate the main facilities in a third country which is not close to either its sources of physical inputs or its markets. Clearly, however, the main consideration in this situation is the availability of relatively inexpensive labor in Indonesia. The additional costs associated with transporting materials to Indonesia and finished goods to the U.S. are offset by the savings in labor costs. The specific choice of Indonesia, rather than another low-labor-cost country, would be based assessing the actual transportation costs and the reliability of transportation, as well as other benefits and risks associated with alternative locations.

Concentrated versus Dispersed

A concentrated production strategy implies a small number of facilities in a few locations, whereas a dispersed strategy implies a large number of facilities in many locations. Companies can either produce all their products in one location and supply all markets from this location, locate plants strategically in a variety of locations, or produce in each market for that market only. These choices form a continuum, with varying degrees of concentration or dispersion between the extremes. Each strategy has benefits and costs associated with it.

The benefits of a concentrated approach are efficiency and standardization. In concentrated strategy with one, or a few, production facilities, larger quantities are produced in these facilities and efficiencies of scale result in a lower per-unit cost. This strategy usually allows for standardized production processes and procedures, and these result in a simplified administrative system. A concentrated strategy, in some ways, is therefore easier to establish and operate than a dispersed strategy.

From a logistical view, a concentrated strategy means that inputs must be transported to central facilities and final products from these facilities transported to markets. This can add time, expense, and complexity to the production system. The efficiencies and simplicity associated with concentration can be nullified by countering inefficiencies and complexities. The degree to which these offsetting pressures will affect a particular company depends on the specifics of its product and production processes. If its inputs and markets are relatively concentrated, and adaptations are not needed, concentration of production facilities will likely be attractive. If its inputs and/or markets are dispersed, or adaptations are needed, concentration of production facilities will be less attractive.

From a national cultural view, there can be noneconomic considerations that eliminate the benefits of centralization. It can be politically beneficial to engage in local production for some markets and politically unwise to do so in others. A concentrated strategy also means that the company relies on one, or only a few, locations for its production. If these locations should become less attractive for some reason (for example, a negative change in exchange rates, government, employee attitudes, and so on), it can be difficult to shift operations quickly to other locations. If sources of inputs and markets are not politically sensitive and are relatively safe, a concentrated strategy will be attractive. If the reverse is the case, a concentrated strategy will be less attractive.

The benefits of a dispersed production strategy are adaptation and flexibility. Where inputs from suppliers in different countries vary, or products have to be adapted for different markets, standardization is no longer an advantage. In this situation it can be more effective to have production facilities in a variety of locations. This allows the company to take advantage of the opportunities offered by different sources of supply and to cater to the needs of different markets. This strategy can also provide more flexibility because production can be increased or decreased at different locations as circumstances change. If a location becomes less attractive, production can be decreased and the difference made up in another location. This strategy means that the company is less dependent on any one location. In addition, a growing trend appears to be the use of smaller production runs, closer to the user to allow customization of the product for a particular buyer's needs.

The negative side of a dispersed production strategy are possibly higher per-unit costs associated with smaller production quantities and greater administrative complexity because of the need to manage multiple facilities. These disadvantages must be weighed against the benefits. The appropriate choice depends on the specific product, production processes, sources of supply, and markets.

Where firms produce a standardized product for a region or for the entire world market, they may adopt a rationalized production system. In such a system each plant specializes in a particular component which is then provided to the final assembly. This system allows each plant to produce larger quantities and benefit from economies of scale and efficiencies of standardization. Such a system needs to be carefully coordinated because the final product depends on each subsidiary facility providing the appropriate quantity of components, of an acceptable quality, and at the expected time. The system is only as strong as its weakest link.

Type of Facilities

Depending on a firm's choice of production strategy, the appropriate design for facilities will often differ. Centralized strategies will call for large, efficient, standardized, and, probably, automated designs. Dispersed strategies will mean that facilities are smaller and each may be unique in design to meet the special needs of a particular location and product adaptation.

The distinctive characteristics of any location selected need to be considered prior to designing the facilities for that location. These characteristics may be climatic, cultural, physical, or governmental:

- Different climatic conditions can affect the appropriate design of facilities. In the tropics, particularly in developing countries where air conditioning is expensive and unusual, facilities need to be designed to take advantage of cooling breezes. An unfortunate example of a design that fails to do this is a hospital in a small Caribbean island designed by a Canadian architect. The building does not face in an appropriate direction so there is little air circulation. This combined with a black roof, causes temperatures often to soar to well over 100 degrees inside even though the outside temperature is only 80 degrees. Local people joke that the Canadian thought he was designing a hospital to be warm in Canada's north. Unfortunately, patients are often too uncomfortable to consider it a joking matter.

- Different cultural conditions can affect the appropriate design of facilities. In certain Muslim countries, men and women are not permitted to work together, so that facilities have to be designed so that those tasks done by women are separate from those done by men.

- Different physical characteristics of people have to be taken into account in designing appropriate facilities. People in the Far East are, on the whole, relatively short in comparison to North Americans. Facilities that are comfortable for North American employees would likely be unsuitable for employees in the Far East.

- Government regulations can affect the appropriate design of facilities. Some countries require employers to provide separate toilet facilities for male and female employees. In other locations this would be considered wasteful and unnecessary.

L O G I S T I C S

The logistics network or system is the means by which inputs get to the production site and the product gets to the customer. Logistics networks can range from simple to complex. Where inputs are close to production facilities and production takes place close to the market, logistics are likely to be relatively simple. Where production is distant from both sources of supplies and markets, the network is likely to be more complex.

The issues associated with international transportation of finished goods from production site to market are essentially the same as those discussed for transportating inputs to production facilities. It is important to recognize, however, that the specific regulations and requirements that apply to finished goods may be different from those that apply to raw materials or components. For example, shoes imported into Canada at one point were not considered finished goods if they did not have laces and, without laces, they qualified for a lower import duty. One manufacturer reportedly discovered this only at the U.S.–Canada border and quickly hired local high-school students to remove the laces from a shipment of shoes before bringing them into Canada.

The development of reliable, efficient, low-cost transportation such as bulk ocean carriers and air cargo planes has made it possible to move both intermediate goods and finished goods around the world relatively easily. This has increased the flexibility that companies have in selecting sites for their production facilities. Managers in developed countries have come to expect and take for granted the existence of reliable and effective transportation systems, but, in reality, they do not always exist or function as international companies would like. In many of the remote parts of the world and in the less-developed countries, transportation can be inefficient and unreliable. Logistical systems, like rationalized production systems, are only as good as their weakest link. It is important, therefore, that companies examine the details of planned logistical systems to identify the potential problems and bottlenecks. The increased flexibility offered by improved transportation has made logistical networks an integral part of doing business internationally, and these networks can be designed and costed by trained technicians so that efficient choices can be made by global companies. These networks are effective only if all parts fit together and run smoothly. Beautifully designed systems can turn into nightmares when one part ceases to work as it was intended. Delays and problems are common to all transport, and logistical networks need to build in enough slack to accommodate these delays and potential problems.

DIFFERENTIATING GOODS FROM SERVICES

Although goods and services differ in some respects as products, broad operational issues are similar for both. Throughout our discussion in this chapter we have used the term "product" to refer to both goods and services. Nevertheless, it is important for managers to consider the differences between the two because specific operational decisions may be influenced by these differences.

The industrial revolution of the early twentieth century transformed the world from a craft-oriented to an industrial economy. The industrial economy was devoted to producing physical goods in large quantities whereas the craft economy had focused on small-scale production. Many people believe that the current Western economy is a postindustrial one, often described as a service economy devoted to providing intangible benefits, or services. Services are an increasingly important component of the world's economy, and trade in services increased dramatically in the last decades of the twentieth century. This is particularly important to multinational managers because services are especially subject to the impact of cultural and national variations.

Products are a firm's salable outputs. They can be anything: screws and widgets, high-tech medical equipment, costume masks, technical expertise, management services, or energy. A helpful way to differentiate among so many products is to categorize them as goods or services.

Goods are generally thought of as physical products, while services are intangible products. This distinction, as well as some of the relationships between the two, is illustrated by the following:

- Services often accompany goods. If you buy a home computer, you usually purchase software to go with it, and you may buy a service contract that agrees to provide you with maintenance and repair on the machine. The computer is a physical product that you can see and touch; therefore it is a good. The software and the service contract are intangible services.

- Services may compete with goods. You can choose to purchase your own physical computer or you can pay for a computer service to fill your computer needs.

- Some services are by their nature distinct from goods. Management consulting services fall into this category. When you purchase the services of a management consultant, there may be no physical product associated with the service.

The difference between goods and services is not always clear because they can be closely connected. For example, computer software is generally thought of as an intangible and thus is a service. But it is often contained on a disk, which can be thought of as a physical product. In the case of the management consultant, a report may be produced that could be considered a physical product.

Services are sometimes described in terms of the personal character of these products: that is, services are very often carried out by people. The personal nature of services is important in the global operational context. Expectations regarding "good service" are likely to differ from one location to another because of national and cultural characteristics. Similarly, expectations regarding service characteristics and service levels may differ. For example, the service contract on your personal computer might include regular maintenance, emergency repair, and replacement of faulty parts (these would be the characteristics of the service). This could mean monthly maintenance, one-day repairs, and no-cost replacement of parts, or it could mean yearly maintenance, two-week repairs, and replacement of parts at cost—depending on the location.

Consider the following illustrations of how services may differ because of national and cultural variations:

- In the case of the computer and computer service, the computer (physical good) will be relatively similar from one location to another except for technical changes. Modifications may be needed for use in different countries, but because of the physical nature of the modifications, they can be objectively identified. The service (intangible good) that is expected and accepted, because of national and cultural characteristics, tends to be more subjective, and, therefore, the modifications may be more difficult to identify. For example, in some locations, a lone serviceman may be allowed into the home to service the machine; in other locations this would violate a social norm. In some locations a woman as service person would be welcomed; in others she would not be accepted. In some locations immediate service would be expected; in others it would not.

- In the case of management consulting services, approaches can differ strikingly depending on local management practices. Access to information, interactions between consultant and client employees, consultant-client relationships, issues of confidentiality, and the like may all vary. These unique aspects to providing this intangible good are inherent to its success or failure. For example, in some places talking about sensitive issues over the telephone is considered undesirable. A consultant from a culture where this was not the case might easily make the unforgivable mistake of doing this and thus alienate a client.

SUMMARY

Operational decisions can be both strategic and tactical, and they usually involve trade-offs. The effective international manager recognizes the need for trade-offs and seeks the optimum balance. Throughout the chapter the suggestion has been made that managers begin with models intended to design efficient systems then temper these with judgments about the political and cultural realities of the world.

The chapter considered operations from the supply side and from the production side. The supply side was discussed in terms of procurement of needed inputs. The production side was discussed in terms of locating and coordinating facilities. Finally logistical networks were examined. The chapter concluded by drawing attention to differences between goods and services and illustrating how these differences might affect global operational decisions. Throughout, the cost/benefit trade-offs inherent in various choices were examined.

DISCUSSION QUESTIONS

1. Both goods and services can be imported or exported. Identify and discuss some of the likely differences in exporting a good (physical product) versus a service.

2. Discuss how the North American Free Trade Agreement is likely to influence decisions regarding facility locations within North America.

3. Assume you are exporting a perishable product from the United States to the People's Republic of China. Identify the various options available and discuss the advantages and disadvantages of each.

REFERENCES

Boddewyn, J.J., M.B. Hallbrich, & A.C. Perry. 1986. Service multinationals: Conceptualization, measurement and theory. *Journal of International Business Studies*, 17 (3), pp. 41–58.

Cohen, M.A., M. Fisher, & R. Jaikumar. 1989. "International manufacturing and distribution networks: A normative model framework," in K. Ferdows (ed.) *Managing International Manufacturing*. Amsterdam: North-Holland.

Dunning, J. 1981. *International Production and the Multinational Enterprise*. London: George Allen and Unwin.

Dunning, J. 1981. "The eclectic paradigm of international production: Restatement and some possible extensions." *Journal of International Business Research*, 19 (1), pp. 1–32.

Foulkes, F.K. & J.L. Hirsch. 1984. "People make robots work." *Harvard Business Review*, January–February, pp. 94–102.

Garvin, D.A. 1983. "Quality on the line." *Harvard Business Review*, September–October, pp. 64–75.

Kotabe, M. & G.S. Omura. 1989. "Sourcing strategies of European and Japanese multinationals: A comparison." *Journal of International Business Studies*, 20 (1), pp. 113–130.

Mascarenhas, B. 1984. "The coordination of manufacturing interdependence in multinational companies." *Journal of International Business Studies*, 15 (3), pp. 91–106.

Mefford, R.N. 1986. "Determinants of productivity differences in international manufacturing." *Journal of International Business Studies*, 17 (1), pp. 63–82.

Poynter, T.A. & A. Rugman. 1982. "World product mandates: How will multinationals respond?" *Business Quarterly*, October, pp. 54–61.

Prahalad, C. & Y. Doz. 1987. The *Multinational Mission: Balancing Local Demands and Global Vision*. New York: The Free Press.

Ricks, D.A. 1983. Homewood, IL: Dow-Jones Irwin.

Ricks, D.A., M. Fu & J. Arpan. 1974. *International Business Blunders*, Columbus, OH: Grid.

Tenner, A.R. & I.J. DeToro. 1992. *Total Quality Management.*, pp. 24; 53; 99. Reading, MA: Addison-Wesley Publishing Company, Inc. Reprinted by permission of the publisher.

11

ORGANIZING

AND CONTROL

IN GLOBAL

ORGANIZATIONS

LEARNING OBJECTIVES

IN THIS CHAPTER WE WILL EXPLORE:

- The relationship of organizational structure to control systems

- North American international organizational structures

- Non-North American organizational structures

- Reasons for control systems

- How effective controls change because of national and cultural differences

- International differences in accounting and auditing

- International differences in plans, policies, and procedures

- The role of bureaucracy in international control

- The role of organizational culture in international control

- Benefits and drawbacks of international centralization

- Adapting information systems to international needs

- Components of effective performance evaluation in international firms

KEY DISCUSSION TOPICS:

- The rationale for different organizational structures

- The typical development of North American international firms

- The nature of control in international contexts

- The determinants of effective control systems

- Fitting control systems to management structures

- Mechanisms for implementing controls

- The effective use of information systems

- The effective use of performance evaluation systems

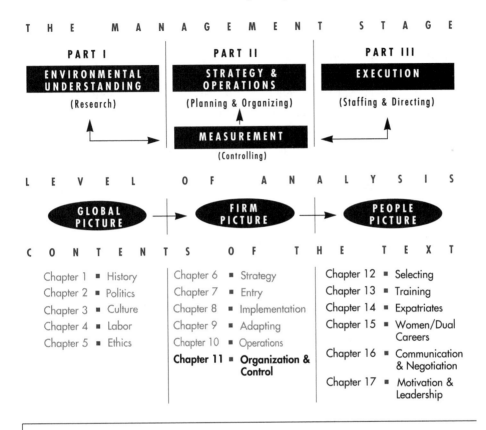

THE MANAGEMENT STAGE

PART I
ENVIRONMENTAL UNDERSTANDING
(Research)

PART II
STRATEGY & OPERATIONS
(Planning & Organizing)

PART III
EXECUTION
(Staffing & Directing)

MEASUREMENT
(Controlling)

LEVEL OF ANALYSIS

GLOBAL PICTURE → FIRM PICTURE → PEOPLE PICTURE

CONTENTS OF THE TEXT

INTRODUCTION

Organizational structure and effective control systems are considered together in this chapter because we believe that they are closely related. Typically, the management process is described as consisting of planning, organizing, staffing, and controlling. While we include discussions of all these aspects of management, we have focused largely on planning (with organizing and controlling as part of this) and staffing.

Organizing may be thought of as providing the framework that allows strategy to be carried out, and controlling as providing the mechanisms that allow management to ensure that strategies are accomplished. The controls used in an international firm will, to some extent, be determined by the organizational structure a firm chooses. This chapter will describe these two functions of the management process and relate them to each other.

First we will consider the typical development of organizational structure in North American firms and examine a number of different international structures that are fairly common among global organizations. We also look at alternative ways of structuring organizations and the relationship of structure to the control process. The second main topic of this chapter is the issue of control. The control process is intended to compare actual activities with planned activities. Organizations use the control process to keep them on track in achieving their objectives. Planning and controlling are therefore closely linked. The planning process sets forth the strategies and goals of the organization as well as the means for attaining them. The control process measures progress toward goals, identifies deviations, and attempts to identify their causes. The control process alerts management when corrective action is needed or when strategies and goals, or the means for attaining them, need to be reevaluated.

Control is fundamental to effective operations in any organization because it keeps the enterprise within a manageable range of planned results. It is of particular importance in international firms because of the complexity of their operations and the physical and cultural distance between their parts. The international business, operating in a variety of locations, can easily find its varying operations acting on their own with little regard for the business as a whole. A good control system can help minimize the degree to which this occurs.

Control systems consist of a variety of measures that are designed to systematically evaluate actual performance relative to desired or planned performance. This evaluation can employ personal observations and written and verbal communication. Choosing the best control methods for an international firm includes considering the complexities of the cultural and national differences that exist. Control systems need to be designed so that they are compatible with cultural and national requirements in different locations.

We begin with a general discussion of the need for and importance of international controls, as well as the characteristics of effective control systems. We will then identify accounting and auditing controls; discuss plans, policies, and procedures as control mechanisms; compare bureaucratic controls with control through corporate culture; and look at the issues of centralization and decentralization of control. Information flows and their importance in effective control are also discussed. Finally, managerial performance evaluation and some of the complexities associated with evaluation on a global scale is reviewed.

ORGANIZATIONAL STRUCTURE

The structure of an organization is fundamental to its ability to achieve its goals effectively; thus, the structure provides a framework for control for the firm. The structure of the organization ensures that the work to be performed is identified and broken into manageable units, that these units are meaningfully related to each other, and that desired communication among these units can take place. Organizations need a defined structure in order to accomplish their chosen strategy. Designing the formal structure of an organization is like designing the structure of a building. A building's structure depends on the purpose of the building, and a building functions well when its structure is appropriate for its purpose. For example, a hospital needs to be different from a school, which, in turn, must be different from a home. In much the same way, organizations can be structured in different ways to accomplish varied purposes. An organization that is primarily a distributor will have a different structure from one predominately focused on research. This will be true of domestic organizations as well as international ones. International structures are further differentiated by the need to standardize or adapt various aspects of the organization and its outputs around the world.

TYPICAL DEVELOPMENT OF NORTH AMERICAN INTERNATIONAL COMPANIES

Although organizations have unique structures, a structural development typical in North American companies consists of four stages: export structures, international division, global structures, and multidimensional structures. These are presented here as sequential, in fact, and they follow in sequence for many companies, though this is necessary. Some companies do not move beyond stage one or two; others bypass these altogether.

Export Structures. From a structural point of view, exports may be either fortuitous or intentional. Each of these alternatives suggests a different structure to be effective. In many instances, fortuitous exports lead to intentional exports, and many companies begin with the former and move to the latter.

With Fortuitous exports, the exporting company does not seek export opportunities. Rather, it is approached by foreign customers, and the company decides to take advantage of a specific export opportunity. In the case of fortuitous exports, there is little need for a formal, permanent adjustment to the company's structure. There is, however, a need to make sure that the exports are taken care of in a timely and efficient manner. Most companies think of this as a temporary situation and delegate someone in marketing or operations to deal with fortuitous exports.

The choice between marketing and operations is an interesting one. If the export function is seen as lying within marketing, this indicates that the company will focus on selling its product in foreign markets. If the export function is seen as lying within the operations, this indicates a concern with allocating production for exports, with little focus on selling in these markets. The first may lead to a greater emphasis on developing foreign markets. The second may be more appropriate where modifications in the product are necessary to make it appropriate for foreign markets.

Once a company has been successful in supplying foreign markets that became available fortuitously, it often begins to see the potential opportunities in export markets and seeks out new ones. Once the export strategy becomes deliberate, a company is likely to make a formal, permanent adjustment in its organizational structure: most often, it creates an export function or department that coexists with the traditional organizational structure. This new unit can be added to either a functional or a divisional structure as illustrated in Exhibit 11.1.

EXHIBIT 11.1

STRUCTURE INCORPORATING EXPORTS

C E O

Marketing & Sales	Operations	R&D		Finance & Admin.
				Exports

C E O

Paper Cups	Laundry Detergent	Light Bulbs
		Exports

In either case, although exports may appear to be on a level with other important functional or divisional priorities, this is often not the case in reality. Exports at this stage of organizational development may receive a lower priority than other organizational considerations. In this structure, the primary business is still domestic, and this is seen as the main priority.

In a functional organization, each function is primarily concerned with its specialization relative to domestic interests, and little attention goes to the export opportunities. In a divisional organization, similarly, the concern is with the product in a domestic context (or with a particular region, in a regionally organized company), and less attention is likely to be paid to the export context. Executives in this situation see little need to develop expertise in foreign markets. This is appropriate for a company that is almost fully occupied by domestic interests. Where a company's strategy recognizes foreign opportunities but is not currently anxious to pursue these, then an export structure is often appropriate.

International Division. Many companies move to an international division structure as foreign opportunities become more interesting from a strategic point of view. An international division structure implies a change in strategic focus to an increased emphasis on international opportunities. This means a conscious intent to seek not only exports but other international involvement as well. A typical international division structure is pictured in Exhibit 11.2.

EXHIBIT 11.2

STRUCTURE INCORPORATING

INTERNATIONAL DIVISION

C E O

| Product A | Product B | Product C | International Division |

International divisions are generally on the same level as other corporate divisions. This structure implies a fair degree of power for the international division, and it concentrates the international expertise in the company. In many cases, international opportunities remain relatively less important than domestic ones; in effect, they are separated and somewhat isolated and may lose out to their domestic counterparts when corporate trade-offs are required.

The international division structure increases the focus on international opportunities, but the international division is responsible for all product groups marketed or produced outside of the domestic area. This generally means that intensive development of international opportunities is complex because of the need to coordinate international requirements with domestic divisions and functional activities. Product development, research, and marketing resources are often scarce for the international arena. The focus of such firms remains on domestic interests and opportunities.

Many companies establish an international division and retain this structure for an extended period of time. This structure is appropriate for a company that recognizes there are international opportunities that require specialized attention, but believes there are better domestic opportunities yet to be exploited. This structure is an intermediary stage between the essentially domestic company and the international company.

Global Structures. A global structure can take the same forms as the domestic ones described earlier, except that the company's strategic view now includes the entire world not just the domestic realm. A global regional structure pictured in Exhibit 11.3 illustrates this international focus. In this structure, the world as a whole is divided into regions, and domestic interests are one of many.

A global product division structure would look identical at the top level to the structure for a domestic one, but each product would have a foreign as well as domestic mandate. Similarly, a global functional structure would have similar

EXHIBIT 11.3

GLOBAL REGIONAL STRUCTURE

CEO

| North America | South East Asia | Africa | Europe |

functions to those in a domestic company, but functional responsibilities would be worldwide.

A global structure becomes appropriate when global opportunities and interests become as important as domestic ones. This can become visible in several ways:

- International sales or profits are increasing faster than domestic sales or profits.

- International sales account for 50 percent of total sales;

- The international division is as large (in terms of investment, employees, assets, or other appropriate measures of size) as the largest product division.

- International experience and expertise have been developed by top executives.

Three primary types of global structures can be identified: a global functional structure, a global product structure, and a global area structure. Each of these is discussed in the following sections in terms of their advantages and disadvantages.

1. A global functional structure is typical of extractive industries (mining, oil, and gas) where the need for functional know-how is paramount to success, and functional expertise is appropriate on a worldwide basis. For example, exploration and refining of oil tends to be the same around the world, and oil companies depend extensively on this expertise. Thus, a global functional structure is appropriate for a company in one of these industries.

   Global functional structures tend to be cumbersome and ineffective for most companies because functional needs tend to differ by product and by geographic region in most situations. For example, production processes tend to vary and need different expertise from product to product and region to region. Similarly, marketing differs from product to product and region to region. These differing needs lead many companies to adopt a global divisional structure, focused on products or geographic areas.

2. A global product structure is typical of companies with a varied product line in which each product can be produced and marketed in a similar fashion around the world. The varied product line suggests a need for differentiated technologies and different end users for each product line, but global standardization within product lines. For example, a company that produces and sells calculators and coffee beans would likely find that these two products needed separate expertise to produce and sell, but that each could be produced and sold in a similar fashion globally.

The global product structure allows the company to focus on the differing needs of each product group and to put primary emphasis on serving these product needs. It encourages the company to overlook regional and cultural differences and may thus create problems. This structure can also lead to duplication of corporate activities, and consequent inefficiencies, within regions. In the example above, the company could have separate facilities for calculators and coffee beans in the same location, and these might duplicate each other in some ways.

3. A global area (or regional) structure is typical of companies with relatively narrow product lines that need to be differentiated regionally. The narrow product line suggests that all products require essentially the same expertise, but that in different regions the same product has varied uses and so needs to be distributed and marketed differently. For example, a company that produces and markets bicycles and small wagons could use the same technology for making each product around the world, but would find that the uses and appropriate marketing practices differ depending on region. Bicycles would have to be marketed as a recreational vehicle in some areas and as a primary means of transportation in others. Similarly, wagons might be considered toys in some areas and work tools in others.

The global area structure allows the company to focus on regional differences and integrate facilities regionally. It optimizes operations in any region and allows the company to develop approaches that are consistent with regional conditions. At the same time this structure encourages a focus on areas rather than products. This entails less focus on product groups and their needs. Therefore R&D may be duplicated, and products developed in one area may not be introduced in other areas. Overall, the area focus may discourage a globally integrated approach to operations.

In the case of bicycles and wagons, in an area structure the company would likely produce and market both products in every region. Insofar as production and marketing required similar expertise, this would be effective. But this approach becomes less effective if this is not so. If, for example, wagons are sold as toys for children and bicycles are sold as transportation for adults, then the marketing approaches might differ. In fact, global structures can be a mixture of functions, product groups, and geographic regions depending on the company's global strategy.

Multidimensional Structures. The need to coordinate functional, product, and area needs leads to trade-offs and modifications in the organization. The choices are usually pragmatic and may not be simple and straightforward. A company may have some product lines where a functional structure would seem appropriate, others where a product structure would be the best choice, and still others where an area structure might be preferred. In addition, more than one priority—function, product, or area—may exist at the same time. This has led to multidimensional structures which attempt to give equal weight to more than one organizational activity or to coordinate action among activities.

The matrix structure is one such multidimensional structure. The most common international matrix combines product and area priorities. A matrix structure allows the company to focus on its product groups and the associated efficiencies while still acknowledging the need for differentiation among different geographic areas. An example of a matrix structure is presented in Exhibit 11.4.

Coordinating committees are an alternative choice to the matrix. In a global product structure an area committee would provide input and advice to product decisions regarding regional needs. In a global area structure a product committee would provide input and advice to area decisions regarding product needs.

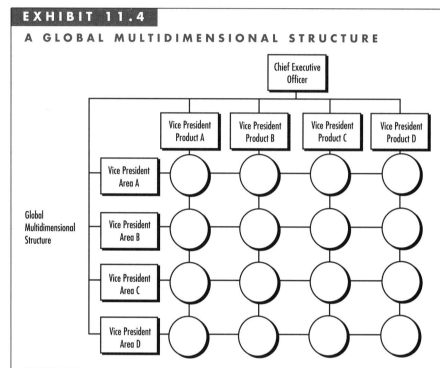

EXHIBIT 11.4

A GLOBAL MULTIDIMENSIONAL STRUCTURE

Global Multidimensional Structure

ALTERNATIVE STRUCTURES

The previous discussion focused on organizational structures likely to occur in North American international companies. It is important, however, for North American managers to realize that other cultures may have different ways of controlling through systems of power, responsibility, and authority, and therefore organizations can be structured in different but equally valid ways.

For example, European companies tend to use a national subsidiary ("mother-daughter") structure (Ronen 1986). This structure treats each subsidiary as a separate entity and each subsidiary reports directly to top management. This approach allows each subsidiary substantial autonomy. The drawback is the difficulty in adequately integrating activities.

Centrally planned economies such as China have organizational structures that interweave various levels of government with the industrial organization. It is difficult for Westerners to understand what, if any, organizational structure exists in some less developed countries. For example, the owner may be the only manager in a vast enterprise, or the extended family of the owners may "manage" the firm even though they don't actually work there.

Actually, the concept of a formal structure appears to some extent to be a Western organizational concept. In some countries the hierarchy, responsibility, and accountability can be implicit and flexible. This approach gives a company flexibility that is often not available in more structured organizations. The lack of formal structure is often frustrating to a foreigner because it is difficult to identify who has responsibility and authority for particular decisions and who reports to whom. In fact, in an unstructured organization, these relationships may change from day to day depending on circumstances which a North American can have difficulty interpreting.

A lack of formal organizational structure in a foreign location should not be construed as a lack of organization. It means only that the basis for organization is different and needs to be understood and interpreted within the cultural environment.

Furthermore, the typical hierarchy found in a North American company may not be found elsewhere. It is conceivable to have a corporate dictatorship with one person in charge, no middle management, and all employees at the same level. It is equally conceivable that power at the top level might be shared by several people, or that middle management (in North American terms) would be fat while other levels were thin. Communication and reporting relationships can also differ: top management can communicate directly with low-level employees; top management can be made up of several individuals who communicate with each other—then one of these persons communicates with lower levels; or top management can wait for communication from lower levels then respond.

RELATING ORGANIZATIONAL STRUCTURE TO CONTROLS

An organization's structure to a large extent determines what types of control systems will be effective. A structure appropriate for the organization's strategy facilitates implementing appropriate controls. The structure of the organization also influences the direction and flow of information.

A control system needs, therefore, to be designed in the context of the whole organization's structure. The organization's structure evolves as the firm's strategy evolves, and control systems need to change to be compatible with this evolution.

The complex issues faced by international firms both in designing an appropriate structure and an effective control system require that the two must be carefully constructed to be complementary and contribute to the overall effectiveness of the organization. An international firm may occasionally achieve its chosen strategy by chance, but it needs to rely on careful planning to be consistently successful. Effective design of international organizational structure and control systems enables the international firm to control its own destiny rather than rely on chance.

THE IMPORTANCE OF CONTROLS

Controls increase in importance as firms increase in internal complexity and face increasingly complex external environments. In addition, control is particularly relevant where a substantial degree of delegation of authority is required and where the environment is changing frequently. All of these factors contribute to a need for a formal system of controls to ensure that the firm is moving in the desired direction.

A complex internal organization that involves substantial delegation of authority provides many opportunities for individuals or groups to act in ways that are not consistent with the organization's goals, either intentionally or unwittingly. An effective system of controls limits the likelihood of this happening by measuring deviations from plans and alerting managers to these deviations. A complex external environment that is changing can make it difficult to achieve desired targets, but can also provide new and unforeseen opportunities. An effective system of controls identifies deviations in time to take corrective action or to change goals to take advantage of new opportunities.

Global business, by its nature, embodies these characteristics. Companies are complex internally because of differing activities in locations around the world. Authority has to be delegated to managers in foreign locations. The external environment is complex because of varying cultural and national characteristics, and the overall environment is likely to be constantly changing because changes in any location can affect operations in other locations. In addition, shifting currency relationships can alter the enterprise's priorities and choices. The nature of global business, therefore, underscores the need for effective control systems in global companies.

The global firm operates in distant countries with diverse and changing environments and relies on people of many nationalities to achieve its plans. This underscores the need for control to an even greater degree than for its domestic counterpart. These conditions also make it more difficult to achieve effective control. In order to design a good international control system, several characteristics of control systems, in general, need to be kept in mind.

CHARACTERISTICS OF AN EFFECTIVE CONTROL SYSTEM

Certain characteristics contribute to the effectiveness of organizational controls. We will discuss seven characteristics that have an international emphasis.

1. *Accuracy*. Information on performance clearly must be accurate if it is to identify whether actual performance conforms with expected performance. Inaccurate information can lead to a false sense of security or corrective action where none is needed. What is measured and how it is measured must therefore be clearly defined in an effective control system.

   Accuracy can be difficult to achieve in international operations because accuracy can mean different things to different people or different groups. For example, the head office may expect subsidiaries to report exact expenditures, while managers and employees at some subsidiaries may be accustomed to rounding all expenditures upwards. Changes in uncontrollable variables such as exchange rates and inflation can also influence accuracy. For example, a subsidiary may forecast its budget needs in local currency;

the U.S. head office translates this figure into U.S. dollars and puts aside U.S. dollars for subsidiary use. If a devaluation of the U.S. dollar relative to the local currency occurs, the amount put aside is no longer adequate when translated to local currency.

In addition, systems of measurement vary and particular measurement approaches may be unfamiliar to some people. As a result, "what is measured" and "how it is measured" may have to be defined differently for different locations. Before selecting a system of measurement for a particular location, a pre-test is often appropriate to discover if problems associated with its use.

2. *Timeliness*. Information is only useful if it is available in time for managers to take corrective action or make appropriate changes in strategy. Late information can result in inappropriate responses or no action at all. When results are measured and how quickly they are reported is therefore critical to an effective control system.

Timeliness can be difficult to achieve in international companies because of geographic distance and cultural or national differences. There may be delays in getting information because of the physical distance that the information has to travel (for example, mail delays, telephone delays, airline delays). Delay is further complicated by time zone shifts that affect when different parts of the enterprise are open for business.

Delays can also be attributed to cultural attitudes regarding time or local restrictions and regulations. For example, Latin Americans are often described as more relaxed about time than North Americans. (This is often referred to as a *"mañana"* approach which implies putting off until tomorrow whatever does not have to be done today.) These different attitudes toward time are reflected in public clocks in the United States and various Latin American countries: U.S. clocks are significantly more accurate than those in Latin America. U.S. managers often appear overanxious, rushed, and insensitive to those who do not see exact time schedules as important. North Americans and Latin Americans are likely to disagree about what constitutes timeliness in a given situation.

Decisions regarding when information is measured and how it is reported should take these potential delays into account in order to ensure timeliness. Many iterations of the process may be needed to work out appropriate time frames.

3. *Objectivity*. Information must be as objective as possible to be useful in indicating corrective action: that is, it should reflect observable facts as much as possible rather than be limited to personal descriptions and opinions. Personal opinions can be biased, either consciously or unconsciously, and can affect the accuracy of information. Wherever possible, therefore, objective measures are preferred. Where subjective measures are needed because of the nature of the information, then the possibility of bias should be kept in mind.

Objectivity may be difficult to ensure internationally because perceptual biases are likely to exist and to influence even seemingly objective measures of performance. Cultural and national differences can make it particularly hard to identify when and in what direction information may be biased. Special care needs to be taken to identify measures of performance that are not easily influenced by personal opinions and to evaluate the information provided for possible inaccuracies.

4. *Acceptability*. A control system works only as well as the people who maintain it. If a system is unacceptable to the members of the organization, they may ignore or sabotage it, or comply with it unwillingly. In any of these cases the information provided is likely to be inaccurate, untimely, and subjective. A good control system, therefore, is designed with the users in mind.

This may be complex in a global company. Because of cultural and national differences, what is acceptable in one location may not be in another. For example, written reports may be normal in North America but unusual in a country where literacy is low or where paper is scarce. Control systems may have to be tailored to the specific needs of different locations in order to be accepted and thus useful. If this is the case, then the company faces the challenge of finding ways of making the different forms of information comparable.

5. *Understandability*. Information is only useful if it is understandable and can be readily interpreted by those who will use it. Information that is difficult to understand is frustrating and annoying. It can be misunderstood and lead to mistaken actions, or it may be ignored. Ensuring that the information provided by a control system is clear is thus an important aspect of designing an effective system.

This can be complex. Different locations have varied ways of collecting and reporting information, and what is clear and easy to understand in one location may be virtually incomprehensible in another location. For example:

- One system can report all sales and costs as total figures where another breaks these down item by item.

- Sales and costs can be reported as currency amounts or as percentages.

- Budgets can be in currency amounts or expressed as percentages.

- Transactions may be completed in currencies of the local company or of the head office, in U.S. $, or in some combination of these.

The effective international control system must be designed to overcome these variations, either by translating information into appropriate formats or by training people to understand a standard format. In some cases both translation and training may be required.

6. *Cost Effectiveness*. A good control system needs to provide greater benefits than the cost of implementing and maintaining the system. Benefits include improved management decisions based on the information the system provides. The system should also be compatible with the organization: that is, the effort of maintaining the system needs to be reasonable. If the costs in terms of employees' time and effort are excessive, there is no gain from the system. Therefore, these should be carefully evaluated.

The fit between the control system and the management structure it is designed to support is important. To evaluate this fit, costs associated with implementing and maintaining an international control system must be carefully evaluated. These are not always obvious because of the complications associated with such systems. The system may therefore have to modified over time as the costs become clear and a realistic cost/benefit evaluation can be made.

7. *Firm specificity*. An effective control system is designed in response to a firm's unique characteristics. Information is provided on performance areas that are important to the firm's overall success but not on other areas. The information is derived from the firm's normal work patterns and does not disrupt operations.

Global firms can have vastly different operations around the world, and the appropriate controls are likely to vary around the world because of this. At the same time, a global company is concerned with controlling its overall operations. An effective control system incorporates a delicate balance between standardization and adaptation. Such a system adapts to local needs as necessary, but still maintains an overall global view of the company.

Creating a control system involves these basic steps:

- Decide on desired final results.

- Identify interim results that will lead to desired final results.

- Establish standards for interim results.

- Collect data and compare with standards.

- Identify causes of deviations.

- Take corrective action.

- Compare actual results with expectations.

- Review plans and goals for the next cycle.

Although this sounds as though the control system has a beginning and end, it is really a continuous system because actual results at any stage can lead to changes in plans or activities, and shorter-term results serve to modify or change longer-term plans. In addition, the control system itself is constantly monitored for effectiveness and can be modified or changed to increase its usefulness.

CONTROL MECHANISMS

A company has many ways to control operations. Some of these mechanisms involve accounting. Other mechanisms include planning or the use of policies and procedures.

INTERNATIONAL ACCOUNTING AND AUDITING CONTROLS

Accounting and auditing controls are a fundamental part of any company's control system. They are designed to measure the financial results of activities over a period of time and to identify and evaluate resources at a particular point in time. These financial measures allow managers to compare actual results with anticipated ones.

Accounting information is historical in nature. It is based on activities that have already occurred and it documents past performance. It reports assets, revenues, and inflows of money into an organization and liabilities, costs, and outflows of funds. The basic purpose of accounting information is to provide a picture of the firm's financial position, so that the firm's managers can evaluate and monitor its financial performance. As such, accounting systems are clearly control systems. Their function is the same in an international company as in a domestic company. However, in international situations controls are much more complex because accounting procedures and standards vary around the world.

An audit checks or verifies the information provided by accounting statements. The audit information is intended to determine whether operational and financial controls are being followed and serves the shareholders. Audits focus on the reliability and validity of reported financial information. An audit, therefore, is essentially a control mechanism to check on the firm's control systems. Audits are used for the same purpose worldwide, though auditing and accounting procedures and standards can vary widely around the world.

It is beyond the scope of this text to discuss international accounting and auditing in any depth. Rather, our discussion will point out some of the complex issues relative to international accounting and auditing controls.

Legal requirements for the reporting of financial information vary from country to country. Variations occur in the specific information that a firm is required to document, the timing of information gathering, and the public availability of such information. The international company must comply with different regulations in different countries. At the same time the company needs to ensure that it has access to the information required to make informed decisions. Here are two excerpts from articles in *The Bottom Line* that indicate some of the changes that are taking place in the area of reporting:

> . . . the U.K. accounting profession is putting together what are potentially the most radical changes to financial reporting for decades. The Accounting Standards Board, which reports to Eearing's Financial Reporting Council, is now having bi-weekly meetings to work out what the basic changes should be. The results of this period of brainstorming will filter through early next year and be translated into practical suggestions (Bruce 1990, p. 6).

> Some of the themes emerging at this year's conference were increasing globalization, the drive toward harmonized standards and the need to provide training and development for accounting professionals that can adapt to changing needs (Streuck 1990, p. 19).

Cultural differences can result in different attitudes toward collecting and documentating of financial information. These differences influence the ease with which information can be obtained, and sometimes its reliability. For example, in some Asian countries asking for proof of someone's statement is insulting because it implies that he or she could be dishonest. This makes it difficult to obtain objective evidence to corroborate stated assertions.

A comparison of Ford's collection and reporting of information in Australia and in the United States provides a good example of how cultural differences can affect financial reporting. Ford monitors gasoline prices as an indicator of motor car demand and sales. While Ford Australia collects data in terms of Australian cents per liter, Ford U.S. collects data in U.S. cents per U.S. gallon (which is different from an Imperial gallon formerly used in Australia). Ford Australia collects sales figures in monthly reporting periods while Ford U.S. collects them in ten-day periods. Ford Australia classifies cars into five categories—small-light, large-light, medium, upper-medium, and luxury/specialty—on the basis of size, engine power, and weight. Ford U.S., using the same factors, has six classes, A through F.

Business practices that differ from one location to another make uniform accounting practices impossible. The same information may simply not be available in different locations. For example, cancelled checks are normally returned to the issuer in some countries but in others they become the property of the bank. Similarly, receipts can be difficult to obtain in countries where they are infrequently required.

Illegal activities create additional difficulties. In some countries it may be normal to engage in black-market or unreported activities of various kinds. By their nature these transactions will not be formally reported in those countries by local managers. In addition, the Foreign Corrupt Practices Act (FCPA) in the U.S., and similar legislation elsewhere, requires that all transactions, including illegal ones, be reported. The FCPA also makes such activities on the part of a U.S. company or U.S. national illegal, no matter where they occur.

Communication difficulties can be numerous, ranging from different spoken and written languages, to mail delays and inadequate telephone service, to different time zones with little effective overlap. Any or all of these can make the gathering of accounting and auditing information complex, particularly when the information claims to be accurate as of a specific point in time.

International companies often have peculiar financial information needs that differ from their domestic counterparts. Financial information is often required on a country, regional, and global basis. Performance in each distinct location may need to be assessed as well as the impact of one location's performance on other locations. Finally, these all have to be integrated in order to judge the company's global performance. Performance at all levels is partially a function of allocated costs between units or from the parent. Currency fluctuations can determine where profits appear without regard for actual management performance.

While accounting and auditing reports form a substantial part of most company's control system, they are by no means the only part. The next section of the chapter examines additional control mechanisms.

INTERNATIONAL CONTROL THROUGH PLANS, POLICIES, AND PROCEDURES

Companies rely on a their formal plans as well as a system of policies and procedures to ensure that activities throughout the organization conform to expectations and accepted standards. Global companies can also achieve a degree of control through plans, policies and procedures.

Plans and control. Planning and control are closely linked. The firm's plan is the yardstick by which success or failure is often measured. Achieving planned objectives is interpreted as success while failing to achieve these must be explained by those responsible for the results.

Global firms frequently have long-term strategic plans stretching ten, twenty, or more years into the future; these plans guide their activities. They also have shorter-term business plans for the immediate future, which serve as a specific guide for the activities of each unit of the organization. It is primarily these short-term plans that serve as a control mechanism.

Plans incorporate specific objectives and goals as well as time frames for achieving them. Typically, objectives and goals are stated and measured in terms of profitability, market share, sales growth, levels of expenditure, production volumes, quality levels, employment levels, investments, and other similar items. These are identified for the company as a whole and for the individual units. The degree of autonomy and authority in various locations is often identified as well, and a budget allocated for each unit. This budget may be allocated to specific activities within a given unit.

Performance on the stated objectives and goals can be measured at predetermined intervals when actual achievements are compared with expectations. The plan, combined with periodic measurement of results, functions as a control system. If actual results differ from those needed to achieve the plan, corrective action can be taken in a timely manner.

Plans of this type are developed specifically for each unit or location, and therefore the differing characteristics of each can be taken into account. These plans are usually best developed with input from top management, regional managers, and managers at the local level. This ensures that all viewpoints are represented and that all levels have agreed to the specific objectives and goals identified in the plan. Top management provides the global view of the firm and ensures that a particular unit's activities contribute to the firm's global objectives. Regional managers are acutely aware of the interactions among units at the regional level and can ensure that the activities of various units contribute positively, where possible, to regional performance and do not negatively impact on others. Local managers are likely to be best informed about local conditions and able to decide what is or is not possible given the local environment.

Policies and procedures and control. Policies and procedures are established by management to channel the thinking and behavior of organization members so that it is consistent with global organization objectives. Policies and procedures thus act as a control over organizational activities. A policy is a general guideline that directs decision making. A procedure is a detailed set of instructions for carrying out a series of activities that occur regularly.

There are advantages to standardizing policies and procedures on a worldwide basis. Such standardization means that all units follow similar practices, which facilitates communication, coordination, and transfers of personnel, resources, and services among units. Standardization can also contribute to a uniform global image. The use of standardized policies and procedures throughout a global business reduces confusion and simplifies the control process for headquarters.

A standardized set of policies and procedures is often not practical in an international setting. This is partly because units of the organization may be involved in quite different businesses and may be organized in varied forms. In addition, the contrasting customs and regulations associated with different cultural and national environments often militate against the use of standard-ized policies and procedures. North American management relies on accurate and precise control information, and its lack often leads to the imposition of tighter controls. What may be needed is not tighter controls but different forms of control that are locally acceptable and reflect local laws, customs, and prac-tices. In such a situation appropriate controls may need to be developed for each unit of the organization. Of course, this complicates the processes of com-munication, coordination, and transfer, and generally makes the control process more complex and varied. International managers must become accus-tomed to managing in this multifaceted environment.

OTHER DIMENSIONS OF INTERNATIONAL CONTROL

In addition to the choice among the various control mechanisms available to international organizations, control systems can vary in other dimensions. Two dimensions of control are considered here: bureaucratic versus corporate cul-ture and centralization versus decentralization.

BUREAUCRATIC VERSUS CORPORATE CULTURE CONTROL

Bureaucratic control systems rely on formal, explicit stipulations regarding expected levels of performance and acceptable activities and behaviors. Many of the control mechanisms previously discussed fall into this category. These mechanisms tend to be relatively rigid and quantitative.

Corporate culture control systems rely on more qualitative and personal means to maintain control. International firms that emphasize control through the establishment of a global corporate culture deliberately seek to institute a sim-ilar corporate culture in all units worldwide. This is achieved through careful selection and training of personnel and frequent international transfers of key personnel. Key managers from the head office take the head office culture with them to units around the world, and key managers from foreign locations spend time at the head office to learn and absorb the head office culture.

The choice between bureaucratic and corporate culture controls is not an either/or choice, and most international firms employ a mix of the two. The particular mix depends on the company's operations and country of origin. U.S.-based international companies have historically favored bureaucratic controls; Japanese and European firms have used the corporate culture approach more often

CENTRALIZATION VERSUS DECENTRALIZATION

International control systems also vary in terms of the degree of centralization associated with the system. Centralization in this context refers to the degree of control maintained by corporate headquarters (the parent) relative to the degree of control allocated to the subsidiary units of the organization. Highly centralized international companies maintain a high degree of control through headquarters while decentralized companies give more freedom to subsidiary units. Note that this discussion refers to the international organization as a whole and does not consider centralization/decentralization at the local level. It is possible that an international firm, as a whole, is described as decentralized because each subsidiary unit makes its own plans and selects its own controls. Individual units might themselves be centralized if decisions are made and controls enforced by one or a few individuals within that unit.

International companies seek a mix of centralization and decentralization that suits the specific firm and the management styles of its leaders. Many factors influence this decision and the degree of control retained by headquarters varies from firm to firm. Among the major factors influencing this decision are:

1. *Industry.* Certain industries tend toward centralized controls because they require product consistency (for example, the pharmaceutical industry) or because they can achieve substantial economic advantages through standardized operations (for example, the oil and gas industry).

2. *Type of subsidiary.* Certain types of subsidiaries are amenable to central control while others need to be decentralized in order to adapt to local conditions. In general, manufacturing is more likely to be centrally controlled to allow for product standardization while marketing may be decentralized to reflect local market characteristics.

3. *Function.* Certain functional areas of international firms tend to be centrally controlled while others are left to the subsidiary units. Financial controls are usually centralized while local human resource issues are usually controlled at the subsidiary level. Research and development is usually centrally controlled while public relations may be locally controlled.

4. *Parent philosophy.* Some companies believe in centralization while others feel that decentralization is more effective. This philosophy is often related to the company's business and its previous international experience, as well as to the management style of its chief executive officer. Global firms are more likely to be centrally controlled while multidomestics may be more decentralized. The greater the interdependency among units, the greater the need for central coordination and control.

5. *Parent confidence in the subsidiary.* The more confidence that a parent has in the subsidiary's management the more likely it is to decentralize controls. Confidence is likely to develop over time. Therefore controls may be more centralized initially and decentralized later on.

6. *Cultural similarity.* Cultural similarity affects centralization because people tend to trust others who express similar cultural values and attitudes. Units that are culturally similar to the parent may therefore be given more freedom. Alternatively, if a unit is very dissimilar culturally from the parent, the decision may be made that it can function best on its own.

7. *Firm-specific advantage.* A firm generally wants to maintain centralized control over those factors which contribute substantially to its competitive position. If a company's technology is its main advantage, then it is likely to control technology centrally. If its training of employees is a key strength, it is likely to control training centrally.

The task for international executives is to find the appropriate balance between headquarters control and subsidiary freedom. Inadequate central control can result in an ineffective system, but too much central control inhibits local initiative and development. The right balance will depend on the firm and its particular subsidiaries. The degree of centralization maintained by an international firm will often vary from one subsidiary to another. Also, a firm's philosophy, relative to centralization, also may change over time as it experiences varying reactions to and results from centralization or decentralization. A firm's business will change over time and this will also influence its choice of control techniques. Centralization or decentralization choices are, therefore, continually reevaluated.

INFORMATION SYSTEMS

The flow of information from headquarters to subsidiaries, from subsidiaries to headquarters, and between subsidiaries is instrumental to the effectiveness of the control system. Designing an effective information system is therefore integral to designing a control system.

Information systems are important to any company's control system but critical for the global company. The physical and cultural separation between units makes it vital that information be understood by all parties to maintain control throughout the organization. Of course, this separation also makes designing an effective system a major challenge. A good information system provides understandable and usable information. In an international company it may have to be understandable to and usable by people who work in different countries, speak different languages, and view their information needs differently.

The specifics of each information system will differ depending on the organization's needs; however, to design an effective system the following questions need to be considered:

1. *What information is needed?* The precise information that is needed at the various levels in the organization must be identified and systems put into place to accumulate the data required to provide this information.

2. *Who will accumulate the data?* Responsibility must be assigned for data collection and needed authority delegated to ensure that the data can be collected. Raw data often has to be transformed into more meaningful information, and responsibility and authority for this also need to be defined and allocated.

3. *Who will receive the data and information?* People only need to receive information that relates to the decisions they have to make or contribute to. Only relevant information should be supplied to appropriate people. This might vary from manager to manager, depending on the style of management and the location.

4. *What form will the information take?* Data must be converted to information that supports decision making; therefore, information should be provided in a form that is useful and understandable to the receiver. User input is particularly important in deciding on the format for presenting information.

5. *When will information be available?* Information is only useful if it is available in a timely manner. Identifying and reducing the time lag between an event and the availability of information describing it is therefore important.

These questions need to be asked to design any information system, but they are particularly relevant to the international system. The complexity of the international firm, its geographic and cultural distances, and varying regulations will affect the answers to all of these questions; therefore, the answers must be thought through carefully. In addition, the ability to collect and process the underlying data can vary because of differences in languages, literacy levels, and the availability of appropriate equipment and supplies. These complicating factors often mean that an effective information flow will have to evolve over time.

PERFORMANCE EVALUATION

An important purpose of any control system is the evaluation of people's performance. People within the organization are expected to perform certain activities and achieve certain results. To ensure these activities are adequately performed and objectives reached, most organizations periodically review and evaluate people's performance.

From a control perspective, the focus is frequently on evaluating managers of subsidiary units to determine if their units are accomplishing expected results. In a U.S. noninternational firm, managers are typically evaluated on the basis of growth in sales, market share, and profits. Managers of various domestic groups (for example, product groups) are often evaluated comparatively on these variables.

Effective performance evaluation focuses on factors within the scope of control of the person being evaluated. In a global firm evaluation can therefore be more difficult because managers may sometimes have little control over the results of their unit. Many decisions in a global company are made above the subsidiary level (at a regional or headquarters level) yet can impact a subsidiary's performance. For example:

- Prices for transfers of goods and/or services among corporate units are often not determined by the subsidiary. Profitability and costs may therefore be outside of the subsidiary manager's control.

- Sales to other corporate units are often not a function of the market but are determined by corporate requirements. Sales and market share may therefore be outside of the subsidiary manager's control.

- A subsidiary may be established for strategic or tactical reasons relating to global returns rather than the subsidiary's returns. The subsidiary manager has little control over sales, costs, or profits.

- Sudden and unexpected changes in local government policy may affect a subsidiary's performance. If the local manager had no reason to expect these changes, he or she cannot be held responsible for results associated with the changes.

- Environmental changes that affect economic factors such as currency values, inflation rates, levels of exports or imports may be unpredictable. A local manager cannot be held responsible for results stemming from these economic impacts.

Evaluation of subsidiary managers should be based on performance within their control. This often means a goal-based evaluation system as opposed to one based largely on financial performance. A goal-based evaluation system is similar to a plan, as described earlier. Such a system establishes goals for the subsidiary that are agreeable to the subsidiary manager as well as to regional and headquarters managers. Performance is then measured in relation to goal achievement.

The goal-based approach focuses on results that can be attributed to the manager's activities at the subsidiary level. The critical factor is to identify and distinguish controllable factors from uncontrollable ones. Financial goals will form part of the evaluation, but nonfinancial goals (those reflecting government relations, employee satisfaction, communications with other subsidiaries) are included as well.

SUMMARY

In this chapter we considered issues related to organizational structure and control in international firms. Structure provides the framework that allows international strategies to be carried out, and control is important effective management because it helps ensure that the enterprise achieves the results it hopes to achieve. Effective organizational structures and control systems are particularly important to the management process in companies that face a complex internal and external environment. International companies clearly fall into this category and therefore need to pay close attention to the control process.

The internal and external environment of international firms makes control particularly important for these companies. But the complexity of the environment also means that it can be more difficult to design and implement an effective control system. This chapter identified and discussed some of the major factors influencing the effectiveness of international control systems.

This chapter examined specific international control mechanisms as well as variations in control systems. It also considered information systems, performance evaluation, and organization structure as integral to achieving international control. The purpose of the chapter is to alert readers to the factors that need to be considered in the control process in international companies. The chapter does not deal in depth with issues such as accounting or auditing practices; rather, it gives a general overview of the international control process.

Control systems tell the international firm how well it is doing in meeting its objectives and achieving its chosen strategies. Results can indicate where a better understanding of the global environment is needed, suggest when political and cultural factors have to be re-examined, and pinpoint firm-specific decision-making and functional areas that need improvement.

Managing an international business effectively, like managing any business, depends on a thorough understanding of the internal and external environment of the firm and the opportunities and threats posed by the interaction of these environments. The management process in an international company is particularly germane to effectiveness because of the complex internal and external environment faced by the international company. A sound control system gives the company command over information that improves this management process.

DISCUSSION QUESTIONS

1. Discuss how the formation of regional trading blocks is likely to be reflected in the organizational structures of international firms.

2. Discuss how a strategy of globally rationalization is likely to be reflected in a firm's choice of international organizational structure.

3. In a multidomestic firm (i.e., one that operates each national subsidiary as a separate entity), identify and discuss some of the challenges associated with achieving effective control.

REFERENCES

Adler, N. 1990. *International Dimensions of Organizational Behavior.* Boston: PWS-Kent.

Baliga, D.R. & A.M. Jaeger. 1984. "Multinational corporations: Control systems and delegation issues," *Journal of International Business Studies*, 15 (2), pp. 25–40.

Bata, T.J. with S. Sinclair. 1990. *Bata, Shoemaker to the World.* Toronto: Stoddart. p. 285.

Brooke, M. & H. Remmers. 1978. *The Strategy of Multinational Enterprise* London: Pitman.

Bruce, R. 1990. "UK Working on radical changes to financial reporting." *The Bottom Line,* December, p. 6.

Cray, D. 1984. "Control and coordination in multinational corporations." *Journal of International Business Studies*, 15 (2), pp. 85–98.

Daniels, J.D., R.A. Pitts & M.J. Tretter. 1984. "Strategy and structure of U.S. multinationals." *Academy of Management Journal*, pp. 292–307.

Doz, Y. & C.K. Prahalad. 1984. "Patterns of strategic control within multinational corporations." *Journal of International Business Studies*, 15 (2), pp. 55–72.

——1981. "Headquarters influence and strategic control in MNCs." *Sloan Management Review,* Fall, pp. 15–29.

Egelhoff, W.G. 1988. "Strategy and structure in MNCs: A revision of the Stopford and Wells model." *Strategic Management Journal*, 9 (1), pp. 1–14.

Kane, M. & D. Ricks. 1989. "The impact of transborder data flow regulations on large United States-based corporations." *Columbia Journal of World Business.*

Kiggundu, M. 1989. *Managing Organizations in Developing Countries.* West Hartford, CO: Kumavian Press, p. 120.

Laaksonen, O. 1988. *Management in China.* New York: Walter de Gruyter.

Prahalad, C. & Y. Doz. 1987. *The Multinational Mission: Balancing Local Demands and Global Vision.* New York: The Free Press.

Ricks, D.A. 1983. *Big Business Blunders.* Columbus, OH: Grid.

Ronen, S. 1986. *Comparative and International Management,* New York: John Wiley & Sons, Inc.

Samiee, S. 1984. "Transnational data flow constraints: A new challenge for multinational corporations." *Journal of International Business Studies,* 15 (1), pp. 141–150.

Selig, G. 1982. "A framework for multinational information systems planning." *Information and Management,* 5, June, pp. 95–115.

Stopford, J.M. & L.T. Wells. 1972. *Managing the Multinational Enterprise.* New York: Basic Books.

Stueck, W. 1990. "Pacific rim accounting conference stresses ethics, controls, and cooperation." *The Bottom Line,* December, p. 19.

"Thought Control," *The Economist,* 1990, July 7, p. 68.

PART TWO:
MAJOR
REFERENCES

Adler, N. 1990. *International Organizational Behavior*. Boston: PWS-Kent.

Adler, N. & J.L. Graham. 1987. "Business negotiations: Canadians are not just like Americans." *Canadian Journal of Administrative Science*, 4(3), pp. 211–238.

Argaval, S. & S.N. Ramaswami. 1992. "Choice of foreign market entry mode: Impact of ownership, location and internationalization factors." *Journal of International Business Studies*, 23(1), First Quarter, pp. 1–28.

Bailey, E. & O. Shenkar. 1993. "Management education for international joint venture managers." *Leadership and Organization Development Journal*, 14(3), pp. 15–20.

Baliga, D.R. & A.M. Jaeger. 1984. "Multinational corporations: Control systems and delegation issues." *Journal of International Business Studies*, Fall, pp. 25–40.

Bar, F. & M. Borrus. 1992. "Information networks and competitive advantage: Issues for government policy and corporate strategy." *International Journal of Technology Management*, 7(6-8), pp. 398–408.

Bartlett, C.A. 1986. "Building and managing the transnationals: The new organizational challenge." In M. Porter (ed.) *Competition in Global Industries*. Boston: Harvard Business School Press.

Bartlett, C. & S. Ghoshal. 1987. "Managing across borders: New strategic requirements." *Sloan Management Review*, 28, Summer, pp. 7–17.

Bartlett, C. & S. Ghoshal. 1988. "Organizing for worldwide effectiveness: The transnational solution." *California Management Review*, 31(1), pp. 54–74.

Beamish, P.W. 1985. "The characteristics of joint ventures in developed and developing countries." *Columbia Journal of World Business*, 20(3), pp. 13–19.

Beamish, P.W. 1987. "Equity joint ventures and the theory of the multinational enterprise." *Journal of International Business Studies*, 18(2), pp. 1–16.

Beamish, P.W. 1987. "Joint ventures in LDCs: Partner selection and performance." *Management International Review*, 27(1), pp. 23–27.

Beamish, P.W. 1988. *Multinational Joint Ventures in Developing Countries*, London: Routledge.

Beamish, P.W. & J. Banks. 1987. "Equity joint ventures and the theory of the multinational enterprise." *Journal of International Business Studies*, Summer, pp. 1–16.

Benito, G.R. & G. Gripsrud. 1992. "The expansion of foreign direct investments: discrete rational location choices or a cultural learning process?" *Journal of International Business Studies*, 23(3), Third Quarter, pp. 461–476.

Bilkey, W.J. 1978. "An attempted integration of the literature on export behavior of firms." *Journal of International Business Studies*, Summer, pp. 33–46.

Blodgett, L.L. 1991. "Partner contributions as predictors of equity share in international joint ventures." *Journal of International Business Studies*, 22(1), First Quarter, pp. 63–78.

Boddewyn, J.J. 1983. "Foreign direct divestment theory: Is it the reverse of FDI theory?" *Weltwirtschfliches Archiv.*, pp. 345–355.

Borys, B. & D.B. Jemison. 1989. "Hybrid arrangements as strategic alliances: Theoretical issues in organizational combinations." *Academy of Management Review*, 14(2), pp. 234–249.

Boyacigillar, N.A. & N.J. Adler. 1991. "The parochial dinosaur: Organizational science in a global context." *Academy of Management Review*, 16, pp. 262–290.

Bradford, M. 1993. "Communication, control are crucial to managing risks of overseas units." *Business Insurance*, 27(6), February 8, p. 10.

Brannen, M.Y. 1991. "Culture, the critical factor in the successful implementation of statistical quality control." *Business Horizons*, 35(6), pp. 59–67.

Brooke, M. & H. Remmers. 1978. *The Strategy of Multinational Enterprise.* London: Pitman.

Calvet, A. 1981. "A synthesis of foreign direct investment theories and theories of the multinational firm." *Journal of International Business Studies*, Spring–Summer, pp. 43–59.

Capon, N., C. Chrisrodoulou, J. Farley, & J. Hulbert. 1987. "A comparative analysis of the strategy and structure of U.S. and Australian corporations." *Journal of International Business Studies*, 18(1), pp. 51–74.

Chakravarthy, B. & H. Perlmutter. 1985. "Strategic planning for a global business." *Columbia Journal of World Business*, 20(3), pp. 3–10.

Contractor, F.J. 1988. "Competition vs. cooperation: A benefit/cost framework for choosing between fully-owned investments and cooperative relationships." *Management International Review*, (28), Special Issue, pp. 5–18.

Contractor, F.J. 1981. "In defense of licensing: Its increased role in international operations." *Columbia Journal of World Business*, Vol. 16.

Contractor, F.J. 1985. *Licensing in International Strategy: A Guide for Planning and Negotiations*. Westport, CT: Greenwood Press.

Contractor, F.J. 1990. "Ownership patterns of U.S. joint ventures abroad and the liberalization of foreign government regulations in the 1980's: Evidence from the benchmark surveys." *Journal of International Business Studies*, 21(1), First Quarter, pp. 55–74.

Contractor F.J. 1984. "Strategies for structuring joint ventures: A negotiations planning paradigm." *Columbia Journal of World Business*, Summer, pp. 30–39.

Contractor, F.J. & P. Lorange (eds.). 1988. *Cooperative Strategies in International Business*. Lexington, MA: Lexington Books.

Cray, D. 1984. "Control and coordination in multinational corporations." *Journal of International Business Studies*, 15(2), pp. 85–98.

Czinkota, M.R. & W.J. Johnston. 1983. "Exporting: Does sales volume make a difference?" *Journal of International Business Studies*, Spring–Summer, pp. 147–153.

Daniel, S.J. & W.D. Reitsperger. 1991. "Management control systems for J.I.T.: An empirical comparison of Japan and the U.S." *Journal of International Business Studies*, 22(4), Fourth Quarter, pp. 603–618.

Daniels, J.D., J. Krug, & D. Nigh. 1985. "U.S. joint ventures in China: motivation and management of political risk." *California Management Review*, 27(4), pp. 46–58.

Daniels, J.D., R.A. Pitts, & M.J. Tretter. 1984. "Strategy and structure of U.S. multinationals: An exploratory study." *Academy of Management Journal*, 27(2), pp. 292–307.

Davidson W. & J. de la Torre. 1989. *Managing the Global Corporations*: Case Studies in Strategy and Management. New York: McGraw-Hill.

Doz, Y. 1980. "Strategic management in multinational companies." *Sloan Management Review*, Winter, pp. 27–45.

Doz, Y. & C.K. Prahalad. 1981. "Headquarters influence and strategic control in MNCs." *Sloan Management Review*, Fall, pp. 15–29.

Doz, Y., C.K. Prahalad, & G. Hamel (eds.). 1990. *Managing the Global Firm*. London: Routledge Chapman & Hill.

DuBois, B. Toyne, & M.D. Oliff. 1993. "International manufacturing strategies of U.S. multinationals: A conceptual framework based on a four-industry study." *Journal of International Business Studies*, 24(2), Second Quarter, pp. 307–334.

Dunning, J. 1981. *International Production and the Multinational Enterprise*. London: George Allen & Unwin.

Dunning, J. 1988. "The eclectic paradigm of international production: Restatement and some possible extensions." *Journal of International Business Research*, 19(1), pp. 1–32.

Dunning, J. 1980. "Toward and eclectic theory of international production: Some empirical tests." *Journal of International Business Studies*, Spring–Summer, pp. 9–31.

Egelhoff, W.G. 1988. *Organizing the Multinational Enterprise*. Cambridge, MA: Ballinger Publishing Company.

Egelhoff, W.G. 1984. "Patterns of control in the U.S., U.K. and European multinational corporations." *Journal of International Business Studies*, 15(2), pp. 73–83.

Egelhoff, W.G. 1988. "Strategy and structure in MNCs: a revision of the stopford and Wells model." *Strategic Management Journal*, 9(1), pp. 1–14.

Encarnation, D. & L. Wells. 1986. "Competitive strategies in global industries: A view from host government. In M. Porter (ed.) *Competition in Global Industries*. Boston: Harvard Business School.

England, G.W. 1978. "Managers and their value systems: A five country comparative study." *Columbia Journal of World Business*, 13(2), pp. 35–44.

Erramilli, M.K. 1991. "The experience factor in foreign market entry behavior of service firms." *Journal of International Business Studies*, 22(3), Third Quarter, pp. 479–502.

Evans, W., H. Lane, & S. O'Grady. 1992. *Border Crossing—Doing Business in the U.S.* Scarborough, Ont.: Prentice-Hall Canada.

Fannin, W. & A. Rodriques. 1986. "National or global?—control vs. flexibility." *Long Range Planning*, 19(5), pp. 84–88.

Ferdows, K., J.G. Miller, J. Nakane, & T.E. Vollman. 1986. "Evolving global manufacturing strategies: Projections into the 1990's." *International Journal of Operations and Production Management*, 6(4), pp. 6–16.

Ferraro, G.P. 1990. *The Cultural Dimensions of International Business*. Englewood Cliffs, NJ: Prentice-Hall.

Ferrel, O.C. & John Fraedrich. 1991. "International business ethics." In *Business Ethics—Ethical Decision Making and Cases*. Boston: Houghton Mifflin.

Fleetwood, E. & B. Molleryd. 1992. "Parent-subsidiary relationships in transnational companies: Aspects of technical development and organization." *International Journal of Technology Management*, 7(1-3), pp. 97–110.

Franko, L.G. 1971. *Joint Venture Survival in Multinational Corporations*. New York: Praeger.

Furino, A. (ed.). 1988. *Cooperation and Competition in the Global Economy: Issues and Strategies*. MA: Ballinger Publishing Company.

Furino, A. 1987. "New forms of investment in developing countries by U.S. companies: A five industry comparison." *Columbia Journal of World Business*, Summer, pp. 39–56.

Galbraith, J. & R. Kazanjian. 1986. "Organizing to implement strategies of diversity and globalization: The role of matrix design." *Human Resource Management*, 25(1), pp. 37–54.

Garland, J., R.N. Farmer, & M. Taylor. 1990. *International Dimensions of Business Policy and Strategy* (2nd ed.). Boston: PWS-Kent.

Gates, S.R. & W.G. Egelhoff. 1986. "Centralization in parent headquarters—subsidiary relationships." *Journal of International Business Studies*, 17(2), pp. 71–92.

Geringer, J.M. 1991. "Strategic determinants of partner selection criteria in international joint ventures." *Journal of International Business Studies* 22(1), First Quarter, pp. 41–62.

Geringer, J.M. & L. Hebert. 1989. "Control and performance of international joint ventures." *Journal of International Business Studies* 20(2), pp. 234–254.

Geringer, J.M. & L. Hebert. 1991. "Measuring performance of international joint ventures." *Journal of International Business Studies*, 22(2), Second Quarter, pp. 249–264.

Gerwin, D. & J. Tarondeau. 1989. "International comparisons of manufacturing flexibility. In K. Ferdows" (ed.) *Managing International Manufacturing*. Amsterdam: North-Holland.

Ghemawat, P. 1986. "Sustainable advantage." *Harvard Business Review*, 64(3), pp. 53–58.

Ghertman, M. 1988. "Foreign subsidiary and parents' roles during strategic investment and divestment decisions." *Journal of International Business Studies*, 19(1), pp. 47–67.

Ghosal, S. 1987. "Global strategy: An organizing framework." *Strategic Management Journal*, 8, pp. 365–388.

Ghoshal, S. & C. Bartlett. 1988. "Creation, adoption, and diffusion of innovation by subsidiaries of multinational corporations." *Journal of International Business Studies*, 19(3), pp. 365–388

Ghoshal, S. & C. Bartlett. 1988. "The multinational corporation as a network: Perspectives from inter-organizational theory." Paper presented at the Academy of International Business Meeting, San Diego.

Ghoshal, S. & C. Bartlett. 1990. "The multinational corporation as in interorganizational network." *Academy of Management Review*, October, pp. 603–625.

Gomes-Casseres, B. 1990. "Firm ownership preferences and host government restrictions: An integrated approach." *Journal of International Business Studies*, 21(1), First Quarter, pp. 1–22.

Gomes-Casseres, B. 1987. "Joint venture instability: Is it a problem?" *Columbia Journal of World Business*, 22(2), pp. 97–102.

Graham, J.L. 1981. "A hidden cause of America's trade deficit with Japan." *Columbia Journal of World Business*, Fall, pp. 5–15.

Graham, J.L. 1985. "The influence of culture on the process of business negotiations: An exploratory study." *Journal of International Business Studies*, 16(1), pp. 81–96.

Grosse, R. 1980. *Foreign Investment Codes and Location of Direct Investment*. New York: Preager.

Habib, G.M. 1987. "Measures of manifest conflicts in international joint ventures." *Academy of Management Journal*, 30(4), pp. 808–816.

Hamel, G., Y.L. Doz, & C.K. Prahalad. 1989. "Collaborate with your competitors—and win." *Harvard Business Review*, 67(1), pp. 133–139.

Hamel, G. & G.K. Prahalad. 1985. "Do you really have a global strategy?" *Harvard Business Review*, 63(4), pp. 139–148.

Harrigan, K.R. 1984. "Joint ventures and global strategies." *Columbia Journal of World Business*, Summer, pp. 7–16.

Harrigan, K.R. 1986. "Matching vertical integration strategies of competitive conditions." *Strategic Management Journal*, 7, pp. 535–555.

Harrigan, K.R. 1988. "Strategic alliances and partner asymmetries." *Management International Review*, 28, Special Issue, pp. 53–72.

Harrigan, K.R. 1987. "Strategic alliances: Their new role in global competition." *Columbia Journal of World Business*, 22(2), pp. 67–69.

Harrigan, K.R. 1985. *Strategies for Joint Ventures.* Lexington, MA: Lexington Books.

Harrigan, K.R. 1985. "Vertical integration and corporate strategy." *Academy of Management Journal*, 28, pp. 397–425.

Hedlund, G. 1986. "The hypermodern MNC—a heterarchy?" *Human Resource Management*, 25(1), pp. 9–35.

Hedlund, G. 1984. "Organization in-between: The evolution of the mother–daughter structure of managing foreign subsidiaries in Swedish MNCs." *Journal of International Business Studies*, 15(2), pp. 109–123.

Hennart, J.F. 1989. "Can the new forms of investment' substitute for the 'old forms'?: A transaction costs perspective." *Journal of International Business Studies*, 20, pp. 1–23.

Hennart, J.F. 1988. "A transaction cost theory of equity joint ventures." *Strategic Management Journal*, 9(4), pp. 361–374.

Herbert, T. 1984. "Strategy and multinational organization structure: An interorganizational relationships perspective." *Academy of Management Review*, 9, pp. 259–271.

Hladik, K.J. 1985. *International Joint Ventures.* Lexington, MA: Lexington Books.

Hood, N. & J.E. Vahlne (eds.). 1988. *Strategies in Global Competition.* London: Croom Helm Ltd.

Hout, T., M.E. Porter, & E. Rudden. 1982. "How global companies win out." *Harvard Business Review*, September–October, pp. 98–103.

Hung, C.L. 1992. "Strategic business alliances between Canada and the newly industrialized countries of Pacific Asia." *Management International Review*, 32(4), Fourth Quarter, pp. 345–361.

Huo, Y.P. & W. McKinley. 1992. "Nation as a context for strategy: The effects of national characteristics on business-level strategies." *Management International Review*, 32(2) Second Quarter, pp. 103–113.

Hymer. S.H. 1976. *The International Operations of National Firms: A Study of Direct Investment.* Cambridge, MA: MIT Press.

Jacquemin, A. (ed.). 1984. *European Industry: Public Policy and Corporate Strategy*. Oxford, England: Clarendon Press.

Jarillo, J.C. 1988. "On strategic networks." *Strategic Management Journal*, 9(1), pp. 34–41.

Jonsson, C. 1986. "Interorganization theory and international organization." *International Studies Quarterly*, 30(1), pp. 39–57.

Kiggundu, Moses N. 1989. *Managing Organizations in Developing Countries: An Operational and Strategic Perspective*. West Hartford, CT: Kumarian Press.

Killing, J.P. 1982. "How to make a joint venture work." *Harvard Business Review*, 60, pp. 120–127.

Killing, J.P. 1983. *Strategies for Joint Venture Success*. New York: Praeger.

Kim, W.C. & P. Hwang. 1992. "Global strategy and multinationals entry mode choice." *Journal of International Business Studies* 23(1), First Quarter, pp. 29–54.

Kim, W.C. & R.A. Mauborgne. 1993. "Effectively conceiving and executing multinationals worldwide strategies." *Journal of International Business Studies*, 24(3), Third Quarter, pp. 419–448.

Kim, W.C. & R.A. Mauborgne. 1993. "Procedural justice, attitudes and subsidiary top management compliance with multinationals' corporate strategic decisions." *Academy of Management Journal*, 36(3), pp. 502–526.

Kimura, U. 1989. "Firm specific strategic advantages and FDI behavior of firms: The case of Japanese semiconductor firms." *Journal of International Business Studies*, 20(2), pp. 293–315.

Kobrin, S.J. 1981. "Ownership structures of foreign subsidiaries: theory and evidence." *Journal of Economic Behavior and Organization*, January, pp. 1–25.

Kobrin, S.J. 1988. "Trends in ownership of American manufacturing subsidiaries in developing countries: An inter-industry analysis." *Management International Review*, 28, Special Issue, pp. 73–84.

Kogut, B. 1985. "Designing global strategies: Comparative and competitive value-added chains." *Sloan Management Review*, 26(4), pp. 15–28.

Kogut, B. 1985. "Designing global strategies: Profiting from operational flexibility." *Sloan Management Review*, 26(1), pp. 27–38.

Kogut, B. 1988. "Joint ventures: Theoretical and empirical perspectives." *Strategic Management Journal*, 9(4), pp. 319–333.

Kogut, B. 1988. "A study of the life cycle of joint ventures." *Management International Review*, 28, Special Issue, pp. 39–52.

Kotabe, M. 1992. *Global Sourcing Strategies, R&D Managing, and Marketing Interfaces*. New York: Quorum Books.

Kotabe, M. & G.S. Omura. 1989. "Sourcing strategies of European and Japanese multinationals: A comparison." *Journal of International Business Studies*, 20(1), pp. 113–130.

Kriger, M.P. & E.E. Solomon. 1992. "Strategic mindsets and decision-making autonomy in U.S. and Japanese MNCs." *Management International Review*, 32(4), Fourth Quarter, pp. 327–343.

Kurland, O.M. 1992. "Intelligencer: A review of RIMS new international strategies course." *Risk Management*, 39(12), December, p. 69.

Laaksonen, O. 1988. *Management in China*. New York: Walter de Gruyter.

Lane, H. & D. Simpson. 1988. "Bribery in international business: Whose problem is it?" *International Management Behavior*, Scarborough, Ont.: Nelson Canada. p. 236.

Lemak, D. & J. Bracker. 1988. "A strategic contingency model of multinational corporate structure." *Strategic Management Journal*, 9(5), pp. 521–526.

Leong, S.M. & C.T. Tan. 1993. "Managing across borders: An empirical test of the Bartlett and Shoshal (1989) organizational typology." *Journal of International Business Studies*, 24(3), Third Quarter, pp. 449–464.

Leontiades, J. 1986. "Going global — global strategies vs national strategies." *Long Range Planning*, 19(6), pp. 96–104.

Lester, T. 1992. "The rise of the network." *International Management*, 47(6), June, pp. 72–73.

Lyles, M.A., 1987. "Common mistakes of joint venture experienced firms." *Columbia Journal of World Business*, Summer, pp. 79–85.

Martinez, J.I. & J.C. Jarillo. 1991. "Coordination demands of international strategies." *Journal of International Business Studies*, 22(3), Third Quarter, pp. 429–444.

Mascarenhas, B. 1984. "The coordination of manufacturing interdependence in multinational companies." *Journal of International Business Studies*, 15(3), pp. 91–106.

Mascarenhas, B. 1986. "International strategies of non-dominant firms." *Journal of International Business Studies*, 17(1), pp. 1–26.

Mascarenhas, B. 1986. "Strategic group dynamics." *Academy of Management Journal*, 3292, pp. 333–352.

McCarthy, M., M. Pointer, D. Ricks, & R. Rolfe. 1993. "Managers' views on potential investment opportunities." *Business Horizons*, July–August, pp. 54–58.

Mefford, R.N. 1986. "Determinants of productivity differences in international manufacturing." *Journal of International Business Studies*, 17(1), pp. 63–82.

Merrifield, D.B. 1992. "Global strategic alliances among firms." *International Journal of Technology Management*, 7(1-3), pp. 77–83.

Meyers, G.C. with J. Holusha. 1986. *When It Hits the Fan—Managing the Nine Crises of Business*. New York: Mentor books.

Morrison, A.J., 1990. *Strategies in Global Industries: How U.S. Businesses Compete*. New York: Quorum Books.

Morrison, A. & K. Roth. 1988. "Interntional business level strategy: The development of a holistic model." In A. Negundhi & A. Savara (eds.) *International Management*. Lexington, MA: Lexington Books.

Morrison, A., K. Roth, & D. Ricks. 1991. "Globalization versus regionalization: Which way for the multinational?" *Organizational Dynamics*, Winter, pp. 17–29.

Mowery, D.C. 1988. *International Collaborative Ventures in U.S. Manufacturing*. Cambridge, MA: Ballinger Publishing Company.

Nehandhi, A.R. 1975. "Comparative management and organization theory: A marriage needed." *Academy of Management Review*, 18(2), pp. 334–344.

Newman, W.H. 1992. "Focused joint ventures in transforming economies." *Academy of Management Executive*. 69(1), pp. 67–75.

Ohmae, K. 1985. *Triad Power: The Coming Shape of Global Competition*. New York: The Free Press.

Osbaldeston, M. & K. Barham. 1992. "Using management development for competitive advantage." *Long Range Planning*, 25(6), December, pp. 18–24.

Parkhe, A. 1991. "Interfirm diversity, organizational learning, and longevity in global strategic alliances." *Journal of International Business Studies*, 22(4), Fourth Quarter, pp. 579–602.

Parkhe, A. 1993. " 'Messy' research, methodological predispositions, and theory development in international joint ventures." *Academy of Management Review*, 18(2), pp. 227–268.

Parkhe, A. 1993. "Strategic alliance structuring: A game theoretic and transaction cost examination of interfirm cooperation." *Academy of Management Journal*, 36(4), pp. 794–829.

Perlmutter, H. & D. Heenan. 1986. "Cooperate to compete globally." *Harvard Business Review*, 64(2), pp. 136–152.

Peterson, R.B. & J.Y. Shimada. 1978. "Sources of management problems in Japanese–American joint ventures." *Academy of Management Review*, 3(4), pp. 790–804.

Picard, J. 1980. "Organizational structures and integrative devices in European multinational corporations." Columbia *Journal of World Business*, 15(1), pp. 30–35.

Pitts, R.A. & J.D. Daniels. 1984. "Aftermath of the matrix mania." *Columbia Journal of World Business*, 19(2), pp. 48–54.

Porter, M.E. 1986. "Changing patterns of international competition." *California Management Review*, 28(1), pp. 9–40.

Porter, M.E. 1980. *Competitive Strategy*, New York: The Free Press.

Porter, M.E. 1986. "Competition in global industries: A conceptual framework." In M. Porter (ed.) *Competition in Global Industries*. Boston: Harvard Business School.

Porter, M.E. & M.B. Fuller. 1986. "Coalitions in global strategy." In M.E. Porter (ed.) *Competition in Global Industries*. MA: Harvard Business School Press.

Poynter, T.A. 1982. "Government intervention in the less developed countries: The experience of multinational companies." *Journal of International business Studies*, Spring–Summer, pp. 19–26.

Poynter, T.A. & A. Rugman. 1992. "World product mandates: How will multinationals respond?" *Business Quarterly*, October, pp. 54–61.

Prahalad, C. & Y. Doz. 1987. *The Multinational Mission: Balancing Local Demands and Global Vision*. New York: The Free Press.

Prasad, S.B. 1989, 1980. *Advances in International Comparative Management*, Vol. 4, 5. Greenwich, CT: JAI Press.

Pucik, V. 1988. "Strategic alliances, organizational learning, and competitive advantage: The HRM agenda." *Human Resource Management*, 27(1), pp. 77–93.

Reitsperger, W.D., S.J. Daniel, S.B. Tallman, & W.B. Chrismar. 1993. "Product quality and cost leadership: Compatible strategies?" *Management International Review*, 33, First Quarter, pp. 7–21.

Ricks, D.A. 1983. *Big Business Blunders: Mistakes in Multinational marketing*. Homewood, IL: Dow-Jones Irwin.

Ricks, D.A., J. Arpan, J. Clamp, H. Hand, & B. Toyne. 1986. "Global challenges and strategies for increasing the international competitiveness of the U.S. man-made fibers industry." *Columbia Journal of World Business*, 21(2), pp. 89–96.

Robinson, R.D. 1978. *International Business Management—A Guide to Decision Making*. Hinsdale, IL: Dryden Press.

Rokeach, J. 1973. *The Nature of Human Values*. New York: The Free Press.

Rolfe, R.J., D.A. Ricks, M.M. Pointer, & M. McCarthy. 1993. "Determinants of FDI incentive preferences of MNEs." *Journal of International Business Studies*, 24(2), Second Quarter, pp. 335–356.

Root, F.R. 1994. *Entry Strategies for International Markets*. New York: Lexington Books.

Roth K. & A.J. Morrison. 1990. "An empirical analysis of the integration-responsiveness framework in global industries." *Journal of International Business Studies*, 21(4), Fourth Quarter, pp. 541–564.

Roth K. & A.J. Morrison. 1992. "Implementing global strategy: Characteristics of global subsidiary mandates." *Journal of International Business Studies*, 22(4), Fourth Quarter, pp. 715–736.

Roth, K. & D. Ricks. 1994. "Goal configuration in a global industry context." *Strategic Management Journal*, 1591), pp. 103–120.

Roth, K. & D. Ricks. 1990. "Objective setting in international business: An empirical analysis." *International Journal of Management* March, pp. 13–19.

Roth, K., D.M. Schweiger, & A.J. Morrison. 1991. "Global strategy implementation at the business unit level: Operational capabilities and administrative mechanisms." *Journal of International Business Studies*, 2293), Third Quarter, pp. 369–402.

Rugman, A.M. 1985. "Internationalization is still a general theory of foreign direct investment." *Weltwirlschaftliches Archiv.*, September, pp. 570–575.

Rugman, A.M. 1985. "Multinationals and global competitive strategy." *International Studies of Management and Organization*, 15(2), pp. 8–18.

Rugman, A.M. & A. Verbeke. 1992. "A note of the transnational solution and the transaction cost theory of multinational strategic management." *Journal of International Business Studies*, 23(4), Fourth Quarter, pp. 761–772.

Ryans, A. 1988. "Strategic market entry factors and market share achievement in Japan." *Journal of International Business Studies*, 19(3), pp. 389–410.

Salacuse, W. 1991. *Making Global Deals*. Boston: Houghton-Mifflin.

Schmiegelow, M. & H. Schmiegelow. 1989. *Strategic Pragmatism: Japanese Lessons in the Use of Economic Theory*. New York: Praeger.

Selig, G. 1982. "A framework for multinational information systems planning." *Information and Management*, 5, June, pp. 141–150.

Shahrokhi, M. 1987. *Reverse Licensing: International Technology Transfer to the United States*. New York: Praeger.

Shan, W. 1991. "Environmental risks and joint venture sharing arrangement." *Journal of International Business Studies* 22(4), Fourth Quarter, pp. 555–578.

Shapiro, S. 1993. "Communication overseas is a passport to success." *Business Insurance*, 27(20), May 10, pp. 20–22.

Shenkar, O. & S. Ronen. 1987. "The cultural context of negotiations: The implications of Chinese interpersonal norms." *Journal of Applied Behavioral Science*, 23(20), pp. 263–275.

Shenkar, O. & Y. Zeira. 1988. "Human resource management in international joint ventures: Direction for research." *Academy of Management Review*, 12(3), pp. 546–557.

Shenkar, O. & Y. Zeira. 1987. "International joint ventures: Implications for organization development." *Personnel Review*, 16(1), pp. 30–37.

Siddall, P., K. Willey, & J. Tavares. 1992. "Building a transnational organization for PB Oil." *Long Range Planning*, 25(1), February, pp. 37–45.

Snodgrass, C.R., 1993. "The use of networks in cross border competition." *Long Range Planning*, 26(2), pp. 41–50.

Steinbart, PJ. & R. Nath. 1992. "Problems and issues in the management of international data communications networks: The experience of American companies." *MIS Quarterly*, 1691, March, pp. 55–76.

Stopford, J.M. 1976. "Changing perspective on investment by British manufacturing multinationals." *Journal of International Business Studies*, Winter, pp. 15–27.

Sundaram, A.K. & J.S. Black. 1992. "The environment and internal organization of Multinational enterprises." *Academy of Management Review* 1794, pp. 729–757.

Sullivan, D. 1992. "Organization in American MNCs: The perspective of the European Regional Headquarters." *Management International Review*, 32(3), Third Quarter, pp. 237–250.

Sullivan J. & R.B. Peterson. 1982. "Factors associated with trust in Japanese–American joint ventures." *Management International Review*, 2292, pp. 30–40.

Swamidass, P.M. 1990. "A comparison of the plant location strategies of foreign and domestic manufacturers in the U.S." *Journal of International Business Studies* 21(2), Second Quarter, pp. 301–318.

Swamidass, P.M. & M. Kotabe. 1993. "Component sourcing of multinationals: An empirical study of European and Japanese multinationals." *Journal of International Business Studies*, 2491, First Quarter, pp. 81–100.

Thorne, P. 1992. "Takeover misery." *International Management*, 47(5), May, pp. 88.

United Nations Centre on Transnational Corporations. 1988. *Transnational Corporations in World Development—Trends and Prospects*. New York: UNCTC.

Vachani, S. 1991. "Distinguishing between related and unrelated international geographic diversification: A comprehensive measure of global diversification." *Journal of International Business Studies*, 2292, Second Quarter, pp. 307–322.

Weigand, R. 1983. "International investments: Weighing the incentives." *Harvard Business Review*, July–August, pp. 146–152.

Weiss, S. 1987. "Creating the GM-Toyota joint venture: A case in complex negotiation." *Columbia Journal of World Business Summer*, pp. 23–37.

Weiss-Wik, S. 1983. "Enhancing negotiators successfulness." *Journal of Conflict Resolution*, 27(4), pp. 706–739.

Wells, L.T. 1977. "Negotiating with third world governments." *Harvard Business Review*, January–February, pp. 72–80.

Wheelwright, S.C. 1984. "Manufacturing strategy: Defining the missing link." *Strategic Management Journal*, 59(1), pp. 77–91.

Whybark, D.C. 1989. *International Operations Management: A Selection of IMEDE Cases*. IL: Irwin.

Woodward, D.P. & R.J. Rolfe. 1993. "The location of export-oriented foreign direct investment in the Caribbean Basin." *Journal of International Business Studies*, 2491, First Quarter, pp. 121–144.

Wortzel, H.V. & L.H. Wortzel. 1985. *Global Strategy Management: The Essentials* (2nd ed.). New York: John Wiley & Sons, Inc.

Young, S.M. 1992. "A framework for successful adoption and performance of Japanese manufacturing practices in the United States." *Academy of Management Review*, 17(4), pp. 677–700.

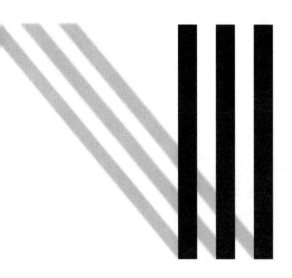

THE PEOPLE PICTURE: EXECUTING INTERNATIONAL DECISIONS THROUGH STAFFING AND DIRECTING

12

HUMAN

RESOURCE

SELECTION

LEARNING OBJECTIVES

IN THIS CHAPTER YOU WILL EXPLORE:

- Labor force distinctions in the international arena

- Issues of expatriate productivity

- The problem of international adjustment

- The cross-cultural adjustment process

- Determinants of international adjustment

KEY DISCUSSION ISSUES:

- How can companies reduce expatriate failure?

- How can expatriates overcome adjustment challenges?

- How can expatriates increase skills that relate to adjustment?

- What role does work play in adjustment?

- What family issues arise around adjustment?

- What can companies do to facilitate adjustment?

- How can companies improve their international selection process?

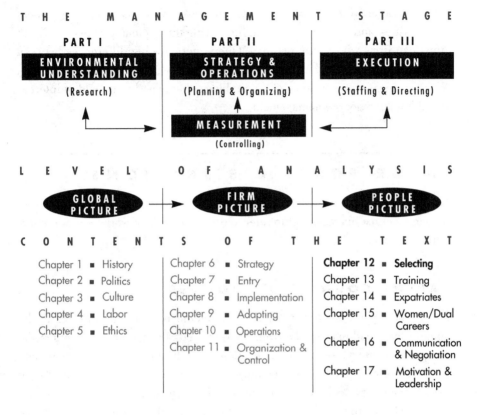

T H E   M A N A G E M E N T   S T A G E

PART I | **PART II** | **PART III**

ENVIRONMENTAL UNDERSTANDING | **STRATEGY & OPERATIONS** | **EXECUTION**

(Research) | (Planning & Organizing) | (Staffing & Directing)

MEASUREMENT

(Controlling)

L E V E L   O F   A N A L Y S I S

GLOBAL PICTURE → **FIRM PICTURE** → **PEOPLE PICTURE**

C O N T E N T S   O F   T H E   T E X T

INTRODUCTION

Whenever companies set up subsidiaries overseas, engage in joint ventures or contract manufacturing projects, license or franchise their technology and business know-how to foreigners, or expand their market with overseas sales, challenges will arise in the human resource realm. Executives in firms engaged in global operations confront questions about human resources such as to what extent should the top management and middle management of the foreign subsidiary consist of employees from headquarters? What are the advantages and disadvantages of sending managers from headquarters overseas? If managers are sent, who should go? These are just a few of the human resource questions that arise when a firm "goes global."

In this chapter we cover what management researchers have found out about these issues and contrast their findings with the typical practice of North American firms who operate abroad. Often, there are big differences between what research shows to be effective practices and what companies actually do. We propose solutions to some of the problems that exist in the field of international human resource management.

LABOR FORCE DISTINCTIONS

We begin this chapter by defining and discussing some common terms used in human resource management to refer to different types of workers in the international arena.

PARENT COUNTRY NATIONALS

Parent country nationals (PCNs) refers to employees who are citizens of the country that headquarters the firm: "parent" refers to the headquarters of the company, "country" refers to the location of the headquarters, and "national" refers to the citizenship of the employee. In international business, PCNs are usually managers, technicians, trouble-shooters, subsidiary heads, and experts who travel from the home office to assist overseas subsidiaries and operations. Missionaries, diplomatic and government personnel, military personnel, and foreign aid workers who travel to a foreign country to work are likewise classified as PCNs.

Some advantages of sending PCNs overseas to staff foreign subsidiaries are that they are expert in how the parent company operates, they know what headquarters wants, and thus they can pass on this knowledge to local workers. By spending time overseas, PCNs can learn in an intimate way how foreign markets operate, and how foreign consumers and clients react to the products or services the company offers. They also gain skills in cross-cultural management and generally get a better sense of the "ins and the outs" of global business. PCNs tend to be assigned overseas when the subsidiary operates in countries high in political risk: that is, where there is political uncertainty and instability, headquarters of global firms prefer to have PCNs in top positions so they can be conduits of information, provide advice, control what is going on in the subsidiary, and provide inputs to headquarters about strategy and policy considerations (Boyacigiller 1991).

Some companies send PCNs to overseas subsidiaries to make sure that the operation runs smoothly and according to headquarters' desires. Thus they are there to perform a "policeman" or "control" function. When PCNs return to the home office, the skills they have learned overseas can be utilized by top management during strategic planning, new product design and innovation, marketing, and allocating financial resources among the firm's subsidiaries.

Also, PCNs tend to be sent to countries that have significantly different cultural values, business systems, and societal norms than those of the home country. Boyacigiller (1991, p. 150) states that "strategically placed (PCNs) play an important interpretative role between the host-country culture and the headquarters offices."

There are disadvantages to staffing a foreign subsidiary with PCNs as well. Perhaps the most obvious one is that PCNs are costly. In addition to increasing domestic salaries, companies must pick up the costs of relocation, cost-of-living allowances, family benefit packages (such as housing and school), and costs of protection against terrorism. It has been estimated that a PCN manager costs the company three times the amount a local manager would cost for the same position (O'Boyle 1989). Also, PCNs have a "cultural learning curve": they must learn the nuances, intricacies, and norms of working in a foreign business culture. In other words, the PCN will not be able to step off the plane and perform well immediately. It takes time to learn how to be effective with people from diverse cultures—especially if foreign language skills are important. Because of this, the PCN may actually, in the short term, cost the company money in terms of real business: lost contracts, poor community relations, personal offenses to key government officials, poor relations with customers and suppliers, and poor morale at the office (Copeland & Griggs 1985).

Because of these disadvantages, many North American firms have in the past tried to move away from sending great numbers of PCNs overseas (Kobrin 1988). Some business people and researchers see this as a short-sighted strategy for North American companies to follow. The danger of staffing over-seas subsidiaries primarily with local managers is that top management of North American firms with international operations will only be able to identi-fy and understand domestic business issues and will be unable to formulate valid worldwide strategies and operating policies because of a lack of interna-tional experience. Simply taking the easy way out by not sending PCNs over-seas may come back to haunt companies later, and cause unforeseen obstacles to a company's global competitiveness.

HOST COUNTRY NATIONALS

Host country nationals (HCNs) refers to employees of the organization who work in an overseas subsidiary and are natives of the country in which the sub-sidiary is located. "Host country" refers to the country that hosts the sub-sidiary, and "national" refers to the citizenship of the worker. An example of a HCN would be a Peruvian who works for American Express in the Lima, Peru, subsidiary. Sometimes HCNs are simply called "host nationals" by researchers in the area of international human resource management. The term "native" or "native worker" is generally not used because of its negative connotation (a negative emotional holdover from colonial periods of countries' histories where people were ruled and employed by PCNs from powerful countries).

A clear advantage of employing HCNs at all levels of a subsidiary's operation is that they are familiar with local business norms and practices, already speak the local language and dialects, may be more adept at motivating and manag-ing workers from the host culture, and do not cost as much as PCNs to employ. Disadvantages of employing only HCNs are that they may not be aware of head-quarters' needs since they have never worked at the home office, may take a local rather than a global view of how the subsidiary should operate, and may have cultural problems when communicating and interacting with executives from the parent company.

Also, it may be difficult to train and develop managers in third world countries where views about achievement, equity, the work ethic, and productivity can differ vastly from Western views. Often international firms expect training to be quick and efficient in the international context. But if training programs are not designed to match how people from the culture in question are used to learning, they fail. Employing a totally HCN work force may or may not make sense, depending on the culture and the industry of the subsidiary.

For many years there was a stereotype view that HCN managers were not as sophisticated, well trained, or technically capable as PCNs. Thus PCNs were sent in great numbers to run overseas subsidiaries. In many countries there is now a large pool of well-educated and highly motivated HCNs to choose from when staffing an overseas subsidiary. Also, some governments require a certain percentage of HCNs to make up the managerial staff of foreign firms operating within their borders. Thus, in some cases, North American firms have no choice but to hire large numbers of HCN managers (Dowling & Schuler 1990).

THIRD COUNTRY NATIONALS

Third country nationals (TCNs) are employees of an organization that work outside the country of their birth and outside of the country where the parent company is headquartered. For example, a Swedish manager who works for a Canadian multinational's Tokyo subsidiary is a TCN. Similarly, a Nigerian manager who works for a U.S. company in Saudi Arabia is also a TCN. TCNs are transferred or hired mainly because of their expertise or because they are able to work more cheaply than either PCNs or HCNs.

In Europe it is common to meet professionals who have skills that firms covet (like software design or engineering expertise) and who move around the world following their company's (or another firm's) next lucrative offer. Some of these TCNs in Europe are being called "Euro-Managers," because they view the European continent as their domain, not just their home country. They rotate around European subsidiaries and are comfortable working virtually anywhere in Europe. Even so, at the managerial level, they are still a minority compared to PCNs and HCNs.

The main advantage for North American firms in employing TCNs is that they cost less and often have international experience along with foreign language skills. In other words, there is less risk in hiring a Swedish TCN who speaks English fluently to work in Norway than to send over a PCN who has no foreign language skills and no experience working in the Scandinavian business environment. However, the pool of potential TCNs is smaller than that of PCNs and

HCNs. Thus TCNs, while attractive, are not always an easy solution to overseas staffing problems. Also, local governments tend to view TCNs in the same way they do PCNs—as outsiders who are taking potential jobs away from their own people. Thus, government policies often limit the number of TCNs who can be employed in their country.

EXPATRIATES

Another common term in international human resource management is *expatriate*, referring to anyone living or working in a country of which they are not a citizen. Thus, PCNs and TCNs are expatriates. Our discussion of expatriates focuses mainly on PCNs and some TCNs—those employees who can be classified as possessing skills critical to the success of the performance of foreign subsidiaries.

Because work that expatriates perform can be critical to the success of their organizations, most researchers in the field of international human resource management have studied the key success factors for expatriates. Researchers have tried to isolate both the exact nature of international adjustment and the key skills that contribute to the expatriate's adjustment to a new social and business culture. If these cross-cultural management skills can be isolated, then companies can select people based on the degree to which they possess them. Also, a large number of expatriates seem to have adjustment problems overseas. Therefore if the important skills were known, companies could train expatriates already overseas and help them adjust to the culture and their jobs.

Some expatriates adjust so poorly that they simply abort their assignments and return home before their assignments are completed. No valid statistics are readily available as to how many expatriates return early from their assignments yearly, either because firms are reluctant to give out such information or because they simply do not keep records on employees who wind up leaving the company. Thus, researchers have had to estimate early returns of expatriates based on their own research data. Estimates generally range from 15 to 40 percent (see Bird & Dunbar 1991; Black 1988; Dunbar & Ehrlich 1986; Tung 1981; Zeira & Banai 1987).

It should be noted that "an additional 30 to 50 percent of American expatriates stay in their international assignments, but are regarded as either marginally effective or ineffective by their organization. According to evidence accumulated over the past twenty years, roughly one in three managers sent overseas gets the job done the way headquarters wanted it done" (Bird & Dunbar 1991; pp. 145–56). One in three is a good batting average in baseball, but in the business world, it is definitely below par. Before valid personnel selection criteria can be set up for expatriates, the skills and challenges that expatriates face overseas must be known.

INTERNATIONAL ADJUSTMENT

International adjustment is the degree to which the expatriate feels comfortable living and working in the host culture. This significantly influences job performance (Black & Mendenhall 1990). International adjustment begins when expatriates leave their familiar environment and other countries. Literally overnight, expatriates find themselves in a new world. They have to get used to the fact that the host nationals think, behave, and believe differently from people in their home country. It is often not easy to adjust to such foreign behaviors as belching during a dinner, driving on the left side of the road, bathing in public, being treated as a minority, having your motives viewed with suspicion, and not being able to read signs, menus, or newspapers. Yet expatriates who are sent to Japan, among other countries, have to deal with all of these concerns—and more.

Because the expatriate does not know all of the social rules or norms that dictate what is and is not acceptable behavior at work and in society, he or she will experience psychological uncertainty. This anxiety surfaces when people are in situations where they feel out of control, do not know how they should behave, or are unable to predict how other people will behave toward them. Psychologists, anthropologists, and human resource specialists agree that expatriates have a strong desire to reduce psychological uncertainty whenever it occurs.

Another term that is often used to describe this psychological uncertainty is "culture shock." Nancy Adler (1991) defines culture shock as "the frustration and confusion that result from being bombarded by uninterpretable cues." As we interact during the day with others in our culture, we respond to behavioral cues that let us know what we should do next. For example, if I meet an acquaintance on the street and he extends his hand to me, that is a cue that I should extend my hand to shake his. In a different culture, however, a host national may do something that he/she perceives as being a cue, while the expatriate, not knowing the rules of social behavior, may not respond appropriately, leading the host national to conclude that the expatriate is rude or backward. When people are in a new culture and do not know how to respond appropriately to behavioral cues, they experience culture shock.

THE CYCLE OF CULTURE SHOCK AND CROSS-CULTURAL ADJUSTMENT

Many researchers have investigated the dynamics of culture shock and have found that to a large degree culture shock follows the general pattern of a U-shaped curve (Black & Mendenhall 1991). Exhibit 12.1 illustrates the relationship between culture shock and the length of time the expatriate has been living and working in the host culture. The cycle is divided into four stages: honeymoon, culture shock, adjustment, and mastery.

In the honeymoon stage the expatriate is fascinated by the host culture. During this stage the expatriate and her/his family usually are living in a hotel until their housing can be arranged, or they may have moved directly into a new home or luxury apartment. Everything is new and exciting, and the host nationals seem exotic and interesting. Generally during this stage the company is providing plenty of support for the expatriate and his/her family, such as help with getting the children enrolled in school, transportation, and so forth. In short, everything is new, fun, and adventurous. This stage generally lasts up to two or three months after arrival.

EXHIBIT 12.1

THE U-CURVE OF CROSS-CULTURAL ADJUSTMENT

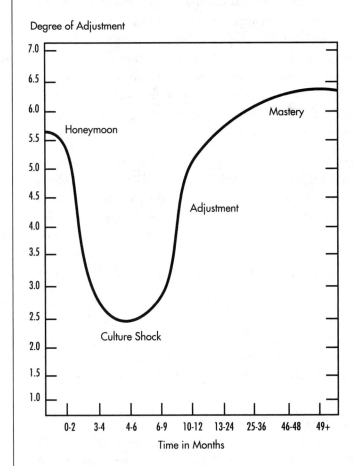

Degree of Adjustment

SOURCE:

Black, J.S. & M. Mendenhall. 1991. "The U-Curve adjustment hypothesis revisited: A review and theoretical framework." *Journal of International Business Studies*, Vol. 22 second quarter, pp. 225–247.

During the culture shock stage the expatriate changes from being infatuated with the host culture to being disillusioned, frustrated, confused, or unhappy with living and working overseas. After a month or two, the company's official support system fades into the background (because the support personnel must turn their attention to new expatriates who are arriving), and the expatriate and his/her family are left to fend for themselves in their daily activities. The manager is on his/her own, and the spouse similarly must figure out how and where to shop, how to communicate with doctors and dentists, where to go for entertainment, and how to build friendships. In other words, expatriates must begin settling into a daily rhythm of living. As they do this, they run into the difficulty of sorting through cultural differences. As shown in Exhibit 12.1, from about three months to upwards of nine or ten months after arrival, the "adjustment" or "satisfaction" curve dips, indicating the expatriate is struggling to adapt to the norms of the host culture.

Before describing the adjustment stage it should be noted that many expatriates never get beyond the culture shock stage, and either return home early from their assignment or simply "gut it out" and complete their assignment but are never completely effective in their assignment or happy about living in the host culture. For these expatriates there is no U-curve, or at best the right arm of the U-curve is shorter than the left arm, indicating that some adjustment has taken place but not enough to offset their frustrations with the host culture.

The *adjustment stage* occurs as the expatriate begins to learn the norms and ways of getting things done in the new culture and in the job. This is a gradual adaptation that occurs generally from the nine-to-ten month point and continues throughout the rest of the overseas assignment. This gradual learning of the host culture requires intensive effort on the part of expatriates—it does not occur naturally.

Eventually the expatriate may enter the *mastery stage* when he/she can function effectively in and enjoy the nuances of the host culture and its institutions, norms, traditions, and activities. Expatriates may not like some of values and norms of the host culture. But at this stage of adjustment, they are able to understand why aspects of the host culture that they find unattractive exist and also realize that different, but just as apparently unpleasant, aspects of their own culture also exist. This stage involves a high level of cross-cultural maturity, and it is only reached after diligent study, effort, and desire to understand a host culture.

Not all expatriates go through this cycle in the same way, though there is evidence that expatriates do generally go through each phase of the cycle. Expatriates who have undergone cross-cultural training (either company-sponsored or on their own) before they depart for their overseas assignment tend to adjust better than those who undergo no training. The downward cycle from the honeymoon phase to culture shock is less steep for those who have had training because they have anticipated the challenges and have begun to acculturate themselves before they leave their home country. This process is called *anticipatory socialization*. (Black & Mendenhall 1991).

Another variable influencing the U-curve's slope and shape is individual differences. Expatriates who possess superior skills in self-efficacy, willingness to communicate, willingness to establish relationships with host nationals, tolerance for ambiguity, and many other skills that will be discussed later in this chapter adjust better and more quickly than expatriates who possess fewer of these skills.

In summary, to reduce the stress and anxiety of culture shock and increase international adjustment, an expatriate must learn the host culture's social rules, and the reasons why these exist within that culture. As this increases, so does the level of adjustment to the host culture. And as adjustment increases, expatriate's productivity and quality of life increase as well.

DETERMINANTS OF INTERNATIONAL ADJUSTMENT

Recent research on international adjustment shows that it consists of at least three dimensions: adjustment to the overseas workplace, adjustment to interacting with the host nationals, and adjustment to the general overseas environment. (Black, Mendenhall & Oddou 1991). This research has uncovered skills that assist both individual expatriates and international organizations in dealing with each of the three dimensions of international adjustment. Some of the skills are necessary for adjustment in all three of the dimensions, while some are skills that enable adjustment to only one or two of the dimensions. These relationships are portrayed in Exhibit 12.2, and we will review the areas that influence international adjustment as identified in this exhibit.

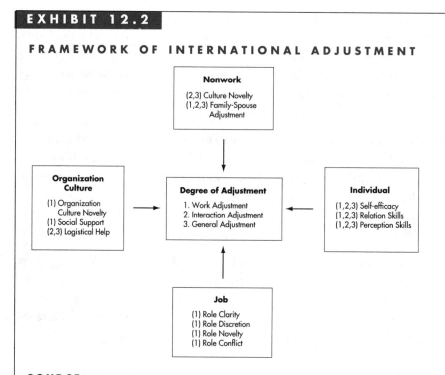

EXHIBIT 12.2

FRAMEWORK OF INTERNATIONAL ADJUSTMENT

Nonwork

(2,3) Culture Novelty
(1,2,3) Family-Spouse
Adjustment

Organization Culture

(1) Organization
Culture Novelty
(1) Social Support
(2,3) Logistical Help

Degree of Adjustment

1. Work Adjustment
2. Interaction Adjustment
3. General Adjustment

Individual

(1,2,3) Self-efficacy
(1,2,3) Relation Skills
(1,2,3) Perception Skills

Job

(1) Role Clarity
(1) Role Discretion
(1) Role Novelty
(1) Role Conflict

SOURCE:

Adapted from: Black, J.S., M. Mendenhall, & G. Oddou. 1991. "Toward a comprehensive model of international adjustment: An integration of multiple theoretical perspectives." *Academy of Management Review*, 16(2), pp. 291–317.

INDIVIDUAL DIMENSION

The individual dimension includes cross-cultural skills that the expatriate possesses. These are perhaps the most important set of skills that contribute to international adjustment because they are in the control of the expatriate and no one else. To a large degree, all the other sets of skills depend upon forces outside the expatriate. There are three general sets of individual skills: self-efficacy, relational, and perception skills (Mendenhall & Oddou 1985). Within these three skill domains, there are, of course, a multiplicity of specific skills that could be discussed; we have chosen those that have emerged from the research literature more often than others. More research is needed to be able to outline with confidence the complete set of skills necessary for international adjustment. However, enough research has been done to identify the critical skills in international adjustment.

Self-Efficacy Skills

Many researchers have found that the ability to possess and retain a state of stable mental health and a confidence in one's own ability to deal with unforeseen cross-cultural occurrences in the new environment are critical to all three dimensions of international adjustment. This ability includes skills and activities that "serve to strengthen the expatriate's self-esteem, self-confidence, and mental hygiene" (Mendenhall & Oddou 1985). It is essential that the expatriate be able to keep mentally and socially healthy with a feeling of being able to control or deal with surprises from the host cultural environment. Stress reduction, technical competence, and reinforcement substitution are three skills in this domain.

1. *Stress reduction.* This ability to deal with such frustrations as interpersonal conflict, financial difficulties, differing business systems, social alienation, pressure to conform, loneliness, and differences in housing, climate, and cuisine is critical to the productive functioning of the expatriate. This finding is true of expatriates of all nationalities (Abe & Wiseman 1983; Bardo & Bardo 1980). No one method of dealing with stress seems to manifest itself from the research findings. What is important is simply having an ongoing stress-reduction program that works for the individual. Indrei Ratiu (1983) found that well-adjusted expatriates have "stability zones." These are mental activities that expatriates resort to when the overseas assignment becomes stressful, such as meditation, religious worship, writing in diaries, and engaging in hobbies. Expatriates need to have an ongoing, clear strategy to reduce the stress that will inevitably occur when living in an unfamiliar culture.

2. *Technical competence.* It should come as no surprise that the ability to get the job done overseas is an important predictor of international adjustment. If an expatriate is unsure of how to accomplish the overseas task, he/she will not be effective until confidence and expertise are gained. A number of researchers have found this rela-

tionship between technical competence and adjustment; one example is the work of Hawes and Kealey (1981), who studied 160 technical advisors and 90 spouses working in 26 projects in 6 countries. Their data revealed that technical competence had a significant effect on whether the technicians and their spouses were comfortable and productive in the overseas assignments.

3. *Reinforcement substitution.* This skill involves "replacing activities that bring pleasure and happiness in the home culture with similar—yet different—activities that exist in the host culture" (Mendenhall & Oddou 1985, p. 40). For example, no matter what country or culture one travels to, the following human interests exist: sports, cuisine, music, art, dance, architecture, and family organizations. Yet, in each culture, the way these interests are manifested differs. For example: in New Zealand, the interest in sports is manifested in rugby, cricket, horse racing, soccer, rowing, softball, and track and field; in the U.S. the main manifestations are baseball, football, basketball, ice hockey, and car racing. An example of reinforcement substitution, for an American expatriate in New Zealand, is the ability to replace love of baseball, with love of rugby—literally to replace the form of reinforcement.

Relational Skills

This domain encompasses skills that enhance the expatriate's ability, desire, and tendency to interact and develop relationships with host nationals. Relational skills are necessary for all three dimensions of international adjustment. While a few expatriates may find that they can get by without interacting with many host nationals, most expatriates will confront host nationals on a daily basis in a variety of settings such as work, grocery stores, public transportation, church, and the neighborhood. Expatriates basically have to make a conscious decision whether they will or will not interact beyond a surface level with the host nationals. While there are many specific skills that relate to developing relationships with host nationals, two skills consistently emerge in the research: finding mentors and being willing to communicate with host nationals.

1. *Finding mentors.* Researchers have found that expatriates who develop close relationships with host nationals are better adjusted and more productive in their overseas assignment than expatriates who do not try to develop such friendships. Establishing friendships with host nationals seems to have "the same effect on the expatriate that a mentor has on a new employee; that is, the experienced person guides the neophyte through the intricacies and complexity of the new organization or culture, protecting him/her against faux pas and helping him/her enact appropriate behaviors" (Mendenhall & Oddou 1985, p. 42). In other words, it is beneficial for an expatriate to develop and nurture a relationship with a host national who can explain things that confuse the expatriate.

Developing such relationships takes time, and the benefit to the expatriate may not show up for a year or so. Ingemar Torbiorn (1982) found that satisfaction with living overseas was different for expatriates based upon their friendships. Expatriates who limited their friendships to other expatriates were more satisfied during the first year than were expatriates who sought out host nationals as friends. However, this changed at the one-year point of the overseas assignment; from then on expatriates who had friendships with host nationals experienced higher levels of satisfaction and adjustment than did expatriates who limited their friendships to fellow expatriates. This relationship is portrayed in Exhibit 12.3.

2. *Willingness to communicate.* Many people assume that being fluent in a foreign language is necessary in order to be a successful expatriate; however, that is not necessarily the case. While complete fluency is a desired goal, it is not a precondition in and of itself to international adjustment. Researchers have found that in developing relationships with host nationals it is not the level of fluency that is important, but rather that the expatriate makes the effort to learn the language in order to get to know and become more familiar with the host nationals and their culture.

Fluency becomes a powerful tool when used strategically by expatriates to create and foster relationships with host nationals. The strategic use of foreign language skills can take many forms, but generally it takes the form of what Brein and David (1971) call "conversational currency." Conversational currency involves collecting cultural information such as proverbs, lyrics to popular songs, famous incidents from history, information about sports and media celebrities, and jokes. The expatriate can insert these tidbits of information into daily conversations with host nationals; this has the effect of showing the host nationals that the expatriate is interested in them and their culture and makes the expatriate more trustworthy in their eyes.

EXHIBIT 12.3

THE ADJUSTMENT PROCESS AND FRIENDS

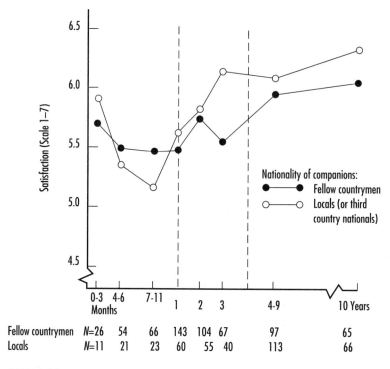

Fellow countrymen	N=26	54	66	143	104	67	97	65
Locals	N=11	21	23	60	55	40	113	66

SOURCE:

Torbiorn, Ingemar. 1982. *Living Abroad: Personal Adjustment and Personnel Policy in the Overseas Setting.* NY: John Wiley & Sons, Inc. Reprinted by permission of John Wiley & Sons, Ltd.

Perception Skills

The third set of skills under the individual domain is perception skills. These have to do with the expatriate's ability to understand why host nationals behave and think the way they do and to make correct inferences as to the motives behind these behaviors. If expatriates understand why host nationals do what they do, they are able to a large degree to reduce the psychological uncertainty associated with cross-cultural experiences. If the expatriate knows the reasons or motives for host nationals' behavior, he/she can feel comfortable in their presence.

The more understanding an expatriate has about the way people think and behave, the more likely the expatriate will be able to predict how people are likely to behave in the future; this reduces psychological uncertainty. Unfortunately, the ability to understand what goes on in other people's minds is not a skill that comes naturally to a lot of people. Even in one's own culture many people find this skill difficult to attain. Research shows that people from different cultures often misinterpret each other's behavior because of the way they have been socialized about how they should perceive and evaluate the behavior of others.

Most important is the ability to be nonjudgmental when faced with confusing situations. This means not labeling people "backward" or "stupid" or "unsophisticated" when they do or say things that would be viewed that way at home. The expatriate's ability to hold back his/her natural evaluations of people until collecting more information about why they behave as they do is critical for international adjustment. Researchers have generally found that being nonjudgmental, accepting the host national's norms as being legitimate for them, and not evaluating host national's behavior according to one's home culture's criteria for acceptable behavior all assist the expatriate to interact with host nationals in a more productive, effective, and emotionally satisfying way.

THE NONWORK DIMENSION

The upper box in Exhibit 12.2 illustrates the relationship between "nonwork" variables and international adjustment. There are two main nonwork variables that influence the expatriate's degree of adjustment: culture novelty and family/spouse adjustment.

Culture novelty includes the basic differences in values, norms, religious beliefs, sex roles, and so on of the host country compared to those of the home country. The greater the difference, the more novel the culture will be for the expatriate; and the greater the novelty in the host culture, the more difficult it will be for the expatriate to adjust.

Experts who have reviewed studies on international adjustment have found this to be a consistent and important aspect of international adjustment. For example, Ingemar Torbiorn studied 641 male and 474 female Swedish expatriates who were living and working in 26 countries (Torbiorn 1982). His results given in Exhibit 12.4 show a rank ordering of countries in terms of the expatriates' satisfaction with living and working in those countries. While there are exceptions within each region, his findings on culture novelty can be summarized by these groupings: high culture novelty (North Africa, Middle East, East Africa); moderate culture novelty (Latin America, Southeast Asia, South Pacific); and low culture novelty (Southern Europe, Central Europe, North America). No one to date has done similar research on North American expatriates; however a rough approximation of culture novelty for Americans can be gained by comparing the index scores of Hofstedes' dimensions (as discussed in Chapter 3) between the U.S. and other countries. Again, while the index scores should not be generalized across all citizens in each country, Hofstede's findings may provide a rough approximation of culture novelty.

The other nonwork variable is *family-spouse adjustment*. The expatriate may have excellent cross-cultural skills and be doing very well on the job, but research shows that if that expatriate's spouse and/or family members are having trouble adjusting, then the expatriate will have problems—which could lead to a premature departure from the overseas assignment. This is an important issue since approximately 85 percent of American expatriates are married. Black and Stephens (1989) found a relationship between expatriates' adjustment and the adjustment of their spouses for a large group of American expatriates in several different countries. These findings are consistent with other researchers who have found that the inability of the spouse or the children to adjust can negatively affect the expatriate's job performance and can increase the likelihood of an aborted overseas assignment (Black & Gregersen 1991; Gaylord 1979; Harvey 1985; Walker 1976).

EXHIBIT 12.4

HOST COUNTRIES RANKED ACCORDING TO
EXPATRIATE SATISFACTION (ARITHMETIC MEAN)

MEN	WOMEN	TOTAL
1. Switzerland	1. South Africa	1. Switzerland
2. Belgium	2. Switzerland	2. Belgium
3. England	3. France	3. South Africa
4. South Africa	4. USA	4. England
5. Portugal	5. England	5. Portugal
6. Colombia, Ecuador, Venezuela	6. Colombia, Ecuador, Venezuela	6. Colombia, Ecuador, Venezuela
7. Canada	7. Brazil	6. USA
8. Australia, New Zealand	8. Belgium	8. Brazil
9. USA	8. Mexico	9. France
10. Brazil	8. Portugal	10. Canada
11. Mexico	8. South East Asia	11. Mexico
12. Spain	12. Spain	12. Spain
13. France	13. Canada	13. Holland
14. Holland	14. Holland	13. South East Asia
15. South East Asia	15. Liberia	15. Australia, New Zealand
16. West Germany	16. West Germany	16. West Germany
17. Austria	17. Italy	17. Liberia
18. Italy	18. Austria	18. Austria
19. Chile, Peru	19. Japan	19. Italy
20. East Africa (Kenya, Tanzania, Uganda)	20. Argentina, Uruguay	20. East Africa (Kenya, Tanzania, Uganda)
21. India, Pakistan	21. Australia, New Zealand	21. Argentina, Uruguay
22. Liberia	22. India, Pakistan	22. India, Pakistan
23. Argentina, Uruguay	23. Middle East	23. Chile, Peru
24. Japan	24. East Africa (Kenya, Tanzania, Uganda)	24. Japan
25. Middle East	25. Chile, Peru	25. Middle East
26. North Africa (Algeria, Egypt, Morocco, Tunisia)	26. North Africa (Algeria, Egypt, Morocco, Tunisia)	26. North Africa (Algeria, Egypt, Morocco, Tunisia)

SOURCE:

Torbiorn, Ingemar. 1982. *Living Abroad: Personal Adjustment and Personnel Policy in the Overseas Setting.* NY: John Wiley & Sons, Inc. Reprinted by permission of John Wiley & Sons, Ltd.

An important question, then, is "Are the factors of adjustment different for spouses than for managers?" To date, no research studies have tried to answer this question, but a recent study has turned up some interesting findings. Black and Gregersen (1991) found that the following factors predict positive spouse adjustment:

- The spouse was in favor of accepting the assignment from the start.

- The spouse engaged in self-initiated, cross-cultural training.

- The spouse had a social support network of HCNs.

- The standard of living in the overseas assignment was acceptable to the spouse.

- The firm sought the spouse's opinion regarding the international assignment from the beginning of the selection process.

- The spouse could adjust to the degree of culture novelty (the higher the culture novelty the less likely the spouse would adjust to the new culture).

THE JOB DIMENSION

It is obvious that to be successful overseas expatriates must adjust, master, and perform at acceptable levels in their jobs. Researchers in international human resource management are just beginning to study in detail the relationship between job variables and international adjustment. Many studies have looked at how the nature of a job can influence performance for people who are transferred within the United States, and many of these findings should theoretically hold true for expatriates as well. The "job" box of Exhibit 12.2 shows four variables that can hamper or help the expatriate adjust to an overseas assignment. The first, *role clarity*, deals with the issue of how clearly the expatriate understands the new job's tasks, demands, and roles. Does the expatriate have a clear idea about what is expected on the job, or is the expatriate basically in the dark about the duties? High role clarity reduces the amount of uncertainty associated with the work situation, and this helps the expatriate adjust to the new workplace.

The second issue, *role discretion*, involves the degree to which the work place is flexible in its rules, expectations, procedures, and policies. In a situation where the work place is flexible, the expatriate can influence his/her role in the office rather than having to adapt and conform to rigid work restrictions. The greater degree of role discretion, the lower the level of adjustment the expatriate will experience in the job.

The third variable, *role novelty*, refers to how different the new job's duties, tasks, and responsibilities are from the previous job back home. The greater the degree of role novelty, the greater the difficulty the expatriate will have in adjusting to the new job. In this sense role novelty is similar to culture novelty that was discussed previously in this chapter.

The fourth variable that influences job adjustment overseas is *role conflict*. Role conflict inhibits international adjustment and occurs when the expatriate gets conflicting signals from people at work regarding his/her role, duties, and performance standards. When this happens, the expatriate will become stressed and will not adapt to the new job in a timely and effective manner.

THE ORGANIZATIONAL CULTURE DIMENSION

All organizations have cultures of their own as evidenced in the rules, norms, expectations, sanctions, and operating procedures—both written and unwritten—that influence how employees get the work done. When an expatriate takes on a new assignment in a foreign country, he/she will likely have to learn a new organizational culture. Adjusting to the overseas organizational culture is necessary to performing the job well.

Organizational culture novelty is similar to culture novelty and role novelty. If the overseas job is high in organizational culture novelty, the expatriate will have a difficult time adjusting to the work situation and will in turn have a more difficult time adjusting to the culture in general. Also, an organizational culture that encourages social support from co-workers and superiors provides new expatriates with clear information about what is and is not acceptable work behavior. Support systems that clarify work rules and procedures for the expatriates, and thus reduce uncertainty, help the expatriate to adjust.

Similarly, if the firm offers support for the expatriate and family in the form of housing, payment of school tuition, practical information about shopping, and so forth, the expatriate will feel a part of the larger social group. If such support does not exist, the expatriate may become frustrated, alienated, and lonely because of a lack of information about the social options available.

APPLICATIONS OF RESEARCH FINDINGS TO GLOBAL COMPANIES

The process of accepting an overseas job and then performing well in that job is a complex issue. Many variables can complicate the good intentions of the expatriate to do a good job overseas: a stressed spouse, an unwillingness to interact with the host nationals, a rigid or unclear work environment, the local culture itself, communication barriers, the challenge of new job demands. The list could go on and on. Thus, it is clear that companies should carefully select the manager to be sent to the overseas office. How do most North American firms select people to go overseas? What criteria do they use to select expatriates?

While it is clear from the research is that to be successful overseas one must possess a variety of individual, interpersonal, and organizational skills, usually only one criterion is used to assess whether candidates go overseas or not: their performance track record. This tendency to use only one criterion to select expatriates has been evidenced since the 1970s. Perhaps one respondent in Baker and Ivancevich's 1971 research study best summarizes the attitude: "Managing a company is a scientific art. The executive accomplishing the task in New York can surely perform as adequately in Hong Kong (p. 40)." This executives felt that other skill dimensions were of little importance: what worked in North America would work anywhere in the world.

Tung found that only five percent of the firms she studied administered tests to determine the relational, cross-cultural, and interpersonal skills of their candidates for overseas assignments. She concluded that:

> It is surprising that an overwhelming majority of the firms included in the study failed to assess the candidate's relational abilities when they clearly recognize that relational abilities are important for overseas work and when research has shown "relational abilities" to be crucial to success in overseas assignments. Given the increasing

demand for personnel who could function effectively abroad and the relatively high incidence of failure, there certainly appears to be room for improvement in this area. (Tung 1981, p. 75)

Not only the candidate, but the candidate's spouse and family need to be included in the selection process. This should be clear based upon research findings that show that the inability of the spouse to adjust often causes expatriate managers to fail. However, studies in the 1970s and 1980s that looked at how firms dealt with the family of the expatriate during selection found that only 40-to-52 percent interviewed the candidates' wives. It should be noted that these interviews were not part of an in-depth screening process, but were designed to get a general feeling for the spouse's willingness to accompany the employee overseas. Raymond Stone (1991, p. 10) of Asia Pacific Management Pty., Ltd., found that "technical know-how remains, in practice, the most important selection factor."

A more comprehensive approach to expatriate selection, which takes into account many of the issues discussed in this chapter, was proposed by Rosalie Tung in 1981 (see Exhibit 12.5). She suggests that the selection decision should be based on answering important questions that relate to expatriate adjustment. The issues of interacting with host nationals, technical competence, culture novelty, family situation, and communication skills all are combined into Tung's decision-making framework. Tung's framework also takes into consideration the fact that overseas jobs differ, and that some jobs may require more interaction with host nationals than others; thus thecriteria for selection need not be the same for all overseas assignments. The framework is general and does not specify exactly how candidates can be measured and evaluated on the criteria she proposes as being important in the selection process.

An important issue to consider when selecting expatriates is how to measure candidates on all of the variables that are important for international adjustment. Some are easier to measure than others, but with effort, all of the dimensions in the four boxes in Exhibit 12.2 (individual, job, organizational culture, nonwork) can be measured and used to assist top management in carefully selecting expatriates.

EXHIBIT 12.5

FLOW CHART OF THE
SELECTION-DECISION PROCESS

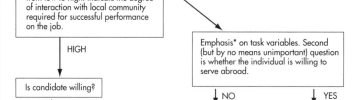

START THE SELECTION PROCESS

Can the position be filled by a local national? ──YES──▶ Select local national and subject him to training basically aimed at improving technical and managerial skills.

NO

Identify degree of interaction required with local community— using a 7- or 9-point scale, ranging from low to high. Indicate the degree of interaction with local community required for successful performance on the job.

LOW

HIGH

Emphasis* on task variables. Second (but by no means unimportant) question is whether the individual is willing to serve abroad.

Is candidate willing?

NO   YES

Probably not suitable for position   Start orientation (moderate-to-low rigor)

NO

YES

Probably not suitable for position

Identify degree of similarity/ dissimilarity between cultures— using a 7- or 9-point scale, ranging from similar to highly diverse. Indicate the magnitude of differences between the two cultures.

VERY SIMILAR

HIGHLY DIVERSE

Emphasis* on task variables

*Emphasis on "relational abilities" factor. "Family situaition" factor must also be taken into consideration.

Start orientation (moderate-to-high rigor)

Start orientation (most rigorous)

*"Emphasis" does not mean ignoring the other factors. It only means that it should be the dominant factor.

SOURCE:

R.L. Tung, 1981. "Selection and training of personnel for overseas assignments." *Columbia Journal of World Business*, Vol.16, No.1, pp. 68-78.

1. *The individual dimension.* Many instruments can be used to measure the candidates' self-efficacy, relational skills, and perception. In the self-efficacy area, the company probably already has detailed records on technical competence and job performance. Also, there are numerous stress tests to evaluate a candidate's stress-reduction skills. Reinforcement substitution is more difficult to measure, but could be approximated through careful interviews and questionnaires that measure attitudes toward experimentating with new behaviors.

   Relational skills could be evaluated through role playing, assessment centers, and in-depth interviews by psychologists and the applicant's superiors. Role playing allows trained observers to measure and calculate the candidate's abilities and predispositions in a variety of hypothetical cross-cultural situations. Assessment centers are off-site testing centers where candidates run through a battery of tests to measure their overall ability for a job. The tests could include role plays, job simulations, in-depth interviews, and tests of job skills (such as interviewing, working in teams, giving feedback, and so on). Ability and desire to learn foreign languages can also be ascertained through testing and biographical data. Work samples are another vehicle for measuring relational skills. They involve doing a part of the actual overseas job as part of the selection process. This can be done at home or during a short-term overseas assignment. Overseas job simulations can also be developed for testing use in the home country.

   Finally, perception can be evaluated by a number of existing psychological tests, most notably for U.S. citizens the California F-Test, the Guilford-Zimmerman Temperament Survey, and the Allport-Vernon Study of Values (Howard 1974; Tung 1981).

2. *The nonwork dimension.* As previously mentioned, culture novelty can be ascertained to some degree by using Hofstede's index scores on the countries in his study. Also, it can be evaluated through an

in-depth study of the host country's religious, social, cultural, soci-
ological, historical, political, and economic systems and comparisons to home-country systems. Countries that are dissimilar to
North America would be considered high in culture novelty for
North Americans. Thus, companies would have a good sense of how
challenging a foreign assignment is likely to be and can conduct a
selection with that clearly in mind. Also, for family adjustment, all
the procedures described for individuals could be applied to spouses and children of the candidate. This makes sense since the family can derail the expatriate's adjustment.

3. *The job dimension.* A thorough job analysis should be conducted so
that those involved in the selection process have a clear idea what
the overseas assignment requires. When false assumptions are
made about the job and a candidate is selected based on those
assumptions, failure at some level is likely to ensue. The human
resource staff may even need to travel on a short-term assignment to
analyze what exact skills would be necessary to accomplish an overseas job. Then the work samples or assessment center techniques
could be used to evaluate a candidate's ability to work well in the
overseas assignment.

4. *The organizational culture dimension.* The human resource staff can
easily analyze the quality of logistical and social support for expatriates in an overseas subsidiary by talking to current expatriates. If
there are no expatriates in the subsidiary, systems will need to be
created through working with the HCN staff of the subsidiary.
Analyzing the organizational culture novelty of a subsidiary is difficult to do well because it takes much time, effort, and observation.
This may be the most difficult factor to evaluate in the selection
process. Human resource staff can approximate the organizational
culture of the overseas subsidiary by interviewing current and past
expatriates who work or have worked in that subsidiary, then analyzing the results of the interview. The analysis would reveal how the
subsidiary gets things done, what formal and informal procedures are
in place, and what challenges the new expatriate is likely to face.

The selection matrix in Exhibit 12.6 illustrates the options that human resource specialists have in constructing a valid selection process for expatriates. It should be emphasized that most North American companies use very few cells of this matrix when they select people for overseas assignments.

SUMMARY

This chapter has focused on the different types of employees that work in the international work place (parent country nationals, host country nationals, third country nationals, foreign guestworkers, and expatriates), and the advantages and disadvantages of each type on overseas assignments. Various challenges that expatriate managers and their families confront overseas were discussed, such as the problem of adjusting to a new culture, culture shock, and the essential skills needed for overseas productivity.

The culture shock cycle and its stages were covered in detail. Each stage and its attendant challenges and problems were outlined and illustrated. Knowing the process humans undergo when shifting cultures is an important factor in one's ability to successfully acculturate in an overseas environment.

The dimensions of international adjustment (individual, nonwork, organizational culture, and job) were discussed in depth, along with the skills and important issues that fall within each dimension. Each of these skills acts as an important determinant of the level of future satisfaction the expatriate will have in living and working overseas. Thus, it is critical that human resource managers understand the skills associated with expatriate success before they become involved in assisting companies evaluate candidates for overseas assignments.

Finally, applications of this knowledge to selecting expatriates was considered, and suggestions were made that would assist companies who are international in nature or who are thinking of going international to select the right candidates for international assignments. Tung's model of expatriate selection was reviewed, and a selection matrix was offered as a tool for human resource managers to consider in aiding their decisions when selecting candidates for overseas assignments.

EXHIBIT 12.6   SELECTION MATRIX

Expatriate	Biographical Data	Standardized Tests	Work Samples	Assessment Centers	Interviews	References
Strategic Factors						
▪ Coordination and Control	✓				✓	✓
▪ Information and Technology Exchange	✓				✓	✓
▪ Executive Development	✓			✓	✓	✓
Assignment Required Professional Skills	✓	✓	✓	✓	✓	✓
General Managerial Skills						
▪ Conflict Resolution Approach		✓	✓	✓	✓	
▪ Leadership Style		✓	✓	✓	✓	
Communication Skills						
▪ Foreign Language Skills	✓	✓				
▪ Willingness to Communicate		✓	✓	✓	✓	
▪ Relationship Development		✓		✓	✓	✓
Individual Characteristics						
▪ Ethnocentricity		✓		✓	✓	
▪ Cultural Adaptability		✓		✓	✓	
▪ Stress Reduction Skills		✓		✓	✓	
Spouse Career Considerations					✓	
Children's Educational Needs					✓	

SOURCE:
Black, J.S., H.B. Gregersen, & M. Mendenhall. 1992. *Global Assignments: Succussfully Expatriating and Repatriating International Managers*. CA: Jossey-Bass, Inc.

DISCUSSION QUESTIONS

1. From the student's perspective, discuss how culture shock is likely to influence a person studying in a foreign location.

2. Select from the characteristics identified in the chapter that are important to international managers the one which you believe is most important. Discuss why this characteristic is especially important to international success as a manager.

3. Discuss the relationship between effective selection of managers and culture shock.

REFERENCES

Abe, H. & R.L. Wiseman. 1983. "A cross-cultural confirmation of the dimensions of intercultural effectiveness." *International Journal of Intercultural Relations*, 7, pp. 53–68.

Adler, N. 1991. *International Dimensions of Organization Behavior*, 2nd ed. Boston: PWS-Kent Publishing Company.

Baker, J.C. & J.M. Ivancevich. 1971. "The assignment of American executives abroad: Systematic, haphazard, or chaotic." *California Management Reveiw*, 13(3), pp. 39–41.

Bardo J.W. & D.J. Bardo. 1980. "Dimensions of adjustment for American settlers in Melbourne, Australia." *Multivariate Experimental Clinical Research*, 5, pp. 23–28.

Barrett, G.V. & B.M. Bass. 1976. "Cross-Cultural Issues in Industrial and Organizational Psychology." In the *Handbook of Industrial and Organizational Psychology*, M.D. Dunnette (ed.) pp. 1639–1686. Chicago: Rand-McNally College Publishing.

Bird, A. & R. Dunbar. 1991. "Getting the job done over there: Improving expatriate productivity," *National Productivity Review*, Spring, pp. 145–156.

Black J.S. & M. Mendenhall. 1990. "Cross-Cultural training effectiveness: A review and a theoretical framework for future research." *Academy of Management Review*, 15(1) pp. 113–136.

Black, J.S. & G.K. Stephens. 1989. "The Influence of the Spouse on American Expatriate Adjustment in Overseas Assignments." *Journal of Management*, 15, pp. 529–544.

Black, J.S. & H. Gregersen. 1991. "The Other Half of the Picture: Antecedents of spouse cross-cultural adjustment." *Journal of International Business Studies*, 22(3), pp. 461–478.

Black, J.S., H. Gregersen, & M. Mendenhall. 1992. *Global Assignments: Successfully Expatriating and Repatriating International Managers.* San Francisco: Jossey-Bass.

Black, J.S. & M. Mendenhall. 1991. "The U-Curve hypothesis revisited: A review and a theoretical framework." *Journal of International Business Studies*, 22(2), pp. 225–247.

Black, J.S. 1988. "Work role transitions: A study of American expatriate managers in Japan." *Journal of International Business Studies*, 19, pp. 277–294.

Black, J.S., M. Mendenhall, & G. Oddou. 1991. "Toward a comprehensive model of international adjustment: An integration of multiple theoretical perspectives." *Academy of Management Review*, 16(2), pp. 291–317.

Boyacigiller, N. 1991. "The international assignment reconsidered." In *Readings and Cases in International Human Resource Management*, M. Mendenhall and G. Oddou (eds.). Boston: PWS-Kent.

Brein, M. & K.H. David. 1971. *Improving Cross-Cultural Training and Measurement of Cross-Cultural Learning*, Vol. 1. Denver: Center for Research and Education.

Copeland, L. & L. Griggs. 1985. *Going International.* New York: Random House.

Dowling, P. & R.S. Schuler. 1990. *International Dimensions of Human Resource Management*. Boston: PWS-Kent Publishing Company.

Dunbar E. & M. Ehrlich, 1986. "International practices, selection, training, and managing the international staff: A survey report." New York: Columbia University, Teachers College, Project on International Human Resources.

Gaylord, M. 1979. "Relocation and the Corporate Family," *Social Work*, May, pp. 186–191.

Graham, M.A. 1983. "Acculturative stress among Polynesian, Asian, and American students on the Brigham Young University—Hawaii campus." *International Journal of Intercultural Relations*, 7, pp. 79–100.

Gudykunst, W.B. & M.R. Hammer. 1984. "Dimensions of intercultural effectiveness: Culture specific or culture general." *International Journal of Intercultural Relations*, 8(1), pp. 1–10.

Hammer, M.R., W.B. Gudykunst, & R.L. Wiseman. 1978. "Dimensions of intercultural effectiveness: An exploratory study." *International Journal of Intercultural Relations*," 2, pp. 382–393.

Harris, J.G., Jr. 1973. "A science of the South Pacific: Analysis of the character structure of the Peace Corps Volunteer." *American Psychologist*, 28, pp. 232–247.

Harvey, M.G. 1985. "The executive family: An overlooked variable in international assignments." *Columbia Journal of World Business*, Spring, pp. 84–92.

Hautaluoma, J.E. & V. Kaman. 1975. "Description of Peace Corps Volunteers' experience in Afghanistan." *Topics in Culture Learning*, 3, pp. 79–96.

Hawes, F. & D.J. Kealey. 1981. "An empirical study of Canadian technical assistance." *International Journal of Intercultural Relations*, 5, pp. 239–258.

Hays, R.D. 1971. "Ascribed behavioral determinants of success-failure among U.S. expatriate managers." *Journal of International Business Studies*, 2, pp. 40–46.

Howard, C.G. 1974. "A model for the design of a selection program for multinational executives. *Public Personnel Management*, March/April, pp. 138–145.

Kobrin, S. 1988. "Expatriate reduction and strategic control in American multinational corporations." *Human Resource Management*, 27(1), pp. 63–76.

Major, R.T. Jr. 1965. "A review of research on international exchange." Unpublished Manuscript. Putney, VT: The Experiment on International Living

Mendenhall, M. & G. Oddou. 1985. "The dimensions of expatriate acculturation: A review." *Academy of Management Review*, 10, pp. 39–48.

O'Boyle, T. 1989. "Grappling with the Expatriate Issue." *The Wall Street Journal*, December 11, p. B1.

Oddou, G. & M. Mendenhall. 1984. "Person perception in cross-cultural settings: A review of cross-cultural and related literature." *International Journal of Intercultural Relations*, 8, pp. 77–96.

Ratiu, I. 1983. "Thinking internationally: A comparison of how international executives learn." *International Studies of Management and Organization*, 13, pp. 139–150.

Stening, B.W. 1979. "Problems in cross-cultural contact: A literature review." *International Journal of Intercultural Relations*, 3, pp. 269–313.

Stone, Raymond. 1991. "Expatriate selection and failure." *Human Resource Planning*, 14(1), pp. 9–18.

Torbiorn, Ingemar. 1982. *Living Abroad: Personal Adjustment and Personnel Policy in the Overseas Setting*. New York: John Wiley & Sons, Inc.

Triandis, H.C., R.S. Malpass, & A.R. Davidson. 1973. "Psychology and culture." *Annual Review of Psychology*, 24, pp. 355–378.

Triandis, H.C., V. Vassilou, & M. Nassiakou. 1968. "Three cross-cultural studies of subjective culture." *Journal of Personality and Social Psychology*, 8, (4, Part 2).

Tung, R.L. 1981. "Selecting and training of personnel for overseas assignments." Columbia *Journal of World Business*, 16(1), pp. 68–78.

Tung, R.L. 1982. "Selection and training procedures of U.S., European, and Japanese multinationals." *California Management Review*, 25(1), pp. 57–71.

Walker, E.J. 1976. "'Til business us do part?" *Harvard Business Review*, pp. 94–101.

Zeira, Y. & M. Banai. 1987. "Selecting managers for foreign assignments." *Management Decision*, 25, pp. 38–40.

13

TRAINING FOR

INTERNATIONAL

ASSIGNMENTS

LEARNING OBJECTIVES

IN THIS CHAPTER YOU WILL EXPLORE:

- North American MNCs' approaches toward cross-cultural training

- The effectiveness of cross-cultural training programs

- The variables associated with cross-cultural training effectiveness

- The various types of cross-cultural training programs

- Important aspects of cross-cultural training programs

- Major cross-cultural training frameworks

- Strategies for selecting cross-cultural training programs

KEY DISCUSSION QUESTIONS:

- Why do companies approach training the way they do?

- What are the most effective types of training programs?

- Where and when should training be conducted?

- Who should receive cross-cultural training?

- How should training programs be evaluated?

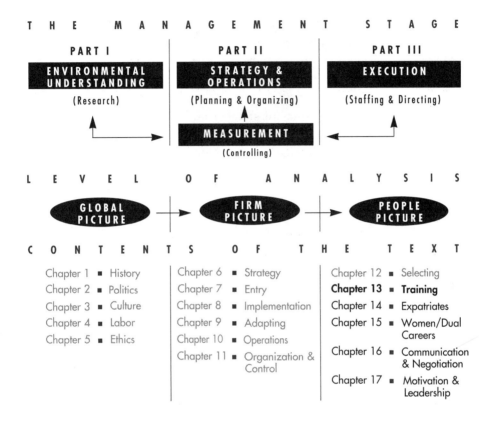

INTRODUCTION

In practically any complex undertaking or profession, training is required before an individual is allowed to perform his/her assigned duties. However, most U.S. firms do not train their expatriates before they send them overseas. The basic attitude of these firms is that their expatriate managers are bright people who shouldn't need any help.

This chapter examines the need for cross-cultural training, research that illustrates its effectiveness, various approaches to training, and important aspects of training. Recognizing that training can be expensive and time-consuming, we consider ways for assessing how rigorous such training needs to be. A number of models for selecting training methods are presented and illustrated. We conclude by arguing that cross-cultural training is a necessity not a luxury and that it is not just for long-term expatriates. We also look at the importance of the family in the training process and examine issues of ethics and cross-cultural training.

THE NEED FOR CROSS-CULTURAL TRAINING

Cross-cultural training programs are designed to educate the trainee in the key cultural norms, values, behaviors, beliefs, and other important aspects of the country to which he/she is assigned. The assumption is that an expatriate who is taught about these things will be able to use knowledge when overseas, to understand the host nationals' behavior and adjust his/her own behavior to fit the requirements of the host culture's social system. Another assumption is that if expatriates are able to transfer the knowledge gained in cross-cultural training programs into new cognitive and physical behaviors, then they will be more satisfied with their overseas assignment, more productive in their jobs, and better able to interact with host nationals. Many U.S. companies do not believe in these assumptions. In fact, researchers have found that approximately 65 percent of U.S. firms do not offer any kind of training to their expatriates before sending them overseas. The situation in Canada is similar. When training is offered, it is often inadequate. We will discuss why that is so later in this chapter. To begin it is important to understand why North American firms do not offer training to their expatriates.

There are four general reasons given by companies for not offering such training (Schnapper, 1973; Mendenhall & Oddou, 1985):

1. A belief that such training programs are ineffective.

2. Past dissatisfaction with such training programs on the part of the trainees.

3. Lack of time between selection and departure.

4. The expense of training.

Trainee dissatisfaction is correctable with better training program design and experienced trainers. The time problem is also correctable through better human resource planning methods. Also, people can be trained once they arrive overseas. Finally, the expense of training won't be an issue if training programs are effective; in other words, if top management sees such training is worth its cost, training will likely be sponsored. Thus, the key issue is the effectiveness of training programs.

RESEARCH ON CROSS-CULTURAL TRAINING

Before the 1990s, research on the effectiveness of cross-cultural training programs had not been gathered into one data base or otherwise systematically reviewed. Black and Mendenhall (1990) reported their findings based on an exhaustive survey of studies that evaluated the effectiveness of a variety of cross-cultural training programs. They found 29 studies that empirically evaluated cross-cultural training programs. The studies were analyzed to find out whether or not cross-cultural training programs effectively fostered the development of self-oriented, relationship-oriented, and perceptual cross-cultural skills, adjustment to the new culture, and improved work performance.

Of the 29 studies, 10 examined the relationship between cross-cultural training and self-oriented skills and all 10 found a positive relationship between

EXHIBIT 13.1

VARIABLES OF CROSS-CULTURAL TRAINING EFFECTIVENESS				
CROSS-CULTURAL			**ADJUSTMENT**	**PERFORMANCE**
Self	Relationship	Performance	9/9	11/15
9/9	19/9	16/16		

these two variables. Nineteen of the 29 studies examined the relationship between cross-cultural training and fostering relationships with host nationals, and each of these found a significant relationship between cross-cultural training and relationship skills. A total of 16 studies investigated the relationship between cross-cultural training and the development of perceptual skills, and all 16 studies found a positive relationship. Nine out of nine studies found a positive relationship between training and adjustment, and 11 of the 15 studies that looked at the work performance and training found a significant relationship. These results are illustrated in Exhibit 13.1.

The authors concluded their analysis by stating that:

> . . . it is important to note that those studies that included rigorous research designs (for example, control groups, longitudinal designs, independent measures) . . . found support for a positive relationship between cross-cultural training and the following variables: cross-cultural skill development, cross-cultural adjustment, and performance in a cross-cultural setting. Thus, the empirical literature gives guarded support to the proposition that cross-cultural training has a positive impact on cross-cultural effectiveness (Black & Mendenhall 1990, pp. 119–20).

Deshpande and Viswesvaran (1991) have replicated Black and Mendenhall's findings. Thus, the belief that cross-cultural training programs are ineffective is not supported by research and should not be used as an argument against training programs for expatriates. In fact, many firms are now beginning to spend more money on cross-cultural training programs for their expatriates (Black, Mendenhall, & Gregersen 1992).

APPROACHES TO CROSS-CULTURAL TRAINING

It appears that cross-cultural training programs are generally effective. The next subject to explore is various appraches to the general design of different cross-cultural training programs. Within each of these approaches a wide variety of individualized programs in terms of design and content is possible. The following list of approaches is taken from Landis and Brislin's (1983) categorization of training methods.

- *Information or fact-oriented training.* The most common approach to cross-cultural training in the business world is to present expatriate candidates with briefing lectures about the country to which they will be assigned. In addition, videotapes, reading materials, pamphlets, and panels of returned expatriates or host nationals can relay information about a country's culture.

- *Attribution training.* This approach is aimed at helping trainees understand why the host nationals behave as they do. The goal is to learn the values, norms, and perceptual maps by which the host nationals evaluate behavior in their own country, so that the expatriate can better understand how host nationals think, evaluate the behavior of others, and respond to various cross-cultural scenarios. Once a culture is understood, the trainees are encouraged to adapt their behavior to the norms of the host country.

- *Cultural awareness training.* The focus in this approach is to teach trainees about the values, attitudes, and behaviors that are common in their own culture; this has the effect of making the trainees more aware of how their own behavior is culturally determined. Once this occurs, it is assumed that the trainees can better understand how culture affects the behavior of host nationals.

- *Cognitive-behavior modification training.* The goal of this approach is to help trainees link what they find to be rewarding and punishing in their own culture and then to learn about the reward/punishment norms of the host country. By comparing reward and punishment in the two countries, the trainees are assisted in constructing their own personal strategy to obtain rewards—and avoid negative experiences—in the host culture.

- *Experiential training.* The purpose of this approach is to expose the trainees to real life in the host country through field trips, visits to the host country, complex role-plays, and cross-cultural simulations. This approach gives the trainees the opportunity to practice the skills learned from the other types of training. By practicing cross-cultural skills in hypothetical situations, the trainees can get a sense of what living and working overseas might really be like, instead of extrapolating what it would be like from information gained in the other training approaches.

Within each of these approaches trainers can use a variety of specific training techniques. Common training techniques include:

1. Area briefings

2. Lectures

3. Books and other reading materials

4. Films

5. Classroom language training

6. Case studies

7. Culture assimilators

8. Sensitivity training

9. Interactive language training

10. Role plays

11. Field trips

12. Simulations

Most of these techniques are familiar, but a few might be new to students. For example, students may have never run across the term "culture assimilator." A culture assimilator is a questionnaire that requires the trainee to respond to a number of cross-cultural scenarios. After reading a hypothetical cross-cultural scenario, the trainee chooses from between five and seven behavioral responses. The trainee must choose the response he/she would make as if in that situation "right now," not the one that he/she appropriate response. Then, the trainee is given instructions based upon his/her choice to turn to a certain page in an accompanying booklet where the trainee's choice is evaluated for cultural appropriateness. Next, the trainee is given feedback about what would likely occur later if that behavioral response was chosen. In other words, the trainee learns the consequences of that action.

Sensitivity training programs assist the trainee in coming to a greater awareness of his/her values, assumptions, behavioral tendencies, interpersonal strengths and weaknesses, relational perceptions, and prejudices and biases. This type of training often involves a trainer who is expert at eliciting information from people that they would not normally disclose to others. This training requires significant amounts of time away from work to be successful; thus, it is not used much by corporations for their expatriate candidates.

Another new training approach involves simulations, which are highly complex role plays. For example, for a while the Peace Corps operated a "third world village" for their expatriate candidates in Hawaii. Peace Corps candidates were assigned to live in this village for a few weeks to get an idea of what life might generally be like in such a setting. Host nationals populated the village and lived as they normally would in their home country. No English was spoken, exposing the candidates to what their future two years might be like. This type of training is very costly both in terms of time and money, so few businesses use it.

IMPORTANT ASPECTS OF CROSS-CULTURAL TRAINING

Some of these training approaches are more rigorous than others: that is, some approaches (for example, simulations) require the trainee to participate directly in the learning experience while others (listening to an area briefing) simply

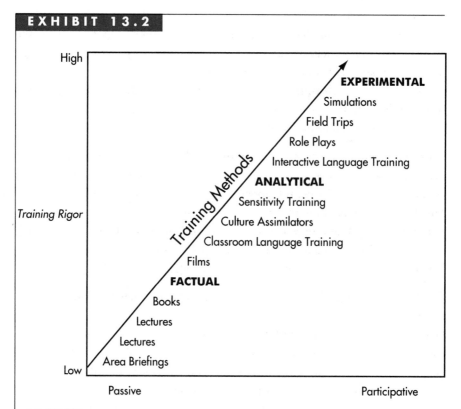

EXHIBIT 13.2

SOURCE:
Black, J.S. & M. Mendenhall. 1989. "A practical but theory-based framework for selecting cross-cultural training programs." *Human Resource Management*, 28(4), pp. 511–539.

require the trainee to passively absorb information with little mental and emotional effort on his/her part. This relationship between training rigor and level of trainees participation is illustrated in Exhibit 13.3.

More rigorous approaches that require the trainee to exert significant cognitive, behavioral, and emotional effort are more effective than less rigorous approaches (Black & Mendenhall 1989). However, it takes significant amounts of time and money to conduct rigorous training programs effectively, and most companies cannot afford to take a manager off the job for two months of off-site training.

ASSESSING THE NEED FOR RIGOR

An important issue for human resource directors is determining when to offer rigorous training and when not to. Three models have been developed by researchers to address this issue. Each model analyzes this problem from different perspectives, but all generally cover at least two of the following three variables: how novel the overseas job is compared to the expatriate's current job; the degree to which the expatriate's success is predicated on interacting with host nationals; and the culture novelty involved in the assignment. Before we discuss the training selection models, we will define these three important variables.

Job novelty refers to the degree to which a new job is different from the current job. The more novel the tasks of the new job, the more assistance the expatriate will need to be effective overseas. Expatriate assignments usually offer the manager higher levels of decision-making power, job autonomy, strategy design and implementation, and general responsibility. An overseas assignment that rates high in job novelty will be challenging for the expatriate. Thus, such managers need to be prepared in the cross-cultural managerial skills necessary for success in their overseas position.

The *degree of interaction with the host nationals* in an overseas job assignment also influences training choices. If an expatriate is going to be assigned overseas for a long time, yet will be living in an American compound and will have relatively little exposure to a wide variety of host nationals (for example, an oil-rig technician in Saudi Arabia), then highly rigorous training is not needed. However, if a manager will be required to manage a host-national work force, interact with host-national customers, suppliers, government officials, and industry leaders, then he/she needs to understand how that culture operates. Other issues to be considered are:

- How culturally familiar are the interaction norms of the host culture.

- How frequently (daily, weekly, rarely) will the expatriate need to interact with host nationals.

- How important are the interactions to the subsidiary's success: that is, if there are cross-cultural misunderstandings, will they potentially cost the company large or small amounts of money?

The concept of *culture novelty* was discussed at length in Chapter 12. It basically deals with the notion that some cultures are more closely aligned with other cultures in their value systems, behavioral norms, and so on. Cultural systems that are highly novel are more difficult to adjust to than cultures that are low in novelty. Also, the more novel the culture the more difficult it will be for the expatriate to absorb the information given in training programs. Thus, if an expatriate is assigned to a country that is high in culture novelty, that expatriate will need more rigorous training.

We will now discuss three models of selecting a cross-cultural training program. Each model is based upon studies that investigated expatriate effectiveness, yet each takes a slightly different slant on the issue of training program selection. While these models are well-known among academics working in this field, to date, few human resource directors use these models when selecting and designing cross-cultural training programs for their companies. Training program design and selection in the global context of human resource management is still done informally, with little regard to findings in the research literature.

TUNG'S FRAMEWORK

In 1981, Rosalie Tung published a framework that included a selection rationale for cross-cultural training methods based on rigor. She concluded that there were two main dimensions that should be used in selecting cross-cultural training methods: the degree of interaction required in the host culture and the similarity between the expatriate's home culture and the host culture (or culture novelty). Of the companies that did engage in cross-cultural training, there was no agreed-upon selection criteria for training methods, and methods were mostly chosen based upon the biases of the trainers. Tung's framework (see Chapter 12) was a first attempt at developing a framework that would enable companies to select valid training methods more carefully.

Tung proposed that if degree of interaction with host nationals was low and culture novelty was low, then the content of the training should focus on task- and job-related issues. The rigor needed for this training would be moderate to low. Conversely, if there was a high level of interaction with the host nationals and culture novelty was also high, then she proposed that the content of the training should focus mainly on cultural issues and cross-cultural skill development in addition to task-related training. The level of rigor for this training would range from high to moderate.

Tung's framework was the first to outline a method for selecting cross-cultural training; the outcomes from her framework yielded useful though general recommendations. She did not define what constitutes rigorous training, and she did not specify which methods would be more rigorous than others.

MENDENHALL AND ODDOU'S FRAMEWORK

In 1986, Mendenhall and Oddou presented a framework that built upon the foundation laid by Tung. They kept the criteria of "degree of interaction" and "culture novelty" and introduced a more complex relationship between training method and these two variables. Exhibit 13.4 shows their grouping of specific training methods into a three-part classification of methods that are low,

EXHIBIT 13.3

Length of Training		CROSS-CULTURAL TRAINING APPROACH
		IMMERSION APROACH
1-2 Months+	HIGH	Assessment Center Field Experiences Simulations Sensitivity Training Extensive Language Training
		AFFECTIVE APROACH
1-4 Weeks	LEVEL OF RIGOR	Culture Assimilator Training Language Training Role Playing Critical Incidents Cases Stress Reduction Training Moderate Language Training
		INFORMATION GIVING APPROACH
Less than a Week	LOW	Area Briefings Cultural Briefings Films/Books Use of Interpreters "Survival-level" Language Training

LOW   MODERATE   HIGH

DEGREE OF INTEGRATION

Length of stay	1 Month or less	2-12 Months	1-3 Years

SOURCE:

Mendenhall, M. & Oddou, G. 1986. "Acculturation profiles of expatriate managers: implications for cross-cultural training programs." *Columbia Journal of World Business.* Winter, pp. 73-79.

medium, or high in rigor. Their framework builds on Tung's in that it provides a grouping of specific training methods by level of rigor, and proposes a relationship between degree of interaction, culture novelty, and training rigor with the needed duration of time for the training program. However, despite these refinements, this model lacks the following elements:

1. The model does not explain how the level of rigor of a specific cross-cultural training method or group of methods is determined.

2. The content of the training methods categorized seems to be limited to "cultural" content and overlooks job-related training.

3. Both Tung's and Mendenhall and Oddous' models do not specify the theoretical basis for their frameworks. In other words, they do not substantiate why their frameworks are useful and valid.

BLACK AND MENDENHALL'S MODEL

In 1989, Black and Mendenhall constructed a framework based on social learning theory. (It is beyond the scope of this chapter to review social learning theory; the interested reader is referred to Bandura 1977 and Black, Mendenhall, & Oddou 1991.) Based upon this theory, Black and Mendenhall logically linked and integrated the variables of culture novelty, job novelty, and training rigor. They argued that the greater the culture novelty, required degree of interaction with host nationals, and job novelty, the greater the need for rigorous cross-cultural training. They further noted that each of these three dimensions are not equal; research suggests that adjusting to the host culture and interacting with host nationals are more difficult tasks than adjusting to the overseas job. The decision-tree model given in Exhibit 13.5 is a simplification of their framework.

EXHIBIT 13.4

DECISION TREE FOR SELECTING APPRPRIATE TRAINING METHODS

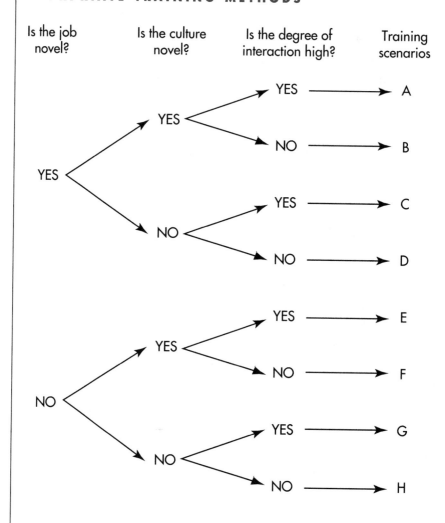

| Is the job novel? | Is the culture novel? | Is the degree of interaction high? | Training scenarios |

EXHIBIT 13.5

TRAINING SCENARIO

A   Level of Rigor: High
    Duration: 60-180 hours
    Approach: lecture, factual briefing, books, culture assimilator, role plays, cases, simulations, field experiences

    Training Content: Equal emphasis on job and culture. Stress job demands, constraints, and choices Include economic, political, historical, and religious topics

B   Level of Rigor: Moderate
    Duration: 20-60 hours
    Approach: Lecture, film, books, culture assimilator, cases
    Training Content: Equal emphasis on job and culture

C   Level of Rigor: Moderate
    Duration: 20-60 hours
    Approach: Lecture, film, books, cases, role plays, and simulations
    Training Content: Strong emphasis on job demands, constraints, and choices; less on culture

D   Level of Rigor: Low to moderate
    Duration: 20-40 hours
    Approach: Lecture, factual briefing, cases
    Training Content: Strong emphasis on job but little emphasis on culture

E   Level of Rigor: Moderate
    Duration: 40-80 hours
    Approach: Lecture, films, books, culture assimilator, cases, role play, simulation
    Training Content: Little emphasis on job; most emphasis on culture, including economic, political, historical, and religious aspects

F   Level of Rigor: Low to moderate
    Duration: 20-60 hours
    Approach: Lectures, films, books, cases
    Training Content: Little emphasis on job more emphasis on culture

G   Level of Rigor: Low to moderate
    Duration: 30-60 hours
    Approach: Lecture, films, books, cases, role plays
    Training Content: Little emphasis on job but more emphasis on culture

H   Level of Rigor: Low
    Duration: 4-8 hours
    Approach: Lecture, films, books
    Training Content: Little emphasis on either job or culture

A CASE EXAMPLE

To illustrate how a decision-tree works, we will go through a short example. Consider the problem of Brent Hall, the human resource director for METER Aerospace's TelKorea Project. METER had focused mainly on the U.S. market but is now engaged in a joint venture with KaeWoo Electronics to develop satellite guidance transmitters. Six engineers and their families will be transferred to Seoul in two months. They will be there for 18 months. Mr. Hall is uncertain what should be covered in their predeparture training since he knows nothing about Korea and has never managed a group of expatriates. Despite Mr. Hall's lack of knowledge about Korea and its culture, he can still arrive at a valid training approach by focusing on the variables of the decision tree and working through the following steps.

Step 1: Job Novelty. While the technical aspects of their job situations will not likely change, the expatriates must work in multicultural R&D teams with Korean engineers. Since the Koreans have been given control over management procedures in the joint-venture agreement, it is safe to assume that there may be differing expectations as to how the work should be conducted. The answer to step one is "yes."

Step 2: Culture Novelty. Despite his lack of knowledge about the Korean culture, Mr. Hall is able to arrive at an answer to this question in a relatively short time. First, the dominant language is not English, and he knows that the Koreans have hired a few interpreters for the R&D team. Second, the Korean language is not related to Indo-European language groups, thus it would probably be difficult for the engineers to learn it quickly enough with enough fluency to communicate without interpreters. Also, the culture, values, heritage, and ethical system of Korea is derived from Asian historical and philosophical systems that differ in their foundations from Western systems. Finally, by making a few phone calls to university professors and others with experience in Korea, Mr. Hall finds that the Korean culture would pose some challenges for the engineers. His answer to step two is "yes."

Step 3: Degree of Interaction. These engineers will be working intimately with Koreans, will be involved in reporting the results to Korean governmental and industrial agencies, and will be engaging in public-relations on behalf of the home office. Thus, their level of interaction with Koreans from a variety of societal levels is important for their performance to be successful. Mr. Hall's answer to step three is "yes."

The appropriate training scenario for Brent Hall's group of expatriates is training scenario A. He needs to provide training that is high in rigor, that will require between 60 and 180 hours of training. A variety of training approaches will be needed. Simply providing short area briefings will not be adequate for his expatriates given their mission. Scenario A requires major cross-cultural training.

FAMILY ISSUES

As discussed in Chapter 12, the spouse's level of adjustment overseas often determines whether an assignment will be completed or aborted. A manager may be performing well in his/her job, but if the spouse cannot adapt, the manager must return early to preserve their relationship. Though it is rarely done, spouses of managers being sent overseas should be given cross-cultural training as well.

The decision-tree model in Exhibit 13.5 can be used for spouses and children as well as for managers. The only adjustment required is a slight rewording of step one of the model. For spouses and children it should be asked if the role requirements are novel. The behavioral roles of the new culture for dual-career couples, homemakers, and students may be very different. In some countries, the spouse may not be able to work due to visa restrictions. A child entering a school where he/she must wear a uniform, show unquestioning respect for authority, be exposed to corporal punishment, or be a minority will no doubt experience culture shock. Even if the child attends a private school that limits enrollment to expatriate children, the norms of the school will probably be different from those of his/her previous school. The child must learn a new student role, just as his/her mother and father might have to learn what it means to be a manager or a homemaker or a career woman in the host country. Rigorous predeparture training will likely be needed for the families of expatriates as well.

USING TRAINING PROGRAMS

Because of time constraints it is not always possible for a company to offer quality training for the employees they send overseas, and they may need to hire consulting firms that specialize in cross-cultural training to conduct three- to four-day rigorous programs. After this initial training, follow-up training can be offered to the expatriates in the host country, where more rigorous methods, such as simulation techniques can be used. In addition, a staff member from the home office can be assigned to keep close contact with the expatriates during the first months. The staff member's role would be to monitor problems so they can be solved before they reach the crisis stage. Each problem should be handled as it comes up, and the staff member should be responsible for making recommendations to the home office about what should be done and how much it would cost.

Of the 30 percent of North American companies that offer cross-cultural training, the majority of that training is limited to techniques that are low in rigor (Oddou & Mendenhall 1991). More research needs to be done on cross-cultural training programs and implement them for maximum assistance to expatriates before they go overseas. Researchers need to investigate which combination of training methods and what sequence are most effective in aiding in job, culture, and interaction adjustment for expatriates. The research of Gudykunst, Hammer, and Wiseman (1977) shows that using more than one method is superior to using just one, and that different combinations of methods cause varying levels of positive results.

Cross-cultural trainers are also discussing the usefulness of predeparture versus in-country training programs. Some trainers support "survival level" aspects of predeparture training (such as how to open a bank account, understanding the monetary systems, and so on). They feel that it would be more effective to offer more rigorous training methods to expatriates once they have been overseas and gained some experience in the host culture. The rationale is that it is difficult to envision complex cross-cultural situations when one has not had any experiences in the new culture. Once the expatriate has gained some "real world" experiences over a period of four-to-six months in the host country, then more rigorous training could be more readily understood and absorbed by the expatriate, since he/she can "hang" the training content onto these experiences. Also, a cross-cultural skill learned overseas can immediately be practiced, whereas if that same skill is learned in the U.S., there is a lag time of at least a couple of months before the expatriate can begin to use it. Such a lag time can cause skills to be lost if they are not immediately used and practiced. For example, learning a language in the country in which it is spoken can produce quicker and longer lasting results because one interacts with natives, in their own tongue, on their own turf. This same principle may apply to cross-cultural skills as well.

THE IMPORTANCE OF CROSS-CULTURAL TRAINING

Cross-cultural training clearly helps expatriates adjust to the new culture and to the overseas job. Those who do not receive such training are not as effective overseas as those who do, all other things being equal. However, if top management does not realize its importance, the training will not occur.

Cross-cultural training is not just for long-term expatriates. Many expatriates go on short-term assignments that are crucial to their companies' future well-being. Sending people on important short-term assignments with no training increases the risk of failure. According to the models discussed in this chapter, if a person is going on a short-term assignment and the degree of interaction and the culture novelty is high, then that person does need some predeparture training—at least at the moderate level of rigor. Research literature strongly indicates that failures tend to ensue when cross-cultural neophytes cross borders to negotiate contracts, seek out customers, train subsidiary personnel, and so on (Triandis 1992). Here are a few true cases of such failures, taken from Ricks (1983):

- The new American owners of a Spanish company changed the firm's previous prestigious Spanish name to that of the U.S. parent, flew the American flag from the company flagpole . . . the company even suggested that those who had managed the company prior to the takeover by the Americans were incompetent . . . The blunder was so serious that it resulted in a general slowdown of work (strikes were then officially banned) . . . The result: The newly acquired subsidiary lost a great deal of its previous business (p. 123).

- An executive from Lucerne, Switzerland, negotiating a business venture with a Japanese firm failed to recognize the importance of personal sentiment to the Japanese and he paid the price. The president of the Japanese company sponsored a party in Tokyo and exclaimed, "I will not do business with a man who does not like us!" The executive believed he had concealed his dislike for the Japanese during his stay, but the president of the Japanese company had seen through his mask (p. 107).

- An American manager who understood little German was sent to Germany to discuss marketing plans with the local German subsidiary managers. The local managers, however, spoke little English. Both sides tried to understand each other, but neither nationality did very well. Eventually they parted, thinking they were in agreement. It was later discovered that during the meeting many important points were overlooked, and the company subsequently lost numerous sales opportunities (p. 58).

- A Brazilian expatriate executive created major problems for his firm when he treated his secretaries in America as personal servants. Not only did he ask them to do his personal shopping, but he even asked them to mend his clothes!

- An American executive was to conduct a presentation for the Prime Minister and his cabinet of a small Caribbean country. The meeting was held in the Prime Minister's conference room, and the executive began his presentation with, "Honorable Mr. Tollis and esteemed members of the cabinet." The Prime Minister interrupted him several times and asked him to start over. Eventually, someone advised the bewildered and then embarrassed businessman that Mr. Tollis had been deposed six months earlier!

As we stated previously, most spouses and children of expatriates do not receive any cross-cultural preparation before moving overseas. However, it is also necessary to train family members in cross-cultural skills for them to adjust to the new life styles, roles, and norms that they will encounter overseas. A case in point is the response of the spouse of an expatriate manager who finally received rigorous cross-cultural training after having lived for 15 months in a foreign country. She said:

I think that one of the most valuable things I'm taking away [from the program] is a more relaxed attitude toward learning the language. I've been approaching it . . . feeling I had to be perfect before I could open my mouth. I have already been using what I know more frequently and it's been fun! [I] was a bit resentful that this course was being offered so far into our assignment. I have been *most* pleased with all I have learned at all levels—culture, history, business, awareness.

Many problems can be buffered when the expatriate family gets training before or shortly after they arrive overseas. The adjustment process can be shortened, and the attendant stress associated with the adjustment process lessened, when such rigorous training is offered (Black & Mendenhall 1989). Cross-cultural training needs to be a family affair.

It could even be said that companies have an ethical responsibility to provide their employees with basic cross-cultural survival skills before they send them into foreign cultures. One of the common findings in the research literature is that expatriates often experience more stress in their overseas life than they do in their home countries because they lack knowledge about how basic aspects of society and business function overseas—especially in countries that are high in culture novelty. If North American firms are to compete globally, they need professional internationalists in their overseas subsidiaries, not confused and stressed employees.

SUMMARY

This chapter considered issues related to cross-cultural training for people who have been assigned to work in a culture that is different from their home culture. The chapter reviewed research studies that investigated the extent to which North American companies utilized cross-cultural training programs for employees that work in foreign cultures. Then, studies that investigated the effectiveness of cross-cultural training programs were reviewed.

Various approaches to designing cross-cultural training programs were discussed as well as important design features to ensure valid content. Design issues of rigor, the degree to which employees will need to interact with host-nationals, job novelty, and culture novelty all must be taken into consideration when designing valid cross-cultural training programs.

Three prominent frameworks that aid human resource managers in selecting cross-cultural training programs to fit their companies' needs were described, as were the advantages and disadvantages of conducting cross-cultural training before expatriates depart on their assignment as opposed to while they are overseas were discussed.

Other important issues discussed were the importance of cross-cultural training to expatriate productivity—that cross-cultural training is not a luxury, but a necessity for companies with overseas operations; that such training would benefit employees who must travel overseas on short term assignments—especially those who will be involved in business negotiations; that family members need cross-cultural training just as much as company employees do; and finally, that it may be ethically wrong not to train employees who are being sent overseas.

Cross-cultural training is an important aspect of preparing managers and others to succeed in their overseas assignments. The purpose of this chapter was to examine this issue in all of its complexity, yet provide future human resource managers and other managers with a basic understanding of practical approaches that can be undertaken to ensure their subordinates are adequately prepared before entering another culture.

DISCUSSION QUESTIONS

1. Many firms do not advocate training for international assignments because of the time and expense involved. Evaluate this approach.

2. Assume you are human resource manager of a Canadian firm arranging the transfer of an Australian manager to the United States. Discuss the need for training for this assignment.

3. Assume that you have been assigned to a post in a foreign country that you believe is culturally very different from your home country. Your firm does not typically provide in-depth training for such assignments. Prepare an argument to present to your boss outlining what training you feel is appropriate and explaining why this is needed.

REFERENCES

Baker, J.C. & J.M. Ivancevich. 1971. "The assignment of American executives abroad: Systematic, haphazard, or chaotic?" *California Management Review*, 13(3), pp. 39–41.

Bandura, A. 1977. *Social Learning Theory*. Englewood Cliffs, NJ: Prentice-Hall.

Black, J.S., M. Mendenhall, & H. Gregersen. 1992. *Global Assignments: Successfully Expatriating and Repatriating International Managers*. San Francisco, CA: Jossey-Bass.

Black, J.S. & G.K. Stephens. 1989. "The influence of the spouse on american expatriate adjustment in overseas assignments." *Journal of Management*, 15, pp. 529–544.

Black, J.S. 1988. "Work role transitions: A study of American expatriate managers in Japan." *Journal of International Business Studies*, 19, pp. 277–294.

Black, J.S. & M. Mendenhall. 1989. "A practical but theory-based framework for selecting cross-cultural training programs." *Human Resource Management*, 28(4), pp. 511–539.

Black, J.S. & M. Mendenhall. 1990. "Cross-cultural training effectiveness: A review and a theoretical framework for future research." *Academy of Management Review*, 15(1), pp. 113–136.

Black, J.S., H. Gregersen, & M. Mendenhall. 1992. *International Assignments*. San Francisco, CA: Jossey-Bass.

Black, J.S., M. Mendenhall, & G. Oddou. 1991. "Toward a comprehensive model of international adjustment: An integration of multiple theoretical perspectives." *Academy of Management Review*, 16(2), pp. 291–317.

Brislin, R.W. 1979. "Orientation programs for cross-cultural preparation." In A.J. Marsella, G. Tharp, & T.J. Ciborowski (eds.) *Perspectives on Cross-cultural Psychology*. Orlando, FL: Academic Press. pp. 207–304.

Deshpande, S.P. & C. Viswesvaran. 1991. "The effectiveness of cross-cultural training: A meta-analysis." Paper presented at the Academy of Management Meetings, Miami, August 13, 1991.

Gudykunst, W.B., M.R. Hammer, & R.L. Wiseman. 1977. "An analysis of an integrated approach to cross-cultural training." *International Journal of Intercultural Relations*, 1, pp. 99–110.

Landis, D. & R.W. Brislin. 1983. *Handbook of Intercultural Training*, Vol. 1. New York: Pergamon Press.

Mendenhall, M. & Oddon, G. 1986. "Acculturation profiles of expatriate managers: Implications for cross-cultural training programs." *Columbia Journal of World Business*. Winter, 73-79.

Oddou, G. & M. Mendenhall. 1991. "Succession planning in the 21st century: How well are we grooming our future business leaders?" *Business Horizons*, January-February, 34(1), pp. 26–34.

Ricks, D. 1983. *Big Business Blunders: Mistakes in Multinational Marketing*, Homewood IL: Dow-Jones Irwin.

Schnapper, M. 1973. "Resistances to intercultural training." Paper presented at the 13th annual conference of the Society for International Development, San Jose, Costa Rica.

Triandis, H.C. 1992. "Cross-cultural industrial and organizational psychology", In M.D. Dunnette (ed.) *Handbook of Industrial and Organizational Psychology*, Vol. 4. Palo Alto, CA: Consulting Psychologists Press.

Tung, R.L. 1981. "Selection and training of personnel for overseas assignments." *Columbia Journal of World Business*, 16(1), pp. 68–78.

Zeira, Y. 1975. "Overlooked personnel problems of multinational corporations." *Columbia Journal of World Business*, 10(2), pp. 96–103.

14

MANAGING THE

EXPATRIATE

MANAGER

LEARNING OBJECTIVES

IN THIS CHAPTER YOU WILL EXPLORE:

- The key variables that ensure expatriate productivity

- The challenges of managing an expatriate cadre

- The "dual loyalty" paradox

- The "unlearned expert" paradox

- The "identification/acculturation" paradox

- The positive and negative role of strereotyping in acculturation

- Various institutional aids that can combat expatriate challenges

- Performance appraisal issues in the expatriate work force

- Compensation packages of expatriate managers

- Repatriation adjustment process

KEY DISCUSSION ISSUES:

- Why is it difficult to manage expatriates?

- Why do expatriates experience a divided sense of loyalty?

- Can expatriate compensation packages be improved?

- Why is it diffficult to readjust to one's home culture?

- How can companies ease the repatriation process?

- How can expatriate mangement programs be improved?

- What is the emotional impact of poor acculturation?

- Can expatriate performance appraisal systems be improved?

THE MANAGEMENT STAGE

PART I	PART II	PART III
ENVIRONMENTAL UNDERSTANDING	**STRATEGY & OPERATIONS**	**EXECUTION**
(Research)	(Planning & Organizing)	(Staffing & Directing)

MEASUREMENT

(Controlling)

LEVEL OF ANALYSIS

GLOBAL PICTURE	→	FIRM PICTURE	→	PEOPLE PICTURE

CONTENTS OF THE TEXT

INTRODUCTION

Once an expatriate manager has been selected and trained, the company cannot assume that the firm's responsibility to that expatriate's adjustment has ended. Consider the following case example:

> A major U.S. food manufacturer was seeking someone from corporate staff to head its Japanese marketing division. Mr. X was selected because he was clearly one of the company's bright young talents . . . Prior to his 18-month assignment, Mr. X was given some literature pertaining to Japan's geography, climate, banking, and educational institutions and was asked to share this material with his family. However, during the initial six months in Japan, Mr. X was unable to devote much time to company activities because he was preoccupied with problems he and his family were having in adapting to the new environmental setting. . . . he often worried about his upcoming job

change. He heard that a peer and rival at home had just been promoted to a position for which both men had aspirations. What must he do to get back into the race? . . . The result: in the course of Mr. X's 18-month assignment to Japan, his company lost 98 percent of its existing market share to a major European competitor (Tung 1987, pp. 117–26).

Mr. X was obviously a capable manager with a proven track record. What more could the company have done to facilitate his success?

Based on the information contained in the previous chapter, rigorous cross-cultural training would be one variable that Mr. X's company overlooked in his preparation. However, training alone is not sufficient to guarantee success in an overseas assignment. The research literature suggests that other variables are important to expatriate productivity as well: overseas support systems, mentoring, planning for repatriation, valid performance appraisal systems, and adequate compensation packages (Dowling & Schuler 1994). Each of these important considerations will be discussed in this chapter. But first, in order to place these variables in their proper perspective, the paradoxes and dilemmas that expatriates face in their overseas assignments need to be discussed.

UNDERSTANDING THE CHALLENGES OF LIVING AND WORKING OVERSEAS

Once an expatriate is assigned overseas, it is a common practice for the company's regional human resource executive to oversee the family's and the expatriate manager's transition into life in the host country. It is not uncommon, however, for these human resource executives to be of little help regarding the challenges the expatriates face in the host country for at least one of two reasons. First, human resource executives may themselves be expatriates—just like those whom they are assigned to support—and thus they are struggling with the same challenges that their fellow employees are trying to overcome. It can be a case of "the blind leading the blind": that is, the human resource executive may not really know how to best aid and assist the expatriates who fall under his/her assignment. Second, the human resource executive may have the assignment to monitor and support expatriates, yet be stationed back at the home office. If this is the case, the geographic distance—as well as a lack of knowledge about the host country on the part of the human resource executive—may hinder the expatriates from receiving needed support.

Ideally, the human resource executive in charge of monitoring and supporting the expatriate work force in a specific region should possess the following characteristics:

1. Have been on an overseas assignment to a country or countries in the region for which he/she is now responsible.

2. Have an in-depth knowledge of the challenges that expatriates face in each of the countries in the region.

3. Have a staff and budget large enough to ensure that expatriates' needs can be met in a timely manner.

Each country presents expatriates with unique challenges, but there are some common one that expatriates must wrestle with no matter where they are assigned. At a minimum, human resource executives need to understand these challenges and construct organizational mechanisms that will assist expatriates to meet them. We will discuss the challenges, dilemmas, and paradoxes that are inherent in international assignments.

THE "DUAL LOYALTY" PARADOX

Virtually all expatriate managers run into situations where the home office wants them to do one thing, while local situations dictate that another thing should be done instead. For example, in Japan, local conditions dictate that market share growth should be the main criterion of a subsidiary's performance, while the home office may force the subsidiary managers into focusing on quarterly profits as the main criterion of organizational performance.

The expatriate manager is often caught in a dillemma: on one hand, he or she can see the folly of implementing a home office policy that is not based on an understanding of local conditions; on the other hand, the manager is employed by the home office and feels a sense of loyalty to superiors at headquarters. Knowing that implementing the policy will cause problems such as strife, a loss of competitiveness, and low morale, the expatriate manager may do what is in the best interests of the subsidiary and ignore, alter, or sabotage the orders from the home office. However, expatriate managers do not want to lose their jobs, be seen as "going native," or receive low performance appraisals—all of which can happen if the home office disapproves of their implementation of home office policies.

Expatriate managers can be grouped into one of four categories based on their allegiance: they can be overly committed to the parent firm or to the local operation, or they can be highly committed to both firms, or to neither. These four allegiances are illustrated in Exhibit 14.1.

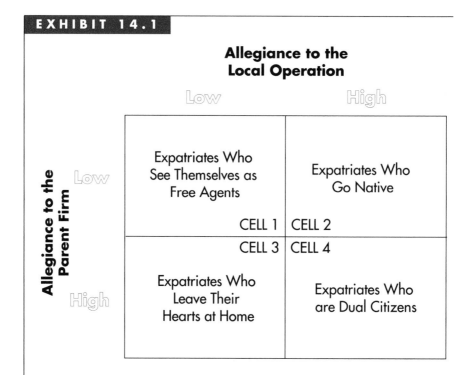

EXHIBIT 14.1

Allegiance to the Local Operation

Low — High

Allegiance to the Parent Firm

Low — High

	Low	High
Low	Expatriates Who See Themselves as Free Agents — **CELL 1**	Expatriates Who Go Native — **CELL 2**
High	**CELL 3** — Expatriates Who Leave Their Hearts at Home	**CELL 4** — Expatriates Who are Dual Citizens

SOURCE:
Black, J.S., H.B. Gregersen & M. Mendenhall. 1992. *Global Assignments: Successfully Expatriating and Repatriating International Managers.* San Francisco: Jossey-Bass, Inc.

1. Free agents are expatriates who are more committed to their careers than to the firm. A respondent manager in a recent research study typifies this category in saying: "I can't really relate to your question about which organization I feel allegiance to [the parent firm or the subsidiary]. I do my job, and I do it well. I play for whatever team needs me and wants me. I'm like a free agent in baseball or a hired gun in the old West" (Black, Gregersen, & Mendenhall 1992, p. 140). This manager was part of a "free agent" network of executives in the Far East. It consisted of about ten American managers who were either bi- or trilingual and had spent significant amounts of time working in the Far East. Whenever one of them learned that the home office was preparing to transfer him back to the U.S., he would contact everyone in the network and pick up job leads. Or, whenever one of the members of this network heard about a good opportunity in a firm, he/she passed it along the network for anyone to follow up on if they so desired.

2. Expatriates who "go native" have high levels of allegiance to the local operation but low levels of allegiance to the home office. These expatriates closely identify with the local customs, ways of doing business, values, and language and form a strong attachment to the larger culture of the host country. For example, an American executive stationed in Paris, whose daughters go to regular French schools and are completely fluent in French, said:

My first commitment is to the unit here. In fact, half the time I feel like corporate [the home office] is more a competitor I must fight than a benevolent parent I can look to for support. . . Sometimes I would simply ignore their directives if I didn't think they were appropriate or relevant to our operations. If it is really important, eventually someone from regional or corporate will hassle me and I have to respond. If it isn't important or if they think I implemented what they wanted, they just leave me alone. As long as the general results are good, it doesn't seem like there are big costs to this approach (Black, Gregersen & Mendenhall 1992, p. 144).

Sometimes, an issue cannot be dealt with in this way, and the expatriate manager who has gone native will choose to confront corporate headquarters directly over policy directives. While this may cost the expatriate manager "points" at corporate headquarters, it usually increases the loyalty of his/her subsidiary staff, which in turn can increase the expatriate's ability to be productive in the overseas assignment. Thus, by fighting headquarters, the expatriate may end up being even more productive overseas—an organizational irony that is not lost on many headquarters executives, who tolerate such behavior because it produces positive results.

3. "Homebound" expatriates have a high level of loyalty to headquarters and feel little allegiance to the local subsidiary. These expatriates, for one reason or another, never integrate deeply into the operations of the local firm and thus are happy to implement corporate policy without reservations. Generally, if managers have had a long tenure in working for the parent firm in the home country, they may not easily transfer that loyalty to a foreign subsidiary. The parent firm has taken care of them, and they expect to be rewarded for continuing to work hard for that parent firm.

There is a correlation between poor adjustment to the host country and strong allegiance to the parent company; the inability to adjust seems to block any transfer of allegiance from the parent to the subsidiary. Also, when expatriates have a formal sponsor back in the home office, they tend to value that relationship and focus their emotional ties on the home office. This type of expatriate is particularly useful for ensuring that headquarters gets what it wants overseas; choosing this type can backfire, however, if headquarters' wants are based on faulty data or ignorance of local conditions. Be that as it may, this type of expatriate can make it easier for the home office to coordinate activities with the subsidiary.

4. Expatriates who are "dual citizens" have a high level of loyalty to both the parent firm and to the local operation, and they feel a responsibility to serve the interests of both. When the home office and the local subsidiary are in opposition, these expatriates work to arrange an acceptable compromise or trade-off. A research study reported in Black, Gregersen, and Mendenhall (1992) indicates

that about one-fourth of American expatriate managers fall into this category. The most powerful factor is "role discretion"—the freedom to decide what needs to be done and then being empowered to take the necessary action to get it done. According to this study:

"The more discretion expatriate managers have, the more they feel responsible for what happens at work, and the more they feel committed to the local operation. . . [and] because they generally view the parent firm as ultimately responsible for the amount of freedom they enjoy, this translates into a greater sense of obligation and commitment to the parent firm" (p. 154).

This category of expatriate is ideal for any firm with an overseas operation. But to facilitate dual loyalty the company must decentralize power, giving it to the expatriate, and maintain clear communications with the expatriate. Also, the home office must listen to and trust the expatriate and be willing to follow his/her evaluations, advice, cautions, and ideas. Without this kind of relationship, dual citizens will not emerge in a firm's overseas work force.

THE "UNLEARNED EXPERT" PARADOX

Expatriate managers are selected because they are intelligent and highly skilled in their area of expertise. Thus, when they go abroad, they are seen by the host-national staff, as well as by the home office, as an expert who should have all the answers to any problem that may arise. Unfortunately, the world of globalized business is becoming very complex for managers in multinational firms. Consider the example of ASEA Brown Boveri (ABB).

ABB is a $20 billion company that was formed via the merger of Combustion Engineering and various units of Westinghouse (American firms), BBC (a Swiss company), and ASEA (a Swedish firm). ABB has subsidiaries in 145 countries and employs over 190,000 people worldwide. Most of its 3,500 subsidiaries are run as profit centers. According to Prahalad (1990, p. 29), expatriate managers who work in large multinationals are faced with a number of complex issues, including:

- Integration of large international acquisitions.

- Understanding the meaning of performance and accountability in a globally integrated system of product flows.

- Building and managing a worldwide logistics capability.

- Developing country-specific corporate strategies.

- Managing of products and services around the world with differing competitive dynamics in each market.

- Forming and managing collaborative agreements (OEM contracts, licensing, joint ventures).

- Balancing the need for global integration, as simultaneously responding to local demands.

- Managing a multicultural workforce.

Prahalad notes that a firm with a large portfolio of diverse businesses creates a world for the expatriate manager where:

> . . . variety, complex interaction patterns among various subunits, host governments, and customers, pressures for change and stability, and the need to re-assert individual identity in a complex web of organizational relationships are the norm. This world is one beset with ambiguity and stress. Facts, emotions, anxieties, power and dependence, competition and collaboration, individual and team efforts are all present. The. . . logical and the intuitive, data and judgment, the analytical and the emotional coexist. Managers have to deal with these often conflicting demands simultaneously (p. 30).

Thus, expatriate managers must play two roles, simultaneously: the role of expert and the role of apprentice. The danger of staying in the expert role is that, in actuality, the manager does not know everything, and if self-confidence is not tempered by knowledge, the manager will make serious blunders. Conversely, if the expatriate manager constantly acknowledges inadequacies, weaknesses, and knowledge gaps in public, the host-national subordinates will come to view the manager as weak and incompetent. When this occurs, morale lessens, loyalty diminishes, conflicts escalate, and cooperation decreases among the workers and between the workers and the manager. The expatriate who can balance these two roles and not become fixed in either one, will be more productive in the overseas assignment. There are no agreed-upon methods for achieving this balance; each expatriate manager must learn this individually, through trial and error.

THE "IDENTIFICATION/ ACCULTURATION" PARADOX

Expatriates must decide how much of their identity, values, beliefs, behavior, and personality to give up in order to adjust to the norms of the host country. Giving up one's entire value system in order to give the host nationals a good impression or to be productive and happy overseas is termed "going native." An expatriate who goes native essentially begins to see the host country as superior in almost every cultural category compared to the home country. The home country becomes exemplified in the expatriate's mind by "a lack of culture," "being excessively materialistic," "ridden with crime and the break down of social order," or some other negative overgeneralization. In contrast, the host country is seen as a place where near ideal states exist in all the important dimensions of life.

Going native is an extreme form of acculturation; on the other extreme is the expatriate who chooses to maintain a lifestyle and behavior pattern that makes no concessions to the host culture's norms. In this case, the expatriate simply decides the home culture's way is best, treats all host nationals like they are inferiors, sees any cross-cultural encounter that is not pleasant as the fault of the host nationals, and spends significant amounts of leisure time with other expatriates.

The basic dilemma is this: "At the same time that expatriates are becoming more cross-culturally sophisticated in their thoughts and their behaviors, they must also decide how much of that cross-cultural world they will take in and how they will make sense out of it (Osland 1991, pp. 5–6)". Those who go native take all of their new cross-cultural world into their personalities; those who are on the other extreme, take none of their new world into their personalities.

Knowing what to change about one's mental and behavioral repertoire overseas is personal and individual and causes much stress and frustration in expatriates and their families. Neither of the above extremes is healthy if the expatriate wants to be productive. A balanced adjustment, where important cultural norms and personal beliefs are maintained while simultaneously accepting new ways of thinking and doing things, is a difficult process to undertake. Yet expatriates who can find this balanced state of adjustment are the high performers overseas.

THE "BELIEVING, YET DISBELIEVING IN STEREOTYPES" PARADOX

Adler (1974) wrote that an individual who possesses superior cross-cultural skills will be committed to seeing the essential similarities among people from different cultures while paradoxically maintaining an equally strong commitment to valuing their differences. Indrei Ratiu (1983) found that managers who possess superior cross-cultural skills deal with host nationals from an informed set of stereotypes: that is, they study as much as they can about the host culture and develop a mental pattern of the behavior, thoughts, and values of the average host national in the host country.

This knowledge allows them to have a number of reference points by which they can understand and gauge host nationals' behavior. These reference points are stereotypes—general categorizations of people's behavior and motives. However, they also know that people deviate from the average: for example, that some Nigerians are perhaps more North American in their behavior and some more traditionally African when compared to the average Nigerian. When they encounter behavior that departs from the stereotye, they are able to adjust their own behavior to ensure good interpersonal relations.

This approach to "believing, yet disbelieving in stereotypes" is graphically represented in Exhibit 14.2. The bell-shaped curve represents the normal distribution of behavior from the mean or average behavior studied. Ratiu's sample of expatriates, after developing a "personal data set" of cultural information, used that data set as the standard for their conceptual mean or average behaviors for the host culture. If a host national's behavior was fairly consistent with the stereotype, then the expatriate's strategy was to deal with the host national according to the norms of that culture. If a host national's behavior deviated substantially from the host culture, then the expatriate would make a decision on how to best interact with this specific host national.

EXHIBIT 14.2

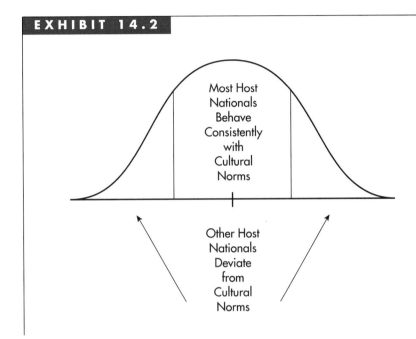

Joyce Osland (1991, p. 5) summarizes this paradox in the following statement: "Expatriates must work to see as valid the general stereotype about the other culture but also realize that many host country nationals do not fit that stereotype." Thus, expatriates have to employ stereotypes to understand the culture around them, but must be willing to throw away those stereotypes when they meet host nationals who do not fit the stereotype. This is difficult to do and takes much effort and practice.

INSTITUTIONAL AIDS TO COMBAT THE PARADOXES

Each of the problems of expatriate life we have discussed can be intensified, mitigated, or sometimes avoided completely if firms will create institutional mechanisms to assist expatriates in dealing with the challenges of their overseas assignments. Some organizational mechanisms that can help expatriates work out their own problems overseas more quickly and effectively are overseas support systems, mentors, preparing for repatriation, valid performance appraisal systems, and adequate compensation packages.

OVERSEAS SUPPORT SYSTEMS

Briody and Chrisman (1991) found that one of the principal barriers to overseas adjustment was the lack of a way for expatriates—and especially their nonworking spouses and family members—to become members of a social network. Working spouses often find a social network in their work situation, which provides them with a daily sense of structure in their interpersonal relationships. Nonworking spouses do not have such structures available to them immediately upon arrival. Briody and Chrisman found that these networks:

> . . . serve a wide variety of functions: friendship, emotional support, business connections, information gathering about the new location, and creating or enhancing an appreciation for the new culture, among others. They may consist of both host country nationals and expatriates in varying combinations. By gaining access to both expatriate and host country national networks, cultural adaptation can be facilitated and the overseas experience broadened for [expatriate] families . . . Without the integration . . . into such networks, adjustment may be slowed, if not permanently hampered (1991, p. 277).

There is no ideal overseas support system, though there are some general organizational principles that firms can adapt to meet the needs of their expatriates. Integration programs and mentor programs are two approaches we will discuss.

INTEGRATION PROGRAMS

For the newly arrived expatriate, there are two types of survival—physical survival and emotional survival. Most large firms take care of the expatriates' physical needs, such as housing, schooling, and transportation. While this is important, it does not necessarily contribute to the expatriate's emotional needs. For example, information can be given to the expatriate or a nonworking spouse about where to shop and how to get there, but the shopping experience itself can be highly stress-provoking, as the following statements made by expatriates in Briody and Chrisman's study (1991, p. 277) illustrate:

I felt like I was dropped there [in the foreign country]. You are starting at base zero. I felt like a kid. I did my pantomimes and pointed to things that I wanted when I went shopping.

I would go every day to the store but I wouldn't talk to anyone there. I was afraid that they would start speaking to me in [the host-country language].

Shopkeepers were not very patient with American buying habits. I started buying groceries on a weekly [rather than a daily] basis . . . A lot of women waiting in line would either sigh as I was coming through the checkout or ask if they could go ahead of me. I would let a few go ahead of me but I couldn't be doing that all day.

Companies can do a variety of things to help expatriates feel emotionally secure shortly after they arrive in the host country. Companies should include as part of the local managing director or CEO's job description the responsibility to ensure that expatriates adjust not only to work, but to the local culture as well. By formalizing this in the job description, adequate resources will more likely be deployed to this task than otherwise. Also, companies should employ a nonworking spouse from inside or outside the firm to fill a part-time or full-time position as a "family coordinator" (Brody & Chrisman 1991). This individual should be one who has been in the country for a lengthy period of time, adjusted well to the host country, developed a network of friends—both in the expatriate and in the host-national communities—and has good interpersonal skills.

The duties of the family coordinator and other human resource staff members would be to:

- Provide informal counseling or arrange for professional counseling for expatriates with questions or problems.

- Sponsor social gatherings to discuss problems and successes among the expatriate employees and their spouses.

- Publish a weekly or biweekly newsletter that offers tips, short cuts, baby-sitting trade-off opportunities, helpful practical information, cross-cultural success stories, and other information of aid to the expatriates.

Furnish information about local churches, volunteer organizations, clubs, and cultural opportunities along with the names of contact people in the company who can act as intermediaries in helping expatriates to feel comfortable in these groups.

Another important goal of the support staff is to provide opportunities for expatriates to merge into the local culture and to develop relationships with host nationals. Research indicates that expatriates who develop relationships and interact often with host nationals reach high levels of adjustment in the host country. Briody and Chrisman (1991, p. 278) propose that "some host-country national spouse or family work with the family coordinator. Perhaps it would be possible to find interested host-country nationals through some local civic group, university, or church. Together the [family coordinator] and the host-country national spouse or family could serve as mediators or cultural brokers, easing the transition of the arriving [expatriate] families into the new culture."

In order for such organized cross-cultural interaction to take place, either the host nationals involved would need to be able to speak the language of the expatriates, or the expatriates would need to be able to speak the local language. Probably, organizing opportunities to interact with English-speaking host nationals and with host nationals that speak little or no English would be important for the expatriates' integration into the host national community; otherwise, expatriates may tend to "camp out" in the expatriate community, isolating themselves from the host nationals.

Research studies clearly show that language skills are important to adjustment; but fluency in the language is not required—willingness and desire to use the language are the keys to adjustment. Thus, expatriates need to develop conversational fluency within the first six months of arrival. This can be done, but it takes a commitment by the company and the expatriate to accomplish.

For example, GM offers its expatriates 180 hours in language lessons. However, most expatriate managers only participate in roughly 80 hours of language training before departure, and most of their spouses do not participate at all. A GM personnel administrator found that most families GM sends overseas do not have language training prior to departure, and a recent internal GM survey indicated that expatriate families were highly dissatisfied with the predeparture language training program (Briody & Chrisman 1991).

GM is no different on this score than the vast majority of North American multinationals. Though GM offers predeparture language training, few managers and no spouses seem to make use of it. Then, once the expatriates are overseas, and realize how helpful it would be to know the language, they complain. Unfortunately, once safely ensconced in the expatriate community, expatriates realize that they can get by in the host country without knowing the local language, and their motivation to learn the language decreases. However, their ability to adjust and to enjoy living and working in a foreign culture depends on the ability to converse at basic levels with the local populace.

A variety of scholars in this area recommend that companies take a long-term approach to language study by giving expatriates several months of language training before their departure. This training should focus on conversational ability and strategies for building conversational and vocabulary skills rather than on grammatical correctness. If an expatriate can get off the plane in the host culture and be able to converse at a "survival level" of fluency, that expatriate will be able to solve many future challenges individually, without the help of the company.

MENTOR PROGRAMS

Expatriates need a formalized link back to the home office and a host-national mentor to help them understand the workings of the local business culture. We will discuss three types of mentors: host-national mentors, home-office mentors, and fellow-expatriate mentors.

Host-National Mentors

Osland (1990) compared expatriates who had developed a relationship with a host-country national with those who did not seek out such mentors. She found that those who did:

- Reported themselves as being better adapted to work and general living conditions abroad.

- Were more aware of the paradoxes, challenges, and frustrations of expatriate life and were better able to cope with them.

- Had higher performance appraisal ratings and evaluated their own performance as being more effective.

- Became more fluent in the foreign language.

Mentors can be formally assigned by the company, but truly effective host-country mentors usually cannot be dictated by the company. Rather, such relationships need to form naturally between the expatriate and the host national in order for the appropriate level of trust, compatibility, and friendship to exist.

Home Office Mentors

Expatriates need someone in the home office who is responsible for maintaining frequent contact with them. Often expatriates feel like the home office has forgotten them while overseas, and concerns build up over whether the overseas assignment has been detrimental to their career path in the firm. Oddou and Mendenhall, after surveying numerous expatriates, believe that ideally the home-office mentor: "should be the individual's former or future line manager. This responsibility needs to be part of the line manager's formal performance responsibilities so there is some level of reward and punishment attached to how well the line manager is updating and consulting with the expatriate" (1991, p. 32).

The home-office mentor can assist the expatriate in the following ways:

- Ensure that the expatriate's successes overseas are communicated among the executive staff at the home office.

- Bring up the expatriate's name in meetings when succession planning, promotion, and organizational restructuring discussions occur.

- Keep the expatriate informed of power shifts in the home office so the expatriate can keep in contact with key personnel in the home office.

- Arrange for the expatriate to be involved in relevant meetings when the expatriate is back on home leave.

- Indicate to the expatriate what job openings are available within the company.

- Make sure the expatriate is kept up to date on the home office's operations.

Fellow-Expatriate Mentors

In Oddou and Mendenhall's 1991 study, a common observation on the part of their expatriate respondents was the importance of having fellow-expatriate mentors. A formally or informally assigned mentor can assist the newly arrived expatriate by:

- Clarifying performance expectations.

- Giving advice regarding the informal culture of the subsidiary and the best ways to get things done within the subsidiary.

- Sharing knowledge about the local culture.

- Giving personal advice and tips on how to survive emotionally in the host country.

Price Waterhouse is an example of a company that assigns fellow-expatriate mentors. The mentor meets the new expatriates at the airport, assists them in getting settled in at work, and generally helps them in any way possible (Osland 1990). The concept really is simple, but its institutionalization requires that it be part of the mentor's job description, that clear expectations regarding mentoring activities be communicated to the mentor, and that mentoring activities be included in the mentor's performance evaluation. As with any performance criteria, if top management views it as being important and rewards it, it will get done. If it is merely mentioned in a company handbook and is not rewarded, it will not get done.

PERFORMANCE APPRAISAL

Another aspect of managing expatriates is measuring their performance while in the overseas assignment. The research done on this area of international human resource management indicates that often performance appraisal measures are not carefully implemented for expatriate managers. One issue involved in measuring performance is whether the host national or the home office is measuring the expatriate's performance.

When host-national managers are involved in the performance appraisal process, there is always the danger that they will evaluate the expatriate from their own cultural frame of reference and not take into account that the expatriate is struggling to learn a new cultural/business system. An expatriate's experience in France illustrates this problem:

> In France, women are legally allowed to take six months off for having a baby. They are paid during that time but are not supposed to do any work related to their job. This expatriate had two of the three secretaries take maternity leave. Because they were going to be coming back, they were not replaced with temporary help. The same amount of work, however, still existed. The American expatriate asked them to do some work at home, not really understanding the legalities of such a request. The French women could be fired from their job for doing work at home. One of the women agreed to do it because she felt sorry for him. When the American's French boss found out one of these two secretaries was helping, he became very angry and intolerant of the American's actions. As a result, the American felt he was given a lower performance evaluation than he deserved (Mendenhall & Oddou 1991, p. 372).

The outcome of this case is interesting. The French manager persisted in believing that the American was incompetent and unethical despite the American's explanation of his ignorance of French law. The American asked his former boss in the subsidiary, an American, to intercede and resolve the dispute. The French manager finally updated the American's performance rating more positively.

Having the home office evaluate expatriate performance raises some problems, too, because the home office is geographically, culturally, and organizationally distanced from foreign subsidiaries. Ignorance about the reality of the subsidiaries' workings can cause problems in performance evaluation. This communication gap can be compounded by the fact that the expatriate might be evaluated in the home office by individuals who lack international experience themselves and thus do not have a sense of the environment in which the expatriate is working.

If the home office simply uses traditional North American measures of success (such as quarterly profits, return on investment, and so on) the home office may not be measuring the key criteria for success in a particular foreign country (such as the ability to deal with strikes, developing good relationships with key government officials, increases in market share). Take, for example, an American expatriate manager's experience in Chile:

> . . . he almost singlehandedly stopped a strike that would have shut down their factory completely for months and worsened relations between the Chileans and the parent company in the U.S. In a land where strikes are commonplace, numerous meetings and talks with labor representatives, government officials, and local management required an acute understanding of their culture and a sensitivity beyond the ability of most expatriates. However, at the time, because of exchange rate fluctuations with its primary trading partners in South America, the demand for their ore temporarily decreased by 30 percent during the executive's tenure. [Thus, sales went down.] Rather than applauding the efforts this expatriate executive made to avert a strike and recognizing the superb negotiation skills he demonstrated, the home office saw the expatriate as being only somewhat better than a mediocre performer (Mendenhall & Oddou 1991, p. 29–30).

Expatriates who were surveyed regarding what companies should do in terms of overseas performance evaluations made the following three points (taken from Oddou & Mendenhall 1991).

1. Modify the normal performance criteria to fit the overseas position and site characteristics: This involves doing an in-depth study of what the key factors of success are for the overseas operation. Once those factors are isolated, the company can use a performance evaluation program that is designed especially for each subsidiary. For example, expatriates in Japan have complained that the home office in North America insists on using measures based on profit gains for the Japanese subsidiaries and their managers, though in the Japanese market it would make more sense to use measures based on market share growth. Companies need to pay close attention to the culture of the overseas industry, country, and competitor companies when designing strategy and performance measures for their overseas subsidiaries.

2. Include the expatriate's insights as part of the evaluation: The expatriate should have the chance to communicate insights as to how the overseas operation can better coordinate with the parent company. For example, if a subsidiary in India needs supplies by specific dates in order to accommodate local laws and customs, passing on the details of that state of affairs to the home office is important; the home office needs to understand why the plant in India demands delivery on different schedules than their U.S. suppliers. Whenever expatriate managers are able to iron out such differences, they should be rewarded—even if such behaviors are not listed on a performance evaluation sheet.

3. Use both the on-site manager and a former expatriate who is now assigned to headquarters to evaluate the expatriate's performance: An expatriate is usually evaluated by someone from the home office. The home office evaluator and the on-site manager should be in communication with each other and discuss the expatriate's performance. These evaluators can act as a check and balance for each other, and both should be educated in the cross-cultural dilemmas regarding the reality of work life for expatriate managers. This will lead to less biased evaluations and the expatriate will feel that he/she has been evaluated equitably.

EXPATRIATE COMPENSATION PACKAGES

Each company's expatriate compensation package differs in its details, but most companies include the following provisions in their compensation packages for expatriates.

1. *Base salary.* The base salary for the overseas position is usually determined by comparing the overseas position with comparable domestic positions in the parent company. Because the expatriate is usually moving to an overseas position that is a promotion from his/her current position, the base salary often is, in essence, a pay raise for the expatriate. The purpose of the base salary is to allow

the expatriate to maintain the same personal buying power while overseas; the base salary usually covers the costs of goods and services, savings, and income taxes.

2. *Foreign service premium.* This is extra pay that companies provide to expatriates for working outside the country of their citizenship. It is "compensation for the inconveniences of having to live in a new environment isolated from family and friends, for difficulty in language and cultural barriers, for greater responsibility and reduced access to home-office resources, and for the effort of dealing with different work habits" (Helms 1991, p. 380). Foreign service premiums range from 10 to 30 percent of base salary, and are usually tax free (Stone 1986).

3. *Hardship or site allowance.* This payment is given to expatriates who relocate to a country that is designated as a "hardship" country. Many companies consider some countries as being more difficult to live in and adjust to than others. As a reward for accepting an assignment in such a country, companies sometimes give lump sum payments as bonuses. For example, in 1986, the monthly site allowance for Hong Kong ranged up to $200, but for Beijing, China, it ranged from $500 to $900 (Stone 1986, p. 67).

4. *Cost of living allowance.* The cost-of-living allowance (COLA) is to help expatriates maintain their domestic standard of living while overseas. It is basically a salary adjustment because it is virtually impossible to find living conditions overseas that perfectly reflect the expatriate's domestic housing conditions and costs. The COLA is a buffer that makes sure that the expatriate has enough spendable income to take care of food, clothing, entertainment, and other day-to-day expenses. The COLA changes based upon exchange rate fluctuations and cost-of-living index fluctuations.

5. *Housing allowance.* The housing allowance is the most significant aspect of the compensation package next to the base salary. Marilyn Helms (1991) notes that "companies usually adopt one of three housing choices: (1) provide a tax-free housing allowance with a

maximum limit computed as a specified percentage of base salary, (2) provide housing free of charge, or (3) make a statistical housing deduction based on the home location market rate" (1991, p. 382).

6. *Taxation.* Companies usually handle taxation of expatriates in two ways (Gaffney & Hitchings 1985, p. 84). Because expatriates must pay taxes both to their home country and to the host country, companies either make up the difference in the expatriate's net pay (called "tax protection"), or the company pays the expatriate's foreign taxes that are in excess of the expatriate's home-country tax rate (called "tax equalization").

7. *Incidental benefits.* Beyond the compensation benefits listed above, companies often provide other kinds of allowances based upon company philosophy and the needs of their expatriates. These other benefits include paying for private schooling for the expatriate's children, all medical expenses, home leave (all-expense-paid vacations back to the home country), automobile allowance, furniture allowance, country club allowance, and language lesson allowance.

Compensating expatriates with base salaries, housing allowances, and incidental benefits are common practices among North American, European, and Asian multinational companies, though on average, North American companies tend to include more allowances than companies from other regions of the world (J.S. Black, personal communication).

REPATRIATION

Repatriation means to return to one's own country, and planning and preparing for this event is important—for expatriates and the home office alike. Unfortunately, what expatriates think will happen to them when they get home and what actually takes place are more often than not two separate things. Before discussing what expatriates bring home with them that benefits the parent company, it is first necessary to understand the following about the nature of international assignments (Oddou & Mendenhall 1991):

1. Expatriates experience more autonomy and independence in their overseas jobs than in the jobs they previously held in the home office.

2. Expatriates have more direct impact on the performance of the subsidiary organization than on the parent company in their previous assignments before moving overseas.

3. Expatriates have wider and more important job responsibilities in the overseas assignment than in the positions they held in the home office.

4. Expatriates' overseas positions are a promotion from the ones previously held in the parent company.

What affect do these four factors have on an expatriate? The answer to this question also answers the question of what expatriates bring home with them that benefits the parent company. Oddou and Mendenhall (1991, p. 30) asked a large number of "repatriates" (expatriates who had returned home) what their international assignments had done for them, and found that:

1. Nearly 90 percent said their overseas experience significantly increased their global perspective of their firm's business operations.

2. Over 85 percent reported being able to communicate more effectively with people of diverse backgrounds.

3. Almost 80 percent said that they could conceptualize and comprehend business trends and events better because of their exposure to contrasting cultural, political, and economic work systems.

4. 50 percent reported their experience overseas helped them become better planners.

5. Nearly 60 percent said they are better motivators of subordinates as a result of working with culturally diverse personnel overseas.

Given the benefits of an overseas assignment to management development, one would assume that these expatriates would be put on the "fast track" upon returning home, in positions commensurate with the skills they have developed; however, this is not the case. A variety of scholars have found the following to be generally true of North American companies in regards to the policies they have toward repatriates:

1. In a study conducted by Organization Resources Counsellors (ORC), it was found that only 4.3 percent of North American firms gave more than six months notice to expatriates that they would be returning home; 30 percent received three months notice; and 64 percent received random notice that they would be returning home. These percentages indicate that the firms had not been spending a great deal of time planning for their repatriation.

2. In some studies, half of the repatriates reported that they did not know what their job assignments would be upon return. Thus many repatriates are put into a "holding pattern" until the company can find a job for them (Black, Gregersen, & Mendenhall 1992).

3. When compared to the repatriates' overseas positions, their new positions have less autonomy, less authority, less job responsibility, and are usually lateral career moves or straight demotions compared to the overseas assignment. One study shows that as many as 77 percent of American expatriates receive a demotion upon return (Black, Gregersen, & Menhenhall 1992). These general trends hold true for American, Japanese, and Finnish repatriates in large multinational firms.

4. The international business expertise repatriates gained while overseas is not effectively utilized by the home office; studies show that only about 40 percent of American repatriates feel that their international skills are utilized by the firm (Black, Gregersen, & Mendenhall 1992).

5. Looking back on their overseas assignment, only 29 percent of repatriates in one study felt that it had been helpful to their careers (Oddou & Mendenhall 1991).

THE REPATRIATION ADJUSTMENT PROCESS

The whole process of adjusting to one's home culture after having lived abroad is complex; dealing with disappointments in the return job is just one aspect of the process. Exhibit 14.3 illustrates the four major variables that affect repatriation adjustment: individual, job, organization, and nonwork. In each of these classifications are a subset of issues that can positively or negatively influence repatriation adjustment. The return job issue, discussed above, is generally viewed by researchers in the field as being the most significant indicator of level of repatriation adjustment; however, the other factors shown in exhibit 14.3 play important roles in repatriation adjustment as well.

EXHIBIT 14.3

POST RETURN ADJUSTMENT

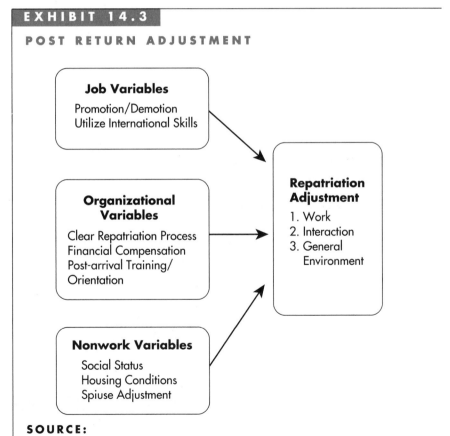

SOURCE:
Black, J.S., H.B. Gregersen & M. Mendenhall. 1992. *Global Assignments: Successfully Expatriating and Repatriating International Managers*. San Francisco: Jossey-Bass, Inc.

ORGANIZATIONAL FACTORS

The way in which a company structures its human resource policies regarding repatriates can have a significant effect on their repatriation adjustment. Very few companies have clearly articulated repatriation programs in place, causing expatriates to be unsure about what will happen to them when they return to the parent company. The expatriates are uncertain about what their pay will be upon return, how they will fit into the company's succession planning, where they will be assigned, and how their tax situation will be affected.

Virtually all expatriates experience a reduction in their standard of living upon return to their home country because they lose the numerous perquisites they were given for living overseas. This reduction of living standard and quality of life adds to the stress regarding their job assignments upon return. As one respondent put it: "When you are overseas you receive many benefits such as maybe a free car, or free petrol, or a nicer home than you have had back in your home country. You become accustomed to these benefits; then, when you return to your home country things return to normal and lots of these benefits you were accustomed to disappear. It's like being Cinderella and midnight has struck!" (Black, Gregersen, & Mendenhall 1992, p. 239). The stress of having to adjust to a new standard of living—in essence to being poorer—happens not only to North American repatriates, but for Japanese and European repatriates as well.

Just as cross-cultural training is beneficial to expatriates before they arrive in a foreign country, similar training given to expatriates before they are repatriated would likely be useful (Harvey 1989). Intuitively this may not make sense to most people; after all, these expatriates are returning to the country of their birth, where they were raised, where their extended families reside. Why do they need training? Consider for a moment what has happened while an expatriate is on a long-term overseas assignment.

While the expatriate is away, the home culture has not remained frozen. North American values, fads, laws, norms, music, sports, cuisine, and other basic aspects of life undergo change. The home office changes too: people are transferred, strategic emphases are altered, organizational restructurings occur. In the meantime the expatriate has been busy learning a new culture, and if the expatriate adjusted well, has learned to value certain aspects of this new culture. When it comes time to return home, the expatriate develops expectations about what it will be like living and working back home, relating with old friends and family, and enjoying aspects of the home culture enjoyed before the overseas assignment.

Upon return, the expatriate realizes the following: the home country is not the same country as when the expatriate left. The country has changed. The company is not the same company. Familiar faces are gone, policies are different, and the work culture has changed. Old friends and relatives are not the same. They have undergone a variety of life changes and they no longer are the same people that the expatriate has frozen in his/her memory. It is like going back to one's childhood home after being gone for years. Everything's changed, and the childhood town exists only in the individual's memory, not in reality.

Coming home to a place that is supposed to be familiar, but is not, is stressful. The remarks of an Austrian expatriate summarize this problem:

> I am Austrian by birth and lived in Austria until I was 18 years old. Then, I moved to the U.S. and my ties to Austria and Germany have remained strong all these years. When I had the opportunity to work in England and Germany for the last two years, I happily accepted the German part of the assignment, it seemed like going home. When I went back I took with me all the expectations about a country that I remember mostly through holiday visits and through the eyes of my parents and relatives. . .Then came a Germany I didn't recognize! I found the people very rigid and inflexible. I felt a foreigner in a country I expected to feel very much at home in . . . The differences which caused me the most difficulties were the ones between the Germany that I had lived in years ago and the Germany I was returning to (Black, Gregersen, & Mendenhall 1992, pp. 248–49).

A major problem in repatriation adjustment is developing inaccurate expectations about what life will be like. Training programs can assist expatriates realign their expectations about life "back home" with more realistic assumptions about what is likely to occur upon repatriation. Simply understanding the process of repatriation adjustment would be of immense aid to expatriates. Most repatriates, when surveyed, indicated that cross-cultural training to help them adjust upon returning home would have been significantly helpful to their own personal situations (Black, Gregersen, & Mendenhall 1992).

NONWORK VARIABLES

Studies show that changes in social status levels and housing conditions impact the manager's repatriation adjustment. While overseas, the expatriate manager is often a "big fish in a little pond": that is, the expatriate has a lot of power in the overseas job position, and is used to being treated with respect and consideration at work. While overseas, it is not unusual for expatriates to feel "special," "unique," and sometimes even superior to many of the host nationals. Then, to come home and be treated like everyone else in the mass of society can be a blow to the ego and self-esteem.

One study found that 54 percent of Americans and 47 percent of the Japanese experienced significant drops in status upon repatriation. Such losses had a direct negative impact on adjustment to work and the general environment for Americans and a negative impact on all three dimensions of adjustment (work, interaction, and general environment) for Finnish and Japanese repatriates (Black & Gregersen 1991).

For nonworking spouses, significant changes in housing conditions affected repatriation adjustment (Black & Gregersen 1991). When American expatriates who had rented out their homes returned home, on average they had to spend 2-to-15 weeks in a hotel while they had their homes repaired. Destruction by renters over a period of two years could reach over $15,000 for some families, and few companies picked up the tab for this problem. If the families had sold their houses and had to purchase new houses upon return, companies often did not provide an adequate hotel allowance. The time allowed to find a house was often too short for the families to conduct a careful search of the housing market and then take care of the financial and other paperwork that is necessary in purchasing a home.

Another shock was the fact that home prices had increased significantly while the expatriates were overseas. That being the case, the expatriates expected their companies to assist them with a housing allowance, but 60% of them (according to an ORC survey) found that their companies were unwilling to assist them in this challenge. Japanese expatriates especially experience a significant decline in housing conditions: 70 percent of Japanese expatriates feel a major loss in quality of life due to housing conditions upon repatriation. It is difficult to return to a cramped apartment when one has become accustomed to a large house on three acres, bordered by a forest. Such is the lot of many Japanese who have served their overseas assignments in Tennessee, Kentucky, Georgia, and other parts of the United States.

The repatriation process is normally a difficult one for many expatriate managers and their families, and the current research literature indicates that most companies do not manage this process well. It behooves companies to utilize their repatriate managers, to draw upon their skills and international expertise, and not to ignore this valuable organizational resource.

SUMMARY

When employees are sent overseas to work, someone winds up managing them. Often, it is a human resource manager who is either stationed abroad or at the home office. Just as often, the expatriate may be managed by someone in a line position, who finds him/herself suddenly in charge of a variety of human resource concerns relating to the needs of expatriate subordinates. The purpose of this chapter is to provide insight into the issues involved in managing an expatriate work force.

One of the key issues to understand about expatriates is the paradoxes they face in their new positions overseas—particularly in regards to their sense of allegiance and the way in which they deal with uncertainty of their role in the overseas environment. Working and managing overseas brings with it additional challenges that must be met, challenges that domestic managers do not face. After these problems were discussed, ways in which companies can deal with them were delineated.

The way in which performance appraisal differs overseas was discussed in detail. Many perceptual problems can confuse the performance appraisal process in cross-cultural contexts; ways in which these problems can be overcome were discussed. Expatriates, of course, must be paid, so expatriate compensation packages were discussed. These compensation packages differ from domestic compensation packages in many ways.

Returning home should be a joyous occasion for expatriates, but it often is not. A review of studies that have investigated this problem revealed that repatriation involves culture shock, and the nature of that process was discussed in detail. Ways in which companies can assist repatriates in their adjustment, and make use of their abilities and international skills was covered in the chapter as well.

DISCUSSION QUESTIONS

1. As a manager born in India, educated in the United Kingdom, and currently working for a U.S.–headquartered firm in its Canadian subsidiary, identify the loyalty conflicts that you would likely encounter.

2. Identify and discuss the kinds of expertise that a parent country national (PCN) is likely to have that makes it appropriate to send him/her on foreign assignments.

3. Discuss the advantages and disadvantages of compensating an expatriate, working outside of the parent country on the basis of prevailing compensation systems in the parent country.

REFERENCES

Adler, N.J. 1981. "Reentry: Managing cross-cultural transitions." *Group & Organization Studies*, 6, pp. 341–356.

Adler, P. 1974. "Beyond cultural identity: Reflections on culture and man." *Topics in Culture Learning*, 2, pp. 23–40.

Black, J.S. & H. Gregersen. 1991. "When Yankee comes home: Factors related to expatriate and spouse repatriation adjustment." *Journal of International Business Studies*, 22, pp. 671–695.

Black, J.S., H.B. Gregersen & M. Mendenhall. 1992. *Global Assignments: Successfully Expatriating and Repatriating International Managers.* San Francisco: Jossey-Bass.

Briody, E.K. & J.B. Chrisman. 1991. "Cultural adaptation on overseas assignments." *Human Organization*, 50(3), pp. 264–282.

Clague, L. & N.B. Krupp. 1978. "International personnel: The repatriation problem." *Personnel Administrator*, pp. 29-45.

Dowling, P.J., R.S. Schuler, & D.E. Welch. 1994. *International Dimensions of Human Resource Mangement* (2nd ed.) Belmont, CA: Wadsworth Publishing Company.

Gaffney, C. & B. Hitchings. 1985. "How to make a foreign job pay." *Business Week*, December 23, p. 84.

Harvey, M.G. 1989. "Repatriation of corporate executives: An empirical study." *Journal of International Business Studies*, 20, pp. 121–144.

Helms, M. 1991. "Cross-National Comparisons of Executive Pay." In M. Mendenhall, & G. Oddou. (eds.), *Readings and Cases in International Human Resource Management*. Boston: PWS-Kent.

Mendenhall, M. & G. Oddou. 1988. "The overseas assignment: A Practical Look." *Business Horizons*, September–October, pp. 78–84.

Mendenhall, M. & G. Oddou. (eds.). 1991. *Readings and Cases in International Human Resource Management*. Boston: PWS-Kent.

Napier, N.K. & R.B. Peterson. 1990. "Expatriate reentry: What do repatriates have to say?" *Human Resource Planning*, 14, pp. 19–28.

Oddou, G. & M. Mendenhall. 1991. "Succession planning in the 21st century: How well are we grooming our future business leaders?" *Business Horizons*, January–February, 34(1), pp. 26–34.

Osland, J. 1991. "The overseas experience of expatriate business people: Paradox and cultural involvement." Paper presented at the annual meeting of the Academy of Management, Miami Beach, August.

Osland, J.S. 1990. "The myth of the hero's adventure: Practical implications for managing the expatriate experience." Unpublished manuscript.

Prahalad, C.K. 1990. "Globalization: The intellectual and managerial challenges." *Human Resource Management*, 29(1), pp. 27–37.

Ratiu, I. 1983. "Thinking internationally: A comparison of how international executives learn." *International Studies of Management and Organization*, 13, pp. 139–150.

Stone, R.J. 1986. "Pay and perks for overseas executives." *Personnel Journal*, January, pp. 64, 67.

Tung, R.L. 1987. "Expatriate assignments: Enhancing success and minimizing failure." *Academy of Management Executive*, 1(2), pp. 117–126.

15

SPECIAL ISSUES

FOR GLOBAL

FIRMS: WOMEN

AND DUAL-CAREER

COUPLES

LEARNING OBJECTIVES

IN THIS CHAPTER WE WILL EXPLORE:

- How women's roles differ from men's internationally

- How women's roles are changing around the world

- Different interpretations of equality

- Women's contributions to management around the world

- Reasons for increases in dual-career couples

- The role of the spouse in foreign assignments

- Special issues affecting male spouses in foreign assignments

- Using dual-career couples effectively internationally

KEY DISCUSSION TOPICS:

- The traditional role of women in business and management

- The changing role of women in business and management

- The management of women around the world

- The meaning of equality

- The role of the spouse in expatriate assignments

- Strategies for dealing with male spouses in international assignments

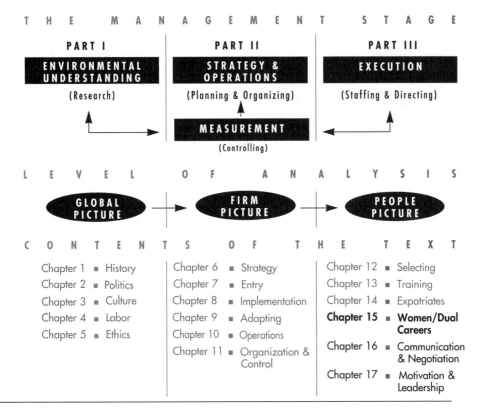

THE MANAGEMENT STAGE

INTRODUCTION

This chapter considers issues associated with both women and dual-career couples in international organizations. There are several dimensions to this discussion:

- Focusing on women, there are two main considerations: the role of women in different countries (both as employees and as managers) and the effectiveness of women as international managers in various locations.

- Focusing on dual-career couples, there are three main considerations: the role of spouses, challenges for men and women as international spouses, and the effective use of dual-career couples.

Women and dual-career couples are discussed together because issues associated with one are often closely linked to issues associated with the other.

International organizations often find that employing women leads to questions regarding their spouses, who often have careers. Similarly, dealing with dual-career couples in many cases involves finding productive activities for the female half of the couple.

These issues have only recently received much attention, either from practicing managers or from academic researchers. They are particularly important current issues, however, for North American organizations, and their importance is growing in other parts of the world as well, particularly in Europe. Women are entering the work force in increasing numbers. Many of these women have careers that they are following, and, more and more, women expect to have the same opportunities as their male counterparts. International organizations need to consider the role of women and plan for dual-career couples.

THE ROLE OF WOMEN IN BUSINESS AROUND THE WORLD

The role of women in society varies from country to country and even from region to region within a country. It also varies over time. This variation affects women in business and women as managers. Consider some possibilities:

- Women may be largely excluded from the general workforce and expected to work only in the home.

- Women may be excluded from management jobs but accepted in lower-level jobs.

- Certain work may be considered acceptable for women and not men, and vice versa.

- Women may be expected to work before they marry but not after.

- Women and men may work at the same jobs but women are compensated at a lower rate.

A United Nations study in the 1980s reported (Ramachandran 1992) that women do two-thirds of the world's work and produce 60-to-80 percent of

Africa and Asia's food. Yet they earn only ten percent of the world's income and own less than one percent of the world's property.

Some illustrations of the role of women in selected countries gives a sense of the barriers that women may face:

- In Saudi Arabia, restrictions on women's freedom to move around make it difficult for women to work. For example, women are not permitted to drive, to travel on an airplane alone, or to stay in a hotel without a male family member.

- In Japan women seldom work after marriage; consequently, women are unlikely to progress far within organizations.

- In the U.S., women have attained a degree of equality in business, but they are seldom found in top management positions.

- In Ireland, the constitution has been interpreted to mean that a woman should only join the work force if her husband is not able to look after the family economically.

- In St.Vincent, a West Indian island country, the minimum wage for women is lower than for men, regardless of the work performed.

- In Canada, the great majority of nurses and secretaries are women while the majority of fire fighters, construction workers, and foresters are men.

- In the People's Republic of China women hold many of the same positions as men, but they are required to retire at an earlier age.

- Ramachandran (1992) gives this example of the role of women in parts of India: in Rajasthan, when a social work organization wanted to establish a hospital for women, there was a great deal of hostility and resistance. The village men could not understand why so much fuss should be made over women; they insisted that what they really needed was a hospital for their farm animals

International managers, whether they are men or women, cannot avoid dealing with the question of the role of women in business. They must often decide if to employ women, when to employ them, which ones to employ, where to employ them; then they must decide how to manage the women employed. In addition, international managers need to recognize that men and women may view roles differently, and different treatment can be interpreted in a variety of ways. Different treatment of women can be considered protection or discrimination. It can be readily accepted or contested. It may be regulated by law or culturally accepted. It may be conscious or unconscious.

Understanding and working with the role of women in a new country is complicated by the biases that managers bring from home. As discussed in terms of culture and ethnocentrism, people often find it difficult to accept that values which contradict those held in their home society can be anything but wrong. This is often particularly true of issues associated with sexual roles and the place of women in society. The role of women is generally well known in the home culture, and a manager's reactions to this role are defined at an early age. When faced with contradictory views of gender roles, many people are especially disquieted and find these differences hard to accept. For example, managers who strongly believe in equality and whose training has emphasized nondiscrimination may find it very difficult to accept and adjust to a situation where women are generally treated as inferior in business. Women managers may find it particularly challenging to deal with this situation.

International managers need to pay particular attention to understanding the role of women in society and business in each country where they do business. They also need to assess consciously their reactions to this role. A manager in a country where women's role in business is unfamiliar can react in a number of different ways. Foreign managers can accept the new and unfamiliar role and adjust to the host country's view of the role of women, or they can try to influence people in the host country to change the role. Alternatively, foreign managers may seek out colleagues and employees who see the role of women in a way that is similar to that at home because they will be more comfortable interacting with these people. In most cases, some acceptance and adjustment will be necessary, but input that may help change the role is possible, as is seeking colleagues and employees whose views on the role of women are not typical of the host country.

SOME EXAMPLES OF
WOMEN'S ROLE IN BUSINESS

We will present some general descriptions of the role of women in business in selected countries or regions. These are intended to give students a feel for some of the differences that may be encountered. A detailed examination is not practical here, and it is important to recognize that the situation in any country or region will change over time.

Managers moving from the more-developed countries to developing ones may be particularly struck by differences in the status of women. The United Nations Center on Transnational Corporations (UNCTNC 1988) reported that international firms employ about two million women in the developing countries. This represents a very small proportion of the total labor force in these countries, and only about three percent of the worldwide employment by international firms. The typical role of women in these countries can be seen in a number of comments from the report:

- In some countries, women are employed, frequently with the whole family, in plantations owned by TNCs which often date from colonial times and grow such crops as tea and rubber. Their position in the plantation labor force is inferior to that of men.

- In the service sector, a small proportion of the total employment of women by TNCs work in white-collar occupations in transnational banks and commercial establishments. However, most women employed in services hold low-level jobs as maids, cleaners, waitresses, and salesgirls in hotels, offices, and retail establishments.

- TNCs in export processing zones (EPZs) have become significant employers of women, who work as low-paid, unskilled, or semi-skilled workers. Wages tend to be low, and they are often below those earned by men. Therefore, the practices of TNCs largely reflect prevailing local circumstances.

Firms often favor employing women in EPZs because they are seen as more efficient and stable than men. At the same time, their wages are lower than those for men, and it is easier to hire and lay off women. It is important to recognize that many of these women would otherwise be unemployed, and that they probably prefer to be employed in these jobs than unemployeed. Their inferior role is also probably accepted by most of the women. This illustrates the dilemma faced by many international managers. The balance between providing employment and exploiting female workers is not always clear-cut.

The role of women in business in the Arabian peninsula is often difficult for Westerners to understand and accept. Women are described as equal, but with different responsibilities. Once married, for example, women in Saudi Arabia go out only to visit close friends and relatives or to shop, and then they must be accompanied by a male relative. Women make up only about ten percent of the work force in Saudi Arabia, not because they are prohibited from working or from certain occupations, but because they are not permitted to work with men. The sexes must be kept segregated. Consequently, most organizations prefer not to employ women. Women who do work are in education, medicine, or social work, where contacts with males can be avoided. The situation is not very different in other countries in the region, even those with less stringent rules governing women's conduct. In Bahrain, for example, women are well educated and given equal opportunity, but affluence and social beliefs have discouraged women from seeking employment. This is changing somewhat with the emergence of a middle class and women interested in entering the professions. In Oman, as well, there are steps being taken to encourage women's participation in the work force.

Countries of the Far East vary in their acceptance of women in business. According to *The Economist*, "South-East Asia on Business," 1988:

- In Hong Kong women are found relatively frequently at all levels of organizations, and they are accepted as effective business people. Nevertheless, they are found most often in secretarial positions, and males are not found in traditionally female jobs.

- In Malaysia, women have "equal opportunity," but in reality they are sheltered and business is considered the preserve of males.

- In Singapore, increasing numbers of women are entering the work force, with 80 percent of those between the ages of 20 and 24 working. Professional women are more likely to advance in firms linked with the government. But, generally, their role is subordinate to that of men.

- In South Korea it is rare for women to be in positions of authority, and their prospects for advancement are slim as many companies have a policy of employing women only until they are 30 or marry.

- In Thailand women are seen as "the hind legs of the elephant"—powerful but following—and are generally in subordinate positions. This is tempered by educational and social background, which allows some women to hold top positions in government and private industry.

The situation in the People's Republic of China is somewhat mixed. Virtually all women work, but women in upper-level positions are rare. Traditionally, women were not expected to partake in business activities, but the Communist Party promoted the idea that "women hold up half of heaven" and implemented educational programs that have led to a substantial increase in the numbers of women at work and in scientific professions and government. Women, however, are required to retire at an earlier age than men for "physical reasons," and their advancement and lifetime earnings are consequently diminished.

Japanese organizations have traditionally seen women as serving in lower-paid, lower-level positions, and even graduates of top universities were hired for clerical positions. More Japanese women have been and are entering the workforce, however, and in 1986 Japan passed a law prohibiting discrimination on the basis of sex. Antidiscrimination legislation is better enforced in the public sector than the private, and women are more likely to be treated equally in government and public offices. While the situation for working women may be improving in Japan, the traditional role of the woman remaining at home after marriage is still accepted by most Japanese.

In the countries of the European Union (EU) the situation also varies from country to country. For example, in Denmark, women in the public sector receive their full wage for 32 weeks of maternity leave. Fathers are entitled to 2 weeks and may take the last 10 weeks of the 32 in place of the mother. In comparison, in Greece maternity leave is 15 weeks and in Spain 16.

Most EU countries are, at least in theory, promoting equal opportunities for women. Considerable progress regarding equal pay, treatment, access to education, and training for women has been made in the past 20 years, and there have been significant developments in legislation, antidiscrimination procedures and changing attitudes toward women in the work force. The current focus is on positive actions for equality and integrating women's issues into all areas of decision making. Specific programs are aimed at:

1. Facilitating access to the labor market through education and training.

2. Improving the quality of women's employment through reevaluation of their contribution, career development, and social protection.

3. Reconciling work and family through childcare, family services, housework sharing.

4. Improving the status of women through involvement in all levels of the decision process and their portrayal in the media.

In spite of, or sometimes because of, some of these efforts, women remain predominantly in lower-level, lower-paid positions. A particular result of efforts to allow women to combine work and family noted by Barry and Kelleher (1991) has been increased flexibility in the work place. While demanded by the women themselves, it has had the negative effect of putting these women outside of the traditional employer–employee contract and often outside of labor legislation protection.

THE MEANING OF EQUALITY

International managers need to understand the reasons for varying roles for men and women, as well as contrasting interpretations of equality. As with other cross-cultural variations, understanding helps managers adjust to unusual practices.

Most cultures differentiate between appropriate roles for men and women. This can probably be attributed to women being the child bearers and, consequently, the child rearers in most societies. Women traditionally have stayed in the home and carried out activities associated with the home or activities that could be combined with homemaking. Men, in contrast, have performed activities that occurred away from home. As a result, men were seen as more important in the business world.

These traditions have persisted even when it is no longer necessary for women to remain at home. The result has been that women who work outside the home often work in subordinate positions. In addition, the traditional role of women as care givers and supporters persists. Women work more often in a supportive capacity, such as secretarial positions, and care-giving professions, such as nursing, than do males.

These traditions are deeply ingrained. Consider Hofstede's cultural model discussed in Chapters 3 and 4. One dimension of this model described traditional masculine and feminine values. Masculine values encompassed competition, assertiveness, achievement, and material possessions while feminine values included nurturing, concern for others, and concern with the quality of life. Many people would see these masculine values as contributing to success in business while the feminine values would contribute to success in a supportive and caring role. Changing these traditional views is not easy, but changes are occurring around the world.

Achieving equality in the work force in Canada and the United States has focused on demonstrating the equal abilities of men and women. Legislation and social pressure has encouraged organizations to treat men and women largely in the same manner: that is, men and women should be given the same opportunities, training, compensation, and so on for equivalent jobs. An alternative approach is to look at the unique contributions that men and women can make in the work force. This approach focuses on the differences between men and women and assumes that they will be most effective in different roles, but that these different roles are equally important.

The distinction between these interpretations of equality is that, in the first, equality implies standardized, thus equitable, treatment for men and women; in the second it implies equitable valuation of different contributions. Those who believe in the first argue that focusing on differences tends to support the traditional view of women. Those who believe in the second argue that ignoring differences does not make the best use of the varying abilities and interests of the sexes.

This distinction needs to be recognized because managers who believe in equality for women do not always mean the same thing. A European manager who believes in equality for women may feel that female employees are different from male employees and thus better at some jobs. This manager may be surprised when working in the United States to find that U.S. employees reject this idea as discriminatory.

WOMEN AS MANAGERS IN DIFFERENT COUNTRIES

International managers often need to focus on the role of women as managers as well as their more general role in business. In most parts of the world, women make up a relatively small percentage of management; however, this seems to be changing. There are a number of reasons for this change: an increasing number of women in the work force generally, better educational opportunities for women, government regulations mandating equal treatment of women, and changing social and cultural values, among others.

The issue of women as managers is faced in foreign countries when hiring or promoting local women to management levels. It is necessary to assess the legal and cultural factors that may militate against women managers. As discussed earlier, legal provisions in some countries, such as Saudi Arabia, may make it onerous for local women to function effectively as managers. In other countries, such as Japan, local customs can make it equally onerous for different reasons. It is important to recognize these restrictions and make decisions within this framework. The international manager needs to be aware of the potential difficulties for the women as well as others in the organization and outside. If women agree to accept management positions under such circumstances, special provisions may have to be made to enable them to function productively.

THE ROLE OF WOMEN AS MANAGERS IN SELECTED LOCATIONS

We will now briefly discuss the role of women as managers in selected locations around the world. Exhibits 15.1, 15.2, and 15.3 present statistics on women in the work force as well as their participation in a variety of occupations. These are summary statistics and give only an overview of the situation in any country. Managers will want a more complete breakdown than this for any foreign country of interest. For example, data are given for managerial and administrative positions, but do not differentiate among top management, middle management, and supervisory positions. Similarly, data are given for sales positions and do not differentiate between retail and commercial sales positions.

Canada and the United States

The situation is better for women managers in Canada and the United States than in many other locations. Nevertheless, women are more likely to serve in jobs that are subordinate to men. They are usually the secretaries rather than the bosses, the nurses rather than the doctors, the teachers rather than the principals, the assistants rather than the politicians, and so on. Legislation in both countries prohibits discrimination on the basis of sex, and this has encouraged women to seek management positions and organizations to fill these positions with women. At lower- and middle-management levels women are well represented; at top levels, however, there are still relatively few women. The lack of women in top management has been attributed to several factors, including past discrimination, ongoing discrimination, a lack of interest on the part of some women, and a shortage of women with appropriate education and training. Whatever the causes, it seems likely that the situation is changing and that there will be increasing pressure on organizations to admit women to top management ranks.

EXHIBIT 15.1

CHANGES IN WORK FORCE PARTICIPATION
1969–1989: CANADA, JAPAN, UNITED STATES

	CANADA		JAPAN		UNITED STATES	
Year	% Male	% Female	% Male	% Female	% Male	% Female
1969	66.8	33.2	62.7	37.3	60.0	39.4
1970	66.4	33.6	62.3	37.7	60.7	39.3
1971	65.8	34.2	62.2	37.8	61.3	38.7
1972	65.4	34.6	62.0	38.0	61.8	38.2
1973	64.8	35.2	61.5	38.5	61.5	38.5
1974	64.3	35.7	61.1	38.9	62.3	37.7
1975	63.6	36.4	60.4	39.6	62.6	37.6
1976	62.9	37.1	59.9	40.1	62.5	37.5
1977	62.5	37.5	59.5	40.5	61.9	38.1
1978	61.6	38.4	58.8	41.2	61.5	38.5
1979	61.2	38.8	58.3	41.7	61.4	38.6
1980	60.3	39.7	57.6	42.4	61.3	38.7
1981	59.6	40.4	57.2	42.8	61.3	38.7
1982	58.7	41.3	56.5	43.5	61.0	39.0
1983	58.1	41.9	56.3	43.7	60.5	39.5
1984	57.7	42.3	56.3	43.7	60.4	39.6
1985	57.3	42.7	55.9	44.1	60.3	39.7
1986	57.0	43.0	55.6	44.4	60.2	39.7
1987	56.6	43.4	55.2	44.8	60.1	39.9
1988	56.2	43.8	55.0	45.0	59.9	40.1
1989	55.9	44.1	54.8	45.2	59.6	40.4

SOURCE:
Yearbook of labour Statistics 89/90. 1990. Geneva: International Labour Organization.

EXHIBIT 15.2

WOMEN AND MEN IN THE WORK FORCE (1990)—SELECTED COUNTRIES

Total Work Force	% Male	% Female
Brazil	66.2	33.8
Canada	55.7	44.3
Israel	60.4	39.6
Japan	59.9	40.1
Korea	60.2	39.8
Nigeria	67.8	32.2
Portugal	58.0	42.0
United States	55.5	44.5

SOURCE:

Yearbook of labour Statistics 89/90. 1990. Geneva: International Labour Organization.

Western Europe

Women are not as well represented in management ranks in Europe as in Canada and the United States. The situation varies from country to country and each country has its own regulations and socially accepted views. Integration of the European Union and standardization of regulations likely to result in a more uniform role for women managers throughout the Union, although social dissimilarities will probably continue to influence this role in individual countries. The European Union's Foundation for the Improvement of Living and Working Conditions has recently emphasized the need to take positive action for equality in the work place, and this will likely have a positive impact on women's participation in management throughout the community.

EXHIBIT 15.3

WOMEN AND MEN IN DIFFERENT OCCUPATIONS (1990)—SELECTED COUNTRIES

Country	Prof. Tech. %M	%F	Adm. Mgr. %M	%F	Cleric. %M	%F	Sales %M	%F	Servc. %M	%F	Agr. %M	%F	Prod. %M	%F
Canada	13.1	20.1	13.1	10.4	5.9	30.2	8.8	9.7	10.6	17.4	7/0	2.3	41.5	9.3
Israel	18.2	29.8	0.3	2.3	9.8	28.0	8.9	6.8	0.8	18.2	5.6	1.8	37.3	8.3
Japan	9.8	11.0	5.7	0.7	12.0	25.2	15.7	14.2	6.3	11.2	6.7	9.0	40.9	25.7
Korea	6.5	6.0	2.2	0.0	12.1	11.0	12.8	16.6	0.8	16.1	18.3	22.4	38.2	26.1
Nigeria	6.3	4.0	0.4	0.0	4.4	2.8	13.4	43.8	4.0	1.6	48.4	35.1	16.2	5.3
Portugal	5.3	8.6	1.9	0.5	10.3	13.1	8.8	0.1	6.0	16.4	17.6	24.5	40.5	18.8

SOURCE:
Yearbook of labour Statistics 89/90. 1990. Geneva: International Labour Organization.

Africa

Women's roles in Africa depend to a large extent on the particular ethnic group to which they belong. In a number of cases the role is clearly secondary and inferior to that of men, as the following illustrate:

- Parkin (1978) described one African group as defining women's status as "the producers of men's children" and "confined to domestic activities" while men were the "political leaders and wage earners" (p.168).

- An executive who had worked in Africa described one location where female employees sat on the floor facing the wall when speaking with their male superiors.

- Ferraro (1990) described Kenya as one of the most Westernized and progressive African countries but said that the role and status of women remained characterized by traditional distinctions of inferiority.

- Ferraro (1990) described African men as having "considerable difficulty seeing women as anything other than wives, mothers, and food producers" (p.114).

Japan

The Japanese social system has encouraged Japanese women to work full-time only until marriage; following marriage, they may work part-time when needed by a firm. This system has resulted in virtually no Japanese women currently in management positions. There is some evidence of a growing desire on the part of Japanese women to participate more fully in Japanese business. But this movement is in its early stages, and it is not possible to say what its impact will be.

The People's Republic of China

Top positions in China are almost entirely filled by men. The government has encouraged equal opportunity for women, however, and women have been encouraged to become entrepreneurs and managers. Nevertheless, there are relatively few women in business school programs, and women largely accept their secondary role in business.

The Middle East

The role of women in the Arab countries of the Middle East as described previously largely precludes women being managers. Even in situations where women run their own businesses, they generally employ a man as a "front" according to *The Economist* (1988). The situation in Israel is somewhat different from other Middle Eastern countries. Women in Israel are well-educated, and they have been relatively well-accepted as managers. Nevertheless, as Exhibit 15.3 indicates, only a very small percentage of women in the Israeli work force are in administrative and managerial positions. The picture in Israel is similar to that in most Western countries: management positions are dominated by men and clerical positions by women.

WOMEN AS INTERNATIONAL MANAGERS

The numbers of women undertaking international assignments in the early 1980s was relatively low according to Adler (1984). This did not change dramatically through the 1980s according to Kirk & Maddox (1988). There is, however, an expectation that the situation will change in the 1990s and beyond. There are a number of reasons to expect more women international managers in the next decades.

There are an increasing number of women domestic managers, particularly in Canada and the United States. As a result, more women are candidates for foreign assignments. In the past, firms may have had a limited number of qualified women to select for international jobs. This picture is changing, and, in turn, firms will likely find that they are sending more and more women to fill foreign posts.

Many global firms want their top executives to have international experience. If women are to reach the top they need to accept expatriate assignments. In the past, some firms have hesitated to ask women to go overseas because of the potential hardships associated with some locations. Women do not share this hesitancy, however. Among MBA students surveyed by Nancy Adler (1984) women were equally as willing as males to accept international assignments and pursue international careers.

CHALLENGES FOR WOMEN INTERNATIONALLY

There is growing evidence that women make good expatriate managers. This suggests that firms will want to use more women in foreign locations. Particularly interesting is the evidence that women make good expatriate managers even in locations where local women would generally not be well accepted as managers. Many organizations are concerned about assigning women to countries such as Japan in case they would not be accepted by males. A paper by Jelinek and Adler (1988) reports that this is not the case. They found that North American women managers in Japan were viewed as "foreigners" rather than as "women" and that their sex was not an impediment to competent management. Nancy Adler quotes one woman who works successfully in Hong Kong as saying: "It doesn't make any difference if you are blue, green, purple, or a frog, if you have the best product at the best price, the Chinese will buy," and she concludes that in global business pragmatism wins out over prejudice.

While the information currently available suggests that women make effective international managers, they clearly face difficulties. The previous reports of women's effectiveness are based on the small number of women who were offered, and accepted, international assignments. Given the general biases against female candidates, it is likely that these women were particularly good candidates. It is to be expected, therefore, that their performance would also be good.

MAKING EFFECTIVE USE OF WOMEN IN INTERNATIONAL ORGANIZATIONS

It is only practical for firms, and women seeking expatriate assignments, to investigate the reality of the foreign work environment for a woman manager. By realistically assessing the environment the expatriate can be appropriately prepared, and the firm can provide the needed support to allow for high performance. For example, if the woman cannot legally drive in a foreign country, she must be prepared to accept this limitation, and the firm must provide a driver to give her needed mobility. If a woman will not be admitted to clubs where business is often conducted, she will need to develop alternative venues for making business contacts, and the firm should provide the necessary funding, contacts, and so on to accomplish this.

In spite of potential obstacles, *The Economist's* "Doing Business In" series generally suggests that foreign women can overcome local biases against women managers relatively easily. For example, they note that Saudi men are uncomfortable working with women but treat foreign women with respect because of their assumed high status. In Saudi Arabia where the man must precede the woman into a room, they note that he will generally apologize to the foreign woman first. In most countries where local women are not typically part of the business world, women are expected to be conservative and to view marriage as a desirable achievement. *The Economist* suggests that foreign women managers will find it helpful not to contradict these values.

The view that foreign women can be effective as managers where it would be difficult for local women is supported by a study reported by Dawson, Ladenburg, and Moran (1987). A majority of the women surveyed described themselves and their professional positions as outside the cultural norms in the foreign environment, but they were "challenged and happy with their lives overseas" (p. 81). Rossman (1990) also illustrates the potential for women managers internationally in a series of profiles of women. Some selected excerpts from Rossman's work show that virtually anywhere in the world it is possible for women to succeed:

> Barbara Stewart has successfully conducted business in Saudi Arabia, Tunisia, Jordan, Iraq, and Egypt.

> Diane Simpson, president of a small New York-based management consulting firm, specializes in U.S.–Japanese business.

> Linda Pakh has negotiated loans in Budapest, Bucharest, Moscow, Prague, Warsaw, and East Berlin.

> Jane Altschuler successfully produced and directed a film shot in Nigeria entitled *Nigeria: The Unknown Giant.*

> Pat Winters, at 24, has made sales trips to the United Kingdom, Norway, France, Germany, and Italy.

The author has worked as a marketing consultant in Latin America, Europe, and the Far East.

Legislation in North America, and in a number of other countries, prohibits discrimination on the basis of certain personal characteristics, including gender. This applies to international assignments as well as those at home. Nevertheless, this legislation is tempered by the requirements of particular jobs. For example, the Roman Catholic Church does not accept women for ordination as priests and is not required by this law to do so. Similarly, in foreign locations, there may be legislation governing the assignment of women to certain jobs, positions, or locations. In these circumstances the firm has to abide by the foreign legislation. This creates a dilemma for the firm because it may be breaking the law at home, and possibly its own internal policies, in order to comply with the foreign legislation.

Situations such as these may need to be considered on a case-by-case basis to determine the most appropriate way of resolving the dilemma. In some situations, a female candidate may prefer not to accept a posting to such a location; in others, it may be possible to make special arrangements that provide a means to bypass the foreign requirements; in still others, a job title, duties and so on may need to be modified. Perhaps a lesson can be taken from the Saudi women entrepreneurs who employ a man as a front. From the perspective of the firm, the important outcome is the effective use of women managers. From the woman's perspective, the important outcome is her ability to perform at an appropriate level.

The actual experience of women expatriates can vary widely. Some women find an international posting a successful and rewarding experience both from a career and personal perspective. Others find it unsuccessful, resulting in career setbacks and family breakups. Still others have mixed experiences. Interviews with women executives suggest that there is a substantial number of women in foreign locations with careers (both women expatriates and married women accompanying their spouses on an international transfer), and that there are going to be increasing numbers. Organizations that recognize this and pay attention to their concerns will likely benefit.

DUAL-CAREER COUPLES

International firms in Canada and the United States are finding, more and more, that their married employees are part of a dual-career couple. While the trend is not as dramatic, there is a growing number of such couples in Europe as well in dual-career couples both partners work, and both see their work as not simply providing financial remuneration. These people see their work as representing an important occupation which they wish to pursue for personal achievement and advancement.

Exhibits 15.4 and 15.5 illustrate the increases in professional and managerial women and dual-career couples in North America. Coinciding with these trends is a likely increase in the numbers of women who are being offered, and accepting, expatriate assignments. These trends all imply that international firms in the 1990s and the twenty-first century will need to pay close attention to dual-career couples. A survey of directors of human resource management of U.S. multinationals by Rosalie Tung (1988) found that a majority believed that the issue of dual-career families will be a major problem confronting their companies in the next decade; similarly, Canadian surveys have found that this issue was a major concern for human resource executives in Canada (Punnett 1989; Punnett, Crocker, & Stevens 1992).

In spite of the apparent importance, many companies are not yet addressing the issues related to dual-career couples and international assignments directly. Tung found that many companies believed that problems associated with the relocation of spouses in dual-career couples was a family or personal matter; consequently, the company should adopt a "hands-off" policy. Other firms seek more host-country nationals, third-country nationals, or single home-country nationals for expatriate positions to avoid the issues associated with dual-career couples. These are not entirely effective choices because companies limit the pool of candidates from which they choose, and some managers lose the opportunity to develop international expertise. It seems that international firms that want to attract and retain the best employees and make the best possible use of them around the world need to develop policies for dual-career couples, including women expatriates whose spouses have careers.

EXHIBIT 15.4

WOMEN EMPLOYED IN
PROFESSIONAL OCCUPATIONS 1971-1986

	Total number of women			Percentage increase	Woman as a % of total growth in profession	Woman as a % of total employment in profession	
	1971	1981	1986	1981–1986	1981-1986	1981	1986
Male-dominated professions							
Management occupations, natural sciences, and engineering	70	800	1,225	53.1	23.8	6.6	8.8
Management occupations, social sciences, and related fields	760	3,805	6,090	60.1	85.9	48.2	57.7
Administrators in teaching and related fields	6,445	9,120	12,425	36.2	76.7	25.0	30.5
Chemists	895	1,975	3,080	55.9	63.5	20.4	27.0
Geologists	145	795	1,005	26.4	35.6	10.3	12.1
Physicists	45	65	95	46.2	*	5.0	7.9
Meteorologists	40	90	120	33.3	24.0	9.0	10.7
Agriculturists and related scientists	330	1,220	2,420	98.4	37.6	13.2	19.5
Biologists and related scientists	830	2,330	3,000	28.8	80.7	31.9	36.9
Architects	125	560	850	51.8	48.7	7.7	10.8
Chemical engineers	65	340	560	64.7	62.9	5.9	9.2
Civil engineers	235	980	1,490	52.0	*	3.0	4.6
Electrical engineers	205	1,000	1,655	65.5	14.4	3.7	5.2
Mechanical engineers	100	380	710	86.6	8.6	1.9	3.0
Metallurgical engineers	15	50	100	100.0	*	2.8	6.1
Mining engineers	20	105	155	47.6	*	2.9	4.3
Petroleum engineers	15	225	285	26.7	*	1.1	6.5
Nuclear engineers	—	40	70	75.0	*	4.8	9.5
Other architects and engineers	140	1,640	2,640	61.0*	36.8	12.2	16.3
Mathematicians, statisticians, and actuaries	`1,010	2,070	2,305	11.4	54.0	34.7	36.0
Economists	640	2,570	4,345	69.1	62.2	20.5	28.3
Sociologists, anthropologists, and related social scientists	170	540	685	26.9	290.0	39.0	47.7
Judges and magistrates	75	220	320	45.5	27.4	10.5	-120.0
Lawyers and notaries	860	5,390	9.140	74.6	51.2	15.5	-22.0
Ministers of religion	900	1,785	2,590	45.1	65.7	7.6	10.5
University teachers	5,190	9,785	11,470	17.2	48.7	26.5	28.4
Other university teaching and related occupations	1,525	6,170	8,640	40.0	44.1	45.8	45.3
Community college and vocational school teachers	3,280	13,770	16,945	23.1	57.1	41.6	43.8
Physicians and surgeons	3,150	7,255	10,175	40.2	47.3	17.4	-21.2
Dentists	330	860	1,670	94.2	44.1	8.1	13.5
Veterinarians	75	605	1,510	149.6	114.6	17.2	35.1
Osteopaths and chiropractors	80	340	520	52.9	25.7	14.9	17.5
Pharmacists	2,540	6,090	8,755	43.8	91.1	41.8	-50.1
Optometrists	105	365	840	130.1	37.2	17.7	32.2
Total male-dominated professions	30,410	83,340	118,155	41.8	52.1	18.6	22.9
Other professions							
Psychologists	2,035	4,600	7,075	53.8	79.6	52.6	59.7
Social workers	7,230	21,020	31,005	47.5	78.5	63.5	67.7
Supervisors in library, museum, and archival sciences	600	1,440	1.700	18.1	85.2	62.1	64.8
Librarians and archivists	6,120	13,575	15,315	12.8	80.6	80.9	80.9
Educational and vocational counselors	1,690	3,050	4,285	40.5	84.0	49.3	55.9
Elementary and kindergarten teachers	140,500	152,335	163,505	7.3	79.0	81.5	81.3
Secondary school teachers	56,615	63,320	62,745	-0.9	*	43.8	45.7
Postsecondary school teachers	5,730	4,445	3,850	-13.4	*	63.9	74.1
Teachers of exceptional students	4,420	15,315	18,710	22.2	97.7	72.1	75.7
Physiotherapists, occupational and other therapists	5,895	12,525	16,855	34.6	86.0	85.0	85.2
Dietitians and nutritionists	2,010	3,280	4,250	29.6	100.0	94.3	95.5
Translators and interpreters	1,395	4,340	5,175	19.2	92.8	61.9	65.4
Total other professions	234,240	299,250	334,470	11.8	9.7	66.2	68.6
Total all professions	264,650	382,590	452,610	18.3	68.5	42.5	45.1

* Total employment in this profession declined between 1981 and 1986
** Amount to small to be expressed

SOURCE:

Statistics Canada, Census of Canada.

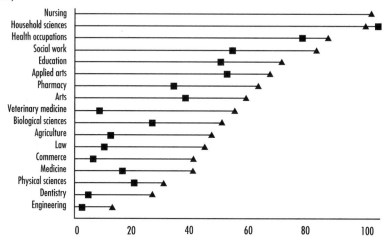

EXHIBIT 15.5

BACHELOR AND FIRST PROFESSIONAL DEGREES OBTAINED BY WOMEN AS A PROPORTION OF TOTAL

Field of Study

Note: In almost every discipline, women's share of all degrees granted increased sharply—e.g., from 39% to 62% in pharmacy.

SOURCE

Women and Education: A Canadian Perspective (Edited Edition). 1987. Calgary: Detselig Enterprises.

Revised papers from Women and Education Conference held at the University of British Columbia June, 1986.

THE ROLE OF THE SPOUSE INTERNATIONALLY

Previously, when the role of the spouse in the success or failure of an expatriate was acknowledged firms usually assumed that the spouse would be a non-working female. Not surprisingly, their concern was with the typical expatriate who was male. In the past, the expatriate couple was a working husband and a wife, who, if she had a career, was willing to forgo immediate career advancement in favor of the foreign assignment. Companies were concerned with finding productive activities, such as volunteer opportunities for the wife.

The problem of an expatriate's spouse is magnified for women expatriates and their spouses, most of whom, in the current social system, have careers. The situation is more complex when the husband must make the decision to accompany his wife because the current social system makes it difficult for many men to adjust to the role of secondary breadwinner or homemaker, if they do not work in the foreign location. These roles are still more socially acceptable for women. Women, even those with careers, may make the transition to these roles more easily than men. Society generally judges men by their careers more so than it does women; thus, a negative or even neutral career move can be especially troublesome for many males. Also, because most expatriate managers are male, the nonworking expatriate spouse group is largely female, and the nonworking husband may find himself the lone man in a group of wives. Finally, the traditional volunteer activities of wives may not be available or appropriate for males in some countries. Thus, husbands may be barred from the productive activities that wives have available.

MAKING EFFECTIVE USE OF DUAL-CAREER COUPLES

North American studies of domestic transfers have generally revealed that companies need to take a proactive approach to dual-career couples to attract and retain the best employees, concluding that "companies with successful family-related policies will be able to increasingly attract the cream of the crop in future workers" (Potter 1989, p. 29). The same is true for international transfers.

The cost of expatriate failure and poor performance is difficult to estimate. It includes much more than the actual costs associated with the transfer. Copeland and Griggs (1988) estimated that American companies lose $2 billion a year in direct costs due to expatriate failure. Furthermore, while there is no figure for the costs of lost business and damage to the company's reputation caused by expatriate failure, they assume the numbers to be "frightening."

This high cost suggests that global organizations should be concerned with improving their performance in this area. One means may be greater attention to the dual-career issue.

Assigning dual-career couples within North America is often difficult, but the problems are magnified across national boundaries. Work permit restrictions of some host societies make it difficult if not impossible for a spouse to work. Countries such as the United States, Australia, and Switzerland seldom grant work permits to both spouses unless they possess expertise and skills in short supply. The restrictions to be placed on individuals by foreign countries fall into the following three basic categories:

1. Prohibition of the nontransferring spouse from working.

2. Restrictive regulations similar to restrictions faced by any individual applying to work in the foreign country; whereby country nationals have priority for jobs over foreigners.

3. Very few restrictions which amounts to an almost open-door policy.

In countries with no work permit restrictions, there may be a bias against women working in predominantly male occupations or vice versa. Or, it may be socially unacceptable for the husband to be the homemaker.

Keeping both careers on track while abroad is also hard. Even if the spouse can work, career advancement may be less likely in a foreign environment. For example, professional requirements and designations can vary from country to country. One spouse may have to make career sacrifices.

As discussed in Chapters 12, 13, and 14, research on expatriate transfers has identified the family, and particularly the spouse, as critical to the expatriate's success overseas. Spouses who are well prepared for the foreign environment and receive support while overseas adjust well generally, and this increases the likelihood of successful transfers. The adjustment is often more difficult for spouses because they lack the focus and support provided by work. Spouses accustomed to working may be particularly frustrated if they cannot work or if they encounter difficulties finding work. These difficulties may add to the already stressful transfer and perhaps increase the possibility of failure. Add to this the stress engendered when male is the spouse in this position, and it is not surprising if some couples have concerns about foreign assignments.

PROACTIVE APPROACHES TO DUAL-CAREER COUPLES

There are a number of alternative approaches that firms can adopt to activity assist dual-career couples facing international transfers. These deal specifically assist the spouse. For example, an interesting initiative has recently been implemented by Aluminum Company of Canada according to the *Globe and Mail* (April 15, 1991). It has reached an agreement with Immigration Canada to waive the requirement that employers first try to find a Canadian to fill a job that the expatriate would like—on condition that the expatriate manager's country agrees to make a reciprocal arrangement. The following points illustrate some proactive approaches for companies to help alleviate the concerns of dual-career couples moving internationally:

- Provide more time for the move so that the spouse can investigate job opportunities and provide a premove trip to make initial contacts.

- Develop career-oriented employment networks; for example, public sector organizations can coordinate employment opportunities with other public and private sector organizations.

- Provide letters of introduction, office space, telephone and secretarial support, and other similar services for spouses seeking foreign employment.

- Provide the services of an international job-search firm.

- Consider opportunities for job sharing when both spouses are in the same field, and give the spouse preference for available jobs within the organization overseas.

- Provide realistic predeparture information on foreign job opportunities and help in obtaining requisite visas, permits, and so on.

- Consider the reentry problem: spouses again have to seek employment and need the same support as when going overseas. In addition, recognize that those who meet spouses overseas and return home with them will need similar, additional, assistance.

- Address questions of unemployment, benefits, pensions, and so on as they relate to the accompanying spouse.

- Provide, or help identify and apply for, research money for which spouses could apply. This would provide funding to do research in a career area while overseas and would allow a spouse to further his career without undertaking paid employment. For example, an accountant could study the accounting system in a foreign location (say, Japan), and later use this information for career advancement.

- Establish education funds to provide the opportunity to further a current career or change careers.

- Provide help (such as networking) focused on professional employment opportunities, rather than lower-level employment. Executive search services could also be provided.

- Provide more recognition for the work that the spouse does to assist the employee (for example, hosting social functions).

Many women feel that in today's North American economy it is necessary for both parties to work. Therefore, international transfers can have substantial financial implications if one spouse has to give up working. Career-oriented women are also likely to be married to career-oriented men and vice versa.

Male spouses who have accompanied their wives on foreign assignments have some specific concerns as well. In interviews, a male spouse group consisting of a cross-section of careers—a landscape architect, a sculptor, a banker, an advocate for the handicapped, a foreign service officer, and a lawyer—made the following comments:

- Spouses have to be flexible and fend for themselves in terms of finding appropriate employment. If they can't find appropriate employment, then the transfer won't be successful.

- Organizations have to realize that most spouses have careers and are not interested in just any job. It needs to be something that contributes to a sense of self-worth and future career opportunities.

- The expatriate lifestyle and their wives' advancement is positive. But the specifics of the situation can be negative, for example, being the only male spouse, being streamed into traditional spouse activities, and being ignored.

- Spouses want activities that benefit their careers and provide interest while in a foreign location.

In general, the male spouses expressed a sense of being overlooked. Yet they felt they were important to the success of the assignment. They wanted organizations to recognize that there were many things that could alleviate their situation. They were willing to go overseas under somewhat difficult circumstances and to talk about the experience. One could conjecture that spouses with less transportable careers, and who were less willing to go, may have found the experience more difficult.

Overall, the research on dual-career couples abroad suggests that the number of such couples is increasing and that this trend is likely to continue in Canada and the United States and possibly to escalate elsewhere. These couples are therefore a significant group for international firms. Firms that respect the concerns of these couples may benefit by attracting, retaining, and motivating these employees. There are a variety of actions that firms can undertake to deal with concerns often expressed by these couples.

SUMMARY

This chapter has given an overview of some of the issues associated with women and dual-career couples that international managers must consider. Women are participating in the work force in increasing numbers in most countries. The role of women varies considerably from place to place, however. International managers need to understand these variations and their implications for human resource policies and practices as well as for management style. Dual-career couples are also an increasing force international firms need to be aware of. These couples face a number of difficulties, particularly related to international transfers. In this chapter we considered a variety of concerns as well as approaches for addressing these concerns.

DISCUSSION QUESTIONS

1. Identify recent trends regarding women in management in your home country and discuss how they are likely to influence firms from your country sending managers on foreign assignments.

2. Discuss the unique challenges faced by male spouses of expatriates and suggest ways of managing these challenges.

3. Discuss the impact of the changing role of women in North American firms on international staffing decisions by North these firms.

REFERENCES

Adler, N.J. 1984. "Women do not want international careers: And other myths about international management." *Organizational Dynamics*, pp. 66–78.

Adler, N.J. 1986. "Women in management worldwide." *International Studies of Management and Organizations*, Fall–Winter.

Adler, N.J. 1987. "Pacific Basin managers: A Gaijin, not a woman." *Human Resource Management*, 26(2), pp. 169–191.

Adler, N.J. 1991. *International Dimensions of Organizational Behavior.* Boston: PWS-Kent Publishing Company.

Barry, U. & P. Kelleher. 1991. *Review of the Foundation's Work 1985–92 and Its Implications for Women.* Loughlinstown House, Shankill, Co. Dublin: European Foundation for the Improvement of Living and Working Conditions.

Bielby, D.D. & W.T. Bielby. 1988. "Women's and men's commitment to paid work and family: Theories, models and hypotheses." *Women and Work: An Annual Review*, 3.

Black, J.S. & G.K. Stephens. 1989. *The influence of the spouse on American expatriate adjustment and intent to stay in Pacific Rim overseas assignments. Journal of Management*, 15(4) pp. 529–544.

Burke, R. & C.A. McKeen. 1988. "Work and family: What we know and what we need to know." *Canadian Journal of Administrative Sciences*, 5(4) pp. 30–40.

Colwill, N.L. & L. Temple. 1987. "Three jobs and two people: the dual-career dilemma." *Business Quarterly*, 52(3) pp. 12–15.

Copeland, L. & L. Griggs. 1988. "The internationable employee." *Management Review*, pp. 52–53.

Dawson, G., E. Ladenburg, & R. Moran. 1987. "Women in international management." In *Businesswoman—Present and Future*, D. Clutterbuck & M. Devine (eds.). London: The Macmillan Press Limited. pp. 76–90.

Dowling, P.J. & R.S. Schuler. 1990. *International Dimensions of Human Resource Management*. Boston: PWS-Kent Publishing Company.

Ferraro, G.P. 1990. *The Cultural Dimension of International Business*. Englewood Cliffs, NJ: Prentice-Hall.

Gibb-Clark, M. April 15, 1991. "Career move may include spouse's job." *Globe and Mail*. Report on Business, B4.

Jelinek, M. & N.J. Adler. 1988. "Women: World-class managers for global competition." *Academy of Management Executive*, 11(1), pp. 11–20.

Kirk, W.Q. & R.C. Maddox. 1988. "International management: The new frontier for women." *Personnel*, 65(2), pp. 46–49.

Kobrin, S.J. 1988. "Expatriate reduction and strategic control in American multinational corporations." Human Resource Management, 27(1), pp. 63–75.

Lewis, S., D.N. Izraeli, & H. Hootsmans (eds.). 1992. *Dual-Earner Families— International Perspectives*. London: Sage Publications.

Paddock, J.R. & K.M. Schwartz. 1986. "Rituals for dual-career couples." *Psychotherapy*, 23(3), pp. 453–459.

Parkin, D. 1978. *The Cultural Definition of Political Response: Lineal Destiny among the Luo*. London: Academic Press.

Potter, J.M. 1989. "Family-related programs: Strategic issues." *Canadian Business Review*, 16(3), pp. 27–30.

Punnett, B.J. 1989. "Human resource management in international Canadian companies." In *Canadian Dimensions of International Business: A Strategic Approach*. Toronto: Prentice-Hall Canada, p. 330–346.

Punnett, B.J., O. Crocker, & M. Stevens. 1992. "The challenge for women expatriates and spouses: Some empirical evidence." *International Journal of Human Resource Management*, 3(3).

Ramachandran, R. 1992. "The silenced majority: Sex ratio and the status of women in India." *Canadian Women Studies*, 13(1), pp. 60–66.

Report on Social Developments Year 1989. 1991. Brussels-Luxembourg: Commission of the European Communities.

Rossman, M.L. 1990. *The International Businesswoman of the 1990s—A Guide to Success in the Global Marketplace*. New York: Praeger.

Sekaran, U. 1986. *Dual-Career Families: Contemporary Organizational and Counseling Issues*. San Francisco: Jossey-Bass.

Taylor, A.S. & J.W. Lounsbury. 1988. "Dual-career couples and geographic transfer: Executives reaction to commuter marriage and attitude toward the move." Human Relations, 41(5), pp. 407–424.

The Economist. 1988. *Business Travellers Guides: Arabian Peninsula On Business*. London: The Economist.

The Economist. 1988. *Business Travellers Guides: China On Business*. London: The Economist.

The Economist. 1988. *Business Travellers Guides: South-East Asia On Business*. London: The Economist.

Tung, R.L. 1988. *The New Expatriates: Managing Human Resources Abroad.* Cambridge, MA: Ballinger.

Yearbook of Labour Statistics 89/90. 1990. Geneva: International Labour Organization.

16

COMMUNICATION

AND NEGOTIATION

IN GLOBAL

MANAGEMENT

LEARNING OBJECTIVES

IN THIS CHAPTER YOU WILL EXPLORE:

- The process of human communication

- How culture affects communication

- Various cross-cultural communication challenges

- The barriers to cross-cultural communication

- The role of perception in cross-cultural communication

- Body language and other non-verbal forms of communication

- The stages of the negotiation process

- Cross-cultural differences in negotiation styles

KEY DISCUSSION ISSUES:

- How do the six dimensions of communication affect us daily?

- Why is it so easy to misunderstand when communicating?

- How can you train yourself to become a better communicator?

- Explore the differences between high versus low context cultures.

- How do spatial and architectural features influence communication?

- Explore the nature of perceptual biases and faulty attributions.

- Why do cultures differ in their orientation towards negotiation?

- How can one prepare to negotiate in another culture?

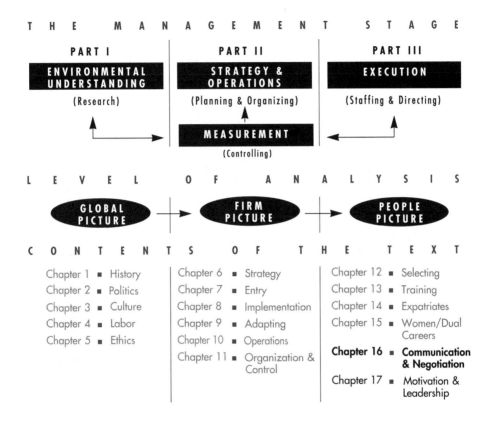

T H E   M A N A G E M E N T   S T A G E

PART I

| ENVIRONMENTAL UNDERSTANDING |
(Research)

PART II

| STRATEGY & OPERATIONS |
(Planning & Organizing)

| MEASUREMENT |
(Controlling)

PART III

| EXECUTION |
(Staffing & Directing)

L E V E L   O F   A N A L Y S I S

GLOBAL PICTURE → FIRM PICTURE → PEOPLE PICTURE

C O N T E N T S   O F   T H E   T E X T

INTRODUCTION

All of us know what it feels like to be misunderstood by someone we are trying to communicate with. In fact, it is probably impossible that any other person can feel and understand completely what another person feels and understands because the only way we can share our feelings, thoughts, attitudes, beliefs, and emotions is through verbal and nonverbal language.

The process by which verbal and nonverbal language is shared is communication. There are five fundamental dimensions of human communication we describe in this chapter. We explore the difficulties of communicating across cultures and the barriers to effective cross-cultural communication. Negotiations are a major aspect of international management and are fundamentally influenced by communication as well. We will consider various aspects of negotiations and how these can differ from location to location.

Before we describe the dimensions of communication, consider the following examples of cross-cultural communication failures; they will be used later to illustrate the five aspects of human communication in cross-cultural contexts. (These examples are from Haworth & Savage 1989.)

- An American expatriate in Seoul beckons to a Korean store clerk with the typical U.S. "come-here" wave of the hand. The Korean store clerk is amazed and appalled and avoids the American. The American waits, sees he is being avoided, and angrily walks out of the store. The Korean store clerk was offended that the American would use a gesture to call him that is used in Korea to call only dogs. The American was incensed that the clerk would ignore and refuse to assist him.

- A British student and an American student were assigned to be lab partners in a chemistry class. The British student complained that "she would tell me exactly step-by-step to do things. I'm on the same level as she is, and I felt that she thought I was an idiot and didn't know what the difference between a test tube and a thermometer was."

- An Israeli immigrant to the U.S. owned a chain of stores. An American employee of the Israeli was promoted to be a store manager. The American was used to taking orders from the owner and carrying them out. After awhile, the American manager's store began to lose sales because the manager did not cut prices enough. The Israeli owner blamed the manager for not cutting prices more. The American manager was confused because no directives had been given to cut prices. The American assumed that the communication relationship would be the same with the Israeli as it would be with an American—receiving and carrying out orders. The Israeli assumed that now the American was a manager, he would make decisions on his own, just like the owner did.

- While on assignment in Japan some years ago, an American soldier had a Japanese houseboy. The soldier bought a pair of brown shoes to augment his current collection, which was limited to black shoes only. The American soldier was surprised to find the next morning that the houseboy had shined his new brown shoes with black shoe polish.

- A Korean company contracted with an American toy company to manufacture model trains. After sending the first shipment to the American company, the Korean owner was surprised to receive a letter from the American company with detailed a list of manufacturing flaws, modeling errors, and other problems with the product. Feeling that the American company was trying to justify a reduction in price for the shipment, the owner formulated a price-cutting plan for the American company. He was surprised when, not long thereafter, the American company cancelled the order, returned the shipment, and withdrew the letter of credit that had been established.

- A male Chinese student studying in the United States earned money tutoring American students. A female student he tutored, thanks in part to his efforts, received a good grade on her test. She was so happy she embraced the Chinese student, praised and thanked him for his efforts, and was surprised at the subsequent look of amazement, consternation, and embarrassment on his face.

THE FIVE DIMENSIONS OF HUMAN COMMUNICATION

Dimension #1: Communication is a process. "Communication has no determinate beginning or end; rather, it is an ongoing exchange of messages between two or more people" (Haworth & Savage 1989, p. 234). If we assume that our communication relationships with the same people will always remain the same, misunderstandings are bound to happen because people change, the circumstances around the relationship change, and topics of communication change. In the case of the Israeli owner and the American manager, their organizational roles changed, and the American manager simply assumed that the communication relationship would stay the same. The promotion of the American changed the communication relationship, and neither the owner nor the manager adjusted to that change.

Dimension #2: Communication involves purposive and expressive messages. When people communicate they exchange verbal and nonverbal messages with each other. One kind of message is a purposive message, that is, a message that communicates the direct intention of the sender of the message. In contrast, expressive messages are those unintentionally sent along with a spoken message: for example, anger in one's voice along with the spoken words, "That's okay, just don't let it happen again." The speaker, in this case, is saying that he/she forgives the other person explicitly. But because of the tone of the speaker's voice, the receiver of the message is unsure whether to believe the intended message. In the example of the British and American lab partners, the American student gave clear directions to her partner, but the high level of specificity of the directions themselves caused the British student to interpret them in a way unintended by the American. Thus, for clear communication to occur and for the receiver to interpret the message correctly, purposive and expressive messages must be in harmony with each other.

Dimension #3: Communication is made up of multi-unit signals. Human communication travels through a variety of signals, not just words. Kinesic, proxemic, olfactory, and other signals picked up by the five senses are methods or "units" of human communication. These do not occur one at a time in human communication, but simultaneously. A receiver of someone's communication simultaneously hears words, sees body positions, observes nonverbal signals (such as hand gestures), observes proximity of the sender to the receiver, smells or does not smell body odor or perfume, and so on. Purposive and expressive messages are sent through these signals. Thus, if the combined package of these units is comfortable, understandable, and known to the receiver, clear communication takes place. However, if the units present confusing stimuli to the receiver, misunderstanding will occur, as in the case of the bewildered Chinese tutor and his pupil.

Dimension #4: Communication depends on the context for its meaning. "Context" means the degree to which the communicator and the listener share a common background of knowledge and experience. This occurs when both individuals have a common history or, at least a shared understanding, of each others' lives, intentions, and experiences. When a context is understood to a great degree between two communicators, much can be said even though little is actually spoken: they can "read between the lines" of each other's statements. Consider the example of a husband and wife's communication in Exhibit 16.1. In this example, more communicating going on than would be apparent to someone who was overhearing the conversation.

EXHIBIT 16.1

What was said	What was understood
Husband: Dana succeeded in putting a penny in a parking meter today without being picked up.	This afternoon as I was bringing Dana, our four-year-old son, home from the nursery school, he succeeded in reaching high enough to put a penny in a parking meter when we parked in a meter zone, whereas before he had always had to be picked up to reach that high.
Wife: Did you take him to the record store?	Since he put a penny in a meter that means that you stopped while he was with you. I know that you stopped at the record store either on the way to get him or on the way back. Was it on the way back, so that he was with you or did you stop there on the way to get him and somewhere else on the way back?
Husband: No, to the shoe repair shop.	No, I stopped at the record store on the way to get him and stopped at the shoe repair shop on the way home when he was with me.
Wife: What for?	I know of one reason why you might have stopped at the shoe repair shop. Why did you in fact?
Husband: I got some new shoe laces for my shoes.	As you will remember, I broke a shoe lace on one of my brown oxfords the other day, so I stopped to get some new laces.
Wife: Your loafers need new heels badly.	I was thinking of something else you could have gotten. You could have taken in your black loafers, which need heels badly. You'd better get them taken care of pretty soon.

Garfinkel, H. 1967. *Studies in Ethno-Methodology*. NJ: Prentice-Hall. pp. 34. Reprinted by permission of Prentice-Hall, Englewood Cliffs, New Jersey.

cultures are *high-context* cultures: their members those share many cultural norms, and thus do not really need to talk that much to communicate. Canada and the U.S. are considered to be *low-context cultures*. Because there are many subcultures in these countries, people do not widely share the exact same norms regarding communication. In high-context cultures, because everyone understands the nature of and requirements for communication, a simple nod, grunt, sigh, or wave of the hand may communicate a lot of information. Japan is a high-context culture, and the term used there for such high-context communication is hara-gei, which translates as "belly-language." Traditionally, emotions in Japan were seen as residing in the stomach; thus, when people's emotions are naturally understood because of shared norms, there is little need for high levels of dicussion to aid in communication.

In the cross-cultural examples at the beginning of the chapter, a lack of mutual understanding of the context of the communication is seen most strikingly in the model train fiasco. Neither side understood how the other was viewing the business context. The Korean manufacturer remained puzzled by the cancellation of the contract until he ran into an American serviceman stationed in Korea who was a model train enthusiast. He invited the American to visit his factory. The serviceman explained to the owner that in North America, serious model train enthusiasts would not buy trains that had the kind of defects in them that the manufacturer was producing. The owner asked the American to visit his factory from time to time and oversee his quality control program to ensure his product would be marketable in North America. Once the context was revealed, understanding occurred.

Dimension #5: Communication depends on the competence of the communicators. If a person is able to send and express messages clearly and receive and interpret messages correctly, communication is enhanced. The degree to which a message is poorly expressed and incorrectly interpreted is the degree to which misunderstandings occur. These can happen at different levels of communication. For example, if an expatriate cannot speak the local language very well, misunderstanding may occur due to the expatriate's inability to express basic sentences clearly. If the expatriate is fluent in the language, misunderstandings may still occur because the host nationals may interpret the purposive message correctly but also pick up an unintended expressive message negative in nature. Or, the expatriate's words may be perfectly understood, but the body odor of the expatriate may be unpleasant to the host national. If this is the case, the message's importance may be downplayed, the expatriate judged adversely, or the communication may even be cut off entirely by the host national. All of the cross-cultural examples cited earlier involve instances where both parties lacked the competence necessary to communicate cross-culturally.

Each of the these five dimensions of human communication apply to any culture. However, *how* each dimension is manifest and carried out in each culture is unique to each culture. That is why living and working with people from diverse cultures can be both irritating and interesting. It is almost as if to communicate with someone from a different culture, one must first learn not only the language, but also the rules for how the language is used in differing contexts and situations.

BARRIERS TO CROSS-CULTURAL COMMUNICATION COMPETENCE

To communicate effectively with someone from a different culture, there are certain barriers that must be understood and surmounted. These are ignorance of cultural rules of communication, perceptual biases, faulty attributions, and stereotypes.

IGNORANCE OF CULTURAL RULES OF COMMUNICATION

It has been estimated that approximately 65 percent of much of our communication is nonverbal in nature. Each culture has different rules regarding nonverbal communication. We will consider five types of nonverbal communication: kinesics, proxemics, fixed features of space, semifixed features of space, and personal space.

Kinesics

Kinesics refers to gestures, facial expressions, body positions, body movements, and their relation to communication. Consider the following cross-cultural differences in kinesics (taken from Dodd 1977, pp. 53–4):

- When North Americans use hand gestures to "say good-bye," they typically place the palm of the right hand down, extend the fingers, and move the fingers up and down. In India, West Africa, and Central America such a gesture would be interpreted as beckoning one to come toward you. In these countries the gesture is often used for beckoning taxi cabs.

- It is common in Indonesia to converse with someone, while in their home, by sitting on the floor and talking. As one sits down on the floor great care must be taken not to point the soles of one's shoes or feet toward the host. Doing this is a grave offense, for the gesture indicates that the person is seen as being inferior.

- During the Cold War, Soviet Premier Nikita Kruschev visited the United States. As he emerged from the airplane, officials, news reporters, and other visitors greeted him cordially. In response, Kruschev clasped his hands together and raised them above his shoulders. To television viewers and observers in the U.S., the gesture appeared like a boxer signaling victory. However, Kruschev intended the gesture to represent a clasping of hands in friendship.

Without a knowledge of basic kinesics for the culture in which one is operating, misunderstandings and bad feelings can be caused rather easily—just as when the American expatriate and the Korean store owner both became incensed over a simple hand gesture. Edward T. Hall, a noted anthropologist, believes by holding that kinesics is one of the most basic of all modes of communication and is only partially readable across cultural boundaries. Further, "in new and unknown situations, in which one is likely to be most dependent on reading non-verbal cues, the chances of one's being correct decrease as cultural distance increases" (Hall 1977, pp. 75–6). The only way this barrier can be overcome is to study the kinesics of the culture in which one will be living and to memorize the behavioral patterns.

Proxemics

Proxemics is the study of the spatial relationships in human communication. The field includes the study of fixed features of space (such as, architecture and buildings) and how they influence human relationships semifixed features of space (such as, seating arrangements, office layouts) and how they influence communication; and dynamic space, or human's use of personal space when communicating (Dodd 1977, p. 55).

Fixed Features of Space

One example of a fixed feature of space that influences organizational behavior is room size. Different cultures design offices and work room layouts differently to reflect cultural preferences. For example: "A large office in the United States communicates status and perhaps power. The smaller the office, the less status appears connected with the occupant of the office. In contrast, in India, high government officials may share a room with six other lesser employees in a room perhaps 15 feet by 20 feet" (Dodd 1977, p. 56). If a business person or government official visiting from a country such as the U.S.—where size of office indicates the status, prestige, power, and authority of its occupant—was ushered into an office in India to meet his/her host, the visitor may make incorrect judgments regarding the host's true position and power.

Also, buildings themselves can embody a value, emotion, or belief system. For Americans, visiting the Lincoln Memorial and the Vietnam War Memorial arouses emotions related to the values of justice, freedom, sacrifice, and gratitude. Similarly, a visit to the Sengakuji Shrine in Tokyo, the burial place of the ashes of the 47 samurai, arouses emotions in the Japanese that relate to the values of duty, sacrifice, obligation, and honor.

The following case exemplifies how the use of buildings can effect business and political relationships. As a background to this case, it is important to understand that traditionally in many Latin American countries universities were not supposed to be used by politicians to support their own political agendas if they were invited to speak. Academia and politics were seen as separate. Also, because many Latin American countries have histories of military dictatorship, the presence on campus of military personnel was seen as threatening to academic freedom and was almost always avoided. When Richard Nixon was Vice President of the United States, he visited Latin America. At one stage of his visit, he desired to give a speech at a university. Unfortunately, he spoke on politically related topics and employed an interpreter from the local military who was in full-dress uniform. While hoping to improve the relationship between his country and the host country, the setting, the kinesics of the military uniform of the interpreter, and the subject matter of the speech all combined to have the opposite effect from the one Nixon intended (Smith 1966, p. 13).

Semifixed Features of Space

How companies lay out office furniture and work space directly influences how people communicate with each other. High-context cultures tend to have more open, less private work spaces. For example, Exhibit 16.2 illustrates a typical office in a large Japanese company. If a Westerner was to walk into this Japanese office looking for a particular individual, he/she would be confronted with a large room wherein desks are linked together in long rows. Without understanding the reason behind the layout, it would be difficult for the visitor to find the person he/she was seeking.

Japanese norms reinforce working groups and being part of a group. There are no partitions separating desks, so everyone can overhear what everyone else is saying on the telephone or in work-related conversations. Compare this with the strong perceived need for privacy in North American companies. Large work spaces are partitioned and subdivided with movable "walls" in such a way that cubicles are formed. In each cubicle a person has his/her own desk, often surrounded with personal items marking that territory as the worker's private working space. North American cultural values of independence, individualism, and privacy dictate to a large degree how work space is arranged, and the resulting structures reinforce the norms associated with those values. Interestingly, in Japan, there is no word that translates the value of "privacy" adequately; that value is simply not as strong in Japanese culture as it is in North America.

EXHIBIT 16.2

LAYOUT OF A TYPICAL JAPANESE OFFICE

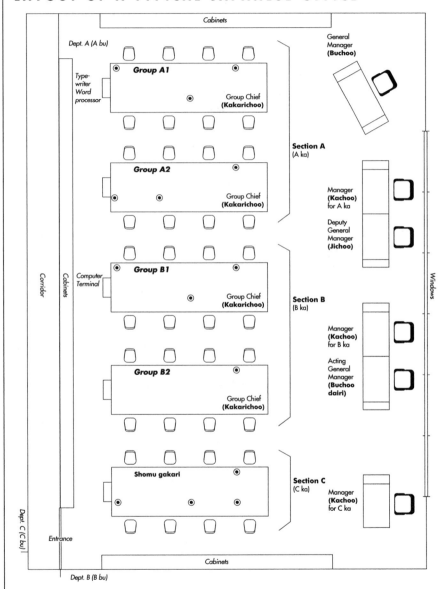

SOURCE:
Adapted from *Business Japanese* 1984. Tokyo: Nissan Motor Corporation. p. 64.

Personal Space

Researchers have found that humans unconsciously structure and measure the space around their bodies. This invisible measuring that allows us to make sense out of the communications of those with whom we are interacting. Edward T. Hall notes that:

> ... the flow and shift of distance between people as they interact with each other is part and parcel of the communication process. The normal conversational distance between strangers illustrates the importance of the dynamics of space interaction. If a person gets too close, the reaction is instantaneous and automatic—the other person backs up. I have observed an American backing up the entire length of a long corridor while a Latin American whom he considered pushy tried to catch up with him. (1977, p. 58)

This illustration shows that different cultures have different measurements of personal space. For North Americans, there is a radius of 18 inches around them that they view as "intimate space": people who physically are allowed to enter that space are people whom the North American knows and trusts and is comfortable with. Conversely, Latin Americans and people from the cultures of the Middle East have relatively small intimate space. In some of these countries, "being close enough to breathe on another person during a conversation is deemed appropriate. In fact, the breath is like one's spirit and life itself, so sharing your breath in close conversation is like sharing your spirit" (Dodd 1977, p. 58). If interacting with a North American who is consistently backing up in order to retain a comfortable sense of his/her personal space, an individual from Latin America or the Middle East may consider the North American to be cold, aloof, or not interested in the conversation. Conversely, the North American may indeed be interested in the topic of conversation, but view the other person as being pushy, backward, uneducated, uncivilized, or dangerous.

PERCEPTUAL BIASES

Researchers studying cognition have found that in order to store information, make sense out of what we perceive in the world around us, and simplify the world around us, humans develop mental categories. For example, although there are reported 7,500,000 colors in the world, there are only about 4,000 English words to represent them. Of the 4,000 words, only 8 (the primary colors) are commonly used to represent all the colors—a ratio of one word to 937,000 colors (Oddou & Mendenhall 1984, p. 79). There are four important reasons why humans have developed this capacity for information categorization (see Bruner 1957, Oddou & Mendenhall 1984):

1. To reduce the complexity of the environment. There is no way humans could remember 7,500,000 different words for different colors—we would undergo information overload.

2. To identify objects and behaviors in the environment. English speakers have chosen over time to rely on the primary colors or variants of them (for example, "light" and "dark" green) to identify the color of objects.

3. To reduce the necessity of constant learning and reclassifying. Simplifying colors to the primary colors and their general variants enables English speakers to classify the color of something quickly without having to undergo long mental-processing episodes.

4. To construct a ready knowledge of appropriate and inappropriate action to take in any situation. For example, a yellow light on a traffic signal means "slow down to stop"; the driver doesn't have to think about the shade of the color before taking the appropriate action.

The mental categories by which a person sorts out and responds to the world reflect the culture into which that individual was born (Bruner 1957, p. 10). Thus, people from different cultures attach meaning and expect certain responses in various situations according to learned experience and socialization. In other words, our categories are to a large degree taught to us by others (parents, teachers, peers). The research seems clear that people from different cultures process and categorize information differently; it is almost as if people's "software" is different based upon the culture in which they were raised. For example, it is known that the Inuit (or Eskimo) have 26 different words to describe different kinds of snow. Obviously, survival in their environment demands a more specific knowledge of snow and its forms than in the typical American's environment, where snow generally is seen on a continuum of wet to dry. A conversation about snow between an Eskimo and an American might well lead to erroneous conclusions and misattributions.

It seems that categorizing what we see in the world around us into more simple, workable frameworks allows us to live more efficiently and effectively. However, the danger is that since we oversimplify the reality of the world, we might tend to misperceive it and make mistakes in our mental processing. Regarding the possible effect that culture-based categories may have on one's ability to effectively interact with people from other cultures, Szalay said: "The more we consider our views and experiences [our categories of the world] to be absolute and universal, the less prepared we are to deal with people who have different backgrounds, experiences, culture, and therefore different views [categories] of the universe" (1981, p. 138).

Triandis (1964) notes that as we utilize the categories in our minds to make sense out of the world around us, we have positive and negative experiences associated with those categories. Thus, emotions attach to them. For example, even if an Indonesian knew that Westerners might not be expected to know that they should not show the soles of their feet to him, if the Westerner did do so, he would still feel a revulsion, shame, or other negative emotions associated with his/her mental category of "appropriate nonverbal behaviors."

To conclude, another barrier to effective cross-cultural communication is the way we make sense of the world around us. While our categorization helps us live by allowing us to make sense out of, and predict what will happen in, the world, when we take our categories into a new culture, they may not be the same as those widely shared by the host nationals. And if we misperceive the behavior of host nationals, this will lead to faulty attributions.

FAULTY ATTRIBUTIONS

When we judge the motives behind why people do what they do, we attribute reasons to their behavior. For example, if while you are driving down the freeway, a car races up to you from behind, passes you, and then continues to weave in and out of traffic while exceeding the speed limit, you may attribute the driving behavior of that person to a number of reasons: the driver has no regard for the rights of others, is drunk, is late for an important appointment, or has a pregnant wife in the backseat and is speeding to the hospital. The possible attributions you could make are numerous.

Similarly, if while on an overseas assignment an expatriate observes behavior in business that is strange to him/her, the expatriate will make attributions about why that behavior occurred. In the case involving the American expatriate and the Korean store clerk, both made inaccurate attributions about the motives behind the other's behavior based upon their respective categories. When the American saw the clerk refuse to wait on him, he probably attributed that behavior to the fact that the Korean was rude or hated Americans; while the Korean attributed the American's hand gesture to arrogance, prejudice, or rudeness.

A simplified version of how easily attributions in a cross-cultural context can be made in error is portrayed in Exhibit 16.3. We will review the steps involved in attributions.

Step 1: Perception. The first step in attributing motive or reason behind a behavior is to observe that behavior. The Korean clerk would not have reacted the way he did if he had not seen the American beckon to him.

Step 2: Category retrieval. Once a behavior is observed, in milliseconds our brain goes through a kind of "library index card" retrieval until it finds the category in our mind that makes sense out of the behavior we observed. The Korean accessed his category of "appropriate nonverbal behaviors for humans" and found that the American's gesture did not meet the criteria for that category. As was mentioned before, once a category is accessed, emotions that are linked with it are triggered as well. Exhibit 16.3 shows that linked to emotions are evaluations of what we observe. The Korean store clerk, might evaluate the American's hand gesture as bad, immoral, dirty, condescending. Again, it is important to note that all of this takes place in milliseconds, virtually automatically.

Step 3: Estimation of motives. Once evaluations about, and emotions toward, the observed behavior have been triggered, the next phase is to estimate why that behavior occurred. Humans seem to have a strong need to understand why things happen. The evaluations and emotions kindled will likely influence the correctness of the attribution. Researchers have found that humans make two general kinds of attributions about behaviors they observe: internal and external attributions.

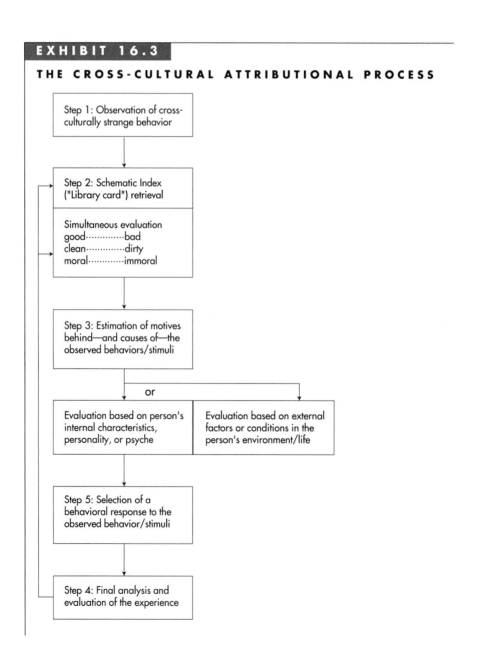

EXHIBIT 16.3

THE CROSS-CULTURAL ATTRIBUTIONAL PROCESS

Step 1: Observation of cross-culturally strange behavior

Step 2: Schematic Index ("Library card") retrieval

Simultaneous evaluation
good··············bad
clean··············dirty
moral··············immoral

Step 3: Estimation of motives behind—and causes of—the observed behaviors/stimuli

or

Evaluation based on person's internal characteristics, personality, or psyche

Evaluation based on external factors or conditions in the person's environment/life

Step 5: Selection of a behavioral response to the observed behavior/stimuli

Step 4: Final analysis and evaluation of the experience

Internal attributions are made when the behavior is viewed as being caused by the other individual's internal characteristics, personality, or psyche. This was the kind of attribution both the American and the Korean made about each other. Each viewed the reason for the other's behavior as being connected to the character or the personality of the other person. External attributions are made when the behavior is viewed as being caused by external factors or conditions that impinge on the other individual. For example, in the case of the erratic car driver, if you attributed that driving behavior to a pregnant wife in the back seat, you would have been making an external attribution; the pregnant wife was an external factor that influenced the behavior.

Culture is an external factor that influences to a large degree why people do what they do. It influences hand gestures, tones of speech, clothing, an so on. Thus, if the Korean store clerk had been more aware of the fact that culture influences hand gestures, he would have made an external attribution about the expatriate. Similarly, if the American expatriate had been more attuned to culture as an external influence of behavior, instead of making an internal attribution about the Korean, he might have made an external attribution about the Korean's behavior. He may have considered that since it was not logical for the Korean to refuse to wait on him, then maybe the Korean's behavior resulted from something he was doing that offended the Korean.

Step 4: Behavioral response. Based upon the attribution made, the observer selects a behavioral response. In the case of the American, he stormed out of the store. In the case of the Korean clerk, he avoided the American. Based upon one's personality traits, one chooses a response. If that response is inappropriate in a cross-cultural business setting, such as during a negotiation, devastating results can occur.

Step 5: Final analysis. Once attributions have been made, that information is fed back to the category, and the category is updated. If the category is fed with faulty information, the category will not be accurate. Then, when a similar incident occurs, the category will cause inaccurate evaluations and trigger inappropriate emotions in the individual. Conversely, the more accurate the information fed back into the category, the more effectively the individual will be able to deal with his/her environment.

To make correct attributions cross-culturally, it is important to put one's attributions on hold and not automatically assume that one's evaluation of the situation has been correct. Research shows that successful expatriates compare their evaluations with host nationals to make sure they are accurate before they permanently store them in their memory categories: that is, they consult an expert on the culture. That expert can be a secretary, an interpreter, a manager—virtually anyone who can guide the expatriate through the norms of the local culture.

STEREOTYPES

Another barrier to cross-cultural communication is stereotyping—categorizing a group of people based upon some feature they hold in common, such as nationality, race, or religion. Studies show that once the categorization takes place, "an individual tends to favor his/her own group in nearly every respect and disfavors the other group, attributing more positive attributes to one's own group and more negative ones to the other. Furthermore, such research has firmly established that the favoring of one's group can be attributed to the existence of a perceived out-group, regardless of any actual differences among people that would merit division (Oddou & Mendenhall 1984, p. 86).

Once one feels part of an in-group, individuals not part of that group are categorized on a variety of issues (intelligence, industriousness, education, accent) and are seen as similar to one another. Stereotyping is a powerful barrier to cross-cultural communication because interactions with people from out-groups is processed through the categories that make up the stereotype. If a group is classified as being dishonest, for example, whenever one interacts with a member of that group, it will be difficult for the holder of the stereotype to trust anything the outsider does or says. Prejudice and racism are difficult to eradicate because the categories that make up discrimination interpret the world in such a way that the categories are reinforced, even if reality is different.

CROSS-CULTURAL NEGOTIATION

One of the most important arenas of cross-cultural communication for international business people is negotiation. Business will not occur unless negotiations are successful. Yet if both parties come to the negotiating table without having done some serious thinking about the barriers to and complexities of cross-cultural communication, there is a low probability that the negotiations will be successful.

One important finding about cross-cultural negotiation is that within any culture, people go through four stages in the negotiation process. These stages are relationship building, exchanging task-related information, persuasion, and making concessions and agreements (see Adler 1991; Graham 1989; Graham & Herberger 1983). However, cultures differ in the degree to which value is placed on each stage of the negotiation relationship. Exhibit 16.4, compares the importance of each step in negotiations between U.S. nationals and the Japanese. Importance is also reflected by the amount of time that is spent on each stage of the negotiation.

RELATIONSHIP BUILDING

The first stage of negotiations involves building interpersonal relationships between the negotiating parties. As Exhibit 16.4 indicates, to Japanese this is a very important part of the negotiation process, and they spend considerable time in building relationships with the other party. Conversely, Americans rate building relationships as less important and thus spend much less time on this phase than do the Japanese. For the Japanese, it is important to spend a lot of time after the official meetings out on the town, eating and drinking with the members of the other party. In this way formal barriers are broken down between the parties, and a sense of trust slowly develops. During the first meetings when Americans may want to get down to business, the Japanese will likely talk in generalities, for in their minds the preliminary sessions are simply to assist in building relationships. The "power breakfast" and the "power lunch"—making deals over meals—were invented in the U.S. Thus, when Americans who are eager to cut through the small talk and get down to business meet Japanese who desire to build a trusting relationship before doing business, frustration and failure can occur.

EXHIBIT 16.4

U.S./JAPANESE STAGES OF NEGOTIATIONS

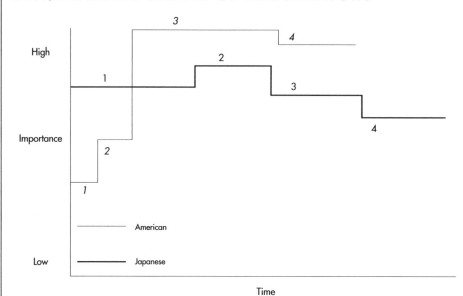

Negotiation Stage Legend
1 = Non-task Time (Building Relationship)
2 = Information Exchange
3 = Influence Bidding
4 = Conclusion and Contact

INFORMATION EXCHANGE

The second phase of cross-cultural negotiations involves information exchange: stating one's "situation and needs and . . . understanding the opponent's situation and needs" (Adler 1991, p. 197). It is difficult enough to understand the other party's situation, interests, and needs in a negotiation situation in one's own culture, but understanding these issues when the other party is from another culture adds to the difficulty of this phase. As was stated previously in this chapter, people from differing cultures commonly view problems, reality, and business operations in different ways. It takes a sustained, sincere effort both to clearly articulate one's own situation and to understand that of the other party in a cross-cultural negotiation.

As can be seen in Exhibit 16.4, the Japanese rate this step as important and spend a fair amount of time on the issue. Americans, conversely, rate it as moderate importance and spend relatively little time on this phase. Therefore, misunderstandings and problems may well occur based on the different ways these cultures value this phase.

PERSUASION

Persuasion involves influencing the other party to adopt one's viewpoint, position, or beliefs. Exhibit 16.4 indicates that Americans like to "cut to the chase" and quickly begin to persuade the other party to agree with their offer, bid, contract, and so forth. Americans view this phase as the most important part of the negotiation process and spend quite a bit of time in the use of persuasive tactics. The Japanese also rate this phase as important and spend a fair amount of time on it as well. However, for the Japanese, persuasion should only take place after mutual trust has been established; for Americans, persuasion can take place quickly with appeals to logic and rationality overriding the need for warm interpersonal relationships.

CONCESSION AND AGREEMENT

Exhibit 16.4 suggests that the Japanese value this phase less than Americans do, though they spend about the same amount of time in this phase as Americans. Adler notes that "Americans negotiate sequentially: they discuss and attempt to agree on one issue at a time. Throughout the bargaining process, Americans make many small concessions, which they expect their opponents to reciprocate; then they finalize the list of concessions into an overall agreement" (1991, pp. 199–200).

The Japanese do not tend to spend a lot of time and energy on making small concessions that reciprocate their opponent's concessions. Instead they like to view the process holistically, trying to understand each side's views and needs, build trust, and then make concessions, if any, at the end as a form of wrapping up the negotiations.

DIFFERENT NEGOTIATING STYLES

The four phases of cross-cultural negotiation indicate that beneath cultural differences in negotiation norms are differences in underlying values and philosophies about the negotiation process. Understanding this is an important first step for the international negotiator. An important second step is to learn the specific negotiation norms of the culture of the firm with whom one is negotiating. It is impossible to cover the negotiating norms of all the cultures in this chapter, but a few will be highlighted in order to convey the importance of doing one's "cultural homework" before negotiating abroad.

BRAZIL

A variety of researchers have done work on the negotiating approach used by Brazilians, and their findings point to clear preferences Brazilian managers have during negotiations. Their studies indicate that though Brazilian managers do use persuasive tactics, a more dominant tendency is to use a "receptive" style of influence involving linking and seducing approaches. Linking involves the desire to understand the frame of reference of the other party and is manifested by encouraging the participation of others, searching for points of agreement, listening, and empathetic behaviors. "Seducing" is a term used to describe an approach that has at its heart the desire to win the opponent over to one's side by ingratiating oneself. It is manifested by sharing information, admitting mistakes, motivating others, praising them, and raising their spirits through gracious behavior.

These two approaches are reflected in Exhibit 16.5, which compares the cross-cultural differences in nonverbal negotiating behavior of Brazilian, Japanese, and Americans. Notice that Brazilians talk more, touch more, and look directly at the other party more than do Japanese and Americans. These nonverbal behaviors reflect active linking and seducing activities.

Amado and Brasil conclude from the studies of Brazilian negotiating behavior that: "everything seems to happen [during negotiations] in such a way that Brazilian managers somehow try to fix things up in order to avoid direct confrontation, which is experienced as dangerous, thus [the tendency of] establishing personal relationships and giving signs of an open mind and empathy" (1991, p. 41). Further, Graham and Herberger note that while Americans value persuasion in the negotiation process, Brazilians do not. They state that "Brazilians cannot depend on a legal system to iron out [business] conflicts, so they depend on personal relationships" (1983, p. 163). This situation fosters linking and seducing behaviors aimed at forming trust, obligation, and friendship between negotiating parties.

EXHIBIT 16.5

DIFFERENCES IN NEGOTIATING BEHAVIOR AMONG JAPANESE, NORTH AMERICAN AND BRAZILIAN NEGOTIATORS

Behavior (Tactic)	Japanese	Brazilian	N. American
Silent Periods (Number of periods greater than 10 seconds, per 30 minutes)	5.5	0	3.5
Conversational Overlaps (More than one person speaking at the same time; number per 30-minute periods)	12.6	28.6	10.3
Facial Gazing (Minutes of gazing at other party's face per 10-minute periods)	1.3	5.2	3.3
Touching (Not including handshaking, per 30-minute periods)	0	4.7	0

SOURCE:
Adapted from Graham, J.L. 1985. "The influence of culture on the process of business negotiations: an exploratory study." *Journal of International Business Studies*, Spring. pp. 81–96.

Finally, the negotiating preferences of Brazilians can be said to mirror their basic values of organizational behavior. After reviewing the research literature, Amado and Brasil state that: "the results of these different research projects are consistent and allow us to define a certain identity of both the Brazilian organization and the behaviors of the employees in it: . . . Brazilian organizations seem to be comprised of members who are faced with the fear of unbearable conflicts, sensitive to the human dimension of work, and who are accustomed to avoiding difficulties" (p. 42). In summary, Brazilian negotiators are open-minded, cooperative, and receptive (linking and seducing), while their tendency to direct persuasion and exertion of pressure is weak.

PEOPLE'S REPUBLIC OF CHINA

The People's Republic of China (PRC) offers companies over a billion potential consumers for their products and services. While many Western businesses left after the suppression of dissent in the summer of 1989, they are now returning. The Chinese government under Li Peng continues to focus on attracting Western business into the country; thus it behooves companies interested in doing business there to study the Chinese style of business negotiations.

At the beginning stages of negotiations, Chinese negotiators prefer to seek agreement on generalities with the other party and try to avoid dealing with specific details altogether. They prefer to leave the details for later meetings, which is to some degree due to the Chinese cultural value that interpersonal conflict is inappropriate and should be avoided (Kirkbride & Tang 1990; Kirkbride, Tang, & Westwood 1988). This approach of agreeing on general principles allows the Chinese to adopt a mental framework for the negotiation process from which to work, and many Westerners mistake this seeking after general principles as only rhetoric, and thus they often easily agree to the Chinese position (Frankenstein 1986). As Kirkbride and Tang point out, however: "For the Chinese side, these declarations are an important step; they establish a framework for the negotiations and provide ammunition should the foreign negotiators go beyond the boundaries" (1990, p. 4). Lucien Pye also notes an advantage foreign negotiators give up when they agree too quickly to general principles, when he observes that at times the Chinese can "quickly turn an agreement on principles into an agreement on goals and then insist that all discussion on concrete arrangements must foster those agreed upon goals" (1982, p. 42).

HOLISTIC VERSUS SEQUENTIAL THINKING

Graham and Herberger note that American negotiators tend to approach negotiations sequentially: they "separate the issues and settle them one at a time . . . in an American negotiation the final agreement is a sum of the several concessions made on individual issues" (1983, p. 164). However, in the PRC concessions are not made sequentially throughout the course of the negotiation, they come at the end.

Yang has noted that "Chinese people, especially adults, tend to display a cognitive style of seeing things . . . in wholes rather than in parts while Westerners tend to do the reverse" (1986, p. 147). Yang further notes that the Chinese "will try to synthesize the constituent parts into a whole so that all parts blend into a harmonious relationship at this higher level of perceptual organization" (p. 148). The result of this cognitive style is that the Chinese will not concede things that they have not integrated into their perception of what the final settlement should look like. Thus, once the perception of the final settlement is in place in their minds, then and only then can they make the unimportant concessions.

CONFRONTATION

The Chinese consider harmonious interpersonal relationships to be of great importance in life and in business. Thus, it is not surprising that conformity is a value that is highly regarded in Chinese society. Kirkbride and Tang note that "this conformity . . . leads individuals to consider the relationship between themselves and the other party as one of the crucial factors in any conflict or negotiation situation" (1990, p. 7).

To preserve harmonious interpersonal relationships, Chinese will avoid confronting the other party in negotiations at all costs. If Western negotiators engage in confrontational tactics, their Chinese counterparts experience deep levels of personal shame at being treated in such a manner. What may not seem to be overly aggressive, argumentative, or pushy behavior to Westeners is highly likely to be viewed that way by Chinese. Negotiating a contract in the PRC requires an in-depth knowledge of both negotiation norms and cultural protocol on the part of the expatriate negotiator.

RUSSIA

Conversely, Russia is a country where the negotiating style has been considered confrontational by Westerners (Rajan & Graham 1991). The recent political turmoil in what was once the Soviet Union makes it difficult for researchers to chart any trends and changes in the way the Russians will go about conducting business negotiations—so far, historical trends seem to be holding, but this may change. Thus, though the research quoted here is recent, it may not reflect the future. The fast pace of change in the international environment is what makes international business exciting, but also so challenging to those engaged in it.

Historically, Russian negotiators have been secretive about themselves, their motives, and their goals for negotiations. Many feel this is because they have lived in a society that is isolated from the international business community and thus are reluctant to reveal their ignorance of common capitalist business practices or, simply, because they have a general distrust of foreigners.

Their negotiating behavior has been variously characterized by Western business people as rigid, stubborn, inflexible, confrontational, and competitive. Some scholars note that Americans and Russians are influenced by two different types of ethical systems (Lefebvre & Lefebvre 1986; Rajan & Graham 1991). Within Western ethical systems, it is positive to seek compromises in order to resolve conflicts and come to agreement. However, Russians come from an ethical background where "it is positive for individuals to create new conflicts with adversaries and to exacerbate existing ones . . . the very word 'deal' itself has negative associations in the Russian language, because anyone seeking compromises is considered cowardly, weak, and unworthy" (Rajan & Graham 1991, p. 48).

Rajan and Graham have studied managers negotiating behavior in a variety of countries and found that Russian managers did not focus on cooperative or creative solutions that would enable both parties to profit from the negotiations. Interestingly, the Russian word for "profit," *pribyl*, has a negative connotation in Russian. It connotes exploitation and the sense that profits are always gained at the expense of another human being. In English it can have that connotation as well; but it can also imply monetary success that comes from hard work and creativity and can be a boon to one's quality of life. Rajan and Graham note that Russian negotiators do not view negotiation "as a means of achieving higher profits for their organization nor as a vehicle for furthering personal goals—unlike Americans. Instead, to [them] the negotiation process represents an opportunity for 'right" (their world view) to succeed over . . . the American perspective; thus they assume inflexible, uncompromising, conflictual stances" (p. 47).

At this point in our discussion, the Russian negotiating style appears, from the Western standpoint, to be unattractive. However, there is another side to the coin. Historically, they have been extremely reliable in honoring all contractual arrangements. John Minneman, Chase Manhattan's vice-president and representative in Moscow, stated that his Russian banking counterparts were "sophisticated and tough, but they never lie and always pay on time;" another international business person concurred by saying: "Although [they] drive a very hard bargain in contract negotiations, they will faithfully abide by its provisions, and expect the other party to do the same. They have an excellent record in honoring their financial commitments" (Rajan & Graham 1991, p. 50). Thus, while Westerners may not like the way Russians bargain, once a contract is in force, for many Western business people the ramifications of doing business in Russia are positive in nature. Exhibit 16.6 summarizes some of the difference in negotiating behavior between North Americans and Russians.

SUMMARY

The importance of effective communication in order to manage well and be successful in business overseas is self-evident. The purpose of this chapter was to review the important aspects of cross-cultural communication to prepare students for working with people from other cultures.

EXHIBIT 16.6

NORTH AMERICANS AND RUSSIANS

	North Americans	Russians
Primary Negotiating Style and Process	Factual: Appeals made to logic	Axiomatic: Appeals made to ideals
Conflict: Opponent's Arguments Countered with . . .	Objective facts	Asserted ideals
Making Concessions	Small concessions made early to establish a relationship	Few, if any, small concessions made
Response to Opponent's Concessions	Usually reciprocate opponent's concessions	Opponent's concessions viewed as weakness and almost never reciprocated
Relationship	Short term	No continuing relationship
Authority	Broad	Limited
Initial Position	Moderate	Extreme
Deadline	Very important	Ignored

SOURCE:
Reprinted with permission. E.S. Glenn, D. Witmeyer, & K.A. Stevenson. 1984. "Cultural styles of persuasion." *International Journal of Intercultural Relations*, Vol. 1.

This figure is used with permission from J. Stewart Black.

Basic dimensions of human communication were covered, along with examples of how they operate in cross-cultural contexts. Barriers to cross-cultural communication were then discussed, and ways in which those barriers can be surmounted were introduced. The role that kinesics, proxemics, fixed and semifixed features of space, and personal space play in communicating ideas across cultures were covered in detail.

The role of perception, and how it links with how we evaluate others and in turn behave towards them was covered in depth in this chapter. To aid students understanding of this process, a model of how humans evaluate the cross-cultural stimuli they perceive in their overseas environment was reviewed. Practical suggestions were derived from the model as to how to better communicate with host nationals.

As a component of the communication process, negotiations in cross-cultural contexts were covered in this chapter. The purpose of this portion of the chapter was to explore the similarities of certain aspects of the negotiation process across cultures as well as the dissimilarities in negotiation norms across cultures.

To do this, the basic stages of the negotiation process were discussed, followed by a comparison of how negotiations are undertaken in three separate cultures: Brazil, Peoples' Republic of China, and Russia.

DISCUSSION QUESTIONS

1. Discuss how "noise" is likely to enter the communication process when Japanese managers talk to their U.S. counterparts.

2. Identify specific nonverbal aspects of communication that are important in communicating in your home country. Discuss how these nonverbal activities influence communication effectiveness.

3. Discuss your home country and a contrasting country in terms of their approach to the various stages of communication.

REFERENCES

Adler, N.J. 1991. *International Dimensions of Organizational Behavior.* Boston: PWS-Kent Publishing Company. pp. 195–200.

Allen, V., & D. Wilder. 1975. "Categorization, belief similarity, and intergroup discrimination." *Journal of Personality and Social Psychology,* 32, pp. 971–977

Amado, G. & H.V. Brasil. 1991. "Organizational behaviors and cultural context: The Brazilian 'Jeitinho'." *International Studies of Management and Organization*, 21(3), pp. 38–61.

Amado, G. & M. Cathelineau. 1987. "Estudo sobre os comportamentos na negociacao." *Tendencias Do Trabalho*, December, pp. 12–6; January 1988, pp. 23–27; February 1988, pp. 15–18.

Billig, M. & H. Tajfel. 1973. "Social categorization and similarity in intergroup behavior." *European Journal of Social Psychology*, 3, pp. 27–52.

Bruner, J. 1957. "On perceptual readiness." *Psychological Review*, 64, pp. 123–152.

Dodd, C. 1997. *Perspectives on Cross-Cultural Communication*. Dubuque: Kendall Hunt Publishing Company.

Frankenstein, J. 1986. "Trends in Chinese business practice: Changes in the Beijing wind." *California Management Review*, 29(1), pp. 148–160.

Graham, J.L. 1989. "An exploratory study of the process of marketing negotiations using a cross-cultural perspective." In R.Scarcella, E. Andersen, and S

Graham, J.L. & R.A. Herberger. 1983. "Negotiators abroad —Don't shoot from the hip." *Harvard Business Review*, July–August. pp. 160–168.

Hall, E.T. (1977). *Beyond Culture*. New York: Anchor.

Haque, A. & E. Lawson. 1980. "The mirror image phenomenon in the context of the Arab-Israeli conflict." *International Journal of Intercultural Relations*, 4, pp. 107–115.

Haworth, D.A. & G.T. Savage. 1989. "A channel-ratio model of intercultural communication: The trains won't sell, fix them please." *Journal of Business Communication*, 26(3), pp. 231–254.

Howard, J.W. & M. Rothbart. 1980. "Social categorization and memory for ingroup and outgroup behavior." *Journal of Personality and Social Psychology*, 38, pp. 301–310.

Kirkbride, P.S., S.F.Y. Tang, & R.I. Westwood. 1988. "Chinese bargaining behavior and negotiating behaviour: The cultural effects." Working Paper No. 23, City Polytechnic of Hong Kong.

Kirkbride, P.S. & S.F.Y. Tang. 1990. "Negotiation: Lessons from behind the bamboo curtain." *Journal of General Management*, 16(1), pp. 1–13.

Krashen (eds.), *Developing Communicative Competence in a Second Language*. Rowley, MA: Newbury House Publishers.

Lefebvre, V.A. & V.D. Lefebvre. 1986. *Soviet Ways of Conflict Resolution and International Negotiations*, Vol. 1 and 2. Irvine, CA: School of Social Sciences, University of California, Irvine.

Oddou, G. & M. Mendenhall. 1984. "Person perception in cross-cultural settings: A review of cross-cultural and related cognitive literature." *International Journal of Intercultural Relations*, 8(1), pp. 77–96.

Pye, L. 1982. *Chinese Commercial Negotiating Style*. New York: Oelgeschlager, Gunn, and Hain. p. 42.

Rajan, M.N. & J.L. Graham. 1991. "Nobody's grandfather was a merchant: Understanding the Soviet commercial negotiating process and style." *California Management Review*, Spring, pp. 40–57.

Schneider, M. & W. Jordan. 1981. "Perception of the communicative performance of Americans and Chinese in intercultural dyads." *International Journal of Intercultural Realtions*, 5, pp. 175–191.

Smith, A. 1966. *Communication and Culture*. New York: Holt, Rinehart, & Winston.

Szalay, L. 1981. "Intercultural communication—A process model." *International Journal of Intercultural Relations*, 5, pp. 133–146.

Triandis, H. 1964. "Cultural influences upon cognitive processes." In L. Berkowitz (ed.), *Advances in Experimental and Social Psychology*, Vol. 1. New York: Academic Press.

Wey, V.L. 1987. "Pesquisa revela quem e negociador brasileiro." *Tendencias Do Trabalho*, July, pp. 9–11.

Yang, K.S. 1986. "Chinese personality and its change." In M.H. Bond (ed.), *The psychology of the Chinese People*. Hong Kong: Oxford University Press.

LEADERSHIP AND

MOTIVATION IN

A GLOBAL

CONTEXT

LEARNING OBJECTIVES

IN THIS CHAPTER YOU WILL EXPLORE:

- The history of the study of leadership and motivation

- Cross-cultural issues that pertain to leadership and motivation

- How leaders differ from followers

- Different leadership styles across a variety of cultures

- The validity of North American theories in other countries

KEY DISCUSSION ISSUES:

- What are the assumptions that underly these theories?

- To what extent do these theories apply across cultures?

- What constitutes "leadership"?

- How can expatriates apply these principles in their work?

- Which theory seems to best explain motivation?

- What is the practicality of these theories?

- What implications does the literature hold for future research?

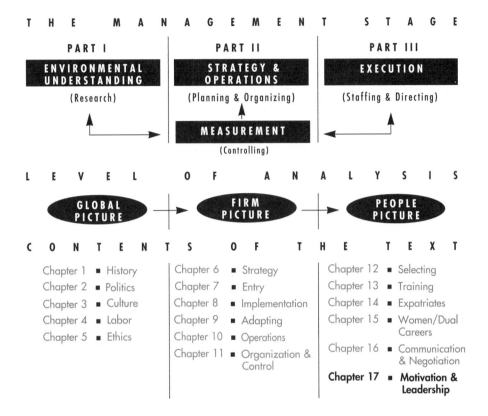

T H E   M A N A G E M E N T   S T A G E

PART I

ENVIRONMENTAL UNDERSTANDING

(Research)

PART II

STRATEGY & OPERATIONS

(Planning & Organizing)

MEASUREMENT

(Controlling)

PART III

EXECUTION

(Staffing & Directing)

L E V E L   O F   A N A L Y S I S

GLOBAL PICTURE

FIRM PICTURE

PEOPLE PICTURE

C O N T E N T S   O F   T H E   T E X T

Chapter 1 ▪ History
Chapter 2 ▪ Politics
Chapter 3 ▪ Culture
Chapter 4 ▪ Labor
Chapter 5 ▪ Ethics

Chapter 6 ▪ Strategy
Chapter 7 ▪ Entry
Chapter 8 ▪ Implementation
Chapter 9 ▪ Adapting
Chapter 10 ▪ Operations
Chapter 11 ▪ Organization & Control

Chapter 12 ▪ Selecting
Chapter 13 ▪ Training
Chapter 14 ▪ Expatriates
Chapter 15 ▪ Women/Dual Careers
Chapter 16 ▪ Communication & Negotiation
Chapter 17 ▪ Motivation & Leadership

INTRODUCTION

One of the most difficult tasks for international managers is to motivate and lead people from cultural backgrounds different from their own. In this chapter we begin by examining the study of leadership in general, then we consider the impact of culture on effective leadership. Different approaches to leadership are illustrated using varied countries. We will also discuss how various theories of motivation apply cross-culturally. These are essentially Western theories of motivation, and where cross-cultural research is available we draw on this to evaluate the theories.

THE STUDY OF LEADERSHIP

The study of leadership is an ancient practice. Dorfman and Ronen observe:

> Great leaders have existed throughout history and can be found in all cultures. Skillful leadership predates the construction of pyramids in Egypt, notably in the construction of the massive temples at Thebes (3500 B.C.), and pre-Columbian civilizations of the Americas . . . The practice and philosophy of leadership can be gleaned from writings as diverse in content, philosophy, and time as those from Moses to Confucius, to Machiavelli (1468–1527) and John Stuart Mill (1806–1873). Thus, the process of leadership has existed before formal history, and words and symbols for leaders have existed for thousands of years. (1991, p. 4)

Since World War II, leadership has been a hot topic within the social sciences, with over 3,500 studies and numerous books written on the subject (Bass 1990). Numerous social scientific theories of leadership have been constructed, but so few studies have been done to test their effectiveness in cross-cultural settings we have decided not to review these models here. Perhaps one reason few studies have cross-culturally tested these models is that studies done in the countries in which the models were developed have not found strong support for the models' effectiveness. The "universal" theories of McGregor, Likert, Blake and Mouton, Misumi, and others have not been adequately substantiated by the research literature. After reviewing these theories, Yukl (1989, p. 90) noted that "the empirical research provides only limited support for the universal [theories]."

Exhibit 17.1 presents a summary of the major situational leadership models that have been developed since World War II and the general results of studies that have tested them. As can be seen, few have received much support and few have been tested internationally. The Vroom and Yetton model, though promising, deals only with only a small part of leadership (decision making), and more research is needed to test each of the model's elements. (For an in-depth review of these theories, see Yukl 1989, and Bass 1990.) Despite the lack of testing of Western leadership models, much writing and research has been done on differences of leadership in different cultures.

CROSS-CULTURAL DIFFERENCES IN LEADERSHIP

Historically, writings on leadership have always had a cross-cultural flavor. Consider the books about and the writings of great leaders such as Winston Churchill, Niccolo Machiavelli, Joan of Arc, and Mohandas Ghandi in the political arena; Jesus Christ, the Prophet Mohammed, Confucius, and Moses in the religious world; and Sun Tzu, Patton, Alexander the Great, and Miyamoto Mushashi in the military affairs.

EXHIBIT 17.1

SUMMARY OF EMPIRICAL SUPPORT FOR SITUATIONAL LEADERSHIP MODELS

Leadership Model	Validation Results
Path-Goal Theory	Many studies, partial support
Hersey and Blanchard's Situational Leadership Model	Few studies, inconclusive
Leadership Substitutes	Few studies, inconclusive
Vroom-Yetton Model	Few studies, most were supportive
Fiedler's Contingency Model	Many studies, partial support
Cognitive Resource Theory	Few studies, inconclusive

SOURCE

Yukl, G., *Leadership in Organizations*, 3rd ed. Copyright © 1994. Englewood Cliffs, NJ: Prentice-Hall, pp. 311. Adapted by permission of Prentice-Hall, Englewood Cliffs, New Jersey.

While leadership is exhibited in all societies, cultural norms influence what kinds of leadership behaviors are appropriate in a particular culture. By definition, leaders stand out from their peers, yet they stand out without pushing the constraints of cultural norms too far. If leaders attempt to behave too differently from cultural norms, they will be rejected; however, if they adhere to all cultural norms to the letter, they will not be leaders—for leaders must break some norms to be seen as different by their fellow men and women.

Leaders tend to differ from the masses in these ways:

1. They have a vision, an obsession of what needs to be achieved in the organization, their group, or society. They envision where the group should go.

2. They inspire others to follow their vision, to work to make it a reality. Generally, the vision energizes the leader to work hard and have high levels of physical energy in seeking to make it a reality. This energy and excitement are picked up by the followers. Also, the leader is able to persuade the majority in his/her group to work to achieve the vision.

3. They are able to organize their followers into cohesive, loyal groups, and they reward their followers in many ways to keep them focused on the goal of the vision.

While these general observations about leaders hold true across cultures, the manner in which the leaders inspire others to follow their vision, motivate them to work to accomplish the vision, communicate the vision to elicit followers, organize their followers, and reward their followers differs among cultures. The following excerpts from Bass (1990, p. 785) make this point:

- The aggressive, efficient, ambitious Manus leader in Oceania would have been rejected by the Dakota Indians, who valued mutual welfare, conforming to the group, generosity, and hospitality.

- With their consciousness of position and conformity to rank in a clear hierarchy, the Samoans followed a completely different style of leadership from that pursued by the individualistic Inuits, who considered no person's importance relative to another.

- Leadership among the Iroquois was achieved through behavior that was socially rewarding to others . . . but among the Kwakiutl, the ideal chieftain was one who could successfully compete financially against the other chiefs.

- Thus, it is not surprising that the patterns of leader-subordinate behavior in industrialized societies vary considerably across countries and across cultures. Although such extreme effects of cultural differences may not be seen in the modern industrialized world, nevertheless considerable differences emerge in what managers think is required for success in the top . . . levels of management.

In discussing the differences in leadership across cultures, we note that the research has largely been driven by the economic success (or potential for economic success) of various nations. For example, we know more about the leadership styles of Japanese executives than the leadership styles of executives in Bhutan. The leadership norms of all of the countries of the industrialized world cannot be discussed in this chapter. Therefore, the leadership styles in France, the Arab world, and Japan have been selected as useful contrasts in the way leadership is manifest in differing cultures.

FRANCE

Leadership in business and government organizations in France is heavily based on belonging to the cadre. Obtaining cadre status is important, for it changes social and legal status relating to pension entitlement, self-perception, and the way others perceive a person.

One attains cadre status in three ways, the most common being to excel in high school and be admitted to one of the *grandes ecoles*—professional schools that admit only the best and the brightest of France's high school graduates. Upon graduation from such a school individuals are automatically positioned for success in a company or in the government (Barsoux & Lawrence 1991). The second way to obtain cadre status is to get a job after or before graduation from a university other than one of the *grandes ecoles* and wait five to ten years to gain cadre status. Thus, cadre status must be earned "on the job." The third way is to enter a firm without any higher-education and, over a period of several years, prove oneself to be outstanding.

This system of producing leaders from the cream of the crop has predictable effects on leadership style. Barsoux and Lawrence observe that: "French managers see their work as an intellectual challenge, requiring the remorseless application of individual brainpower. They do not share the Anglo-Saxon view of management as an interpersonally demanding exercise, where plans have to be constantly 'sold' upward and downward using personal skills. The bias is for intellect rather than for action" (1991, p. 60).

The design of French organizations reinforces the isolationist, intellectual, and analytical orientation of the cadre. French organizations are highly centralized, have rigid hierarchies, and positions of authority are respected. At the top of the firm in France is the PDG (president-directeur-general). In U.S. terms, this position is akin to the chairman of the board and the CEO together. The person who inhabits this position in a French organization has complete decision-making power and control of the company.

> There is a clear connection between the intellectual manager and organizational centralization. Senior executives in France believe they owe their high position to their intelligence and cunning. It therefore follows that they should make all the critical decisions and that they should be told everything so they can check other people's decisions. When Bernard Attali became PDG of Air France, he told his assembled directors, "I want to be at all times informed of every notable event in your different sectors of activity" (Barsoux and Lawrence, 199?).

Because of this rigid organization, French managers resist adopting a more flexible organizational system. Andre Laurent, a noted academic and consultant in international management, once tried to explain the concept of matrix management (where a manager may have to report to more than one superior); he found that:

> The idea of reporting to two bosses was so alien to these managers that mere consideration of such organizing principles was an impossible, useless exercise. What was needed first was a thorough examination and probing of the holy principle of the single chain of command and

the managers' recognition that this was a strong element of their own belief system rather than a constant element in nature (Laurent 1983, pp. 75–6).

French leaders are expected to make decisions based on careful, quantitative analysis and prefer to communicate by memo and letter. All of this reinforces norms of formality and authoritarianism. French executives command respect and obedience from their subordinates and in turn give their own superiors the same. Such norms reflect the larger national organizational culture where leaders are expected to display behaviors that relate to intellect, analysis, and independence in thinking. Barsoux and Lawrence note that:

> . . . unlike Britons or Americans, the French are inclined to favor the intellectual politician. One can see it in their choice of presidents, especially throughout the Vth Republic (since 1958). The idea of someone who left school at 16 (like John Major), much less an ex-actor, ever becoming President of France is unthinkable. French politicians seeking election will often boast of their intellectual (and even literary) accomplishments—for these are trumps to be played not skeletons to be concealed. In short, the French do not adhere to the Anglo-Saxon view that qualities of thought and action are mutually exclusive. Intellect, then, does not arouse suspicion or fear in France. Rather, it is regarded as the prime criterion for leadership in any field—including business (1991, pp. 2–3).

If a French manager who desired to lead his work group attempted to engage in more participative and democratic approaches to decision making and goal setting, and relied on his/her intuition in making decisions, that manager would most likely not be seen as a leader.

Similarly, if an expatriate manager from a culture that valued work norms of group decision making and participative management tried to superimpose that style of leadership on his/her French subordinates, disaster may well ensue. For example, in 1988, General Electric (GE) bought the French medical-equipment maker Cie. Generale de Radiologie. Because the French company had been struggling, GE attempted to boost the morale of their newly acquired co-workers in the following ways (quoted from Nelson 1990):

- GE's culture is an extension of the strong personality of its combative chairman, John F. Welch, Jr. He preaches a philosophy of self-reliance, hard work and big profits—a sort of evangelical capitalism. At company meetings in Paris, gung-ho American staffers would chant his credo—"speed, simplicity, and self-confidence"—to skeptical French managers.

- GE called a training seminar for French and other European managers. In their hotel rooms, the company left colorful T-shirts emblazoned with the GE slogan "Go For One." A note urged the managers to wear the T-shirts "to show that you are members of the team." The French wore them, grudgingly, to the seminar, but, as one of the French managers recalls: "It was like Hitler was back, forcing us to wear uniforms. It was humiliating."

- Soon after the takeover, GE set out to fix CGR's financial-control system. U.S. computer specialists are said to have imposed a GE system that was unsuited to French financial-reporting requirements or to the way CGR kept records, and the company spent months seeking a workable compromise.

- GE managers plastered English language posters everywhere, flying GE flags and otherwise making GE's culture ubiquitous. "They came in here bragging, We are GE, we're the best and we've got the methods," says a CGR union leader.

The result of this approach was a conflict in leadership styles between the Americans and the French. Morale after the takeover was low, the best French managers and engineers left for other firms, and it was difficult to recruit qualified replacements. GE-CGR's expected losses for 1991 were $25 million dollars. GE leaders did not communicate their vision, inspire others to work for achieving the vision, and did not organize their French work force to work effectively toward the vision because they engaged in leadership behaviors that did not fit with French expectations of organizational leadership.

THE ARAB WORLD

Leadership behaviors in Arab societies are closely linked to tribal traditions as well as Western influences. Ali (1990, p. 14) notes that the tribal-kinship influence is felt heavily among Arab managers today, and many Arab managers tend to:

> . . . behave as fathers, i.e., as protectors, caregivers, and those who should shoulder all the responsibilities of business. While the above characteristics are not necessarily negative...they do suggest an authoritarian management style. The authoritarian structure is particularly apparent in large organizations. Most Arab organizations, whether public or private, are highly centralized and adopt an authoritarian structure (functional-type), regardless of corporate strategy or technology.

Ali (1988) observes that the tribal-kinship influence on managers does not facilitate a willingness to work with groups outside the family, engage in creative problem solving, seek alliances with outsiders, or break or test established organizational norms. It is not unusual for organizational problems to be solved according to cultural values of the tribal-kinship group. For example, according to Ali (1990, p. 15), "in Iraq . . . a conflict between two powerful senior managers in a state enterprise was solved by the creation of two companies headed by each of them—a typical tribal practice of treating equally and pleasing favored rivals (sons or relatives)."

The legacy of being ruled by the Ottoman and Europeans has left a strong tradition of ruling by administration in the Arab countries. This legacy left administrative orientations toward centralization, rigid rules, clear divisions of labor, low tolerance for ambiguity, and little tolerance of autonomy. These systems, combined with tribal-kinship values, have developed into the leadership style of "sheikocracy" (Ali, 1990). The characteristics of sheikocracy are:

- Hierarchical authority.

- Rules and regulations contingent on the personality and power of individuals who make the rules.

- Subordination of efficiency goals to human relations and personal friendships.

- Indecisiveness in decision making.

- A patriarchal approach to leadership.

- Nepotism at upper levels of organizations.

- Open-door policies.

Western influences in management methods have also influenced Arab managers, but the use of participative and other more democratic approaches to leading workers is difficult because of resistance on the part of political rulers, conservative segments in society, and other managers who are not as Westernized in their approach to management. Ali has shown that these influences have produced a "duality" in Arab managers' approaches to leadership, described as "the Arabs love to invest in the modern sector . . . and to invest simultaneously in the traditional sector in order to maintain it . . . (e.g., using Majlis or open house to hear [subordinates'] requests and solve their problems outside the formal organizational channels)" (Ali 1990, p. 20). He further notes that this duality is translated into the following behaviors by Arab leaders:

- Creating numerous rules and regulations without making strong attempts to implement them; they are created as symbols of being modern.

- Creating systems for selection and promotion based on performance, while selecting and promoting based on personal relationships, social ties, and nepotism.

- Creating organizational structures and then not abiding by them or abiding by them only on an exceptional basis; again, the structure is a symbol of being modern, while organizational life continues on the basis of traditional cultural values.

Bashir Khadra (1990) has developed an Arabian leadership model called the "prophetic-caliphal" model. It is based on the assumptions that there is a continuity of traditional forms of behavior in Arab society in organizations and that leadership in Arab society is interrelated with the political, social, economic, and other ideological systems of Arab cultures. As shown in Exhibit 17.2, Khadra's model has four dimensions: personalism, individualism, lack of institutionalization, and expectations of the "great man."

EXHIBIT 17.2

KHADRA'S "PROPHETIC-CALIPHAL" LEADERSHIP MODEL

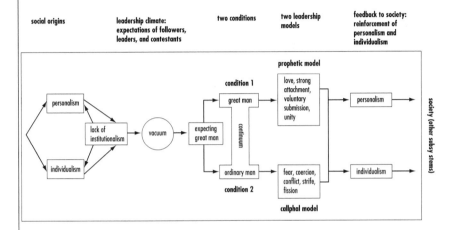

SOURCE:

Khadra, B. 1990. "The Prophetic-Caliphal model of leadership: An empirical study." *International Studies of Management and Organization*, 20(3), pp. 37-51; p. 38.

Personalism involves how the manager/leader views his relationships with other people. The tendency toward personalism involves viewing one's relationships with others from an egocentric perspective: the person subjectively analyzes the relationship from his own sets of needs and does not try to view the relationship from an objective viewpoint. Personalism also reflects a strong emotional attachment to others with whom relationships have been built.

The term "individualism" is used differently by Khadra from the way Hofstede defines it. To Khadra, "individualism" refers to the "tendency to make decisions regardless of the opinions of the group, or in spite of such opinions" (p. 39). The effects of the cultural values of personalism and individualism in Arab society create organizations where systems of rules, procedures, regulations, and protocol do not solve problems readily. In other words, organizational problems are viewed subjectively by managers, and when managers feel they have a solution, they tend to be rigid in their decision-making processes.

In Khadra's model, lack of institutionalization means "the ineffectiveness of the means of solving the leadership problems of accession, succession, and conflict, which are resolved instead outside the institutional arrangements created for such purposes" (p. 39). When control devices such as committees, rules, and handbooks are ignored in Arab organizations, a kind of leadership vacuum exists. Someone or something must enter the vacuum and restore order and guidance. According to Khadra, in the Arab cultural context, seeking out new management ideas, new training programs, and so on are not thought of to solve organizational stagnation. Neither are groups of workers looked to as the solution. In Arab cultures, the most important element in filling the vacuum is a person, "a great man," who will make things right. Thus, a great man is expected to emerge and is waited for by all the organization's members, and there will be a predisposition to accept him in his role once he emerges.

Khadra (pp. 39–40) emphasizes that stability, progress, and growth of the system depend on whether the leader is an ordinary man or a great man. If the leader happens to be an ordinary man, the model of leadership is the "caliphal model"; if the leader happens to be a great man, the model becomes a "prophetic model." The factor that distinguishes the leader who emerges between becoming a great man or an ordinary man is the ability to accomplish a superior feat. Other members of the organization will perceive the leader to be a "great man" if he is able to accomplish an extraordinary feat of some kind; if he is unable to do this, he will be classified as an ordinary leader, similar to other members of the organization, incapable of miracles and possessing no traits that are superior to any one else.

In order for the ordinary man to lead the group, he must use coercion and authoritarian measures, as well as ingrate himself, to maintain his status as leader. The fear, conflict, and strife this creates in the organization will usually eventually cause another organizational leadership vacuum to emerge as his power slowly wanes. For the great man, however, a different situation exists. His power and influence depend on showing love, a minimum use of coercion, and his followers' freely given submission to his instructions. Followers feel free to express their opinions and emotions to a great man because such a leader by nature and custom must show his interest and concern in diverse ideas.

JAPAN

Some societies focus more on rules and regulations as a way of compelling people to comply with organizational expectations for worker behavior, while other societies focus more on cultural norms and values as mechanisms to influence people to comply with organizational expectations. Norms are generally not written down but are assumed—that is, they are not made manifest through control systems. Norms are obeyed out of a sense of duty because others in the group expect one to obey the norm and out of fear that if the norm is not obeyed, the group will punish the member who breaks the norm.

All societies have both norms and organizational rules, but some societies have stronger tendencies to be norm-oriented rather than rule-oriented. Sullivan, Suzuki, and Kondo's research found that in Japan performance is controlled by the workers in the work group. Japanese workers will not miss work because they would let down others in the group, not because there is an organizational rule about not missing work. The work group in Japan, not the individual, is monitored, rewarded, and punished by management. Dorfman and Ronen (1991, p. 16) observe that influence to achieve high performance levels in Japanese work groups "flows from the norms themselves, [and] not from an active or hands-on directive leadership style . . . Detailed organizational charts and job descriptions are not the norm in Japan, but procedures for formalizing the structure of an organization are ubiquitous in U.S. companies. In Japan organizations do have rules, but they are not as important as the underlying norms of organizational behavior in the workplace. Rules are seen as flexible in nature, easily bent to meet different situations, and not ironclad and dangerous if broken."

One of the basic values that influences Japanese leadership behaviors is that of *amae*. *Amae* is a noun form of the intransitive verb *amaeru* which refers to the desire to depend upon the love and patience of others, or to presume upon another's benevolence, or to bask in another's indulgence, or to depend on another's kindness. A prominent Japanese psychologist, Takeo Doi, observed that all humans exhibit *amae* behavior in the mother-infant relationship. The infant is totally dependent on the mother, desires to be completely and passively loved by the mother, and does not desire to be separated from the mother. However, in many other cultures, *amae* is socialized out of infants as they are taught very early to be independent and self-reliant, and are rewarded by parents when they are able to do things on their own. In Japan, *amae* is not socialized out of infants, children, teenagers, or adults; rather it is reinforced.

Another Japanese researcher, Kumagai (1981), notes that in Japan *amae* is regarded as a positive thing; other researchers have observed that *amae* is prolonged and diffused throughout Japanese society. Relationships in Japan (manager-subordinate, husband-wife, teacher-pupil, leader-follower) to one degree or another, are affected by *amae* (Mendenhall & Oddou 1986).

Two other important cultural norms that influence leadership behavior in Japan are *on* and *giri*. Befu (1983c) defines *on* as "the debt or obligation one incurs upon receiving a favor or gift from another." Thus, human relationships in Japan become bound in a network of reciprocal obligations. *Giri* is a word that reflects the norm of duty to pay back debts—whether one wants to or not. Befu (1983a, p. 34) defines *giri* as:

> . . .[the] norm that obliges the observance of reciprocal relationships . . . [*Giri* is] a moral force that compels members of society to engage in socially expected reciprocal activities even when their natural inclination (*ninjo*) may be to do otherwise. In Japan, to be observant of *giri* is an indication of high moral worth. To neglect the obligation to reciprocate is to lose the trust of others expecting reciprocation, and eventually lose their support.

The model in Exhibit 17.3 outlines the relationship of these three cultural values at work. The model begins with the existing *amae* relationship between leader and follower. Chie Nakane, a noted Japanese sociologist, states that:

> . . . the relationship between two individuals of upper and lower status is the basis . . . of Japanese society. This important relationship is expressed in the traditional terms *oyabun* and *kobun*. *Oyabun* means

the person with the status of *oya* (parent) and *kobun* means with the status of *ko* (child) . . . The traditional *oyabun-kobun* relationship took the form of . . . master and disciple. The expressions are still used today, although more informally. *Oyabun* may be one in a senior position at a [person's] place of work, with whom has grown a close personal relationship over the years . . . the *kobun* receives benefits or help from his *oyabun*, such as assistance in securing [a] promotion, and advice on the occasion of important decision-making. The *kobun*, in turn, is ready to offer his services whenever the oyabun requires them . . . Most Japanese, whatever their status or occupation, are involved in *oyabun-kobun* relationships (1970, pp. 42–43).

EXHIBIT 17.3

VALUES-BASED MODEL OF THE LEADER-FOLLOWER RELATIONSHIP IN JAPAN

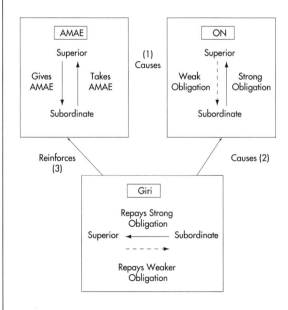

At work, the *oyabun-kobun* relationship is sometimes referred to as *sempai-kohai*, which can be roughly translated as "senior-junior." When an employee in Japan goes to his/her manager and seeks the manager's advice about a personal problem, the manager will take the time to listen, advise, and help the subordinate. In other words, the employee is engaging in *amae* behavior (depending on the benevolence of the *oyabun*) and the manager is replying with *amae* behavior (allowing someone to be dependent on him/her). The employee presumes upon the manager's benevolence out of *amae* emotions, and the manager gives time, attention, and concern out of *amae* emotions.

The next step in the model refers to the obligation (*on*) that the employee incurs because of this incident. Since the manager was willing to help, the employee is in debt to the manager. The manager is also somewhat in debt to the employee, except not as much (this is implied by a broken-line arrow in the model), because that the employee allowed the manager to express *amae* in their relationship.

In the *giri* phase of the model, the employee will seek ways to repay the debt later, usually through obeying and being loyal to all requests the manager asks of the employee. The manager will repay the debt owed to the employee in more subtle ways, such as bending a rule for him/her. The result of this process is that the *amae* relationship between the two is reinforced; thus the cultural values associated with the process remain intact.

Research findings generally confirm the model. Bass, et. al. (1979) found that among 12 national groups, Japanese managers expressed more tendencies to listen to others with understanding and to accept warmth and affection from others. They also scored highest in their willingness to discuss feelings with others, cooperate with peers rather than compete against them, and seeing the need for top management to be tolerant. Bolon and Crain (1985) found that Japanese managers take more steps when dealing with a problem subordinate, and spend more time in trying to understand the situation compared to American managers. Ivancevich, Schweiger, and Ragan (1986) found the Japanese managers in their study reported that they obtained more social support from their superiors than did American and Indian managers; the latter two reported receiving social support from spouses and relatives. Other studies found that among Japanese managers, consideration is expected from superiors, and in return subordinates should accept the guidance of superiors (see Hall & Hall 1987; Yokochi 1989).

Attributes commonly seen as necessary for leadership in Japan are:

- *Majime:* being serious, exhibiting hard work and consistent performance.

- *Kyochosei:* exhibiting cooperation and harmony with others and being able to facilitate close interpersonal relationships.

- *Kuro:* having experienced hardship—it is necessary to have gone through trials and tribulations to become wise and experienced.

- *Seishin-shugi:* being self-disciplined—only someone who has learned to control his/her ambitions, intellect, personal desires, and emotions is mature enough to be a leader.

- *Onjo-shugi:* showing paternalism, the sympathy felt by the leader toward his/her subordinates.

Though Japanese society is undergoing shifts in its values, business, and economic systems, traditional leadership norms are holding firm. Nakane (1970, pp. 65–71) summarizes the issues of Japanese leadership by stating the following general principles:

1. In comparison to leaders in other societies, Japanese leaders have less authority and control. Because Japanese leaders are expected to have good, warm relations with their followers, their followers (because of *amae*), are allowed to influence the decisions of the leader to a great degree. Thus, leaders in Japan are obligated to modify their opinions as a result of their followers' inputs—the greater the leader, the more this type of behavior is manifested.

2. The loyalty of a subordinate to a superior is a virtue in Japanese ethics, thus leaders must allow subordinates to show this loyalty. The leader, to a large degree, is expected to be dependent on the followers—it is seen as positive if the leader has some weaknesses that the followers can compensate and make up for.

3. Leaders must keep conflict, contention, anxiety, and tension to a minimum among the workers they lead. An important value in Japanese intra-group relations is conflict avoidance; in fact, the push for harmony is born out of a loathing of interpersonal conflict.

4. More than anything else, a leader's effectiveness in Japan is based on the ability to understand and attract his/her subordinates.

LEADERSHIP ISSUES SUMMARIZED

An important issue to remember when thinking about leadership styles across cultures is that not all French, Arab, and Japanese managers will behave exactly like what has been described in this chapter. While researchers have found general tendencies in leadership behaviors within countries, there is variation between individuals within those same countries. Companies develop their own corporate cultures, and some of these may not mirror traditional leadership values of the society in which the organizations exist. Thus, managers from such companies will naturally have a different leadership style compared to many of their fellow citizens. Part of the art of international management is to discern the style of leadership and motivation most effective for one's company in a specific country. Whether that style should reflect national leadership norms, be exactly the same as headquarters' corporate culture norms, or be a hybrid of headquarters' and local culture's leadership norms is an important question for multinational companies to answer.

CROSS-CULTURAL ISSUES IN MOTIVATION

Motivation is probably one of the most researched areas of management, and it is easy to understand why. If a manager can grasp what will motivate his/her employees, then that manager will have a more productive work force. Being able to understand what motivates employees is thus a key diagnostic skill for a manager to possess. The actions a manager takes to motivate his/her subordinates depend on that manager's assumptions about what motivates people.

Issues to consider are what causes people to work hard, to work together, and to work effectively. Most of the research undertaken in this area has been carried out in the U.S., Canada, and Great Britain. Thus, the motivation theories we will review are Western in their origin and have not been tested extensively in other countries. We will also discuss cross-cultural issues that influence how valid these theories are for other cultures, as well as cross-cultural research findings that give insight into motivation around the world.

The most common approach, historically, to answer the question of what motivates workers has been to focus on satisfaction of need. The assumption is that humans act to satisfy their inner needs; for example, humans are motivated to eat because they experience hunger. Thus hunger causes a need and eating satisfies that need. Much research in management has been undertaken to understand how various needs people have at work might be met, to increase their motivation.

One of the earliest researchers that took this approach was Frederick Taylor. He believed that workers were motivated to work by the need for money. His model is based on the idea that people work harder when they are given more money. He held that a company should break work down into its most efficient components to use workers' time on the job more productively. By doing this, profits would increase, and the company would have more money to increase workers' pay, which, in turn, would keep them motivated to work hard.

Taylor's ideas seem to work best when the nature of the job is routine and predictable (such as basic assembly-line work), when little judgment is required from managers, and when workers are willing to comply with organizational rules. Motivation is not really that simple. People seem to be motivated by more than just money; and individual differences exist in workers—some may be more interested in receiving more leisure time instead of money, for example.

In reaction to Taylor's ideas, a new approach to worker motivation developed: the "human relations" school. This assumes that individuals are motivated by more than just money and that more people would have higher levels of motivation at work if they could get more of their needs met there.

MASLOW'S HIERARCHY OF NEEDS

The famous psychologist Abraham Maslow contributed to the human relations school. Despite the fact that he did not develop a theory of management, his work in psychology was applied by others to the organizational context. He believed that people can understand others' behavior if they know what needs others are trying to satisfy. Maslow viewed humans as having a relatively small set of basic needs, which form a hierarchy, shown in Exhibit 17.4.

Lowest on the hierarchy is the *physiological* category—needs that have to do with satisfying hunger, thirst, shelter, and sex. Next on the hierarchy is *safety*— needs that involve ensuring personal safety and income. Following this need is the category of *belongings* needs; these have to do with the need for social acceptance as shown by rewarding interpersonal relationships. *Esteem* is the next category on the hierarchy, and this involves the desire for prestige, to feel valuable in the eyes of only self and others. Finally, the highest needs of all are those of *self-actualization*; these needs involve the desire to feel competent, authentic, self-expressive, creative, and unique.

EXHIBIT 17.4

MASLOW'S HIERARCHY OF NEEDS

Fulfillment off the Job	Need Heirarchy	Fulfillment on the Job
Eduacation, religion, hobbies, personal growth	Self-Actualization Needs	Opportunities for training, advancement, growth, and creativity
Approval of family, friends, community	Esteem Needs	Recognition, high status, increased responsibilities
Family, friends, community groups	Belongings Needs	Work groupps, clients, coworkers, supervisors
Freedom from war, pollution, violence	Safety Needs	Safe work, fringe benefits, job security
Food, water, sex	Physiological Needs	Heat, air, base salary

SOURCE:

Excerpts from *Management*, Second Edition by Richard L. Daft, Copyright © 1991 by The Dryden Press, reproduced by permission of the publisher.

Maslow assumed that an individual will not be concerned with higher needs in the hierarchy until lower needs in the hierarchy are met. For example, if you have a job that you enjoy and meets your needs for esteem, and suddenly that job is threatened by cutbacks, Maslow would contend that you would forget about what others think of you, how well you get along with your colleagues at work, and other higher needs. Instead, you would focus on security needs—having a job and a steady income. You will likely try to protect your job or make plans to find a new one.

Maslow's ideas were applied to organizational settings by a variety of academics, writers, and consultants, and the need for self-actualization was elevated as the ideal state for people to seek. Much attention was paid to how organizations could facilitate conditions that allow people to pursue self-actualization at work. It was believed that if organizations could foster this, they would have more highly motivated managers and workers.

One problem with this theory is that individuals often pursue self-actualization outside of work, as is shown in Exhibit 17.4. Many people may not want to be self-actualized at work, and programs that promote such an environment may, therefore fail. Nevertheless, Maslow's model of needs has had a powerful effect on how training programs and management education programs are conducted. The content of such programs often have, assumed, that if a manager meets workers' needs, they will be motivated.

Maslow's hierarchy was the first motivation model to be tested internationally. Compared to the number of studies that tested Maslow's model in the U.S. and in Canada, the number that tested his model internationally is relatively small. We will present two general findings.

1. The studies are not definitive in their support or refutation of Maslow. Thus, scholars in the field have been arguing for quite awhile about the general validity and universality of Maslow's hierarchy of needs. Exhibit 17.5 illustrates the mixed nature of the research findings. Some studies found that Maslow's hierarchy was the same or very similar across cultures, while other studies found some similarities along with significant differences in needs hierarchies across cultures.

EXHIBIT 17.5

STUDIES THAT INVESTIGATED MASLOW'S HIERARCHY OF NEEDS INTERNATIONALLY AND THEIR GENERAL FINDINGS

Supported	Partially Supported	Refuted
Reitz, 1975	Invancevich & Baker, 1970	Hofstede, 1980
Ronen, 1979	Kao & Leven, 1978	Howell, et.al., 1975
Salman, 1978	Nambudiri & Saiyadain, 1978	Buera & Glueck, 1979
Herbert, et.al., 1979		Redding, 1976, 1977
Haire, et.al., 1966		Whitehill, 1964
Clark & McCabe, 1970		Kanugo, 1983
Mozina, 1969		Redding & Martyn-Johns, 1979
		Badawy, 1979
		At-Twaijri, 1989
		Ali & Al-Shakhis, 1988

2. While complete support was not found for Maslow's hierarchy, there is clear evidence that the need types in his model do manifest themselves across cultures. Adler noted in her review of this research that "numerous research studies testing Maslow's hierarchy demonstrate similar but not identical rank ordering of needs across cultures" (1991, p. 154).

Thus, while Maslow's hierarchy itself may not be universal, the needs within that hierarchy do seem to reflect universal needs. For example, Badawy (1979; 1980) found that among Arab managers in Saudi Arabia, Kuwait, Abu Dhabi, Bahrain, Oman, and the United Arab Emirates, the highest need was autonomy. Closely tied to autonomy was interpersonal relationships—these Arab managers preferred to do business with people whom they knew and trusted. Another study by At-Twaijri (1989) found similar results when Saudi and

American expatriate managers working in Saudi Arabia were compared on Maslow's needs hierarchy. The Saudis were much more concerned about issues in the social needs category and less concerned about self-actualization needs than the Americans.

Thus, in a Middle-Eastern hierarchy of needs, the esteem and social categories may be at the top of the pyramid, with self-actualization in the middle, followed by safety and physiological needs. Such a hierarchy of Middle-Eastern needs cannot be built based upon the findings of two studies, however. A study that investigated school administrators' need orientations in Saudi Arabia found that autonomy and security were the highest-valued needs (Ali & Al-Shakhis 1988). This means that managers and school administrators within the same culture may have different hierarchies of needs. Unfortunately, researchers have not pursued efforts to define culture-specific need hierarchies and differences in those hierarchies based on occupation. If such culture-specific hierarchies do exist, knowing them would greatly aid expatriate managers and multinational companies in designing motivational, reward, and control systems for their subsidiaries.

HERZBERG'S TWO-FACTOR THEORY

Frederick Herzberg developed a different needs-oriented theory. He believed that when an organization satisfies a worker's lower-order needs, the worker will reach a "zero-level" of motivation. In other words, if a company pays a fair wage and has a safe work place and decent interpersonal relationships between supervisors and employees, then the worker will show up to work on time. Doing all that isn't enough to motivate the worker. Rather, it is a prerequisite for motivation to occur. Herzberg labeled these lower order needs "hygiene factors." When they are not present, or are inadequate, they create dissatisfaction. When these needs are met, they create "motivational neutrality."

Herzberg believed that higher-order needs must be met in order for motivation to occur in the work place. He argued that jobs must allow for a sense of individual achievement, challenge, and recognition in order for a person to feel motivated at work. He advised companies to take care of the lower-order needs first and then to enrich the nature of jobs, so that they will allow workers to meet their higher-order needs.

EXHIBIT 17.6

HERZBERG'S TWO-FACTOR THEORY

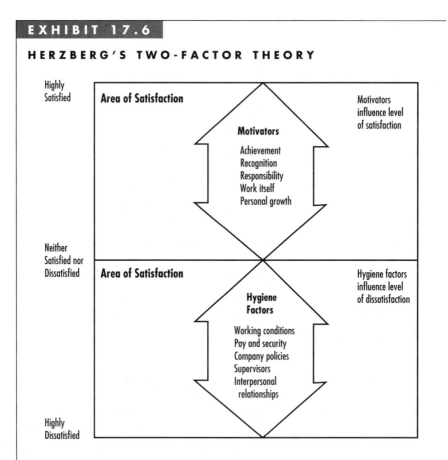

SOURCE:

Excerpts from *Management*, Second Edition by Richard L. Daft. Copyright © 1991 by The Dryden Press, reproduced by permission of the publisher.

Herzberg's model has been tested outside of the U.S. (though less often than Maslow's model) and support for it cross-culturally is mixed, as is illustrated in Exhibit 17.7. Though some studies found support for the model, others did not When added to the general lack of research support for the model in North America, the model is questionable in terms of its general validity across cultures.

In general, not enough of the studies found that people across cultures view the same kinds of work-related issues as motivators and as hygiene factors. In some cases, people viewed hygiene factors as being highly motivating to them at work. Herzberg's model has not found clear support in North America either. It seems even for North Americans that there great diversity about what is motivating and what is dissatisfying at work. As an idea managers can use to analyze individual worker's attitudes, the theory may be useful as a diagnostic tool for tailoring specific motivation programs in the work place.

MCCLELLAND'S NEED THEORY

David McClelland's research findings support the facts that humans tend to have dominant need clusters and that those needs may not exist in any kind of hierarchical ordering. McClelland's work would suggest that individuals acquire dominant need groupings as they grow up, and these are influenced both by nature and nurture. People are not necessarily born with these needs, but can acquire them over time and through experience. The three needs he studied were the need for power, the need for achievement, and the need for affiliation.

EXHIBIT 17.7

STUDIES THAT INVESTIGATED HERZBERG'S TWO-FACTOR THEORY INTERNATIONALLY AND THEIR GENERAL FINDINGS

Supported	Partially Supported	Refuted
Ronen, 1979	Simonetti & Weitz, 1972	Kao & Levin, 1978
Machungwa & Schmitt, 1983	White & Leon, 1976	Hofstede, 1980
Macarov, 1972		Kanugo, 1983
		Hines, 1972, 1973
		Crabbs, 1973
		Cant & Woods, 1968
		Griew & Philipp, 1969
		Watson, 1971

People who have a strong need for achievement desire to accomplish challenging tasks, seek success, and always try to excel. They are often entrepreneurs. People who have a high need for affiliation seek to have rewarding interpersonal relationships, develop friendships, and avoid conflict. These individuals often work as "integrators" whose role is to facilitate the work of several departments or work groups. This role requires communication skills and the ability to develop good working relationships with a diverse group of people. Finally, people who have a high need for power desire to influence others, to be in authority over others, and to influence organizations. These individuals often become managers, executives, teachers, and ministers. None of these need types is inherently good or bad—they simply reflect dominant and not-so-dominant needs in people's personalities.

In a review of the research on McClelland's need theory (most of which focused on studying the "need for achievement"), Ronen (1986, p. 153) observes that "McClelland has presented evidence that the achievement motive is a fairly consistent trait developed in early childhood and persisting into adult life." Numerous studies have been conducted worldwide (Japan, Great Britain, Italy, Poland, Turkey, United States, Nigeria, Iran, South Africa, Mexico, France, Afghanistan, Kuwait, Jordan, Czechoslovakia, India) to test the general validity of McClelland's work. These studies provide strong support for the cross-cultural general validity of his model and indicate that the need for achievement exists to varying degrees across cultures.

Many of the studies also found a relationship between the degree to which achievement orientation was socialized into people and the economic growth of the nation or subculture. For example, McClelland and his fellow researchers were able to teach Indians and Mexicans to increase their achievement orientation and found promising results from such training in subsequent entrepreneurial activities on the part of the participants (McClelland 1965, McClelland & Winter 1969).

However, linking economic growth to the degree to which achievement orientation is manifest among individuals in a society is simplistic. In 1972, Iwawaki and Lynn found that though British and Japanese workers had approximately the same orientation toward achievement, the two nations differed dramatically in their economic growth. Further studies found similar discrepancies, and Ronen notes that these studies were interpreted at the time as being evidence that discredited McClelland's ideas. He observed:

> [these] studies made one crucial assumption—that motivation is manifested similarly across cultures—which is not necessarily correct. Perhaps achievement motivation takes on different forms in different cultures . . . For instance, the Japanese have a high need for affiliation, and many Japanese workers' need for achievement expresses itself as a need to belong and to cooperate with others. The motive is not 'I did it for myself' but rather 'I did it for others' (Ronan 1986, pp. 153–154).

Hofstede found that nationalities in his study that were high in assertive, aggressive, and action orientations and also high in risk taking, tended to correlate with nations that were high in economic growth. But even in Hofstede's work this pattern did not hold for the Japanese; the Japanese in his study scored very low in risk taking.

Thus, the manner in which the need for achievement is manifested is probably due to cultural norms and predispositions. Further, the degree to which individuals in a society are achievement oriented should not be viewed as the main cause of the economic success of that society—too many variables in addition to achievement orientation come into play in the economic success of a nation. However, all this does not dilute the model's strengths when applied to individuals. McClelland's work has proven to be strong in predicting entrepreneurial activities and differences in individual need orientations across cultures.

Other theorists began to look at motivation from a different angle, in part because need theories seemed to lack the ability to explain motivation in a comprehensive manner. Two of the most popular of these theories are expectancy theory and equity theory.

EXPECTANCY THEORY

The expectancy theory (illustrated in Exhibit 17.8) assumes that individual motivation level is a function of perceived probability that one's work will, in fact, result in the desired performance. If a worker feels that, "if I try, I can finish the job," then the "effort (E) and performance (P) link" will be strong. If the worker does not believe that his/her effort will lead to high performance, for whatever reason, the link will be weak. This link is affected not only by self-confidence, but by the worker's actual ability, his/her understanding of what is involved in accomplishing the task, and the clarity of the task requirements.

Another important relationship illustrated in Exhibit 17.6 is the performance-outcome linkage. This linkage assumes that a worker also takes into account whether the performance will bring the desired outcomes. In other words, the worker calculates the pay-off. Thus, the "performance (P) and outcome (O) link" is strong if the worker believes that achieving the performance goal will actually lead to a desired outcome (a bonus, a promotion, a company car). The link will be weak if the worker does not believe that achievement of the performance goal will lead to the desired outcome.

Another variable affects this model—"valence." Valence is the degree to which the outcome (the bonus, the promotion, the company car) is valued by the worker. If the employee does not desire the outcome, it has a "low valence", and the employee will not be motivated to work hard.

EXHIBIT 17.8

THE MAJOR ELEMENT OF EXPECTANCY THEORY

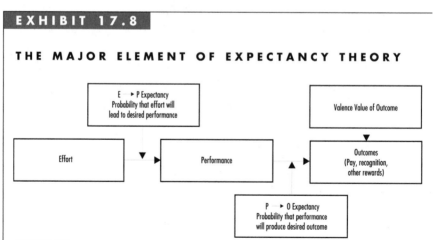

SOURCE:

Excerpts from *Management*, Second Edition by Richard L. Daft. Copyright © 1991 by The Dryden Press, reproduced by permission of the publisher.

Expectancy theory does not try to define specific needs of people; rather, it acknowledges that employees value different kinds of outcomes and that once organizations understand the expectancy mind set of each employee, the correct outcomes can be held up as goals. The employee must not only desire the outcome, but believe that he/she can do the job and that once the job is accomplished, the outcome will in fact be given to him/her. For a worker to be highly motivated, all three aspects—the E-P, P-O, and valence factors—must be high.

EQUITY THEORY

Another model that has received a lot of attention by management researchers is equity theory by J. Stacy Adams. The principle behind it is straightforward:

> "if people perceive their compensation as equal to what others receive for similar contributions, they will believe that their treatment is fair and equitable" (Daft 1991, p. 410). Whenever perceived inequity exists, dissatisfaction, anger, frustration, and other conditions that do not contribute to motivation occur; when perceived equity does exist, people are motivated to work hard. When workers compare themselves to one another, they take into consideration differences in terms of experience, age, education, performance, and a host of other variables. Equity theory holds that as employees we calculate our level of performance in relationship to our "inputs" (experience, education, effort, ability, potential) against the level of our "outputs" (actual performance, status, pay). Whenever our ratio of inputs to outputs equals or nearly approximates the ratios of others we feel that justice has been done and we continue to work hard. If our ratio is higher than others— and those others receive organizational rewards we do not receive— then a state of inequity exists, and our motivation decreases.

Equity theory has many implications for managers. Some are:

- Employees evaluate the perceived equity of their rewards compared to those of others. An increase in salary will have no effect on motivation if it is perceived to be inequitable relative to other employees.

- Employees may try to change their outcomes in order to create equity;

for example, employees may demand salary increases, better perquisites, and other conditions. Unions may get involved and the whole process can change everyone's focus from getting the job done to "getting my fair share."

▪ Employees who are doing a good job and feel that their input-output ratio is not being rewarded enough compared to others may leave the firm. Sometimes people who perceive they are being overpaid may leave—or be low in motivation—became of the persecution they suffer at the hands of those who feel underpaid.

Very few studies have been done on expectancy and equity theory internationally, so it is difficult to comment on their cross-cultural general validity. The few studies that have been done have supported both equity and expectancy theory (see Eden 1975, Yuchtman-Yaar 1972).

MOTIVATIONAL ISSUES SUMMARIZED

Some scholars have criticized the validity of all research done on motivational issues. They claim that superimposing a model that has inherent Western assumptions about the nature of human needs may not apply to non-Western cultures. For example, a Cambodian manager may understand concepts such as self-actualization differently from a North American or a European manager.

One problem for researchers is that it is often difficult to translate survey questionnaires so that the meaning of critical words like "achievement" are understood by the reader of the questionnaire. Hofstede has argued that in some languages Western concepts like achievement cannot even be translated, that there is no word in those languages that captures the meaning of the concept. Therefore, critics of these studies feel that the findings might be worthless because all of the respondents in the studies do not interpret the questions in similar ways.

So, what can be said about motivating people across cultures? While there is no magical or universal equation that will motivate anyone, anywhere, at anytime, the findings from the research that people seek to have their needs met, and when they have these needs met, they are motivated.

McClelland found that no matter where one travels, there are people to a larger or smaller degree who will be motivated by the need to achieve. In cultures where achievement is not a primary value, the likelihood of having a work force with an innate orientation to work hard and achieve goals will be low. Thus, in such cultures, expatriate managers will need to focus on ways to meet their workers' needs and link those needs to motivation. Expatriate managers must learn the strengths of their host-national employees, and adjust their motivational strategy accordingly. The key for expatriates is to learn under what circumstances their employees perform well and under what circumstances they perform poorly and to learn what kind of tasks they like and dislike. Though it is difficult, expatriate managers must learn to understand the real nature of their workers and then manage accordingly.

Consider this example of an expatriate manager of a ranching operation in New Zealand in the late 1960s: the Maoris who worked on the farm did not possess a strong work ethic. Under McClelland's theory they would have scored low in need for achievement, low in need for power, and very high in need for affiliation. They often loafed when the manager was not around—work and money were not that important to them. Rather than stereotype them as lazy, the manager hit on an idea. He told them that if they got a certain project completed, they could take the afternoon off and have a rifle-shooting competition. They worked hard, got the job done, and they—along with the expatriate manager—had a shooting match.

In this case, focusing on project completion instead of hourly work, as well as linking a reward the worker's valued to the completion of the project, worked. Other cross-cultural work situations may require different managerial approaches. Another way to describe the success of this manager's approach among his Maori work force was that, in terms of expectancy theory, he crafted a strong performance-outcome relationship (P-O) with a strong valence attached to it. Thus, he was able to influence his workers to complete the task in a timely and effective manner. Expectancy theory seems to hold a strong potential for application in the cross-cultural work setting once a manager understands the needs of his/her subordinates. In cross-cultural settings, it requires significant study, observation, and insight to be able to clearly understand the needs of one's work force.

SUMMARY

The purpose of this chapter was to review important principles associated with leading and motivating people in cross-cultural and comparative contexts. Leadership was discussed from a cross-cultural perspective, and leadership issues that seem to transcend cultures and conversely seem to be culture-specific were delineated. Then, a review of leadership theories from the management literature suggested that since World War II, the vast majority of these theories were created in the U.S., and that subsequent empirical testing of these theories did not produce compelling support for them.

Since the literature had little to offer in terms of general principles, studies that focused on leadership in specific cultures were reviewed, and leadership practices and philosophies of three cultural regions (France, Arabic cultures, and Japan) were discussed in detail. A summary of what was learned from the literature concluded this portion of the chapter.

The concept of motivation was introduced by reviewing the major theories of motivation since World War II, and studies that tested the cross-cultural general validity of these theories were reviewed. General findings in this literature were summarized, and again, no one theory stood out as warranting unrestricted use by people working in cross-cultural contexts.

Criticisms of these theories were reviewed as well, and illustrations were used to help students understand the potential application of the underlying concepts of the theories to the real world of living and working overseas.

The chapter indicates that from a social-scientific viewpoint, we know relatively little about leadership and motivation in cross-cultural contexts. Much more research needs to be done before conclusive prescriptions can be made for expatriates. However, the findings do suggest some fruitful areas for expatriates to consider when faced with the daunting task of motivating and leading people who come from a different culture from themselves.

DISCUSSION QUESTIONS

1. Compare and contrast leadership in France with leadership in the Arab World.

2. In a country that is high on power distance, people generally expect and accept differences in power as appropriate. Discuss equity theory in the context of a high power difference society.

3. Discuss the relationship of differences in leadership and motivation across cultures to the need for careful selection of expatriate managers.

REFERENCES

Abd-Al-Khaliq, N. 1984. "Al-Abaad Al-Biyha le-albureaucrata Al-Kuwaita" [Environmental dimensions of bureaucracy in Kuwait]. *Studies in the Gulf and Arab Island*, 10 (38), pp. 13-65.

Adler, N. 1991. *International Dimensions of Organizational Behavior* (2nd ed.). Boston: PWS-Kent Publishing Company.

Ali, A. & M. Al-Shakhis. 1988. "Hierarchy of needs among school administrators in Saudi Arabia." *Journal of Social Psychology*, 127(2), pp. 183-189.

Ali, A. 1988. A cross-national perspective on managerial work value systems. In R. Farmer and E. McGoun (eds.) *Advances in International Comparative Management*. Greenwich, CT: JAI Press.

Ali, A. 1990. "Management theory in a transitional society: The Arab's experience." *International Studies of Management and Organization*, 20(3), pp. 7–35.

Angelini, A.L. 1966. "Measuring the achievement motive in Brazil." *Journal of Social Psychology*, 68, pp. 35–44.

At-Twaijri, M.I. 1989. "A cross-cultural comparison of American-Saudi managerial values in U.S.-related firms in Saudi Arabia: An empirical investigation." *International Studies of Management and Organization*, 19(2), pp. 58–73.

Ayoubi. In N. Al-Saigh (ed.) *Administrative Reform in the Arab World: Readings*, Amman, Jordan: Arab Organization of Administrative Sciences, pp. 313–329.

Badawy, M.K. 1979. "Managerial attitudes and need orientations of Mid-Eastern executives: An empirical cross-cultural analysis." *Proceedings of the 39th Annual Meeting of the Academy of Management*, Atlanta, GA, August.

Badawy, M.K. 1980. "Styles of Mideastern managers." *California Management Review*, 22(3), pp. 51–58.

Barsoux, J. & P. Lawrence. 1991. "In search of intelligence." *Journal of General Management*, 17(2), pp. 1–12.

Barsoux, J. & P. Lawrence. 1991. "The making of a French manager." *Harvard Business Review*, July–August, pp. 58–67.

Bass, B., P.C. Burger, R. Doktor, & G.V. Barrett. 1979. *Assessment of Managers: An International Comparison*. New York: The Free Press.

Bass, B.M. 1990. *Bass and Stogdill's Handbook of Leadership*, (3rd ed.). New York: The Free Press.

Befu, H. 1983a. *Giri* and *ningo*. In *Kodansha Encyclopedia of Japan*. Vol. 3. Tokyo: Kodansha International. pp. 34.

Befu, H. 1983c. *On*. In *Kodansha Encyclopedia of Japan*. Vol. 6. Tokyo: Kodansha International. pp. 105.

Bhagat, R.S. & S.J. McQuaid. 1982. "Role of subjective culture in organizations: A review and direction for future research." *Journal of Applied Psychology Monograph*, 67(5), pp. 635–685.

Bhagat, R.S. & S.J. McQuaid. 1982. "Role of subjective culture in organizations: A review and direction for future research." *Journal of Applied Psychology Monograph*. 67(5), pp. 635–685.

Bolon, D.S. & C.R. Crain. 1985. "Decision sequence: A recurring theme in comparing American and Japanese management." *Proceedings*, Academy of Management, San Diego, CA, pp. 88–92.

Bradburn, N.M. N "Achievement and father dominance in Turkey." *Journal of Abnormal and Social Psychology*, 67, pp. 464–468.

Cole, R.E. 1979. *Work, Mobility, and Participation: A Compariative Study of American and Japanese Industry*. Berkeley and Los Angeles: Univeresity of California Press.

Conner, J.W. 1976. "*Joge Kankel*: A key concept for an understanding of Japanese-American achievement." *Psychiatry*, 39, pp. 266–279.

Daft, R.L. *Management.* (2nd ed.). Dryden Press.

Dol, T. 1986. *The Anatomy of Self: The Individual Versus Society.* Tokoyo: Kodansha International.

Dol, T. 1973. *The Anatomy of Dependence*. Tokyo: Kadansha International.

Dorfman, P.W. & S. Ronen. 1991. "The universality of leadership theories: Challenges and paradoxes." Paper presented at the annual Academy of Management meeting, Miami, August.

Eden, D. 1975. "Intrinsic and extrinsic rewards and motives: Replication and extension with kibbutz workers." *Journal of Applied Social Psychology*, 6, pp. 348–361.

Hall, E.T. & M.R. Hall. 1989. *Hidden Differences: Doing Business with the Japanese*. New York: Doubleday.

Hamady, S. 1960. *Temperament and Character of the Arabs*. New York: Twayne Publishers.

Heckhausen, H. 1967. *The Anatomy of Achievement Motivation*. New York: Academic Press.

Hines, G.H. 1973. "Achievement motivation, occupations, and labor turnover in New Zealand." *Journal of Applied Psychology*, 58(3), pp. 313–317.

Ivancevich, J.M., D.M. Schweiger, & J.W. Ragan. 1986. "Employee stress, health, and attitudes: A comparison of American, Indian, and Japanese managers." Paper presented at the Academy of Management meeting, Chicago, August.

Iwaki, S. & R. Lynn. 1972. "Measuring achievement motivation in Japan and Great Britain." *Journal of Cross-Cultural Psychology*, 3, pp. 219–220.

Jasim, A. 1987. *Studies in Culture and Alienations*. Beirut: Dar Alandls.

Kanugo, R.N. & R. Wright. "A cross-cultural comparative study of managerial job attitudes." *Journal of International Business Studies*, 14, pp. 115–129.

Khadra, B. 1990. "The prophetic-caliphal model of leadership: An empirical study." *International Studies of Management and Organization*, 20(3), pp. 37–51.

Krus, D.J. & J.A. Rysberg. 1976. "Industrial managers and Nach: Comparable and compatible?" *Journal of Cross-Cultural Psychology, December*, pp. 491–496.

Kumagal, H. 1981. "A dissection of intimacy: A study of "bipolar posturing" in Japanese social interaction—*Amaeru* and *amayakasu*, indulgence and deference." *Culture, Medicine and Psychiatry*, 5, pp. 249–272.

Laurent, A. 1983. "The cultural diversity of Western conceptions of management." *Interntional Studies of Management and Organization*, 13(1-2), pp. 75–96.

Lebra, T.S. 1976. *Japanese Patterns of Behavior*. Honolulu: University of Hawaii Press.

LeVine, R. 1968. *Dreams and Deeds: Achievement Motivation in Nigeria*. Chicago: University of Chicago Press.

McClelland, D.C. 1961. *The Achieving Society*. Princeton, NJ: Van Nostrand.

McClelland, D.C. 1965. "Achievement motivation can be developed." *Harvard Business Review*, 43(6), pp. 6–24.

McClelland, D.C. 1971. The two faces of power. In *Organizational Psychology*, D.A. Colb, I.M. Rubin, & J.M. McIntyre (eds.). Englewood Cliffs, NJ: Prentice-Hall.

McClelland, D.C., & D.G. Winter. 1969. *Motivating Economic Achievement*. New York: The Free Press.

Melikian, L., A. Ginsberg, D.M. Cuceloglu, & R. Lynn. 1971. "Achievement motivation in Afghanistan, Brazil, Saudi Arabia, and Turkey." *Journal of Social Psychology*, 83, pp. 183–184.

Mitchell, D.D. 1976. *Amaeru: The Expression of Reciprocal Dependency Needs in Japanese Politics and Law*. Boulder, CO: Westview Press.

Morsbach, H. "A cross-cultural study of achievement motivation and achievement values in two South African groups." *Journal of Social Psychology*, 79, pp. 267–268.

Nakane, C. 1970. *Japanese Society*. Berkeley and Los Angeles: University of California Press.

Nelson, M.M. & E.S. Browning. 1990. "GE's culture turns sour at French unit: Woes at CGR show how big, mature firms can stumble abroad." *Wall Street Journal*, July 31, p. A10.

Ronen, S. 1986. *Comparative and Multinational Management*. New York: John Wiley & Sons.

Singh, N.P. 1970. "N/Ach among agricultural and business entrepreneurs of Delhi." *Journal of Social Psychology*, 81, pp. 145–149.

Storm, T., W.S. Anthony, & R.D. Porsolt. 1965. "Ethnic and social class differences in performance for material and nonmaterial rewards: New Zealand children." *Journal of Personality and Social Psychology*, 2, pp. 759–762.

Sullivan, J., T. Suzuki, & Y. Kondo. 1984. "Managerial theories of the performance control process in Japanese and American work groups." *Proceedings of the Academy of Management*. Boston, pp. 98–102.

Tedeschi, J.T. & M. Kian. "Cross-cultural study of the TAT assessment for achievement motivation: Americans and Persians." *Journal of Social Psychology*, 58, pp. 227–234.

Tyler, W. 1983. *Amae*. In Kodansha Encyclopedia of Japan. Vol. 1. Tokyo: Kodansha International. pp. 350–352.

Yasin, M.M. & M.J. Stahl. 1990. "An investigation of managerial effectiveness in the Arab culture." *International Studies of Management and Organization*, 20(3), pp. 69–78.

Yokochi, N. 1989. *Leadership Styles of Japanese Business Executives and Managers: Transformational and Transactional.* Doctoral dissertation, United States International University, San Diego, CA.

Yukl, G.A. 1980. *Leadership in Organizations.* (2nd ed.). Englewood Cliffs: Prentice-Hall.

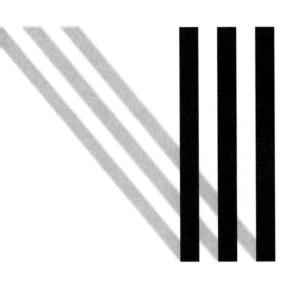

PART THREE:

MAJOR

REFERENCES

Acuff, F.L. 1993. *How to Negotiate Anything with Anyone Anywhere Around the World*. New York: AMACOM.

Adler, N.J. 1993. "Competitive frontiers: Women managers in the triad." *International Studies of Management and Organizations*, 23(2), Summer. pp. 3–23.

Adler, N.J. 1991. *International Dimensions of Organization Behavior*. Boston: PWS-Kent.

Adler, N.J. 1987. "Pacific Basin managers: A Gaijin, not a woman." *Human Resource Management*, 26(2), pp. 169–191.

Adler, N.J. 1981. "Reentry: managing cross-cultural transitions." *Group and Organization Studies*, vol. 6, no. 3, pp. 342–356.

Adler, N.J. 1979. "Women and androgynous managers: A conceptualization of the potential for American woman in international management." *International Journal of Intercultural Relations*, 3(4), pp. 407–436.

Adler, N.J. 1984. "Women do not want international careers: And other myths about international management." *Organizational Dynamics* 13(2), pp. 66–79.

Adler, N.J. 1984. "Women in international management: Where are they?" *California Management Reviews*, 269(4), pp. 78–89.

Adler, N.J. 1986/1987. "Women in management worldwide." *International Studies of Management and Organization*, 16(3-4), pp. 3–32.

Adler, N.J. & S. Bartholomew. 1992. "Academic and professional communities of discourse: Generating knowledge on transnational human resource management." *Journal of International Business Studies*, 23(3), Third Quarter, pp. 551–569.

Adler, N.J. & S. Bartholomew. 1992. "Managing globally competent people." *Academy of Management Executive*, 6(3), pp. 52–65.

Adler, N.J. & J.L. Graham. 1987." Business negotiations: Canadians are not just like Americans." *Canadian Journal of Administrative Sciences*, 4(3), pp. 211–238.

Agarval, S. 1992. "Influence of formalization on role stress, organizational commitment, and work alienation of salespersons: A cross-national comparative study." *Journal of International Business Studies*, 24(4), Fourth Quarter, pp. 715–740.

Ali, A. 1990. "Management theory in a transitional society: The Arab's experience." *International Studies of Management and Organization*, 20(3), pp. 7–35.

Amado, G. & H.V. Brasil. 1991. "Organizational behaviors and cultural context: The Brazilian 'Jeitinho'." *International Studies of Management and Organization*, 21(3), pp. 38-61.

Antal, A.B. & C. Krebsbach-Gnath. 1993. "Women in management in Germany: East, West, and reunited." *International Studies of Management and Organization*, 23(2), Summer, pp. 49–69.

At-Twaijri, M.I. 1989. "A cross-cultural comparison of American-Saudi managerial values in U.S.-related firms in Saudi Arabia: An empirical investigation." *International Studies of Management and Organization*, 19(2), pp. 58–73.

Baglioni, G. 1991. "An Italian mosaic: collective bargaining patterns in the 1980's." *International Labour Review*, 130(1), pp. 81–112.

Baker, J.C. 1984. "Foreign language and predeparture training of U.S. multinational firms." *Personnel Administrator*, 29(7), pp. 68–72.

Bakke, E.W. 1992. "The human resource function." *Management International Review*, 32, First Quarter, pp. 74–82.

Baliga, G.M. & J.C. Baker. 1985. "Multinational corporate policies for expatriate managers: Selection, training, evaluation." *Advanced Management Journal*, 50(4), pp. 31–38.

Banai, M. & W.D. Reisel. 1993. "Expatriate managers loyalty to the MNC: Myth or reality?" An exploratory study. *Journal of International Business Studies*, 24(2), Second Quarter, pp. 233–248.

Barsoux, J. & P. Lawrence. 1991. The making of a French manager. *Harvard Business Review*, July–August, pp. 58–67.

Bass, B.M. 1990. *Bass and Stodgill's Handbook of Leadership* (3rd ed.). New York: The Free Press.

Bass, B., P.C. Berger, R. Doktor, & G.V. Barrett. 1979. *Assessment of Managers: An International Comparison*. New York: The Free Press.

Beatty, J., J.T. McCune, & R.W. Beatty. 1988. A policy-capturing approach to the study of United Stated and Japanese managers' compensation decisions. *Journal of Management*, 14(3), pp. 465–474.

Bhagat, R.S. & S.J. McQuaid. 1982. "Role of subjective culture in organizations: A review and direction for future research." *Journal of Applied Psychology Monograph*, 67(5), pp. 635–685.

Bielby, D.D. & W.T. Bielby. 1988. "Women's and men's commitment to paid work a family: Theories, models and hypothesis." *Women and Work: an Annual Review*, 3.

Bird, A. & R. Dunbar. 1991. "Getting the job done over there: Improving expatriate productivity." *National Productivity Review*, Spring, pp. 145–156.

Black, J.S. 1988. "Work role transistions: A study of American expatriate managers in Japan." *Journal of International Business Studies*, 19(2), pp. 277–294.

Black, J.S. & H.B. Gregerson. 1991. "The other half of the picture: Antecedents of spouse corss-cultural adjustment." *Journal of International Business Studies*, 22(3), Third Quarter, pp. 461–478.

Black, J.S. & H.B. Gregerson. 1991. "When Yankee comes home: Factors related to expatriate and spouse repatriation adjustment." *Journal of International Business Studies*, 22(4), Fourth Quarter, pp. 471–494.

Black, J.S. & H.B. Gregerson. 1993. "Resolving conflicts with the Japanese: Mission impossible?" *Sloan Management Review*, 34(3), Third Quarter, pp. 49–59.

Black, J.S., H. Gregerson, & M. Mendenhall. 1992. *Global Assignments*. San Francisco: Jossey-Bass.

Black, J.S., H. Gregerson, & M. Mendenhall. 1991. "The U-curve adjustment hypothesis revisited: A review and theoretical framework." *Journal of International Business*, 22(2), Second Quarter, pp. 225–248.

Black, J.S., M. Mendenhall, & G. Oddou. 1991. "Toward a comprehensive model of international adjustment: An integration of multiple theoretical perspectives." *Academy of Management Review*, 16(2), pp. 291–317.

Black, J.S. & L.W. Porter. 1991. "Managerial behaviors and job performance: A successful manager in Los Angeles may not succeed in Hong Kong." *Journal of International Business Studies*, 22(1), First Quarter, pp. 99–114.

Black, J.S. & G.K. Stephens. 1989. "The influence of the spouse on American expatriate adjustment and intent to stay in Pacific Rim overseas assignments." *Journal of Management*, 15(4), pp. 529–544.

Bohning, W. 1991. "Integration and immigration pressures in Western Europe." *International Labour Review*, 130(4), pp. 445–458.

Bottger, P.C., I.H. Hallein, & P.W. Yetton. 1985. "A cross-national study of leadership: Participation as a function of problem structure and leader power." *Journal of Management Studies*, 22(4), pp. 358–368.

Bournoise, F. 1992. "The impact of 1993 on management development in Europe." *International Studies of Management and Organization*, 22(1), Spring, pp. 7–29.

Bowie, N.E. 1990. "Business Ethics and cultural relativism." In P. Madsen & J.M. Shafritz (eds.) *Essentials of Business Ethics*. New York: Meridian.

Boyacigiller, N. 1990. "The role of expatriates in the management of interdependence, complexity and risk in multinational corporations." *The Journal of International Business Studies*, 21(3), Third Quarter, pp. 357–382.

Brady, F.N. 1990. *Ethical Managing: Rules and Results*. New York: Macmillian.

Briggs, N. & G. Harwood. 1982. "Training personnel in multinational businesses." *International Journal of Intercultural Relations*, vol. 6, pp. 341–354.

Briody, E.K. & J.B. Chrisman. 1991. "Cultural adaptation on overseas assignments." *Human Organization*, 50(3), pp. 264–282.

Bronstein, A.S. 1991. "Temporary work in Western Europe: Threat or complement to permanent employment?" *International Labour Review*, 130(3), pp. 291–310.

Brown, R. 1987. "How to choose the best expatriates." *Personnel Management*, June, p. 67.

Burke, R. & C.A. McKeen. 1988. "Work and family: What we know and what we need to know." *Canadian Journal of Administrative Sciences*, 59(4), pp. 30–40.

Business International Corporation. 1982. *Worldwide Executive Compensation and Human Resource Planning*. New York: Business International Corporation.

Campbell, A., A. Sorge, & M. Warner. 1990. "Technological change, product strategies and human resources: Defining Anglo-German differences." *Journal of General Management*, 159(3), pp. 39–54.

Child, J. 1972. "Organizational structure, environment and performance." *Sociology*, 6(1), pp. 1–22.

Colwill, N.L. & L. Temple. 1987. "Three jobs and two people: The dual career dilemma." *Business Quarterly*, 51, pp. 12–15.

Copeland, L. & L. Griggs. 1985. *Going International: How to Make Friends and Deal Effectively in the Global Marketplace*. New York: New American Library.

Cotton, J.L., D.B. McFarlin, & P.D. Sweeney. 1993. "A cross-national comparison of employee participation." *Journal of Managerial Psychology*, 8(1), pp. 10–19.

Daniels, J.D. 1986. "Approaches to European regional management by large U.S. multinational firms." *Management International Review*, 26(2), pp. 27–42.

De la Torre, J. & B. Toyne. 1978. "Cross-national managerial interaction: A conceptual model." *Academy of Management Review*, 3(3), pp. 462–474.

De la Torre, J. & B. Toyne. 1981. "Foreign investment conflict, regulations and negotiation." *Journal of International Business Studies*, 12(2), pp. 151–162.

Dorfman, P.W. & J.P. Howell. 1988. "Dimensions of national culture and effective leadership patterns: Hofstead revisited." *Advances in International Comparative Management*, 3, pp. 127–150.

Douglas, M. & J. Douglas. 1989. "Institutions of the third kind: British and Swedish labor markets compared." *Journal of General Management*, 14(4), pp. 34–52.

Dowling, P.J. & T.W. Nagel. 1986. "Nationality and work attitudes: A study of Australian and American business majors." *Journal of Management*, 12(1), pp. 121–128.

Dowling, P.J. & R.S. Schular. 1990. *International Dimensions of Human Resource Management*. Boston: PWS-Kent.

Doz, Y. & C.K. Prahalad. 1986. "Controlled variety: A challenge for human resource management in the MNC." *Human Resource Management*, 25(1), pp. 55–71.

Earley, P.C. 1993. "East meets West meets Mideast: Further explorations of collectivistic and individualistic work groups." *Academy of Management Journal*. 36(2), pp. 319–348.

Earley, P.C. 1987. "Interculture training for managers: A comparison of documentary and interpersonal methods." *Academy of Management Journal* 30(4), pp. 685–698.

Ebrahimpour, M. & J.B. Cullin. 1993. "Quality management in Japanese and American firms operating in the United States: A comparative study of styles and motivational beliefs." *Management International Review*, 33, First Quarter, pp. 23–38.

Edstron, A. & P. Lorange. 1984. "Matching strategy and human resources in multinational corporations." *Journal of International Business Studies*, 15(2), pp. 125–137.

Erden, D. 1988. "Impact of multinational companies on host countries: Executive training programs." *Management International Review*, 28(3), pp. 39–47.

Erez, M. & P.C. Earley. 1993. *Culture, Self-Identify and Work.* New York: Oxford University Press.

Evans, P. 1992. "Developing leaders and managing development." *European management Journal*, 10(1), March, pp. 1–9/

Evans, W.A., D. Sculli, & W.S. L. Yau. 1987. "Cross-cultural factors in the identification of managerial potential." *Journal of General Management*, 13(1), pp. 52–57.

Farmer, R. & E. McGoun (eds.). 1988. *Advances in International Comparative Management.* Greenwich, CT: JAI Press.

Feldman, D.C. & D.C. Thomas. 1992. "Career management issues facing expatriates." *Journal of International Business Studies*, 23(2), Second Quarter, pp. 271–294.

Feldman, D.C. & H.B. Thompson. 1993. "Expatration, repatriation, and domestic geographical relocation: An empirical investigation of adjustment to new job assignments." *Journal of International Business Studies*, 24(3), Third Quarter, pp. 507–530.

Ferraro, G.P. 1990. *The Cultural Dimension of International Business.* Englewood Cliffs, NJ: Prentice-Hall.

Fontaine, G. 1989. *Managing International Assignments: The Strategy for Success.* Englewood Cliffs, NJ: Prentice-Hall.

Furnham, A. & P. Stringfield. 1993. "Personality and occupational behavior: Myers-Briggs type indicator correlates of managerial practices in two cultures." *Human Relations*, 46(7), pp. 827–848.

Garland, J., R.N. Farmer, & M. Taylor. 1990. *International Dimensions of Business Policy and Strategy* (2nd ed.). Boston: PWS-Kent.

Gomez-Meija, L.R. 1984. "Effect of occupation on task related, contextual, and job involvement orientation: A cross-cultural perspective." *Academy of Management Journal* 27(4), pp. 706–720.

Gomez-Meija, L.R. & D.B. Bolkin. 1987. "The determination of managerial satisfaction with the expatriation and repatriation process." *Journal of Management Development*, 3(1), pp. 7–17.

Graham, J.L. 1992. "An empirical comparison of Soviet and American business negotiations." *Journal of International Business Studies*, 23(3), Third Quarter, pp. 387–418.

Graham, J.L. 1985. "The influence of culture on business negotiations: An exploratory study." *Journal of International Business Studies*, 16(1), pp. 81–96.

Graham, J.L. 1983. "Foreign corrupt practices: A manager's guide." *Columbia Journal of World Business*, Fall, pp. 89–94.

Graham, J.L. & R.A. Herberger. 1983. "Negotiators abroad—don't shoot from the hip." *Harvard Business Review*, July–August, pp. 160–168.

Gregersen, H.B. & J.S. Black, 1992. "Antecedents to commitment to a parent company and a foreign operations." *Academy of Management Journal*, 35(1), pp. 65–90.

Grove, C.L. & I. Torbiorn. 1985. "A new conceptualization of intercultural adjustment and the goals of training." *International Journal of Intercultural Relations*, 9(2), pp. 205–233.

Gutteridge, T.G., Z.B. Leibowitz, & J.E. Shore. 1993. *Organizational Career Development: Benchmarks for Building a World-Class Workforce*. San Francisco: Jossey-Bass.

Hall, E.T. 1977, *Beyond Culture*. New York: Anchor.

Hall, E.T. 1960. "The silent language in overseas business." *Harvard Business Reviews*, May–June, p. 87.

Harpaz, I. 1990. "The importance of work goals: An international perspective." *Journal of International Business Studies*, 21(1), pp. 75–93.

Harvey, M. 1993. "Empirical evidence of recurring international compensation problems." *Journal of International Business Studies*, 24(4), Fourth Quarter, pp. 785–800.

Harvey, M. 1985. "The executive family: An overlooked variable in international assignments." *Columbia Journal of World Business*, Spring, pp. 84–92.

Harvey, M. 1989. "Repatriation of corporate executives: An empirical study." *Journal of International Business Studies*, 20, pp. 121–144.

Haworth, D.A. & G.T. Savage. 1989. "A channel-ratio model of intercultural communication: The trains won't sell, fix them please." *Journal of Business Communications*, 26(3), pp. 231–254.

Heller, J.E. 1980. "Criteria for selecting an international manager." *Personnel*, May–June, pp. 47–55.

Hendon, D. & R.A. Hendon. 1990. *World Class Negotiating*. New York: John Wiley & Sons, Inc.

Heskin, A.D. & R.A. Heffner. 1987. "Learning about bilingual, multicultural organizing." *Journal of International Business Studies*, 14(2), pp. 75–90.

Hofstede, G. 1985. "The interaction between national and organization value systems." *Journal of Management Studies*, 22(4), pp. 347–357.

Howard, C.G. 1987. "Out of sight—not out of mind." *Personnel Administrator*, June, pp. 82–90.

Illman, P.E. 1980. "Motivating the overseas workforce." In *Developing Overseas Managers and Managers Overseas*. New York: AMACOM.

Ishidi, H. 1986. "Transferability of Japanese human resource management abroad." *Human Resource Management*, 259(1), pp. 103–120.

Ivancevich, J.M., R.S. DeFrank, & P.R. Gregory. 1992. "The Soviet enterprise director: An important resource before and after the coup." *Academy of Management Executive*, 6(1), pp. 42–54.

Izraeli, D.M. & Y. Zeira. 1993. "Women managers in international business: A research review and appraisal." *Business and the Contemporary World*, Summer, pp. 35–64.

Jaeger, A.M. 1984. "The appropriateness of organization development outside North America." *International Studies of Management and Organization*, 12(1), pp. 23–35.

Jaeger, A.M. 1984. "The transfer of organizational culture overseas: An approach to control in the multinational corporation." *Journal of International Business Studies*, 14(2), pp. 91–114.

Jelilnek, M. & N.J. Adler. 1983. "Women: world-class managers for global competition." *Academy of Management and Organization*, Spring–Summer, pp. 75–96.

Khardra, B. 1990. "The prophetic-caliphal model of leadership: An empirical study." *International Studies of Management and Organization*, 20(3), pp. 37–51.

Kirk, W.Q. & R.C. Maddox. 1988. "International management: The new frontier for woman." *Personnel*, 65, pp. 46–49.

Kirkbridge, P.S. & S.F.Y. Tang. 1990. "Negotiation: lessons from behind the bamboo curtain." *Journal of General Management*, 16(1), pp. 1–13.

Kobrin, S.J. 1988. "Expatriate reduction and strategic control in American multinational corporations." *Human Resource Management*, 27(1), pp. 63–75.

Kolodney, H. & T. Stjernberg. 1986. "The change process of innovative work designs: New design and redesign in Sweden, Canada, and the U.S." *Journal of Applied Behavioral Science*, 229(3), pp. 287–301.

Kremenyuk, V.A. (ed.). 1991. *International Negotiation: Analysis, Approaches, Issues*. San Francisco: Jossey-Bass.

Laabs, J.J. 1993. "Building a global management team." *Personnel Journal*, 72(8), August, p. 75.

Laaksonen, O. 1988. *Management in China*. New York: Walter de Gruyter.

Landis, D. & R.W. Brislin. 1983. *Handbook of Intercultural Training*, Vol. 1. New York: Pergamon Press.

Lane, H.W. & J.J. Distefano. 1992. *International Management Behavior* (2nd ed.). Boston: PWS-Kent.

Laurent, A. 1986. "The cross-cultural puzzle of international human resource management." *Human Resource Management*, 25(1), pp. 91–102.

Laurent, A. 1983. "The cultural diversity of Western conceptions of management." *International Studies of management and Organization*, Spring–Summer, pp. 75–96.

Lewis, S., D.N. Izraeli, & H. Hootsmans (eds.). 1992. *Dual-Earner Families—International Perspectives*. London: Sage Publications.

Lorange, P. 1986. "Human resource management in multinational cooperative ventures." *Human Resource Management*, 2591), pp. 133–148.

Luthans, F., H.S. McCaul, & N.G. Dodd. 1985. "Organizational commitment: A comparison of American Japanese, and Korean employees." *Academy of Management Journal*, 28(1), p. 213–219.

Martinez, J.I. & J.C. Jarillo. 1989. "The evolution of research on coordination mechanisms in multinational corporations." *Journal of International Business Studies*, 20(3), pp. 489–514.

Martinez, Z.L. & D.A. Ricks. 1989. "Multinational parent companies' influence over human resource decisions of affiliates: U.S. forms in Mexico." *Journal of International Business Studies*, 20(3), pp. 465–487.

Mautner-Markhof, F. 1989. *Processes of International Negotiations*. Boulder, CO: Westview Press.

McClelland, D.C. 1965. "Achievement motivation can be developed." *Harvard Business Review*, 43(6), pp. 6–24.

McClelland, D.C. & D.G. Winter. 1969. *Motivating Economic Achievement*. New York: The Free Press.

McCreary, D.R. 1986. *Japanese–U.S. Business Negotiations: A Cross-cultural Study*. New York: Praeger.

Mendenhall, M., E. Dunbar, & G. Oddou. 1989. "Expatriate selection, training and career-pathing: A review and critique." *Human Resource Management*, Fall, pp. 331–345.

Mendenhall, M. & G. Oddou. 1986. "Acculturation profiles of expatriate managers: Implications for cross-cultural training programs." *Columbia Journal of World Business*, Winter, pp. 73–79.

Mendenhall, M. & G. Oddou. 1985. "The dimensions of expatriate acculturation: A review." *Academy of Management Review*, 10(1), pp. 39–47.

Mendenhall, M. & G. Oddou. (1991). *International Human Resource Management*. Boston: PWS-Kent.

Mendenhall, M. & G. Oddou (eds.). 1991. *Readings and Cases in International Human Resource Management*. Boston: PWS-Kent.

Mendenhall, M. & C. Wiley. 1994. "Strangers in a strange land: The relationship between expatriate adjustment and impression management." *American Behavioral Scientist*, 37(5), pp. 605–620.

Moran, R.T. 1986. "Forget about gender, just get the job done." *International Management*, March, p. 72.

Napier, N.K. & R.B. Peterson. 1990. "Expatriate reentry: What do repatriates have to say?" *Human Resource Planning*, 14, pp. 19–28.

Naumann, E. 1992. "A conceptual model of expatriate turnover." *Journal of International Business Studies*, 23(3), Third Quarter, pp. 499–532.

Naumann, E. 1993. "Organizational predictors of expatriate job satisfaction." *Journal of International Business Studies*, 24(1), First Quarter, pp. 61–80.

Oddou, G. & M. Mendenhall. 1984. "Person perception in cross-cultural settings: A review of cross-cultural and related cognitive literature." *International Journal of Intercultural Relationa*, 8(1), pp. 77–96.

Oddou, G. & M. Mendenhall. 1994. "Succession planning for the 21st century: How well are we grooming our future business leaders?" *Business Horizons*, 34(1), pp. 26–34.

Okubayashi, K. 1989. "The Japanese industrial relations system." *Journal of General Management*, 14(3), pp. 67–88.

Ondrack, D. 1985. "International human-resource management in European and North American firms." *International Studies in Management and Organization*, 159(1), pp. 6–32.

Ondrack, D. (1985). "International transfers of managers in North American and European MNCs." *Journal of International Business Studies*, 16(3), Fall, pp. 1–19.

Ondrack, D. 1992/1993. "Internationalizing management education: Human resource management." *Journal of Business Administration*, 21(1,2), pp. 237–249.

Peterson, R.B. & H.F. Schwind. 1977. "A comparative study of personnel problems in international companies and joint ventures in Japan." *Journal of International Business Studies*, 8(1), pp. 796–804.

Peterson, R.B. & J. Sullivan. 1991. "Japan's lifetime employment: Wither is goest?" In S.B. Prasad *Advances in International Comparative Management*, Vol. 5. Greenwich, CT: JAI Press.

Popp, G.E., H.J. Davis, & T.T. Hebert. 1986. "An international study of intrinsic motivation composition." *Management International Review*, 26(3), pp. 28–35.

Poole, M. 1986. "Managerial strategies and 'styles' in industrial relations: A comparative analysis." *Journal of General Management*, 12(1), pp. 40–53.

Prahalad, C.K. 1990. "Globalization: the intellectual and managerial challenges." *Human Resource Management*, 29(1), pp. 27–37.

Prahalad, C.K. & Y. Doz. 1989. *The Multinational Mission: Balancing Local Demands and Global Vision*, New York: The Free Press.

Pucik, V. 1984. "White collar human resource management: a comparison of the U.S. and Japanese automobile industries." *Columbia Journal of World Business*, 19(3), pp. 87–94.

Pucik, V. & J.H. Katz. 1986. "Information, control, and human resource management in multinational firms." *Human Resource Management*, 25(1), pp. 121–132.

Puffer, S.M. 1994. "Understanding the bear: A portrait of Russian business leaders." *Academy of Management Executive*, 8(1), pp. 41–54.

Pulatie, D. 1985. "How do you ensure success of managers going abroad?" *Training & Development Journal*, December, pp. 22–24.

Punnett, B.J. 1989. *Experiencing International Management*. Boston: PWS-Kent.

Punnett, B.J. 1989. "International human resource management." In A. Rugman (ed.), *International Business in Canada.* Toronto: Prentice-Hall Canada.

Punnett, B.J. 1991. "Language, cultural values and preferred leadership style: A comparison of Anglophones and Francophones in Ottawa." *Canadian Journal of Behavioral Sciences*, 23(2), pp. 241–244.

Punnett, B.J., J. Singh, & G. Williams. 1994. "The relative influence of economic development and Anglo heritage on expressed values: Empirical evidence from a Caribbean country." Forthcoming in *International Journal of Intercultural Relations*.

Punnett, B.J. & S. Moore. 1993. "Expatriates and their spouses: A pilot study in the Limerick region, and direction for future research." *Irish Business Administration Research*, 14(2).

Punnett, B.J., O. Crocker, & M.A. Stevens. 1992. "The challenge for women expatriates and their spouses: Some empirical evidence." *International Journal of Human Resource Management*, 3(3), pp. 585–592.

Rajan, M.N. & J.L. Graham. 1991. "Nobody's grandfather was a merchant: Understanding the Soviet commercial negotiating process and style." *California Management Review*, Spring, pp. 40–57.

Randall, D.M. 1993. "Cross-cultural research on organizational commitment: A review and application of Hofstede's value survey module." *Journal of Business Research*, 26(1), January, pp. 91–110.

Reiss, M. 1987. "Diagnosis in management: A comparative analysis of approaches to management integration." *Management International Review*, 27(1), pp. 67–79.

Ronen, S. 1986. *Comparative and Multinational Management.* New York: John Wiley & Sons, Inc.

Ronen, S. & A.I. Kraut. 1977. "Similarities among countries based on employee work values and attitudes." *Columbia Journal of World Business*, 12(2), pp. 89–96.

Ronan, S. & O. Shenkar. 1985. "Clustering countries on attitudinal dimensions: A review and synthesis." *Academy of Management Review*, 10(3), pp. 435–454.

Ronen, S. & O. Shenkar. 1988. "Using employee attitudes to establish MNC regional divisions." *Personnel*, 65(8), pp. 32–39.

Rossman, M.L. 1990. *The International Businesswoman of the 1990s—A Guide to Success in the Global Marketplace*. New York: Praeger.

Scarcella, R., E. Andersen, & S. Krashen (eds.). 1989. *Developing Communicative Competence in a Second Language*. Rowley, MA: Newbury House Publishers.

Schular, R.S. 1993. "World class HR departments: Six critical issues." *The Singapore Accounting and Business Review*, Inaugural Issue, September.

Schular, R.S. 1994. "Human resource management: Domestic to global." Forthcoming in M. Warner (ed.) *International Encyclopedia of Business and Management*. London: Routeledge.

Schwind, H.F. & R.B. Peterson. 1985. "Shifting personal values in the Japanese management system." *International Studies of Management and Organization*, 15(2), pp. 60–74.

Sekaran, U. 1986. *Dual-Career Families: Contemporary Organizational and Counseling Issues*. San Francisco: Jossey-Bass.

Shama, A. 1993. "Management under fire: The transformation of managers in Soviet Union and Eastern Europe." *Academy of Management Executive*, 7(1), pp. 22–34.

Shenkar, O. & S. Ronen. 1987. "The cultural context of negotiations: The implications of Chinese interpersonal norms." *Journal of Applied Behavioral Science*, 23(2), pp. 263–275.

Shenkar, O. & Y. Zeira. 1987. "Human resource management in international joint ventures: Directions for research." *Academy of Management Review*, 12(3), pp. 546–557.

Shumsky, N.J. 1993. "Keeping track of global managers." *Human Resource Professional*, 5(4), Spring, pp. 6–9.

Stening, B.W. & M.R. Hammer. 1992. "Cultural baggage and the adaption of expatriate American and Japanese managers." *Management International Review*, 329(1), First Quarter, pp. 77–89.

Stone, R. 1991. "Expatriate selection and failure." *Human Resource Planning*, 14(1), pp. 9–18.

Sullivan J.J. 1986. "Human nature, Organizations, and management theory." *Academy of Management International Review*, 11(3), pp. 6–10.

Sullivan, J., R.B. Persons, N. Kameda, & J. Shimada. 1981. "The relationship between conflict resolution approaches and trust: A cross-cultural study." *Academy of Management Journal*, 24(4), pp. 803–815.

Szalay, L. 1981. "Intercultural communication—a process model." *International Journal of Intercultural Relations*, 5, pp. 133–146.

Taylor, A.S. & J.W. Lounsbury. 1988. "Dual-career couples and geographic transfer: Executives reaction to commuter marriage and attitude toward the move." *Human Relations*, 41(5), pp. 407–424.

Teargarden, M.B. & M.A. Von Glinow. 1990. "Contextual determinants of HRM effectiveness in cooperative alliances: Mexican evidence." *Management International Review*, 30, Special Issue, pp. 23–36.

Thomas, R.R., Jr. 1990. "From affirmative action to affirming diversity." *Harvard Business Review*, March–April, pp. 107–117.

Torbiorn, I. 1982. *Living Abroad: Personal Adjustment and Personnel Policy in the Overseas Setting*. New York: John Wiley & Sons.

Torrington, D. & N. Holden. 1992. "Human resource management and the international challenge of change." *Personnel Review*, 2(2), pp. 19–30.

Towsend, A.M., K.D. Scott, & S.E. Markham. 1990. "An examination of country and culture-based differences in compensation practices." *Journal of International Business Studies*, 21(4), Fourth Quarter, pp. 541–564.

Toyne, B. 1987. *Host Country Managers of MNCs*. New York: Arno Press.

Toyne, B. & R.J. Kuhne. 1983. "The management of the international executive compensation and benefits process." *Journal of International Business Studies*, 14(32), pp. 37–50.

Triandis, H.C. "Cross-cultural industrial and organization psychology." In M.D. Dunnette (ed.) *Handbook of Industrial and Organizational Psychology*, 4. Palo Alto, CA: Consulting Psychologists Press, in press.

Tung, R. 1988. "Career issues in international assignments." *Academy of Management Executive*, August, pp. 241–244.

Tung, R. 1987. "Expatriate assignments: Enhancing success and minimizing failure." *Academy of Management Executive*, May, pp. 117–126.

Tung, R. 1984. "How to negotiate with the Japanese." *California Management Review*, Summer, pp. 62–77.

Tung, R. 1984. "Human resource planning in Japanese multinationals: A model for U.S. firms." *Journal of International Business Studies*, Fall, pp. 139–149.

Tung, R. 1988. *The New Expatriates: Managing Human Resources Abroad*, Cambridge, MA: Ballinger.

Tung, R. 1981. "Selection and training of personnel for overseas assignments." *Columbia Journal of World Business*, 16(1), pp. 68–78.

Tung, R. 1984. "Strategic management of human resources in the multinational enterprise." *Human Resource Management*, 23(2), pp. 129–143.

Ueno, I., R.R. Blake, & J.S. Mouton. 1984. "The productivity battle: A behavioral science analysis of Japan and the United States." *Journal of Applied Behavioral Science*, 20(1), pp. 49–56.

Ulrich, W.L. 1984. "HRM and culture: History, ritual, and myth." *Human Resource Management*, 23(2), pp. 117–128.

Von Glinow, M.A. & M.B. Teagarden. 1988. "The transfer of human resource management technology in Sino-U.S. cooperative ventures: Problems and solutions." *Human Resource Management*, 27(2), pp. 201–227.

Watanabe, S. (1991). "The Japanese quality control circles: Why it works." *International Labour Review*, 130(1), pp. 57–80.

Watson, W.E., K. Kumar, & L.K. Michaelsen. 1993. "Cultural diversity impact on interaction process and performance: Comparing homogeneous and diverse task groups." *Academy of Management Journal*, 36(3), pp. 590–602.

Weiss, S.E. 1994. "Negotiating with 'Romans' — Part I." *Sloan Management Review*, 35(2), pp. 51–61.

Weiss, S.E. 1994. "Negotiating with 'Romans' — Part II." *Sloan Management Review*, 35(3).

Weiss-Wik, S. 1983. "Enhancing negotiators successfulness." *Journal of Conflict Resolution*, 27(4), pp. 706–739.

Welsh, D.H.B., F. Luthans, & S.M. Sommer. 1993. "Managing Russian factory workers: The impact of U.S.-based behavioral and participative techniques." *Academy of Management Journal*, 36(1), pp. 58–79.

West, M. & E. Moore. 1989. "Undocumented workers in the United States and South Africa: A comparative study of changing control." *Human Organization*, 48(1), pp. 1–10.

Wiersema, M.F. & A. Bird. 1993. "Organizational demography in Japanese firms: Group heterogeneity, individual dissimilarity, and top management team turnover." *Academy of Management Journal*, 36(5), pp. 996–1025.

Zeira, Y. & M. Banai. 1984. "Present and desired methods of selecting expatriate managers for international assignments." *Personnel Review*, 13(2), pp. 29–35.

Zeira, Y. & M. Banai. 1987. "Selecting managers for foreign assignments." *Management Decision*, 25(4), pp. 38–40.

Zeira, Y. & M. Banai. 1985. "Selection of expatriate managers in MNC's: The host environment point of view." *International Studies of Management and Organization*. 15(1), pp. 33–51.

CAREERS IN

INTERNATIONAL

BUSINESS

CULTURE AND
CAREER MANAGEMENT

CAREER OPPORTUNITIES
IN INTERNATIONAL
BUSINESS

LEADING BUSINESS
SCHOOLS IN THE U.S.

LEADING BUSINESS
SCHOOLS IN SELECTED
COUNTRIES OUTSIDE OF
THE U.S.

SPECIALTY PROGRAMS

JOB PROSPECTS

REFERENCES

627

CULTURE AND CAREER MANAGEMENT

Companies' career-management systems often reflect cultural values of the nation where the company is headquarted. Some cultures assume that people can be evaluated on individual performance measures while other cultures assume that only groups of people—not individuals—can and should be evaluated. Cultures that share assumptions that individuals should be evaluated may construct career-management systems that differ due to differences in cultural values regarding privacy. For example, the British feel that performance information about people is too personal to input into a computer file where who knows who would have access to it (Schneider 1988). Conversely, many French companies make use of highly technical computer programs to track the career progress and evaluations of their managers. Thus, it should not be surprising to see differences between countries in terms of how managers' careers are managed. Brooke Derr (1987) studies how companies in Germany, France, Great Britain, Sweden, and Switzerland managed their "fast-track" managers. His results (given below) reflect different cultural philosophies.

1. GERMANY: Companies have fewer institutionalized career-management programs due to the bureaucratic nature of their organizational structures. Innovation and "standing out from the crowd" disrupts the clear, bureaucratic chain of command; thus people progress in their careers based upon their ability to move up the chain of command, not on their ability to challenge it with innovative ideas. Innovation comes from within set, organizational units, such as R&D, not from individuals. German firms tend to focus on accountability for performance and ensuring the organization runs smoothly.

Germans value technical expertise, thus it is possible for someone who is a technical specialist (such as an engineer) to rise on the corporate ladder to the highest levels. Such people demonstrate their technical expertise over long time periods in the firm compared to other countries. This approach also reflects a stricter merit system for career advancement compared to other countries—German specialists must prove their worth by performance.

2. FRANCE: Derr found that French firms value the career paths of managers, and often have complex, highly computerized systems to gather and evaluate information about fast-track managers. French companies strongly value certain academic backgrounds for their fast-track managers; however, once a manager fails or somehow loses status, he/she is no longer considered as being on the fast track. In France, it seems there is little margin for career setbacks if one is trying to climb to the upper echelons of the company. French companies rely on performance reviews, succession planning, and career-pathing systems to track their fast trackers. Thus, the French take a systems approach rather than an "informal, personal-recommendation" approach to career management.

French managers interviewed in another study "felt that their careers had been mapped out for them on the day they completed their higher education. They could also foresee how their careers would unfold and where their promotional ceiling would be, irrespective of their career aspirations" (Barsoux & Lawrence 1991, p. 6). For a manager to continue to rise in a French firm, it is necessary to start out as a specialist, but then fairly early in one's career branch out and be seen as a generalist, with a general-manager perspective.

3. GREAT BRITAIN: Firms have typically valued the generalist type of manager. Typically, the manager would come from an elite university, be a "gentleman," able to converse about philosophy, classical literature, and history, and approach business problems from a broad perspective. However, Great Britain is in a transition time regarding career-management systems, and some companies are looking at on the job individual performance and downplaying social, academic background, and traits not related specifically to the job. For years British management has been skeptical of technical business or engineering training as an important prerequisite for effective management—a classical education was seen as a more appropriate training for a general manager.

Derr found that most British firms do have technical career-management systems in place, but that informal career-management systems are also in place.

For example, a manager with a proven track record measured by the technical career-management system may not be promoted because he/she may not have a proper speech accent, highly refined table manners, or conversational skills. Fitting into a strong corporate culture still holds some sway in climbing the ladder in Great Britain.

4. SWEDEN: Swedish companies have the fewest technical career-management programs, compared to all other national groups Derr studied. If a manager is valued for his/her potential, Swedish companies will spend money on sending the manager to training and development programs. Social democracy is a strong value in Swedish companies, thus the idea of isolating a group of fast trackers is seen as a negative organizational practice, elevating people in status over others. Derr goes on to observe that in Sweden social equality is are strong value, and many people prefer not to become a manager because there are few rewards—the job often comes with little power and authority. In Sweden, having more authority than other people is not seen as being particularly desirable.

5. SWITZERLAND: The Swiss value fast-track managers and keep track of them with technical career-management systems. The unique aspect to Swiss career management, however, is the degree to which the Swiss keep separate career and personal issues. Derr found the Swiss scored the lowest in valuing an employee who balances his/her professional career against his/her private life. Swiss companies also scored the highest in neglecting to take into account a manager's personal life issues when making career decisions about that manager.

As the country-specific information above shows, different cultures require different traits for successful careers in business. However, there are similarities between cultures as well. Sally Stewart and Chong Chung Him (1990) looked at what made for successful careers in the People's Republic of China and the United States. For the PRC, the traits were:

1. Interpersonal relationship skills; an ability to maintain harmonious relationships with all the people with whom managers come into contact.

2. Training; especially in the areas of engineering, management, and foreign languages.

3. Hard work; being willing to sacrifice personal enjoyment and leisure and give extra effort to work.

4. Luck; career advancement as a result of unforeseen external and internal opportunities.

5. Willingness to take risks and make personal commitments.

6. Competence.

7. Loyalty and seniority in the organization.

8. Aggressiveness; a strong desire to achieve and a determination to get to the top.

Now consider the top ten key elements of career development in the U.S. that were found by Margerison and Kakabadse (1993):

1. A need to achieve results.

2. An ability to work easily with a wide range of people.

3. The desire to take on challenges.

4. A willingness to take risks.

5. Early overall responsibility for important tasks.

6. A breadth of experience in many functions prior to age 35.

7. A desire to seek new opportunities.

8. Leadership experience early in one's career.

9. An ability to develop more ideas than other colleagues.

10. A basic desire to determine the central strategy of an organization according to one's own principles.

It is important to note the overlap between the cultures in terms of key career skills (willingness to take risks, "people" skills, achievement orientation) and those that did not overlap (luck, loyalty, seniority).

CAREER OPPORTUNITIES IN INTERNATIONAL BUSINESS

Students often ask the following types of questions about working in international business: Are there entry-level positions in international business for students? In what fields do they exist, and which companies are prone to hire international business majors? What are the chances of receiving an overseas assignment? Do the same opportunities exist for foreign graduates as for North American graduates? Do the same opportunities exist for women as well as for men? What skills in the international business areas are employers most interested in? (Gillespie 1986).

For students interested in pursuing careers in international business, there are a variety of approaches that can fulfill their goals. There is no one best way to achieve this aim—one can chart a highly individualized course toward the goal. However, with this flexibility comes a lack of institutional guidance—both from universities and from companies—as to how to best prepare oneself to work internationally. Consider the following strategies, which have worked for gaining employment in the global business arena.

Strategy 1: Start your own business.

For those of the entrepreneurial bent, there are a variety of ways to work internationally. Starting an import/export business, or manufacturing products offshore and then selling them in the home country are two ways in which entrepreneurs and small businesses can operate in the international realm. For example, the owner of an antique reproduction store in Georgia travels twice a year to Taiwan to restock his inventory. In the past he has also travelled to Hong Kong and South Korea, and in the future plans to visit the PRC. His work requires that he be in frequent contact with Southeast Asian merchants, understand how to negotiate with people from other cultures, and be knowledgeable about the worldwide industry in which his business operates. Though he spends most of his time in the U.S., his business is strongly linked to others in foreign countries.

Strategy 2: Work in a not-for-profit organization.

There are a variety of not-for-profit organizations that operate internationally, many of which are human aid, religious, or human rights organizations. One such organization is World Vision, whose mission is to give relief and various kinds of assistance to others all over the world. It has significant numbers of expatriates all over the world overseeing its operations, as well as a corporate headquarters staff who ensure that financial and administrative controls are in place and working. Additionally, a fundraising arm of the organization seeks contributions so that the organization's work can continue. Obviously, such an organization gives one ample opportunity to be involved in working in the international arena, as well as the benefit of knowing that one's work is making a difference in the lives of others.

Strategy 3: Work for a governmental agency.

Government agencies in the areas of national security, defense, foreign aid, intelligence, and diplomacy all require people who are proficient in knowledge of international affairs. The most straightforward way to work internationally in this approach would be to join the military and seek specialized training there, in areas that would increase the probability of a foreign posting. Another direct approach (if you are American) would be to join the Peace Corps or a similar volunteer organization that would train you and send you overseas to work. Many North Americans find themselves living and working overseas because their careers are in government-related industries.

Strategy 4: Work in a company that has international operations.

Many students want to work for a multinational corporation (or a firm with overseas subsidiaries) that will allow them to live and work overseas or will assign them to work in areas requiring travel overseas from time to time. There is no agreed-upon approach among North American companies about who they will groom to become their international business specialists. A student who is full of desire to work on international projects can be hired by such a company but may never be assigned to work in an internationally-related area of the company. Conversely, in many European and Asian companies, a overseas assignment is an important step to moving up the management hierarchy, and it is clear what one has to do to merit an overseas assignment. North American companies are now gradually making more strategic use of expatriates.

It is important to understand that now and in the future, it is probable that business students will have many chances to work in a cross-cultural/international context in their jobs. Gary F. Kohut summarizes this condition of the business world:

> . . . few careers exist today that have no international implications. Over 40,000 businesses people from the United States and Canada now live and work overseas. many more are employed by the 35,000 North American businesses involved in exporting. About 2 million people work in the United States and Canada for foreign employers. Whether students plan to or not, chances are good that at some point in there careers, they will be involved in some kind of international business activity. (1986, p. 4)

If one adds family members to the expatriates Kohut mentions, and also includes expatriates and their families who are in the government and not-for-profit industries, the number of North Americans who live and work overseas reaches the hundreds of thousands. Also not included in his statement are the thousands of North Americans who travel overseas on short-term business trips.

With so much foreign investment in the U.S., it is difficult to avoid doing business with people from other countries and cultures, even if one never leaves the confines of Canada and the U.S. Numerous companies who manufacture parts for a variety of industries are having to make adjustments to how they do business. For example, there are over 600 Japanese companies in the state of Tennessee alone who do business differently from their American clients. Thus, many people in North America will find themselves dealing with foreign business people as a matter of course.

We list here two specific approaches (both regarding Strategy 4) to prepare for international work, though neither approach can be said to ensure that one will work and live overseas, or even that one will find work that is significantly international in nature. The reader must evaluate these strategies against his/her personality characteristics, risk-orientation, financial resources, and career goals.

1. After completion of an undergraduate degree, seek employment in a large multinational firm and be patient. Over the years as promotions ensue, volunteer or let it be know that you are interested in working in the international division of the company or in some area in the company that is heavily involved in international business. This approach requires patience and the gradual building of technical expertise on the part of the person who desires to work internationally, but for many this approach will pay off.

2. Another approach is to take graduate study at a school of business that has a strong international dimension to its curriculum. Then, upon graduation, seek employment with a firm that will utilize your knowledge and expertise in international business. Historically, most North American MBA programs have focused on how domestic businesses operate; relatively few programs have strong international elements in this course work.

LEADING BUSINESS SCHOOLS IN THE U.S.

It is difficult to objectively measure quality in MBA programs, though some studies are reported to give the student a starting point in his/her research about graduate work in international business. There are many issues that must be considered when selecting a graduate program, and an advisor in university job-placement offices or career-advisory centers can discuss these issues in depth with the interested student.

Ball and McCulloch (1988) surveyed international business professors across the U.S. to get their opinions about which colleges offered the best international business programs. They were asked to rank the top ten schools in the U.S., based on the quality of international business programs at the graduate level. The survey results yielded the following ranking of graduate programs in international business:

1. New York University

2. University of South Carolina

3. Wharton (University of Pennsylvania)

4. Columbia University

5. Harvard University

6. University of Michigan

7. American Graduate School of International Management (Thunderbird)

8. Indiana University

9. UCLA

10. University of Washington

11. George Washington University

12. MIT

13. Stanford

14. University of Texas, Austin

15. Berkeley

16. University of Southern California

17. Georgia State University

18. Ohio State University

19. Pennsylvania State University

20. Northwestern

21. Georgetown University

22. University of North Carolina

23. University of Illinois

24. University of Miami

25. Florida International University

It should be noted that this survey was published in 1988; if the survey was conducted today, the rankings would probably change. Nevertheless, it is a good starting point for the student interested in researching international business programs at the graduate level. The rankings are based on how many first place votes, second place votes, and so on, each program garnered in the survey. There are excellent MBA programs in countries outside of the U.S., and Ball and McCulloch asked their respondents to rank these programs separately. Some of these institutions are located in countries where the primary language is not English although their courses are taught in English (for example, INSEAD, and International University of Japan).

Lee Nehrt (1987) attempted to devise a study that would rely less on faculty perceptions of excellence and more on other criteria when ranking international business programs. Nehrt used a wide range of criteria and the results are given in Exhibit A.1.

This study's findings came under some criticism, and, in 1989, Nehrt offered a summary of his updated findings, based upon some of these criticisms only to the lack of data, New York University, Baylor, and Northwestern were dropped from the study. His summary table is given in Exhibit A.2, showing the rank of each school in each category, with 1 being highest and 27 the lowest.

Based upon his study, in 1989 Nehrt gave his overall rankings of international business graduate programs as follows:

1 . University of South Carolina

2 . American Graduate School of International Management (Thunderbird)

3 . George Washington University

4 . Indiana University

5 . Georgia State University

6 . University of New Mexico

7 . Georgetown University

8 . Brigham Young University

EXHIBIT A.1

THE RANKING OF MASTERS PROGRAMS IN INTERNATIONAL BUSINESS

School	GMAT Average	% Foreign Students	Average Age	% of 1985 Grads MBA	% of 1985 MBA Grads with IB Majors	Other	Intro to IB	Int'l Mgmt.	Int'l Mktg.	Int'l Corp. Fin.	Int'l Acctg.	Int'l Banking	Comp. Mgmt.	Comp. Labor	Comp. Bus. Sys.	Area Studies	IB Law	IB Negotiations	IB Seminar	Int'l Transportation	IB Strategy	IB Courses Required for Major	Required Non-Business Courses
AISTM (Thunderbird)	510	26%	25	—	—	MIM — 893	x	x	x	x	x	x	x	x	x	8	x	x	x	x	x	5	Cross-cultural courses + 3 area courses in Pol. Sci. history, econ. dev., etc.
Alabama	550	9%	25	40	2	None	x	x	x	x	x						x					5	None
American University	525	18%	27	219	18	7 grads MS in IB	x	x	x	x	x	x					x		x			4	None
Baylor	532	5%	25	107	?	6 grads MIM			x	x		x	x									3	4 courses in pol. sci.
Brigham Young	563	7%	27	295	7	None	x	x	x	x	x		x									3	None
Columbia	620	16%	25	639	57	None	x	x	x	x	x					2			x		x	4	None
CUNY (Baruch)	510	9%	28	378	11	3 grads MBA in IM	x	x	x	x			x				x	x	x	x	x	5	None
Georgetown	579	22%	26	62	58	None		x	x	x	x		x			4		x				3	None
George Washington	531	17%	26	670	84	18 grads MA in IB	x	x	x	x	x		x					x	x			5	None
Georgia State	538	40%	28	?	31	None	x	x	x	x	x				x		x		x			5	None
Hawaii	546	13%	29	104	?	None	x	x	x	x	x			x		x						4	None
Houston	556	12%	27	550	40	None	x	x	x	x	x					3	x		x			3	None
Indiana University	576	12%	25	271	30	None	x	x	x	x	x	x	x	x		5		x	x			4	None
MIT	640	20%	26	?	?	MS in IB	x	x	x	x						x						4	None
Monterey	528	20%	25	48	48	None	x	x	x	x	x	x	x		x	3	x	x	x		x	5	One regional course
New Mexico	540	15%	30	112	9	4 grads IB in Lat. Amer.	x	x	x	x	x	x	x	x			x		x			5	For IB in Lat. Amer. needs 2 Lat. Am. courses
NYU	591	25%	28	998	120	None	x	x	x	x	x	x				x	x					4	None
Northwestern	619	11%	28	300	50	None	x	x	x	x	x											3	None
Notre Dame	533	25%	23	142	27	None	x	x		x		x	x			x			x			6	None
Ohio State	584	21%	25	150	5	6 grads MBA in IB	x	x	x	x	x	x	x	x				x			x	3	None
Pennsylvania State	?	14%	25	140	5	1 grad MS in IB		x		x			x						x		x	3	None
St. Louis	494	12%	26	200	12	None		x	x	x	x	x				x	x					5	None
Southern California	583	14%	26	400	7	None		x			x	x	x			3			x			3	None
South Carolina (MIBS)	556	19%	28	305	None	138 grads MIBS	x	x	x	x	x	x	x	x			x	x	x	x	x	8	2 courses
Temple	550	10%	28	241	12	2 grads MS in IB — 7 courses	x	x	x	x	x	x	x	x		3	x		x	x		4	None
Texas-Austin	599	10%	25	376	40	None	x	x	2	x	x	x	x			3	3		x		x	3	None
Texas-Dallas	521	35%	25	380	8	31 grads MA in IB	x	x	x	x	x		x			6			x	x		5	None
Toledo	500	11%	29	136	5	None	x	x		x	x	x				3		x	x	x		3	None
Washington	586	16%	28	225	15	None	x	x	x	x	x		x			x	x		x			3	None
Wisconsin	567	11%	25	400	14	None	x	x	x	x	x			x								3	None

EXHIBIT A.1 (continued)
THE RANKING OF MASTERS PROGRAMS IN INTERNATIONAL BUSINESS

School	IB Computer Games?	Foreign language Required?	# of IB Executives as visiting lecturers	Special Programs for IB Majors	Majors	Minors	No. of IB faculty?	% of faculty with Ph.D. major in IB	% of faculty with Ph.D. minor in IB	% with work experience minor in IB	Average years teaching abroad	% with Foreign Language Competence	Average No. of IB books published	Average No. of IB articles published
AGSIM (Thunderbird)	FORAD; MARK STRAT; AGRIBUS; IB Policy Game; Int'l Bank Mgmt.	15 credit hours	75	Winterim seminars on selected IB subjects	No	No	29	10%	14%	55%	1.0	55%	0.3	2.1
Alabama	Multinat'l Mgmt/Hoskins	No	3		No	4	5	20%	20%	20%	0	60%	0	2
American University	None	No	30	IB coop Educ. Placements	No	No	6	33%	0%	83%	2.3	83%	1	9
Baylor	None	Yes	10	—	No	No	3	?	?	83%	?	?	?	?
Brigham Young	INTOP	No	5	—	No	No	5	40%	20%	100%	1	100%	1.8	3
Columbia	None	No	?	—	No	No	8	25%	0%	38%	1.5	38%	0.2	6.2
CUNY (Baruch)	None	No	5	—	No	No	8	25%	13%	75%	0.5	75%	3.5	21
Georgetown	GETI ONE	No	8	NCEIS Internships & Fellowships	No	No	3	33%	67%	33%	0.1	67%	4	17
George Washington	None	No	45	—	28	17	11	45%	18%	55%	3	82%	1.5	17
Georgia State	Multi-nat. Mgt. Game	No	6	—	11	0	2	50%	0%	50%	3	100%	0.5	8.5
Hawaii	Multi-nat. Bus. Game	No	?	Study in Japan; Certificate for study in PAMI	No	No	10	8%	8%	42%	3	67%	0.8	18
Houston	None	No	4	Summer courses in UK	No	No	2	0%	0%	?	1	?	1.5	7
Indiana University	INTOP	No	10	—	15	15	7	57%	0%	29%	1.8	71%	4	5.5
MIT	None	No	6	—	4	0	2	50%	0%	100%	0.4	100%	1.5	19
Monterey	None	12 credit hours	10	—	No	No	4	25%	0%	50%	0.8	75%	0	17
New Mexico	INTOP	Yes	15	—	No	No	6	0%	0%	67%	2.5	83%	0.8	1.5
NYU	None	No	?	—	30	20	18	?	?	?	?	?	?	4
Northwestern	None	No	3	—	No	No	3	?	?	?	?	?	?	?
Notre Dame	None	No	4	1 year at London, Eng., campus	No	No	1	0	0%	0%	1	100%	0	0.8
Ohio State	None	No	3	—	11	6	5	60%	0%	80%	0.4	80%	1.8	7
Pennsylvania State	None	No	4	—	3	1	3	100%	0%	67%	0.3	100%	1	14
St. Louis	FORAD	No	10	—	3	2	4	50%	0%	25%	0	25%	0.8	5

EXHIBIT A.1 (continued)
THE RANKING OF MASTERS PROGRAMS IN INTERNATIONAL BUSINESS

School	IB Computer Games?	Foreign language Required?	Special Programs for IB Majors	# of 18 Executives as visiting lecturers	PH. D Majors	DBA Majors	No. of 18 faculty?	% of faculty with Ph.D. major in 18	% of faculty with Ph.D. minor in 18	% with work experience in 18	Average years teaching abroad	% with Foreign Language Competence	Average No. of 18 books published	Average No. of 18 articles published
Southern California	Strategic Planning Simulator	No	Pacific Rim Mgmt. programs	?	No	No	8	13%	0%	75%	1.5	63%	1.2	6
South Carolina (MIBS)	MARKSTRAT	18 weeks intensive — 6 ct. hrs.	6-month Overseas internships	30	17	17	11	55%	9%	64%	1	82%	2.2	16
Temple	None	Yes	—	6	5	4	6	17%	33%	17%	0.1	67%	1	4.5
Texas-Austin	INTOP	No	—	4	5	3	9	11%	11%	33%	2.2	89%	0.6	7
Texas-Dallas	None	No	Summer courses in China	20	11		7	29%	0%	57%	0	71%	0.6	4
Toledo	None	No	No	12	No	No	6	67%	0%	67%	0.3	100%	1.2	10
Washington	None	No	—	10	4	12	4	50%	0%	25%	2	50%	2	13
Wisconsin	None	No	—	8	8	2	4	0%	0%	75%	0.5	100%	0.5	7

A number of schools have unique courses that are not included in the table, as follows:

AGSIM (Thunderbird): International Marketing Research; International Industrial Marketing (2); Cross-Cultural Communications (2); Managing MNC-Government Conflict; Political Risk and Global Change; International Consumer Marketing (2); International Insurance (2); Export-Import Management; International Advertising.

Alabama: Import-Export Management.

CUNY (Baruch): Export-Import Documentation and Finance; International Commodity Trading; Comparative Marketing Systems; International Financial Markets.

George Washington: International Financial Markets; International Marketing Systems; International Portfolio Management.

Georgia State: International Insurance; International Real Estate.

Hawaii: International Capital Markets; Japanese Financial Markets.

MIT: International Transfer of Technology.

Monterey: International Trade Management; International Advertising; International Marketing Research.

New Mexico: Cross-Cultural Organizational Behavior.

NYU: International Taxation; Economics of MNC Operations; International Financial Marketing; International Treasury Management; International Security Analysis; International Advertising Management; International Marketing Research.

Temple: International Insurance.

Texas-Austin: Taxation of International Business; Cross-Cultural Management; I.B. Communications.

Washington: Competitive National Policies.

2 In counting the number of I.B. faculty, only regular, full-time faculty who have taught on I.B. course during the past 3 years are included.

3 In counting publications, only those books and articles which were on the subject of I.B., using the same definition as that used by JIBS, were included. Also, only articles published in journals or proceedings were included.

4 The data taken from the questionnaires received, refers to student data for 1985, and course and faculty data for the academic year 1985-86. The questionnaire was administered in the Spring of 1986.

SOURCE:
Nehrt, L.C. 1987. "The Ranking of Master Programs in International Business." *Journal of International Business Studies*, Fall. pp. 91-99.

EXHIBIT A.2

THE RANKING OF MASTERS PROGRAMS IN INTERNATIONAL BUSINESS

Universities (columns): 1 AACSM · 2 Alabama · 3 American · 4 Brigham Young · 5 Columbia · 6 CUNY · 7 Georgetown · 8 Geo Washington · 9 Georgia State · 10 Hawaii · 11 Houston · 12 Indiana · 13 MIT · 14 Monterey · 15 New Mexico · 16 Notre Dame · 17 Ohio State · 18 Penn State · 19 St. Louis · 20 So. Cal. · 21 So. Carolina · 22 Temple · 23 Tex-Austin · 24 Tex-Dallas · 25 Toledo · 26 Washington · 27 Wisconsin

Rankings for Each Criterion	1	2	3	4	5	6	7	8	9	10	11	12	13	14	15	16	17	18	19	20	21	22	23	24	25	26	27
Size of Ph.D. Program in I.B.	27	12	27	27	27	27	1	6	27	27	3	12	27	27	4	27	12	11	27	2	9	10	6	27	5	27	8
Aver No. of I.B. Articles per Faculty	25	26	10	24	17	1	4	1	3	14	19	2	4	27	22	14	7	20	18	6	21	14	22	9	8	14	
Aver No. of I.B. Books per Faculty	23	27	14	6	27	3	1	9	21	17	9	1	9	27	17	6	14	17	11	4	14	19	19	11	5	21	
% of I.B. Faculty with Foreign Lang Ability	22	22	9	4	24	14	18	11	4	18	27	16	4	14	9	4	13	4	25	21	11	18	8	16	4	23	4
Average No. of Years I.B. Faculty have Taught Abroad	12	27	4	12	8	17	23	12	1	1	12	7	19	16	3	12	19	21	27	8	12	23	5	27	21	6	17
% of I.B. Faculty with Work Experience in I.B.	13	24	3	1	18	6	19	13	15	17	27	21	1	15	9	27	4	9	22	6	11	25	19	12	9	22	6
% of I.B. Faculty with Ph.D. in I.B.	20	14	16	6	18	15	1	5	11	22	27	8	11	18	27	6	2	11	23	4	11	15	17	3	11	27	
No. of I.B. Full-Time Faculty	1	16	12	16	7	7	22	2	25	4	25	9	25	19	12	27	16	22	19	7	2	12	5	9	12	19	19
I.B. Execs as Guest Speakers	1	24	3	17	26	17	12	2	15	25	21	9	15	9	6	21	24	21	9	26	3	15	21	5	7	9	12
Special I.B. Programs	2	27	5	27	27	27	9	27	27	3	6	27	27	27	4	27	27	8	1	27	6	27	27	27			
No. of Intl Non-Business Courses Required	1	27	27	27	27	27	27	27	27	27	27	3	4	27	27	27	27	2	27	27	27	27	27	27			
No. of I.B. Courses Required	7	7	15	22	14	7	7	7	7	14	23	14	14	7	7	2	22	22	7	22	1	14	7	22	22	22	
Foreign Language Required	2	27	27	4	27	27	27	27	27	27	3	27	27	27	27	1	4	27	27	27	27	27	27				
No. of I.B. Games	1	6	27	6	27	27	6	27	6	6	27	6	6	6	27	6	6	6	27	27	27	27					
No of I.B. Courses Available	2	24	10	24	10	10	17	4	8	17	26	17	24	6	17	17	24	17	26	3	10	6	1	6	17		
No. of I.B. Majors	1	25	13	21	4	15	5	12	10	26	7	11	26	6	18	12	20	23	19	21	2	17	9	24	14	15	
Age	21	9	21	9	21	5	12	12	5	2	9	21	12	1	27	21	21	21	21	12	21	5	21	21	2	5	21
Average GMAT	23	13	21	10	2	23	7	19	17	15	11	8	1	20	16	18	5	27	26	6	11	13	3	22	25	4	9

SOURCE:

Nehrt, L.C. 1989. "The Ranking of Master Programs in International Business—Reply." *Journal of International Business Studies*, Spring. pp. 163-168.

9. American University

10. University of Washington

11. University of Texas, Austin

12. CUNY, Baruch

13. MIT

14. University of Texas, Dallas

15. University of Hawaii

16. Temple University

LEADING BUSINESS SCHOOLS OUTSIDE OF THE U.S.

The following is contact information for a selection of business schools in selected countries outside the United States.

CANADA

University of Western Ontario

Attention: MBA Admissions Office
School of Business Administration
London, Ontario, N6A 3K7
Canada

McGill University

School of Business Administration
1001 Rue Sherbrooke Ouest
Montreal, Quebec H3A 1G5
Canada

University of Windsor

Faculty of Business Administration
401 Sunset Ave.
Windsor, Ontario, N9B 3P4
Canada

York University

Faculty of Administrative Studies
North York
Ontario, M35 1P3

University of Calgary

Faculty of Management
Calgary
AB T2N 1N4

Dalhousie University

School of Business
Halifax NS B3H 1Z5

University of Toronto

Faculty of Management
Toronto, Ontario, M5S 1V4

Simon Fraser University

Faculty of Business
Burnaby, BC V5A 1S6

FRANCE
ISA
(Institut Superieur des Affaires)

Centre HEC-ISA

78350 Jouy-en-Josas
France

INSEAD

Attention: MBA Information Service
Boulevard De Constance
77305 Fountainebleau Cedex

ITALY
SDA Bocconi

Via Bocconi 8
20136 Milan
Italy

JAPAN
International University of Japan

Attention: MBA Program Director
Yamato-Machi, Ninami Uonuma-Gun
Niigata, 949-72, Japan

THE NETHERLANDS
Rotterdam School of Management Erasmus University

Burgemeester Oudlaan 50
3000 DR Rotterdam
The Netherlands

SPAIN
IESE

Avenida Pearson 21
08034 Barcelona
Spain

SWEDEN
Stockholm School of Economics

Box 6501
Stockholm 11383
Sweden

SWITZERLAND
IMD

P.O. 915
Ch 1001 Lausanne
Switzerland

UNITED KINGDOM
London Business School

Sussex Place, Regent's Park
London NW1 4SA
United Kingdom

Manchester Business School

Attention: MBA Information Service
Booth Street West
Manchester M15 6PB
United Kingdom

SPECIALTY PROGRAMS

Internationally oriented MBA programs, in addition to classroom requirements, often offer specialty programs that can be intellectually stimulating as well as provide students with valuable experiences that will make them more attractive to employers. The most common specialty program is that of an internship. An international internship usually involves working overseas, and it is not unusual for students to be offered jobs after graduation by the companies in which they interned.

It would be impossible to list all of the creative approaches MBA programs use to internationalize their students; the following is a sampling of what is available. Loyola Marymount University, located in Los Angeles, offers a unique capstone course, whereby students travel overseas to visit companies that are in the same industry but in different countries. Company executives and workers are interviewed at each stop, and student groups that are organized by business function, collect data and analyze each company's operation. The trip takes three weeks, and upon return, each group writes a detailed report of their findings. The final product is a comprehensive analysis of business functions, across cultures, within the same industry.

The MBA Enterprise Corps is a kind of Peace Corps for business students (see Roman & Reichlin 1991). It was formed in 1990 by a 16-school consortium and is headquarted at the Kenan-Flagler Business School at the University of North Carolina, Chapel Hill. This is an opportunity for interested MBA student to work in Eastern Europe (specifically, Czechoslovakia, Poland, and Hungary) for government agencies and newly privatized businesses. Their duties include such things as developing business plans, locating financing, and developing exporting operations. Each MBA volunteer receives a modest stipend, but the real value is the chance to live and work overseas, and help managers who know little about capitalism develop expertise. Before going overseas, the students receive six weeks of training that includes language training, history courses, and cultural studies.

JOB PROSPECTS

Students usually want to know about the international job prospects available to them after graduation from an internationally oriented MBA program. This is difficult to answer because business researchers have largely neglected this topic. One study attempted to gain insight into this issue, however, and it offers some interesting findings.

Kate Gillespie (1986) surveyed 271 graduates of the Masters program in International Business Studies Program at the University of South Carolina. The graduates of this program were required to gain proficiency in a foreign language and serve a six-month internship overseas. Exhibit A.3 shows the graduates' descriptions of their initial employers (the companies that hired them upon graduation). Note that over 70 percent found employment with an international company. Gillespie also notes that not all graduates went to work for U.S. corporations; a substantial number (18.44 percent) were employed by foreign-based enterprises.

Exhibit A.4 describes the nature of the first job these graduates accepted upon graduation. Note that the largest group, over 40 percent, said their job was "truly international" in that it required them to work extensively with more than one national market. Also, more than one-third reported that their job

---

EXHIBIT A.3

DESCRIPTION OF INITIAL EMPLOYER

"Best Description of Employer"	Number Responses	Percent Responses
An organization exclusively concerned with its home market.	16	6.78%
An organization primarily concerned with its home market although it did some international business.	35	14.83%
An organization with relatively little international business but committed to increasing its international involvement.	17	7.20%
An organization already substantially involved in international business.	168	71.19%
	n = 236	100%

SOURCE:

Gillespie, K. 1986. "MBA and International business: a study of position opportunity for graduates and the importance of foreign language and internship." *Issues in International Business*, Vol. 3, No. 1, Winter/Spring. pp 7-16.

required them to live and work overseas, and 55 percent felt that if they stayed with their company they would be assigned overseas in the future.

Gillespie's study also found the following facts:

1. The U.S. graduates who found work in foreign-based companies, almost exclusively, were individuals who were proficient in French and German.

2. Of the graduates who sought jobs in finance, 74.14 percent received at least one job offer, and 89.54 percent of this group accepted their offers. Of those graduates who sought 60 percent jobs in marketing received an offer, and 73.47 percent of this group accepted their offers. No data was collected on those who sought jobs in other business disciplines.

3. When graduates were asked which aspects of their Master's program were most significant in getting them jobs, they responded as follows: first, foreign language ability; a close second, having had an international internship; and third, the fact that they had more international business training than other MBA graduates. The language skills that seemed to be most critical in getting the job were: first, Portuguese; second, German; third, Spanish; and fourth, French.

4. Female graduates were hired at the same rate as male graduates, thus there was no indication of gender discrimination in hiring; however, female graduates' salaries were somewhat lower on average, than those of male graduates.

This study would be more valuable if its findings could be compared against other studies' findings on the same topic; unfortunately, no other studies exist.

EXHIBIT A.4

TASKS INVOLVED WITH INITIAL JOB

Job Description	Number Responses	Percent Responses
The job required that I deal exclusively with my native home market.	56	24.24%
The job required that I deal primarily with my native home market, but there was some international work involved.	48	20.78%
The job required that I deal primarily or exclusively with a single market which was not my native home market.	34	14.72%
The job was truly international, requiring that I work extensively with more than one national market.	93	40.26%
	n = 231	**100%**

However, Beamish and Calof (1989) published a study that sheds more light on which concentrations within MBA programs might be more important in terms of career issues. They surveyed 122 Canadian executives to ascertain what areas, skills, qualities, and knowledge were necessary to remain globally competitive. Their attitudes about the importance of specific skills and international business courses were examined, and they felt that the following areas were most important: (1) international marketing and sales; (2) international finance/capital markets; and (3) international trade/export management.

Gillespie's study does indicate that many companies do value specialized international business training at the graduate level, especially if that training is linked with language skills and an international internship experience. Thus, when evaluating the graduate programs listed in this appendix, students should consider whether or not the program offers internships and language training in its curriculum.

REFERENCES

Ball, D.A. & W.H. McCulloch, Jr. 1988. "International business education programs in American and non-American schools: How they are ranked by the Academy of International Business." *Journal of International Business Studies*, 19(2), pp. 295–299.

Barsoux, J. & P. Lawrence. 1991. "In search of intelligence." *Journal of General Management*, 17(2), pp. 1–12.

Beamish, P.W. & J.L. Calof. 1989. "International business education: A corporate view". *Journal of International Business Studies*, 20(3), pp. 553–564.

Black, J.S., H. Gregersen, & M. Mendenhall. 1992. "Global assignments: Successfully expatriating and repatriating international managers." San Francisco: Jossey-Bass.

Derr, C.B. 1987. "Managing high potentials in Europe." *European Management Journal*, 5(2), pp. 72–80.

Gillespie, K. 1986. "MBA in international business: A study of position opportunities for graduates and the importance of foreign language and internship." *Issues in International Business*, 3(1), Winter–Spring, pp. 7–16.

Kakabadse, A. & C. Margerison. 1988. "Top executives: Addressing their management development needs." *Leadership and Organization Development Journal*, Vol. 9 (4). pp. 17–21.

Kohut, G.F. 1986. "Internationalizing business communication." *The Diary of Alpha Kappa Psi*, July, pp. 4–5.

Nehrt, L. 1987. "The ranking of Masters programs in international business." *Journal of International Business Studies*, Fall, pp. 91–99.

Nehrt, L. 1989. *The ranking of Masters programs in International Business— Reply*. Journal of International Business Studies, 20(1), pp. 163–168.

Roman, M. & I. Reichlin. 1991. "From the halls of U.S. B-schools to the mills of Hungary". *Business Week*, August 12, p. 26.

Schneider, S. C. 1988. "National vs. corporate culture: Implications for human resource management." *Human Resource Management.* 27(2) pp. 231–246

Stewart, S. & Chong Chung, Nim. 1990. "Chinese winners: Views of senior PRC managers on the reasons for their success." *International Studies of Management and Organization.* Vol. 20, (1), 2, pp. 57–68

EXPERIENTIAL

EXERCISES

651

INTRODUCTION

Students may grasp the importance of international issues intellectually but need to experience the difficulties associated with international transactions personally; experiential exercises provide an opportunity for this personal involvement. These exercises also provide students an opportunity to test newly learned theories and concepts and to make decisions in a realistic framework. Students find experiential learning especially helpful in terms of new attitudes, communication skills, and self-awareness. This is particularly relevant in international management, where these skills are critical to moving effectively from one country to another. Of course, practical knowledge of business is also important in the learning context. The exercises provided here have been designed to focus on realistic issues so they can be used to impart concrete business knowledge as well as new attitudes, communication skills, and self-awareness.

These exercises are intended to supplement other teaching methods, including lectures, readings, case studies, research, and computer simulations. A combination of teaching methods incorporates theoretical concepts with a practical understanding of the complex issues that international managers face.

Experiential exercises take many forms: some are completed individually, others in groups; some can be entirely conducted in class, others involve outside work; some take a few minutes, others several hours. The exercises provided here follow a number of different formats; they are flexible in terms of class size, outside preparation, and completion time. There are guidelines, but each instructor will adapt them to the needs of his or her class. The exercises here parallel the issues discussed in the text, and they often illustrate more than one idea.

EXERCISE 1:
RISK ASSESSMENT AND MANAGEMENT

Background

The purpose of this exercise is to consider assessing and managing risk where risk is seen as substantial. Students select a country where they believe there is a substantial degree of risk and determine how they would manage a firm's exposure to risk in this country.

Each student is asked to do a preliminary risk assessment, based on published risk indices, recent events, and news reports, to identify three potentially risky countries.

In Class

Students form groups of four. Group members share information on the countries they have identified, and select one to examine in detail. Assume that the group represents the political-risk department of a medium-sized firm called International Management Incorporated (IMI). IMI has decided to establish a subsidiary in the country being examined in spite of the high level of risk (the benefits have been assessed as outweighing the risks). IMI is a consulting firm specializing in market assessment, using a variety of proprietary computer simulation programs. As a group, your tasks are to:

1. Identify the risks that IMI faces in the country (government takeover, local hostility, onerous regulations, terrorism, currency collapse, and so on).

2. Decide how to structure the subsidiary to minimize IMI's exposure to risk. Consider, but do not limit your discussion to, the following:

   - Ownership structure

   - Management makeup

   - Legal protection of proprietary assets

   - Debt/equity structure

   - Relationships to parent company, other subsidiaries

- Insurance

- Human resource policies

- Marketing policies

- Financial policies

- Public relations issues

3. Prepare a brief written summary of your risk-management strategy to be handed in at the end of the class period.

EXERCISE 2:
CULTURAL SCENARIOS

Background

The purpose of this exercise is to illustrate that the way we react "at home" to various situations may be considered incorrect in other locations. The simple scenarios described provide an opportunity to discuss the differences one may encounter in other locations.

Assignment (5 minutes)

Individually, respond to the following situations. For each scenario choose the answer that best describes how you believe you would react.

1. You meet a Japanese colleague for the first time and exchange business cards. What do you do with the Japanese business card?

    a. Put it in your pocket.

    b. Place it on the table in front of you.

    c. Study it carefully then put it where you can see it.

2. You are at a Chinese banquet and your host keeps helping you to food from the central platter. How do you react?

    a. Eat what you are given to be polite.

    b. Eat some of what you are given but not all because you know there are more courses to come.

   c. Politely refuse, because you are concerned about the germs, saying that you are waiting for the other courses that you know will be coming.

3. You are meeting an Arab colleague whom you have met before but do not know well. After you have greeted him you would:

   a. Accept the coffee that you are offered.

   b. Ask politely about his wife and family.

   c. Get down to business immediately.

4. You are in Mexico for a brief business meeting with a company representative at a local bar. When the representative arrives, you would expect:

   a. To have a couple of drinks and talk about Mexico.

   b. To order drinks then get down to business so that you can get it out of the way.

   c. To have one quick drink then adjourn to an office to discuss business.

5. You are visiting the Far East and are being shown around by a business associate and her family. Her daughter, a small child, makes a cute comment. You would:

   a. Pat her on the head and say something like, "What a cute comment."

   b. Kiss her on both cheeks to express your appreciation of her comment.

   c. Ignore her because children should not speak in the company of adults.

6. You are in Australia, talking on the phone, when your joint-venture partner comes into your office and says excitedly, "We have just got the contract."

   a. You nod vigorously sideways to indicate your approval.

b. You give a "thumbs-up" signal.

c. You immediately hang up the phone.

(20 minutes)

Your instructor will have you vote on various options and discuss why some are considered appropriate and others are unacceptable. The discussion can be extended to deal with additional cultural differences that students have encountered.

EXERCISE 3:
CROSS-CULTURAL MOTIVATION

Background

Consider a lesser-developed country called "Gamma," where people are relatively poor. Some facts about Gamma follow:

- In Gamma people like to work closely in groups. They do not believe people should make decisions on their own; rather, they seek consensus of all group members. Gammans are often seen in groups discussing what they should do next.

- In Gamma strict hierarchies are observed. People are born to a certain level or station in life and are expected to remain there. In organizations, managers are expected to make decisions and instruct their subordinates. Lower-level Gammans accept orders without question.

- In Gamma people believe that they have little control over their environment. The expression "God willing" describes the general attitude toward taking action. Gammans behave in ways they think are acceptable to society and higher authority.

Assignment   (20 minutes)

In small groups you will discuss how a particular motivational theory would apply in the country Gamma described above. The process will be as follows:

1. Choose one of the motivational theories—Maslow, Equity, Expectancy, Reinforcement—to consider.

2. Briefly describe the major elements of that theory as presented in an organizational behavior text.

3. Examine each element of the theory in light of the description of Gamma and try to identify how the culture of Gamma, as described, would influence the theory.

4. Does your group think the theory could be used to motivate people in such a society?

5. If you think it could be used, would you propose any modifica tions? If you think it could not be used, what do you see as the main limitations?

(20 minutes)

Develop a role-playing skit to illustrate your theory in Gamma. In your skit, one person will represent a North American and one person a Gamman. The North American will try to explain the theory to the Gamman, and the Gamman will respond from that cultural background.

(15 minutes)

Groups will present their skits to the class.

EXERCISE 4:
EXPERIMENTING WITH FOREIGN PRACTICES

Background

The purpose of this exercise is to try doing things in ways that are unusual for you. Each student, prior to class, identifies three or four practices from foreign cultures which are different from the norm at home. These should be relatively simple practices that can be tried by everyone in the class within the classroom setting.

In Class

The instructor may devote an entire class to this exercise, or may devote a short period of several classes, throughout the semester. In class, students identify a foreign practice and explain where and how it is used; then some, or all, students in the class experiment with the foreign practice. The following are examples a North American might identify:

- In parts of Latin America people conversing stand closer together than they do in North America. Students can talk to each other and establish a "normal" distance, then try standing a few inches closer to see how they feel.

- In parts of the Far East it is not considered polite to meet the eyes of the person to whom you are speaking. Students can try talking to each other while looking at the floor instead of at each other.

- In parts of the Middle East it is common to sit cross-legged on the floor for extended periods. Students can try sitting in this position and see for how long it is comfortable (this may have to be done outside of class and reported later).

EXERCISE 5:
INTERNATIONAL STRATEGIC CHOICE: COUNTRY ANALYSIS FOR FOREIGN EXPANSION

Background

The purpose of this exercise is to examine a number of foreign countries as potential sites for foreign expansion. A firm from the home country (that is, the country where you live) is considering foreign expansion and wishes to compare a number of countries and rank them in terms of attractiveness. The class as a whole represents the firm which is called "The Home Firm." Groups of students represent task forces within the firm who gather information on various aspects of the foreign countries under investigation. The following is preparation for this exercise.

Step One:

The instructor selects two or more countries for the class to study (the number of countries depends on the size of the class). If time permits, this may be done in class; students suggest countries, then vote to decide which they will study.

Step Two:

The class is divided into groups of four or five people. Each group is assigned one of the following topics for one country:

- Political environment

- Cultural environment

- Legal environment

- Economic environment

- Current events

Step Three:

Each group researches the assigned topic for one country; gathering information from books, journals, magazines, and newspapers: country reports may be particularly helpful. In addition, interviews with people who are familiar with the foreign country and information from the foreign country's trade representatives can be very useful.

Step Four:

Each group prepares a brief summary for presentation to the class. This should take the form of a five-minute slide (overhead or computer) presentation, highlighting the main issues, and a typed handout for the class. Groups should focus on factors that will influence the foreign-expansion business decision.

In Class

One or more class periods is devoted to reviewing the country analyses (depending on the number of countries investigated). Each task-force group presents its analysis and provides the class with a typed handout.

Working with their task-force group, students review all the material outside of class and prepare a summary of the positive and negative aspects for each country. On the basis of this summary, the class compares and ranks countries in terms of attractiveness.

In a subsequent class students discuss and synthesize the summaries. The instructor may take the summaries and prepare a synthesis for discussion in class. Alternatively, the instructor may call on each group to identify benefits and drawbacks for the countries, and prepare a synthesis in class which serves as the basis for discussion. The final output is an overall ranking of the countries investigated. Students must bear in mind that this ranking is in the context of an international-expansion decision for The Home Firm.

EXERCISE 6:
ASSESSING FOREIGN OPPORTUNITIES: COUNTRY EXHIBITS/PRESENTATIONS

Background

The purpose of this exercise is to expose students to the business opportunities in a variety of countries, and to consider how these opportunities relate to foreign-entry decisions. Each student is assigned a country to investigate (this may be done in groups, depending on the size of the class). The instructor assigns countries to ensure that a wide range of countries is covered. Students may be asked to select from a list of countries, or each student may be assigned a specific country.

Students play the role of a trade representative from the assigned country. Each student researches her/his assigned country and prepares a brief presentation for the class. The presentation can take the form of a visual exhibit, or a brief slide (overhead or computer) presentation. The role of the trade representative is to provide information that would interest prospective businesses in considering that country as a place to do business.

In Class

One or more classes can be devoted to country presentations, depending on the format selected.

If visual exhibits are used, the class is organized as a "Country Exhibit Fair" (similar to a science fair or a trade fair). Each student or group sets up an exhibit that describes business opportunities in the assigned country. The exhibit should be able to stand on its own; that is, students should not need to explain it. Students spend the class period examining the various country exhibits and evaluating the apparent opportunities for doing business in each country. Each student selects one country (not her/his own), from those exhibited, that seems to offer the most opportunities, and prepares a brief written report of the advantages and disadvantages of various forms of entry (exports/imports, licenses, franchises, contracts, turnkeys, joint ventures, sole ownership) into this country.

If presentations are used, each student or group presents a brief overview, describing the business opportunities in this country. Each student selects one country (not her/his own) from those exhibited, that offers the most opportunities, and prepares a brief written report of the advantages and disadvantages of various forms of entry (exports/imports, licenses, franchises, contracts, turnkeys, joint ventures, sole ownership) into this country.

EXERCISE 7:
NEGOTIATIONS

Background

The purpose of this exercise is to illustrate the complexities of negotiating in an unfamiliar setting. The situation is simple—students represent two firms meeting for the first time to begin negotiating an agreement. The firms have been in contact by mail, fax, phone, and so on. They believe that they can work together for mutual benefit and are meeting to work out the contractual details.

In Class

Students are assigned to groups, or to act as observers, by the instructor. Each group receives instructions regarding its approach to the negotiations. Observers are briefed by the instructor.

(10 minutes)

Group members discuss their assignment and prepare for negotiations. Observers watch and take notes.

(30 minutes)

Groups meet with counterparts and attempt to work out an agreement. Observers watch and make notes.

(20 minutes)

Observers report on the negotiations.

EXERCISE 8:
EVALUATING SUBSIDIARY PERFORMANCE

Background

The purpose of this exercise is to illustrate some of the complexities of evaluating performance in different locations. Consider the following scenario:

- A large international firm, BJP, is headquartered in Paris, France. BJP has affiliations with other companies in other countries as well as subsidiaries. Top management in Paris is almost entirely French. BJP recently established a majority-owned subsidiary, Assembly Incorporated, in a small developing country in the Caribbean. BJP owns 65 percent of Assembly; a wealthy local business woman owns 35 percent.

- Assembly Incorporated assembles automotive parts that are sold to other subsidiaries of BJP. Materials are provided by BJP and billed to Assembly. BJP also provides Assembly with machinery and supplies that are not available locally, as well as consulting advice.

▪ Management at Assembly consists of three locals and one French national. The expectation is that the French national will remain until she is confident the local managers are capable of running operations on their own. The French national was expected to stay in the Caribbean for one year, but after a year of operations she has indicated that she should remain for a second year. The local partner is not involved in day-to-day operations of Assembly, but provides advice and assistance on local matters when requested.

▪ Assembly has completed one year of operations, and performance is being reviewed by a top management group in France. Costs have been higher than anticipated, and Assembly has lost money (see Exhibit B.1). The loss is relatively small but unexpected, and it rais-

EXHIBIT B.1

ASSEMBLY INC. - SUMMARY INCOME STATEMENT

		Actual	Projected
Net Sales		1,555,800	1,250,000
Less:			
	Materials	575,000	450,000
	Direct labor	350,000	300,000
	Import duties*	100,000	—
	Depreciation	70,000	70,000
Total		1,095,000	820,000
Gross Profit		460,000	430,000
Administrative Expenses			
	Management salaries and expenses	260,000	230,000
	Staff expenses**	110,000	100,000
	Other expenses	110,000	90,000
Total		480,000	420,000
Net Profit/Loss		(20,000)	10,000

* A request is being considered by the government for a refund of import duties.

** The local partner received a $60,000 consultation fee; the balance was for services from headquarters.

es a number of issues that BJP needs to resolve. Most importantly, BJP needs to decide how, indeed if, operations at Assembly should continue. The decision is complicated by the fact that there has been a recent change of government in the Caribbean country, and BJP is unsure of its relationship with the new government. In addition, there are rumors of an impending devaluation of the country's currency.

In Class

Form groups of four to discuss the following questions.

1. What factors account for most of Assembly's loss?

2. How badly/well is Assembly's performing?

3. Should BJP continue operations at Assembly?

4. What problems are typically associated with the evaluation of subsidiaries (use the case study as an illustration)? What solutions to these problems can you suggest?

The board will be divided and labeled "Problems" and "Solutions." Following individual group discussions, groups take turns coming to the board and writing up a problem and solution statement until the major issues have been covered.

EXERCISE 9:
THE BATA SHOE ORGANIZATION AND INTERNATIONAL MANAGEMENT

Background

The Bata Shoe Organization (BSO) is the world's largest manufacturer and marketer of footwear. The company is headquartered in Toronto, Canada, but 95 percent of its business is outside Canada, in more than 100 countries around the world. BSO is a family-owned business that establishes wholly-owned subsidiaries wherever possible. In spite of this, the company is usually thought of as a local business whenever it operates. In fact, in at least one African country, the word *bata*, means "shoe."

At the heart of this combination of globalization and localization is a somewhat unique approach to management issues. Executives at BSO developed an agenda of issues they believed affect managers and supervisors no matter where they operate (for example, all managers and supervisors need to reward people). While the executives believe that the issues affect all managers and supervisors everywhere, they also believe that different cultures deal differently with issues (for example, monetary rewards may be effective in one location while special privileges work better in another).

In Class

Form groups of four and try to replicate the BSO executives' approach using the following steps.

- Develop a list of issues you believe all managers and supervisors face. To get started, motivation, assigning work, and discipline are possibilities.

- Define in simple language the meaning of each of the issues identified. Using examples may be helpful.

- Describe how effective managers address each issue "at home" (meaning, in the country where you are).

- Discuss alternative ways of addressing each issue. If there are foreign students in the class, draw on their experiences. If there are no foreign students, use your imagination and information from the chapters on culture.

Groups hand in a written summary, or, if time permits, report to the class as a whole.

EXERCISE 10:
EXPATRIATE ASSIGNMENTS

Background

Imagine that you are an employee (named Sandy) in a large international company. The following are some personal facts.

- You are married to a financial analyst who works in a bank located in the same city.

- You have two children—a boy, aged 10, and a girl, aged 8.

- You and your family are actively engaged in a variety of volunteer activities sponsored by your church, which include environmental activities and providing food for the needy.

- You and your spouse enjoy sports activities together—you jog, play tennis, and golf on a regular basis. You also enjoy cultural events together, such as concerts and plays.

You have just received the following letter from your company.

> Dear Sandy,
>
> We are pleased to be able to tell you that you have been selected as a candidate for an overseas position in our subsidiary in Kenya. Please contact M. Jones, our international human resources manager, as soon as possible to discuss this opportunity further.

Assignment

(10 minutes)

Individually, consider this situation and how you would react to it. Identify your major concerns as well as reasons why you would want to accept or decline such an offer.

(20 minutes)
Meet in groups to discuss the issue of expatriate assignments from the point of view of the expatriate. Using the ideas generated individually as a beginning, develop some general concepts regarding expatriate assignments. Feel free to go beyond the information provided in the profile, and discuss other issues that might influence people's reactions to such assignments.

(10 minutes)
Each group is asked to outline their thoughts about expatriate assignments.

EXERCISE 11:
CROSS-CULTURAL TRAINING

Background
Anthropologists describe societies in terms of how they relate to nature, to time, and to other people. These ideas will be applied in this exercise.

Anglo societies (including Australia, Canada, New Zealand, the United Kingdom, and the United States) are generally described as wanting to master nature, while other societies are seen as living in harmony with nature. Anglo societies focus on the present, while some others focus on the past. Anglo societies believe in equality, while some others subscribe to clear hierarchies and distinctions of power. For this exercise, imagine a society called Zeta, which is comprised of the opposite qualities of Anglo societies.

Assignment   (30 minutes)
In small groups, discuss the following situation: You have been asked to develop a computer training program for employees who are not familiar with computers. How would your program in Zeta differ from one you might develop for North American employees?

(15 minutes)
Each group will either present its conclusions briefly or prepare a brief written summary to hand in.

EXERCISE 12:
FACING DISCRIMINATION IN INTERNATIONAL ASSIGNMENTS

Background

Patricia O'Neill is manager of the building construction division of Quantum Corporation. Quantum is a U.S.-headquartered multinational firm with offices and subsidiaries around the world. Patricia has worked hard to reach this position, having been encouraged to go into the cosmetics division when she joined Quantum ten years earlier. Her boss, John Salmond, has supported her throughout her career.

Quantum is currently filling a position in the United Kingdom from headquarters. It is important to advancement within Quantum that managers serve in foreign locations. Patricia is directly involved in filling the position and has recommended Bob Jones, a subordinate of whom she thinks very highly. There is an alternative candidate, James Perry, who has been considered, but Patricia does not believe his experience qualifies him for the U.K. position.

Patricia believes that Bob's assignment is essentially concluded when she receives a telephone call from her counterpart in the U.K., Albert Smith. Albert expresses grave concerns about the choice of Bob Jones, and eventually admits that it is because Bob is of African descent. Albert says that "others like him" have run into racial discrimination in the U.K. and have had difficulty functioning effectively. Albert feels that James would be a better choice for the U.K. position.

United States legislation forbids discrimination on the basis of race and Quantum has specific guidelines encouraging equal opportunity, regardless of factors such as race and gender.

In Class   (30 minutes)

Form groups of four and discuss the situation described. Consider the following questions:

1. If you were Patricia O'Neill, which candidate would you recommend? Why?

2. If you were Bob Jones, would you want to be recommended? Why? Why not?

3. How should Quantum deal with this situation?

4. Is it ever appropriate to take race (or gender, or other similar characteristics) into account in selecting someone for a foreign assignment?

(30 minutes)

Each group reports on its decisions on one or more of these questions.

C

MITSUHOSHI FRANCE, S.A.

THE ROAD TO HELL

MITSUHOSHI FRANCE, S.A.

SUSAN SCHNEIDER

RYUKICHI INOUE

CHRISTINE MEAD

Satoshi Suzuki has been lost in thought for more than an hour in front of a telex from the foodstuffs division in Tokyo. Its subject is a new project proposed for France. The telex read as follows:

> TO MITSUHOSHI PARIS FOODSTUFFS DEPT
> COPY MITSUHOSHI LONDON FOOD DIV
> FROM MITSUHOSHI TOKYO FOODSTUFFS DIV
>
> RE HEALTHY FOOD PROJ IN FRANCE
>
> OKAMOTO RESEARCH INSTITUTE ONE OF TOP BIOTECH COMP IN JPN
> PLANS TO MAKE J/V IN FRANCE TO PRODUCE HEALTHY PRODUCTS OF
> "TOFU" OR FOOD FROM SOY BEANS STP THEY ASKED US TO COOPER-
> ATE IN FINDING FRENCH PARTNER AS WELL AS PARTICIPATING J/V
> STP ACDGTO PLANS NOT ONLY "TOFU" BUT ALSO DIET FOODS BASED
> ON SOY BEANS AND VITAMIN FOODS BE PRODUCED STP IF RESULT OF
> F/S SATISFACTORY WE ARE READY TO INVEST AS MUCH AS ONE BIL-
> LION YEN STP PLS IMMEDIATELY ARRANGE FORMATION AT YOUR
> SIDE TO PROCEED ZS PROJ STP RPLY IMMEDIATELY STP RGDS

He thought through what this project would mean for him. It would be a new venture, something that would be his responsiblity, which could be useful for him when he returned to Japan in a few years time.

In thinking about who to hire for this project, he remembers recent discussions with his superior, President Tanaka, about the problems of Japanese expatriates and French nationals working at Mitsuhoshi, France. He knows that these problems reflect a deeper concern—the internationalization of Mitsuhoshi Corporation

Company Background

Mitsuhoshi Corp. Tokyo is one of the leading Japanese general trading houses (*sogoshosha*). It has more than 150 offices around the world and the volume of information it exchanges daily through its telex channel network is the equivalent of some 1,600 pages of the *New York Times*. The total turnover in 1987 was more than 590 billion. The corporation employed 8,000 Japanese staff and 5,000 local staff around the world.

Mitsuhoshi France S.A. is a wholly owned subsidiary of Mitsuhoshi Tokyo. Its activity ranges from importing Japanese steel and machinery into France and exporting French goods to Japan, to organizing a huge refinery complex in Francophone Africa. Its turnover reached 1,800 million French francs in 1987.

Mitsuhoshi France is tightly controlled by Tokyo, although legally independent in France. Mitsuhoshi's European Regional Center is in London, where Mitsuhoshi Tokyo's senior managing director acts as a general manager of Europe and Africa operations.

Employees

Of its fifty employees, ten are expatriate Japanese managers who have been appointed by Tokyo headquarters. They are the president, two vice presidents, and seven department managers. In addition, there are fifteen locally employed Japanese, only one of whom is scheduled to be promoted to manager. The expatriate Japanese return to Tokyo after five or six years; the locally employed Japanese always stay in France. The remaining thirty-five are all French. Some of them have worked more than ten years to obtain the title of manager.

Yuuji Tanaka is the 52-year-old president of Mitsuhoshi France. He has worked for Mitsuhoshi for thirty years, joining them straight after university graduation. He will retire in eight years. Through on-the-job training, he has become a specialist in chemical trading. Before Paris, he was posted in London and Dusseldorf.

Susumu Sato is the 45-year-old vice president of Mitsuhoshi France. He has been appointed to France for the second time because he studied French at the Tokyo University of Foreign Studies. This time he chose to come to France alone. He cannot sacrifice the future career of his only son, who is 14 years old. His son must study in the Japanese way to win entry in a good Japanese university. His wife has remained in Tokyo with the son to help him prepare for difficult examinations. In four years' time, after the boy has passed his examinations and has secured a place at the university, he might reconsider calling his wife back to Paris.

He is in charge of administration in Mitsuhoshi France, including accounting and personnel, which are particularly important. His assignment is not easy. Managing the complaints of the French staff is one of his headaches; he often finds himself caught between the two fires of Tokyo headquarters and the French office.

Owing to the slow growth of the world economy, the business of Mitsuhoshi France has been stagnating recently. This means that salaries cannot be raised sharply or constantly. Mr. Sato submitted a draft proposal to London for a wage hike that would fit the French employees' expectations. London required that the French subsidiary implement the same policy as the British, German, Belgian, Italian, and Scandinavian subsidiaries, to keep the average wage hike below 2 percent. Mr. Sato understands that the motivation for keeping the French staff is largely through salary increases, since it is clear that they are not promoted to posts where they have decision-making power. He was almost swallowed by complaints from the French staff when he announced the salaries for the coming year. A bone of contention has been the traditional Japanese *Bonenkai*; the equivalent of the western company Christmas party. Many of the French staff made it clear that they would rather be paid more money than have such an absurd party sponsored by the company.

Satoshi Suzuki is the 38-year-old Japanese expatriate manager in charge of the foodstuffs department of Mitsuhoshi France. He was sent by company order from Tokyo in April 1986, along with his wife Keiko (36) and two children (6 and 10).

Before Paris, he spent three years (1979-1982) as the company's chief representative in Khartoum. Although regarded as the worst place to work among Mitsuhoshi's overseas offices, he had enjoyed the responsibility of being the only manager, in charge of the whole operation. Had he stayed in Tokyo, he would have waited ten years for such responsibility. In Khartoum he performed well, getting contracts financed by the Japanese government's official aid programs.

Returning to Tokyo, he was assigned to work on imports of foodstuffs from the U.S. and the EC. In addition, he was appointed vice chairman of Mitsuhoshi's employees' union, and negotiated with Mitsuhoshi Tokyo for the wage hike of some 5,000 union members. This was a vital experience in giving Mr. Suzuki a global view of the company and its activities.

Mr. Suzuki studied French for two years at the University of Tokyo, but realizes that his French is far from perfect when it comes to communicating with his French clients and subordinates. He is confident in conducting daily business in English.

He wakes up ever morning at 7 A.M., has a Japanese breakfast, leaves his cozy apartment paid for by the company near the Bois de Boulogne in the 16e arrondissement in Paris, and arrives at work at 8:45 A.M. He reads telexes—mostly in Japanese—until 10 A.M., and then he plans and suggests to his subordinates what to do for the day.

Satoshi Suzuki has three subordinates: Mr. Vincent and two secretaries. Mr. Vincent is a senior member of the staff who has worked there for twelve years. After finishing high school, he worked as a salesman for a leading French foodstuffs company, but he decided to change to Mitsuhoshi France to practice his English. Working in a Japanese company was a bit like living on a different planet for him, but he learned through his twelve years in the company how to be patient with his bosses. He is considered a reliable member of the staff in his field of trading French wines, brandies, and cookies.

Overseas Assignments

At last year's *Bonenkai* party, President Tanaka and Mr. Suzuki discussed the differences in the older and younger Japanese managers' attitudes toward international assignments—hardship or privilege? President Tanaka reminisces about the days when he was sent to London in 1961. The Japanese economy had then just recovered from the effects of World War II and was concentrating on the development of heavy industry and chemicals. As very few companies had overseas activities, any person who went abroad was considered part of an elite, called "glorious representative abroad," and sought after by young girls as an ideal husband.

> Tanaka: I heard that there have come to be more employees, especially in the younger generation in Tokyo headquarters, who do not want to work abroad. This might indicate the devaluation of the

status of overseas representatives of *sogoshosha*. Mr. Suzuki, what do you think of this tendency?

Suzuki: Well, frankly speaking, I think we cannot find anything better than Tokyo, even in the cities of the U.S. or Europe. It is true that in Tokyo the cost of living is higher than anywhere else in the world, but we can endure life without the horror of terrorism or holdups in the street. Goods are abundant, service is quick and precise. For the younger generation, candidly speaking, not only Paris but also New York is ranked below Tokyo.

Tanaka: But can't you recognize the superior quality of life in Paris? In Tokyo, we have no Louvre and no opera. Those who enjoy the classical arts are regarded as a privileged minority, whereas in Paris, everyone is very much accustomed to enjoying the artistic life after work.

Suzuki: In my opinion, that is the evidence that French culture has entered a period of decline—longing for the good old days. Your generation, President Tanaka, may understand the feeling of adoring the "made in France" products, but we know that most of them are not of better quality than Japanese goods.

Tanaka: By the way, what do you think of *sogoshosha's* young employees who no longer wish to work abroad?

Suzuki: Working abroad is not reserved for the elites today. In fact, if we think of the importance of good education for our children, working abroad as a representative might not be an advantage for us any more. Vice President Sato seems to be clear that he is living here, apart from his family, just because he has a boy who has to study in Japan, preparing for entering the better universities.

What is worse is that even an independent subsidiary like Mitsuhoshi France is not allowed to initiate action. It is always Tokyo that makes the final decision. Even though we have a hard time abroad, it is said that people who remain in Tokyo have more chance of being promoted more quickly. For a rational person, his heart is not in working abroad, even if it is in the developed countries.

The Role of the Local Staff

At Mitsuhoshi Tokyo headquarters, a new strategy regarding HRM abroad became one of the main issues to be addressed immediately. Mr. Takahashi, the General Manager of the Overseas Coordinating Division, came to Paris on the way back to Tokyo from his visit to African offices to discuss his plan—that excellent local staff should play a more important role. Mr. Takahashi asked President Tanaka to talk more informally after office hours, at the Japanese restaurant Takara, near the opera.

> Takahashi: In the 1960s when you first went to London, the English who applied for jobs with Mitsuhoshi had a high school education. We were obviously a second choice for those who could not find work in a good English company. Now, as the Japanese economy grows and Mitsuhoshi's reputation increases, even Oxbridge boys are coming knocking on our doors. We cannot, of course, make their salaries equal to those with a high-school level education. It is moreover much more economical for us if they do the work previously done by Japanese representatives. I believe that in the future we should make the most of the power of local employees. Or we might abolish the differentiation between Japanese representatives who were employed in Tokyo and others.

> Tanaka: General Manager Mr. Takahashi, I understand what you say in theory; however, there would be a lot of trouble if this new policy is introduced in practice. For example, if we employed a graduate of the top *grandes écoles*, I cannot believe they would work for us for a long time. How then would they function as well as the Japanese expatriate managers in the very hierarchical Japanese organization?

> In addition, they probably do not understand Japanese. You know that 90 percent of our telexes are in Japanese. It is out of the question that directors could use an interpreter to communicate with Tokyo.

> Takahashi: Language problems can be solved if Tokyo headquarters would change. As you know, until we acquired a worldwide network in the late 1960s, we traded by telegram in English. Why can't the younger generation do as we did?

Tanaka: What about the relations between Tokyo and offices abroad? Do you think the local manager would understand the limit of his power, even though he was general manager of Mitsuhoshi France? Although we are an independent company by law, we cannot undertake any business without Tokyo's full assistance.

It happened quite recently that the general merchandising division in Tokyo decided not to work in France any more. We, therefore, have to do our own risk assessment and accounting if we want to stay in that line of business. But it is almost impossible with our limited number of staff to assess the reliability of each client and to manage the shipments one by one. I am considering abandoning all our business in the general merchandising field, but it will be very troublesome to persuade the French staff to change their assignment or to quit Mitsuhoshi.

Takahashi: At Tokyo headquarters, we are facing a critical situation. We should be flexible enough to adapt to fundamental changes in the structure of Japanese industry. We hope that, as a means of survival in the twenty-first century, every subsidiary in the U.S. and in Europe should act independently, without any help from Tokyo. As you know, we have established the President's Prize for the overseas subsidiary who has performed well in these fields of offshore or local transactions.

Tanaka: The mentality of the Japanese will not change so quickly. This month I had twenty guests from Japan, many of whom were not clients of Mitsuhoshi France but were somehow related to the corporation as a whole. When asked by Tokyo to "Please attend to them carefully," I could not find any other way but to do it. Can you imagine that there are times when I have two guests in one night, manage to have dinner twice, and after dinner take them to the Moulin Rouge? Yesterday, too, I came home at 2 A.M., and this morning I went to my office at half past eight. I cannot imagine that any French manager would be willing to do this.

Takahashi: I am sure that sooner or later the Japanese mentality will change. At least I can say that it will be internationalized, as we have to survive in the international business world and cannot keep our company closed. The labor environment should be much more open to anyone who is capable. This will be a key success factor for *sogoshosha* very soon.

A New Challenge

Coming back to the telex, Suzuki believes that success in this project requires the hiring of a business elite—a highly qualified French manager who had attended the top schools (*grandes écoles*) with a degree in bioengineering and experience in management as well as marketing. Before proposing his plan to President Tanaka, he decides to talk to the vice president in charge to personnel affairs, Mr. Sato:

> Sato: It seems to me that your plan to employ a French manager in the new project would incur great risks for us. The salary of the new manager would be double that of them. This would lead to great dissatisfaction among them. In your department, Mr. Vincent, who has worked with us for twelve years, would surely claim that he should get as high a salary as the new manager.

> As you know, it is almost impossible to fire a man once employed in France. If Mr. Vincent undertakes legal proceedings to support his claim—or even hints at them—President Tanaka cannot help accepting his claim because Tokyo headquarters does not like any legal proceedings, especially in personnel affairs. It would be a black mark against President Tanaka. Do you think that President Tanaka would risk his future post in Tokyo, his promotion, for such a project?

> Suzuki: I don't believe it is all so bad. I heard that the overseas coordination division in Tokyo recently adopted a new strategy of encouraging local managers. Besides this, I can say that Mr. Vincent is not properly qualified to run this new project. He is lacking in knowledge of biotechnology and he is not from the *grandes écoles* or from a university. Do you imagine that Mr. Vincent, considering his background, could promote the project successfully with top management in French companies who are all from the *grandes écoles*?

> Sato: If you are so concerned you should do it yourself.

> Suzuki: We cannot expect to encourage local staff by continuing in our traditional way. I am sure that even Mr. Vincent would accept

the difference in salaries because the new director is from the *grandes écoles*.

Sato: After employing someone from the *grandes écoles*, imagine if we find out that this new project is not feasible. What will you do with him? We cannot dismiss him, except at huge cost to us and he would not accept being in charge of, say, the machinery department. We would have to keep him employed for life without any suitable assignment!

Suzuki: Perhaps you are referring to the case of Mr. Dupont, of the general merchandise department. But once we decide to abandon the department, we should dismiss him at any cost. Whether President Tanaka might be regarded as incapable by Tokyo headquarters is not relevant if we consider the benefit of the whole Mitsuhoshi group.

In any case, even without your consent, I shall ask President Tanaka to employ a manager from the *grandes écoles* as I already have a favorable opinion from Tokyo's foodstuffs division, who strongly support this project.

Mr. Suzuki leaves the conversation thinking that President Tanaka will probably agree immediately. However, the Tokyo foodstuffs division considers the success of this project critical to their continued good relationship with the Okamoto Research Institute in other business fields and have already approved the appointment of an elite French manager. If need be, he can appeal directly to the managing director of the Mitsuhoshi Corporation in London. This is not the traditional Japanese way of respect for seniors. But he must also consider his duty to the foodstuffs division in Tokyo. He knocks on President Tanaka's door at once with qualms of conscience and confidence in his plan.

EXHIBIT C.1

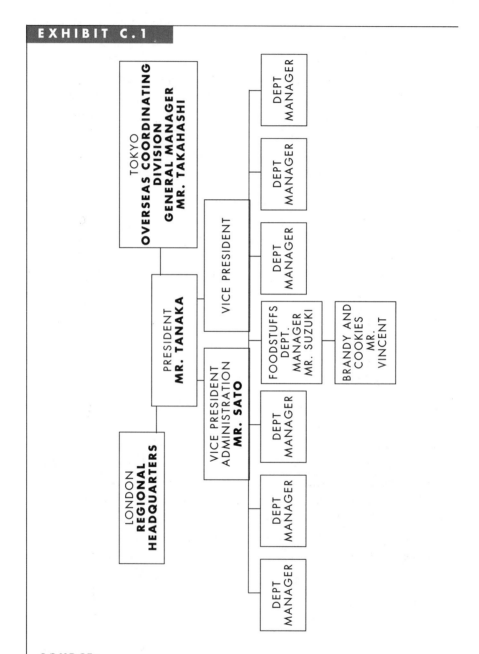

SOURCE:
Gillespie, K. 1986. "MBA and International Business: A Study of Position Opportunity for Graduates and the Importance of Foriegn Language and Internship." *Issues in International Business*, Winter/Spring. Vol. 3 No. 1. pp.7-16.

THE ROAD TO HELL

GARETH EVANS

John Baker, chief engineer of the Caribbean Bauxite Company, of Barracania, in the West Indies, was making his final preparations to leave the island. His promotion to production manager of Keso Mining Corporation, near Winnipeg—one of Continental Ore's fast-expanding Canadian enterprises— had been announced a month before and now everything had been tidied up except that last vital interview with his successor, the able young Barracanian, Matthew Rennalls. It was vital that this interview be a success and that Rennalls leave his office uplifted and confident to face the challenge of his new job. A touch on the bell would have brought Rennalls walking into the room but Baker delayed the moment and gazed thoughtfully through the window, considering exactly what he was going to say and, more particularly, how he was going to say it.

John Baker, an English expatriate, was 45 years old and had served his 23 years with Continental Ore in many different places: in the Far East; several countries of Africa; Europe; and, for the last two years, in the West Indies. He hadn't cared much for his previous assignment in Hamburg and was delighted when the West Indian appointment came through. Climate was not the only attraction. Baker had always preferred working overseas ("in what were termed the developing countries") because he felt he had an innate knack— better than most other expatriates working for Continental Ore—of knowing just how to get on with regional staff. Twenty-four hours in Barracania, however, soon made him realize that he would need all of this "innate knack" if he was to deal effectively with the problems in this field that now awaited him.

At his first interview with Hutchins, the production manager, the whole problem of Rennalls and his future was discussed. There and then it was made quite clear to Baker that one of his most important tasks would be to "groom" Rennalls as his successor. Hutchins had pointed out that, not only was Rennalls one of the brightest Barracanian prospects of the staff of Caribbean Bauxite—at London University he had taken first-class honors in the B.Sc. Engineering degree—but, being the son of the Minister of Finance and Economic Planning, he also had no small political pull.

The company had been particularly pleased when Rennalls decided to work for them rather than for the government in which his father had such a prominent post. They ascribed his action to the effect of their vigorous and liberal regionalization program, which, since the Second World War, had produced eighteen Barracanians at mid-management level and given Caribbean Bauxite a good lead in this respect over all other international concerns operating in Barracania. The success of this timely regionalization policy led to excellent relations with the government—a relationship that was given added importance when Barracania, three years later, became independent, an occasion which encouraged a critical and challenging attitude toward the role foreign interests would have to play in the new Barracania. Hutchins therefore had little difficulty convincing Baker that the successful career development of Rennalls was of the first importance.

The first interview with Hutchins was now two years ago and Baker, leaning back in his office chair, reviewed just how successful he had been in the "grooming" of Rennalls. What aspects of the latter's character had he helped and what had he hindered? What about his own personality? How had that helped or hindered? The first item to go on the credit side without question, would be the ability of Rennalls to master the technical aspects of his job. From the start he had shown keenness and enthusiasm, and had often impressed Baker with his ability in tackling new assignments and the constructive comments he invariably made in departmental discussions. He was popular with all ranks of Barracanian staff and had an ease of manner which stood him in good stead when dealing with his expatriate seniors. These were all assets, but what about the debit side?

First and foremost, there was his racial consciousness, his four years at London University had accentuated this feeling and made him sensitive to any sign of condescension on the part of expatriates. It may have been to give expression to this sentiment that, as soon as he returned home from London, he threw himself into politics on behalf of the United Action Party, who were later to win the pre-independence elections and provide the country with its first Prime Minister.

Rennall's ambitions—and he certainly was ambitious—did not, however, lie in politics for, staunch nationalist that he was, he saw that he could serve himself and his country best (for was not bauxite responsible for nearly half of the value of Barracania's export trade?) by putting his engineering talent to the best possible use. On this account, Hutchins found that he had an unexpectedly easy task in persuading Rennalls to give up his political work before entering the production department as an assistant engineer.

It was, Baker knew, Rennalls's well-repressed sense of race consciousness which had prevented their relationship from being as close as it should have been. On the surface, nothing could have seemed more agreeable. Formality between the two men was at a minimum; Baker was delighted to find that his assistant shared his own peculiar "shaggy dog" sense of humor, so that jokes were continually being exchanged. They entertained each other at their houses and often played tennis together—and yet the barrier remained invisible, indefinable, but ever present. The existence of this "screen" between them was a constant source of frustration to Baker since it indicated a weakness which he was loath to accept. If successful with all other nationalities, why not with Rennalls?

But at least he had managed to "break through" to Rennalls more successfully than any other expatriate. In fact, it was the young Barracanian's attitude— sometimes overbearing, sometimes cynical—toward other company expatriates that had been one of the subjects Baker had raised last year when he discussed Rennalls's staff report with him. He knew, too, that he would have to raise the same subject again in the forthcoming interview because Jackson, the senior draftsman, had complained only yesterday about the rudeness of Rennalls. With this thought in mind, Baker leaned forward and spoke into the intercom. "Would you come in Matt, please? I'd like a word with you," and later, "Do sit down," proffering the box, "have a cigarette." He paused while he held out his lighter and continued.

"As you know, Matt, I'll be off to Canada in a few days' time, and before I go, I thought it would be useful if we could have a final chat together. It is indeed with some deference that I suggest I can be of help. You will shortly be sitting in this chair doing the job I am now doing, but I, on the other hand, am ten years older, so perhaps you can accept the idea that I may be able to give you the benefit of my longer experience."

Baker saw Rennalls stiffen slightly in his chair as he made this point so added in explanation, "You and I have attended enough company courses to remember those repeated requests by the personnel manager to tell people how they are getting on as often as the convenient moment arises and not just the automatic 'once a year' when, by regulation, staff reports have to be discussed."

Rennalls nodded his agreement, so Baker went on. "I shall always remember the last job performance discussion I had with my previous boss back in Germany. He used what he called the 'plus and minus' technique. His firm belief was that when a senior, by discussion, seeks to improve the work performance of his staff, his prime objective should be to make sure that the latter leaves the interview encouraged and inspired to improve. Any criticism must, therefore, be constructive and helpful. He said that one very good way to encourage a person—and I fully agree with him—is to tell him about his good point—the plus factors—as well as his weak ones—the minus factors—so I though, Matt, it would be a good idea to run our discussion along these lines."

Rennalls offered no comment, so Baker continued: "Let me say, therefore, right away, that, as far as your own work performance is concerned, the plus far outweighs the minus. I have, for instance, been most impressed with the way you have adapted your considerable theoretical knowledge to master the practical techniques of your job—that ingenious method you used to get air down to the fifth-shaft level is a sufficient case in point—and at departmental meetings I have invariably found your comments well taken and helpful. In fact, you will be interested to know that only last week I reported to Mr. Hutchins that, from the technical point of view, he could not wish for a more able man to succeed to the position of chief engineer."

"That's very good indeed of you, John," cut in Rennalls with a smile of thanks. "My only worry now is how to live up to such a high recommendation."

"Of that I am quite sure," returned Baker, "especially if you can overcome the minus factor which I would like now to discuss with you. It is one which I have talked about before so I'll come straight to the point. I have noticed that you are more friendly and get on better with your fellow Barracanians than you do with Europeans. In point of fact, I had a complaint only yesterday from Mr. Jackson, who said you had been rude to him—and not for the first time either."

"There is, Matt, I am sure, no need for me to tell you how necessary it will be for you to get on well with expatriates because until the company has trained up sufficient people of your caliber, Europeans are bound to occupy senior positions here in Barracania. All this is vital to your future interests, so can I help you in any way?"

While Baker was speaking on this theme, Rennalls had sat tensed in his chair and it was some seconds before he replied. "It is quite extraordinary, isn't it, how one can convey an impression to others so at variance with what one intends? I can only assure you once again that my dispute with Jackson—and you may remember also Godson—have had nothing at all to do with the color of their skins. I promise you that if a Barracanian had behaved in an equally peremptory manner I would have reacted in precisely the same way. And again, if I may say it within these four walls, I am sure I am not the only one who has found Jackson and Godson difficult. I could mention the names of several expatriates who have felt the same. However, I am really sorry to have created this impression of not being able to get on with Europeans—it is an entirely false one—and I quite realize that I must do all I can to correct it as quickly as possible. On your last point, regarding Europeans holding senior positions in the company for some time to come, I quite accept the situation. I know that Caribbean Bauxite—as they have been doing for many years now—will promote Barracanians as soon as their experience warrants it. And, finally, I would like to assure you, John—and my father thinks the same too— that I am very happy in my work here and hope to stay with the company for many years to come."

Rennalls had spoken earnestly and, although not convinced by what he had heard, Baker did not think he could pursue the matter further except to say, "All right, Matt, my impression may be wrong, but I would like to remind you about the truth of that old saying, 'What is important is not what is true but what is believed.' Let it rest at that."

But suddenly Baker knew that he didn't want to "let it rest at that." He was disappointed once again at not being able to "break through" to Rennalls and having yet again to listen to his bland denial that there was any racial prejudice in his makeup. Baker, who had intended ending the interview at this point, decided to try another tack.

"To return for a moment to the 'plus and minus technique' I was telling you about just now, there is another plus factor I forgot to mention. I would like to congratulate you not only on the caliber of your work but also on the ability you have shown in overcoming a challenge which I, as a European, have never had to meet."

"Continental Ore is, as you know, a typical commercial enterprise—admittedly a big one—which is a product of the economic and social environment of the United States and Western Europe. My ancestors have all been brought up in this environment for the past two or three hundred years and I have, therefore, been able to live in a world in which commerce (as we know it today) have been part and parcel of my being. It has not been something revolutionary and new which has suddenly entered my life. In your case the situation is different because you and your forebears have only had some fifty or sixty years' experience of this commercial environment. You have had to face the challenge of bridging the gap between fifty and two or three hundred years. Again, Matt, let me congratulate you—and people like you—once again on having so successfully overcome this particular hurdle. It is for this very reason that I think the outlook for Barracania—and particularly Caribbean Bauxite—is so bright."

Rennalls had listened intently and when Baker finished, replied, "Well, once again, John, I have to thank you for what you have said, and, for my part, I can only say that is gratifying to know that my own personal effort has been so much appreciated. I hope that more people will soon come to think as you do."

There was a pause and, for a moment, Baker thought hopefully that he was about to achieve his long awaited "breakthrough," but Rennalls merely smiled back. The barrier remained unbreached. There remained some five minutes' cheerful conversation about the contrast between the Caribbean and Canadian climate and whether the West Indies had any hope of beating England in the Fifth Test before Baker drew the interview to a close. Although he was as far as ever from knowing the real Rennalls, he was nevertheless glad that the interview had run along in the friendly manner and, particularly, that it had ended on such a cheerful note.

This feeling, however, lasted only until the following morning. Baker had some farewells to make, so he arrived at the office considerably later than usual. He had no sooner sat down at his desk than his secretary walked into the room with a worried frown on her face. Her words came fast. "When I arrived this morning I found Mr. Rennalls already waiting at my door. He seemed very angry and told me in quite a peremptory manner that he had a vital letter to dictate which must be sent off without any delay. He was so worked up that he couldn't keep still and kept pacing about the room, which is most unlike him. He wouldn't even wait to read what he had dictated. Just signed the page where he thought the letter would end. It has been distributed and your copy is in your 'in tray.'"

INDEX